THE ESSENTIAL E. P. THOMPSON

THE ESSENTIAL
E. P. THOMPSON

EDITED BY DOROTHY THOMPSON

The New Press, New York

The editor is grateful for permission to reprint the following copyrighted material:
"Preface," "Exploitation," "The Weavers," and "Class Consciousness" reprinted from *The Making of the English Working Class* by E. P. Thompson, copyright © 1963 by E. P. Thompson. Reprinted by permission of Pantheon Books, a division of Random House, Inc.
"Rejections and Reconciliations" reprinted from *"Alien Homage": Edward Thompson and Rabindranath Tagore* by E. P. Thompson, copyright © 1993 by E. P. Thompson. Reprinted by permission of Oxford University Press (India).
"History from Below" reprinted from the *Times Literary Supplement* (7 April 1966). Reprinted by permission of the *Times Literary Supplement*.

Excerpts from previously published works:
"The Anti-Scrape," "The River of Fire," and "Postscript 1976" reprinted from *William Morris: Romantic to Revolutionary* by E. P. Thompson (New York: Pantheon Books, 1955, 1977).
"The Rule of Law" reprinted from *Whigs and Hunters: The Origin of the Black Act* by E. P. Thompson (New York: Pantheon Books, 1975).
"The Moral Economy of the English Crowd" reprinted from *Customs in Common* by E. P. Thompson (New York: The New Press, 1991).
"Mary Wollstonecraft," "The Grid of Inheritance," and "Agenda for Radical History" reprinted from *Making History: Writings on History and Culture* by E. P. Thompson (New York: The New Press, 1994).
"The Crime of Anonymity" reprinted from *Albion's Fatal Tree: Crime and Society in Eighteenth-Century England* by Douglas Hay, Peter Linebaugh, John G. Rule, E. P. Thompson, and Cal Winslow (New York: Pantheon Books, 1975).
"Historical Logic" and "Marxism and History" reprinted from *The Poverty of Theory and Other Essays* by E. P. Thompson (New York and London: Monthly Review Press, 1978).

Published in the United States by The New Press, New York, 2001
Distributed by W. W. Norton & Company, Inc., New York

LIBRARY OF CONGRESS CATALOGING-IN-PUBLICATION DATA
Thompson, E. P. (Edward Palmer), 1924–1993
[Selections. 2000]
The essential E. P. Thompson / edited by Dorothy Thompson.
p. cm.
Includes bibliographical references.
ISBN 1-56584-621-4 (hc.)—ISBN 1-56584-622-2 (pbk.)
1. Great Britain—History—18th century— 2. Great Britain—History—19th century. 3. Great Britain—Social conditions—18th century— 4. Great Britain—Social conditions—19th century. I. Thompson, Dorothy, 1923– II. Title.
DA480 .T46 2000
941.07—dc21   00–042701

The New Press was established in 1990 as a not-for-profit alternative to the large, commercial publishing houses currently dominating the book publishing industry. The New Press operates in the public interest rather than for private gain, and is committed to publishing, in innovative ways, works of educational, cultural, and community value that are often deemed insufficiently profitable.

The New Press, 450 West 41st Street, 6th floor, New York, NY 10036
www.thenewpress.com

Printed in Canada

2 4 6 8 9 7 5 3 1

CONTENTS

INTRODUCTION

By Dorothy Thompson

Edward Palmer Thompson (1924–1993) was one of the most influential historians of his generation. As well as major volumes of social history, he published pieces on contemporary politics and squibs, arguments, and polemics on a wide range of academic and nonacademic subjects. The selection of his writing in this volume is in the main confined to his work as a historian of eighteenth- and nineteenth-century England, though the final extract, which is from a study based partly on family papers, moves into the wider area of the empire and takes the period covered into the twentieth century. At the end of the collection, two short pieces written almost a generation apart give his own view of the traditions in which he was writing and of other work with which he felt in sympathy.

Thompson did not see himself primarily as a scholarly or academic writer or, for that matter, only as a historian. In addition to his historical works, he published a novel and a number of poems, most of which have been collected in a posthumously published volume. He also wrote extensively on the writers of the early romantic period, and his last completed work was a study of William Blake.

The family into which E. P. Thompson was born in 1924 had until then lived and worked mainly outside Britain. His father, Edward John Thompson, was coming to the end of a career as a Methodist educational missionary working mainly in India. He was a poet and scholar who had served during World War I as an army chaplain in Mesopotamia and had been awarded the Military Cross for bravery in the front line. While on leave in wartime Palestine he had met and married Theodosia Jessup, daughter of an American missionary family who had grown up in Beirut, although she had returned to the United States to study and for a short time to teach at Vassar College.

When they returned to India, Edward resumed his study of Bengali literature and culture and his contacts with many writers and artists. By the time of

Edward junior's birth they were back in England with a four-year-old son, William Frank, and Edward senior had just taken up an appointment teaching Bengali at Oxford University. During the years between the wars he maintained and increased his contacts with Indian culture and politics and became one of the chief voices in Britain in support of the movement for Indian independence.

E. P. Thompson, therefore, grew up in an atmosphere of internationalism. As a child he spent time in Lebanon and in the United States as well as the usual family holidays in Europe. He was called up into the army at the age of seventeen and in 1942 was sent to Africa and from there to Italy, where he took part in the battle of Cassino. He spent his twenty-first birthday on duty on an Italian mountainside. He returned to England in 1945 and went up to Corpus Christi College at Cambridge University in the autumn term of that year.

His upbringing, his wartime experience, and probably his temperament made him profoundly critical of the establishment and its institutions. A wartime degree could be gained by only two years' academic study, so he opted for a wartime BA and spent the scholarship which his first-class result earned him on individual study for the third year of his course. This year was spent working on Elizabethan and Jacobean literature and history and also in exploring a wide range of historical philosophers including Vico and Marx. Although his degree was in history, his first love was probably always literature, especially poetry and drama. When he began taking adult education classes during 1946 and '47 it was as often literature as history that he taught. He never regarded history as a "background" to the study of literature, or literature as a simple referential source of historical data. He did however, consider the context as essential to the understanding of works of art as it was to the study of any of the other aspects of past societies.

His first full-sized book, *William Morris: Romantic to Revolutionary*, was published in 1955. It was one of the first and remains one of the most thorough examinations of Morris's politics, which saw his poetry and design as inseparable from his political and philosophical ideas. It was also the beginning of what became a lifetime's occupation, the exploration of English romanticism in art and politics. The work on Morris was his first move toward an engagement with certain mechanistic and teleological forms of historical presentation which he found not only in mainstream economic and political history but in aspects of the Marxist tradition within which he was writing. Looking back many years later in an interview published in *Radical History Review*, he answered the question "How did the author of a biography of William Morris come to write about the ecology of Windsor Forest in *Whigs and Hunters*?" with:

> This arises from a preoccupation that runs through all my work, even before I saw its . . . significance. . . . This preoccupation is with what I

regard as a real silence in Marx, which lies in the area that anthropologists would call value systems.

The problem, as he saw it, lay in:

> the degeneration of the theoretical vocabulary of mainstream Marxism—the impoverishment of its sensibility. . . . the extrusion (if you like) of that whole area of imaginative passion that informs the later writings of William Morris. . . . The injury that advanced industrial capitalism did, and that the market society did, was to define human relations as being primarily economic. Marx . . . proposed revolutionary economic man. But it is also implicit, particularly in the early Marx, that the injury is in defining man as "economic" at all.[1]

William Morris was written when Edward was five years into his first job as tutor/organizer in the extramural department at the University of Leeds. Initially he saw this as a short-term occupation—he had first given it five years—to provide an income while he gained the experience and contacts to become a freelance writer. In fact, he stayed for seventeen years, during which time all three Thompson children were born.

Adult teaching in the West Riding of Yorkshire, left-wing politics, the experience of the wartime army, and his deep interest and respect for spoken and written culture at all levels found expression in his second book, *The Making of the English Working Class*, published in 1963. This remains his best-known piece of writing, and it has never been out of print since it was published.

After *The Making* was published, Thompson took an internal university post at the newly founded University of Warwick, where he was the first director of the Centre for the Study of Social History. After seven years at Warwick, where he did his most concentrated graduate and undergraduate teaching, he was finally able to turn freelance when the children were old enough for his wife to take a full-time job. Freed from the demands of a teaching post, however, he was caught up in the European peace movement which came into being at the end of the 1970s, and by the time he was able to stand back from this work his health had begun to fail. His last five years were a struggle against the clock when he had to publish work that he did not feel was ready and to republish pieces that he had hoped to expand into major studies.

The extracts below give some idea of the quality of his work. He wrote very little about historiography or historical theory, preferring to let the theory emerge from the historical and literary writing itself. The exception was the long essay "The Poverty of Theory," which was evoked by the fashion for a particular set of theoretical texts which he felt were seriously inhibiting the creative exploration of the subject, from which we have included two short extracts. The title of the 1966 essay "History from Below," which was given to the piece by the editor, became the common term for the sort of history Edward wrote, but it was one about which he had doubts, since he always resisted any kind of history which neglected the structures of power in society. He always acknowledged the debt that he and the historical profession in general owed to Marx, but he increasingly hesitated to call himself a Marxist. He preferred to say that he wrote within a Marxist tradition. He always insisted that class was a concept and a tool for the examination of social structures that was of immense value, but he distrusted many of the closed and self-validating theoretical systems in which it was used. He once said, "It would be strange, wouldn't it, if all we have been talking about through the centuries has been the struggle of the poor against the rich. . . ." However, as his work shows, he did find Marx's definition of class conflict of value in the analysis of many areas of history, although there were others—he used to use the example of Fascism—for which he felt it had no explanatory power.

There are several books in print which discuss Edward Thompson's work, and most of his major works are still in print. This brief introduction is intended to give some context to the extracts published here. A list of further reading is included on page 497.

Note

1. MARHO, The Radical Historians Organization, *Visions of History* (New York: Pantheon Books, 1984), pp 20, 21–22.

I

Politics and Culture

PREFACE

FROM *THE MAKING OF THE ENGLISH WORKING CLASS*

This book has a clumsy title, but it is one which meets its purpose. *Making*, because it is a study in an active process, which owes as much to agency as to conditioning. The working class did not rise like the sun at an appointed time. It was present at its own making.

Class, rather than classes, for reasons which it is one purpose of this book to examine. There is, of course, a difference. "Working classes" is a descriptive term, which evades as much as it defines. It ties loosely together a bundle of discrete phenomena. There were tailors here and weavers there, and together they make up the working classes.

By class I understand an historical phenomenon, unifying a number of disparate and seemingly unconnected events, both in the raw material of experience and in consciousness. I emphasise that it is an *historical* phenomenon. I do not see class as a "structure," nor even as a "category," but as something which in fact happens (and can be shown to have happened) in human relationships.

More than this, the notion of class entails the notion of historical relationship. Like any other relationship, it is a fluency which evades analysis if we attempt to stop it dead at any given moment and anatomise its structure. The finest-meshed sociological net cannot give us a pure specimen of class, any more than it can give us one of deference or of love. The relationship must always be embodied in real people and in a real context. Moreover, we cannot have two distinct classes, each with an independent being, and then bring them *into* relationship with each other. We cannot have love without lovers, nor deference without squires and labourers. And class happens when some men, as a result of common experiences (inherited or shared), feel and articulate the identity of their interests as between themselves, and as against other men whose interests are different from (and usually opposed to) theirs. The class experience is

From *The Making of the English Working Class* by E. P. Thompson (New York: Vintage Books, 1963).

largely determined by the productive relations into which men are born—or enter involuntarily.

Class-consciousness is the way in which these experiences are handled in cultural terms: embodied in traditions, value-systems, ideas, and institutional forms. If the experience appears as determined, class-consciousness does not. We can see a *logic* in the responses of similar occupational groups undergoing similar experiences, but we cannot predicate any *law*. Consciousness of class arises in the same way in different times and places, but never in *just* the same way.

There is today an ever-present temptation to suppose that class is a thing. This was not Marx's meaning, in his own historical writing, yet the error vitiates much latter-day "Marxist" writing. "It," the working class, is assumed to have a real existence, which can be defined almost mathematically—so many men who stand in a certain relation to the means of production. Once this is assumed it becomes possible to deduce the class-consciousness which "it" ought to have (but seldom does have) if "it" was properly aware of its own position and real interests. There is a cultural superstructure, through which this recognition dawns in inefficient ways. These cultural "lags" and distortions are a nuisance, so that it is easy to pass from this to some theory of substitution: the party, sect, or theorist, who disclose class-consciousness, not as it is, but as it ought to be.

But a similar error is committed daily on the other side of the ideological divide. In one form, this is a plain negative. Since the crude notion of class attributed to Marx can be faulted without difficulty, it is assumed that any notion of class is a pejorative theoretical construct, imposed upon the evidence. It is denied that class has happened at all. In another form, and by a curious inversion, it is possible to pass from a dynamic to a static view of class. "It"—the working class—exists, and can be defined with some accuracy as a component of the social structure. Class-consciousness, however, is a bad thing, invented by displaced intellectuals, since everything which disturbs the harmonious co-existence of groups performing different "social roles" (and which thereby retards economic growth) is to be deplored as an "unjustified disturbance-symptom."[1] The problem is to determine how best "it" can be conditioned to accept its social role, and how its grievances may best be "handled and channelled."

If we remember that class is a relationship, and not a thing, we can not think in this way. "It" does not exist, either to have an ideal interest or consciousness, or to lie as a patient on the Adjustor's table. Nor can we turn matters upon their heads, as has been done by one authority who (in a study of class obsessively concerned with methodology, to the exclusion of the examination of a single real class situation in a real historical context) has informed us:

> Classes are based on the differences in legitimate power associated with
> certain positions, i.e. on the structure of social roles with respect to their
> authority expectations. . . . An individual becomes a member of a class by
> playing a social rôle relevant from the point of view of authority. . . . He
> belongs to a class because he occupies a position in a social organisation;
> i.e. class membership is derived from the incumbency of a social rôle.[2]

The question, of course, is how the individual got to be in this "social role,"
and how the particular social organisation (with its property-rights and structure
of authority) got to be there. And these are historical questions. If we stop
history at a given point, then there are no classes but simply a multitude of
individuals with a multitude of experiences. But if we watch these men over an
adequate period of social change, we observe patterns in their relationships,
their ideas, and their institutions. Class is defined by men as they live their
own history, and, in the end, this is its only definition.

If I have shown insufficient understanding of the methodological preoccupations
of certain sociologists, nevertheless I hope this book will be seen as a contribution to the understanding of class. For I am convinced that we cannot understand class unless we see it as a social and cultural formation, arising from
processes which can only be studied as they work themselves out over a considerable historical period. This book can be seen as a biography of the English
working class from its adolescence until its early manhood. In the years between
1780 and 1832 most English working people came to feel an identity of interests
as between themselves, and as against their rulers and employers. This ruling
class was itself much divided, and in fact only gained in cohesion over the same
years because certain antagonisms were resolved (or faded into relative insig-
nificance) in the face of an insurgent working class. Thus the working-class
presence was, in 1832, the most significant factor in British political life.

The book is written in this way. In Part One I consider the continuing
popular traditions in the 18th century which influenced the crucial Jacobin agitation of the 1790s. In Part Two I move from subjective to objective influences—the experiences of groups of workers during the Industrial Revolution
which seem to me to be of especial significance. I also attempt an estimate of
the character of the new industrial work-discipline, and the bearing upon this
of the Methodist Church. In Part Three I pick up the story of plebeian Radicalism, and carry it through Luddism to the heroic age at the close of the
Napoleonic Wars. Finally, I discuss some aspects of political theory and of the
consciousness of class in the 1820s and 1830s.

This is a group of studies, on related themes, rather than a consecutive
narrative. In selecting these themes I have been conscious, at times, of writing

against the weight of prevailing orthodoxies. There is the Fabian orthodoxy, in which the great majority of working people are seen as passive victims of *laissez-faire*, with the exception of a handful of far-sighted organisers (notably, Francis Place). There is the orthodoxy of the empirical economic historians, in which working people are seen as a labour force, as migrants, or as the data for statistical series. There is the "Pilgrim's Progress" orthodoxy, in which the period is ransacked for forerunners—pioneers of the Welfare State, progenitors of a Socialist Commonwealth, or (more recently) early exemplars of rational industrial relations. Each of these orthodoxies has a certain validity. All have added to our knowledge. My quarrel with the first and second is that they tend to obscure the agency of working people, the degree to which they contributed, by conscious efforts, to the making of history. My quarrel with the third is that it reads history in the light of subsequent preoccupations, and not as in fact it occurred. Only the successful (in the sense of those whose aspirations anticipated subsequent evolution) are remembered. The blind alleys, the lost causes, and the losers themselves are forgotten.

I am seeking to rescue the poor stockinger, the Luddite cropper, the "obsolete" hand-loom weaver, the "utopian" artisan, and even the deluded follower of Joanna Southcott, from the enormous condescension of posterity. Their crafts and traditions may have been dying. Their hostility to the new industrialism may have been backward-looking. Their communitarian ideals may have been fantasies. Their insurrectionary conspiracies may have been foolhardy. But they lived through these times of acute social disturbance, and we did not. Their aspirations were valid in terms of their own experience; and, if they were casualties of history, they remain, condemned in their own lives, as casualties.

Our only criterion of judgement should not be whether or not a man's actions are justified in the light of subsequent evolution. After all, we are not at the end of social evolution ourselves. In some of the lost causes of the people of the Industrial Revolution we may discover insights into social evils which we have yet to cure. Moreover, this period now compels attention for two particular reasons. First, it was a time in which the plebeian movement placed an exceptionally high valuation upon egalitarian and democratic values. Although we often boast our democratic way of life, the events of these critical years are far too often forgotten or slurred over. Second, the greater part of the world today is still undergoing problems of industrialisation, and of the formation of democratic institutions, analogous in many ways to our own experience during the Industrial Revolution. Causes which were lost in England might, in Asia or Africa, yet be won.

Finally, a note of apology to Scottish and Welsh readers. I have neglected these histories, not out of chauvinism, but out of respect. It is because class is a cultural as much as an economic formation that I have been cautious as to generalising beyond English experience. (I have considered the Irish, not in Ireland, but as immigrants to England.) The Scottish record, in particular, is quite as dramatic, and as tormented, as our own. The Scottish Jacobin agitation was more intense and more heroic. But the Scottish story is significantly different. Calvinism was not the same thing as Methodism, although it is difficult to say which, in the early 19th century, was worse. We had no peasantry in England comparable to the Highland migrants. And the popular culture was very different. It is possible, at least until the 1820s, to regard the English and Scottish experiences as distinct, since trade union and political links were impermanent and immature.

This book was written in Yorkshire, and is coloured at times by West Riding sources. My grateful acknowledgements are due to the University of Leeds and to Professor S. G. Raybould for enabling me, some years ago, to commence the research which led to this book; and to the Leverhulme Trustees for the award of a Senior Research Fellowship, which has enabled me to complete the work. I have also learned a great deal from members of my tutorial classes, with whom I have discussed many of the themes treated here. Acknowledgements are due also to the authorities who have allowed me to quote from manuscript and copyright sources: particular acknowledgements will be found at the end of the volume.

I have also to thank many others. Mr. Christopher Hill, Professor Asa Briggs, and Mr. John Saville criticised parts of the book in draft, although they are in no sense responsible for my judgements. Mr. R. J. Harris showed great editorial patience, when the book burst the bounds of a series for which it was first commissioned. Mr. Perry Anderson, Mr. Denis Butt, Mr. Richard Cobb, Mr. Henry Collins, Mr. Derrick Crossley, Mr. Tim Enright, Dr. E. P. Hennock, Mr. Rex Russell, Dr. John Rex, Dr. E. Sigsworth, and Mr. H. O. E. Swift, have helped me at different points. I have also to thank Mrs. Dorothy Thompson, an historian to whom I am related by the accident of marriage. Each chapter has been discussed with her, and I have been well placed to borrow not only her ideas but material from her notebooks. Her collaboration is to be found, not in this or that particular, but in the way the whole problem is seen.

Halifax, August 1962

Notes

1. An example of this approach, covering the period of this book, is to be found in the work of a colleague of Professor Talcott Parsons: N.J. Smelser, *Social Change in the Industrial Revolution* (1959).

2. R. Dahrendorf, *Class and Class Conflict in Industrial Society* (1959), pp. 148–9.

EXPLOITATION
FROM *THE MAKING OF THE ENGLISH WORKING CLASS*

John Thelwall was not alone in seeing in every "manufactory" a potential centre of political rebellion. An aristocratic traveller who visited the Yorkshire Dales in 1792 was alarmed to find a new cotton-mill in the "pastoral vale" of Aysgarth—"why, here now is a great flaring mill, whose back stream has drawn off half the water of the falls above the bridge":

> With the bell ringing, and the clamour of the mill, all the vale is distub'd; treason and levelling systems are the discourse; and rebellion may be near at hand.

The mill appeared as symbol of social energies which were destroying the very "course of Nature." It embodied a double threat to the settled order. First, from the owners of industrial wealth, those upstarts who enjoyed an unfair advantage over the landowners whose income was tied to their rent-roll:

> If men thus start into riches; or if riches from trade are too easily procured, woe to us men of middling income, and settled revenue; and woe it has been to all the Nappa Halls, and the Yeomanry of the land.

Second, from the industrial working population, which our traveller regarded with an alliterative hostility which betrays a response not far removed from that of the white racialist towards the coloured population today:

> The people, indeed, are employ'd; but they are all abandon'd to vice from the throng. . . . At the times when people work not in the mill, they issue out to poaching, profligacy and plunder. . . .[1]

From *The Making of the English Working Class* by E. P. Thompson (New York: Vintage Books, 1963).

The equation between the cotton-mill and the new industrial society, and the correspondence between new forms of productive and of social relationship, was a commonplace among observers in the years between 1790 and 1850. Karl Marx was only expressing this with unusual vigour when he declared: "The hand-mill gives you society with the feudal lord: the steam-mill, society with the industrial capitalist." And it was not only the mill-owner but also the working population brought into being within and around the mills which seemed to contemporaries to be "new." "The instant we get near the borders of the manufacturing parts of Lancashire," a rural magistrate wrote in 1808, "we meet a fresh race of beings, both in point of manners, employments and subordination . . ."; while Robert Owen, in 1815, declared that "the general diffusion of manufactures throughout a country generates a new character in its inhabitants . . . an essential change in the general character of the mass of the people."

Observers in the 1830s and 1840s were still exclaiming at the novelty of the "factory system." Peter Gaskell, in 1833, spoke of the manufacturing population as "but a Hercules in the cradle"; it was "only since the introduction of steam as a power that they have acquired their paramount importance." The steam-engine had "drawn together the population into dense masses" and already Gaskell saw in working-class organisations an " 'imperium in imperio' of the most obnoxious description."[2] Ten years later Cooke Taylor was writing in similar terms:

> The steam-engine had no precedent, the spinning-jenny is without ancestry, the mule and the power-loom entered on no prepared heritage: they sprang into sudden existence like Minerva from the brain of Jupiter.

But it was the human consequence of these "novelties" which caused this observer most disquiet:

> As a stranger passes through the masses of human beings which have accumulated round the mills and print works . . . he cannot contemplate these "crowded hives" without feelings of anxiety and apprehension almost amounting to dismay. The population, like the system to which it belongs, is *new*; but it is hourly increasing in breadth and strength. It is an aggregate of masses, our conceptions of which clothe themselves in terms that express something portentous and fearful . . . as of the slow rising and gradual swelling of an ocean which must, at some future and no distant time, bear all the elements of society aloft upon its bosom, and float them Heaven knows whither. There are mighty energies slumbering in these masses. . . . The manufacturing population is not new in its formation alone: it is new in its habits of thought and action, which have been formed by the cir-

cumstances of its condition, with little instruction, and less guidance, from external sources. . . .[3]

For Engels, describing the *Condition of the Working Class in England in 1844*, it seemed that "the first proletarians were connected with manufacture, were engendered by it . . . the factory hands, eldest children of the industrial revolution, have from the beginning to the present day formed the nucleus of the Labour Movement."

However different their judgments of value, conservative, radical, and socialist observers suggested the same equation: steam power and the cotton-mill = new working class. The physical instruments of production were seen as giving rise in a direct and more-or-less compulsive way to new social relationships, institutions, and cultural modes. At the same time the history of popular agitation during the period 1811–50 appears to confirm this picture. It is as if the English nation entered a crucible in the 1790s and emerged after the Wars in a different form. Between 1811 and 1813, the Luddite crisis; in 1817 the Pentridge Rising; in 1819, Peterloo; throughout the next decade the proliferation of trade union activity, Owenite propaganda, Radical journalism, the Ten Hours Movement, the revolutionary crisis of 1831–2; and, beyond that, the multitude of movements which made up Chartism. It is, perhaps, the scale and intensity of this multiform popular agitation which has, more than anything else, given rise (among contemporary observers and historians alike) to the sense of some *catastrophic* change.

Almost every radical phenomenon of the 1790s can be found reproduced tenfold after 1815. The handful of Jacobin sheets gave rise to a score of ultra-Radical and Owenite periodicals. Where Daniel Eaton served imprisonment for publishing Paine, Richard Carlile and his shopmen served a total of more than 200 years imprisonment for similar crimes. Where Corresponding Societies maintained a precarious existence in a score of towns, the post-war Hampden Clubs or political unions struck root in small industrial villages. And when this popular agitation is recalled alongside the dramatic pace of change in the cotton industry, it is natural to assume a direct causal relationship. The cotton-mill is seen as the agent not only of industrial but also of social revolution, producing not only more goods but also the "Labour Movement" itself. The Industrial Revolution, which commenced as a description, is now invoked as an explanation.

From the time of Arkwright through to the Plug Riots and beyond, it is the image of the "dark, Satanic mill" which dominates our visual reconstruction of the Industrial Revolution. In part, perhaps, because it is a dramatic visual image—the barrack-like buildings, the great mill chimneys, the factory children, the clogs and shawls, the dwellings clustering around the mills as if spawned by them. (It is an image which forces one to think first of the industry, and only secondly of the people connected to it or serving it.) In part, because the cotton-mill and the new mill-town—from the swiftness of its growth, ingenuity of its techniques, and the novelty or harshness of its discipline—seemed to contemporaries to be dramatic and portentous: a more satisfactory symbol for debate on the "condition-of-England" question than those anonymous or sprawling manufacturing *districts* which figure even more often in the Home Office "disturbance books." And from this both a literary and an historical tradition is derived. Nearly all the classic accounts by contemporaries of conditions in the Industrial Revolution are based on the cotton industry—and, in the main, on Lancashire: Owen, Gaskell, Ure, Fielden, Cooke Taylor, Engels, to mention a few. Novels such as *Michael Armstrong* or *Mary Barton* or *Hard Times* perpetuate the tradition. And the emphasis is markedly found in the subsequent writing of economic and social history.

But many difficulties remain. Cotton was certainly the pace-making industry of the Industrial Revolution,[4] and the cotton-mill was the pre-eminent model for the factory-system. Yet we should not assume any automatic, or over-direct, correspondence between the dynamic of economic growth and the dynamic of social or cultural life. For half a century after the "break-through" of the cotton-mill (around 1780) the mill workers remained as a minority of the adult labour force in the cotton industry itself. In the early 1830s the cotton hand-loom weavers alone still outnumbered all the men and women in spinning and weaving mills of cotton, wool, and silk combined.[5] Still, in 1830, the adult male cotton-spinner was no more typical of that elusive figure, the "average working man," than is the Coventry motor-worker of the 1960s.

The point is of importance, because too much emphasis upon the newness of the cotton-mills can lead to an underestimation of the continuity of political and cultural traditions in the making of working-class communities. The factory hands, so far from being the "eldest children of the industrial revolution," were late arrivals. Many of their ideas and forms of organisation were anticipated by domestic workers, such as the woollen workers of Norwich and the West Country, or the small-ware weavers of Manchester. And it is questionable whether factory hands—except in the cotton districts—"formed the nucleus of the Labour Movement" at any time before the late 1840s (and, in some northern and Midland towns, the years 1832–4, leading up to the great lock-outs). Jacobinism, as we have seen, struck root most deeply among artisans. Luddism was the work of skilled men in small workshops. From 1817 onwards to Chartism, the outworkers in the north and the Midlands were as prominent in every radical agitation as the factory hands. And in many towns the actual nucleus from which the labour movement derived ideas, organisation, and leadership, was made up of such men as shoemakers, weavers, saddlers and harnessmakers, booksellers, printers, building workers, small tradesmen, and the like. The vast area of Radical London between 1815 and 1850 drew its strength from no major heavy industries (shipbuilding was tending to decline, and the engineers only made their impact later in the century) but from the host of smaller trades and occupations.[6]

Such diversity of experiences has led some writers to question both the notions of an "industrial revolution" and of a "working class." The first discussion need not detain us here.[7] The term is serviceable enough in its usual connotations. For the second, many writers prefer the term working *classes*, which emphasises the great disparity in status, acquisitions, skills, conditions, within the portmanteau phrase. And in this they echo the complaints of Francis Place:

> If the character and conduct of the working-people are to be taken from reviews, magazines, pamphlets, newspapers, reports of the two Houses of Parliament and the Factory Commissioners, we shall find them all jumbled together as the "lower orders," the most skilled and the most prudent workman, with the most ignorant and imprudent labourers and paupers, though the difference is great indeed, and indeed in many cases will scarce admit of comparison.[8]

Place is, of course, right: the Sunderland sailor, the Irish navvy, the Jewish costermonger, the inmate of an East Anglian village workhouse, the compositor on *The Times*—all might be seen by their "betters" as belonging to the "lower classes" while they themselves might scarcely understand each others' dialect.

Nevertheless, when every caution has been made, the outstanding fact of the period between 1790 and 1830 is the formation of "the working class." This is revealed, first, in the growth of class-consciousness: the consciousness of an identity of interests as between all these diverse groups of working people and as against the interests of other classes. And, second, in the growth of corresponding forms of political and industrial organisation. By 1832 there were strongly-based and self-conscious working-class institutions—trade unions, friendly societies, educational and religious movements, political organisations, periodicals—working-class intellectual traditions, working-class community-patterns, and a working-class structure of feeling.

The making of the working class is a fact of political and cultural, as much as of economic, history. It was not the spontaneous generation of the factory-system. Nor should we think of an external force—the "industrial revolution"—working upon some nondescript undifferentiated raw material of humanity, and turning it out at the other end as a "fresh race of beings." The changing productive relations and working conditions of the Industrial Revolution were imposed, not upon raw material, but upon the free-born Englishman—

and the free-born Englishman as Paine had left him or as the Methodists had moulded him. The factory hand or stockinger was also the inheritor of Bunyan, of remembered village rights, of notions of equality before the law, of craft traditions. He was the object of massive religious indoctrination and the creator of new political traditions. The working class made itself as much as it was made.

To see the working class in this way is to defend a "classical" view of the period against the prevalent mood of contemporary schools of economic history and sociology. For the territory of the Industrial Revolution, which was first staked out and surveyed by Marx, Arnold Toynbee, the Webbs, and the Hammonds, now resembles an academic battlefield. At point after point, the familiar "catastrophic" view of the period has been disputed. Where it was customary to see the period as one of economic disequilibrium, intense misery and exploitation, political repression and heroic popular agitation, attention is now directed to the rate of economic growth (and the difficulties of "take-off" into self-sustaining technological reproduction). The enclosure movement is now noted, less for its harshness in displacing the village poor, than for its success in feeding a rapidly growing population. The hardships of the period are seen as being due to the dislocations consequent upon the Wars, faulty communications, immature banking and exchange, uncertain markets, and the trade-cycle, rather than to exploitation or cut-throat competition. Popular unrest is seen as consequent upon the unavoidable coincidence of high wheat prices and trade depressions, and explicable in terms of an elementary "social tension" chart derived from these data.[9] In general, it is suggested that the position of the industrial worker in 1840 was better in most ways than that of the domestic worker of 1790. The Industrial Revolution was an age, not of catastrophe or acute class-conflict and class oppression, but of improvement.[10]

The classical catastrophic orthodoxy has been replaced by a new anti-catastrophic orthodoxy, which is most clearly distinguished by its empirical caution and, among its most notable exponents (Sir John Clapham, Dr. Dorothy George, Professor Ashton) by an astringent criticism of the looseness of certain writers of the older school. The studies of the new orthodoxy have enriched historical scholarship, and have qualified and revised in important respects the work of the classical school. But as the new orthodoxy is now, in its turn, growing old and entrenched in most of the academic centres, so it becomes open to challenge in its turn. And the successors of the great empiricists too often exhibit a moral complacency, a narrowness of reference, and an insufficient familiarity with the actual movements of the working people of the time. They are more aware of the orthodox empiricist postures than of the changes in social relationship and in cultural modes which the Industrial Revolution entailed. What has been lost is a sense of the whole process—the whole political and social context of the period. What arose as valuable qualifications have passed by imperceptible stages to new generalisations (which the evidence can rarely sustain) and from generalizations to a ruling attitude.

The empiricist orthodoxy is often defined in terms of a running critique of the work of J. L. and Barbara Hammond. It is true that the Hammonds showed themselves too willing to moralise history, and to arrange their materials too much in terms of "outraged emotion"[11] There are many points at which their work has been faulted or qualified in the light of subsequent research, and we intend to propose others. But a defence of the Hammonds need not only be rested upon the fact that their volumes on the laborers, with their copious quotation and wide reference, will long remain among the most important source-books for this period. We can also say that they displayed throughout their narrative an understanding of the political context within which the Industrial Revolution took place. To the student examining the ledgers of one cotton-mill, the Napoleonic Wars appear only as an abnormal influence affecting foreign markets and fluctuating demand. The Hammonds could never have forgotten for one moment that it was also a war against Jacobinism. "The history of England at the time discussed in these pages reads like a history of civil war." This is the opening of the introductory chapter of *The Skilled Labourer*. And in the conclusion to *The Town Labourer*, among other comments of indifferent value, there is an insight which throws the whole period into sudden relief:

> At the time when half Europe was intoxicated and the other half terrified by the new magic of the word citizen, the English nation was in he hands of men who regarded the idea of citizenship as a challenge to their religion and their civilization; who deliberately sought to make the inequalities of life the basis of the state, and to emphasise and perpetuate the position of the work people as a subject class. Hence it happened that the French Revolution has divided the people of France less than the Industrial Revolution has divided the people of England. . . .

"Hence it happened. . . ." The judgment may be questioned. And yet it is in this insight —that the revolution which did *not* happen in England was fully as devastating, and in some features more divisive, than that which did happen in France—that we find a clue to the truly catastrophic nature of the period. Throughout this time there are three, and not two, great influences simultaneously at work. There is the tremendous increase in population (in Great Britain, from 10.5 millions in 1801 to 18.1 millions in 1841, with the greatest rate of increase between 1811–21). There is the Industrial Revolution, in its technological aspects. And there is the political *counter*-revolution, from 1792–1832.

In the end, it is the political context as much as the steam-engine, which had most influence upon the shaping consciousness and institutions of the working class. The forces making for political reform in the late 18th century—Wilkes, the city merchants, the Middlesex small gentry, the "mob"—or Wyvill, and the small gentry and yeomen, clothiers, cutlers, and tradesmen—were on the eve of gaining at least some piecemeal victories in the 1790s: Pitt had been cast for the role of reforming Prime Minister. Had events taken their "natural" course we might expect there to have been some show-down long before 1832, between the oligarchy of land and commerce and the manufacturers and petty gentry, with working people in the tail of the middle-class agitation. And even in 1792, when manufacturers and professional men were prominent in the reform movement, this was still the balance of forces. But, after the success of *Rights of Man*, the radicalisation and terror of the French Revolution, and the onset of Pitt's repression, it was the plebeian Corresponding Society which alone stood up against the counter-revolutionary wars. And these plebeian groups, small as they were in 1796, did nevertheless make up an "underground" tradition which ran through to the end of the Wars. Alarmed at the French example, and in the patriotic fervour of war, the aristocracy and the manufacturers made common cause. The English *ancient régime* received a new lease of life, not only in national affairs, but also in the perpetuation of the antique corporations which misgoverned the swelling industrial towns. In return, the manufacturers received important concessions: and notably the abrogation or repeal of "paternalist" legislation covering apprenticeship, wage-regulation, or conditions in industry. The aristocracy were interested in repressing the Jacobin "conspiracies" of the people, the manufacturers were interested in defeating their "conspiracies" to increase wages: the Combination Acts served both purposes.

Thus working people were forced into political and social *apartheid* during the Wars (which, incidentally, they also had to fight). It is true that this was not altogether new. What was new was that it was coincident with a French Revolution: with growing self-consciousness and wider aspirations (for the "liberty tree" had been planted from the Thames to the Tyne): with a rise in population, in which the sheer sense of numbers, in London and in the industrial districts, became more impressive from year to year (and as numbers grew, so deference to master, magistrate, or parson was likely to lessen): and with more intensive or more transparent forms of economic exploitation. More intensive in agriculture and in the old domestic industries: more transparent in the new factories and perhaps in mining. In agriculture the years between 1760 and 1820 are the years of wholesale enclosure, in which, in village after village, common rights are lost, and the landless and—in the south—pauperized labourer is left to support the tenant-farmer, the landowner, and the tithes of the Church. In the domestic industries, from 1800 onwards, the tendency is widespread for small masters to give way to larger employers (whether manufacturers or middlemen) and for the majority of weavers, stockings, or nail-makers to become wage-earning outworkers with more or less precarious employment. In the mills and in many mining areas these are the years of the employment of children (and of women) underground; and the large-scale enterprise, the factory-system with its new discipline, the mill communities—where the manufacturer not only made riches out of the labour of the "hands" but could be *seen* to make riches in one generation—all contributed to the transparency of the process of exploitation and to the social and cultural cohesion of the exploited.

We can now see something of the truly catastrophic nature of the Industrial Revolution; as well as some of the reasons why the English working class took form in these years. The people were subjected simultaneously to an intensification of two intolerable forms of relationship: those of economic exploitation and of political oppression. Relations between employer and laborer were becoming both harsher and less personal; and while it is true that this increased the potential freedom of the worker, since the hired farm servant or the journeyman in domestic industry was (in Toynbee's words) "halted half-way between the position of the serf and the position of the citizen," this "freedom" meant that he felt his *un*freedom more. But at each point where he sought to resist exploitation, he was met by the forces of employer or State, and commonly of both.

For most working people the crucial experience of the Industrial Revolution was felt in terms of changes in the nature and intensity of exploitation. Nor is this some anachronistic notion, imposed upon the evidence. We may describe some parts of the exploitive process as they appeared to one remarkable cotton operative in 1818—the year in which Marx was born. The account—an Address to the public of strike-bound Manchester by "A Journeyman Cotton Spinner"—commences by describing the employers and the workers as "two distinct classes of persons":

"First, then, as to the employers: with very few exceptions, they are a set of men who have sprung from the cotton-shop without education or address, except so much as they have acquired by their intercourse with the little world of merchants on the exchange at Manchester; but to counterbalance that deficiency, they give you enough of appearances by an ostentatious display of elegant mansions, equipages, liveries, parks, hunters, hounds, &c. which they take care to shew off to the merchant stranger in the most pompous manner. Indeed, their houses are gorgeous palaces, far surpassing in bulk and extent the neat charming retreats you see round London . . . but the chaste observer of the beauties of nature and art combined will observe a woeful deficiency of taste. They bring up their families at the most costly schools, determined to give their offspring a double portion of what they were so deficient in themselves. Thus with scarcely a second idea in their heads, they are literally petty monarchs, absolute and despotic, in their own particular districts, and to support all this, their whole time is occupied in contriving how to get the greatest quantity of work turned off with the least expence. . . . In short, I will venture to say, without fear of contradiction, that there is a greater distance observed between the master there and the spinner, than there is between the first merchant in London and his lowest servant or the lowest artisan. Indeed there is no comparison. I know it to be a fact, that the greater part of the master spinners are anxious to keep wages low for the purpose of keeping the spinners indigent and spiritless . . . as for the purpose of taking the surplus to their own pockets.

"The master spinners are a class of men unlike all other master tradesmen in the kingdom. They are ignorant, proud, and tyrannical. What then must be the men or rather beings who are the instruments of such masters? Why, they have been for a series of years, with their wives and their families, patience itself—bondmen and bondwomen to their cruel taskmaster. It is in vain to insult our common understandings with the observation that such men are free; that the law protects the rich and poor alike, and that a spinner can leave his master if he does not like the wages. True; so he can: but where must he go? why to another, to be sure. Well: he goes; he is asked where did you work last: 'did he discharge you?' No; we could not agree about wages. Well I shall not employ you nor anyone who leaves his master in that manner. Why is this? Because there is an abominable *combination existing amongst the masters*, first established at Stockport in 1802, and it has since become so general, as to embrace all the great masters for a circuit of many miles round Manchester, though not the little masters: they are excluded. They are the most obnoxious beings to the great ones that can be imagined. . . . When the combination first took place, one of their first articles was, that no master should take on a man until he had first ascertained whether his last master had discharged him. What then is the man to do? If he goes to the parish, that grave of all independence, he is there told—We shall not relieve you; if you dispute with your master, and don't support your family, we will send you to prison; so that the man is bound, by a combination of circumstances, to submit to his master. He cannot travel and get work in any town like a shoe-maker, joiner, or taylor; he is confined to the district.

"The workmen in general are an inoffensive, unassuming set of well-informed men, though how they acquire their information is almost a mystery to me. They are docile and tractable, if not goaded too much; but this is not to be wondered at, when we consider that they are trained to work from six years old, from five in a morning to eight and nine at night. Let one of the advocates for obedience to his master take his stand in an avenue leading to a factory a little before five o'clock in the morning, and observe the squalid appearance of the little infants and their parents taken from their beds at so early an hour in all kinds of weather; let him examine the miserable pittance of food, chiefly composed of water gruel and oatcake broken into it, a little salt, and sometimes coloured with a little milk, together with a few potatoes, and a bit of bacon or fat for dinner; would a London mechanic eat this? There they are (and if late a few minutes, a quarter of a day is stopped in wages), locked up until night in rooms heated above the hottest days we have had this summer, and allowed no time, except three-quarters of an hour at dinner in the whole day: whatever they eat at any other time must be as they are at work. The negro slave in the West Indies, if he works under a scorching sun, has probably a little breeze of air sometimes to fan him: he has a space of ground, and time allowed to cultivate it. The English spinner slave had no enjoyment of the open atmosphere and breezes of heaven. Locked up in factories eight stories high, he has no relaxation till the ponderous engine stops, and then he goes home to get refreshed for the next day; no time for sweet association with his family; they are all alike fatigued and exhausted. This is no over-drawn picture: it is literally true. I ask again, would the mechanics in the South of England submit to this?

"When the spinning of cotton was in its infancy, and before those terrible machines for superseding the necessity of human labour, called steam engines, came into use, there were a great number of what were then called *little masters*; men who with a small capital, could procure a few machines, and employ a few hands, men and boys (say to twenty or thirty), the produce of whose labour was all taken to Manchester central mart, and put into the hands of brokers. . . . The brokers sold it to the merchants, by which means the master spinner was enable to stay at home and work and attend to his workmen. The cotton was then always given out in its raw state from the bale to the wives of the spinners at home, when they heat and cleansed it ready for the spinners in the factory. By this they could earn eight, ten, or twelve shillings a week, and cook and attend to their families. But none are thus employed now; for all the cotton is broke up by a machine, turned by the steam engine, called a devil: so that the spinners' wives have no employment, except they go to work in the factory all day at what can be done by children for a few shillings, four or five per week. If a man then could not agree with his master, he left him, and could get employed elsewhere. A few years, however, changed the face of things. Steam engines came into use, to purchase which, and to erect buildings sufficient to contain them and six or seven hundred hands, required a great capital. The engine power produced a more marketable (though not a better) article than the little master could at the same price. The consequence was their ruin in a

short time; and the overgrown capitalists triumphed in their fall; for they were
the only obstacle that stood between them and the complete control of the
workmen.

"Various disputes then originated between the workmen and masters as to
the fineness of the work, the workman being paid according to the number of
hanks or yards of thread he produced from a given quantity of cotton, which
was always to be proved by the overlooker, whose interest made it imperative
on him to lean to his master, and call the material coarser than it was. If the
workman would not submit *he must summon his employer before a magistrate*;
the whole of the acting magistrates in that district, with the exception of two
worthy clergymen, being gentlemen who have sprung from the *same* source
with the master cotton spinners. The employer generally contented himself with
sending his overlooker to answer any such summons, thinking it beneath him
to meet his servant. The magistrate's decision was generally in favour of the
master, though on the statement of the overlooker only. The workman dared
not appeal to the sessions on account of the expense. . . .

"These evils to the men have arisen from that dreadful monopoly which
exists in those districts where wealth and power are got into the hands of the
few, who, in the pride of their hearts, think themselves the lords of the universe."[12]

This reading of the facts, in its remarkable cogency, is as much an *ex parte*
statement as is the "political economy" of Lord Brougham. But the "Journeyman Cotton Spinner" was describing facts of a different order. We need not
concern ourselves with the soundness of all his judgments. What his address
does is to itemise one after another the grievances felt by working people as
to changes in the character of capitalist exploitation: the rise of a master-class
without traditional authority or obligations; the growing distance between master and man; the transparency of the exploitation at the source of their new
wealth and power; the loss of status and above all of independence for the
worker, his reduction to total dependence on the master's instruments of production; the partiality of the law; the disruption of the traditional family economy; the discipline, monotony, hours, and conditions of work; loss of leisure
and amenities; the reduction of the man to the status of an "instrument."

That working people felt these grievances at all—and felt them passionately—is itself a sufficient fact to merit our attention. And it reminds us forcibly
that some of the most bitter conflicts of these years turned on issues which are
not encompassed by cost-of-living series. The issues which provoked the most
intensity of feeling were very often ones in which such values as traditional
customs, "justice," "independence," security, or family-economy were at stake,
rather than straight-forward "bread-and-butter" issues. The early years of the

1830s are aflame with agitations which turned on issues in which wages were of secondary importance: by the potters, against the Truck System; by the textile workers, for the 10-Hour Bill; by the building workers, for co-operative direct action; by all groups of workers, for the right to join trade unions. The great strike in the north-east coalfield in 1831 turned on security of employment, "tommy shops," child labour.

The exploitive relationship is more than the sum of grievances and mutual antagonisms. It is a relationship which can be seen to take distinct forms in different historical contexts, forms which are related to corresponding forms of ownership and State power. The classic exploitive relationship of the Industrial Revolution is depersonalized, in the sense that no lingering obligations of mutuality—of paternalism or deference, or of the interests of "the Trade"—are admitted. There is no whisper of the "just" price, or of a wage justified in relation to social or moral sanctions, as opposed to the operation of free market forces. Antagonism is accepted as intrinsic to the relations of production. Managerial or supervisory functions demand the repression of all attributes except those which further the expropriation of the maximum surplus value from labour. This is the political economy which Marx anatomized in *Das Kapital*. The worker has become an "instrument," or an entry among other items of cost.

In fact, no complex industrial enterprise could be conducted according to such a philosophy. The need for industrial peace, for a stable labour-force, and for a body of skilled and experienced workers, necessitated the modification of managerial techniques—and, indeed, the growth of new forms of paternalism— in the cotton-mills by the 1830s. But in the overstocked outwork industries, where there was always a sufficiency of unorganised "hands" competing for employment, these considerations did not operate. Here, as old customs were eroded, and old paternalism was set aside, the exploitive relationship emerged supreme.

This does not mean that we can lay all the "blame" for each hardship of the Industrial Revolution upon "the masters" or upon *laissez-faire*. The process of industrialisation must, in any conceivable social context, entail suffering and the destruction of older and valued ways of life. Much recent research has thrown light upon the particular difficulties of the British experience: the hazards of markets; the manifold commercial and financial consequences of the Wars; the post-war deflation; movements in the terms of trade; and the exceptional stresses resulting from the population "explosion." Moreover, 20th-century preoccupations have made us aware of the overarching problems of economic growth. It can be argued that Britain in the Industrial Revolution was encountering the problems of "take-off": heavy long-term investment—canals, mills, railways, foundries, mines, utilities—was at the expense of current consumption; the generations of workers between 1790 and 1840 sacrificed some, or all, of their prospects of increased consumption to the future.[13]

These arguments all deserve close attention. For example, studies of the fluctuations in the demand of the South American market, or of the crisis in country banking, may tell us much about the reasons for the growth or retardation of particular industries. The objection to the reigning academic orthodoxy is not to empirical studies *per se*, but to the fragmentation of our comprehension of the full historical process. First, the empiricist segregates certain events from this process and examines them in isolation. Since the conditions which gave rise to these events are assumed, they appear not only as explicable in their own terms but as inevitable. The Wars had to be paid for out of heavy taxation; they accelerated growth in this way and retarded it in that. Since this can be shown, it is also implied that this was *necessarily* so. But thousands of Englishmen at the time agreed with Thomas Bewick's condemnation of "this superlatively wicked war."[14] The unequal burden of taxation, fund-holders who profited from the National Debt, paper-money—these were not accepted as given data by many contemporaries, but were the staple of intensive Radical agitation.

But there is a second stage, where the empiricist may put these fragmentary studies back together again, constructing a model of the historical process made up from a multiplicity of interlocking inevitabilities, a piecemeal processional. In the scrutiny of credit facilities or of the terms of trade, where each event is explicable and appears also as a self-sufficient cause of other events, we arrive at a *post facto* determinism. The dimension of human agency is lost, and the context of class relations is forgotten.

It is perfectly true that what the empiricist points to was there. The Orders in Council had in 1811 brought certain trades almost to a standstill; rising timber prices after the Wars inflated the costs of building; a passing change of fashion (lace for ribbon) might silence the looms of Coventry; the power-loom competed with the hand-loom. But even these open-faced facts, with their frank credentials, deserve to be questioned. Whose Council, why the Orders? Who profited most from corners in scarce timber? Why should looms remain idle when tens of thousands of country girls fancied ribbons but could not afford to buy? By what social alchemy did inventions for saving labour become engines of immiseration? The raw fact—a bad harvest—may seem to be beyond human election. But the way that fact worked its way out was in terms of a particular complex of human relationships: law, ownership, power. When we encounter some sonorous phrase such as "the strong ebb and flow of the trade cycle" we must be put on our guard. For behind this trade cycle there is a structure of social relations, fostering some sorts of expropriation (rent, interest, and profit) and outlawing others (theft, feudal dues), legitimising some types of conflict (competition, armed warfare) and inhibiting others (trades unionism, bread riots, popular political organisation)—a structure which may appear, in the eyes of the future, to be both barbarous and ephemeral.

It might be unnecessary to raise these large questions, since the historian cannot always be questioning the credentials of the society which he studies. But all these questions were, in fact, raised by contemporaries: not only by men of the upper classes (Shelley, Cobbett, Owen, Peacock, Thompson, Hodgskin, Carlyle) but by thousands of articulate working men. Not the political institutions alone, but the social and economic structure of industrial capitalism, were brought into question by their spokesmen. To the facts of orthodox political economy they opposed their own facts and their own arithmetic. Thus as early as 1817 the Leicester framework-knitters put forward, in a series of resolutions, an under-consumption theory of capitalist crisis:

> That in proportion as the Reduction of Wages makes the great Body of the People poor and wretched, in the same proportion must the consumption of our manufactures be lessened.
>
> That if liberal Wages were given to the Mechanics in general throughout the Country, the Home Consumption of our Manufactures would be immediately more than doubled, and consequently every hand would soon find full employment.
>
> That to Reduce the Wage of the Mechanic of this Country so low that he cannot live by his labour, in order to undersell Foreign Manufacturers in a Foreign Market, is to gain one customer abroad, and lose two at home. . . .[15]

If those in employment worked shorter hours, and if child labour were to be restricted, there would be more work for hand-workers and the unemployed could employ themselves and exchange the products of their labour directly—short-circuiting the vagaries of the capitalist market—goods would be cheaper and labour better-rewarded. To the rhetoric of the free market they opposed the language of the "new moral order." It is because alternative and irreconcilable views of human order—one based on mutuality, the other on competition—confronted each other between 1815 and 1850 that the historian today still feels the need to take sides.

It is scarcely possible to write the history of popular agitations in these years unless we make at least the imaginative effort to understand how such a man as the "Journeyman Cotton Spinner" read the evidence. He spoke of the "masters," not as an aggregate of individuals, but as a class. As such, "they" denied him political rights. If there was a trade recession, "they" cut his wages. If trade improved, he had to fight "them" and their state to obtain any share in the improvement. If food was plentiful, "they" profited from it. If it was scarce, some of "them" profited more. "They" conspired, not in this or that fact alone, but in the essential exploitive relationship within which all the facts were validated. Certainly there were market fluctuations, bad harvests, and the rest; but the experience of intensified exploitation was constant, whereas these other causes of hardship were variable. The latter bore upon working people, not directly, but through the refraction of a particular system of ownership and power which distributed the gains and losses with gross partiality.

These larger considerations have been, for some years, overlaid by the academic exercise (through which all students must march and counter-march) known as the "standard-of-living controversy." Did the living standards of the bulk of the people rise or fall between 1780 and 1830—or 1800 and 1850?[16] To understand the significance of the argument, we must look briefly at its development.

The debate on values is as old as the Industrial Revolution. The controversy on the standard-of-living is more recent. The ideological *muddle* is more recent still. We may start at one of the more lucid points of the controversy. Sir John Clapham, in his Preface to the first edition of his *Economic History of Modern Britain* (1926) wrote:

> The legend that everything was getting worse for the working man, down to some unspecified date between the drafting of the People's Charter and the Great Exhibition [1837 and 1851: E.P.T.], dies hard. The fact that, after the price fall of 1820–1, the purchasing–power of wages in general— not, of course, of everyone's wages—was definitely greater than it had been just before the revolutionary and Napoleonic wars, fits so ill with the tradition that it is very seldom mentioned, the work of statisticians on wages and prices being constantly ignored by social historians.

To this, J. L. Hammond offered a reply in the *Economic History Review* (1930) of two kinds: first, he criticised Clapham's statistics of agricultural earnings. These had been based on totting up the country averages, and then dividing them by the number of counties in order to reach a national average; whereas the population in the low wage-earning counties of the south was more numerous than that of the high wage-earning counties (where agricultural earnings were inflated by the proximity of industry) so that Hammond was able to show that the "national average" concealed the fact that 60% of the labouring population was in counties where wages were below the "average" figure. The second part of his reply consisted in a switch to discussions of value (happiness) in his most cloudy and unsatisfactory manner. The first part of this reply Clapham, in his Preface to his second edition (1930), accepted; the second part he met with dry caution ("a curve in words," "higher matters") but nevertheless acknowledged: "I agree most profoundly . . . that statistics of material well-being can never measure a people's happiness." Moreover, he asserted that when he had criticised the view that "everything was getting worse"—"I did not meant that everything was getting better. I only meant that recent historians have too often . . . stressed the worsenings and slurred over or ignored the betterings." The Hammonds, for their part, in a late revision of *The Bleak Age* (1947 edition), made their own peace: "statisticians tell us that . . . they are satisfied that earnings increased and that most men and women were less poor when this discontent was loud and active than they were when the eighteenth century was beginning to grow old in a silence like that of autumn. The evidence, of course, is scanty, and its interpretation not too simple, but this general view is probably more or less correct." The explanation for discontent "must be sought outside the sphere of strictly economic conditions."

So far, so good. The most fertile—but loose—social historians of the period had encountered the astringent criticism of a notable empiricist; and in the result, both sides had given ground. And, despite the heat which has subsequently been generated, the actual divergence between the hard economic conclusions of the protagonists is slight. If no serious scholar is now willing to argue that everything was getting worse, no serious scholar will argue that everything was getting better. Both Dr. Hobsbawm (a "pessimist") and Professor Ashton (an "optimist") agree that real wages declined during the Napoleonic Wars and in their immediate aftermath. Dr. Hobsbawm will not vouch for any marked general rise in the standard-of-living until the mid-1840s; whereas Professor Ashton notes a "more genial" economic climate after 1821— a "marked upward movement broken only by the slumps of 1825–6 and 1831"; and in view of increasing imports of tea, coffee, sugar, etc., "it is difficult to believe that the workers had no share in the gain." On the other hand his own tables of prices in the Oldham and Manchester districts show that "in 1831 the standard diet of the poor can hardly have cost much less than in 1791," while he offers no corresponding wage-tables. His conclusion is to suggest two main groups within the working class—"a large class raised well above the level of mere subsistence" and "masses of unskilled or poorly skilled workers—seasonally employed agricultural workers and hand-loom weavers in particular— whose incomes were almost wholly absorbed in paying for the bare necessaries of life." "My *guess* would be that the number of those who were able to share in the benefits of economic progress was larger than the number of those who were shut out from these benefits and that it was steadily growing."[17]

In fact, so far as the period 1790–1830 goes, there is very little in it. The condition of the majority was bad in 1790: it remained bad in 1830 (and forty years is a long time) but there is some disagreement as to the size of the relative groups within the working class. And matters are little clearer in the next decade. There were undoubted increases in real wages among organised workers during the burst of trade union activity between 1832–4: but the period of good trade between 1833 and 1837 was accompanied by the smashing of the trade unions by the concerted efforts of Government, magistrates, and employers; while 1837–42 are depression years. So that it is indeed at "some unspecified date between the drafting of the People's Charter and the Great Exhibition" that the tide begins to turn; let us say, with the railway boom in 1843. Moreover, even in the mid-40s the plight of very large groups of workers remains desperate, while the railway crash led to the depression years of 1847–8. This does not look very much like a "success story"; in half a century of the fullest development of industrialism, the standard-of-living, still remained—for very large but indeterminate groups—at the point of subsistence.

This is not, however, the impression given in much contemporary writing. For, just as an earlier generation of historians who were also social reformers (Thorold Rogers, Arnold Toynbee, the Hammonds) allowed their sympathy with the poor to lead on occasions to a confusion of history with ideology, so we find that the sympathies of some economic historians today for the capitalist entrepreneur have led to a confusion of history and apologetics.[18] The point of transition was marked by the publication, in 1954, of a symposium on *Capitalism and the Historians*, edited by Professor F. A. Hayek, itself the work of a group of specialists "who for some years have been meeting regularly to discuss the problems of the preservation of a free society against the totalitarian threat." Since this group of international specialists regarded "a free society" as by definition a capitalist society, the effects of such an admixture of economic theory and special pleading were deplorable; and not least in the work of one of the contributors, Professor Ashton, whose cautious findings of 1949 are now transmuted—without further evidence—into the flat statement that generally it is now agreed that for the majority the gain in real wages was substantial.[19] It is at this stage that the controversy degenerated into a muddle. And despite more recent attempts to rescue it for scholarship,[20] in many respects it is as a muddle of assertion and special pleading that the controversy remains.

The controversy falls into two parts. There is, first, the very real difficulty of constructing wage-series, price-series, and statistical indices from the abundant but patchy evidence. We shall examine some of the difficulties in interpreting such evidence when we come to the artisans. But at this point a further series of difficulties begins, since the term "standard" leads us from data amenable to statistical measurement (wages or articles of consumption) to those satisfactions which are sometimes described by statisticians as "imponderables." From food we are led to homes, from homes to health, from health to family life, and thence to leisure, work-discipline, education and play, intensity of labour, and so on. From standard-of-life we pass to way-of-life. But the two are not the same. The first is a measurement of quantities: the second a description (and sometimes an evaluation) of qualities. Where statistical evidence is appropriate to the first, we must rely largely upon "literary evidence" as to the second. A major source of confusion arises from the drawing of conclusions as to one from evidence appropriate only to the other. It is at times as if statisticians have been arguing: "the indices reveal an increased *per capita* consumption of tea, sugar, meat and soap, *therefore* the working class was happier," while social historians have replied: "the literary sources show that people were unhappy, *therefore* their standard-of-living must have deteriorated."

This is to simplify. But simple points must be made. It is quite possible for statistical averages and human experiences to run in opposite directions. A *per capita* increase in quantitative factors may take place at the same time as a great qualitative disturbance in people's way of life, traditional relationships, and sanctions. People may consume more goods and become less happy or less free at the same time. Next to the agricultural workers the largest single group of working people during the whole period of the Industrial Revolution were the domestic servants. Very many of them were household servants, living-in with the employing family, sharing cramped quarters, working excessive hours, for a few shillings' reward. Nevertheless, we may confidently list them among the more favoured groups whose standards (or consumption of food and dress) improved on average slightly during the Industrial Revolution. But the hand-loom weaver and his wife, on the edge of starvation, still regarded their status as being superior to that of a "flunkey." Or again, we might cite those trades, such as coal-mining, in which real wages advanced between 1790 and 1840, but at the cost of longer hours and a greater intensity of labour, so that the bread-winner was "worn out" before the age of forty. In statistical terms, this reveals an upward curve. To the families concerned it might feel like immiseration.

Thus it is perfectly possible to maintain two propositions which, on a casual view, appear to be contradictory. Over the period 1790–1840 there was a slight improvement in average material standards. Over the same period there was intensified exploitation, greater insecurity, and increasing human misery. By 1840 most people were "better off" than their fore-runners had been fifty years before, but they had suffered and continued to suffer this slight improvement as a catastrophic experience. In order to explore this experience, out of which the political and cultural expression of working-class consciousness arose, we shall do these things. First, we shall examine the changing life-experience of three groups of workers: the field labourers, the urban artisans, and the hand-loom weavers.[21] Second, we shall discuss some of the less "ponderable" elements in the people's standard-of-life. Third, we shall discuss the inner compulsions of the industrial way of life, and the bearing upon them of Methodism. Finally, we shall examine some of the elements in the new working-class communities.

Notes

1. *The Torrington Diaries*, ed. C. B. Andrews (1936), III, pp. 81–2.

2. P. Gaskell, *The Manufacturing Population of England* (1833), p. 6; Asa Briggs, "The Language of 'Class' in Early Nineteenth-century England," in *Essays in Labour History*, ed. Briggs and Saville (1960), p. 63.

3. W. Cooke Taylor, *Notes of a Tour in the Manufacturing Districts of Lancashire* (1842), pp. 4–6.

4. For an admirable restatement of the reasons for the primacy of the cotton industry in the Industrial Revolution, see E. J. Hobsbawm, *The Age of Revolution* (1962), Ch. 2.

5. Estimates for U.K., 1833. Total adult labour force in all textile mills, 191,671. Number of cotton hand-loom weavers, 213,000. See below, p. 66.

6. Cf. Hobsbawm, op. cit., Ch. 11.

7. There is a summary of this controversy in E. E. Lampard, *Industrial Revolution* (American Historical Association, 1957). See also Hobsbawm, op. cit., Ch. 2.

8. Cit. M. D. George, *London Life in the 18th Century* (1930) p. 210.

9. See W. W. Rostow, *British Economy in the Nineteenth Century* (1948), esp. pp. 122–5.

10. Some of the views outlined here are to be found, implicitly or explicitly, in T. S. Ashton, *Industrial Revolution* (1948) and A. Radford, *The Economic History of England* (2nd edn. 1960). A sociological variant is developed by N. J. Smelser, *Social Change in the Industrial Revolution* (1959), and a knockabout popularisation is in John Vaizey, *Success Story* (W.E.A., n.d.).

11. See E. E Lampard op. cit., p. 7.

12. *Blanck Dwarf*, 30 September 1818.

13. See S. Pollard, "Investment, Consumption, and the Industrial Revolution," *Econ. Hist. Review*, 2nd Series, XI (1958), pp. 215–26.

14. T. Bewick, *Memoir* (1961 edn.), p. 151.

15. H.O. 42.160. See also Hammonds, *The Town Labourer*, p. 303, and Oastler's evidence on the hand-loom weavers, below, pp. 54–55.

16. The futility of one part of this discussion is shown by the fact that if different datum-lines are taken, different answers may come up. 1780–1830 favours the "pessimists"; 1800–1850 favours the "optimists."

17. My italics. T. S. Ashton, "The Standard of Life of the Workers in England, 1790–1830," in *Capitalism and the Historians* (ed. F. A. Hayek), pp. 127 ff.; E. J. Hobsbawm, "The British Standard of Living, 1790–1850," *Economic History Review*, X, August 1957.

18. Lest the reader should judge the historian too harshly, we may record Sir John Clapham's explanation as to the way in which this selective principle may order the evidence. "It is very easy to do this unawares. Thirty years ago I read and marked Arthur Young's *Travels in France*, and taught from the marked passages. Five years ago I went through it again, to find that whenever Young spoke of a wretched Frenchman I had marked him, but that many of his references to happy or prosperous Frenchmen remained unmarked." One suspects that for ten or fifteen years most economic historians have been busy marking up the happy and prosperous evidence in the text.

19. T. S. Ashton, "The Treatment of Capitalism by Historians," in *Capitalism and the Historians*, p. 41. Professor Ashton's essay on "The Standard of Life of the Workers in England," reprinted in this volume, originally appeared in the *Journal of Economic History*, 1949.

20. The most constructive appraisal of the controversy is in A. J. Taylor's "Progress and Poverty in Britain, 1780–1850," *History*, February 1960.

21. These groups have been selected because their experience seems most to colour the social consciousness of the working class in the first half of the century. The miners and metal-workers do not make their influence fully felt until later in the century. The other key group—the cotton-spinners—are the subject of an admirable study in the Hammonds, *The Skilled Labourer*.

THE WEAVERS

FROM *THE MAKING OF THE ENGLISH WORKING CLASS*

The history of the weavers in the 19th century is haunted by the legend of better days. The memories are strongest in Lancashire and Yorkshire. But they obtained in most parts of Britain and in most branches of textiles. Of the Midlands stocking-weavers in the 1780s:

> When the wake came, the stocking-maker had peas and beans in his snug garden, and a good barrel of humming ale.

He had "a week-day suit of clothes and one for Sundays and plenty of leisure"[1] Of the Gloucestershire weavers:

> Their little cottages seemed happy and contented . . . it was seldom that a weaver appealed to the parish for a relief . . . Peace and content sat upon the weaver's brow.[2]

Of the linen-weaving quarter of Belfast:

> . . . a quarter once remarkable for its neatness and order; he remembered their whitewashed houses, and their little flower gardens, and the decent appearance they made with their families at markets, or at public worship. These houses were now a mass of filth and misery. . . .[3]

Dr. Dorothy George, in her lucid and persuasive *England in Transition*, has argued that the "golden age" was in general a myth. And her arguments have carried the day.

They have, perhaps, done so too easily. After all, if we set up the ninepin

---

From *The Making of the English Working Class* by E. P. Thompson (New York: Vintage Books, 1963).

of a "golden age" it is not difficult to knock it down. Certainly, the condition of the Spitalfields silk-weavers in the 18th century was not enviable. And it is true that capitalist organistion of the woollen and worsted industries of the south-west and of Norwich early gave rise to many forms of antagonism which anticipate later developments in Lancashire and Yorkshire. Certainly, also, the conditions of 18th-century weaving communities were idealised by Gaskell in his influential *Manufacturing Population of England* (1833); and by Engels when (following Gaskell) he conjured up a picture of the grandparents of the factory operatives of 1844 "leading a righteous and peaceful life in all piety and probity."

But the fact of 18th-century hardship and conflict on the one hand, and of 19th-century idealisation on the other, does not end the matter. The memories remain. And so does plentiful evidence which does not admit of easy interpretation. The existence of supplementary earnings from small farming or merely slips of garden, spinning, harvest work, etc., is attested from most parts of the country. There is architectural evidence to this day testifying to the solidity of many late 18th-century weaving hamlets in the Pennines. The commonest error today is not that of Gaskell and of Engels but that of the optimist who muddles over the difficult and painful nature of the change in status from artisan to depressed outworker in some such comforting phrases as these:

> The view that the period before the Industrial Revolution was a sort of golden age is a myth. Many of the evils of the early factory age were no worse than those of an earlier period. Domestic spinners and weavers in the eighteenth century had been "exploited" by the clothiers as ruthlessly as the factory operatives were "exploited" by the manufacturers in the 1840s.[4]

We may distinguish between four kinds of weaver-employer relationship to be found in the 18th century. (1) The customer-weaver—the Silas Marner, who lived in independent status in a village or small town, much like a master-tailor, making up orders for customers. His numbers were declining, and he need not concern us here. (2) The weaver, with the status of superior artisan, self-employed, and working by the piece for a choice of masters. (3) The journeyman weaver, working either in the shop of the master-clothier, or, more commonly, in his own home and at his own loom for a single master. (4) The farmer or smallholder weaver, working only part-time in the loom.

The last three groups all run into each other, but it is helpful if the distinctions are made. For example, in the mid 18th century, the Manchester smallware and check trades were largely conducted by weaver-artisans (group 2), with a high degree of organisation. As the cotton industry expanded in the latter half of the century, more and more small farmers (group 4) were attracted by the high wages to becoming part-time weavers. At the same time the West Riding woollen industry remained largely organised on the basis of small working-clothiers employing only a handful of journeymen and apprentices (group 3) in their own domestic unit. We may simplify the experiences of the years 1780–1830 if we say that they saw the merging of all three groups into a group, whose status was greatly debased—that of the proletarian outworker, who worked in his own home, sometimes owned and sometimes rented his loom, and who wove up the yarn to the specifications of the factor or agent of a mill or of some middleman. He lost the status and security which groups 2 and 3 might expect, and the side-earnings of group 4: he was exposed to conditions which were, in the sense of the London artisan, wholly "dishonourable."

Among the weavers of the north memories of lost status were grounded in authentic experiences and lingered longest. In the West Country by the end of the 18th century the weavers were already outworkers, employed by the great gentlemen clothier who "buys the wool, pays for the spinning, weaving, Milling, Dying, Shearing, Dressing, etc.," and who might employ as many as 1,000 workers in these processes. A Yorkshire witness in 1806 contrasted the two systems. In the West Country,

> there is no such thing as what we in Yorkshire call the domestic system; what I mean by the domestic system is the little clothiers living in villages, or in detached places, with all their comforts, carrying on business with their own capital. . . . I understand that in the west of England it is quite the reverse of that, the manufacturer there is the same as our common workman in a factory in Yorkshire, except living in a detached house; in the west the wool is delivered out to them to weave, in Yorkshire it is the man's own property.[5]

But in the Yorkshire domestic industry of the 18th century, the wool was the property, not of the weaver, but of the little master-clothier. Most weavers were journeymen, working for a single clothier, and (however much this was later idealised) in a dependent status. An "idyllic" picture of the clothier's life is to be found in a "Poem Descriptive of the Manners of the Clothiers, written about the year 1730."[6] The weavers—we do not know whether Tom, Will, Jack, Joe and Mary are journeymen, apprentices, or sons and daughters of the "Maister"—are shown eating at a common board, after keeping "time with hand and feet/From five at morn till Eight at *neet!*"

> Quoth Maister—"Lads, work hard, I pray,
> "Cloth mun be pearked next Market day.

"And Tom mun go to-morn to t'spinners,
"And Will mun seek about for t'swingers;
"And Jack, to-morn, by time be rising,
"And go to t'sizing house for sizing,
"And get you web, in warping, done
"That ye may get it into t'loom.
"Joe—go give my horse some corn
"For I design for t'Wolds to-morn;
"So mind and clean my boots and shoon,
"For I'll be up it 'morn right *soon*!
"Mary—there's wool—tak thee and dye it
"It's that 'at ligs i th' clouted sheet!"

Mistress: "So thou's setting me my wark,
"I think I'd more need mend thy sark,
"Prithie, who mun sit at' bobbin wheel?
"And ne'er a cake at top o' the' creel!
"And we to bake, and swing, to blend,
"And milk, and barns to school to send,
"And dumplins for the lads to mak,
"And yeast to seek, and 'syk as that'!
"And washing up, morn, noon and neet,
"And bowls to scald, and milk to fleet,
"And barns to fetch again at neet!"

The picture invites comparison with Cobbett's nostalgic reconstructions of the patriarchal relations between the small southern farmer and his labourers, who shared his board and his fortunes in the 18th century. It is a credible picture of a time when, in the Halifax and Leeds districts, nearly all the processes of cloth manufacture took place within a single domestic unit. By the end of the 18th century it would require some qualification. Master would no longer buy his wool in the Wolds (he might now buy his yarn direct from a spinning-mill) and the finishing processes would be undertaken in specialised shops. Nor was the market for his pieces as "free," although the last of the great yeoman Cloth Halls was built at Halifax as late as 1779, and in the 1790s a new pirate cloth hall was set up at Leeds, where interlopers, unapprenticed "shoemakers and tinkers," and self-employed weavers marketed their cloth. The small clothier was becoming increasingly dependent upon merchants, factors, or mills. He might, if successful, be a small capitalist, employing fifteen or twenty weavers, many of whom worked in their own homes. If unsuccessful, he might find himself being squeezed out of his independence; his profit being lost in a simple payment for the work undertaken, in working yarn into cloth to the specifications of a middleman. In spells of bad trade he might become indebted to the merchant. He was on his way to becoming a mere hand-loom weaver; and, as competition became more intense, so the Mistress's domestic economy was lost in the demands of the trade.

These processes were slow and at first they were not exceptionally painful. Hundreds of yeomen clothiers were among those who rode to York to vote for Wilberforce in 1807. The intricate sub-divisions of the industry enabled some small masters to cling on for fifty more years, while others founded small finishing and cropping shops. Moreover, the great increase in the output of yarn laid a special premium on the weaver's labour; between 1780 and 1820 the clothier's loss of independence and of status was to some degree disguised by the abundance of work. And if Master's status was, in some cases, falling to that of his journeymen, that of Tom, Will, Jack, and Joe appeared to be rising. As the mills and the factors were searching for weavers, so the journeyman gained some independence of the master-clothier. He might now pick and choose his masters. This was, in wool as in cotton, the "golden age" of the journeyman weaver.

In the earlier 18th century the relationships described in the poem are idyllic only in a patriarchal sense. On the debit side, the journeyman had little more independence of his master than the yearly hand on the farm. The parish apprentice, if placed with a bad master, was for years in a position of near-servitude. On the credit side, the journeyman considered himself to be a "clothier" rather than a mere weaver; his work was varied, much of it in the loom, but some of it out and about; he had some hope of obtaining credit to buy wool and of becoming a small master on his own account. If he worked in his own home, rather than in the master's workshop, he was subject to no work-discipline except that of his own making. Relations between small masters and their men were personal and sometimes close: they observed the same customs and owned allegiance to the same community values:

> The "little makers" ... were men who doffed their caps to no one, and recognized no right in either squire or parson to question, or meddle with them. . . . Their brusqueness and plain speaking might at times be offensive. . . . If the little maker . . . rose in the world high enough to employ a few of his neighbours, he did not therefore cease to labour with his own hands, but worked as hard or perhaps harder than anyone he employed. In speech and in dress he claimed no superiority.[7]

The master-clothier was the peasant, or small *kulak*, of the Industrial Revolution; and it is to him that the Yorkshire reputation for bluntness and independence may be traced.

In the cotton industry the story is different. Here the average unit of production was larger, and relationships similar to those in Norwich and the west
of England may be found from the late 18th century. By the 1750s Manchester
small-ware and check-weavers had strongly organised trade societies. Already
they were seeking to maintain their status, by resisting the influx of unapprenticed labour. "Illegal" men began "to multiply so fast as to be one in the Gate
of another." During the summer (the weavers complained) these men "betook
themselves to Out-work, such as Day labouring," and in the autumn:

> would again return to the Loom, and would be content to work upon any
> Terms, or submit to do any Kind of servile Work, rather than starve in
> the Winter; and what they thus submitted to, soon became a general
> Rule. . . .[8]

When the Oldham check-weavers sought, in 1759, to secure legal enforcement of apprenticeship restrictions, the Assize Judge delivered a hostile judgement in which the laws of the land were set aside in favour of the
as-yet-unstated doctrines of Adam Smith. If apprenticeship were to be enforced,
"that Liberty of setting up Trades (the Foundation of the present flourishing
Condition of Manchester) [would be] destroyed":

> In the Infancy of Trade, the Acts of Queen Elizabeth might be well
> calculated for the publick Weal; but now, when it is grown to that Per-
> fection we see it, it might perhaps be of Utility to have those Laws re-
> pealed, as tending to cramp and tye down that Knowledge it was at first
> necessary to obtain by Rule. . . .

As for combinations, "if Inferiors are to prescribe to their Superiors, if the Foot
aspire to be the Head . . . to what End are Laws enacted?" It was the "indispensable Duty of every one, as a Friend to the Community, to endeavour to
suppress them in their Beginnings."[9]

This remarkable judgement anticipated the actual repeal of the Statute of
Artificers by more than half a century. Although their organisations were by
no means extinguished, the weavers were left without any shadow of legal
protection when the vast increase in the output of yarn from the early cotton-
mills led to the amazing expansion of weaving throughout south-east Lancashire.
William Radcliffe's account of these years in the Pennine uplands is well known:

> . . . the old loom-shops being insufficient, every lumber-room, even old
> barns, cart-houses and outbuildings of any description were repaired, win-
> dows broke through the blank walls, and all were fitted up for loom-shops.

> This source of making room being at length exhausted, new weavers
> cottages with loom-shops rose up in every direction. . . .[10]

It was the loom, and not the cotton-mill, which attracted immigrants in their
thousands. From the 1770s onwards the great settlement of the uplands—Middleton, Oldham, Mottram, Rochdale—commenced. Bolton leapt from 5,339 inhabitants in 1773 to 11,739 in 1789: at the commencement of the Wars—

> notwithstanding the great numbers who have enlisted, houses for the
> working class are not procured without difficulty; and last summer many
> houses were built in the skirts of the town, which are now occupied.[11]

Small farmers turned weaver, and agricultural labourers and immigrant artisans entered the trade. It was the fifteen years between 1788 and 1803 which
Radcliffe described as "the golden age of this great trade" for the weaving
communities:

> Their dwellings and small gardens clean and neat,—all the family well
> clad—the men with each a watch in his pocket, and the women dressed
> to their own fancy,—the church crowded to excess every Sunday,—every
> house well furnished with a clock in elegant mahogany or fancy case,—
> handsome tea services in Staffordshire ware . . . Birmingham, Potteries,
> and Sheffield wares for necessary use and ornament . . . many cottage fam-
> ilies had their cow. . . .[12]

Experience and myth are here intermingled, as they are in Gaskell's account of
weaving families earning 4 pounds per week at the turn of the century, and in
Bamford's description of his own *Early Days* in Middleton. We know from an
Oldham diarist that the prosperity did not extend to fustians, the coarsest branch
of the trade.[13] In fact, probably only a minority of weavers attained Radcliffe's
standard; but many aspired towards it. In these fifteen or twenty years of
moderate prosperity a distinct cultural pattern emerges in the weaving communities: a rhythm of work and leisure: a Wesleyanism in some villages softer
and more humanised than it was to be in the first decades of the 19th century
(Bamford's Sunday school taught him to write as well as to read), with class
leaders and local preachers among the weavers: a stirring of political Radicalism,
and a deep attachment to the values of independence.

But the prosperity induced by the soaring output of machine yarn disguised
a more essential loss of status. It is in the "golden age" that the artisan, or
journeyman weaver, becomes merged in the generic "hand-loom weaver." Except in a few specialised branches, the older artisans (their apprenticeship walls

being totally breached) were placed on a par with the new immigrants; while many of the farming-weavers abandoned their smallholdings to concentrate upon the loom. Reduced to complete dependence upon the spinning-mill or the "putters-out" who took yarn into the uplands, the weavers were now exposed to round after round of wage reductions.

Wage cutting had long been sanctioned not only by the employer's greed but by the widely-diffused theory that poverty was an essential goad to industry. The author of the *Memoirs of Wool* had probably the industry of the west of England in mind when he wrote:

> It is a fact well known . . . that scarcity, to a certain degree, promotes industry, and that the manufacturer who can subsist on three days work will be idle and drunken the remainder of the week. . . . The poor in the manufacturing counties will never work any more time in general than is necessary just to live and support their weekly debauches. . . . We can fairly aver that a reduction of wages in the woollen manufacture would be a national blessing and advantage, and no real injury to the poor. By this means we might keep our trade, uphold our rents, and reform the people into the bargain.[14]

But the theory is found, almost universally, among employers, as well as among many magistrates and clergy, in the cotton districts as well.[15] The prosperity of the weavers aroused feelings of active alarm in the minds of some masters and magistrates. "Some years ago," wrote one magistrate in 1818, the weavers were "so extravagantly paid that by working three or four days in the week they could maintain themselves in a comparative state of luxury." They "spent a great portion of their time and money in alehouses, and at home had their tea-tables twice a day provided with a rum bottle and the finest wheaten bread and butter."[16]

Reductions, during the Napoleonic Wars, were sometimes forced by the large employers, sometimes by the least scrupulous employers, sometimes by little masters of self-employed weavers working for "commission houses." When markets were sluggish, manufacturers took advantage of the situation by putting out work to weavers desperate for employment at any price, thereby compelling them "to manufacture great quantities of goods at a time, when they are absolutely not wanted."[17] With the return of demand, the goods were then released on the market at cut price; so that each minor recession was succeeded by a period in which the market was glutted with cheap goods, thereby holding wages down to their recession level. The practices of some employers were unscrupulous to a degree, both in the exaction of fines for faulty work and in giving false weight in yarn. Yet at the same time as wages were screwed lower and lower, the number of weavers continued to increase over the first three decades of the 19th century; for weaving, next to general labouring, was the grand resource of the northern unemployed. Fustian weaving was heavy, monotonous, but easily learned. Agricultural workers, demobilised soldiers, Irish immigrants—all continued to swell the labour force.

The first severe general reductions took place at the turn of the century: there was an improvement in the last year or two of the Wars, followed by further reductions after 1815 and an uninterrupted decline thereafter. The weavers' first demand, from 1790 onwards, was for a legal minimum wage—a demand supported by some employers, as a means of enforcing fair conditions of competition upon their less scrupulous rivals. The rejection of this demand by the House of Commons in May 1808, was followed by a strike, when 10,000 to 15,000 weavers demonstrated on successive days in St. George's Fields, Manchester. The demonstration was dispersed by the magistrates with bloodshed, and the full vindictiveness of the authorities was revealed by the State prosecution and imprisonment of a prominent manufacturer, Colonel Joseph Hanson of the Volunteers, who had supported the minimum wage bill, for the crime of riding among the weavers and uttering "malicious and inflammatory words":

> Stick to your cause and you will certainly succeed. Neither Nadin nor any of his faction shall put you off the field to-day. Gentlemen, you cannot live by your labour. . . . My father was a weaver; I myself was taught the weaving trade; I am a weaver's real friend.

The weavers subsequently presented to Colonel Hanson a tribute, in the form of a silver cup, to which 39,600 persons contributed. "The effects of this ill-advised prosecution," commented the Manchester historian, Archibald Prentice, "were long and injuriously felt. It introduced that bitter feeling of employed against employers which was manifested in 1812, 1817, 1819, and 1826. . . ."[18]

The dates which Prentice singled out are those of the destruction of power-looms (1812, 1826), of the March of the Blanketeers (1817) and Peterloo (1819). With no hope of legal protection the weavers turned more directly towards the channels of political Radicalism. But for some years after 1800 an alliance between Methodism and "Church and King" rowdyism kept most of the weavers as political "loyalists." It was claimed that 20,000 of them joined the Volunteers early in the Wars, and that there was a time when a man would be knocked down if he criticised the monarchy or the Pension List: "I have two or three individuals in my eye," declared a Bolton witness before the Select Committee on Hand-loom weavers in 1834, "who were in serious danger for being reformers of the old school." It was after the Wars that the real Radical tide set in; and in 1818 a second critical confrontation between the weavers and their employers took place. It was the year of the great Manchester cotton-spinners strike, and of the first impressive attempt at general unionism (the "Philan-thropic Hercules"). Once again the weavers struck, collecting the shuttles and locking them in chapels or workshops, not only in Manchester but throughout the weaving towns—Bolton, Bury, Burnley. The strike ended in short-lived concessions on the masters' side, and in the prosecution and imprisonment of several of the weavers' leaders.[19] It was the last effective general strike move-ment of the Lancashire weavers: thereafter wages in most branches continued to be beaten down—9s., 6s., 4s. 6d. and even less per week for irregular work—until the 1830s.

It is an over-simplification to ascribe the cause of the debasement of the weavers' conditions to the power-loom.[20] The status of the weavers had been shattered by 1813, at a time when the total number of power-looms in the U.K. was estimated at 2,400, and when the competition of power with hand was largely psychological. The estimate of power-looms rises to 14,000 in 1820, but even then it was slow and clumsy and had not yet been adapted to the Jacquard principle, so that it was incapable of weaving difficult figured patterns. It can be argued that the very cheapness and superfluity of hand-loom labour *retarded* mechanical invention and the application of capital in weaving. The degradation of the weavers is very similar to that of the workers in the dishonourable artisan trades. Each time their wages were beaten down, their position became more defenceless. The weaver had now to work longer into the night to earn less; in working longer he increased another's chances of unemployment. Even ad-herents of the new "political economy" were appalled. "Did Dr. A. Smith ever contemplate such a state of things?" exclaimed one humane employer, whose honourable practices were the cause of his own ruin:

> It is vain to read his book to find a remedy for a complaint which he could not conceive existed, vis. 100,000 weavers doing the work of 150,000 when there was no demand (as 'tis said) and that for half meat, and the rest paid by Poor Rates, could he conceive that the profits of a Manufacture should be what one Master could wring from the hard earnings of the poor, more than another?[21]

"100,000 weavers doing the work of 150,000"—this is the essence of the dishonourable trades, as later seen by Mayhew in London: a pool of surplus labour, semi-employed, defenceless, and undercutting each other's wages. The very circumstances of the weaver's work, especially in the upland hamlets, gave an additional impediment to trade unionism. A Salford weaver explained these conditions to the Select Committee of 1834:

The very peculiar circumstances in which the hand-loom weavers are situated, preclude the possibility of their having the slightest control over
the value of their own labour. . . . The fact that the weavers of even one
employer may be scattered over an extensive district presents a constant
opportunity to that employer, if he be so minded, to make his weavers
the means of reducing the wages of one another alternatively; to some he
will tell that others are weaving for so much less, and that they must have
no more, or go without work, and this in turn he tells the rest. . . . Now
the difficulty, and loss of time it would occasion the weavers to discover
the truth or falsehood of this statement, the fear that, in the interval, others
would step in and deprive them of the work so offered . . . the jealousy
and resentment enkindled in the minds of all, tending to divide them in
sentiment and feeling, all conspire to make the reduction certain to be
effected. . . .

The decline of the Yorkshire woollen and worsted weavers followed a parallel course, although it often lagged fifteen or more years behind the changes
in cotton. Evidence before the Committee on the Woollen Trade of 1806
showed the domestic system still commanding the woollen industry. But the
"little makers" were on the decrease: 'many which were masters' houses are
now workmen's houses"; while at the same time merchant manufacturers were
bringing a number of hand-looms, as well as the finishing processes, under one
roof in unpowered "factories." ("A factory," said one witness, "is where they
employ perhaps 200 hands in one and the same building.") The factories—
notably those of Benjamin Gott in Leeds—aroused bitter dislike among both
small masters and journeymen, because they were creaming the best customers,
and in the finishing processes—where the cloth-dressers or croppers were highly
organised—they were taking "illegal" men. Wealth, declared one witness, "has
gone more into lumps." The journeymen complained that the factories put out
more work to out-weavers in brisk times, and dismissed them without com-
punction in slack, whereas the small master-clothiers still sought to find employment for their own journeymen. Moreover, even before the use of power,
the hand-loom "factories" offended deep-rooted moral prejudices. A trade
union—the Clothier's Community or "the Institution"—existed among the
croppers and weavers, its avowed purpose being to join with the small clothiers
in petitioning for a restriction upon the factories and for an enforcement of
apprenticeship.

Neither the "little makers" nor the journeymen received any satisfaction from
the House of Commons: their petitions served only to draw attention to their
combination, and to the old paternalist statutes which were soon afterwards
repealed. In the Leeds and Spen Valley clothing districts the small clothiers

were tenacious, and their decline was protracted over a further fifty years. It was in the worsted districts of Bradford and Halifax, and in the fancy woollen district to the south of Huddersfield that the putting-out system was most fully developed by the 1820s; and, just as in cotton, the weavers were the victims of wage-cutting, and of "slaughter-house men" who warehoused stocks of cut-price goods.

Just as the croppers were the artisan elite of the woollen industry, so the woolcombers were the elite workers in worsted. Controlling a bottle-neck in the manufacturing process, they were in a position to uphold their status so long as they could limit entry to their trade. And this they had done with some success, owing to their exceptional trade union organisation which reached back at least to the 1740s. In the early 19th century, despite the Combination Acts, they had effective national organisation, an imposing Constitution, with all the paraphernalia of an underground union, and the reputation for insubordination and lax time-keeping:

> They come on a Monday morning, and having lighted the fire in the comb-pot, will frequently go away, and perhaps return no more till Wednesday, or even Thursday. . . . A spare bench is always provided in the shop, upon which people on the *tramp* may rest. . . .[22]

In Bradford, in February 1825, the festival in honour of Bishop Blaize, the woolcomber's saint, was celebrated on a magnificent scale. In June as if to punctuate the transition to the new industrialism, there commenced the bitterest strike of Bradford's history, in which 20,000 woolcombers and weavers were involved, and which lasted for twenty-three weeks, ending in total defeat for the strikers.[23] The Combination Acts had been repealed in the previous year. Commencing in demands for wage advances and rationalisation, the strike turned into a struggle for union recognition, the employers going so far as to dismiss all children from the spinning-mills whose parents refused to sign a document renouncing the union. The contest was seen to be crucial throughout the country, and up to £20,000 was contributed in support of strike funds. After defeat, the woolcomber was translated almost overnight from a privileged artisan to a defenceless outworker. Apprenticeship restrictions had already broken down, and in the years before 1825 thousands had been attracted by high wages into the trade. While some combers worked in large workshops, it had been customary for others to club together in threes and fours, sharing an independent shop. Now they were supplemented by hundreds of newcomers whose unhealthy trade was carried on in their own homes. Although combing machinery was in existence by 1825 it was of doubtful service in fine combing;

and the cheapness of combers' labour enabled the threat of machinery to be kept above their heads for a further twenty years. Throughout this time the combers remained noted for their independence and their "democratic" politics. The union estimated that 7,000 or 8,000 were employed in the Bradford trade in 1825; twenty years later there were still 10,000 handcombers in the district. Many came, in the 1820s, from agricultural districts:

> They came from Kendal, North Yorkshire, Leicester, Devonshire, and even from the Emerald Isle; so that to spend an hour in a public-house (the comber's calling was a thirsty one) one might have heard a perfect Babel of different dialects. . . . His attachment to rural life was evidenced by the fact that in hay-time and harvest he used to lay aside his wool-combs, take up his scythe . . . and go to his own country a harvesting. . . . He was a bird fancier too, and his comb-shop was often transformed into a perfect aviary. . . . Some combers had a talent for elocution, and could recite with wonderful power. . . . Others again were so clever at dramatic personation that they even went the length of forming themselves into companies. . . .

—so runs one Bradford account.[24] An account from Cleckheaton is in more sombre terms:

> Perhaps a more wretched class of workmen never existed than the old woolcombers. The work was all done in their own houses, the best part of their cottages being taken up with it. The whole family, of sometimes six or eight, both male and female, worked together round a "combpot" heated by charcoal, the fumes of which had a very deleterious effect upon their health. When we add that the workshop was also perforce the bed-room, it will not be wondered at that woolcombers were almost invariably haggard looking . . . many of them not living half their days. . . .

Their wives also had "often to stand at the 'pad-posts' and work from six o'clock in the morning till ten at night like their husbands."

> Another peculiarity about these woolcombers was that they were almost without exception rabid politicians. . . . The Chartist movement had no more enthusiastic adherents than these men; the "Northern Star" was their one book of study.[25]

Perhaps no group was thrown so precipitately as the woolcombers from "honourable" into "dishonourable" conditions. The worsted- and woollen-weavers had not known so privileged a status as the 18th-century combers; and at first they resisted less stubbornly as their wages declined. As late as 1830, the largest employer of hand-loom weavers in Bradford wrote:

> The weavers are of all classes we have to do with the most orderly and steady, never at any period, that I know of, constraining an advance of wages, but submitting to every privation and suffering with almost un-exampled patience and forbearance.[26]

Two years later, Cobbett rode through the Halifax district, and reported that:

> It is truly lamentable to behold so many thousands of men who formerly earned 20 to 30 shillings per week, new compelled to live upon 5s, 4s, or even less. . . . It is the more sorrowful to behold these men in their state, as they still retain the frank and bold character formed in the days of their independence.[27]

The depression in the Huddersfield "fancy" trade had continued without intermission since 1825. In 1826, 3,500 families were on the list of paupers in Delph in the Saddleworth district, and there was some extension of the "in-dustrial Speenhamland" system (already in operation in some Lancashire cotton districts) whereby weavers were relieved out of the poor-rates while still in work, thereby further reducing their wages. (For two days a week road-work in Saddleworth the weavers received 12 lb. of oatmeal per day.) In Huddersfield a committee of the masters established, in 1829, that there were over 13,000 out of a population of 29,000 who—when the wage was divided between all mem-bers of the family—subsisted on 2d. per day per head. But it was a curious "depression," in which the actual output of woollen cloth exceeded that in any previous period. The conditions of the weavers were bluntly attributed to "the abominable system of reducing wages."[28]

Once again the decline preceded serious competition with the power-loom. Power was not introduced into worsted-weaving on any scale until the late 1820s; into "fancy" woollens until the late 1830s (and then only partially); while the power-loom was not effectively adapted to carpet-weaving until 1851. Even where direct power competition existed, the speed of weaving only slowly rose to that by which the hand-loom's output was trebled or quadrupled.[29] But there was undoubtedly a chain reaction, as weavers forced out of plain cottons and fustians turned to fine work or silk or worsted and thence to "fancy" woollen or carpets.[30] Power, indeed, continued in many branches of textiles as an aux-iliary to hand-loom weaving, for ten, fifteen, or twenty years. "In Halifax," one witness informed the Select Committee (somewhat illogically):

there are two very extensive manufacturers, two brothers[Messrs Akroyd];
the one weaves by power-looms and the other by hand-looms. . . . They
have to sell their goods against each other, therefore they must bring their
wages as near in point of comparison as possible . . . to obtain a profit.[31]

Here the power-loom might appear as a lever to reduce the hand-loom
weaver's wages and vice versa. From another aspect, the manufacturer was well
satisfied with an arrangement by which he could base his steady trade upon his
power-loom sheds and in times of brisk trade give out more work to the hand
workers who themselves bore the costs of fixed charges for rent, loom, etc. "In
the event of a decreased demand," reported the Assistant Commissioner enquiring into the West Riding in 1839,

> the manufacturer who employs power, as well as hand-looms, will, of
> course, work his fixed capital as long as possible. Hence the services of
> the hand-loom weaver are first dispensed with.

The conditions of most weavers, from the 1820s (and earlier in cotton) to
the 1840s and beyond, are commonly referred to as "indescribable" or as "well
known." They deserve, however, to be described and to be better known. There
were selected groups of weavers who maintained their artisan-status, owing to
some special skill, until the 1830s; the Leeds stuff weavers were better situated
than most, while the Norwich worsted weavers, whose Jacobin and trade union
traditions were exceptionally strong, succeeded in keeping up wages in the 1830s
by a combination of picketing, intimidation of masters and "illegal" men, municipal politics, and violent opposition to machinery—all of which contributed
to the supersession of the Norwich by the West Riding industry.[32] But the great
majority of the weavers were living on the edge—and sometimes beyond the
edge—of the borders of starvation. The Select Committee on Emigration (1827)
was given evidence of conditions in some districts of Lancashire which read
like an anticipation of the Irish potato famine:

> Mrs. Hulton and myself, in visiting the poor, were asked by a person
> almost starving to go into a house. We there found on one side of the
> fire a very old man, apparently dying, on the other side a young man
> about eighteen with a child on his knee, whose mother had just died and
> been buried. We were going away from that house, when the woman said,
> "Sir, you have not seen all." We went up stairs, and, under some rags,
> we found another young man, the widower; and on turning down the
> rags, which he was unable to remove himself, we found another young

man who was dying, and who did die in the course of the day. I have no
doubt that the family were actually starving at the time. . . .

The evidence came from West Houghton, where half of the 5,000 inhabitants
were "totally destitute of bedding, and nearly so of clothes." Six were described
as being in the actual process of starvation.

It is true that the low wages quoted in these years (from 10s. to 4s.) might
represent only one of several wages in the same family, since many wives, girls,
and youths worked at a second or third loom. But the wages also concealed
further outpayments or deductions. The Bradford worsted weavers in 1835
claimed that from an average wage of 10s. there would be an outlay of 4d. for
sizing, 3d. for looming, 9½d. for winding the weft, 3½d. for light, while 4d.
more should be added for outlay and wear and tear on the loom. If the outlay
for rent (1s. 9d.) and fire and washing (1s. 6d.) were added, this totalled deductions amounting to 5s. 3d., although where the wife or son also worked on
a second loom some of these overheads could be spread over two wages.[33] In
some cases the loom itself was hired by the weaver, in other cases he owned
the loom, but had to hire the gearing or slays for pattern-weaving from the
employer. Many weavers were in a perpetual state of indebtedness to the
"putter-out," working off their debts by instalments upon their work, and in a
condition where they were incapable of refusing any wages however low.

As their conditions worsened, so they had to spend more and more time in
unpaid employments--fetching and carrying work, and a dozen other processes.
"I can remember the time," wrote one observer in 1844,

> when manufacturers hired rooms in districts, and the warps and wefts were
> conveyed to them, by horse and cart, for convenience of the weavers, and
> the employer inquired after the employed; but the case is now diametrically
> opposite, the labourer not only undertakes long journeys in quest of work,
> but is doomed to many disappointments.[34]

An even more graphic description of all this ancillary unpaid work comes
from Pudsey:

> It was quite common when trade was not bad to see weavers and spinners
> going from place to place seeking work. . . . If they succeeded it was
> mostly on the condition that they helped to break the wool for it; that is,
> opened the bales, then the fleeces, taking off the coarse parts called the
> *britch*, put it in sheets, then go to the mill and help to scour it, then "lit"
> or dye it. . . . All this was for *nothing*, except in some cases a small allow-
> ance for a little ale or cheese and bread. . . . When the slubber had doffed

the first set of slubbing, it often became a serious question as to whose turn it was to have it, and casting lots would frequently be the mode of deciding it. . . . When the web was warped there was the sizing process to go through, and the weavers, as a rule, had to buy their own size. . . . After sizing the web, one of the most critical of all the processes is to put it out of doors to dry. . . . A place is chosen, the web-sticks or stretchers are put out, and if frosty, a pick-axe is used to make holes in the ground for posts to hold the ends of the web. . . . Sometimes might be seen a man and his wife up to their knees in snow going out with a web to dry. . . .

After this, the weaving, late into the evening by candle or oil light, with "a boy or girl or perhaps a weaver's wife, standing on one side of the loom watching to see when a thread broke down, whilst the weaver watched the other side, because if a thread broke, and another 'shoit' was picked, a dozen more might be broken." And after the weaving, there were half a dozen odd jobs to do again, before the piece was taken off by the carrier to Leeds:

All this odd jobbing, we say, was done for nothing. . . . It was no uncommon thing, too, when the work was done for the weavers to be unable to get paid for some time after. . . . We cannot wonder that a hand-loom weaver came to be called a "poverty knocker."[35]

Some of these practices did not obtain in cotton, or had long been devolved to specialist processes in worsted. They indicate the obsolescence of the small-scale woollen trade. But in the worsted and fancy woollen weaving districts there were equally time-wasting forms of jobbing. Among the scattered upland hamlets the "human packhorse" was known—the man or woman who hired his or her labour to carry the heavy finished pieces five or even ten miles over the moorland roads. It was in the weaving districts surrounding such centres as Bradford, Keighley, Halifax, Huddersfield, Todmorden, Rochdale, Bolton, Macclesfield, that the largest populations of utterly depressed outworkers were to be found. The Select Committee of 1834 reported that it found "the sufferings of that large and valuable body of men, not only not exaggerated, but that they have for years continued to an extent and intensity scarcely to be credited or conceived." John Fielden, giving evidence to the same Committee in 1835, declared that a very great number of the weavers could not obtain sufficient food of the plainest or cheapest kind; were clothed in rags and ashamed to send their children to Sunday school; had no furniture and in some cases slept on straw; worked "not unfrequently sixteen hours a day"; were demoralised by cheap spirits, and weakened by undernourishment and ill-health. Possessions gained in the "golden age" had passed out of the weaving households. A Bolton witness declared:

> Since I can recollect, almost every weaver that I knew had a chest of drawers in his house, and a clock and chairs, and bedsteads and candle-sticks, and even pictures, articles of luxury; and now I find that those have disappeared; they have either gone into the houses of mechanics, or into houses of persons of higher class.

The same witness, a manufacturer, could not "recollect an instance but one, where any weaver of mine has bought a new jacket for many years." A coarse coverlid, of the value of 2s. 6d. when new, often did service for blankets: "I have seen many houses with only two or three-legged stools, and some I have seen without a stool or chair, with only a tea chest to put their clothes in, and to sit upon."

There is unanimity as to the diet of the poor weaver and his family: oatmeal, oatcake, potatoes, onion porridge, blue milk, treacle or home-brewed ale, and as luxuries tea, coffee, bacon. "They do not know what it is, many of them," declared Richard Oastler, "to taste flesh meat from year's end to year's end . . . and their children will sometimes run to Huddersfield, and beg, and bring a piece in, and it is quite a luxury. . . ." If confirmation was needed, it was brought by the careful investigations of the Assistant Commissioners who toured the country after the appointment of the Royal Commission in 1838. The very worst conditions, perhaps, were those found in the cellar dwellings of the big towns—Leeds and Manchester—where Irish unemployed attempted to earn a few shillings by the loom.

But it is easy to assume that the country weavers in the solid, stonebuilt cottages, with the long mullioned windows of the loom-shops, in the beautiful Pennine uplands—in the upper Calder Valley or upper Wharfedale, Saddle-worth or Clitheroe—enjoyed amenities which compensated for their poverty. A surgeon who investigated a typhus epidemic in a hamlet near Heptonstall (a thriving little woollen township during the Civil War) has left a terrible picture of the death of one such community. Situated high on the moors, nevertheless the water-supplies were polluted: one open stream, polluted by a slaughter-house, was in summer "a nursery of loathsome animal life." The sewer passed directly under the flags of one of the weaver's cottages. The houses were wet and cold, the ground floors beneath the surface of the earth: "It may be fairly said oatmeal and potatoes are well nigh what they contrive to exist upon," with old milk and treacle. If tea or coffee could not be afforded, an infusion of mint, tansy or hyssop was prepared. Even of this diet "they have by no means sufficient. . . . The inhabitants are undergoing a rapid deterioration." Medical attendance and funeral expenses were generally paid from the poor-rates; only one in ten received any medical aid in childbirth:

> What is the situation of the wife of the hand-loom weaver during the parturient efforts? She is upon her feet, with a woman on each side; her arms are placed round their necks; and, in nature's agony, she almost drags her supporters to the floor; and in this state the birth takes place. . . . And why is this the case? The answer is, because there is no change of bedclothing. . . .

"How they contrive to exist at all," exclaimed this humane surgeon, "confounds the very faculties of eyes and ears."[36]

The contemporary reaction against "the Hammonds" has gone so far that it is almost impossible to quote such sources, with which these years are all too plentiful, without being accused of pejorative intentions. But it is necessary to do so because, without such detail, it is possible for the eye to pass over the phrase "the decline of the handloom-weavers" without any realisation of the scale of the tragedy that was enacted. Weaving communities—some in the West Country and the Pennines, with 300 and 400 years of continuous existence, some of much more recent date but with, none the less, their own cultural patterns and traditions—were literally being extinguished. The demographic pattern of Heptonstall-Slack was extraordinary: in a population of 348, over one-half were under twenty (147 under fifteen), while only 30 were over fifty-five; this did not represent a growing community, but a low expectation of life. In the catastrophic years of the 1830s and 1840s, when the power-loom, the Irish influx, and the new Poor Law finished off what wage-cutting had begun, there were—alongside the insurrectionary hopes of Chartist weavers—the more gruesome stories: the children's burial clubs (where each Sunday-school pupil contributed 1d. per week towards his own or a fellow-pupil's funeral); the dissemination and serious discussion of a pamphlet (by "Marcus") advocating infanticide. But this is not the whole story. Until these final agonies, the older weaving communities offered a way of life which their members greatly preferred to the higher material standards of the factory town. The son of a weaver from the Heptonstall district, who was a child in the 1820s, recalled that the weavers "had their good times." "The atmosphere was not fouled by . . . the smoke of the factory."

> There was no bell to ring them up at four or five o'clock . . . there was freedom to start and to stay away as they cared. . . . In the evenings, while still at work, at anniversary times of the Sunday schools, the young men

and women would most heartily join in the hymn singing, while the musical rhythm of the shuttles would keep time. . . .

Some weavers had fruit, vegetables, and flowers from their gardens. "My work was at the loom side, and when not winding my father taught me reading, writing, and arithmetic." A Keighley factory child, who left the mill for a handloom at the age of eighteen, informed Sadler's Committee (1832) that he preferred the loom to the mill "a great deal": "I have more relaxation; I can look about me, and go out and refresh myself a little." It was the custom in Bradford for the weavers to gather in their dinner break at noon:

> . . . and have a chat with other weavers and combers on the news or gossip of the time. Some of these parties would spend an hour talking about pig-feeding, hen-raising, and bird-catching, and now and then would have very hot disputes about free grace, or whether infant baptism or adult immersion was the correct and scriptural mode of doing the thing. I have many a time seen a number of men ready to fight one another on this . . . topic.[37]

A unique blend of social conservatism, local pride, and cultural attainment made up the way of life of the Yorkshire or Lancashire weaving community. In one sense these communities were certainly "backward"—they clung with equal tenacity to their dialect traditions and regional customs and to gross medical ignorance and superstitions. But the closer we look at their way of life, the more inadequate simple notions of economic progress and "backwardness" appear. Moreover, there was certainly a leaven amongst the northern weavers of self-educated and articulate men of considerable attainments. Every weaving district had its weaver-poets, biologists, mathematicians, musicians, geologists, botanists: the old weaver in *Mary Barton* is certainly drawn from the life. There are northern museums and natural history societies which still possess records or collections of lepidoptera built up by weavers; while there are accounts of weavers in isolated villages who taught themselves geometry by chalking on their flagstones, and who were eager to discuss the differential calculus.[38] In some kinds of plain work with strong yarn a book could actually be propped on the loom and read at work.

There is also a weaver's poetry, some traditional, some more sophisticated. The Lancashire "Jone o' Grinfilt" ballads went through a patriotic cycle at the start of the Wars (with Jacobin counter-ballads) and continued through Chartist times to the Crimean War. The most moving is "Jone o' Grinfilt Junior," sung at the close of the Wars:

Aw'm a poor cotton-wayver, as mony a one knaws,
Aw've nowt t'ate i' th' heawse, um' aw've worn eawt my cloas,
Yo'd hardly gie sixpence fur o' aw've got on,
Meh clogs ur' booath baws'n, un' stockins aw've none;
 Yo'd think it wur hard, to be sent into th' ward
 To clem un' do best 'ot yo' con.

Eawr parish-church pa'son's kept tellin' us lung,
We'st see better toimes, if aw'd but howd my tung;
Aw've howden my tung, toll aw con hardly draw breoth,
Aw think i' my heart he meons t'clem me to deoth;
 Aw knaw he lives weel, wi' backbitin' the de'il,
 Bur he never pick'd o'er in his loife.

Wey tooart on six weeks, thinkin' aich day wur th' last,
Wey tarried un' shifted, till neaw wey're quite fast;
Wey liv't upo' nettles, whoile nettles were good,
Un' Wayterloo porritch wur' the best o' us food;
 Aw'm tellin' yo' true, aw con foind foak enoo,
 Thot're livin' no better nur me . . .

The bailiffs break in, and take their furniture after a fight.

 Aw said to eawr Marget, as wey lien upo' th' floor,
 "Wey ne'er shall be lower i' this wo'ald, aw'm sure . . ."

When he takes his piece back to his master, Jone is told that he is in debt for
over-payment on his last piece. He comes out of the warehouse in despair, and
returns to his wife.

Eawr Marget declares, if hoo'd clooas to put on,
Hoo'd go up to Lunnon to see the great mon;
Un' if things didno' awter, when theere hoo had been,
Hoo says hoo'd begin, un' feight blood up to th' e'en,
 Hoo's nout agen th' king, bur hoo loikes a fair thing,
 Un' hoo says hoo con tell when hoo's hurt.[39]

 The other kind of weaver-poet was the auto-didact. A remarkable example
was Samuel Law, a Todmorden weaver, who published a poem in 1772 mod-
elled on Thomson's *Seasons*. The poem has few literary merits, but reveals a
knowledge of Virgil, Ovid, and Homer (in the original), of biology and as-
tronomy:

Yes, the day long, and in each evening gloom,
I meditated in the sounding loom. . . .
Meanwhile, I wove the flow'ry waved web,
With fingers colder than the icy glebe;
And oftentimes, thro' the whole frame of man,
Bleak chilling horrors, and a sickness ran.[40]

Later weaver-poets often convey little more than pathos, the self-conscious efforts to emulate alien literary forms (notable "nature poetry") which catch little of the weaver's authentic experience. A handloom weaver from 1820 to 1850, who then obtained work in a power-loom factory, lamented the effect of the change upon his verses:

I then worked in a small chamber, overlooking Luddenden Churchyard. I used to go out in the fields and woods . . . at meal-times, and listen to the songs of the summer birds, or watch the trembling waters of the Luddon . . . Sometimes I have been roused from those reveries by some forsaken lovesick maiden, who . . . has poured forth her heartwailing to the thankless wind. I have then gone home and have written. . . . But it is all over; I must continue to work amidst the clatter of machinery.

It is sad that years of self-education should result only in a patina of cliché. But it was the attainment itself which brought genuine satisfactions; as a young man in the late 1820s his observation of nature appears far more soundly-based than his observation of lovesick maidens:

I collected insects, in company with a number of young men in the village. We formed a library. . . . I believed I and a companion of mine . . . collected twenty-two large boxes of insects; one hundred and twenty different sorts of British birds' eggs; besides a great quantity of shells (land and fresh water), fossils, minerals, ancient and modern coins. . . .[41]

Samuel Bamford serves as a bridge between the folk traditions of the 18th-century communities (which lingered long into the next century) and the more self-conscious intellectual attainments of the early decades of the 19th. Between these two periods there are two deeply transforming experiences—those of Methodism and of political radicalism. But in accounting for the intellectual leaven, we should also remember the number of small clothiers reduced to the status of weavers,[42] sometimes bringing with them educational attainments and small libraries.

The fullest expression of the values of the weaving communities belongs to the history of the Chartist movement. A high proportion of northern and Mid-lands local Chartist leaders were outworkers, whose formative experiences came in the years between 1810 and 1830. Among such men were Benjamin Rushton of Halifax, born in 1785 and already a "veteran" reformer by 1832. Or William Ashton, a Barnsley linen-weaver, born in 1806, transported in 1830 for alleged complicity in strike-riots, liberated in 1838 and brought back from Australia by the subscriptions of his fellow-weavers, to play a leading part in the Chartist movement, and to suffer a further term of imprisonment. Or Richard Pilling, a hand-loom weaver who had transferred to power-looms, and who was known as the "Father" of the Plug Riots in Lancashire. Or John Skevington, local preacher with the Primitive Methodists, stocking-weaver, and Loughborough Chartist leader; William Rider, a Leeds stuff-weaver; and George White, a Bradford woolcomber.[43]

The career of these men would take us beyond the limits of this study. But the Lancashire Radicalism of 1816–20 was in great degree a movement of weav-ers, and the *making* of these later leaders was in communities of this kind. What they brought to the early working-class movement can scarcely be over-estimated. They had, like the city artisan, a sense of lost status, as memories of their "golden age" lingered; and, with this, they set a high premium on the values of independence. In these respects they provided, in 1816, a natural audience for Cobbett. The vexed question of embezzlement of yarn apart, nearly all witnesses spoke to the honesty and self-reliance of the weavers—"as faithful, moral, and trust-worthy, as any corporate body amongst his Majesty's sub-jects. . . ."[44] But they had, more than the city artisan, a deep social egalitari-anism. As their way of life, in the better years, had been shared by the community, so their sufferings were those of the whole community; and they were reduced so low that there was no class of unskilled or casual labourers below them against which they had erected economic or social protective walls. This gave a particular moral resonance to their protest, whether voiced in Owenite or biblical language; they appealed to essential rights and elementary notions of human fellowship and conduct rather than to sectional interests. It was as a whole community that they demanded betterment, and utopian notions of redesigning society anew at a stroke—Owenite communities, the universal general strike, the Chartist Land Plan—swept through them like fire on the common. But essentially the dream which arose in many different forms was the same—a community of independent small producers, exchanging their prod-ucts without the distortions of masters and middlemen. As late as 1848 a Barns-ley linen-weaver (a fellow transportee with William Ashton) declared at the Chartist National Convention that when the Charter was won "they would divide the land into small farms, and give every man an opportunity of getting his living by the sweat of his brow."[45]

———

At this point we should enquire more strictly into the actual position of the weavers in the 1830s, and possible remedies. It is customary to describe their plight as "hopeless," in a "sick" or "obsolete" trade, fighting a "losing battle" and facing "inevitable decline." It may be said, on the other hand, that until the late 1820s the power-loom was used as *an excuse* to distract attention from other causes of their decline.[46] Until 1830 it is difficult to establish a case for *direct* competition between power and hand; although power-looms in cotton were multiplying, it is sometimes forgotten that the consumption of cotton was leaping upwards at the same time.[47] Something of the same kind is true for the worsted industry until 1835; and in other branches of wool until the 1840s.[48] Thus there were two phases in the hand-loom weavers' decline. The first, up to 1830 or 1835, in which power was a creeping ancillary cause, although it bulked more largely in psychological terms (and was, in this sense, a lever in reducing wages); the second, in which power actually displaced hand products. It was in the first phase that the major reductions in wages (let us say, from 20s. to 8s.) took place.

Were both phases inevitable? In the judgment of most historians, it would appear that they were, although it is sometimes suggested that the weavers might have received more assistance or guidance. In the judgment of a great many contemporaries—including the weavers and their representatives—they were not. In the first phase of decline there were a dozen contributory factors, including the general effects of the post-war deflationary decade: but the underlying causes would appear to be, first, the breakdown of both custom and trade union protection; second, the total exposure of the weavers to the worst forms of wage-cutting; third, the over-stocking of the trade by unemployed to whom it had become "the last refuge of the unsuccessful." A Bolton manufacturer defined the efficient cause succinctly:

> . . . I find that from the very commencement of the manufacture of muslins at Bolton, the trade of weaving has been subject to arbitrary reductions, commencing at a very high rate. One would suppose that the reward of labour would find its proper level; but from the very commencement of it, it has been in the power of any one manufacturer to set an example of reducing wages; and I know it as a fact, that when they could not obtain a price for the goods, such as they thought they ought to get, they immediately fell to reducing the weavers' wages.

But at the same time, in Bolton in 1834—a good year—"there are no weavers out of employment; there is no danger of any being out of employment at this time."[49]

The breakdown of custom and of trade unionism was directly influenced by State intervention. This was "inevitable" only if we assume the governing ideology and the counter-revolutionary tone of these years. The weavers and their supporters opposed to this ideology a contrary analysis and contrary policies, which turned on the demand for a regulated minimum wage, enforced by trade boards of manufacturers and weavers. They offered a direct negative to the homilies of "supply-and-demand." When asked whether wages ought not to be left to find their own "level," a Manchester silk-weaver replied that there was no similarity between "what is called capital and labour":

> Capital, I can make out to be nothing else but an accumulation of the products of labour. . . . Labour is always carried to market by those who have nothing else to keep or to sell, and who, therefore, must part with it immediately. . . . The labour which I . . . might perform this week, if I, in imitation of the capitalist, refuse to part with it . . . because an inadequate price is offered me for it, can I bottle it? can I lay it up in salt? . . . These two distinctions between the nature of labour and capital (viz. that labour is always sold by the poor, and always bought by the rich, and that labour cannot by any possibility be stored, but must be every instant sold or every instant lost) are sufficient to convince me that labour and capital can never with justice be subjected to the same laws. . . .[50]

The weavers saw clearly, Richard Oastler testified, that *capital and property are protected and their labour is left to chance.* Oastler's evidence before the Select Committee, when he was heckled by one of the partisans of "political economy," dramatises the alternative views of social responsibility:

[OASTLER]. The time of labour ought to be shortened, and . . . Government ought to establish a board . . . chosen by the masters and the men . . . to settle the question of how wages shall be regulated. . . .

Q. You would put an end to the freedom of labour?

A. I would put an end to the freedom of murder, and to the freedom of employing labourers beyond their strength; I would put an end to any thing which prevents the poor man getting a good living with fair and reasonable work: and I would put an end to this, because it was destructive of human life.

Q. Would it have the effect you wished for?

A. I am sure the present effect of free labour is poverty, distress and death. . . .

Q. Suppose you were to raise the price very considerably, and . . . could not export your goods?

> A. We can use them at home.
>
> Q. You would not use so much, would you?
>
> A. Three times as much, and a great deal more than that, because the labourers would be better paid, and they would consume them. The capitalists do not use the goods, and there is the great mistake. ... If the wages were higher, the labourer would be enabled to clothe himself ... and to feed himself ... and those labourers are the persons who are after all the great consumers of agricultural and manufacturing produce, and not the capitalist, because a great capitalist, however wealthy he is, wears only one coat at once, at least, he certainly does seldom wear two coats at once; but 1,000 labourers, being enabled to buy a thousand coats, where they cannot now get one, would most certainly increase the trade. ...

As to the commission-houses or "slaughter-houses," Oastler favoured direct legislative interference:

> You never make a Law of this House but it interferes with liberty; you make laws to prevent people from stealing, that is an interference with a man's liberty; and you make laws to prevent men from murdering, that is an interference with a man's liberty. ... I should say that these slaughter-house men shall not do so. ...

The capitalists "seem as if they were a privileged order of being, but I never knew why they were so,"[51]

"There is the great mistake"—weavers, who wove cloth when they themselves were in rags, were forcibly educated in the vitiating error of the orthodox political economy. It was before the competition of power—and while their numbers were still increasing—that the Lancashire weavers sang their sad "Lament":

> You gentlemen and tradesmen, that ride about at will,
> Look down on these poor people; it's enough to make you crill;
> Look down on these poor people, as you ride up and down,
> I think there is a God above will bring your pride quite down.
>
> *Chorus*—You tyrants of England, your race may soon be run,
> You may be brought unto account for what you've sorely done.
>
> You pull down our wages, shamefully to tell;
> You go into the markets, and say you cannot sell;

And when that we do ask you when these bad times will mend,
You quickly give an answer, "When the wars are at an end."

The clothing of the weavers' children is in rags, whilst "yours do dress as manky as monkeys in a show":

You go to church on Sundays, I'm sure it's nought but pride,
There can be no religion where humanity's thrown aside;
If there be a place in heaven, as there is in the Exchange,
Our poor souls must not come near there; like lost sheep they must
    range.

With the choicest of strong dainties your tables overspread,
With good ale and strong brandy, to make your faces red;
You call'd a set of visitors—it is your whole delight—
And you lay your heads together to make our faces white.

You say that Bonyparty he's been the spoil of all,
And that we have got reason to pray for his downfall;
Now Bonyparty's dead and gone, and it is plainly shown
That we have bigger tyrants in Boneys of our own.[52]

The transparency of their exploitation added to their anger and their suffering: nothing in the process which brought troops to Peterloo or enabled their masters to erect great mansions in the manufacturing districts seemed to them to be "natural" or "inevitable."

Historians who assume that wage-regulation was "impossible" have not bothered to present a case which can be answered. John Fielden's proposals for a minimum wage periodically reviewed in each district by trade boards was no more "impossible" than the 10 Hour Bill which was only won after three decades of intensive agitation and in the face of equal opposition. Fielden had on his side not only the weavers but many of the masters who wished to restrict the less scrupulous and the "slaughter-houses." The difficulty lay, not (as Professor Smelser has it) in the "dominant value-system of the day," but in the strong opposition of a minority of masters, and in the mood of Parliament (which Professor Smelser commends for its success in "handling" and "channelling" the weavers' "unjustified disturbance symptoms").[53] In 1834 the House appointed a Select Committee, chaired by a sympathetic Paisley manufacturer, John Maxwell. He and John Fielden (who was a member of the Committee) ensured that it was well supplied with sympathetic witnesses. The Committee, while expressing deep concern at the weavers' plight, came to no firm recommendation in 1834: but in 1835, after taking further evidence, it came out with an unequivocal report in favour of Fielden's Minimum Wage Bill: "the effect of the measure would be to withdraw from the worst-paying masters the power which they now possess of regulating wages." A trial of the measure was essential, and "it will at least show that Parliament has sympathised in their distress, and lent a willing ear to their prayers for relief":

> To the sentiment that Parliament cannot and ought not to interfere in cases of this nature, Your Committee is decidedly opposed. On the contrary, where the comfort and happiness of any considerable number of British subjects is at stake, Your Committee conceive that Parliament ought not to delay a moment to inquire, and, if possible, to institute redress.
>
> Your Committee, therefore, recommend that a Bill of the nature of the one proposed by Mr. Fielden should be immediately introduced. . . .[54]

Pursuant to these recommendations, a Bill was actually introduced on 28 July 1835, by John Maxwell. The strength of the opposition was voiced in a speech by Poulett Thomson:

> Was it possible for the Government of the country to fix a rate of wages? Was it possible that the labour of man should not be free?

Such a measure would be "an act of tyranny." Dr. Bowring and Edward Baines (of the *Leeds Mercury*) advised the weavers to "relieve themselves" by bringing up their children to other employments. John Fielden was written off by *Hansard* as "inaudible." The Bill was rejected by 41 to 129. Raised again by Maxwell in 1836, its second reading was repeatedly postponed and finally dropped. Reintroduced in May 1837, by Maxwell on a motion for the adjournment, leave to introduce a Bill was negatived by 39 to 82. In the teeth of a *laissez-faire* legislature the manufacturers from Paisley and Todmorden (many of whose constituents were on the edge of starvation) continued to fight. John Fielden moved to introduce a fresh Bill on 21 December 1837: negatived by 11 to 73. But Fielden then stood up in his place and served notice that he would oppose every money bill until the House did something. This time he was "audible." A Royal Commission was appointed, firmly in the hands of that doyen of orthodox "political economy," Nassau Senior, and another stage of "handling and channelling" commenced. Assistant Commissioners toured the stricken districts in 1838, forewarned by Senior that they would have to "combat many favorite theories, and may disappoint many vague or extravagant but long-cherished expectations." Humane and intelligent men in some cases, who enquired min-

utely into the weavers' circumstances, they were none-the-less ideologues of
laissez-faire. Their reports—and the final report of the Commission—were
published in 1839 and 1840. The arid report of the Assistant Commissioner for
the West Riding suggests that—unless for the use of future social historians—
his labours need never have been undertaken:

> The general conclusion which I have endeavoured to establish is, that it
> is the business of legislation to remove all checks upon the accumulation
> of capital, and so improve the *demand* for labour; but with the *supply*
> thereof it has nothing to do.

But this had also been his assumption. "The power of the Czar of Russia," it
was reported,

> could not raise the wages of men so situate . . . all that remains, therefore,
> is to enlighten the handloom weavers as to their real situation, warn them
> to flee from the trade, and to beware of leading their children into it, as
> they would beware the commission of the most atrocious of crimes.[55]

All this "handling and channelling" had at least two effects: it transformed the
weavers into confirmed "physical force" Chartists, and in cotton alone there
were 100,000 fewer weavers in 1840 than in 1830. No doubt Fielden's Bill would
have been only partially effective, would have afforded only slight relief in the
1830s as power-loom competition increased, and might have pushed the bulge
of semi-unemployment into some other industry. But we must be scrupulous
about words: "slight relief" in the 1830s might have been the difference between
death and survival. "I think there has been already too long delay," Oastler
told the Select Committee of 1834: "I believe that delay that has been occasioned
in this question has sent many hundreds of British operatives to their graves."
Of the 100,000 weavers lost to Lancashire in that decade, it is probable that
only a minority found other occupations: a part of the majority died in their
natural term while the other part just "died off" prematurely.[56] (Some would
have been supported by their children who had entered the mills.) But it was
in 1834 that the Legislature which found itself unable to offer them any measure
of relief struck directly and actively at their conditions with the Poor Law
Amendment Bill. Out-relief—the stand-by of many communities, sometimes on
a "Speenhamland" scale—was (at least in theory) replaced by the "Bastilles"
from the late 1830s. The effect was truly catastrophic. If Professor Smelser will
examine the "dominant value-system" of the weavers he will find that *all* poor
relief was disliked but to the Malthusian workhouse the values of independence

and of marriage offered an absolute taboo. The new Poor Law not only denied the weaver and his family relief, and *kept* him in his trade to the final end, but it actually drove others—like some of the poor Irish—into the trade. "I cannot contemplate this state of things with any degree of patience," a Bolton muslin-weaver told the Committee of 1834:

> I am in a certain situation; I am now at this moment within a twelvemonth of 60 years of age, and I calculate that within the space of eight years I shall myself become a pauper. I am not capable, by my most strenuous exertions, to gain ground to the amount of a shilling; and when I am in health it requires all my exertions to keep soul and body together. . . . I speak feelingly upon the subject as a man in these circumstances; I view the present Poor Law Amendment Bill as a system of coercion upon the poor man, and that very shortly I shall be under its dreadful operation. I have not merited these things. I am a loyal man, strongly attached to the institutions of my country, and a lover of my country. "England, with all thy faults, I love thee still," is the language of my soul . . .[57]

It was in such weaving districts as Ashton (where the Chartist parson, Joseph Rayner Stevens, made insurrectionary speeches), Todmorden (where Fielden flatly defied the law), Huddersfield and Bradford that resistance to the Poor Law was violent, protracted, and intense.

But when the second phase of the weavers' decline—full competition with the power-loom—was entered, what remedies were there? "What enactment," Clapham wrote, "other than state pensions for weavers, the prohibition of the power-loom, or the prohibition of training in hand-loom weaving, would have been of the least use it is hard to see."[58] These were not among the weavers' own demands, although they protested against:

> . . . the unrestricted use (or rather abuse) of improved and continually improved machinery. . . .
> . . . the neglect of providing for the employment and maintenance of the Irish poor, who are compelled to crowd the English labour market for a piece of bread.
> . . . The adaptation of machines, in every improvement, to *children*, and *youth*, and *women*, to the exclusion of those who ought to labour—*the men*.[59]

The response of the weavers to machinery was, as these resolutions indicate, more discriminating than is often supposed. Direct destruction of power-looms rarely took place except when their introduction coincided with extreme distress and unemployment (West Houghton, 1812: Bradford, 1826). From the late 1820s, the weavers brought forward three consistent proposals.

First, they proposed a tax on power-looms, to equalise conditions of competition, some part of which might be allocated towards the weavers' relief. We should not forget that the hand-loom weaver was not only himself assessed for poor-rates, but paid a heavy burden in indirect taxation:

> Their labour has been taken from them by the power-loom; their bread is taxed; their malt is taxed; their sugar, their tea, their soap, and almost every other thing they use or consume, is taxed. But the power-loom is not taxed—

so ran a letter from the Leeds stuff weavers in 1835.[60] When we discuss the minutae of finance we sometimes forget the crazy exploitive basis of taxation after the Wars, as well as its redistributive function—from the poor to the rich. Among other articles taxed were bricks, hops, vinegar, windows, paper, dogs, tallow, oranges (the poor child's luxury). In 1832, of a revenue of approximately £50 millions, largely raised in indirect taxation on articles of common consumption, more than £28 millions were expended on the National Debt and £13 millions on the armed services as contrasted with £356,000 on the civil service, and £217,000 on the police. A witness before the Select Committee in 1834 offered the following summary of taxation liable to fall annually upon a working man:

> No. 1. Tax on malt, £4. 11s. 3d. No. 2. On sugar, 17s. 4d. No. 3. Tea or coffee, £1. 4s. No. 4. On soap, 13s. No. 5. Housing, 12s. No. 6. On food, £3. No. 7. On clothing, 10s. Total taxes on the labourer per annum, £11. 7s. 7d. Taking a labourer's earnings at 1s. 6d. per diem, and computing his working 300 days in the year (which very many do), his income will be £22. 10s.; thus it will be admitted that at the very least, 100 per cent., or half of his income is abstracted from him by taxation . . . for do what he will, eating, drinking, or sleeping, he is in some way or other taxed.[61]

The summary includes items which few hand-loom weavers could afford, including, only too often, bread itself:

> Bread-tax'd weaver, all can see
> What that tax hath done for thee,
> And thy children, vilely led,
> Singing hymns for shameful bread,

Till the stones of every street
Know their little naked feet.

—so ran one of Ebenezer Elliott's "Corn Law Rhymes."[62]

It is no wonder that Cobbett's attacks on the fund-holders met with a ready reception, and that Feargus O'Connor first won the applause of the "fustian jackets and unshorn chins" of the north by striking the same note:

> You think you pay nothing: why, it is you who pay all. It is you who
> pay six or eight millions of taxes for keeping up the army; for what? for
> keeping up the taxes. . . .[63]

Certainly, a tax on power-looms seems no more "impossible" than taxes on windows, oranges, or bricks.

Two other proposals related to the restriction of hours in power-loom factories, and the employment of adult male power-loom weavers. The first of these was a powerful influence leading many hand-loom weavers to give their support to the 10 Hour agitation. Heavy weather has been made of this, from the 1830s to the present day, with the men coming under the accusation of "sheltering behind the skirts of the women" or of using the plight of the children as a stalking-horse in their own demand for shorter hours. But, in fact, the aim was openly declared by factory operatives and weavers. It was intrinsic to their alternative model of political economy that shorter hours in the factory should at one and the same time lighten the labour of children, give a shorter working day to the adult operatives, and spread the available work more widely among the hand-workers and unemployed. In the second case, whereas mule-spinning was generally reserved to male operatives, the power-loom more often was attended by women or juveniles. And here we must look further at the reasons for the hand-loom weaver's opposition to the factory system.

"Reason" is not the appropriate word, since the conflict is between two cultural modes or ways of life. We have seen that even before the advent of power the woollen weavers disliked the hand-loom factories. They resented, first, the discipline; the factory bell or hooter; the time-keeping which overrode ill-health, domestic arrangements, or the choice of more varied occupations. William Child, a journeyman weaver victimised for his activities with "the Institution" of 1806, refused to enter a hand-loom factory because of his objections to "being confined to go exactly at such an hour and such a minute, and the bad conduct that was carried on there. . . ."

> A tender man when he had his work at home could do it at his leisure;
> there you must come at the time: the bell rings at half past five, and then

again at six, then ten minutes was allowed for the door to be opened; if eleven expired, it was shut against any person either man, woman, or child; there you must stand out of door or return home till eight.[64]

In the "golden age" it had been a frequent complaint with employers that the weavers kept "Saint Monday"—and sometimes made a holiday of Tuesday—making up the work on Friday and Saturday nights. According to tradition, the loom went in the first days of the week to the easy pace of "Plen-ty of time. Plen-ty of time." But at the week-end the loom clacked, "A day t' lat. A day t' lat." Only a minority of weavers in the 19th century would have had as varied a life as the smallholder weaver whose diary, in the 1780s, shows him weaving on wet days, jobbing—carting, ditching and draining, mowing, churning—on fine.[65] But variety of some sorts there would have been, until the very worst days—poultry, some gardens, "wakes" or holidays, even a day out with the harriers:

> So. come all you cotton-weavers, you must rise up very soon,
> For you must work in factories from morning until noon:
> You mustn't walk in your garden for two or three hours a-day,
> For you must stand at their command, and keep your shuttles in play.[66]

To "stand at their command"—this was the most deeply resented indignity. For he felt himself, at heart, to be the real *maker* of the cloth (and his parents remembered the time when the cotton or wool was spun in the home as well). There had been a time when factories had been thought of as kinds of workhouses for pauper children; and even when this prejudice passed, to enter the mill was to fall in status from a self-motivated man, however poor, to a servant or "hand."

Next, they resented the effects upon family relationships of the factory system. Weaving had offered an employment to the whole family, even when spinning was withdrawn from the home. The young children winding bobbins, older children watching for faults, picking over the cloth, or helping to throw the shuttle in the broad-loom; adolescents working a second or third loom; the wife taking a turn at weaving in and among her domestic employments. The family was together, and however poor meals were, at least they could sit down at chosen times. A whole pattern of family and community life had grown up around the loom-shops; work did not prevent conversation or singing. The spinning-mills—which offered employment only for their children—and then the power-loom sheds, which generally employed only the wives or adolescents—were resisted until poverty broke down all defences. These places were held to be "immoral"—places of sexual licence, foul language, cruelty, violent accidents, and alien manners.[67] Witnesses before the Select Committee put now one, now another, objection to the front:

> . . . no man would like to work in a power-loom, they do not like it, there is such a clattering and noise it would almost make some men mad; and next, he would have to be subject to a discipline that a hand-loom weaver can never submit to.
>
> . . . all persons working on the power-loom are working there by force, because they cannot exist any other way; they are generally people that have been distressed in their families and their affairs broken up . . . they are apt to go as little colonies to colonize these mills . . .

A Manchester witness whose own son had been killed in a factory accident declared:

> I have had seven boys, but if I had 77 I should never send one to a cotton factory. . . . One great objection that I have is, that their morals are very much corrupted. . . . They have to be in the factories from six in the morning till eight at night, consequently they have no means of instruction . . . there is no good example shown them. . . .

"I am determined for my part, that if they will invent machines to supersede manual labour, they must find iron boys to mind them."[68]

Finally, we have all these objections, not taken separately, but taken as indicative of the "value-system" of the community. This, indeed, might be valuable material for a study in historical sociology; for we have, in the England of the 1830s, a "plural society," with factory, weaving, and farming communities impinging on each other, with different traditions, norms, and expectations. The history of 1815 to 1840 is, in part, the story of the confluence of the first two in common political agitation (Radicalism, 1832 Reform, Owenism, 10 Hour agitation, Chartism); while the last stage of Chartism is, in part, the story of their uneasy co-existence and final dissociation. In the great towns such as Manchester or Leeds, where the hand-loom weavers shared many of the traditions of the artisans, intermarried with them, and early sent their children to the mills, these distinctions were least marked. In the upland weaving villages, the communities were far more clannish; they despised "teawn's folk"— all made up of "offal an' boylin-pieces."[69] For years, in such areas as Saddleworth, Clitheroe, the upper Calder Valley, the weavers in their hillside hamlets kept apart from the mills in the valley-bottoms, training their children to take their places at the loom.

Certainly, then, by the 1830s, we may begin to speak of a "doomed" occupation, which was in part self-condemned by its own social conservatism. But even where the weavers accepted their fate, the advice of the Royal Commission "to flee from the trade" was often beside the point. The children might find places in the mills, or the growing daughters turn to the power-loom:

> If you go into a loom-shop, where there's three or four pairs of looms,
> They all are standing empty, encumbrances of the rooms;
> And if you ask the reason why, the old mother will tell you plain,
> My daughters have forsaken them, and gone to weave by steam.[70]

But this was not always possible. In many mills, the spinners or the existing labour force had priority for their own children. Where it took place, it added to the weaver's shame his dependence upon his wife or children, the enforced and humiliating reversal of traditional roles.

We have to remember the lack of balance between adult and juvenile labour in the early factory system. In the early 1830s between one-third and one-half of the labour force (all classes of labour) in cotton-mills was under twenty-one. In worsted the proportion of juveniles was a good deal higher. Of the adults, considerably more than half were women. Dr. Ure estimated, from the reports of the Factory Inspectors in 1834, an adult labour force in all textile mills in the United Kingdom of 191,671, of whom 102,812 were women and only 88,859 were men.[71] The male employment pattern is clear enough:

> In the cotton factories of Lancashire, the wages of the males during the period when there is the greatest number employed—from eleven to sixteen—are on the average 4s. 10¾d. a-week; but in the next period of five years, from sixteen to twenty-one, the average rises to 10s. 2½d. a-week; and of course the manufacturer will have as few at that price as he can. . . . In the next period of five years, from twenty-one to twenty-six, the average weekly wages are 17s. 2½d. Here is a still stronger motive to discontinue employing males as far as it can practically be done. In the subsequent two periods the average rises still higher, to 20s. 4½d., and to 22s. 8½d. At such wages, only those men will be employed who are necessary to do work requiring great bodily strength, or great skill, in some art, craft, or mystery . . . or persons employed in offices of trust and confidence.[72]

Two obvious, but important, points must be made about this employment pattern. The first—which we have already made in relation to "dishonourable" trades—is that we cannot artificially segregate in our minds "good" factory wages from bad wages in "outmoded" industries. In a system based upon the discontinuance of the employment of adult males "as far as it can practically be done" the wage of the skilled factory operative and the wage of the unskilled worker displaced from the mill at sixteen or twenty-one must be stamped on different sides of the same coin. Certainly in the wool textiles industries, juvenile workers displaced from the mills were sometimes forced, in their teens, back to the hand-loom. The second point is that the adult male hand-loom weaver, even when hardship overcame his prejudices, had little more chance of employment in a mill than an agricultural worker. He was rarely adapted to factory work. He had neither "great bodily strength" nor skill in any factory craft. One of the best-disposed of masters, John Fielden, recalled of 1835:

> I was applied to weekly by scores of hand-loom weavers, who were so pressed down in their conditions as to be obliged to seek such work, and it gave me and my partners no small pain to . . . be compelled to refuse work to the many who applied for it.[73]

In the artisan trades of Lancashire in the early 1830s wages were reasonably high—among iron-moulders, engineers, shoemakers, tailors, and skilled building workers anything from 15s. to 25s. (and above in engineering). But these rates had been obtained only by the strength of combination, one of whose aims was to keep the discharged factory youth and the hand-loom weaver *out*. If the weaver could have changed jobs—or apprenticed his children—to any *artisan* trade, social conservatism would not have prevented this. Against unskilled labouring there was certainly understandable prejudice: it was seen as a final loss of status:

> But aw'll give o'er this trade, un work wi' a spade.
> Or goo un' break stone upo' th' road . . .

—declares "Jone o' Grinfilt" at the height of his tribulations.

But even here there were difficulties. The Manchester silk-weaver who expounded the elements of a labour theory of value to the House of Commons had failed in his attempts to get work as a porter (wages, 14s. to 15s.). The weaver's physique was rarely up to heavy unskilled labouring (the wages of bricklayer's labourers and "spademen" being 10s. or 12s.), and he competed with Irish labourers who were stronger and willing to work for less.[74] And while weavers in the large towns no doubt found ill-paid odd jobs of many kinds, the middle-aged country weaver could not remove his home and family:

> The change had a terrible effect on the minds of some old hand-loom weavers. . . . We have seen an old Pudsey weaver with tears in his eyes

while . . . recounting the good points of his loom. Yes, it was hung on its
prods as a loom ought to be, and swung to and fro as a loom should do,
the going part easy to put back, yet came freely to its work, and would
get any amount of weft in. When that loom first came from one of the
best makers in England . . . the neighbours all came to see it, and admired
and coveted it. But now for some time both this loom and another . . .
have all been dumb, and are covered with dust and cobwebs. . . .[75]

The story of the hand-loom weavers impinges at a score of points upon the
general question of living standards during the Industrial Revolution. In its first
stages it appears to provide evidence on the "optimistic" side: the spinning-
mills are the multiplyers which attract thousands of outworkers and raise their
standards. But as their standards are raised, so their status and defences are
lowered; and from 1800 to 1840 the record is almost unrelievedly "pessimistic."
If we are to assess standards in these years, not in "futuristic" terms, but in
terms of the living generations who experienced them, then we must see the
weavers as a group who not only did not "share in the benefits" of economic
progress but who suffered a drastic decline. Since textiles were the staple industries of the Industrial Revolution, and since there were far more adults
involved in the weaving than in the spinning branches, this would seem as valid
a way of describing the experience of these years as any. The customary story,
perhaps for reasons of dramatic style, fastens attention upon the multiplyer (the
mule, the mill, and steam): we have looked at the people who were multiplied.
   "Optimists," of course, recognise the plight of the weavers; in every account
there is some saving clause, excepting "a few small and specially unhappy
sections of the people, such as the hand-loom weavers," "a small group among
a prospering community," or "pockets of technological underemployment."[76]
But, as Clapham well knew, the weavers could in no sense be described as a
"small" group before the later 1840s. Weavers were, and had probably been
for some hundreds of years, the largest single group of industrial workers in
England. They were the ploughmen of our staple industries. At any time between 1820 and 1840 they came third in the occupational lists, after agricultural
labourers and domestic servants, and greatly exceeding any other industrial
group. "No census of them [i.e. looms in the U.K.] was ever taken: but there
cannot have been fewer than 500,000 and there may have been very many
more."[77] Estimates for the United Kingdom, taking in looms in cotton, wool,
silk, linen, flax, as well as such specialist branches as ribbon-weaving (but
excluding framework-knitting), sometimes rose as high as 740,000. But in many
families there would be two, three, and four looms. The estimate of the Select
Committee of 1834–5 that 800,000 to 840,000 were wholly dependent upon the
loom (that is, the weavers and their families) may be as close as we can get.

It is the enduring myth of freedom in an obsolete ideology that for the Legislature to do nothing, and to allow "natural" economic forces to inflict harm on a part of the community, constitutes a complete defence. The power-loom provided both the State and the employers with a cast iron alibi. But we might equally well see the story of the weavers as the expression of the highly abnormal situation which existed during the Industrial Revolution. In the weavers' history we have a paradigm case of the operation of a repressive and exploitive system upon a section of workers without trade union defences. Government not only intervened actively against their political organisations and trade unions; it also inflicted upon the weavers the negative dogma of the freedom of capital as intransigently as it was to do upon the victims of the Irish famine.

The ghost of this dogma is still abroad today. Professor Ashton regrets that financial factors retarded investment in power-looms:

> It is sometimes suggested that the "evils" of the industrial revolution were due to the rapidity with which it proceeded: the case of the domestic textile workers suggests the exact opposite. If there had been in weaving a man of the type of Arkwright, if rates of interest had remained low, if there had been no immigration and no Poor Law allowance, the transfer to the factory might have been effected quickly and with less suffering. As it was, large numbers of hand workers continued, for more than a generation, to fight a losing battle against the power of steam.[78]

But, as we have seen, for the power-loom masters it was not a "battle" but a great convenience to have an auxiliary cheap labour force, as a stand-by in good times and as a means of keeping down the wages of the women and girls (8s. to 12s. Manchester, 1832) who minded the power-looms. Moreover, there *was* scarcely no "transfer to the factory." If the introduction of power had been swifter, then—all other things being equal—its consequences would have been even more catastrophic.

Some economic historians appear to be unwilling (perhaps because of a concealed "progressivism," which equates human progress with economic growth) to face the evident fact that technological innovation during the Industrial Revolution, until the railway age, did displace (except in the metal industries) adult skilled labour. Labour so displaced swelled the limitless supply of cheap labour for the arduous work of sheer human muscle in which the times were so spendthrift. There was little or no mechanisation in the mines; in the docks; in brickworks, gasworks, building; in canal and railway building; in carterage and porterage. Coal was still carried on men's backs up the long ladders from ships' holds: in Birmingham men could still, in the 1830s, be hired at 1s. a day to wheel sand in barrows nine miles by road, and nine miles empty back. The disparity between the wages of an engineer (26s. to 30s.) or carpenter (24s.) and the spademan (10s. to 15s.) or weaver (say, 8s.) in 1832 is such that we cannot allow social conservatism alone to explain it. It suggests that it is the skilled trades which are exceptional, and that conditions in unskilled manual labour or in outwork industries, so far from being "specially unhappy," were characteristic of a system designed by employers, legislators, and ideologists to cheapen human labour in every way. And the fact that weaving became over-stocked at a time when conditions were rapidly declining is eloquent confir-mation. It was in the outwork industries, Marx wrote, that exploitation was most "shameless," "because in these last resorts of the masses made 'redundant' by Modern Industry and Agriculture, competition for work attains its maxi-mum."[79]

There is, of course, a "futurist" argument which deserves attention. It is, in fact, an argument which many working men who lived through until better times adopted. However full of suffering the transition, one such working man commented:

> ... power-loom weavers have not to buy looms and a jenny to spin for them; or bobbins, flaskets, and baskets; or to pay rent and taxes for them standing; nor candles, or gas and coal for lighting and warming the work-shop. They have not to pay for repairs, for all wear and tear ... nor have they to buy shuttles, pickers, side-boards, shop-boards, shuttle-boards, picking-sticks, and bands and cords ... They have not to be propped up on the treadles and seatboards ... or have their wrists bandaged to give strength. ... They have not to fetch slubbing, warp their webs, lay up lists, size, put the webs out to dry, seek gears, leck pieces, tenter, teem, dew, and cuttle them; and least of all would they think of breaking wool, scouring, and dyeing it *all for nothing too.*[80]

If we see the hand-loom weaver's work in this light, it was certainly painful and obsolete, and any transition, however full of suffering, might be justified. But this is an argument which discounts the suffering of one generation against the gains of the future. For those who suffered, this retrospective comfort is cold.

Notes

1. W. Gardiner, *Music and Friends* (1838), I, p. 43. See also M. D. George, *England in Transition* (Penguin edn. 1953), p. 63.

2. T. Exell, *Brief History of the Weavers of Gloucestershire*, cited in E. A. L. Moir, "The Gentlemen Clothiers," in (ed.) H. P. R. Finberg, *Gloucestershire Studies* (Leicester, 1957), p. 247.

3. Emmerson Tennant, M. P. for Belfast, in House of Commons, 28 July 1835.

4. Introduction by W. O. Henderson and W. H. Chaloner to F. Engels, *Condition of the Working Class in England in 1844* (1958), p. xiv.

5. Cited by E. A. L. Moir, op. cit., p. 226. For the West of England industry, see also D. M. Hunter. *The West of England Woollen Industry* (1910) and J. de L. Mann, "Clothiers and Weavers in Wiltshire during the Eighteenth Century," in (ed). L. S. Presnell, *Studies in the Industrial Revolution* (1960).

6. The MS. copy in Leeds Reference Library is transcribed by F. B. in *Publications of the Thoresby Society*, XLI. Part 3, No. 95, 1947, pp. 275–9; there are extracts in H. Heaton, *Yorkshire Woollen and Worsted Industries* (1920), pp. 344–7. Professor Heaton's book remains the standard authority on the domestic industry in Yorkshire in the 18th century.

7. Frank Peel, "Old Cleckheaton," *Cleckheaton Guardian*, Jan–April 1884. Peel, a local historian of accuracy, was writing about the 1830s in a region of the West Riding where the master-clothier lingered longest.

8. See A. P. Wadsworth and J. de L. Mann, *The Cotton Trade and Industrial Lancashire* (Manchester, 1931), p. 348.

9. Ibid., pp. 366–7.

10. W. Radcliffe, *Origin of Power Loom Weaving* (Stockport, 1828), p. 65.

11. J. Aikin, *A Description of the Country . . . round Manchester* (1795), p. 262. Note the early use of "working class."

12. Radcliffe, op. cit., p. 167.

13. See S. J. Chapman, *The Lancashire Cotton Industry* (Manchester, 1904), p. 40. There are indications of widespread reductions commencing in about 1797. An Association of Cotton Weavers, based on Bolton, claimed that wages had fallen by ⅓ between 1797 and 1799; Rev. R. Bancroft, 29 April 1799, P.C. A. 155; A. Weaver, *Address to the Inhabitants of Bolton* (Bolton, 1799); Radcliffe, op. cit., pp. 72–7. But wages seem to have reached a peak of 45 to 50 shillings a week in Blackburn in 1802: *Blackburn Mail*, 26 May 1802.

14. J. Smith, *Memoirs of Wool* (1747), II, p. 308.

15. See Wadsworth and Mann, op. cit., pp. 387 ff.

16. Aspinall, op. cit., p. 271.

17. Weavers' petition in favour of a minimum wage bill, 1807, signed—it is claimed—by 130,000 cotton-weavers: see J. L. and B. Hammond, *The Skilled Labourer*, p. 74.

18. Howell's *State Trials*, Vol. XXXI, pp. 1–98; Prentice, op. cit., p. 33.

19. Hammonds, op. cit., pp. 109–21. The Home Office papers on the 1818 strike, drawn upon by the Hammonds, are now available in full in Aspinall, op. cit., pp. 246–310.

20. Similar processes can be seen in the Spitalfields silk-weaving industry in the 18th century, where no power was involved. See M. D. George, *London Life in the 18th Century*, p. 187.

21. Hammonds, op. cit., p. 123. See also the impressive statement of the Manchester weavers in 1823, in the Hammonds, *Town Labourer*, pp. 298–301.

22. *Book of English Trades* (1818), p. 441.

23. For accounts of the strike see J. Burnley, *History of Wool and Woolcombing* (1889), pp. 166 ff.; J. James, *History of the Worsted Manufacture* (1857), pp. 400 ff.; *Trades Newspaper*, June–September, 1826; W. Scruton, "The Great Strike of 1825," *Bradford Antiquary* (1888), I, pp. 67–73.

24. W. Scruton, *Bradford Fifty Years Ago* (Bradford, 1897), pp. 95–6.

25. Frank Peel, op. cit. The plight of the combers in the 1840s is described in J. Burnley, op. cit., pp. 175–85; their sudden extinction by improved combing machinery in Bradford in the late 1840s is described by E. Sigsworth in C. Fay, *Round About Industrial Britain*, 1830–1850 (1952), pp. 123–8; for their extinction in Halifax in 1856, see E. Baines, *Yorkshire Past and Present*, II, p. 415.

26. Cited in W. Cudworth, *Condition of the Industrial Classes of Bradford & District* (Bradford, 1887).

27. *Political Register*, 20 June 1832.

28. W. B. Crump and G. Ghorbal, *History of the Huddersfield Woollen Industry* (Huddersfield, 1935), pp. 120–1.

29. This is a difficult technical argument. Witnesses before the *Select Committee on Hand-Loom Weavers' Petitions* (1834) disagreed as to whether the average ratio of power to hand output in plain cottons should be estimated at 3:1 or 5:1. The dandy-loom, a species of hand-loom operated mechanically in so far as the movement of the cloth through the loom was concerned, to which the weaver must keep time by accelerated movements of the hand-thrown shuttle, was alleged to keep pace with the power-loom, but at great cost to the weaver's health. In worsted, J. James, estimated 2,768 power-looms in the West Riding in 1835, as compared with 14,000 hand-looms estimated in the Bradford district in 1838; by 1841 there were 11,458 West Riding power-looms. Estimates in the *Leeds Times* (28 March, 11 April 1835) suggest that the worsted power-loom weaver (generally a girl or woman minding two looms) could produce two and a half to three times as much work as the hand-loom weaver. But in the next fifteen years the speed of shuttle movements on a six-quarter loom more than doubled. (H. Forbes, *Rise, Progress, and Present State of the Worsted Manufactures* (1852), p. 318). The Crossley Carpet Power Loom, patented in 1851, could weave twelve to fourteen times the speed of hand ("Reminiscences of Fifty Years by a Workman," *Halifax Courier*, 7 July 1888).

30. See *S. C. on Handloom Weavers' Petitions* (1835), p. 148 (2066).

31. Ibid., 1835, p. 60 (465–6).

32. An account of the strength of the Norwich Weavers' Committee in its resistance to "that unclean thing called underprice work" is given (from the master's standpoint) in *First Report of the Constabulary Commissioners* (1839), pp. 135–46. See also J. H. Clapham, "The Transference of the Worsted Industry from Norfolk to the West Riding," *Econ. Journal*, XX.

33. *Leeds Times*, 7 March 1835.

34. R. Howard, Surgeon, *History of the Typhus of Heptonstall-Slack* (Hebden Bridge, 1844).

35. J. Lawson, *Letters to the Young on Progress in Pudsey* (Stanningley, 1887), pp. 26–30.

36. R. Howard, op cit., passism.

37. J. Greenwood, "Reminiscences," *Todmorden Advertiser*, 10 September 1909; J. Hartley, "Memorabilia," *Todmorden and District News*, 1903; W. Scruton, op. cit., p. 92.

38. See also J. F. C. Harrison, *Learning and Living* (1961), p. 45; and M. D. George, op. cit., p. 188 for the Spitalfields weavers. Such traditions were also strong in the West Country, Norwich, and, most notably, among the Scottish weavers. In Spitalfields the silk-weavers supported Mathematical, Historical, Floricultural, Entomological, Recitation, and Musical Societies: G. I. Stigler, *Five Lectures on Economic Problems* (1949), p. 26.

39. J. Harland, *Ballads and Songs of Lancashire* (1865), pp. 223–7.

40. *A Domestic Winter-piece. . . . By Samuel Law, of Barewise, near Todmorden, Lancashire weaver* (Leeds, 1772).

41. W. Heaton, *The Old Soldier* (1857), pp. xxiii, xix.

42. John Fielden declared before the Select Committee of 1835: "I think three-fourths of the manufacturers at least in the neighborhood where I reside have been reduced to poverty."

43. For Ashton, see various sources in Barnsley Reference Library. For Pilling, see *Chartist Trials*
(1843). For Skevington, see J. F. C. Harrison, "Chartism in Leicester," in A. Briggs, *Chartist
Studies* (1959), pp. 130–1. For White and Rider, see Harrison, "Chartism in Leeds," ibid., pp. 70
ff.

44. Radcliffe, op. cit, p. 107.

45. *Halifax Guardian*, 8 April 1848.

46. G. H. Wood, *History of Wages in the Cotton Trade* (1910), p. 112, offers averages for cotton
weavers ranging from 18s. 9d. (1797); 21s. (1802); 14s. (1809); 8s. 9d. (1817); 7s. 3d. (1828); 6s.
(1832). These probably understate the decline: a weekly average of 4s. 6d. was certainly found
in many districts by the 1830s. The decline in most branches of worsted and woollens was much
the same, commencing a little later and rarely falling quite so low. The statistically-inclined may
consult the voluminous evidence in the Reports of the Select Committee and Assistant Commissioners: useful tables are in *S. C. on Hand-loom Weaver's Petitions*, 1834, pp. 432–3, 446: and in
J. Fielden, *National Regeneration* (1834), pp. 27–30.

47. Estimated cotton power-looms in England: 1820, 12,150; 1829, 55,000; 1833, 85,000. Estimated
weight of twist consumed: 1820, 87,096 million lb.; 1829, 149,570 million lb. Estimated number
of cotton handloom weavers in U.K.: 1801, 164,000; 1810, 200,000; 1820, 240,000; 1830, 240,000;
1833, 213,000; 1840, 123,000. See N. J. Smelser, *Social Change in the Industrial Revolution* (1959),
pp. 137, 148–9, 207.

48. In the parish of Halifax, where worsted was predominant, consumption of wool leapt from 1830,
3,657,000 lb. to 1850, 14,423,000 lb. Over the same period, worsted power-looms multiplied from
some hundreds to 4,000. In Bradford worsteds the ratio of power-looms to hand in 1836 was still
about 3,000 to 14,000.

49. *S. C. on Hand-Loom Weavers' Petitions*, 1834, p. 381 (4901), p. 408 (5217).

50. Ibid., 1835, p. 188 (2686).

51. *S. C. on Hand-Loom Weavers' Petitions*, 1834, pp. 283–8.

52. J. Harland, op. cit., pp. 259–61.

53. See N. J. Smelser, op. cit., p. 247. In fairness to Professor Smelser it should be added that his
book, while ponderously insensitive in its general arguments, includes some valuable insights into
the effect of technological changes upon the cotton workers' family relationships.

54. *S.C. on Hand-Loom Weavers' Petitions*, 1835, p. xv. I have quoted this section of the Report in
order to correct the inaccurate accounts in Smelser, op. cit., pp. 263–4, and Clapham, op. cit., I.
p. 552.

55. *Journals of House of Commons and Hansard*, passim; *Reports of Hand-Loom Weavers' Commissioners*,
1840, Part III, p. 590; A. Briggs, *Chartist Studies* pp. 8–9.

56. See the diary of W. Varley, a weaver, in W. Bennett, *History of Burnley* (Burnley, 1948), III,
pp. 379–89; e.g. February, 1827) "sickness and disease prevails very much, and well it may, the
clamming and starving and hard working which the poor are now undergoing. . . . The pox and
measles takes off the children by two or three a house."

57. Loc. cit., 1834, pp. 456–60.

58. Clapham, op. cit., I, p. 552.

59. *Report and Resolutions of a Meeting of Deputies from the Hand-Loom Worsted Weavers residing in
and near Bradford, Leeds, Halifax, &c.* (1835).

60. *Leeds Times*, 25 April 1835.

61. *S.C. on Hand-Loom Weavers' Petitions*, 1834, pp. 293 ff. The witness, R. M. Martin, was author of *Taxation of the British Empire* (1833).

62. E. Elliott, *The Splendid Village, &c.* (1834), I. p. 72.

63. *Halifax Guardian*, 8 October 1836.

64. *Committee on the Woollen Trade* (1806), p. 111 and passim.

65. T. W. Hanson, "Diary of a Grandfather," *Trans. Halifax Antiq. Soc.* 1916.

66. I. Harland, op. cit., p. 253.

67. See statement of the Manchester weavers (1823): "The evils of a Factory-life are incalculable,— There uninformed, unrestrained youth, of both sexes mingle—absent from parental vigilance. . . . Confined in artificial heat to the injury of health,—The mind exposed to corruption, and life and limbs exposed to Machinery—spending youth where the 40th year of the age is the 60th of the constitution. . . ." (Hammonds, *The Town Labourer*, p. 300).

68. *S.C. on Hand-Loom Weavers' Petitions*, 1834, p. 428 (5473), p. 440 (5618); p. 189 (2643–6).

69. Edwin Waugh, *Lancashire Sketches* (1869), p. 128.

70. J. Harland, op. cit., p. 253.

71. A. Ure, *The Philosophy of Manufactures* (1835), p. 481; J. James, *History of the Worsted Manufacture*, pp. 619–20; James *Continuation of the History of Bradford* (1866), p. 227. The reports often underestimate the Juvenile labour force.

72. Ure, op. cit., p. 474.

73. J. Fielden, *The Curse of the Factory System* (1836), p. 68.

74. Wages noted here are those listed as average in 1832 by the Manchester Chamber of Commerce: see *First Annual Report! P.L.C.*, 1836, p. 331, and *British Almanac*, 1834, pp. 31–61.

75. J. Lawson, *Progress in Pudsey*, pp. 89–90.

76. Clapham, *Economic History*, I, p. 565; F. A. Hayek in *Capitalism and the Historians*, p. 28; R. M. Hartwell, "The Rising Standard of Living in England, 1800–1850," *Econ. Hist. Review*, 2nd Series, XIII, April 1961.

77. Clapham, op. cit., I, p. 179.

78. T. S. Ashton, *The Industrial Revolution*, p. 117.

79. *Capital* (1938 edn.), p. 465.

80. J. Lawson, op. cit., p. 91.

CLASS CONSCIOUSNESS
FROM *THE MAKING OF THE ENGLISH WORKING CLASS*

I. The Radical Culture

When contrasted with the Radical years which preceded and the Chartist years which succeeded it, the decade of the 1820s seems strangely quiet—a mildly prosperous plateau of social peace. But many years later a London costermonger warned Mayhew:

> People fancy that when all's quiet that all's stagnating. Propagandism is going on for all that. It's when all's quiet that the seed's a-growing. Republicans and Socialists are pressing their doctrines.[1]

These quiet years were the years of Richard Carlile's contest for the liberty of the press; of growing trade union strength and the repeal of the Combination Acts; of the growth of free thought, co-operative experiment, and Owenite theory. They are years in which individuals and groups sought to render into theory the twin experiences which we have described—the experience of the Industrial Revolution, and the experience of popular Radicalism insurgent and in defeat. And at the end of the decade, when there came the climactic contest between Old Corruption and Reform, it is possible to speak in a new way of the working people's consciousness of their interests and of their predicament *as a class.*

There is a sense in which we may describe popular Radicalism in these years as an intellectual culture. The articulate consciousness of the self-taught was above all a *political* consciousness. For the first half of the 19th century, when the formal education of a great part of the people entailed little more than instruction in the Three R's, was by no means a period of intellectual atrophy.

From *The Making of the English Working Class* by E. P. Thompson (New York: Vintage Books, 1963).

The towns, and even the villages, hummed with the energy of the autodidact. Given the elementary techniques of literacy, labourers, artisans, shopkeepers and clerks and schoolmasters, proceeded to instruct themselves, severally or in groups. And the books or instructors were very often those sanctioned by reforming opinion. A shoemaker, who had been taught his letters in the Old Testament, would labour through the *Age of Reason*; a schoolmaster, whose education had taken him little further than worthy religious homilies, would attempt Voltaire, Gibbon, Ricardo; here and there local Radical leaders, weavers, booksellers, tailors, would amass shelves of Radical periodicals and learn how to use parliamentary Blue Books; illiterate labourers would, nevertheless, go each week to a pub where Cobbett's editorial letter was read aloud and discussed.

Thus working men formed a picture of the organisation of society, out of their own experience and with the help of their hard-won and erratic education, which was above all a political picture. They learned to see their own lives as part of a general history of conflict between the loosely defined "industrious classes" on the one hand, and the unreformed House of Commons on the other. From 1830 onwards a more clearly-defined class consciousness, in the customary Marxist sense, was maturing, in which working people were aware of continuing both old and new battles on their own.

It is difficult to generalise as to the diffusion of literacy in the early years of the century. The "industrious classes" touched, at one pole, the million or more who were illiterate, or whose literacy amounted to little more than the ability to spell out a few words or write their names. At the other pole there were men of considerable intellectual attainment. Illiteracy (we should remember) by no means excluded men from political discourse. In Mayhew's England the ballad-singers and "patterers" still had a thriving occupation, with their pavement farces and street-corner parodies, following the popular mood and giving a Radical or anti-Papal twist to their satirical monologues or Chaunts, according to the state of the market.[2] The illiterate worker might tramp miles to hear a Radical orator, just as the same man (or another) might tramp to taste a sermon. In times of political ferment the illiterate would get their workmates to read aloud from the periodicals; while at Houses of Call the news was read, and at political meetings a prodigious time was spent in reading addresses and passing long strings of resolutions. The earnest Radical might even attach a talismanic virtue to the possession of favoured works which he was unable, by his own efforts, to read. A Cheltenham shoemaker who called punctually each Sunday on W. E. Adams to have "Feargus's letter" read to him, nevertheless was the proud owner of several of Cobbett's books, carefully preserved in wash leather cases.[3]

Recent studies have thrown much light on the predicament of the working-class reader in these years.[4] To simplify a difficult discussion, we may say that something like two out of every three working men were able to read after some fashion in the early part of the century, although rather fewer could write. As the effect of the Sunday schools and day schools increasingly became felt, as well as the drive for self-improvement among working people themselves, so the number of the illiterate fell, although in the worst child labour areas the fall was delayed. But the ability to read was only the elementary technique. The ability to handle abstract and consecutive argument was by no means inborn; it had to be discovered against almost overwhelming difficulties—the lack of leisure, the cost of candles (or of spectacles), as well as educational deprivation. Ideas and terms were sometimes employed in the early Radical movement which, it is evident, had for some ardent followers a fetishistic rather than rational value. Some of the Pentridge rebels thought that a "Provisional Government" would ensure a more plentiful supply of "provisions"; while, in one account of the pitmen of the north-east in 1819, "Universal Suffrage is understood by many of them to mean universal suffering . . . 'if one member suffers, all must suffer.' "[5]

Such evidence as survives as to the literary accomplishment of working men in the first two decades of the century serves only to illustrate the folly of generalisation. In the Luddite times (when few but working men would have supported their actions), anonymous messages vary from self-conscious apostrophes to "Liberty with her Smiling Attributes" to scarcely decipherable chalking on walls. We may take examples of both kinds. In 1812 the Salford Coroner, who had returned a verdict of "Justifiable Homicide" upon the body of a man shot while attacking Burton's mill, was warned:

> . . . know thou cursed insinuater, if Burton's infamous action was "justifiable," the Laws of Tyrants are Reasons Dictates—Beware, Beware! A months' bathing in the Stygian Lake would not wash this sanguinary deed from our minds, it but augments the heritable cause, that stirs us up in indignation.[6]

The letter concludes, "Ludd finis est"—a reminder that Manchester boasted a grammar school (which Bamford himself for a short time attended) as well as private schools where the sons of artisans might obtain Latin enough for this. The other paper was found in Chesterfield Market. It is much to the same purpose but (despite the educational disadvantages of the writer) it somehow carries a greater conviction:

> I Ham going to inform you that there is Six Thousand men coming to you in Apral and then We Will go and Blow Parlement house up and

Blow up all afour hus/labring Peple Cant Stand it No longer/dam all Such Roges as England governes but Never mind Ned lud when general nody and is harmey Comes We Will soon bring about the greate Revelution then all these greate mens heads gose of.

Others of the promised benefits of "general nody" were: "We Will Nock doon the Prisions and the Judge we Will murde whan he is aslepe."[7]

The difference (the critics will tell us) is not only a matter of style: it is also one of sensibility. The first we might suppose to be written by a bespectacled, greying artisan—a cobbler (or hatter or instrument-maker) with Voltaire, Volney, and Paine on his shelf, and a taste for the great tragedians. Among the State prisoners of 1817 there were other men of this order from Lancashire: the seventy-year-old William Ogden, a letter-press printer, who wrote to his wife from prison: "though I am in Irons, I will face my enemies like the Great Caractacus when in the same situation"; Joseph Mitchell, another printing worker, whose daughters were called Mirtilla, Carolina, and Cordelia, and who—when another daughter was born while he was in prison—wrote in haste to his wife proposing that the baby be called Portia: or Samuel Bamford himself, whose instructions to his wife were more specific: "a Reformers Wife ought to be an heroine."[8] The second letter (we can be almost sure) is the work of a collier or a village stockinger. It is of much the same order as the more playful letter left by a pitman in the north-east coalfield in the house of a colliery viewer in 1831, into which he and some mates had broken during a strike riot:

I was at yor hoose last neet, and meyd mysel very comfortable. Ye hey nee family, and yor just won man on the colliery, I see ye hev a greet lot of rooms, and big cellars, and plenty wine and beer in them, which I got ma share on. Noo I naw some at wor colliery that has three or fower lads and lasses, and they live in won room not half as gude as yor cellar. I don't pretend to naw very much, but I naw there shudn't be that much difference. The only place we can gan to o the week ends is the yel hoose and hev a pint. I dinna pretend to be a profit, but I naw this, and lots o ma marrows na's te, that wer not tret as we owt to be, and a great filosopher says, to get noledge is to naw wer ignerent. But weve just begun to find that oot, and ye maisters and owners may luk oot, for yor not gan to get se much o yor own way, wer gan to hev some o wors now ...[9]

"If the Bible Societies, and the Sunday School societies have been attended by no other good," Sherwin noted, "they have at least produced one beneficial effect;—they have been the means of teaching many thousands of children to read."[10] The letters of Brandreth and his wife, of Cato Street conspirators, and of other State prisoners, give us some insight into that great area between the attainments of the skilled artisan and those of the barely literate. Somewhere in the middle we may place Mrs. Johnston, addressing her husband ("My Dear Johnston"), who was a journeyman tailor, in prison:

> . . . believe me my Dear if thare is not a day nor a hour in the day but what my mind is less or more engage about you. I can appeal to the almighty that it is true and when I retire to rest I pray God to forgive all my enimies and change thare heart . . .

Beside this we may set the letter of the Sheffield joiner, Wolstenholme, to his wife:

> Our Minaster hath lent me four vollams of the Missionary Register witch give me grat satisfaction to se ou the Lord is carin on is work of grais in distant contres.

The writing of this letter was attended with difficulties, since "Have broke my spettacles."[11] Such letters were written in unaccustomed leisure. We can almost see Wolstenholme laboriously spelling out his words, and stopping to consult a more "well-lettered" prisoner when he came the to the hurdle of "satisfaction." Mrs. Johnston may have consulted (but probably did not) one of the "professional" letter-writers to be found in most towns and villages, who wrote the appropriate form of letter at 1 penny a time. For, even among the literate, letter-writing was an unusual pursuit. The cost of postage alone prohibited it except at infrequent intervals. For a letter to pass between the north and London might cost one shilling ten pence, and we know that both Mrs. Johnston and Mrs. Wolstenholme were suffering privations in the absence of their husbands— Mrs. Johnston's shoes were full of water and she had been able to buy no more since her husband was taken up.

All the Cato Street prisoners, it seems, could write after some fashion. Brunt, the shocmaker, salted some sardonic verses with French, while James Wilson wrote:

> the Cause wich nerved a Brutus arm
> to strike a Tirant with alarm
> the cause for wich brave Hamden died
> for wich the Galant Tell defied
> a Tirants insolence and pride.

Richard Tidd, another shoemaker, on the other hand, could only muster: "Sir I Ham a very Bad Hand at Righting."[12] We cannot, of course, take such men as a "sample," since their involvement in political activity indicates that they belonged to the more conscious minority who followed the Radical press. But they may serve to warn us against *under*stating the diffusion of effective literacy.[13] The artisans are a special case—the intellectual elite of the class. But there were, scattered throughout all parts of England, an abundance of educational institutions for working people, even if "institution" is too formal a word for the dame school, the penny-a-week evening school run by a factory cripple or injured pitman, or the Sunday school itself. In the Pennine valleys, where the weavers' children were too poor to pay for slates or paper, they were taught their letters by drawing them with their fingers in a sand-table. If thousands lost these elementary attainments when they reached adult life, on the other hand the work of the Nonconformist Churches, of friendly societies and trade unions, and the needs of industry itself, all demanded that such learning be consolidated and advanced. "I have found," Alexander Galloway, the master-engineer, reported in 1824,

> from the mode of managing my business, by drawings and written descriptions, a man is not of much use to me unless he can read and write; if a man applies for work, and says he cannot read and write, he is asked no more questions. . . .[14]

In most artisan trades the journeymen and petty masters found some reading and work with figures an occupational necessity.

Not only the ballad-singer but also the "number man" or "calendar man" went round the working-class districts, hawking chap-books,[15] almanacs, dying speeches and (between 1816 and 1820, and at intervals thereafter) Radical periodicals. (One such "calendar man", who travelled for Cowdrey and Black, the "seditious [i.e. Whig] printers in Manchester," was taken up by the magistrates in 1812 because it was found that on his catalogues was written: "No blind king—Ned Ludd for ever."[16] One of the most impressive features of post-war Radicalism was its sustained effort to extend these attainments and to raise the level of political awareness. At Barnsley as early as January 1816 a penny-a-month club of weavers was formed, for the purpose of buying Radical newspapers and periodicals. The Hampden Clubs and Political Unions took great pains to build up "Reading Societies" and in the larger centres they opened permanent newsrooms or reading-rooms, such as that at Hanley in the Potteries. This room was open from 8 a.m. till 10 p.m. There were penalties for swearing, for the use of indecent language, and for drunkenness. Each evening the London papers were to be "publicly read." At the rooms of the Stockport Union in

1818, according to Joseph Mitchell, there was a meeting of class leaders on Monday nights; on Tuesdays, "moral and political readings"; on Wednesdays, "a conversation or debate"; on Thursdays, "Grammar, Arithmetic, &c" was taught; Saturday was a social evening; while Sunday was school day for adults and children alike. In Blackburn the members of the Female Reform Society pledged themselves "to use our outmost endeavour to instil into the minds of our children a deep and rooted hatred of our corrupt and tyrannical rulers." One means was the use of "The Bad Alphabet for the use of the Children of Female Reformers": B was for Bible, Bishop, and Bigotry; K for King, King's evil, Knave, and Kidnapper; W for Whig, Weakness, Wavering, and Wicked.

Despite the repression after 1819, the tradition of providing such newsrooms (sometimes attached to the shop of a Radical bookseller) continued through the 1820s. In London after the war there was a boom in coffee-houses, many of which served this double function. By 1833, at John Doherty's famous "Coffee and Newsroom" attached to his Manchester bookshop, no fewer than ninety-six newspapers were taken every week, including the illegal "unstamped." In the smaller towns and villages the reading-groups were less formal but no less important. Sometimes they met at inns, "hush-shops," or private houses; sometimes the periodical was read and discussed in the workshop. The high cost of periodicals during the time of the heaviest "taxes on knowledge" led to thousands of *ad hoc* arrangements by which small groups clubbed together to buy their chosen paper. During the Reform Bill agitation Thomas Dunning, a Nantwich shoemaker, joined with his shopmates and "our Unitarian minister . . . in subscribing to the *Weekly Dispatch*, price 8½d., the stamp duty being 4d. It was too expensive for *one* ill-paid crispin. . . ."[17]

The circulation of the Radical press fluctuated violently. Cobbett's *2d. Register* at its meridian, between October 1816 and February 1817, was running at something between 40,000 and 60,000 each week, a figure many times in excess of any competitor of any sort.[18] The *Black Dwarf* ran at about 12,000 in 1819, although this figure was probably exceeded after Peterloo. Thereafter the stamp tax (and the recession of the movement) severely curtailed circulation, although Carlile's periodicals ran in the thousands through much of the Twenties. With the Reform Bill agitation, the Radical press broke through to a mass circulation once more: Doherty's *Voice of the People*, 30,000, Carlile's *Gauntlet*, 22,000, Hetherington's *Poor Man's Guardian*, 16,000, while a dozen smaller periodicals, like O'Brien's *Destructive*, ran to some thousands. The slump in the sale of costly weekly periodicals (at anything from 7d. to 1s.) during the stamp tax decade was to great degree made up by the growth in the sales of cheap books and individual pamphlets, ranging from *The Political House that Jack Built* (100,000) to Cobbett's *Cottage Economy* (50,000, 1822–8), *History of the Protestant 'Reformation,'* and *Sermons* (211,000, 1821–8). In the same period, in most of the great centers there were one or more (and in London a dozen) dailies or weeklies which, while not being avowedly "Radical," nevertheless catered for this large Radical public. And the growth in this very large *petit-bourgeois* and working-class reading public was recognized by those influential angencies—notably the Society for the Promotion of Christian Knowledge and the Society for the Diffusion of Useful Knowledge—which made prodigious and lavishly subsided efforts to divert the readers to more wholesome and improving matter.[19]

This was the culture—with its eager disputations around the booksellers' stalls, in the taverns, workshops, and coffee-houses—which Shelley saluted in his "Song to the Men of England" and within which the genius of Dickens matured. But it is a mistake to see it as a single, undifferentiated "reading public." We may say that there were several different "publics" impinging upon and overlapping each other, but nevertheless organised according to different principles. Among the more important were the commercial public, pure and simple, which might be exploited at times of Radical excitement (the trials of Brandreth or of Thistlewood were as marketable as other "dying confessions"), but which was followed according to the simple criteria of profitability; the various more-or-less organised publics, around the Churches or the Mechanic's Institutes; the passive public which the improving societies sought to get at and redeem; and the active, Radical public, which organized itself in the face of the Six Acts and the taxes on knowledge.

The struggle to build and hold this last public has been admirably told in W. D. Wickwar's *The Struggle for the Freedom of the Press.*[20] There is perhaps no country in the world in which the contest for the rights of the press was so sharp, so emphatically victorious, and so peculiarly identified with the cause of the artisans and labourers. If Peterloo established (by a paradox of feeling) the right of public demonstration, the rights of a "free press" were won in a campaign extending over fifteen or more years which has no comparison for its pig-headed, bloody-minded, and indomitable audacity. Carlile (a tinsmith who had nevertheless received a year or two of grammar school education at Ashburton in Devon) rightly saw that the repression of 1819 made the rights of the press the fulcrum of the Radical movement. But, unlike Cobbett and Wooler, who modified their tone to meet the Six Acts in the hope of living to fight another day (and who lost circulation accordingly), Carlile hoisted the black ensign of unqualified defiance and, like a pirate cock-boat, sailed straight into the middle of the combined fleets of State and Church. As, in the aftermath of Peterloo, he came up for trial (for publishing the Works of Paine), the entire Radical press saluted his courage, but gave him up for lost. When he finally emerged, after years of imprisonment, the combined fleets were scattered beyond the horizon in disarray. He had exhausted the ammunition of the

Government, and turned its *ex officio* informations and special juries into laughing-stocks. He had plainly sunk the private prosecuting societies, the Constitutional Association (or "Bridge-Street Gang") and the Vice Society, which were supported by the patronage and the subscriptions of the nobility, bishops, and Wilberforce.

Carlile did not, of course, achieve this triumph on his own. The first round of the battle was fought in 1817, when there were twenty-six prosecutions for seditious and blasphemous libel and sixteen *ex officio* informations filed by the law officers of the Crown.[21] The laurels of victory, in this year, went to Wooler and Hone, and to the London juries which refused to convict. Wooler conducted his own defence; he was a capable speaker, with some experience of the courts, and defended himself with ability in the grandiloquent libertarian manner. The result of his two trials (5 June 1817) was one verdict of "Not Guilty" and one muddled verdict of "Guilty" (from which three jurymen demurred) which was later upset in the Court of King's Bench.[22] The three trials of William Hone in December 1817 are some of the most hilarious legal proceedings on record. Hone, a poor bookseller and former member of the London Corresponding Society, was indicted for publishing blasphemous libels, in the form of parodies upon the Catechism, Litany, and Creed. Hone, in fact, was only a particularly witty exponent of a form of political squib long established among the newsvendors and patterers, and practised in more sophisticated form by men of all parties, from Wilkes to the writers in the *Anti-Jacobin*. Hone, indeed, had not thought his parodies worth risking liberty for. When the repression of February 1817 commenced, he had sought to withdraw them; and it was Carlile, by republishing them, who had forced the Government's hand. Here is a sample:

> Our Lord who art in the Treasury, whatsoever be thy name, thy power be prolonged, thy will be done throughout the empire, as it is in each session. Give us our usual sops, and forgive us our occasional absences on divisions; as we promise not to forgive those that divide against thee. Turn us not out of our places; but keep us in the House of Commons, the land of Pensions and Plenty; and deliver us from the People. Amen.

Hone was held in prison, in poor health, from May until December, because he was unable to find 1,000 pounds bail. He had aroused the particular and personal fury of members of the Cabinet to whom he had attached names that were never forgotten: "Old Bags" (Lord Chancellor Eldon), "Derry Down Triangle" (Castlereagh), and "the Doctor" (Sidmouth). Not much was expected when it was learned that he intended to conduct his own defence. But Hone had been improving the time in prison by collecting examples, from the past and present, of other parodists; and in his first trial before Justice Abbott he secured an acquittal. In the next two days the old, ill and testy Lord Chief Justice Ellenborough himself presided over the trials. Page after page of the record is filled with Ellenborough's interruptions, Hone's unruffled reproofs to the Chief Justice on his conduct, the reading of ludicrous parodies culled from various sources, and threats by the Sheriff to arrest "the first man I see laugh." Despite Ellenborough's unqualified charge (". . . in obedience to his conscience and his God, he pronounced this to be a most impious and profane libel") the jury returned two further verdicts of "Not Guilty," with the consequence (it is said) that Ellenborough retired to his sick-room never to return. From that time forward—even in 1819 and 1820—all parodies and squibs were immune from prosecution.[23]

Persecution cannot easily stand up in the face of ridicule. Indeed, there are two things that strike one about the press battles of these years. The first is, not the solemnity but the delight with which Hone, Cruikshank, Carlile, Davison, Benbow and others baited authority. (This tradition was continued by Hetherington, who for weeks passed under the noses of the constables, in his business as editor of the unstamped *Poor Man's Guardian*, in the highly unlikely disguise of a Quaker.) Imprisonment as a Radical publisher brought, not odium, but honour. Once the publishers had decided that they were ready to go to prison, they outdid each other with new expedients to exhibit their opponents in the most ludicrous light. Radical England was delighted (and no one more than Hazlitt) at the resurrection by Sherwin of *Wat Tyler*—the republican indiscretion of Southey's youth. Southey, now Poet Laureate, was foremost in the clamour to curb the seditious licence of the press, and sought an injunction against Sherwin for infringement of copyright. Lord Eldon refused the injunction: the Court could not take notice of property in the "unhallowed profits of libellous publications." "Is it not a little strange," Hazlitt enquired, "that while this gentleman is getting an injunction against himself as the author of *Wat Tyler*, he is recommending gagging bills against us, and thus making up by force for his deficiency in argument?"[24] On the other hand, Carlile (who had taken over Sherwin's business) was more than pleased that the injunction was refused—for the sales of the poem were a staple source of profit in his difficult period at the start of business. "Glory be to thee, O Southey!" he wrote six years later: "*Wat Tyler* continued to be a source of profit when every other political publication failed. The world does not know what it may yet owe to Southey."[25]

The incidents of the pirating of *Queen Mab* and the *Vision of Judgement* were part of the same ebullient strategy. No British monarch has ever been portrayed in more ridiculous postures nor in more odious terms than George IV during the Queen Caroline agitation, and notably in Hone and Cruikshank's *Right Divine of Kings to Govern Wrong*, *The Queen's Matrimonial Ladder*, *Non Mi*

Ricordo, and *The Man in the Moon*. The same author's *Slap at Slop and the Bridge-Street Gang* (1822), appeared in the format of the Government-subsidised *New Times*, complete with a mock newspaper-stamp with the design of a cat's paw and the motto: "On Every Thing He Claps His Claw," and with mock advertisements and mock lists of births and deaths:

MARRIAGE

His Imperial Majesty Prince Despotism, in a consumption, to Her Supreme Antiquity, The *ignorance* of Eighteen Centuries, in a decline. The bridal dresses were most superb.

While Carlile fought on from prison, the satirists raked his prosecutors with fire.

The second point is the real toughness of the libertarian and constitutional tradition, notwithstanding the Government's assault. It is not only a question of support in unexpected places—Hone's subscription list was headed by donations from a Whig duke, a marquis, and two earls —which indicates an uneasiness in the ruling class itself. What is apparent from the reports of the law officers of the Crowns, in all political trials, is the caution with which they proceeded. In particular they were aware of the unreliability (for their purposes) of the jury system. By Fox's Libel Act of 1792 the jury were judges of the libel as well as of the fact of publishing; and however judges might seek to set this aside, this meant, in effect, that twelve Englishmen had to decide whether they thought the "libel" dangerous enough to merit imprisonment or not. One State prosecution which failed was a blow at the morale of authority which could only be repaired by three which succeeded. Even in 1819–21 when the Government and the prosecuting societies carried almost every case[26] (in part as a result of their better deployment of legal resources and their influence upon juries, in part because Carlile was at his most provocative and had shifted the battlefield from sedition to blasphemy), it still is not possible to speak of "totalitarian" or "Asiatic" despotism. Reports of the trials were widely circulated, containing the very passages—sometimes, indeed, whole books read by the defendants in court—for which the accused were sentenced. Carlile continued imperturbably to edit the *Republican* from gaol; some of his shopmen, indeed, undertook in prison the editing of another journal, as a means of self-improvement. If Wooler's *Black Dwarf* failed in 1824, Cobbett remained in the field. He was, it is true, much subdued in the early Twenties. He did not like Carlile's Republicanism and Deism, nor their hold on the artisans of the great centres; and he turned increasingly back to the countryside and distanced himself from the working-class movement. (In 1821 he undertook the first of his

Rural Rides, in which his genius seems at last to have found its inevitable form and matter.) But, even at this distance, the *Political Register* was always there, with its columns—like those of the *Republican*—open to expose any case of persecution, from Bodmin to Berwick.

The honours of this contest did not belong to a single class. John Hunt and Thelwall (now firmly among the middle-class moderates) were among those pestered by the "Bridge-Street Gang"; Sir Charles Wolseley, Burdett, the Reverend Joseph Harrison, were among those imprisoned for sedition. But Carlile and his shopmen were those who pressed defiance to its furthest point. The main battle was over by 1823, although there were renewed prosecutions in the late Twenties and early Thirties, and blasphemy cases trickled on into Victorian times. Carlile's greatest offence was to proceed with the unabashed publication of the *Political Works*, and then the *Theological Works*, of Tom Paine—works which, while circulating surreptitiously in the enclaves of "old Jacks" in the cities, had been banned ever since Paine's trial *in absentia* in 1792, and Daniel Isaac Eaton's successive trials during the Wars. To this he added many further offences as the struggle wore on, and as he himself moved from Deism to Atheism, and as he threw in provocations—such as the advocacy of assassination[27]—which in any view of the case were incitements to prosecution. He was an indomitable man, but he was scarcely loveable, and his years of imprisonment did not improve him. His strength lay in two things. First, he would not even admit of the possibility of defeat. And second, he had at his back the culture of the artisans.

The first point is not as evident as it appears. Determined men have often (as in the 1790s) been silenced or defeated. It is true that Carlile's brand of determination ("THE SHOP IN FLEET STREET WILL NOT BE CLOSED AS A MATTER OF COURSE") was peculiarly difficult for the authorities to meet. No matter how much law they had on their side, they must always incur odium by prosecutions. But they had provided themselves, under the Six Acts, with the power to *banish* the authors of sedition for offences far less than those which Carlile both committed and proudly admitted. It is testimony to the delicate equilibrium of the time, and to the limits imposed upon power by the consensus of constitutionalist opinion, that even in 1820 this provision of the Act was not employed. Banishment apart, Carlile could not be silenced, unless he were to be beheaded, or, more possibly, placed in solitary confinement. But there are two reasons why the Government did not proceed to extreme measures: first, already by 1821 it seemed to them less *necessary*, for the increased stamp duties were taking effect. Second, it was apparent after the first encounters that if Carlile were to be silenced, half a dozen new Carliles would step into his place. The first two who did so *were*, in fact, Carliles: his wife and his sister. Thereafter the "shopmen" came forward. By one count, before the battle had ended Carlile had

received the help of 150 volunteers, who—shopmen, printers, newsvendors—
had between them served 200 years of imprisonment. The volunteers were
advertised for in the *Republican*—men "who were free, able, and willing to
serve in General Carlile's Corps":

> It is most distinctly to be understood that a love of propagating the prin-
> ciples, and a sacrifice of liberty to that end . . . *and not gain*, must be the
> motive to call forth such volunteers; for—though R. Carlile pledges him-
> self to . . . give such men the best support in his power—should any great
> number be imprisoned, he is not so situated as to property or prospects
> as to be able to promise any particular sum weekly. . . .[28]

From that time forward the "Temple of Reason" off Fleet Street was scarcely
left untenanted for more than a day. The men and women who came forward
were, in nearly every case, entirely unknown to Carlile. They simply came out
of London; or arrived on the coach from Lincolnshire, Dorset, Liverpool, and
Leeds. They came out of a culture.

It was not the "working-class" culture of the weavers or Tyneside pitmen.
The people most prominent in the fight included clerks, shop assistants, a
farmer's son; Benbow, the shoemaker turned bookseller; James Watson, the
Leeds warehouseman who "had the charge of a saddlehorse" at a drysalter's;
James Mann, the cropper turned bookseller (also of Leeds). The intellectual
tradition was in part derived from the Jacobin years, the circle which had once
moved around Godwin and Mary Wollstonecraft, or the members of the L.C.S.,
the last authentic spokesman of which—John Gale Jones—was one of Carlile's
most constant supporters. In part it was a new tradition, owing something to
Bentham's growing influence and something to the "free-thinking Christians"
and Unitarians, such as Benjamin Flower and W. J. Fox. It touched that vigorous sub-culture of the "editors of Sunday newspapers and lecturers at the
Surrey Institute" which *Blackwood's* and the literary Establishment so scorned—
schoolmasters, poor medical students, or civil servants who read Byron and
Shelley and the *Examiner*, and among whom, not Whig or Tory, but "right
and wrong considered by each man abstractedly, is the fashion."[29]

It is scarcely helpful to label this culture *bourgeois* or *petit-bourgeois*, although
Carlile had more than his share of the individualism which (it is generally
supposed) characterises the latter. It would seem to be closer to the truth that
the impulse of rational enlightenment which (in the years of the wars) had been
largely confined to the Radical intelligentsia was now seized upon by the artisans
and some of the skilled workers (such as many cotton-spinners) with an evangelistic zeal to carry it to "numbers unlimited"—a propagandist zeal scarcely
to be found in Bentham, James Mill, or Keats. The subscription lists for Carlile's

campaign drew heavily upon London; and, next, upon Manchester and Leeds. The artisan culture was, above all, that of the self-taught. "During this twelve-month," Watson recalled of his imprisonment, "I read with deep interest and much profit Gibbon's *Decline and Fall of the Roman Empire*, Hume's *History of England*, and . . . Mosheim's *Ecclesiastical History*."[30] The artisans, who formed the nuclei of Carlile's supporting "Zetetic Societies" (as well as of the later Rotunda), were profoundly suspicious of an established culture which had excluded them from power and knowledge and which had answered their protests with homilies and tracts. The works of the Enlightenment came to them with the force of revelation.

In this way a reading public which was increasingly working class in character was forced to *organise itself*. The war and immediate post-war years had seen a "kept" press, on the one hand, and a Radical press on the other. In the Twenties much of the middle-class press freed itself from direct Government influence, and made some use of the advantages which Cobbett and Carlile had gained. *The Times* and Lord Brougham, who disliked the "pauper press" perhaps as much as Lord Eldon (although for different reasons), gave to the term "Radicalism" a quite different meaning—free trade, cheap government, and utilitarian reform. To some degree (although by no means entirely) they carried the Radical middle-class with them—the schoolmasters, surgeons, and shopkeepers, some of whom had once supported Cobbett and Wooler—so that by 1832 there were *two* Radical publics: the middle-class, which looked forward to the Anti-Corn Law League, and the working-class, whose journalists (Hetherington, Watson, Cleave, Lovett, Benbow, O'Brien) were already maturing the Chartist movement. Throughout the Twenties the working-class press struggled under the crushing weight of the stamp duties,[31] while Cobbett remained loosely and temperamentally affiliated to the plebeian rather than to the middle-class movement. The dividing-line came to be, increasingly, not alternative "reform" strategies (for middle-class reformers could on occasion be as revolutionary in their tone as their working-class counterparts) but alternative notions of political economy. The touchstone can be seen during the field labourer's "revolt" in 1830, when *The Times* (Cobbett's "BLOODY OLD TIMES") led the demand for salutary examples to be made of the rioters, while both Cobbett and Carlile were prosecuted once again on charges of inflammatory writing.

In 1830 and 1831 the black ensign of defiance was hoisted once again. Cobbett found a loophole in the law, and recommenced his *Twopenny Trash*. But this time it was Hetherington, a printing worker, who led the frontal attack. His *Poor Man's Guardian* carried the emblem of a hand-press, the motto "Knowledge is Power," and the heading: "Published contrary to 'Law' to try the power of

'Might' against 'Right.' " His opening address quoted, clause by clause, the laws
he intended to defy:

> ... the *Poor Man's Guardian* ... will contain *"news, intelligence and occur-*
> *rences,"* and *"remarks and observations thereon,"* and *"upon matters of Church*
> *and State tending,"* decidedly, *"to excite hatred and contempt of the Govern-*
> *ment and Constitution of ... this country as* BY LAW *established,"* and also,
> *"to vilify the* ABUSES *of Religion"*. ...

It would also defy every clause of the stamp tax legislation,

> or any other acts whatsoever and despite the "laws" or the will and plea-
> sure of *any tyrant* or *body of tyrants* whatsoever, any thing herein-before,
> or any-where-else ... to the contrary notwithstanding.

His fourth number carried the advertisement, "WANTED, Some hundreds of
POOR MEN out of employ who have NOTHING TO RISK ... to sell to the poor
and ignorant" this paper. Not only were the volunteers found, but a score of
other unstamped papers sprang up, notably Carlile's *Gauntlet*, and Joshua Hobson's *Voice of the West Riding*. By 1836 the struggle was substantially over, and
the way had been opened for the Chartist press.

But the "great unstamped" was emphatically a working-class press. The *Poor
Man's Guardian* and the *Working Man's Friend* were, in effect, organs of the
National Union of the Working Classes; Doherty's *Poor Man's Advocate* was
an organ of the Factory Movement; Joshua Hobson was a former hand-loom
weaver, who had built a wooden hand-press by his own labour; Bronterre
O'Brien's *Destructive* consciously sought to develop working-class Radical theory. These small, closely-printed, penny weeklies carried news of the great
struggle for General Unionism in these years, the lock-outs of 1834 and the
protests at the Tolpuddle case, or searching debate and exposition of Socialist
and trade union theory. An examination of this period would take us beyond
the limits of this study, to a time when the working class was no longer in the
making but (in its Chartist form) already made. The point we must note is the
degree to which the fight for press liberties was a central formative influence
upon the shaping movement. Perhaps 500 people were prosecuted for the production and sale of the "unstamped."[32] From 1816 (indeed, from 1792) until
1836 the contest involved not only the editors, booksellers, and printers, but
also many hundreds of newsvendors, hawkers, and voluntary agents.[33]

Year after year the annals of persecution continue. In 1817 two men selling
Cobbett's pamphlets in Shropshire, whom a clerical magistrate "caused ... to

be apprehended under the Vagrant Act . . . and had *well flogged at the whipping-post*"; in the same year hawkers in Plymouth, Exeter, the Black Country, Oxford, the north; in 1819 even a peep-show huckster, who showed a print of Peterloo in a Devon village. The imprisonments were rarely for more than a year (often newsvendors were committed to prison for a few weeks and then released without trial) but they could be more serious in their effects upon the victims than the more widely-publicised imprisonments of editors. Men were thrown into verminous "Houses of Correction"; often chained and fettered; often without knowledge of the law or means of defence. Unless their cases were noted by Cobbett, Carlile, or some section of the Radicals, their families were left without any income and might be forced into the workhouse.[34] It was, indeed, in the smaller centres that the contest for freedom was most hard-fought. Manchester or Nottingham or Leeds had Radical enclaves and meeting-places, and were ready to support the victimised. In the market town or industrial village the cobbler or teacher who took in Cobbett or Carlile in the Twenties might expect to be watched and to suffer persecution in indirect forms. (Often Cobbett's parcels of *Registers* to country subscribers simply failed to arrive— they were "lost" on the mail.) A whole pattern of distribution, with its own folklore, grew up around the militant press. Hawkers (Mayhew was told), in order to avoid "selling" the *Republican*, sold straws instead, and then *gave* the paper to their customers. In the Spen Valley, in the days of the "unstamped," a penny was dropped through a grating and the paper would "appear." In other parts, men would slip down alleys or across fields at night to the known rendezvous. More than once the "unstamped" were transported under the noses of the authorities in a coffin and with a godly cortege of free-thinkers.

We may take two examples of the shopmen and vendors. The first, a shop-*woman*, serves to remind us that, in these rationalist and Owenite circles, the claim for women's rights (almost silent since the 1790s) was once again being made, and was slowly extending from the intelligentsia to the artisans. Carlile's womenfolk, who underwent trial and imprisonment, did so more out of loyalty than out of conviction. Very different was Mrs. Wright, a Nottingham lace-mender, who was one of Carlile's volunteers and who was prosecuted for selling one of his *Addresses* containing opinions in his characteristic manner:

> A Representative System of Government would soon see the propriety of turning our Churches and Chapels into Temples of Science and . . . cherishing the Philosopher instead of the Priest. Kingcraft and Priestcraft I hold to be the bane of Society. . . . Those two evils operate jointly against the welfare both of the body of mind, and to palliate our miseries in this life, the latter endeavour to bamboozle us with a hope of eternal happiness.

She conducted her long defence herself[35] and was rarely interrupted. Towards the end of her defence,

> Mrs. Wright requested permission to retire and suckle her infant child that was crying. This was granted, and she was absent from the Court twenty minutes. In passing to and fro, to the Castle Coffee House, she was applauded and loudly cheered by assembled thousands, all encouraging her to be of good cheer and to persevere.

Some time later she was thrown into Newgate, on a November night, with her six-months' baby and nothing to lie on but a mat. Such women as Mrs. Wright (and Mrs. Mann of Leeds) had to meet not only the customary prosecutions, but also the abuse and insinuations of an outraged loyalist press. "This wretched and shameless woman," wrote the *New Times*, was attended by "*several females*. Are not these circumstances enough to shock every reflecting mind?*" She was an "abandoned creature" (the conventional epithet for prostitutes) "who has cast off all the distinctive shame and fear and decency of her sex." By her "horrid example" she had depraved the minds of other mothers: "these monsters in female form stand forward, with hardened visages, in the face of day, to give their public countenance and support—*for the first time in the history of the Christian world*—to gross, vulgar, horrid blasphemy." She was a woman, wrote Carlile, "of very delicate health, and truly all spirit and no matter."[36]

The longest sentences endured by a newsvendor were probably those served by Joseph Swann, a hat-maker of Macclesfield. He was arrested in 1819 for selling pamphlets and a seditious poem:

> Off with your fetters; spurn the slavish joke;
> Now, now, or never, can your chain be broke;
> Swift then rise and give the fatal stroke.

Shunted from gaol to gaol, and chained with felons, he was eventually sentenced to two years imprisonment for seditious conspiracy, two years for blasphemous libel, and a further six months for seditious libel to run consecutively. When these monstrous sentences had been passed, Swann held up his white hat and enquired of the magistrate: "Han ye done? Is that all? Why I thowt ye'd got a bit of hemp for me, and hung me." His wife also was briefly arrested (for continuing the sale of pamphlets); she and her four children survived on a parish allowance of 9s. a week, with some help from Carlile and Cobbett. Cobbett, indeed, interested himself particularly in the case of Swann, and when Castlereagh committed suicide it was to Swann that Cobbett addressed his

triumphant obituary obloquies: "CASTLEREAGH HAS CUT HIS OWN THROAT
AND IS DEAD! Let that sound reach you in the depth of your dungeon . . . and
carry consolation to your suffering soul!" After serving his four and a half
years, Swann "passed the gate of Chester Castle . . . in mind as stubborn as
ever," and resumed his trade as a hatter. But he had not yet been discharged
from service. In November 1831 the *Poor Man's Guardian* reported proceedings
at the Stockport magistrate's court, where Joseph Swann was charged with
selling the "unstamped." The Chairman of the Bench, Captain Clarke, asked
him what he had to say in his defence:

DEFENDANT. —Well, Sir, I have been out of employment for some time;
neither can I obtain work; my family are all starving. . . . And
for another reason, the weightiest of all; I sell them for the good
of my fellow countrymen; to let them see how they are misrepresented in Parliament. . . . I wish to let the people know how
they are humbugged. . . .

BENCH. —Hold your tongue a moment.

DEFENDANT. —I shall not! for I wish every man to read these publications. . . .

BENCH. —You are very insolent, therefore you are committed to three
months' imprisonment in Knutsford House of Correction, to hard
labour.

DEFENDANT. —I've nothing to thank you for; and whenever I come out, I'll
hawk them again. And *mind you* [looking at Captain Clarke] the
first that I hawk shall be to your house. . . .

Joseph Swann was then forcibly removed from the dock.[37]

In the 20th-century rhetoric of democracy most of these men and women
have been forgotten, because they were impudent, vulgar, over-earnest, or "fa-
natical." In their wake the subsidised vehicles of "improvement," the *Penny
Magazine* and the *Saturday Magazine* (whose vendors no one prosecuted),
moved in; and afterwards the commercial press, with its much larger resources,
although it did not really begin to capture the Radical reading public until the
Forties and the Fifties. (Even then the popular press—the publications of
Cleave, Howitt, Chambers, Reynolds, and Lloyd—came from this Radical
background.) Two consequences of the contest may be particularly noticed.
The first (and most obvious) is that the working-class ideology which matured
in the Thirties (and which has endured, through various translations, ever since)
put an exceptionally high value upon the rights of the press, of speech, of
meeting and of personal liberty. The tradition of the "free-born Englishman"
is of course far older. But the notion to be found in some late "Marxist"
interpretations, by which these claims appear as a heritage of "bourgeois indi-

vidualism," will scarcely do. In the contest between 1792 and 1836 the artisans and workers made this tradition peculiarly their own, adding to the claim for free speech and thought their own claim for the untrammelled propagation, in the cheapest possible form, of the products of this thought.

In this, it is true, they shared a characteristic illusion of the epoch, applying it with force to the context of working-class struggle. All the enlighteners and improvers of the time thought that the only limit imposed to the diffusion of reason and knowledge was that imposed by the inadequacy of the means. The analogies which were drawn were frequently mechanical. The educational method of Lancaster and Bell, with its attempt at the cheap multiplication of learning by child monitors, was called (by Bell) the "STEAM ENGINE OF THE MORAL WORLD." Peacock aimed with deadly accuracy when he called Brougham's Society for the Diffusion of Useful Knowledge the "Steam Intellect Society." Carlile was supremely confident that "pamphlet-reading is destined to work the great necessary moral and political changes among mankind":

> The Printing-press may be strictly denominated a Multiplication Table as applicable to the mind of man. The art of Printing is a multiplication of mind . . . Pamphlet-vendors are the most important springs in the machinery of Reform.[38]

Owen contemplated the institution, by means of propaganda, of the NEW MORAL WORLD with messianic, but mechanical, optimism.

But if this was, in part, the rationalist illusion, we must remember the second—and more immediate—consequence: between 1816 and 1836 this "multiplication" seemed to *work*. For the Radical and unstamped journalists were seizing the multiplying-machine on behalf of the working class; and in every part of the country the experiences of the previous quarter-century had prepared men's minds for what they now could read. The importance of the propaganda can be seen in the steady extension of Radical organisation from the great towns and manufacturing areas into the small boroughs and market towns. One of the Six Acts of 1819 (that authorising the search for weapons) was specifically confined only to designated "disturbed districts" of the Midlands and the north.[39] By 1832—and on into Chartist times—there is a Radical nucleus to be found in every county, in the smallest market towns and even in the larger rural villages, and in nearly every case it is based on the local artisans. In such centres as Croydon, Colchester and Ipswich, Tiverton and Taunton, Nantwich or Cheltenham, there were hardy and militant Radical or Chartist bodies. In Ipswich we find weavers, saddlers, harness-makers, tailors, shoemakers; in Cheltenham shoemakers, tailors, stonemasons, cabinet-makers, gardeners, a plasterer, and a blacksmith—"earnest and reputable people—much above the average in intelligence."[40] These are the people whom Cobbett, Carlile, Hetherington, and their newsvendors had "multiplied."

"Earnest and reputable people . . ." this autodidact culture has never been adequately analysed.[41] The majority of these people had received some elementary education, although its inadequacy is testified from many sources:

> I well remember the first half-time school in Bingley. It was a cottage at the entrance to the mill-yard. The teacher, a poor old man who had done odd jobs of a simple kind for about 12s. a week, was set to teach the half-timers. Lest, however, he should teach too much or the process be too costly, he had to stamp washers out of cloth with a heavy wooden mallet on a large block of wood during school hours.[42]

This is, perhaps, the "schooling" of the early 1830s at its worst. Better village schools, or cheap fee-paying schools patronised by artisans, could be found in the Twenties. By this time, also, the Sunday schools were liberating themselves (although slowly) from the taboo upon the teaching of writing, while the first British and National schools (for all their inadequacies) were beginning to have some effect. But, for any secondary education, the artisans, weavers, or spinners had to teach themselves. The extent to which they were doing this is attested by the sales of Cobbett's educational writings, and notably of his *Grammar of the English Language*, published in 1818, selling 13,000 within six months, and a further 100,000 in the next fifteen years.[43] And we must remember that in translating sales (or the circulation of periodicals) into estimates of readership, the same book or paper was loaned, read aloud, and passed through many hands.

But the "secondary education" of the workers took many forms, of which private study in solitude was only one. The artisans, in particular, were not as rooted in benighted communities as it is easy to assume. They tramped freely about the country in search of work; apart from the enforced travels of the Wars, many mechanics travelled abroad, and the relative facility with which thousands upon thousands emigrated to America and the colonies (driven not only by poverty but also by the desire for opportunity or political freedom) suggests a general fluency of social life. In the cities a vigorous and bawdy plebeian culture co-existed with more polite traditions among the artisans. Many collections of early 19th-century ballads testify to the fervour with which the battle between Loyalists and Radicals was carried into song. Perhaps it was the melodramatic popular theatre which accorded best with the gusto of the Jacobins and of the "old Radicals" of 1816–20. From the early 1790s the theatre, especially in provincial centres, was a forum in which the opposed factions confronted each other, and provoked each other by "calling the tunes" in the intervals. A "Jacobin Revolutionist and Leveller" described a visit to the theatre, in 1795, in a northern port:

> . . . and as the theatre is generally the field in which the Volunteer Officers fight their Campaigns, these military heroes . . . called for the tune of *God Save the King*, and ordered the audience to stand uncovered . . . I sat covered in defiance of the military.[44]

It was in the years of repression that this song (with its denunciation of the "knavish tricks" of the Jacobins) replaced "The Roast Beef of Old England" as a "national anthem." But as the Wars dragged on, the audience often proved itself to be less easily cowed by "Church and King" bullies than later generations. A riot in Sheffield in 1812 commenced when "the South Devon officers insist on having 'God Save the King' sung, and the mobility in the gallery insist on its not being sung. . . . A disturber has been sent to prison."[45]

Most early 19th-century theatre-riots had some Radical tinge to them, even if they only expressed the simple antagonism between the stalls and the gods. The jealousy of the monopolistic Patent Theatres to their little rivals, with their "burlettas" and their shows "disgraced . . . by the introduction of Horses, Elephants, Monkeys, Dogs, Fencers, Tumblers, and Rope Dancers,"[46] was reinforced by the dislike felt by employers for the dangerous ebullience of the audience. In 1798 the "opulent Merchants, Shipbuilders, Ropemakers" and other employers around London Docks memorialised the Government, complaining that the performances at the Royalty Theatre, near the Tower, encouraged "habits of dissipation and profligacy" among "their numerous Manufacturers, Workmen, Servants, &c."[47] (The complaint had been going on for more than two hundred years.) In 1819 disorder raged through central London, night after night, and week after week, in the notorious "O.P." riots, when the prices were raised at Drury Lane. It was Authority's particular dislike of the theatre's blend of disorder and sedition which enabled the Patent Theatres to preserve at least the forms of their monopoly until as late as 1843.

The vitality of the plebeian theatre was not matched by its artistic merit. The most positive influence upon the sensibility of the Radicals came less from the little theatres than from the Shakespearian revival— not only Hazlitt, but also Wooler, Bamford, Cooper, and a score of self-taught Radical and Chartist journalists were wont to cap their arguments with Shakespearian quotations. Wooler's apprenticeship had been in dramatic criticism; while the strictly trades unionist *Trades Newspaper* commenced, in 1825, with a theatre critic as well as a sporting column (covering prize-fighting and the contest between "the Lion Nero and Six Dogs").[48] But there was one popular art which, in the years between 1780 and 1830, attained to a peak of complexity and excellence—the political print.

This was the age, first, of Gillray and of Rowlandson, and then of George Cruikshank, as well as of scores of other caricaturists, some competent, some atrociously crude. Theirs was, above all, a metropolitan art. The models for the cartoonists drove in their coaches past the print-shops where their political (or personal) sins were mercilessly lampooned. No holds whatsoever were barred, on either side. Thelwall or Burdett or Hunt would be portrayed by the loyalists as savage incendiaries, a flaming torch in one hand, a pistol in the other, and with belts crammed with butchers' knives; while Cruikshank portrayed the King (in 1820) lolling blind drunk in his throne, surrounded by broken bottles and in front of a screen decorated with satyrs and large-breasted trollops. (The Bishops fared no better.) The popular print was by no means an art for the illiterate, as the balloons full of minute print, issuing from the mouths of the figures, testify. But the illiterate also could participate in this culture, standing by the hour in front of the print-shop window and deciphering the intricate visual minutae in the latest Gillray or Cruikshank: at Knight's in Sweeting's Alley, Fairburn's off Ludgate Hill, or Hone's in Fleet Street (Thackeray recalled), "there used to be a crowd . . . of grinning, good-natured mechanics, who spelt the songs, and spoke them out for the benefit of the company, and who received the points of humour with a general sympathising roar." On occasions, the impact was sensational; Fleet Street would be blocked by the crowds; Cruikshank believed that his "Bank Restriction Note" (1818) resulted in the abolition of the death-penalty for passing forged money. In the 1790s the Government actually suborned Gillray into anti-Jacobin service. During the Wars the mainstream of prints was patriotic and anti-Gallican (John Bull took on his classic shape in these years), but on domestic issues the prints were savagely polemical and frequently Burdettite in sympathy. After the Wars a flood of Radical prints was unloosed, which remained immune from prosecution, even during the Queen Caroline agitation, because prosecution would have incurred greater ridicule. Through all its transformations (and despite the crudities of many practitioners) it remained a highly sophisticated city art: it could be acutely witty, or cruelly blunt and obscene, but in either case it depended upon a frame of reference of shared gossip and of intimate knowledge of the manners and foibles of even minor participants in public affairs—a patina of intricate allusiveness.[49]

The culture of the theatre and the print-shop was popular in a wider sense than the literary culture of the Radical artisans. For the keynote of the autodidact culture of the Twenties and early Thirties was moral sobriety. It is customary to attribute this to the influence of Methodism, and undoubtedly, both directly and indirectly, this influence can be felt. The Puritan character-structure underlies the moral earnestness and self-discipline which enabled men to work on by candle-light after a day of labour. But we have to make two important reservations. The first is that Methodism was a strongly *anti-intellectual* influence, from which British popular culture has never wholly recovered. The circle to which Wesley would have confined the reading of Methodists (Southey noted) "was narrow enough; his own works, and his own series of abridgements, would have constituted the main part of a Methodist's library."[50] In the early 19th century local preachers and class leaders were encouraged to read more: reprints of Baxter, the hagiography of the movement, or "vollams of the Missionary Register." But poetry was suspect, and philosophy, biblical criticism, or political theory taboo. The whole weight of Methodist teaching fell upon the blessedness of the "pure in heart," no matter what their rank or accomplishments. This gave to the Church its egalitarian spiritual appeal. But it also fed (sometimes to gargantuan proportions) the philistine defences of the scarcely-literate. "It is *carte blanche* for ignorance and folly," Hazlitt exploded:

> Those . . . who are either unable or unwilling to think connectedly or rationally on any subject, are at once released from every obligation of the kind, by being told that faith and reason are opposed to one another.[51]

From the successive shocks of Paine, Cobbett, Carlile, the Methodist ministers defended their flocks: the evidence was abundant that unmonitored literacy was the "snare of the devil."

Some of the off-shoots from the main Methodist stem—the Methodist Unitarians (an odd conjunction) and notably the New Connexion—were more intellectual in inclination, and their congregations resemble the older Dissenting Churches. But the main Methodist tradition responded to the thirst for enlightenment in a different way. We have already noted the submerged affinities between Methodism and middle-class Utilitarianism. Strange as it may seem, when we think of Bentham and his hatred of "juggical" superstition, the spirit of the times was working for a conjunction of the two traditions. If intellectual *enquiry* was discouraged by the Methodists, the acquisition of *useful* knowledge could be seen as godly and full of merit. The emphasis, of course, was upon the *use*. Work-discipline alone was not enough, it was necessary for the labour force to advance towards more sophisticated levels of attainment. The old opportunist Baconian argument—that there could be no evil in the study of nature, which is the visible evidence of God's laws—had now been assimilated within Christian apologetics. Hence arose that peculiar phenomenon of early Victorian culture, the Nonconformist parson with his hand on the Old Testament and his eye on a microscope.

The effects of this conjunction can already be felt within the working-class culture of the Twenties. Science—botany, biology, geology, chemistry, mathematics, and, in particular, the applied sciences—the Methodists looked upon with favour, provided that these pursuits were not intermixed with politics or speculative philosophy. The solid, statistical, intellectual world which the Utilitarians were building was congenial also to the Methodist Conference. They also compiled their statistical tables of Sunday school attendances, and Bunting (one feels) would have been happy if he could have calculated degrees of spiritual grace with the accuracy that Chadwick calculated the minimum diet that might keep a pauper in strength to work. Hence came that alliance between Nonconformists and Utilitarians in educational endeavour, and in the dissemination of "improving" knowledge alongside godly exhortation. Already in the Twenties this kind of literature is well established, in which moral admonishments (and accounts of the drunken orgies of Tom Paine on his unvisited deathbed) appear side by side with little notes on the flora of Venezuela, statistics of the death-roll in the Lisbon earthquake, recipes for boiled vegetables, and notes on hydraulics:

> Every species . . . requires a different kind of food. . . . Linnaeus has remarked, that the cow eats 276 species of plants and rejects 218; the goat eats 449 and rejects 126; the sheep eats 387 and rejects 141; the horse eats 262 and rejects 212; and the hog, more nice in its taste than any of those, eats but 72 plants and rejects all the rest. Yet such is the unbounded munificence of the Creator, that all these countless myriads of sentient beings are amply provided for and nourished by his bounty! "The eyes of all these look unto Him, and he openeth his hand and satisfieth the desire of every living being."[52]

And already in the Twenties, Political Economy can be seen as a third partner alongside Morality and Useful Knowledge, in the shape of homilies upon the God-given and immutable laws of supply and demand. Capital, even nicer in its taste than the hog, would select only the industrious and obedient worker and reject all others.

Thus Methodism and Evangelicism contributed few active intellectual ingredients to the articulate culture of the working people, although they can be said to have added an earnestness to the pursuit of *information*. (Arnold was later to see the Nonconformist tradition as deeply philistine, and indifferent to "sweetness and light.") And there is a second reservation to be made, when the sobriety of the artisan's world is attributed to this source. Moral sobriety was in fact demonstrably a product of the Radical and rationalist agitation itself; and owed much to the old Dissenting and Jacobin traditions. This is not to say that there were no drunken Radicals nor disorderly demonstrations. Wooler was only one of the Radical leaders who, it was said, was too fond of the bottle; while we have seen that the London taverns and Lancashire hush-shops were important meeting-places. But the Radicals sought to rescue the people from the imputation of being a "mob"; and their leaders sought continually to present an image of sobriety.

Moreover, there were other motives for this emphasis. One of the Rules of the Bath Union Society for Parliamentary Reform (established in January 1817) is characteristic:

> It is earnestly recommended to every Member not to spend his Money at public houses, because half of the said Money goes in Taxes, to feed the Maggots of Corruption.[53]

In the post-war years Hunt and Cobbett made much of the call for abstinence from all taxed articles, and in particular of the virtues of water over spirits or beer. The sobriety of the Methodists was the one (and only) attribute of their "sect" which Cobbett found it possible to praise: "I look upon drunkenness as the root of much more than half the mischief, misery and crimes with which society is afflicted."[54] This was not always Cobbett's tone; on other occasions he could lament the price, for the labourer, of beer. But a general moral primness is to be found in most quarters. It was, particularly, the ideology of the artisan or of the skilled worker who had held his position in the face of the boisterous unskilled tide. It is to be found in Carlile's account of his early manhood:

> I was a regular, active, and industrious man, working early and late . . . and when out of the workshop never so happy anywhere as at home with my wife and two children. The alehouse I always detested . . . I had a notion that a man . . . was a fool not to make a right application of every shilling.[55]

Many a day he had missed out a meal, and "carried home some sixpenny publication to read at night." It is to be found, in its most admirable and moving form, in William Lovett's *Life and Struggles . . . in Pursuit of Bread, Knowledge and Freedom*, a title which, in itself, condenses all that we are seeking to describe.

It was a disposition strengthened, among the republicans and free-thinkers, by the character of the attacks upon them. Denounced in loyalist lampoons and from Church pulpits as disreputable exemplars of every vice, they sought to exhibit themselves as bearing, alongside their unorthodox opinions, an irreproachable character. They struggled against the loyalist legends of revolutionary France, which was presented as a sanguinary thieves' kitchen, whose Temples of Reason were brothels. They were particularly sensitive to any accusation of sexual impropriety, of financial misconduct, or of lack of attachment to the familial virtues.[56] Carlile published in 1830 a little book of homilies, *The Moralist*, while Cobbett's *Advice to Young Men* was only a more hearty and readable essay upon the same themes of industry, perseverance, independence. The rationalists, of course, were especially anxious to counter the accusation that the rejection of the Christian faith must inevitably entail the dissolution of all moral restraints. Alongside Volney's influential *Ruins of Empire* there was translated, and circulated as a tract, his *Law of Nature*, which served to argue— in the form of a dialogue—that the respectable virtues must all be adhered to according to the laws of social utility:

Q. Why do you say that conjugal love is a virtue?
A. Because the concord and union which are the consequence of the affection
   subsisting between married persons, establish in the bosom of their family
   a multitude of habits which contribute to its prosperity and conservation. . . .

So on for the greater part of a page. And so, through chapters on Knowledge, Continence, Temperance, Cleanliness, the Domestic Virtues, which read like a prospectus for the Victorian age. Where heterodoxy appeared on matters of sexual relations, as it did among the Owenite communitarians, it generally did so with a zeal characteristic of the Puritan temperament.[57] The very small group of neo-Malthusians, who with considerable courage propagated among the working people, in the early Twenties, knowledge of the means of contraception did so out of the conviction that the only way in which the "industrious classes" could raise their physical and cultural standards was by limiting their own numbers. Place and his companions would have been utterly shocked if it had been suggested that these means contributed to sexual or personal freedom.[58]

Levity or hedonism was as alien to the Radical or rationalist disposition as it was to the Methodist, and we are reminded of how much the Jacobins and Deists owed to the traditions of old Dissent. But it is possible to judge too much from the written record, and the public image of the orator. In the actual movement, cheerfulness keeps breaking in, not only with Hone, but, increasingly, with Hetherington, Lovett, and their circle, who were softer, more humorous, more responsive to the people, less didactic, but not less determined, than their master, Carlile. It is tempting to offer the paradox that the rationalist artisans on Carlile's or Volney's model exhibited the same behaviour-patterns as their Methodist analogues; whereas in one case sobriety and cleanliness were recommended in obedience to God and to Authority, in the other case they were requisite virtues in those who made up the army which would overthrow Priestcraft and Kingcraft. To an observer who did not know the language the moral attributes of both might have appeared indistinguishable. But this is only partly so. For Volney's chapter-headings continue, "Of the Social Virtues, and of Justice." There was a profound difference between disciplines recommended for the salvation of one's own soul, and the same disciplines recommended as means to the salvation of a class. The Radical and free-thinking artisan was at his most earnest in his belief in the *active* duties of citizenship.

Moreover, together with this sobriety, the artisan culture nurtured the values of intellectual enquiry and of mutuality. We have seen much of the first quality, displayed in the fight for press freedom. The autodidact had often an uneven, laboured understanding, but it was *his own*. Since he had been forced to find his intellectual way, he took little on trust: his mind did not move within the established ruts of a formal education. Many of his ideas challenged authority, and authority had tried to suppress them. He was willing, therefore, to give a hearing to any new anti-authoritarian ideas. This was one cause for the instability of the working-class movement, especially in the years between 1825 and 1835; it also helps us to understand the rapidity with which Owenism spread, and the readiness of men to swing from one to another of the utopian and communitarian schemes which were put forward. (This artisan culture can be seen, also, as a leaven still at work in Victorian times, as the self-made men or the children of artisans of the Twenties contributed to the vigour and diversity of its intellectual life.) By mutuality we mean the tradition of mutual study, disputation, and improvement. We have seen something of this in the days of the L.C.S. The custom of reading aloud the Radical periodicals, for the benefit of the illiterate, also entailed—as a necessary consequence—that each reading devolved into an *ad hoc* group discussion: Cobbett had set out his arguments, as plainly as he could, and now the weavers, stockingers, or shoemakers, debated them.

A cousin of this kind of group was the mutual improvement society, whether formal or informal, which met week by week with the intention of acquiring knowledge, generally under the leadership of one of its own members.[59] Here, and in the Mechanic's Institutes, there was some coming-together of the traditions of the chapel and of the Radicals. But the co-existence was uneasy, and not always peaceful. The early history of the Mechanic's Institutes, from the formation of the London Institute in 1823 until the 1830s, is a story of ideological conflict. From the standpoint of the Radical artisan or trade unionist, the enthusiasm of Dr. Birkbeck and of some Dissenting clergy and Benthamite professional men to assist them to establish centres for the promotion of knowledge was very much to be welcomed. But they certainly were not prepared to have this help *on any terms*. If Brougham appears in some recent writing as a great, but opportunist, Radical, this was not at all how he was viewed by the "old Radicals" of 1823. They had seen him provide apologies for the spy system in 1817 (in a speech which Cobbett raked up again and again); and they were to see him stand up in the House at the climax of Carlile's campaign and declare that he "rejoiced at the result of some recent trials" and regarded the prisoners as having published "a mass of the grossest and most criminal matter."[60] Brougham's zeal for the Institutes was enough to make them suspect at the outset; and Place's attempts to act as go-between between Brougham (whom he secretly despised) and the London trades unionists (who less secretly suspected him) were not likely to dispel this. The crucial conflicts took place on the questions of control, of financial independence, and on whether or not the Institutes should debate political economy (and, if so, *whose* political economy). Thomas Hodgskin was defeated in the latter conflict by Place and Brougham. In the former conflicts Birkbeck, in his zeal to raise money to expand the facilities of the Institute, overruled the advice of Robertson, Hodgskin, and John Gast that—if the matter was undertaken less ambitiously—the artisans themselves could raise the necessary funds, and own and control the whole.

These two defeats, and the inauguration of Brougham's lectures on political economy (1825), meant that control passed to the middle-class supporters, whose ideology also dominated the political economy of the syllabus. By 1825 the *Trades Newspaper* regarded the London Institute as a lost cause, which was dependent upon "the great and wealthy":

> When it was founded, there was such a strong and general feeling excited on its behalf among the Mechanics of the Metropolis, that we felt perfectly convinced, had not that feeling been damped . . . the Mechanics themselves might and would have furnished all the means requisite for ensuring it the most splendid success . . .

In the provinces the history of the Mechanic's Institutes is more chequered. In Leeds (as Dr. Harrison has shown) the Institute was from the outset controlled by sponsors from the middle class, and notably by Nonconformist manufacturers; in Bradford and in Huddersfield it was, for a period, controlled by Radical artisans. After the mid-Twenties the tendency was general for the custom of artisans to give way to that of the lower middle class, and for orthodox political economy to come into the syllabus. But still in 1830 the movement looked unorthodox enough (by reason of its galaxy of Utilitarian and Unitarian sponsors) for many Anglican and Wesleyan clergy to hold aloof. A Yorkshire vicar, in 1826, saw the Institutes as agencies of universal suffrage and "universal free-thinking," which would "in time degenerate into Jacobin clubs, and become nurseries of disaffection." In the early 1830s a curate attacked the management of the Leicester Mechanic's Institute for perverting it into a school "for the diffusion of infidel, republican, and levelling principles." Among the papers taken by its library was Carlile's *Gauntlet*.[61]

We have spoken of the *artisan* culture of the Twenties. It is the most accurate term to hand, and yet it is not more than approximate. We have seen that *"petit-bourgeois"* (with its usual pejorative associations) will not do; while to speak of a "working-class" culture would be premature. But by artisan we should understand a milieu which touched the London shipwrights and Manchester factory operatives at one side, and the degraded artisans, the outworkers, at the other. To Cobbett these comprised the "journeymen and labourers," or, more briefly, "the people." "I am of opinion," he wrote to the Bishop of Llandaff in 1820, "that your Lordship is very much deceived in supposing the People, or the vulgar, as you were pleased to call them, to be *incapable of comprehending argument"*:

> The people do not, I assure your Lordship, at all relish little simple tales. Neither do they delight in declamatory language, or in loose assertion, their minds have, within the last ten years, undergone a very great revolution . . .
>
> Give me leave . . . to say that . . . these classes are, to my certain knowledge, at this time, more enlightened than the other classes of the community. . . . They see further into the future than the Parliament and the Ministers.—There is this advantage attending their pursuit of knowledge.—They have no particular interest to answer; and, therefore, their judgement is unclouded by prejudice and selfishness. Besides which, their communication with each other is perfectly free. The thoughts of one man produce other thoughts in another man. Notions are canvassed without the restraint imposed upon suspicion, by false pride, or false delicacy. And hence the truth is speedily arrived at.[62]

Which argument, which truths?

II. William Cobbett

Cobbett throws his influence across the years from the end of the Wars until the passing of the Reform Bill. To say that he was in no sense a systematic thinker is not so say that his was not a serious intellectual influence. It was Cobbett who *created* this Radical intellectual culture, not because he offered its most original ideas, but in the sense that he found the tone, the style, and the arguments which could bring the weaver, the schoolmaster, and the shipwright into a common discourse. Out of the diversity of grievances and interests he brought a Radical consensus. His *Political Registers* were like a circulating medium which provided a common means of exchange between the experiences of men of widely differing attainments.

We can see this if we look, less at his ideas, than at his tone. And one way to do this is to contrast his manner with that of Hazlitt, the most "Jacobin" of the middle-class Radicals and the one who—over a long period of years—came closest to the same movement as that of the artisans. Hazlitt is using his knife on the fund-holders and sinecurists:

> Legitimate Governments (flatter them as we will) are not another Heathen mythology. They are neither so cheap nor so splendid as the Delphin edition of Ovid's Metamorphoses. They are indeed "Gods to punish," but in other respects "men of our infirmity." They do not feed on ambrosia or drink nectar; but live on the common fruits of the earth, of which they get the largest share, and the best. The wine they drink is made of grapes: the blood they shed is that of their subjects: the laws they make are not against themselves: the taxes they vote, they afterwards devour. They have the same wants that we have: and, having the option, very naturally help themselves first, out of the common stock, without thinking that others are to come after them.... Our State-paupers have their hands in every man's dish, and fare sumptuously every day. They live in palaces, and loll in coaches. In spite of Mr. Malthus, their studs of horses consume the produce of our fields, their dog-kennels are glutted with the food that would maintain the children of the poor. They cost us so much a year in dress and furniture, so much in stars and garters, blue ribbons, and grand crosses,—so much in dinners, breakfasts, and suppers, and so much in suppers, breakfasts, and dinners. These heroes of the Income-tax, Worthies of the Civil List, Saints of the Court calender (*compagnons du lys*), have their naturals and non-naturals, like the rest of the world, but at a dearer rate.... You will find it easier to keep them a week than a month; and at the end of that time, waking from the sweet dream of Legitimacy, you may say with Caliban, "Why, what a fool was I to take this drunken monster for a God."[63]

Hazlitt's was a complex and admirable sensibility. He was one of the few intellectuals who received the full shock of the experience of the French Revolution, and, while rejecting the naiveties of the Enlightenment, reaffirmed the traditions of *liberté* and *égalité*. His style reveals, at every point, not only that he was measuring himself against Burke, Coleridge, and Wordsworth (and, more immediately, against *Blackwood's* and the *Quarterly Review*), but that he was aware of the strength of some of their positions, and shared some of their responses. Even in his most engaged Radical journalism (of which this is an example) he aimed his polemic, not towards the popular, but towards the polite culture of his time. His *Political Essays* might be published by Hone,[64] but, when writing them, he will have thought less of Hone's audience than of the hope that he might make Southey squirm, make the *Quarterly* apoplectic, or even stop Coleridge short in mid-sentence.

This is in no sense a criticism. Hazlitt had a width of reference and a sense of commitment to a *European* conflict of historical significance which makes the plebeian Radicals appear provincial both in space and time. It is a question of roles. Cobbett could never have written a sentence of this passage. He could not admit (even as a figure of speech) that we might *will* to flatter Legitimacy; he could not have accepted the norms of "the world," which Hazlitt assumes, if only to punish; he could not have written "*our* State-paupers," since his every sinew was strained to make his audience see the stock-jobbers and placemen as *them*; and, as a corollary, he could not have written, with this sense of distance, of "the children of the poor,"—he would either have said (to his audience) "*your* children" or he would have given a particular example. He is not likely to have said "they cost us so much a year"; he would have put down a definite figure, even if it was at hazard. "These heroes of the Income-tax" is closer to Cobbett's trick of *naming*[65] but with Hazlitt there is still the drawl of the patrician Friend of the People (like Wilkes or Burdett, a pinch of snuff just at the moment when poised in the House for the most deadly thrust); with Cobbett there is no ironic pretence of ceremony—out come the names, *Parson* Malthus, *Bolton* Fletcher, the *Thing*, with a bluntness which made even Shelley blench ("Cobbett's snuff, revenge").

It is a matter of tone; and yet, in tone, will be found at least one half of Cobbett's political meaning. Hazlitt's style, with its sustained and controlled rhythms, and its antithetical movement, belongs to the polite culture of the essayist. Despite *Rural Rides*, one cannot easily think of Cobbett as an essayist. Indeed, Hazlitt's fertile allusiveness and studied manner, since it belonged to a culture which was not available to the artisans, might well arouse their hostility. When Cobbett wrote about sinecures it was in some such terms as this:

There are of these places and pensions all sizes, from *twenty pounds* to *thirty thousands* and nearly *forty thousand pounds* a year! . . . There are several individual placemen, the profits of *each* of which would maintain a *thousand families.* . . . Mr. PRESTON . . . who is a *Member of Parliament* and has a large estate, says, upon this subject, "Every family, even of the poorest labourers, consisting of five persons, may be considered as paying in *indirect taxes,* at least *ten pounds a year,* or more than half his wages at seven shillings a week!" And yet the insolent hirelings call you the *mob,* the *rabble,* the *swinish multitude,* and say, that your voice is nothing. . . ."[66]

Everything here is solid, and related, not to a literary culture, but to commonly-available experience. Even Mr. Preston is *placed*. Cobbett brought the rhythms of speech back into prose; but of strenuously argumentative, emphatic speech.

Observe him writing on the familiar theme that the clergy should be judged, not by their professions, but their actions:

> There is something unfortunate, to say the least of it, in this perfect union of action between the Church and the Methodist Convocation. Religion is not an abstract idea. It is not something metaphysical. It is to produce effect upon men's conduct, or it is good for nothing. It is to have an effect upon the actions of men. It is to have a good influence in the affairs and on the condition of men. Now, if the Church religion . . .[67]

Cobbett's relationship to his audience in such passages as this (and the example falls from the first *Register* which comes to hand—almost any *Register* would provide the same) is so palpable that one might reach out one's hand and touch it. It is an argument. There is a proposition. Cobbett writes "metaphysical," looks up at his audience, and wonders whether the word communicates. He explains the relevance of the term. He repeats his explanation in the plainest language. He repeats it again, but this time he enlarges the definition to carry wider social and political implications. Then, these short sentences finished with, he commences exposition once more. In the word "Now" we feel is implied: "if all of you have taken my point, let us proceed together. . . ."

It is not difficult to show that Cobbett had some very stupid and contradictory ideas, and sometimes bludgeoned his readers with specious arguments.[68] But such demonstrations are beside the point unless the profound, the truly profound democratic influence of Cobbett's attitude to his audience is understood. Paine anticipates the tone; but Cobbett, for thirty years, talked to his audience like this, until men were talking and arguing like Cobbett all over the land. He assumed, as a matter scarcely in need of demonstration, that every citizen whatsoever had the power of reason, and that it was by argument addressed to the common understanding that matters should be settled. During the past ten years (he wrote in 1820)—

> I have addressed nothing to [the people] which did not rely, for success, upon *fact*, and upon the best arguments which I was able to produce. My subjects have been generally of the most intricate nature . . . I have made use of no means to attract curiosity or to humour the fancy. All has been an appeal to the understanding, the discernment and the justice of the reader.

It is not, of course, true that Cobbett employed no devices to "attract curiosity."
If he treated his readers as equals he treated Ministers, Bishops, and Lords as
something less. ("Wilberforce," one of his open letters began: "I have you
before me in a canting pamphlet.") To this we should add two other devices.
The first is the homely, practical analogy, most commonly taken from rural
life. In this he had an unerring sense of the experience available to the whole
body of his readers. Such figures, with him, were not decorative in function,
or passing allusions. They were taken up, held in the hand, turned over, deliberately deployed to advance the argument, and then set down. We may take
the example of Cobbett's famous description of Brougham and the moderate
reformers as scarecrows or *shoy-hoys*—"and now I will tell you why":

A shoy-hoy is a sham man or woman, made of straw or other stuff, twisted
round a stake, stuck into the ground . . . with a stick or gun put into its
hand. These shoy-hoys are set up for the purpose of driving birds from
injuring the corn or the seeds, and sometimes to frighten them from cherries, or other fruit. The people want a reform of the parliament, and there
has for a long time . . . been a little band, who have professed the desire
to get parliamentary reform. They have made motions and speeches and
divisions, with a view of keeping the hopes of the people alive, and have
thereby been able to keep them quiet from time to time. They have never
desired to *succeed*; because success would put an end to their hopes of
emolument; but they have amused the people. The great body of the
factions, knowing the reality of their views, have been highly diverted by
the sham efforts, which have never interrupted them in the smallest degree
in their enjoyment of the general plunder. Just as it happens with the birds
and the shoy-hoys in the fields or gardens. At first, the birds take the
shoy-hoys for a *real* man or woman; and, so long as they do this, they
abstain from their work of plunder; but after having for some little while
watched the shoy-hoy with their quick and piercing eyes, and perceived
that it never moves hand or foot, they totally disregard it, and are no
more obstructed by it than if it were a post. Just so it is with these political
shoy-hoys; but . . . they *do mischief*. . . . I remember an instance . . . which
very aptly illustrates the functions of these political deceivers. The birds
were committing great ravages upon some turnip-seed that I had at Botley. "Stick up a shoy-hoy," said I to my bailiff. "That will do *no good*,
sir;" . . . he replied . . . telling me, that he had, that morning, in the garden of
his neighbour Morell . . . actually seen a sparrow settled, with a *pod*, upon
the *shoy-hoy's hat*, and there, as upon a dining-table, actually pecking out
the peas and eating them, which he could do with greater security there
where he could look about him and see the approach of an enemy, than

he could have done upon the ground, where he might have been taken by *surprise*. Just exactly such are the functions of our political shoy-hoys. The agricultural . . . shoy-hoys deceive the depredating birds but a very short time; but they continue to deceive those who stick them up and rely upon them, who, instead of rousing in the morning, and sallying upon the depredators with powder and shot, trust to the miserable shoy-hoys, and thus lose their corn and their seeds. Just thus it is with the people, who are the dupes of all political shoy-hoys. In Suffolk, and other eastern counties, they call them *mawkses*. . . .[69]

What is one to make of such writing? From one aspect it is imaginative writing of genius. The analogy commences a little stiffly; politics and agriculture run on converging lines, but we feel the image to be far-fetched. Then—at "quick and piercing eyes"—the two arguments are fused, with an uprush of polemical delight. Cobbett is half in jest, the image grows to surrealist proportions—Brougham with a sparrow on his hat, the reformers with powder and shot, turnip-seed and neighbour Morell (who will probably never make his appearance again). From another aspect, what an extraordinary thing it is, this part of the English political tradition! This is more than polemic: it is also political theory. Cobbett has defined, in terms that a labourer or artisan could well understand, the function of a very English form of reformist accommodation. More than this, he illuminates, across more than a century, the *mawkses* of other parties and other times.

The other device, which we have already noted, is the personalisation of political issues—a personalisation centred upon Cobbett of Botley himself. But if Cobbett was his own subject, he handled this subject with unusual objectivity. His egotism transcended itself to the point where the reader is aware, not of Cobbett's ego, but of a plain-spoken, matter-of-fact observant, sensibility, with which he is encouraged to identify himself. He is asked to look, not *at* Cobbett, but *with* him. The triumph of this manner can be seen in his *Rural Rides*, where not only his contemporaries but successive generations have felt his palpable presence as he talked with labourers in the fields, rode through the villages, and stopped to bait his horses. The force of his indignation is all the more compelling because of his delight at anything which pleased him. At Tenterden—

the afternoon was very fine, and, just as I rose the hill and entered the street, the people had come out of church and were moving along towards their houses. It was a very fine sight. *Shabbily-dressed people do not go to church*. I saw, in short, drawn out before me, the dress and beauty of the town; and a great many very, very pretty girls I saw; and saw them, too, in their best attire. I remember the girls in the *Pays de Caux*, and, really,

I think those of Tenterden resemble them. I do not know why they should not; for there is the *Pays de Caux* only just over the water, just opposite this very place.

Or, in a village in Surrey, the absence of poverty is made into a telling point against its general incidence:

As I came along between Upwaltham and Eastdean, I called to me a young man, who, along with other turnip-hoers, was sitting under the shelter of a hedge at breakfast. He came running to me with his victuals in his hand; and I was glad to see that his food consisted of a good lump of household bread and not a very small piece of *bacon*. . . . In parting with him, I said, "You do get some *bacon* then?" "Oh, yes! Sir," said he, and with an emphasis and a swag of the head which seemed to say, "We *must* and *will* have *that*." I saw, and with great delight, a pig at almost every labourer's house. The houses are good and warm; and the gardens some of the very best that I have seen in England. What a difference, good God! what a difference between this country and the neighbourhood of those corrupt places *Great Bedwin* and *Cricklade*. What sort of *breakfast* would this man have had in a mess of *cold potatoes*? Could he have *worked*, and worked in the wet, too, with such food? Monstrous! No society ought to exist where the labourers live in a hog-like sort of way.

"There is the *Pays de Caux* . . . just opposite this very place," "this country", "this man"—wherever he was, Cobbett always compelled his readers, by the immediacy of his vision, the confusion of reflection and description, the solidity of detail, and the physical sense of place, to identify themselves with his own standpoint. And "standpoint" is the proper word, for Cobbett placed himself firmly in some physical setting—on his farm at Botley or on the road into Tenterden—and then led outwards from the evidence of his senses to his general conclusions. Even during his American exile (1817–19) it was important for him to convey this sense of place:

From one side of my room I look out into a farm yard, full of fodder and of cattle, sheep, hogs, and multitudes of poultry, while, at a few paces, beyond the yard, runs the river Susquehannah, which is wider than the Thames and has innumerable islands lying in it, from a quarter of an acre to five or six acres in extent. From the other side of my room I look into an Orchard of Apples and Peaches of forty acres, lying in a narrow valley, which runs up between two mountains, about a quarter of a mile high, formed precisely like ridge of a house, the gable ends being towards the river. Last night it rained: it froze before morning, and the frost caught the drops hanging upon the trees; so that the sun, which is now shining as bright as in England in the month of May, exhibits these icicles in countless millions of sparkling diamonds.

But this setting was turned to effect to dramatise the more strongly his feelings (expressed in a letter to Hunt) inspired by the news of the execution of Brandreth and his fellows:

> I have, my dear Hunt, the little thatched cottages of Waltham Chase and of Botley Common now full in my mind's eye, and I feel at this day, with more force than ever, that passion, which would make me prefer the occupation of the meanest of those most humble abodes, accompanied with the character of Englishman, to the mastership over, and the actual possession of, all that I have above described, unaccompanied, with that character. As I said, when I left England, so I still say, that I never can like any people so well as I like the people of England.

If Cobbett made, from the struggles of the reform movement, something of a martyrology and demonology, he was himself the central figure of the myth. But we should hesitate before we accuse him too far of personal vanity. For the myth demanded also that William Cobbett be seen as a plain Englishman, unusually belligerent and persevering, but not especially talented—such a man as the reader might think himself to be, or the labourer in the turnip-field, or (given this or that turn of circumstance) as the landlady's son in a small inn in a Sussex village might become:

> The landlady sent her son to get me some cream, and he was just such a chap as I was at his age, and dressed just in the same sort of way, his main garment being a blue smock-frock, faded from wear, and mended with pieces of *new* stuff. . . . The sight of this smock-frock brought to my recollection many things very dear to me. This boy will, I dare say, perform his part at Billingshurst, or at some place not far from it. If accident had not taken me from a similar scene, how many villains and fools, who have been well teazed and tormented, would have slept in peace at night, and have fearlessly swaggered about by day!

His compassion for the poor always had this quality: "there, but for the grace of God, goes Will Cobbett." His affectation was to appear to be more "normal" than he was. He never allowed his readers to forget that he had once followed the plough, and that he had served as a common soldier. As he prospered, so he affected the dress, not of a journalist (which he pretended not to be), but of an old-fashioned gentleman-farmer. In Hazlitt's description, he wore "a scarlet broadcloth waistcoat with the flaps of the pockets hanging down, as was the custom for gentleman-farmers in the last century"; in Bamford's, "dressed in a blue coat, yellow swansdown waistcoat, drab jersey small-clothes, and top boots . . . he was the perfect representation of what he always wished to be— an English gentleman-farmer." It is Hazlitt who gives the justest character to Cobbett on the score of vanity:

> His egotism is delightful, for there is no affection in it. He does not talk of himself for lack of something to write about, but because some circumstance that has happened to himself is the best possible illustration of the subject, and he is not the man to shrink from giving the best possible illustration of the subject from a squeamish delicacy. He likes both himself and his subject too well. He does not put himself before it, and say, "Admire me first," but places us in the same situation with himself, and makes us see all that he does. There is no . . . abstract, senseless self-complacency, no smuggled admiration of his own person by proxy: it is all plain and above-board. He writes himself plain William Cobbett, strips himself quite as naked as anybody could wish—in a word, his egotism is full of individuality and has room for very little vanity in it.[70]

This is a generous literary judgement. But a political judgement must be more qualified. The great change in the tone and style of popular Radicalism, exemplified in the contrast between Paine and Cobbett, was (once again) first defined by Hazlitt:

> Paine affected to reduce things to first principles, to announce self-evident truths. Cobbett troubles himself about little but the details and local circumstances. . . . Paine's writings are a sort of introduction to political arithmetic on a new plan: Cobbett keeps a day-book, and makes an entry at full of all the occurrences and troublesome questions that start up throughout the year.

The personalisation of politics—this labourer in his cottage-garden, this speech in the House of Commons, that example of persecution—was well adapted to the pragmatic approach of an audience only awakening to political consciousness. It also had an opportunist value, in that, by fixing attention upon circumstantial ephemera and particular grievances, and by eschewing theoretical absolutes, it enabled royalists and republicans, Deists and Churchmen, to engage in a common movement. But the argument can be taken too far. Paine's *Rights of Man* had found an equal response in an audience no more literate, and had encouraged a more principled theory of popular rights; while the contemporaneous success of more theoretical journals proves the existence of a large working-class public which could take its politics neat. Cobbett, in fact, helped to create and nourish the anti-intellectualism, and the theoretical opportunism (masked as "practical" empiricism) which remained an important characteristic of the British labour movement.

"I remembered my mother being in the habit of reading Cobbett's *Register*, and saying she wondered people spoke so much against it; she saw nothing bad in it, but she saw a great many good things in it."[71] James Watson's mother was a domestic servant in a clergyman's house, and a Sunday School teacher. "Mr. Cobbett's *Weekly Political Pamphlets*," wrote Hone, in 1817,

> should be bound up, and be on the same shelf with the History of England, the Pilgrim's Progress, Robinson Crusoe, and the Young Man's Book of Knowledge. Every cottage and kitchen library in the kingdom is incomplete without it . . .

It should be "as common and familiar" as the Housekeeper's Instructor and Buchan's Domestic Medicine.[72] This was, in fact, to be much what happened. Wooler or Carlile might, with their more sophisticated and intellectual manner, have given expression to the Radicalism of the city artisans; but only Cobbett could have succeeded, in 1816, in bringing stockingers and weavers into the same dialogue.

The curious way in which he had graduated from Toryism to Radicalism entailed a certain opportunism in his position. He had been able to side-step the anti-Gallican and anti-Jacobin prejudices of the war years. He was able to disown the French Revolution and Tom Paine as things in whose defence he had had no part. Eventually (as he himself acknowledged in generous terms) he came to accept many of Paine's arguments. But he always ducked away from the intransigent Jacobin rejection of the hereditary principle in any form, and thus was able to present himself both as a radical reformer and as a constitutionalist. In the "Address to Journeymen and Labourers" he warned against men who "would persuade you, that, because things have been perverted from their true ends, there is *nothing good* in our *constitution and laws*. For what, then, did Hampden die in the field, and Sydney on the scaffold?" The Americans, in seceding from Britain, had taken care to preserve "Magna Carta, the Bill of Rights, the Habeas Corpus" and the body of the Common Law:

> We want *great alteration*, but we want *nothing new*. Alteration, modification to suit the times and circumstances; but the great principles ought to be and must be, the same, or else confusion will follow.

Even when (in the last year of his life) he urged the people to resist the New Poor Law with force, he did so in the name of constitutional rights and the sanctities of custom. His attitude to the rationalists showed the same blend of Radicalism and traditionalism. He defended with force their right to publish arguments against the Christian religion. But when Carlile went further and committed what was (in Cobbett's eyes) offensive blasphemy by dating the *Republican* "in the year 1822 of the Carpenter's wife's son)," he appealed to mob law. If this had been done in America (he roared)—

> You would . . . be instantly dressed in a coat of tar and feathers, and . . . be ridden *bare-rumped upon a rail*, till you dropped off by the side of some wood or swamp, where you would be left to ruminate on the wisdom (to say nothing of the modesty) of setting up for a maker of span-new governments and religions.[73]

There can scarcely have been another writer in our history who has written so many and such telling attacks upon the Anglican clergy (and, in particular, the rural clergy) as Cobbett. And yet, for no reason which was ever seriously advanced, he frequently announced his attachment, not only to the Throne (which he nearly brought down in the Queen Caroline agitation) and the Constitution (which his followers all but slew in 1819 and 1832) but also to the Established Church. He was even capable of writing, on occasion, of "our duty to hold in abhorrence Turks and Jews," because Christianity was "part and parcel of the law."

Such opportunism made impossible the development of any systematic political theory out of Cobbettism. And his economic prejudices were of a piece with this kind of evasion. Just as he developed, not a critique of a political *system*, nor even of "Legitimacy," but an invective against "Old Corruption," so he reduced economic analysis to a polemic against the *parasitism* of certain vested interests. He could not allow a critique which centred on ownership; therefore he expounded (with much repetition) a demonology, in which the people's evils were caused by taxation, the National Debt, and the paper-money system, and by the hordes of parasites—fund-holders, placemen, brokers, and tax-collectors—who had battened upon these three. This is not to say that this critique was baseless—there was fuel enough for Cobbett's fire, in the grossly exploitive pattern of taxation, and in the parasitic activities of the East India Company and the Banks. But, characteristically, Cobbett's prejudices keyed in with the grievances of the small producers, shopkeepers, artisans, small farmers, and the consumers. Attention was diverted from the landowner or industrial capitalist and focused upon the middleman—the factor or broker who cornered markets, profited from the people's shortages, or lived, in any way not closely attached to land or industry, upon unearned income. The arguments were moral as much as economic. Men were entitled to wealth, but only if they could be *seen* to be hard at work. Next to sinecurists Cobbett hated Quaker speculators.

Deficient in theory he was also sometimes plainly mischievous in his immediate influence upon political strategy, while he was by no means always as straightforward in his personal and public dealings as he asked other men to be. For his failings as a political leader he was not fully responsible. He was a journalist, and not a political leader or organiser, and it was only the accident of the context (the outlawing of effective political organisation) which forced him into the other role. But, if he did not choose to be a political leader, he was (like other men in this predicament) reluctant to see the movement go in any way but the way which he prescribed. When all these—and other—failings are accounted, it is easy to underestimate him, as a nostalgic romantic or a bully.

But the commonplace judgement so often met with, that Cobbett was "really a Tory," is unhelpful. One reason we have sufficiently examined: the democratic character of his tone. His relationship with his audience was peculiarly intimate: we must remember that he was continually talking with his readers. He addressed them at reform meetings. He made "lecture-tours." Even when he was in America, his post-bag was heavy, and deputations of Scottish mechanics and emigré reformers waited upon him on the banks of the Susquehannah. He rode into the countryside to find out how men were thinking and talking. Hence Cobbett's ideas can be seen less as a one-way propagandist flow than as the incandescence of an alternating current, between his readers and himself. "I always say that I have derived from the people . . . ten times the light that I have communicated to them":

> A writer engaged in the instruction of such a people, is constantly upheld, not only by the applause that he receives from them, and by perceiving that his labours are attended with effect; but also by the aid which he is continually deriving from those new thoughts which his thoughts produce in their minds. It is the flint and the steel meeting that brings forth the fire.[74]

How moving is this insight into the dialectical nature of the very process by which his own ideas were formed! For Cobbett's thought was not a system but *a relationship*. Few writers can be found who were so much the "voice" of their own audience. It is possible to follow Cobbett's genius as an indicator of the movement for which he spoke. At times of crisis there is this bright incandescence. At times when the movement flagged, he becomes most cranky and idosyncratic: his style glows only dully. And this is true until his very last years; as his audience changed, so he changed with it.

This is what Raymond Williams has well described as Cobbett's "extraordinary sureness of instinct." And yet, instinct for *what*? In the first place it was an instinct which disclosed the *real* nature of changing relationships of production, which he judged, in part, against an idealised patriarchal past, and in part against an assertion of the worth of every individual labourer which is, in no sense, backward-looking. In the second place, Cobbett was the "free-born Englishman" incarnate. He gathered up all the vigour of the 18th-century tradition and took it forward, with new emphasis, into the 19th. His outlook approximated most closely to the ideology of the *small producers*. The values which he endorsed with his whole being (and he wrote at his best when he gave his prejudices full rein) were those of sturdy individualism and independence. He lamented the passing of small farmers; of small tradesmen; the drawing of the resources of the country together into "great heaps"; the loss by the weavers of "the frank and bold character formed in the days of their independence."[75] The small farmer who resented the great estate of the brewer or absentee Lord; the small clothier who petitioned against the growth of the factory system; the small tailor or bootmaker who found that middlemen were receiving Government contracts or creaming the market- -these were among his natural audience. They also felt the same diffuse hostility to "speculation" and the "commercial system"; but (like Cobbett) they stopped short before any radical critique of property-rights.

If this had been all, Cobbett might have remained as the political spokesman of the little bourgeoisie. But his audience—the Radical movement itself—took him further. "We are daily advancing to the state in which there are but two classes of men, *masters*, and *abject dependants*." When Cobbett considered the position of the artisan or the cotton-spinner, he extrapolated from the experience of the small masters who were being forced down into the working class. He saw the factory proletariat of Manchester less as new fangled men than as little producers who had lost their independence and rights. As such, the work-discipline of the mills was an outrage upon their dignity. They were right to rebel, as he would rebel in the same position. As for child labour, it was simply "unnatural."

His attitude to the field labourers was somewhat different. Although he struggled to understand a commercial and manufacturing society, the essential model of political economy in his mind was drawn from agriculture. And here he accepted a social structure in which the landowner, the good tenant, the petty land-holder, and the labourer all had their part, provided that productive and social relationships were governed by certain mutual obligations and sanctions.

Defending his own conduct as a landlord, he cited the case of an old cottager, living in retirement on the farm at Botley when he took it up:

> The old man paid me no rent; when he died I had a headstone put to his grave to record, that he had been an honest, skillful, and industrious labouring man; and I gave his widow a shilling a week as long as I was at Botley.[76]

Here he is indistinguishable from the better kind of squire whose passing he so often lamented. But this is not all. There is also that uncomfortable sentence: "No society ought to exist where the labourers live in a hog-like sort of way." *No society ought to exist*—the very touchstone of his social criticism is the condition of the labouring man. When, as at the time of the labourers' revolt or the New Poor Law, he judged this condition to be unendurable, then he was willing to challenge the received social order:

> God gave them life upon this land; they have as much right to be upon it as you have; they have a clear right to a maintenance out of the land, in exchange for their labour; and, if you cannot so manage your lands yourselves as to take labour from them, in exchange for a living, give the land up to them. . . .[77]

This was written less than six months before he died.

This is why Cobbett (and John Fielden, his friend and fellow Member for Oldham after 1832) came so close to being spokesmen of the working class. Once the real condition of the working people—for Cobbett, the labourer, for Fielden, the factory child—is made, not *one*, but *the* test of all other political expedients, then we are close to revolutionary conclusions. Concealed within the seemingly "nostalgic" notion of the "historic rights of the poor," which, in different ways, was voiced by Cobbett, Oastler, and Carlyle, there were also *new* claims maturing, for the community to succour the needy and the helpless, not out of charity, but as of right.[78] Cobbett loathed the "comforting system" of charity and moral rescue, and, in his *History of the Protestant 'Reformation,'* he was chiefly intent upon giving historical backing to his notion of social rights. The lands of the medieval Church had been held in trust for the poor. Wrongfully misappropriated or dispersed, nevertheless the poor still had a claim upon them, which (in Cobbett's eyes) was recognised through the mediation of the old Poor Laws. The repeal of those laws constituted the last act in a shameful series of robberies by which the poor had been cheated of their rights:

Among these rights was, the right to live in the country of our birth; the right to have a living out of the land of our birth in exchange for our labour duly and honestly performed; the right, in case we fell into distress, to have our wants sufficiently relieved out of the produce of the land, whether that distress arose from sickness, from decrepitude, from old age, or from inability to find employment. . . . For a thousand years, necessity was relieved out of the produce of the Tithes. When the Tithes were taken away by the aristocracy, and by them kept to themselves, or given wholly to the parsons, provision was made out of the land, as compensation for what had been taken away. That compensation was given in the rates as settled by the poor-law. The taking away those rates was to violate the agreement, which gave as much right to receive in case of need, relief out of the land, as it left the landowner a right to his rent.[79]

This historical myth, which assumes some medieval social compact between the Church and the gentry, on one hand, and the labourers, on the other, was employed to justify claims to new social rights in much the same way as the theory of Alfred's free constitution and of the Norman yoke had been used to justify the claim to new political rights. According to this view, the landowners' tenure of their land was not of absolute right, but was dependent upon their fulfilling their social obligations. Neither Cobbett nor Fielden started from the assumption that the working people had any right to expropriate landed property or capital; but both accepted that if the existing property-relations violated, for the labourer or his child, essential claims to human realisation, then any remedy, however drastic, was open to discussion. (For Fielden it meant that he—the third greatest. "Seigneur of the Twist" in Lancashire—was willing to work with John Doherty in pursuit of a General Strike for the eight-hour day.)

Cobbett's touchstone was at the same time an insurmountable barrier between his kind of political theory and the ideology of the middle-class Utilitarians. If Malthus's conclusions led to the preaching of emigration or of restraints upon the marriage of the poor, then they were faulted by this touchstone. If the "Scotch feelosofers" and Brougham could do no more than destroy the poor man's rights under the old Poor Law, leave the weavers to starve, and sanction the labour of little children in the mills, then this touchstone proclaimed them to be designing rogues. It is sometimes less an argument than an affirmation, an imprecation, a leap of feeling. But it was enough. Cobbett did more than any other writer to preserve the Radicals and Chartists from becoming the camp-followers of Utilitarians or of Anti-Corn Law League. He nourished the culture of a class, whose wrongs he felt, but whose remedies he could not understand.

III. Carlile, Wade, and Gast

Yet we must not forget the inconsistencies, the bullying, the anti-intellectualism, the professions of loyalty to Throne and Church, the theoretical opportunism, the turns and twists of Cobbett's ephemeral political writing. These weaknesses were more than evident to the more articulate Radicals. Already in 1817 he was under sharp fire from other periodicals. By 1820 many Radical artisans had ceased to take Cobbett seriously as a thinker, although they had not ceased to enjoy his gargantuan polemics. They continued to read him, but they began to read some other journal as well. Among these lesser journals, between 1817 and 1832, there was much original and demanding thought, which was to give shape to the political consciousness of the class after 1832. We may select from these four tendencies: the Paine-Carlile tradition; the working-class Utilitarians and the *Gorgon*; the trade unionists around the *Trades Newspaper* of John Gast; and the variety of tendencies associated with Owenism.

We have already examined the main stock of ideas of the first, in *Rights of Man*, and its most important contribution in Carlile's fight for the free press. The derivation from Paine is explicit. It is not only the acknowledgement of a debt, but the assertion of a doctrinal orthodoxy:

> The writings of Thomas Paine, alone, form a standard for anything worthy of being called Radical Reform. They are not Radical Reformers who do not come up to the whole of the political principles of Thomas Paine. . . . There can be no Radical Reform short of . . . a Republican form of Government.[80]

We get a sense of the force and loyalty with which this doctrine was held from an account of a meeting of the Cheltenham Chartist branch, whose Chairman was an old blacksmith:

> One night . . . somebody spoke of Tom Paine. Up jumped the chairman. "I will not sit in the chair," he cried in great wrath, "and hear that great man reviled. Bear in mind he was not a prize-fighter. There is no such person as Tom Paine. Mister Thomas Paine, if you please."[81]

Uncompromising hostility to the hereditary principle and to "Gothic" superstition and survivals, defiant affirmation of the rights of the private citizen—these are among its virtues. But in England, at least by the later Twenties, the Paine-Carlile tradition had acquired a certain stridency and air of unreality. The cry, *à bas les aristos*, has less force when we consider the real structure of power in England as the Industrial Revolution advanced, the complex interpenetration of aristocratic privilege and commercial and industrial wealth. The rationalist lampoons upon the "priesthood," as the hired apologist of privilege and the emissaries of an ignorance designed to hold the people in thrall, are somehow just wide of the mark; they might touch the fox-hunting rural rector or the clerical magistrate, but they flew past the ear of the Evangelicals and the Nonconformist ministers who were already active with British and National schools. The polemic tends to disperse itself in abstractions; it does not *grip* and *engage*, as Cobbett's nearly always does. Carlile's "priest" was depicted as busy with "Kneeling, tenths, pilgrimages, exorcisms, sprinkling, crosses, sacraments, ablutions, circumcision, and gibberish" in the intervals of "lasciviousness . . . and drunkenness."[82] Although Carlile knew more of English goals than any other Radical he continued to confuse them with the Bastille. If George IV *had* been strangled in the entrails of the Bishop of Llandaff it would have been a triumph, but not the triumph which he supposed. He would still have had to deal with the last city alderman and the last local preacher.

As is characteristic of the doctrinaire, at times he tried to manipulate reality so that it might confirm his doctrines. He fed his persecutors with fresh provocations:

> As I consider that the majority of the present Ministers are tyrants and enemies to the interests and welfare of the people of this country, so also am I bold to confess that, if any man that has suffered unjustly under their administration, should be so indifferent about his own life as to slay any one or more of them, I would tune my lyre to sing his praises.

But such a tyrannicide would show "a want of virtue" if he sought companions to perform the act; he should have the resolution to do it single-handed: "I condemn an association for such purposes".[83] And the passage leads us to others of his weaknesses. There is, first, the irresponsibility of his individualism. This is an incitement which he could publish (as he published others) simply *as* an incitement, without thought of the consequences. Like other men who have codified ideas into an orthodoxy, it is not true that he simply passed on the notions of his master. He ossified them *by* turning them into doctrine; he took one part of Paine's ideas (the doctrine of individual rights), and neglected others. And the part which he adopted he pushed to its extremity, the *ne plus ultra* of individualism.

Every citizen owed no deference to authority and should act as if it did not exist. This he did himself, and was ready to take the consequences. But he held that the citizen owed only a duty to his own reason; he was not bound to consult others, even of his own party, nor to submit to their judgement. Indeed, the notion of party was offensive. The power of reason was the only organiser which he admitted, and the press the only multiplier:

> When the political principles laid down by Thomas Paine are well understood by the great body of the people, everything that is necessary to put them in practice will suggest itself, and then plots and delegate meetings will be wholly unnecessary. . . . In the present state of this country the people have no other real duty than to make themselves individually well acquainted with what constitutes their political rights. . . . In the interim, each individual ought to prepare and hold himself ready, as an armed individual, without relation to or consulting with his neighbours, in case circumstances should ever require him to take up arms, to preserve what liberty and property he may already possess against any tyrannical attempts to lessen them. . . . Let each do his duty, and that openly, without reference to what his neighbour does. . . .

The power of popular knowledge he called the "zetetic principle":

> Let us then endeavour to progress in knowledge, since knowledge is demonstrably proved to be power. It is the power of knowledge that checks the crimes of cabinets and courts; it is the power of knowledge that must put a stop to bloody wars and the direful effects of devastating armies.[84]

The first passage was written in the dark year, 1820, and Carlile was in part anxious to protect Radicals from the kind of organisation so easily penetrated by *provocateurs*. But here is this absence of the concrete—"liberty," "knowledge," "bloody wars," and "cabinets and courts." And here also is this serious misunderstanding of his audience: "Let each do his duty . . . without reference to what his neighbour does . . ." Did he not know that the essence of the working-class Radical movement consisted in each man "consulting with his neighbours"? Without this consultation, his shopmen would not have come forward, his country agents would not have held to their posts. The key to his blindness lies perhaps in the phrase: "to preserve what liberty and property he may already possess against any tyrannical attempts. . . ." For this is not only Paine, it is also Locke.

Once again the term arises in the mind: "petit-bourgeois individualism." And, if we make the difficult effort to discard some of the pejorative associations of the term, we can see that, in the case of Carlile, it is helpful. The model in the back of his mind is perhaps that of the little master, the hatter, the brush-maker, the bookseller; we can see, in Carlile, not only the limitations of the little bourgeoisie, but also, in this insurgent time, their strengths. Bewick, if he had been a somewhat younger man, might have read the *Republican*. What Carlile was doing was taking the bourgeois jealousy of the power of the Crown, in defence of their political and property rights, and extending it to the Shoreditch hatter or the Birmingham toy-maker and his artisans.

In terms of rights of press and speech, the results were as dramatic as was Cobbett's democratic tone. But in terms of political and economic theory, the position was either barren or delusive. The strength of the Lockeian ideology lay in the fact that the bourgeois *were* men of large property; the demand for an end to State control or interference was (for them) a liberating demand. But the hatter had little property and his artisans still less. To demand an absence of State regulation meant simply giving their larger competitors (or "market forces") fuller rein. And this was so evident that Carlile, no less than Cobbett, was forced to make a demonology of sinecurists, placemen, the tax-eaters. The great evil afflicting the little masters must be seen to be taxation. There must be as little Government as possible, and that little must be cheap.

This was close to anarchism, but only in its most negative and defensive sense. Every man must be free to think, to write, to trade, or to carry a gun. The first two were his main preoccupation, to the point where the freedom of the press was no longer a means but, in itself, an end. The vista of social proposals opened up in the second part of *Rights of Man* was that part of the master's work which touched him least. He had the self-made man's contempt of the feckless, and the autodidact's impatience with those who did not take up the opportunities of self-improvement which were offered. He served imprisonment to open the gates of Reason: and if the workers did not flock through that was their own fault: "The Alehouse, I know has charms insuperable to the great body of mechanics."[85] He was a minority-minded man.

His rationalism, like his political theory, was made up of negations. He took pleasure in exposing biblical absurdities, and in publishing passages of obscenity to be found in the Bible. When he offered a primer of positive virtues, in the *Moralist*, it was (as we have seen) a tepid rationalist apologia for the virtues of a bourgeois family man. In his attitude to poetry (or towards any imaginative attributes) he showed a "single-vision" as narrow as that of Bentham. Although he pirated *Cain* and *The Vision of Judgement* he was at pains to point out that he did this "not from any admiration of the works, but because I saw them menaced by my enemies." The half-dozen Cantos of *Don Juan* which he had read were "in my opinion *mere slip-slop*, good for nothing useful to mankind." (He does not appear to have noticed that any of them were witty):

> I am not a poet, nor an admirer of poetry beyond those qualities which
> it might have in common with prose—the power of instructing mankind
> in useful knowledge.[86]

"In my opinion . . ."—this reminds us that the culture of the autodidact can also be philistine. The democracy of intellect was in danger of becoming a sort of Bartholomew Fair. Here everyone might set out his stall, anyone's opinions were as good as anyone else's, the strangest sideshows—headless women and poor old dancing bears—might all be on offer. The artisans strayed in and paid their pennies; they were encouraged at once to set up stall for themselves, to argue and debate before they had served any apprenticeship to the trade. The more strenuous minds who offered their work in the same market—Hodgskin or Thompson, O'Brien or Bray—must have many a time cursed the opinionated hucksters bawling all around them.

Nevertheless, when all these criticisms have been made—and they are many, and they go far to explain the stridency of the militant rationalist tradition in the 19th century—when all this has been said, it was Carlile who set up the market. Nor is this a figure of speech. His publications were one market—it was he who published Paine, Volney, Palmer, Holbach and many others. But he also set up the market for spoken debate. In 1830 he founded the Rotunda in which the formative debates of the London working-class movement took place. Its proceedings were published regularly in his *Prompter*. The journal might have been better entitled the *Promoter*, for this is what, in effect, Carlile had become. He was the Showman of Free Thought, and no one had more right to the situation. He cast around for star performers who would draw in the crowds. John Gale Jones, the veteran Jacobin surgeon, still commanded a following. But his greatest success was the promotion of the Reverend Robert Taylor, an apostate Anglican and former chaplain to the King, who preached— in full canonicals—atheistic sermons attacking the "selfish and wicked priest- hood." Taylor was an earnest and scholarly man, who also served his turn in prison, and who did something to bring "her Divine Majesty, the *ignorance* of Eighteen Centuries" into a further decline. But his sermons, copiously illustrated with linguistic criticism of the hebraic text, were, for the audience, something rich and strange: a headless woman. So also was another of the Rotunda show- pieces, Zion Ward, an inheritor of the Southcottian mantle, who spellbound audiences with stupifying harangues upon Revelation and Reform. Despite these attractions, Carlile reported a sad falling-off in the attendances at the weekly religious debates (August 1831). The Rotunda was now being used on Wednes- day evenings by a new tenant, the National Union of the Working Classes. Carlile (once again in prison) was a little irritated that this Union was proposing to *organise* the next round in the fight for press liberties, the "unstamped." "I have nothing to do with any association," he wrote, "and do not seek . . . assistance from anything of the kind." Like other individualists, his egotism had engrossed the cause, and he resented the idea that others might make it theirs.

"Beware of Political Clubs," he wrote a month later. He had the strongest feeling against clubs, societies, and even trade unions or benefit clubs. "Almost every horror of the first French Revolution sprung out of political clubs . . . I pronounce them all to be dastardly associations, contemptible, frivolous, paltry nothings." As the contest for the Reform Bill became week by week more critical, he published information about barricades, hand-grenades, and burning acids: "LET EVERY MAN ORGANIZE HIMSELF." But the National Union continued to meet in the Rotunda, and many of its most impressive leaders—Watson, Hetherington, Lovett, Cleave, Hibbert—were associates of Carlile, who had long left him behind while still holding fast to his first principle: "Free Discussion is the only necessary Constitution—the only necessary Law to the Constitution."[87]

Twenty years of homilies from Hannah More and the Bishop of Llandaff, Wilberforce and the Methodist Conference, had built up a head of anti-clerical pressure among the Radicals. The *Gorgon* could write as a matter of course of "the meek and gentle Moses, who led the scabby and mangy Israelites out of Egypt":

> We will not say that Moses was as subtle and as great an impostor as Mahomet. We will not say that Aaron, the high priest, was as necessary to Moses, as Perigord Talleyrand once was to Buonaparte. We will not say that Joshua was as great a military ruffian as old Blucher or Suvaroff: and that the cruelties and butcheries committed in Canaan were ten times more atrocious than any committed during the twenty-five years of revolutionary warfare . . .[88]

Nevertheless, this *is* what the *Gorgon* managed to say. This is one point where it touches the Carlile tradition; and the two are related, also, by their affinities to Utilitarianism. In Carlile this is implicit; even poetry must be *useful* and impart *knowledge*. The *Gorgon's* intellectual history is more exciting. It was an explicit attempt to effect a junction between Benthamism and working-class experience. It was not (as Place might have made it if he had captured it) an attempt simply to relay the ideas of the middle-class Utilitarians to a working-class audience. John Wade, the former journeyman wool-sorter who edited it (in 1818–19), was a man of originality and great application, who did not take his ideas on trust. He was advised, on one hand, by Place; on the other by John Gast who, as we shall see, was rejecting orthodox political economy as emphatically as Place endorsed it. In the result, the *Gorgon* seems not so much to accept these ideas as to wrestle with them: the enquiry is being made—can Utilitarianism in the context of working-class experience be put to *use?*

The influence of Place was important, and we must come nearer to understanding the man. We have kept a watchful eye upon him throughout this study
because, as an archivist and historian (of the L.C.S., of Westminster Radicalism,
of the repeal of the Combination Acts) his bias has been gravely misleading.
He has risen from being a journeyman breeches-maker into a prosperous shop-
keeper and employer, the close confidant of Bentham and the Mills, and the
adviser of M.P.s. From the early 1800s his emphasis has been upon the building
of bridges between the artisans and the middle class; he has lent his support to
the Lancastrian schools movement and the Mechanic's Institute; his concern has
been with the sober, respectable artisan and his efforts at self-improvement. But
because he was so obviously a founding father of the Fabian tradition (and was
taken uncritically as such by Graham Wallas) we should not see him just as a
"captive" of the middle class, nor should we suppose that he was incapable of
taking up the most intransigent positions. On matters of free thought and expression he was still half a Jacobin; he had helped to publish the first edition
in England of the *Age of Reason*, and even though he came to regard Carlile
as a "fanatic" he gave him a great deal of assistance in his earlier struggles.
We have seen his fury at the repression of 1817 and 1819, and the enormous
application with which he was to work for trade union rights, even though his
zeal for the cause of the unionists was curiously compounded with the political
economy of M'Culloch. In intellectual terms, by 1818 he really was a captive
of Bentham: he *learned* the doctrines of Bentham and the elder Mill rather than
inquiring into them, and in his own writing he added almost nothing to them
except the illustrative facts which he collected with such industry. But in political
terms he was a force in his own right; he gave to the Utilitarians, not just a
seat at Westminster which was within his manipulation, but a point of contact
with the world of the Radical tradesmen and artisans. The very fact that such
a man could perform this role, both ideologically and politically, is a new
phenomenon.

Place's main contribution to the *Gorgon* was the collection of factual material
on the London trades (notably the tailors).[89] John Wade set the tone and emphases of the periodical. Wade was (beside Place) the most impressive fact-
finder among the Radicals. His *Black Book* is greatly superior to any other
Radical investigation of the kind. One can see that he was attracted to the
Benthamites by their solidity of research, and their concern for the practical
particulars of reform—in the law, the prisons, education. From the outset the
Gorgon expressed irritation at the prevailing rhetoric of popular Radicalism. On
the one hand, it struck hard at the specious arguments of constitutional antiquity—most frequently to be found in the *Black Dwarf*, where Major Cartwright
was still writing of witanegemots and perpetuating the theory of the Norman
yoke:

We really think we cannot better advance the cause of Reform than by excluding from the consideration of the subject, all allusions to a former state of society. . . .

Arguments derived from the "good old times," Wade pointed out, came strangely from the mouths of working-class reformers. Much of the "*ancient lore* that has been raked together" was part and parcel of severely repressive legislation *against* the labourers. Can the reformers' leaders (he asked),

> bring nothing to bear against the old rotten borough-mongering system but musty parchment, black letter and latin quotations? Is there nothing in the situation of our finances, in our belated paper system, in the number of paupers—

for comment and indictment? But if he rejected the specious appeal to precedent, he also rejected Paine's confidence in the claims of "natural rights." If it was argued that all men had a *natural* right to the vote, then how could one gainsay the same right in women? For Wade (as for Cobbett) this was the *reductio ad absurdam*. Lunatics and workhouse inmates were (just like women) denied the vote for evident reasons of social utility; and this seemed the soundest basis upon which working-class Radicals (or at least the male half of them) might rest their claims:

> *General Utility* is the sole and ultimate object of society; and we shall never consider either sacred or valuable any natural or prescriptive claims that may be opposed to it.[90]

It was not difficult to justify a claim to the vote upon such a basis. But here came the rub. Wade was refreshingly preoccupied with social reform and trade union organisation. If Utilitarianism was to be extended as an ideology of the working class, it was necessary to have some theory of social structure and of political economy. How was the good of the greatest number to be determined, and might it be that what was useful to employers might be oppressive to working people? Wade's theory of social structure was impressionistic and derivative, but at least he offered more than Cobbett's "Old Corruption" or the rhetoric of the "borough-mongering system." He divided society into the parasitic and the productive classes. In the first group were (a) the upper classes, including the dignitaries of the Church and the Law, and the nobility, and (b) the "middling classes"—loyal parsons, Commissioners of Taxes, officials in the departments of Revenue. These he identified with Corruption. In the second group were the "productive classes": the term was wide enough to include professional men and employers, but the emphasis was upon "those who, by their labours, increase the funds of the community, as husbandmen, mechanics, labourers, &c." Below this group he placed the nondescripts, such as paupers and State creditors:

> The industrious orders may be compared to the soil, out of which every-thing is evolved and produced; the other classes to the trees, tares, weeds and vegetables, drawing their nutriment . . . on its surface. . . .

When mankind attained to a state of "greater perfectibility," then the industri-ous classes alone ought to exist. "The other classes have mostly originated in our vices and ignorance . . . having no employment, their name and office will cease in the social state."[91]

At this point Wade enlisted the help of Place, and the *Gorgon* began to feature material every week on the state of the working classes. It is not clear whose hand is most influential. On the one hand, there is a strong emphasis upon labour as the source of value, an emphasis perhaps strengthened by Ri-cardo's *Principles of Economics*, published in the previous year.[92] "Labour is the superabundant product of this country," wrote the *Gorgon*, "and is the chief commodity we export":

> Of the four staple manufactures, namely, cotton, linen, cloth, and iron, perhaps, on an average, the raw material does not constitute one-tenth of their value, the remaining nine-tenths being created by the labours of the weaver, spinner, dyer, smith, cutler, and fifty others. . . . The labours of these men form the chief article of traffic in this country. It is by trading in the blood and bones of the journeymen and labourers of England that our merchants have derived their riches, and the country its glory. . . .

The statement is emotive rather than exact. It reminds us that the notion of labour as the source of all value was found, not only in Thelwall's *Right of Nature*, but also in an emphatic tone in Cobbett's "Address to the Journeymen and Labourers" of 1816. Cobbett, one feels, had in his mind's eye, while writing, his own farm, and the labourers busy with the stock, at the plough, repairing buildings. Wade (or Place) had in his eye the craftsman and outworker, the wool-sorter or tailor, who was given raw material in some form and, by his labour or skill, processed the material. To the raw material, one-tenth; to the labour and skill the rest.[93]

But the same article in the *Gorgon* at once commenced to instruct trade unionists in the platitudes of political economy. The reward for labour was regulated by demand and supply. "An increase in the wages of journeymen is attended with a proportionate decrease in the profits of masters"—the wages fund. When the price of labour advances it has "a tendency to force capital out of that branch of industry." And (very much in the language of the Place who assisted to repeal the Statute of Artificers)—

> Both masters and journeymen, ought in all cases to act *individually*, not *collectively*. When either party has recourse to *unnatural* or *artificial* expedients, they produce unnatural effects.

The theory of natural laws or rights, shut out by Wade at the front door, has been invited in by Place at the back. For, by this time, it is scarcely possible to think of middle-class Utilitarianism without thinking also of Malthus and of orthodox political economy: the doctrine of utility could only be interpreted in the light of the "laws" of population and those of supply and demand. If Utilitarianism was to enter working-class ideology it would make it captive to the employing class.

And yet the matter was not to be settled so easily. Through September, October, and November 1818 the *Gorgon* carried detailed examinations of the position of some of the London trades: tailors, type-founders, opticians, compositors. At the same time it conducted a defence of the Manchester cotton-spinners, whose strike was attracting the bitterest attacks in both the loyalist and the new-style middle-class Radical press (notably *The Times*). The comparison of wage-rates over the previous twenty years in organised and unorganised trades led to an inescapable conclusion. Whether "natural" or "artificial," combination *worked*:

> ... we had always thought that the prosperity of masters and workmen were simultaneous and inseparable. But the fact is not so, and we have no hesitation in saying that the cause of the *deterioration* in the circumstances of workmen generally, and the different degrees of deterioration among different classes of journeymen, depends entirely on the degree of perfection that prevails among them, which the law has pronounced a crime—namely, COMBINATION. The circumstances of the workmen do not in the least depend on the prosperity or profits of the masters, but on the power of the workmen to *command*—nay to *extort* a high price for their labour. . . .[94]

This can scarcely be Place, in view of the arguments which he is known to have adopted in 1814 and 1824.[95] It would be tempting to see the hand of John Gast, but equally Wade may have been torn between his two advisers. Subsequently Wade did indeed adopt the ideology of the middle-class Utilitarians, and his popular *History of the Middle and Working Classes* (1835) has this characteristic blend of Radical politics and orthodox economics, together with industrious compilation of fact. It is, however, a disappointing work to have come from the author of the *Black Book* and the editor of the *Gorgon*.

Gast's history is different. He was, with Gravener Henson and John Doherty, one of the three truly impressive trade union leaders who emerged in these early years. Each came from industries undergoing greatly different experiences, and the characteristic contribution of each was for this reason different. Henson exemplifies the struggle of the outworkers, touching the fringes of Luddism, organising their illegal union, sharing their advanced political Radicalism, and attempting until 1824 to enforce or enact protective legislation in their favour. Doherty of the cotton-spinners was able to place more emphasis upon the workers' own power to improve their conditions, or to change the entire system, by the force of combination; he was, by 1830, at the heart of the great movements of the northern workers for general unionism, factory reform, co-operative organisation, and "national regeneration." Gast, coming from a smaller but highly organised skilled trade, was constantly concerned with problems of the organisation and mutual support of the London and national *trades*.

Gast was a shipwright, who served his apprenticeship in Bristol, and came to London around 1790. Of his "thirty or forty" years on the Thames (he said in 1825) twenty-eight had been spent in one Deptford yard, in which he was the "leading hand," with sixteen or so men under his charge: "I there assisted in building not less than from twenty to thirty sail of men-of-war . . . exclusive of merchant ships." In 1793 the shipwrights had been organised in the St. Helena Benefit Society—there were "not ten men in the river who were not members." The society failed, but in 1802 there was a shipwright's strike and the Hearts of Oak Benefit Society was formed in which Gast took a leading part. The society was so successful that it not only provided the usual benefits, for sickness, death, and accident, but also erected from its funds thirteen alms-houses for retired shipwrights. When the Thames Shipwrights Provident Union was founded in August 1824, Gast was its first Secretary. He must by this time have been in his mid-fifties.[96]

After the repeal of the Combination Acts the shipwrights were involved in a particularly bitter struggle with their employers, who led the lobby pressing for new anti-trade union legislation in 1825.[97] Thus Gast and his union were thrown into prominence. But long before this he had won respect in London trade union circles. We have seen that he was associated with the *Gorgon*, while he was prominent at the same time in the attempts (in Manchester and London) to form the "Philanthropic Hercules," the first General Union of all trades.[98] It is clear that by 1818 Gast was the leading figure in more than one committee of London "trades." Moreover, an interesting translation took place in London working-class Radicalism between 1819 and 1822. In the former year, Hunt's triumphal entry into London after Peterloo had been prepared by a committee in which such men as Dr. Watson, Gale Jones, Evans, and Thistlewood, were prominent—in the main old Jacobins, professional men, small masters, and a few artisans. When Hunt was released from Ilchester Gaol at the end of 1822 he was welcomed to London by John Gast, on behalf of "The Committee of the Useful Classes."[99] From this time forwards London working-class Radicalism acquires a new cogency: it is more easy to see from which industries its strength is drawn. In Gast's committee it is possible to see an incipient "trades council." In 1825, with the repeal of the Combination Acts, and with the threat of their reimposition, the trades felt strong enough to found their own weekly *Trades Newspaper*.[100]

The *Trades Newspaper*, with its motto, "They helped every one his neighbour," is important not only because it throws a flood of light upon the strength of trade unionism which, until this time, one must follow through the shadows of the Courts and the Home Office papers. It also indicates a point of complete rupture between middle-class Utilitarianism, on one hand, and emergent "trade union theory" on the other. The conflict was quite explicit. It is as if the orthodox parts of the *Gorgon* had gone on with Place and Wade, while the unorthodox claims for the value of combination became the basis for Gast's new venture. Some of the polemics were aimed specifically at Place, and in a manner both unfortunate and unfair; and this may help to explain why Gast and the London trades feature so little in Place's own account of these years. The controversy had in fact been opened in the previous year, in the pages of Wooler's *Black Dwarf*, now in the last year of its life.[101] It was provoked by the wedding which had been solemnised, in the pages of James Mill, between Malthusianism and political economy. Badly stated, this proposed that the problem of unemployment[102] was a natural, rather than artificial one, arising from the "surplus" of population; as such it was insoluble; being insoluble, it was the underlying determinant of wage-rates, since—however much skilled groups might attain to a privileged position by means of restricting entry into their craft—the mass of the workers would find that the natural laws of supply-and-demand would cheapen the value of a service which was in excess supply.

To this Cobbett had long given a passionate and explosive negative ("*Parson Malthus! Scotch feelosofers!*"). The "Black Dwarf" offered more strenuous arguments. "The quantity of employment is unlimited," he wrote:

> I have seen men and women without stockings in this great manufacturing country, which furnishes stockings to all quarters of the world . . . If every one in these islands alone were as well clothed as they could wish to be, the home consumption would be ten times as extensive as it is.

"It is not by diminishing their numbers," he concluded (in replying to objections from Place), "but by sharpening their intellects, that the condition of the human race is to be bettered."[103]

The argument was resumed in the first number of the *Trades Newspaper*, whose first editor was the advanced Radical, J. C. Robertson, the pioneer of the London Mechanic's Institute and colleague of Thomas Hodgskin.[104] The editorial took issue with M'Culloch for adopting Malthusian theory and advising the workers: "Restrict your numbers so as not to overstock the demand for labourers." "This," wrote Gast, "is to conspire against nature, against morality, and against happiness." The available means for such restriction were either abstinence from marriage, or from the enjoyment of marriage, or else the use of contraceptives. Now Place had firmly endorsed the Malthusian position, and had taken it upon himself to propagate it amongst the working class; but, having no confidence in their capacity for sexual abstinence, he had further assisted in the covert dissemination of handbills providing information as to the means of birth control.[105] Place now attempted to defend M'Culloch in the columns of the *Trades Newspaper*.

If Place had taken part in a courageous action for the most wrong-headed of Utilitarian reasons, Gast attacked him bitterly on both counts. On the one hand, he insinuated that Place was associated with a "nameless" and immoral advocacy, too disgusting to be described. (We should remember that this response to contraception was shared on almost every side, and there is no reason to suppose that Gast was not genuinely shocked.) On the other hand, he opened a critique which was of far greater significance:

> If Messrs Malthus, M'Culloch, Place & Co are to be believed, the working classes have only to consider how they can most effectually restrict their numbers, in order to arrive at a complete solution of all their difficulties. . . . Malthus & Co . . . would reduce the whole matter to a question between Mechanics and their sweethearts and wives [rather than] a question between the employed and their employers—between the Mechanic and the corn-grower and monopolist—between the tax-payer and the tax-inflictor.[106]

The note is quite clear. Gast had rejected the model of a "natural" and self-adjusting political economy, which, left unrestrained, would operate to the benefit of employers and employed alike. An essential antagonism of interests is assumed, and its resolution or adjustment must be a matter of force. What might be of utility to capital might well be oppressive to labour. And for this shaping working-class theory there came important intellectual reinforcements.

There was published in 1825 *Labour Defended Against the Claims of Capital* (over the pseudonym "A Labourer") by Thomas Hodgskin, a retired naval lieutenant on half-pay. Gast and Hodgskin had already been associated in the Mechanic's Institute, for which the latter lectured in political economy. In the second half of 1825 the greater part of *Labour Defended* was published in extracts in the *Trades Newspaper*, and a series of editorial articles gave to it a warm, but not uncritical, welcome. Gast selected from Hodgskin's work, with particular approval, the elements of the labour theory of value: "the *only* thing which can be said to be stored up is the skill of *the labourer*":

> All the capitalists of Europe, with all their circulating capital, cannot of themselves supply a single week's food and clothing, . . .[107]

Hodgskin's primitive socialist theory was particularly well adapted to the experience of the London trades—and from this experience his theory was in great part derived. In the face of renewed threats of legislation, he defended trade unionism with strong and common-sense arguments: "Combination is of itself no crime; on the contrary, it is the principle on which societies are held together." His particular fire was directed against the capitalist in his role as entrepreneur or middleman:

> Betwixt him who produces food and him who produces clothing, betwixt him who makes instruments and him who uses them, in steps the capitalist, who neither makes nor uses them and appropriates to himself the produce of both. . . . Gradually and successively has he insinuated himself betwixt them, expanding in bulk as he has been nourished by their increasingly productive labours, and separating them so widely from each other that neither can see whence that supply is drawn which each receives through the capitalist. While he despoils both, so completely does he exclude one from the view of the other that both believe they are indebted to him for subsistence.

In his active technical or managerial role, the capitalist was seen as productive; in this role he also was a labourer, and should be rewarded as such. But as a middleman or speculator he was merely parasitic:

> The most successful and widest-spread possible combination to obtain an argumentation of wages would have no other injurious effect than to reduce the incomes of those who live on profit and interest, and who have no just claim but custom to any share of the national produce.

Hodgskin did not offer an alternative *system* (unless it was the supersession of all systems, in a Godwinian sense) and there is a sense in which he side-stepped the question of property-rights. What he sanctioned was a mounting organised pressure, by all the strength and intellectual and moral resources of the working class, to confiscate the gross wealth of the capitalist interloper. This war of capital and labour, between "honest industry" and "idle profligacy," would not end until the workers received the full product of their own labour, and "till *man* shall be held more in honour than the clod he treads on or the machine he guides."

IV. Owenism

The publication of *Labour Defended*, and its reception in the *Trades Newspaper*, represents the first clear point of junction between the "labour economists" or the Owenites and a part of the working-class *movement*.[108] But of course Owen had preceded him; and even if Owen, Gray, Pare, and Thompson had not been writing, Hodgskin's work was bound to lead on to the further question: if capital was largely parasitic upon labour, might not labour simply dispense with it or replace it by a new system? Moreover, by a curious twist it was possible for Utilitarianism to lead on to the same question: if the only criterion by which a social system might be judged was *use*, and if the greatest number in that society were toilers, clearly no veneration for custom or Gothic notions should prevent one from contriving the most useful possible *plan* by which the masses might exchange and enjoy their own products. Hence Owenite Socialism always contained two elements which never wholly fused: the philanthropy of the Enlightenment, devising "span-new systems" according to principles of utility and benevolence: and the experience of those sections of workers who selected notions from the Owenite stock, and adapted or developed them to meet their particular context.

The story of Robert Owen of New Lanark is well known, even legendary. The model paternalist mill-owner and self-made man who canvassed the royalty, courtiers, and governments of Europe with his philanthropic proposals; the growing exasperation of Owen's tone as he met with polite applause and practical discouragement; his propaganda to all classes and his proclamation of the Millennium; the growing interest in his ideas and promises among some working people; the rise and fall of the early experimental communities, notably Orbiston; Owen's departure to America for more experiments in community-building (1824–29); the growing support for Owenism during his absence, the enriching of his theory by Thompson, Gray, and others, and the adoption of a form of Owenism by some of the trade unionists; the initiative of Dr. King at Brighton with his *Co-operator* (1828–30) and the widely scattered experiments in co-operative trading; the initiative of some London artisans, among whom Lovett was prominent, in promoting national propaganda in co-operative principles (the British Association for Promoting Co-operative Knowledge), in 1829–30; the swelling tide after Owen's return, when he found himself almost despite himself at the head of a movement which led on to the Grand National Consolidated Trades Union.

It is an extraordinary story; and yet there is a sense in which parts of it *had* to be so. We may start at the point of entry, with the paternalist tradition. And we must see that the great experiments at New Lanark were instituted to meet the same difficulties of labour discipline, and the adaptation of the unruly Scottish labourers to new industrial work-patterns that we have already encountered in our discussion of Methodism and of Dr. Ure. "At that time the lower classes in Scotland . . . had strong prejudices against strangers . . . ," "the persons employed at these works were therefore strongly prejudiced against the new director. . . .":

> . . . they possessed almost all the vices and very few of the virtues of a social community. Theft and the receipt of stolen goods was their trade, idleness and drunkenness their habit, falsehood and deception their garb, dissensions, civil and religious, their daily practice; they united only in a zealous systematic opposition to their employers.

These passages, from *A New View of Society* (1813), are much the common run of the new mill-owner or iron-master's experience. The problem was to indoctrinate the youth in "habits of attention, celerity, and order." It is wholly to Owen's credit that he chose neither the psychic terrors of Methodism nor the discipline of the overlooker and of fines to attain his ends. But we must see, all the time, that Owen's later Socialism retained the marks of its origin. He was cast as the kindly Papa of Socialism: Mr. Owen, the Philanthropist, who secured entree to the Court and the Cabinet-room in the post-war years (until he committed his *faux pas* of dismissing, with kindly tolerance, all received religions whatsoever as mischievous irrationalism), merges without any sense of crisis into "the benevolent Mr. Owen" who was addressed by and issued addresses to the working classes. He was in one sense the *ne plus ultra* of Utilitarianism, planning society as a gigantic industrial panopticon; in another, and most admirable and kindly sense, he was an industrial Hanway, who thought a good deal about children, liked to see them happy, and really was outraged at their callous exploitation. But the notion of working-class advance, by its own self-activity towards its own goals, was alien to Owen, even though he was drawn, between 1829 and 1834, into exactly this kind of movement. This can be seen in the tone of all his writings. He wished (he said in 1817) to "remoralize the Lower Orders." Next to "benevolent" the words most commonly encountered in early Owenite writings are "provided for them." Education should "impress on the young ideas and habits which shall contribute to the future happiness of the individual and the State; and this can be accomplished only by instructing them to become rational beings":

> Fourth,—What are the best arrangements under which these men and their families can be well and economically *lodged, fed, clothed trained, educated, employed, and governed?*[109]

This tone presented an almost insuperable barrier between Owen and the popular Radical as well as trade union movement. "The operatives and working classes were at this time strangers to me and to all my views and intentions," Owen noted (in his *Autobiography*) of the immediate post-war years. "Their democratic and much-mistaken leaders taught them that I was their enemy and that I desired to make slaves of them in these villages of unity and mutual cooperation." But in the circumstances this was scarcely surprising. The Philanthropist, Mr. Owen, swam into their view during the desperate post-war depression years. Many of the gentry were themselves appalled at the extent of unemployment and distress, while they were also anxious as to the insurrectionary temper of the unemployed. More than this, the poor-rates had risen to over £6 millions at a time when agriculture had fallen from its war-time prosperity. The poor were unsightly, a source of guilt, a heavy charge on the country, and a danger. The columns of the reviews were full of discussions on the emendation of the Poor Laws, all of which had greater economy as their goal. Mr. Owen (whose extensive properties at New Lanark became a fashionable addition to genteel tours) now came forward with a Plan, which really could not have been nicer. He proposed to put the poor into "Villages of Cooperation," where—after an initial capital grant out of taxes—they would *pay their own way*, and become "useful," "industrious," "rational," self-disciplined, and temperate as well. The Archbishop of Canterbury liked the idea, and Lord Sidmouth went over it quite closely with Mr. Owen. "My Lord Sidmouth will forgive me," Owen wrote in one of his public letters on poor relief which appeared in the London press in the summer of 1817, "for he knows I intend no personal offence. His dispositions are known to be mild and amiable. . . ." This was published a fortnight after the Pentridge rising and the exposure of Oliver.

The Plan smelled of Malthus and of those rigorous experiments of magistrates (like the strangely-named "Nottingham Reformers") who were already working out the Chadwickian plan of economical workhouse relief. Even if Owen was himself (as some of the Radicals were willing to allow) deeply in earnest and dismayed by the distress of the people, his plan, if taken up by Government, would certainly be orientated in this way. Cobbett has been too easily accused of "prejudice" in denouncing Owen's "Villages of Co-operation" as "parallelograms of paupers." Not only did they savour to him of the "comforting system" of patronage and charity which he loathed, but his instinct was probably right—that Owen's ideas, if they *had* been taken up by the authorities in 1817, would probably have given rise to an extension of "productive employment" within the workhouse system. But Cobbett was only voicing the general Radical response. His proposed institutions (wrote Sherwin) would be "prison," "a community of vassals":

> Mr. Owen's object appears to me to be to cover the face of the country with workhouses, to rear up a community of slaves, and consequently to render the labouring part of the People absolutely dependant upon the men of property.[110]

When Owen attempted to interest the Radicals in his proposals, at a crowded meeting in the City of London Tavern, the Radical leaders, one after another—Cartwright, Wooler, Alderman Waithman—opposed him in similar terms. When Gale Jones proposed that the plan at least deserved examination he was shouted down and accused of apostacy.[111]

The debate served only to display the weaknesses of both sides. On the one hand, Owen simply had a vacant place in his mind where most men have political responses. One part of the *New View* was dedicated to the Prince Regent, another to Wilberforce. Fifteen years later his paper, the *Crisis*, sailed blandly through the waters of 1831 and 1832, carrying cargoes of reports on co-operative congresses and on trading stores at Slaithwaite, without noticing that the country was *in fact* in a state of revolutionary crisis. This vacancy had its endearing aspects: when it occurred to Mr. Owen that the royalty was an irrational institution and that Bishops were a costly and unnecessary tribute to Gothic ignorance, he had no hesitation in pointing this out to the present incumbents, being sure that they would see that he intended "no personal offence" and that they would duly liquidate themselves in submission to rational suasion. But this was scarcely endearing to the "old Radicals" of 1817. Their weaknesses, on the other hand, consisted in a lack of any constructive social theory, whose place was taken by a rhetoric in which all ills were attributed to taxation and sinecures, which all could be remedied by Reform.

Hazlitt's response to the *New View* was the most complex, and shows the bruised Jacobin in him struggling against the weight of Burke: "Why does Mr. Owen put the word 'New,' in black-letter at the head of the advertisements of his plan of reform?" "The doctrine of Universal Benevolence, the belief in the

Omnipotence of Truth, and in the Perfectibility of Human Nature, are not new, but "Old, old,' Master Robert Owen":

> Does not Mr. Owen know that the same scheme, the same principles, the same philosophy of motives and actions . . . of virtue and happiness, were rife in the year 1793, were noised abroad then, were spoken on the house-tops, were whispered in secret, were published in quarto and duodecimo, in political treatises, in plays, poems, songs and romances—made their way to the bar, crept into the church, ascended the rostrum, thinned the classes of the universities . . . that these "New Views of Society" got into the hearts of poets and the brains of metaphysicians, took possession of the fancies of boys and women, and turned the heads of almost the whole kingdom: but that there was one head which they never got possession of, that turned the heads of the whole kingdom round again . . . ?

Thus repelled (Hazlitt mocked) it seems that *philosophy* was driven from the country,

> and forced to take refuge and to lie snug for twenty years in the New Lanark mills, with the connivance of the worthy proprietor, among the tow and spindles; from whence he lets us understand that it is coming up again to Whitehall-stairs, like a spring-tide with the full of the moon, and floating on the blood that has flowed for the restoration of the Bourbons, under the patronage of the nobility, the gentry, Mr. Wilberforce, and the Prince Regent, and all those who are governed, like those great person-ages, by no other principle than truth, and no other wish than the good of mankind! This puff will not take with us: we are old birds, not to be caught with chaff. . . .

Hazlitt's insight is extraordinarily acute. For Owen indeed was not the first of the modern Socialist theorists (Hodgskin was much closer to being that) but one of the last of the 18th-century rationalists—he was Godwin, now setting out from New Lanark to claim the Chairmanship of the Board of Directors of the Industrial Revolution. In his new disguise, as a practical and eminently successful man, he had entree where the old philosophers were reviled and spurned. "A man that comes all the way from the banks of the Clyde acquires a projectile force that makes him irresistible":

> He has access, we understand, to the men in office, to the members of parliament, to lords and gentlemen. He comes . . . to batter down all their establishments, new or old, in church or state . . . and he quietly walks

into their houses with his credentials in his pocket, and reconciles them to innumerable Houses of Industry he is about to erect on the site of their present sinecures. . . .

"We do not," continued Hazlitt, "wish him to alter his tone." But he prophesied, with uncanny accuracy, some of the consequences, if he did not:

His schemes thus far are tolerated, because they are remote, visionary, inapplicable. Neither the great world nor the world in general care any thing about New Lanark, nor trouble themselves whether the workmen there go to bed drunk or sober, or whether the wenches are got with child before or after the marriage ceremony. Lanark is distant, Lanark is insignificant. Our statesmen are not afraid of the perfect system of reform he talks of, and, in the meantime, his cant against reform in parliament . . . serves as a practical diversion in their favour. But let the good which Mr. Owen says he has done in one poor village be in danger of becoming general . . . and his dreams of elevated patronage will vanish. . . . Let his "New View of Society" but make as many disciples as the "Enquiry concerning Political Justice," and we shall see how the tide will turn about. . . . He will be marked as a Jacobin, a leveller, an incendiary, in all parts of the three kingdoms; he will be avoided by his friends, and become a bye-word to his enemies . . . and he will find out that it is not so easy or safe a task as to be imagined to . . . make mankind understand their own interests, or those who govern them care for any interest but their own.[112]

The quality in Owen which his patrons discovered with consternation (and into which Hazlitt had some insight) was that of sheer propagandist zeal. He believed, equally with Carlile, in the multiplication of "reason" by means of its diffusion. He spent a small fortune in posting his Addresses to men of influence throughout the country; and a larger fortune upon the experimental communities. By 1819 his patrons had grown weary of him, and he in turn was addressing himself more particularly to the working classes. He had long held the view that working people were the creatures of circumstances; he deplored their "gross ferocity of character" and one feels that (like Shaw) his chief reason for being a Socialist was the desire that they should be abolished. But here there comes a twist in his thought, productive of large consequences. If the workers were creatures of circumstances, so also—the thought may have occurred to him while walking in the park after an unsatisfactory interview—were Lord Sidmouth and the Archbishop. The thought was communicated in an Address to the Working Classes (1819):

From infancy, you . . . have been made to despise and hate those who differ from you in manners, language, and sentiments. . . . Those feelings of anger must be withdrawn before any being who has your real interest at heart can place power in your hands. . . . You will then distinctly perceive that no rational ground for anger exists. . . . An endless multiplicity of circumstances, over which you had not the smallest control, placed you where you are. . . . In the same manner, others of your fellow-men have been formed by circumstances, equally uncontrollable by them, to become your enemies and grievous oppressors. . . . Splendid as their exterior may be, this state of matters often causes them to suffer even more poignantly than you. . . . While you show by your conduct any desire violently to dispossess them of this power, these emoluments and privileges—is it not evident that they must continue to regard you with jealous and hostile feelings . . . ?

"The rich and the poor, the governors and the governed, have really but one interest"—to form a new co-operative society. But the rich no less than the poor, being creatures of circumstance, were unable to see their true interests. (The "sudden admission of strong light" from Owen's writings was in danger of destroying their "infant powers of vision"). The workers (or those of them who had seen the light of reason) should disengage from class conflict. "This irrational and useless contest must cease," and the *avant garde* (by establishing model communities and by propaganda) might blaze a path by means of which the working people could simply *by-pass* the property-rights and power of the rich.[113]

However admirable Owen was as a man, he was a preposterous thinker, and, while he had the courage of the eccentric, he was a mischievous political leader. Of the theorists of Owenism, Thompson is more sane and challenging, while Gray, Pare, Dr. King, and others had a firmer sense of reality. There comes through his writings not the least sense of the dialectical processes of social change, of "revolutionising practice":

> The materialist doctrine that men are products of circumstances and upbringing and that, therefore, changed men are products of other circumstances and changed upbringing, forgets that circumstances are changed precisely by men and that the educator must himself be educated. Hence this doctrine necessarily arrives at dividing society into two parts, of which one towers above society (in Robert Owen, for example)—

So ran Marx's third thesis on Ludwig Feuerbach. If social character was (as Owen held) the involuntary product of "an endless multiplicity of circumstances," how was it to be changed? One answer lay in education, where one of the most creative influences of the Owenite tradition can be seen. But Owen knew that until "circumstances" changed he could not gain access to the schooling of a generation. The answer must therefore lie in the sudden change of heart, the millenarial leap. The very rigour of his environmental and mechanical materialism meant that he must either despair or proclaim a secular Chiliasm.

Mr. Owen, the Philanthropist, threw the mantle of Joanna Southcott across his shoulders. The tone of the ranter was noted, not only by Hazlitt, but by others of his contemporaries. A writer in Sherwin's *Register* compared him to Joanna, who—

> deluded thousands for the moment, by telling them that a Shiloh was about to come into the world; a Prince of Peace, under whose standard all the nations of the earth were to unite; by telling them that . . . swords were to be converted into plough-shares.[114]

It was also to be examined by Engels and by Marx, and the more recent promulgation of the discovery in academic circles is not original.[115] Owen was promising, in 1820, to *"let prosperity loose on the country,"* and in his communities he offered no less than "Paradise." By 1820 an Owenite society was forming in the metropolis, and the hand-bill advertising its periodical, the *Economist*, declared:

> Plenty will overspread the land!—Knowledge will increase!—Virtue will flourish!—Happiness will be recognized, secured, and enjoyed.

Owen frequently used analogies drawn from the great advance in productive techniques during the Industrial Revolution: some individuals "forget that it is a modern invention to enable one man, with the aid of a little steam, to perform the labour of 1,000 men." Might not knowledge and moral improvement advance at the same pace? His followers took up the same imagery:

> . . . the construction of a great social and moral machine, calculated to produce wealth, knowledge, and happiness, with unprecedented precision and rapidity. . . .

A correspondent to the *Economist* noted that "the tone of joy and exultation which pervades your writings is really most infectious."

The members of the London society were aware—

that their proceedings must be comparatively imperfect, whilst they remain in their present dwellings, remote . . . from one another.

With an enthusiasm reminiscent of the early Moravians, they acquired some new houses on Spa Fields (no longer to be a meeting-place), with a schoolroom and common eating-room. The pages of the *Economist* and other early journals were full of speculations as to how capital might be raised—if it were supposed (an odd supposition) that there were 50,000 families of the working classes in the metropolis, these would, if brought into association, have an average income of £50 p.a. or £2½ millions collectively. And so on. The communitarians at Orbiston were enrolled in a "Society of Divine Revelation." By 1830 when Owen, returning from America, found himself at the head of a movement of the masses, this messianic tone had the force of a secular religion. On May 1st, 1833, Owen delivered an Address at the National Equitable Labour Exchange "denouncing the Old System of the World and announcing the Commencement of the New." Not only would the profit motive be displaced by co-operation, the vices of individualism by the virtues of mutuality, but *all* existing social arrangements would give way to the federations of mixed agricultural and industrial villages:

> We . . . abandon all the arrangements to which [sectional] interests have given birth; such as large cities, towns, villages, and universities. . . .
> Courts of law, and all the paraphernalia and folly of law . . . cannot be found in a rational state of society. . . .

Hitherto the world had been "in gross darkness." All ceremonial worship of an unknown Power was "much worse than useless." Marriage will be recognised as a "union of affection only." "Celibacy, in either sex, beyond the period designed by nature, will be no longer considered a virtue," but "a crime against nature." The new society would offer a balance between intellectual and physical labour, entertainment and the cultivation of the physical powers as in Greece and Rome. All citizens would abandon all ambition, envy, jealous, and other named vices:

> I therefore now proclaim to the world the commencement, on this day, of the promised millennium, founded on rational principles and consistent practices.[116]

This proclamation might startle some Women's Co-operative Guilds today. It also appears, at first sight, an unlikely ideology to be accepted by the working people, whose formative experiences have been the subject of this study. And yet, if we look more closely, we will find that it was not some psychic frenzy or "collective paranoia" which gave rise to the rapid spread of Owenism. In the first place, *Owenism* from the late Twenties onwards, was a very different thing from the writings and proclamations of Robert Owen. It was the very imprecision of his theories, which offered, none the less, an image of an alternative system of society, and which made them adaptable to different groups of working people. From the writings of the Owenites, artisans, weavers, and skilled workers selected those parts which most closely related to their own predicament and modified them through discussion and practice. If Cobbett's writings can be seen as a relationship with his readers, Owen's can be seen as ideological raw material diffused among working people, and worked up by them into different products.

The artisans are the clearest case. The editor of the *Economist* admitted, in 1821, that few of his readers were among the working classes. But we gain an idea of the first members of the London "Co-operative and Economical Society" who set up the community on Spa Fields from a circular sent to the Nobility and Gentry, soliciting their patronage for their wares. They offered to execute carving and gilding, boot and shoe-making, hardware (including grates and stoves), cutlery, clothing, sewing and dress-making, cabinet-making, book-selling and book-binding, drawings in water colours and on velvet, and Transparent Landscape Window Blinds. This suggests artisans and self-employed craftsmen, who abounded in two of the greatest co-operative centres—London and Birmingham. The spirit of these endeavours (of which there were a number, some ante-dating Owen) is expressed in a letter sent to the *Economist*:

> . . . the working classes, if they will but exert themselves *manfully*, have no need to solicit the smallest assistance from any *other* class, but have within themselves . . . superabundant resources.[117]

This is not Owen's tone. But it is certainly the tone which we have met repeatedly when following the *political* Radicalism of the artisans. Individualism was only one part of their outlook; they were also inheritors of long traditions of mutuality—the benefit society, the trades club, the chapel, the reading or social club, the Corresponding Society or Political Union. Owen taught that the profit-motive was wrong and unnecessary: this keyed in with the craftsman's sense of custom and the fair price. Owen endorsed the view, held also by Cobbett, Carlile, and Hodgskin, that the capitalist was largely parasitic in his function: "that manual labour, properly directed, is the source of all wealth": this keyed in with grievances of artisans or little craftsmen-masters against the contractors and middlemen. Owen taught that *"the natural standard of human labour"* should be taken as "the *practical* standard of value,"[118] and that products ought to be exchanged according to the labour embodied in them: this keyed in with the outlook of the shoemaker, cabinet-maker, and brushmaker, who lived in the same court and who did in any case on occasion exchange services.

Indeed, the germ of most of Owen's ideas can be seen in practices which anticipate or occur independently of his writings.[119] Not only did the benefit societies on occasion extend their activities to the building of social clubs or alms-houses; there are also a number of instances of pre-Owenite trade unions when on strike, employing their own members and marketing the product.[120] The artisan was only slowly losing his status as a self-employed man, or as a man who did work for several masters; and in doing this or that contract he might enlist the aid of other craftsmen with different skills. The covered market, or bazaar, with its hundreds of little stalls, was an old institution; but at the close of the Wars new bazaars were opened, which attracted attention in phil-anthropic and Owenite circles, where a section of counter was let (by the foot) for the week, the day, or even part of the day. Wares of every type were invited—even artists might exhibit—and one may suppose that the craftsmen and "garret-masters" who were struggling for "an independence" were the tenants.[121] By 1827 a new bazaar was in being, which acted as a centre for the exchange of products made by unemployed members of London trades—car-penters, tailors, shoemakers, and others who were put to work on materials bought out of trade union funds.[122]

Thus the Equitable Labour Exchanges, founded at London and Birmingham in 1832–3, with their labour notes and exchange of small products, were not conjured out of the air by paranoiac prophets. If we list the products which were brought for exchange to the Co-operative Congress in Liverpool in Oc-tober 1832 we can also see the people. From Sheffield, cutlery and coffee-pots; from Leicester, stockings and lace; from Huddersfield, waistcoat pieces and shawls; from Rochdale, flannels. There were diapers from Barnsley, stuffs from Halifax, shoes and clogs from Kendal, and prints from Birkacre. A spokesman of the Birmingham Equitable Labour Exchange said that the people of his district "knew not what to do with their masses of iron, brass, steel and japan wares": why should they not be exchanged for Lancashire cottons and Leicester stockings? The long list of trades who proposed to bring their wares to the Birmingham Exchange includes (in the "Bs") blacking-makers, bell-hangers, birch broom makers, button and trimming makers, brace-makers, braziers, brush-makers, bakers, bellows-makers, bedstead-makers, basket-makers. In the "Ss" we find straw hat and bonnet makers, scale makers, stove grate makers, silk-weavers, blacksmiths and whitesmiths, and stationers. There are not (and could scarcely be) boiler-makers, blast furnace-men, or builders; shipwrights or cotton-spinners; miners or engineers.[123]

The list includes not only the little masters and artisans but also outworkers.

As their position (weavers and stockingers) was the most desperate, so Owenism was only one of the solutions at which they clutched in the Thirties. The appeal of the Labour Exchange was not so immediate in the vicinity of Huddersfield or Burnley, for the obvious reason that in districts where the staple product was weaving, and where hundreds were semi-employed or employed on starvation wages on the same products, there was no obvious mart. Hence the northerners were impelled, at the outset, to look towards a national plan of cooperation. "If our Birmingham friends will engage to appear in our fabrics," wrote a Halifax co-operator:

> We will engage to cut our beef and pudding (when we can get any) with their knives and forks, and sup our broth and oatmeal porridge with their spoons; and if our London brethren will do so too, we will appear, as soon as possible, with their silk handkerchiefs round our necks.[124]

It was in Lancashire and Yorkshire that we find the most rapid development of a *general theory* of a new "system," whereby on a national scale equitable exchange might take place, as well as some of the hardiest and most practical support for "utopian" experiments in community-building. The Manchester and Salford Association for the Promotion of Co-operative Knowledge, founded in 1830, gained immediate support. The weavers hoped to find in co-operation the strength to compete with the power-loom. A great cause of social evils, wrote the *United Trades' Co-operative Journal*, was—

> in the erroneous arrangement of our domestic, social and commercial affairs, by means of which machinery is made to compete with and against human labour instead of co-operating with him.

"We can fairly trace that all the miseries which society suffers are mostly owing to the unfair distribution of wealth," wrote the *Lancashire and Yorkshire Co-operator*.[125] In these districts with their long traditions of trade unionism and and mutual aid, co-operation offered a movement in which rationalists and Christians, Radicals and the politically neutral, could work together. The movement gathered up also the traditions of self-improvement and educational effort, providing reading-rooms, schools, and itinerant lecturers. By 1832 perhaps 500 co-operative societies were in existence in the whole country, with at least 20,000 members.[126]

While Owen (bruised somewhat, despite his optimism, by the failures at Orbiston and New Harmony) was awaiting large capital gifts before further experiments could be risked, the co-operators in scores of centres, from Brighton to Bacup, were impatient to raise themselves immediately by their own efforts. At the Liverpool Congress of 1832 the proceedings offer the contrast between long evangelistic harangues and such interventions as this:

> Mr. Wilson, a delegate from Halifax, stated that in May 1829, he and 8 other persons laid down a shilling each, and . . . commenced business in a small room in a back entry. Their numbers had increased; they . . . were now worth £240 and had begun to find labour for some of their members (*Hear, hear.*)[127]

This juxtaposition of the little store and the millenarial plan is of the essence of the co-operative mood between 1829 and 1834. (It is found also in the diversity of particular grievances and organisations which held up for a brief while the edifice of the Grand National Consolidated Trades Union.)

In the neighbourhood of Huddersfield and Halifax, where co-operation spread among the weavers with such speed, one hope was that the store might purchase the warp and weft for the weaver and then sell the product, short-circuiting the employers. Co-operators might also, by a penny-a-week subscription, accumulate the capital to employ unemployed members. But most of these motives may be better expressed by quoting the rules of a society formed in 1832 in Ripponden, a weaving village in the Pennines:

> From the astonishing changes which the course of a series of years have produced to the labouring classes . . . from competition and the increase of machinery which supersedes hand labour, combined with various other causes, over which, as yet, the labouring classes have no control—the minds of thinking men are lost in a labyrinth of suggestions what plan to adopt in order to better, if possible, their conditions. . . .
>
> By the increase of capital the working classes may better their condition, if they only *unite* and set their shoulder to the work; by uniting we do not mean strikes and turning out for wages, but like men of one family, strive to begin to work for ourselves. . . .
>
> The plan of co-operation which we are recommending to the public is not a visionary one but is acted upon in various parts of the Kingdom; we all live by the produce of the land, and exchange labour for labour, which is the object aimed at by all Co-operative Societies. We labourers do all the work and produce all the comforts of life;—why then should we not labour for ourselves and strive to improve our conditions?

> *Fundamental Principles*

> First.—That labour is the source of all wealth; consequently the working classes have created all wealth.

Secondly.—That the working classes, although the producers of wealth, instead of being the richest, are the poorest of the community; hence, they cannot be receiving a just recompense for their labour.

The objects of the society included the mutual protection of all members against poverty and "the attainment of independence by means of a common capital." The means of obtaining these objects included a weekly subscription into a common fund, the employment of the capital in trade, the employment of its members "as circumstances will permit," and—

Lastly.—By living in community with each other, on the principles of mutual co-operation, united possessions, equality of exertions, and of the means of enjoyments.[128]

This is not just a translation of Owen's doctrines to the context of a weaving village. The ideas have been shaped, laboriously, in terms of the weavers' experience; the emphases have shifted; in place of the messianic stridency, there is the simple question: Why not? One of the small co-operative journals was aptly entitled *Common Sense*: its emphasis was on the "Trading Associations":

The object of a Trading Association is briefly this: to furnish most of the articles of food in ordinary consumption to its members, and to accumulate a fund for the purpose of renting land for cultivation, and the formation thereon of a co-operative community.

A weekly sum from wages could be used for the wholesale purchase of tea, sugar, bread, or oatmeal.[129] From Brighton Dr. King's *Co-operator* was advocating this in greater detail.[130] The idea keyed in with other needs; the need to escape from the "tommy shop" or the profiteer; the need to buy staple foods cheap, and free from the criminal adulteration which was only too common— the flour mixed with "plaster of Paris, burnt bones, and an earthy substance . . . called Derbyshire White."[131]

But this idea had also an appeal to the skilled and organized workers in the larger industries, whose approach to Owenism was more circumspect. The *Trades Newspaper* carried some notes on Orbiston in 1825, but Owen's plans for communities were held to be "impracticable from the dislike that free-born, independent men, must have to be told what they must eat . . . and what they must do."[132] Moreover, the very notion of acquiring an economic independence, which appealed to some small craftsmen and outworkers, offered an objection to the shipwright or the worker in large-scale industry—what use a Village of Co-operation to him?

By the close of the Twenties, however, Gast had declared for Owenism.[133] A more important adhesion was that of the Manchester Cotton Spinners after their six-month strike in 1829. Doherty pioneered, in 1830, the National Association for the Protection of Labour, whose organ, the *United Trades Co-operative Journal*, soon became the *Voice of the People*. Soon after this another skilled body, the Builders' Union, whose products could not possibly be taken to the Equitable Labour Exchange, set its course towards the greatest of all the experiments in co-operative direct action. What made the difference?

One answer may simply be that by the end of the Twenties one variant or another of co-operative and "labour" economic theory had taken hold of the cadre of the working-class movement. Cobbett offered no coherent theory. Carlile's individualism was repellent. Hodgskin, by implication, pointed toward mature socialist theory, but his analysis pulled up before that point, and was in any case compatible with co-operative theory as William Thompson showed. The rationalist propaganda of the previous decade had been effective; but it had also been narrow and negative, and had given rise to a thirst for a more positive moral doctrine which was met by Owen's messianism. Owen's imprecision of thought made it possible for different intellectual tendencies to co-exist within the movement. And we must insist again that Owenism was both saner, and more strenuous in intellectual terms, than the thought of its master. For the skilled workers the movement which began to take shape in 1830 at last seemed to give body to their long-held aspiration—general national unionism. From the Philanthropic Hercules of 1818 to the Combination Acts lobby of 1825 there had been much reaching out for united action. Throughout the summer and autumn of 1825 the *Trades Newspaper* reported each stage of the Bradford wool-combers' strike, and the support flowing in from all parts of the country. It declared emphatically: "It is all the workers of England against a few masters at Bradford."[134] Doherty saw in the failure of the great spinners' strike of 1829 another lesson: "It was then shown that no individual trade could stand against the combined efforts of the masters of that particular trade: it was therefore sought to combine all the trades."[135] One result was the formation of the Operative Spinners of England, Ireland, and Scotland, whose first conference, on the Isle of man in December 1829, showed an impressive attempt to surmount the organizational complexities of united organization in three disparate regions.[136] From this basis, the National Association for the Protection of Labour brought together, for a short time, wool textile workers, mechanics, potters, miners, builders, and many other trades; "but after it had extended about one hundred miles round this town (Manchester) a fatality came upon it that almost threatened its existence."[137] The "fatality" came from divisions and jealousies within the Operative Spinners itself; excessive or premature demands upon the strike funds of the Association; and Doherty's unwise attempt to move the office of the *Voice of the People* to London. But despite its failure, the National Association gave new notations to the idea of co-operation; and while the Manchester movement entered a phase of recriminations, the movement continued to flourish in the Potteries and in Yorkshire.[138] Doherty may have attempted to take the movement forward too precipitately; but he rightly saw, in the growing popularity of Owenite ideas, a means of bringing the organized workers of the country into a common movement. Thenceforward, the history of Owenism and of general unionism must be taken together.[139]

The experimental communities failed, although one or two—like that at Ralahine—were partially successful. While the most ambitious ventures, like that of the builders, collapsed, some of the smaller co-operative ventures did in fact struggle on. Most of the societies and shops of the early Thirties collapsed, only to be re-born on the Rochdale model in a few years time. The Labour Exchange or Bazaar, in Gray's Inn Road, was a spectacular muddle. And yet there is nothing wholly inexplicable in the Owenite ferment. We have seen the way in which artisans, outworkers, and trade unionists all have a place within it. Its most unstable millenarial elements came largely from two sources: the benevolent well-wishers and the very poor. For the first Owenism (since it professed not to be a doctrine of class conflict or expropriation) attracted to it in some numbers philanthropic gentlemen and clergy—Godwinians, Quakers, intellectual rebels, and cranks. Some of these, like Dr. King and, most notably, William Thompson, the Irish landowner and author of the *Inquiry into the Distribution of Wealth* (1824), *Labour Rewarded* (1827), and (with Anna Wheeler) *An Appeal of One-half of the Human Race, Women, against the Pretensions of the Other Half, Men, to retain them in Political and thence in Civil and Domestic Slavery* (1825), greatly enriched the movement. Others gave money without which its experiments could not have been undertaken. Nevertheless in most of the communities there is the figure of one or more cranky gentlemen, whose inexperience in the practice of any collective unit, and whose utopian experimentalism, drove the Owenite artisans to fury. To declare that men must make a new social system was one thing; to declare that men could make any kind of new system they liked was another. One artisan Socialist, Allen Davenport the former Spencean, left a somewhat sardonic picture of the London Labour Exchange:

> The public mind was completely electrified by this new and extraordinary movement. . . . The great assembly room, originally fitted up in the most elegant style . . . the ceiling was magnificently embossed, and the ornamental parts richly gilded with gold; and capacious enough to hold two thousand individuals. But this . . . was not sufficient to satisfy Mr. Owen's ideas of beauty. A splendid platform was raised, on which was placed a

superb and majestic organ. . . . On festival nights . . . the avenues were brilliantly illuminated with . . . costly Grecian lamps. Ten or a dozen musical instruments were employed; and ladies and gentlemen sung to the sweetest airs. . . .

The festivals were opened with a short lecture, on the subjects of social love, universal charity, and the advantages of co-operation. . . . The lecture was followed by a concert, and the concert by a ball. . . .

Meantime every avenue to the Exchange, during the whole week, was literally blocked up by the crowds of people that constantly assembled— some attracted by the novelty of the institution; some to watch its progress . . . ; some to make deposits and exchanges. . . . But alas! it was soon discovered that the beautiful labour notes . . . could not by any means be forced into general circulation, on which account the supply of provisions failed and a complete failure was the result of one of the most extraordinary movements that was ever attempted in this or in any other country. Still, the principles on which the system was founded remain unimpeachable, and ought to be cherished in the public mind. . . .

The Owen of this account is the Owen whom Peacock ridiculed in *Crotchet Castle*. Too many of the Owenite ventures overshot themselves, and ended in this sort of muddle of waste, benevolence, and bad planning. If Owen was the greatest propagandist of Owenism, he was also one of its worst enemies. If the Labour Exchange had been left in the hands of such men as Lovett, the outcome might have been different.[140]

The other aspect of this millenarial instability came, more directly, out of the Chiliasm of the poor. Just as at the time of the French Revolution, there is a revival of messianic movements during the excitement of the Reform Bill agitation and its aftermath. There remained many offshoots from the South-cottian movement, whose sects were now taking peculiar and perverted forms[141] which perhaps require more attention from the psychiatrist than the historian. But three examples of this continuing millenarial instability may be noted.

The first is the enormous following gained, between 1829 and 1836, by a crippled shoemaker, "Zion" Ward, one of the inheritors of Joanna's mantle. Ward, formerly a zealous Methodist, had convinced himself by allegorical acrobatics, that he was the "Shiloh" whose birth the aging Joanna had announced. Soon afterwards, he came to believe that he was Christ (and had formerly been Satan), and that the entire Bible was an allegorical prophecy of his annunciation. (The story in the New Testament of Christ's life was a false report—if the Redeemer had come, "why is not man redeemed?") What was unusual in Ward's paranoia (apart from its surrealist solipsism) was, first, that he buttressed it with arguments derived from Carlie and the Deists; and, second, that he directed his messianic appeal towards the dynamic of Radicalism. His following grew up in Southwark, Hackney, Walworth; in Chatham, Nottingham, Birmingham, Derby, Chesterfield, Leeds—many of these old Southcottian strongholds. At Barnsley he called forth stormy applause when he launched an attack on all the clergy "who from the Archbishop to the least are perjured persons and the False Prophets mentioned in the Bible." This became, more and more, the keynote of his prophecies: "Priestcraft detected! Its Overthrow projected!" The King must "take away the enormous salaries of the bishops, and expend the money for the public good." He launched a weekly periodical, *The Judgment Seat of Christ*—perhaps the only occasion in which Christ has been credited with the week-by-week editorial conduct of a popular journal. Throughout the summer of 1831 he drew enormous audiences for his lectures, often filling the 2,000 places in Carlile's Rotunda:

> N.B. The writings of the Messiah sold at the . . . Rotunda, Blackfriars Road. Preaching at the Rotunda on Thursday evenings at 7:30 and on Sunday afternoons at 3.

Early in 1832 he was found guilty of blasphemy at Derby ("The Bishops and Clergy are Religious Impostors, and as such by the Laws of England liable to Corporal Punishment"—surely risky ground to argue upon?) and with a fellow prophet imprisoned for two years. Despite illness and partial paralysis, he continued his mission until his death in 1837.[142]

The second example is that of the extraordinary "Sir William Courtenay" (or J. N. Tom), who arrived in a startled Canterbury in 1832, wearing Eastern dress and accompanied by rumors of great wealth, received 400 freak votes in the General Election, and, after being sentenced for perjury, published his *Lion*, with the views of:

> Sir William Courtenay . . . King of Jerusalem, Prince of Arabia, King of the Gypsies, Defender of his King and Country . . . now in the City Goal, Canterbury.

Tom, who was a wine-merchant who originally came from Joanna Southcott's West Country, had been for a short time a Spencian. His *Lion* denounced equally all infidels and clergy:

> The Root of all Evil is in the Church.
> Lucre! Lucre!! Lucre!!!
> Heaven protect the Widow, Fatherless and Distressed.

Released from prison and lunatic asylum, he went to live in the homes of the peasantry in villages near Canterbury. In May 1838 he commenced moving around the villages, on horseback and armed with pistols and a sword, at the head of fifty or a hundred labourers, armed with bludgeons. A loaf of bread was carried on a pole beneath a blue and white flag with a rampant lion, and Tom is supposed to have read to his followers from James, Chapter V:

> Go to now, ye rich men, weep and howl for your miseries that shall
> come upon you. . . .
> Behold, the hire of the labourers who have reaped down your fields,
> which is of you kept back by fraud, crieth: . . .

The women, in particular, believed that he had miraculous powers. A labourer said later, "he loved Sir William"—

> He talked in such a manner to them, and was always reading the Scripture,
> that they did not look upon him as a common man and would have
> cheerfully died for his sake.

Like Oastler and Stephens in the north, he denounced the New Poor Law as a breach of divine law. Eventually a constable was sent to arrest him, whom Courtenay (or Tom) killed. But the laboures did not leave him. More than fifty of them retired with him to Blean Wood, where in the dense undergrowth they awaited the military. Tom exhibited the prints of nails in his hands and feet, and announced that if he should be killed he would rise again:

> This is the day of judgment—this is the first day of the Millennium—
> and this day I will put the crown on my head. Behold, a greater than
> Sampson is with you!

To his followers he promised land—perhaps 50 acres each. As the soldiers approached, he sounded a trumpet and said it was heard at Jerusalem where 10,000 were ready to obey his command. At length the battle was joined— perhaps the most desperate on English soil since 1745. Against firearms and bayonets the Kentish labourers had only bludgeons: "I never witnessed more determination in my life," said one witness: "I never saw men more furious or mad-like in their attack upon us in my life." One officer was killed, as well as Courtenay and eleven or twelve of his followers. It was a higher death-roll than Pentridge or Peterloo.[143]

The affair of Blean Wood belongs more to the older cultural patterns than the new. It was the last peasants' revolt. It is interesting that the "ranting"

Bryanites, or Bible Christians, had one of their strongholds in Kent; and at a time when men's psychic world was filled with violent images from hell-fire and Revelation, and their real world filled with poverty and oppression, it is surprising that such explosions were not more frequent. The third example, which takes us closer to Owenism, is that of the extraordinary success of the Mormon propaganda in industrial districts in England in the late 1830s and 1840s. Thousands of converts were baptized in a few years, and thousand of these "Latter-Day Saints" set sail from Liverpool to the City of Zion. The first converts were "mainly manufacturers and other mechanics . . . extremely poor, most of them not having a change of clothes to be baptised in." Many of them, who were aided with passage money, walked and pushed hand-carts all the way from Council Bluffs to Salt Lake City.[144]

These examples all serve to emphasise that it is premature, in the 1830s, to think of the English working people as being wholly open to secular ideology. The Radical culture which we have examined was the culture of skilled men, artisans, and of some outworkers. Beneath this culture (or co-existing with it) there were more obscure levels of response, from which the charismatic leaders like Oastler and O'Connor drew some of their support. (In the Chartist movement, men like Lovett were never finally to find a common outlook and strategy with the "unshorn chins and fustian jackets" of the north.) The instability was particularly to be found where the new rationalist and the older-style Methodist or Baptist patterns impinged upon each other, or were in conflict within the same mind. But, whereas Dissent and rationalism seem to have ordered and tamed the character of the southern artisan, in those parts where the Methodist pattern was dominant during the Wars, emotional energies seem to have been stored or repressed. Strike a spade into the working-class culture of the north at any time in the Thirties, and passion seems to spring from the ground.

Hence Owenism gathered up some of this passion also. With Owen and his lecturers prophesying that "prosperity would be let loose," it was inevitable that they should gather around them the Children of Israel. The communitarian yearning revived, and the language of rationality was translated into that of brotherhood. As in all such phases of ferment, Antinomianism also revived, with its mystical equivalents of the secular notions of sexual liberation held among some Owenite communitarians: "If you love one another," Zion Ward told young people in his "chapels," "go together at any time without any law or ceremony." (Ward also had a scheme for a Land Colony, "where those who are willing to leave the world can live together as one family.") Moreover, for the poor, Owenism touched one of their deepest responses—the dream that, somehow, by some miracle, they might once again have *some stake in the land*.

One feels that, in the 1830s, many English people felt that the structure of industrial capitalism had been only partly built, and the roof not yet set upon the structure. Owenism was only one of the gigantic, but ephemeral, impulses which caught the enthusiasm of the masses, presenting the vision of a quite different structure which might be built in a matter of years or months if only people were united and determined enough. A spirit of combination has grown up, Bronterre O'Brien wrote in 1833, whose object:

> is the sublimest that can be conceived, namely—to establish for the productive classes a complete dominion over the fruits of their own industry. . . . An entire change in society—a change amounting to a complete subversion of the existing "order of the world"—is contemplated by the working classes. They aspire to be at the top instead of at the bottom of society—or rather that there should be no bottom or top at all.[145]

It is easy, in retrospect, to see this spirit as naïve or "utopian." But there is nothing in it which entitles us to regard it with academic superiority. The poor were desperately poor, and the prospects of a community in which they might not only blend intellectual culture with the athletic pursuits of Greece and Rome, but also *eat*, were attractive. Moreover, there was this important difference between Owenism and earlier creeds which gathered millenarial impetus. With the Owenites the Millennium was not to arrive, it was to be *made*, by their own efforts.

And this is where we may gather all the lines of Owenism together: the artisans, with their dreams of short-circuiting the market-economy; the skilled workers, with their thrust towards general unionism; the philanthropic gentry, with their desire for a rational, planned society; the poor, with their dream of land or of Zion; the weavers, with their hopes of self-employment; and all of these, with their image of an equitable brotherly community, in which mutual aid would replace aggression and competition. Maurice wrote in 1838:

> When the poor men say, "we, too, will acknowledge circumstances to be all in all, we will cast away any belief in that which is invisible, this world shall be the only home in which we will dwell," the language may well apall all who hear. . . . Nevertheless . . . it is the "we will" . . . which imparts to the dry chips of Mr. Owen's theory the semblance of vitality.[146]

This "we will" is evidence that working people were approaching maturity, becoming conscious of their own interests and aspirations as a class. There was nothing irrational or messianic in their offering a critique of capitalism as a system, or in projecting "utopian" ideas of an alternative and more rational system. It was not Owen who was "mad," but, from the standpoint of the toilers, a social system in which steam and new machinery evidently displaced and degraded labourers, and in which the markets could be "glutted" while the unshod weaver sat in his loom and the shoemaker sat in his workshop with no coat to his back. These men knew from their experience that Owen was sane when he said that:

> ... the present arrangement of society is the most anti-social, impolitic, and irrational that can be devised; that under its influence all the superior and valuable qualities of human nature are repressed from infancy, and that the most unnatural means are used to bring out the most injurious propensities. . . .[147]

So far from being backward-looking in its outlook, Owenism was the first of the great social doctrines to grip the imagination of the masses in this period, which commenced with an acceptance of the enlarged productive powers of steam and the mill. What was at issue was not the machine so much as the profit-motive; not the size of the industrial enterprise but the control of the social capital behind it. The building craftsmen and small masters, who resented control and the lion's share of the profits passing to master-builders or con-tractors, did not suppose that the solution lay in a multitude of petty entrepre-neurs.[148] Rather, they wished the co-operation of skills involved in building to be reflected in co-operative social control. It is ironic that a movement which is sometimes supposed to have drawn much of its strength from the "petit-bourgeois" should have made more earnest attempts to pioneer new forms of community life than any in our history. "All the fervour and earnestness of the early Co-operative Societies," Holyoake wrote many years later, "was . . . about communistic life. The 'Socialists' . . . hoped to found voluntary, self-supporting, self-controlled industrial cities, in which the wealth created was to be equitably shared by all those whose labour produced it."[149] Those who see, in the failure of these experiments, only a proof of their folly may perhaps be too confident that "history" has shown them to be a dead end.

What was irrational in Owenism (or "utopian" in its common pejorative meaning) was the impatience of the propaganda, the faith in the multiplication of reason by lectures and tracts, the inadequate attention to the means. Above all, there was Owen's fatal evasion of the realities of political power, and his attempt to by-pass the question of property-rights. Co-operative Socialism was simply to displace capitalism, painlessly and without any encounter, by example, by education, and by growing up within it from its own villages, workshops, and stores. Co-operation has no "*levelling* tendency," the *Economist* was anxious to reassure its readers. Its purpose was to "*elevate* all"; its wealth would not be taken from existing possessors but would be "*newly-produced wealth.*"[150] "We . . . do no come here as levellers," declared a Warrington clergyman: "We do not come here to deprive any human being of any of his or her property."[151] In 1834, at the furthest point in the Owenite movement, a "Charter of the Rights of Humanity" declared:

> The present property of all individuals, acquired and possessed by the usages and practices of old society, to be held sacred until . . . it can no longer be of any use or exchangeable value. . . .[152]

This was the vitiating weakness of Owenism. Even the little group of Spencean Philanthropists, at the end of the Wars, could see that Socialism entailed the expropriation of the great landowners. "It is childish," Spence had written in his *Restorer of Society to Its Natural State* (1800):

> . . . to expect ever to see Small Farms again, or ever to see anything else than the utmost screwing and grinding of the poor, till you quite overturn the present system of Landed Property. For they have got more completely into the spirit and power of oppression now than was ever known before . . . Therefore anything short of total Destruction of the power of these Samsons will not do . . . nothing less than the complete Extermination of the present system of holding Land . . . will ever bring the World again to a state worth living in.

It was this which aroused the particular fury of Britain's rulers, who held the mild Thomas Evans, author of *Christian Policy*, without trial for a year, at a time when Lord Sidmouth was discussing the proposals of the enlightened Mr. Owen. In that year one of the last Spenceans, a coloured tailor called Robert Wedderburn, promoted a little ill-printed journal, *The "Forlorn Hope"*:

> Mr. Owen . . . will find that the lower classes are pretty well convinced that he is a tool to the land-holders and Ministers. . . .[153]

The Spenceans and old Radicals of 1817 proved to be wrong in their estimation of Owen; and Spence's and Evans's preoccupation with agrarian Socialism was inadequate for industrial England. But the Spenceans were at least willing to pose the problems of ownership and class power.

It was because Owen refused to look squarely at either that he was able to remain quite indifferent to political Radicalism, and to lead the movement frequently up illusory paths. For years the co-operative movement continued with this co-existence of philanthropists and working-class Radicals. By 1832, however, men like Hetherington, O'Brien, and James Watson had quite different emphases, and were rejecting Owen's dismissal of all political means. Owenism was for them always a great constructive influence. They had learned from it to see capitalism, not as a collection of discrete events, but as a *system*. They had learned to project an alternative, utopian system of mutuality. They had passed beyond Cobbett's nostalgia for an older world and had acquired the confidence to plan the new. They had gained an understanding of the importance of education, and of the force of environmental conditioning. They had learned, from Thompson and Anna Wheeler, to assert new claims for the rights of women. Henceforward, nothing in capitalist society seemed *given* and inevitable, the product of "natural" law. This is all expressed in the Last Will and Testament of Henry Hetherington:

> These are my views and feelings in quitting an existence that has been chequered with the plagues and pleasures of a competitive, scrambling, selfish system; a system by which the moral and social aspirations of the noblest human beings are nullified by incessant toil and physical deprivations; by which, indeed, all men are trained to be either slaves, hypocrites, or criminals. Hence my ardent attachment to the principles of that great and good man—ROBERT OWEN.

V. "A Sort of Machine"

"The present mischief these two men [Owen and Hodgskin] have in some respects done is incalculable," noted Francis Place.[154] The "mischief" is written across the years 1831–5. And at this point the limits of this study have been reached; for there is a sense in which the working class is no longer in the making, but has been made. To step over the threshold, from 1832 to 1833, is to step into a world in which the working-class presence can be felt in every county in England, and in most fields of life.

The new class consciousness of working people may be viewed from two aspects. On the one hand, there was a consciousness of the identity of interests between working men of the most diverse occupations and levels of attainment, which was embodied in many institutional forms, and which was expressed on an unprecedented scale in the general unionism of 1830–4. This consciousness and these institutions were only to be found in fragmentary form in the England of 1780.

On the other hand, there was a consciousness of the identity of the interests of the working class, or "productive classes," *as against* those of other classes; and within this there was maturing the claim for an alternative *system*. But the final definition of this class consciousness was, in large part, the consequence of the response to working-class strength of the middle class. The line was drawn, with extreme care, in the franchise qualifications of 1832. It had been the peculiar feature of English development that, where we would expect to find a growing middle-class reform movement, with a working-class tail, only later succeeded by an independent agitation of the working class, in fact this process was reversed. The example of the French Revolution had initiated three simultaneous processes: a panic-struck counter-revolutionary response on the part of the landed and commercial aristocracy; a withdrawal on the part of the industrial bourgeoisie and an accommodation (on favourable terms) with the status quo; and a rapid radicalisation of the popular reform movement until the Jacobin cadres who were tough enough to survive through the Wars were in the main little masters, artisans, stock-ingers and croppers, and other working men. The twenty-five years after 1795 may be seen as the years of the "long counter-revolution"; and in consequence the Radical movement remained largely working-class in character, with an advanced democratic "populism" as its theory. But the triumph of such a movement was scarcely to be welcomed by the mill-owners, iron-masters, and manufacturers. Hence the peculiarly repressive and anti-egalitarian ideology of the English middle classes (Godwin giving way to Bentham, Bentham giving way to Malthus, M'Culloch, and Dr. Ure, and these giving rise to Baines, Macaulay, and Edwin Chadwick). Hence also the fact that the mildest measure of reform, to meet the evident irrationalities of Old Corruption, was actually *delayed*, by the resistance of the old order on the one hand, and the timidity of the manufacturers on the other.

The Reform Bill crisis of 1832—or, to be more accurate, the successive crises from early in 1831 until the "days of May" in 1832—illustrates these theses at almost every point. The agitation arose from "the people" and rapidly displayed the most astonishing consensus of opinion as to the imperative necessity for "reform." Viewed from one aspect, England was without any doubt passing through a crisis in these twelve months in which revolution was possible. The rapidity with which the agitation extended indicates the degree to which experience in every type of constitutional and quasi-legal agitation was present among the people:

> The systematic way in which the people proceeded, their steady perse-verance, their activity and skill astounded the enemies of reform. Meetings of almost every description of persons were held in cities, towns, and parishes; by journeymen tradesmen in their clubs, and by common work-men who had no trade clubs or associations of any kind. . . .

So Place wrote of the autumn of 1830, adding (of February 1831):

> . . . yet there was not even the smallest communication between places in
> the same neighbourhood; each portion of the people appeared to under-
> stand what ought to be done. . . .[155]

"The great majority" of those who attended the swelling demonstrations, the
King's private Secretary complained in March 1831 to Grey, "are of the very
lowest class." The enormous demonstrations, rising to above 100,000 in Birmingham and London in the autumn of 1831 and May 1832, were over-
whelmingly composed of artisans and working men.[156]

"We did not cause the excitement about reform," Grey wrote a little pee-
vishly to the King, in March 1831: "We found it in full vigour when we came
into office." And, viewed from another aspect, we can see why throughout
these crisis months a revolution was in fact improbable. The reason is to be
found in the very strength of the working-class Radical movement; the skill
with which the middle-class leaders, Brougham, *The Times*, the *Leeds Mercury*
both used this threat of working-class force, and negotiated a line of retreat
acceptable to all but the most die-hard defenders of the *ancien régime*; and the
awareness on the part of the Whigs and the least intransigent Tories that, while
Brougham and Baines were only blackmailing them, nevertheless if a compromise was not come to, the middle-class reformers might no longer be able to
hold in check the agitation at their backs.

The industrial bourgeoisie desired, with heart and soul, that a revolution
should not take place, since they knew that on the very day of its commencement there would be a dramatic process of radicalisation, in which Huntite,
trade unionist, and Owenite leaders would command growing support in nearly
all the manufacturing centres. "Threats of a 'revolution' are employed by the
middle classes and petty masters," wrote the *Poor Man's Guardian*. But—

> a violent revolution is not only beyond the means of those who threaten
> it, but is to them their greatest object of alarm; for they know that such
> a revolution can only be effected by the poor and despised millions, who,
> if excited to the step, might use it for their own advantage, as well as for
> that of themselves, who would thus . . . have their dear rights of property
> endangered: be assured that a violent revolution is their greatest
> dread. . . .[157]

The middle-class reformers fought skillfuly on both fronts. On the one hand
The Times came forward as the actual organiser of mass agitation: "We trust
there is not a county, town, or village in the United Kingdom which will not
meet and petition for a reform. . . ." It even urged upon the people "the solemn
duty of forming themselves into political societies throughout the whole realm."

It supported—as did Edward Baines, before cheering throngs, at Leeds—measures of enforcement which led directly on towards revolution: the run on the Banks, refusal to pay taxes, and the arming of members of Political Unions. On the other hand, the riots at Nottingham, Derby, and Bristol in October 1831 underlined the dual function of the Political Unions on the Birmingham model:

> These Unions were to be for the promotion of the cause of reform, for the protection of life and property against the detailed but irregular outrages of the mob, as well as for the maintenance of *other* great interests against the systematic violences of an oligarchy. . . .[158]

These middle-class incendiaries carried in their knapsacks a special constable's baton. There were occasions when the Tories themselves hoped to outwit them, by encouraging the independent working-class reform movement to display itself in a form so alarming that Brougham and Baines would run to Old Corruption for protection. When the National Union of the Working Classes proposed to call a demonstration in London for manhood suffrage, and in resistance to the Whig Reform Bill, the King himself wrote (4 November 1831):

> His Majesty is by no means displeased that the measures contemplated by the meeting in question are so violent, and . . . objectionable, as he trusts that the manifestation of such intentions and such purposes may afford the opportunity . . . of checking the progress of the Political Unions. . . .[159]

Throughout the country middle-class and working-class reformers maneuverd for control of the movement. In the earliest stages, until the summer of 1831, the middle-class Radicals held the advantage. Seven years before Wooler had closed the *Black Dwarf* with a sadly disillusioned final Address. There was (in 1824) no "public devotedly attached to the cause of parliamentary reform." Where hundreds and thousands had once clamoured for reform, it now seemed to him that they had only "clamoured for bread"; the orators and journalists of 1816–20 had only been "bubbles thrown up in the fermentation of society."[160] Many of the working-class leaders of the late 1820s shared his disillusion, and accepted the anti-political stance of their master, Owen. It was not until the summer of 1830, with the rural labourers' "revolt" and the July Revolution in France, that the tide of popular interest began to turn back to political agitation. And thenceforward the insanely stubborn last-ditch resistance of the die-hards (the Duke of Wellington, the Lords, the Bishops) to *any* measure of reform dictated a strategy (which was exploited to the full by the middle-class Radicals) by which popular agitation was brought to bear behind Grey and Russell, and in support of a Bill from which the majority had nothing to gain.

Thus the configuration of forces of 1816–20 (and, indeed, of 1791–4), in which the popular demand for Reform was identified with Major Cartwright's platform of manhood suffrage, was broken up. "If any persons suppose that this Reform will lead to ulterior measures," Grey declared in the House in November 1831:

> they are mistaken; for there is no one more decided against annual parliaments, universal suffrage, and the ballot, than I am. My object is not to favour, but to put an end to such hopes and projects.

This was clearly enough seen by the older Radicals, the majority of whose articulate spokesmen poured scorn on the Whig Bill until the final "days of May." "It mattered not to him," declared a Macclesfield Radical, "whether he was governed by a boroughmonger, or a whoremonger, or a cheesemonger, if the system of monopoly and corruption was still to be upheld."[161] Hunt, from his place as Member for Preston (1830–2), maintained the same propositions, in only slightly more decorous language. George Edmonds, the witty and courageous Radical schoolmaster, who had chaired Birmingham's first great post-war demonstration on Newhall Hill (January 1817), declared:

> I am not a house-holder.—I can, on a push, be a musket-holder. The nothing-but-the-Bill does not recognise George Edmonds as a citizen!— George Edmonds scorns the nothing-but-the-Bill, except as cut the first at the national robber.[162]

This was the position also of the elite of London's Radical artisans, enrolled in the National Union of Working Classes and Others, whose weekly debates in the Rotunda in 1831 and 1832 were reported in Hetherington's *Poor Man's Guardian*—undoubtedly the finest working-class weekly which had (until that time) been published in Britain. The debates were attended by Hetherington himself (when not in prison), William Lovett, James Watson, John Gast, the brilliant and ill-fated Julian Hibbert, and old William Benbow (the former colleague of Bamford and of Mitchell), now pressing his proposal for a "Grand National Holiday," or month's general strike, in the course of which the productive classes would assume control of the nation's government and resources.[163] The debates increasingly turned upon the definition of class. William Carpenter, who shared with Hetherington the honour of initiating the struggle for the "unstamped" press, offered a dissentient opinion. The Whig Bill ought to be supported as a "wedge." He complained that the *Poor Man's Guardian* used the words "middle men" and "middle class" as "convertible terms," whereas the middle classes "are not only *not* a class of persons having interests different from your own. They are the *same* class; they are, generally speaking, *working* or *labouring* men."[164] Throughout the entire crisis the controversy continued. After the Bill had passed, the *Poor Man's Guardian* recorded its conclusion:

> The promoters of the Reform Bill projected it, not with a view to subvert, or even remodel our aristocratic institutions, but to consolidate them by a reinforcement of sub-aristocracy from the middle-classes. . . . The only difference between the Whigs and the Tories is this—the Whigs would give the shadow to preserve the substance; the Tories would not give the shadow, because stupid as they are, the millions will not stop at shadows but proceed onwards to realities.[165]

It is problematical how far the militant Owenities of the Rotunda represented any massive body of working-class opinion. They commenced by representing only the intelligentsia of the artisans. But they gathered influence most rapidly; by October 1831 they were able to organise a massive demonstration, perhaps 70,000 strong, many wearing the white scarves emblematic of manhood suffrage; perhaps 100,000 joined their demonstrations against the National Fast in March 1832. Place regarded the Rotundists (many of whom he wrote off as "atrocious") as constituting the greatest of threats to the middle-class strategy, and much of his manuscript history of the Reform Bill crisis (upon which historians have placed too much reliance) is devoted to the unscrupulous maneuvres by which he sought to limit their influence, and displace it by that of his rival National Political Union. The Duke of Wellington himself saw the contest as one between the Establishment and the Rotunda, which he compared to two armies *"en présence."* It confused his military mind very much to reflect that he could place no river between the armies, with adequate sentinels and posts on the bridges. The enemy was installed at sensitive points within his own camp.[166]

The procession of October 1831, however, was mainly composed (it seems) of "shopkeepers and superior artisans." And while the numbers called out were impressive, they compare poorly with the even greater demonstrations at Birmingham, drawn from a smaller population. It would seem that, while the London artisans had at last succeeded in building a cohesive and highly articulate leadership, there remained a wide gulf between them and the mass of London labourers, and workers in the dishonourable trades. (This problem was to recur time and again in the history of London Chartism.) The position was caricatured in the pages of a scurrilous and alarmist pamphlet by Edward Gibbon Wakefield. He saw the Rotundists as "Desperadoes" and idealists, whose danger lay in the fact that they might unleash the destructive energies of the criminal classes, "the helots of society," who were crammed in the lanes and alleys off Orchard Street, Westminster, or Whitechapel. Here were the thousands of unpolitical (but dangerous) "costermongers, drovers, slaughterers of cattle, knackers, dealers in dead bodies and dogs' meat, cads, brick-makers, chimney-sweepers, nightmen, scavengers, &c." His attitude to the Owenite Socialists of the Rotunda was ambiguous. On the one hand, they were mostly "sober men, who maintain themselves by industry"—men plainly marked off by superior talents from the dangerous classes. On the other hand, many were "loose single men living here and there in lodgings, who might set fire to London without anxiety for helpless beings at home":

> In manner they are rather gentle than rough; but touch one of them on his tender point;— only say that you think the stimulus of competition indispensable to the production of wealth;—and he will either turn from you in scorn, or . . . tell you, with flashing eyes, that you are paid by the Government to talk nonsense. Any thing like a compromise is what annoys them even more than decided opposition.

Many, he said (with some truth), "are provided with arms":

> If an insurrection of the London populace should take place, they will be found at the most dangerous posts, leading the thieves and rabble, pointing out the most effectual measures, and dying, if the lot fall on them, with cries of defiance.

"These will be the fighting men of our revolution, if we must have one."[167]

The picture is overdrawn; but it is not wholly without truth.[168] The danger, from the point of view of authority (whether Whig or Tory), lay in a possible conjunction between the artisan Socialists and the "criminal classes." But the unskilled masses in London inhabited another world from that of the artisans—a world of extreme hardship, illiteracy, very widespread demoralisation, and disease, which was dramatised by the cholera outbreak of the winter of 1831–2. Here we have all the classic problems, the hand-to-mouth insecurity, of a metropolitan city swollen with immigrants in a period of rapid population-growth.[169]

The unskilled had no spokesmen and no organisations (apart from friendly societies). They were as likely to have followed the lead of a gentleman as of an artisan. And yet the severity of the political crisis which commenced in October 1831 was sufficient to crack the crust of fatalism, deference, and need, within which their lives were enclosed. The riots of that month in Derby, the sacking of Nottingham Castle, the extensive riots at Bristol—all were indicative of a deep disturbance at the foundations of society, which observers anxiously expected to be followed by the uprising of London's East End.

The Birmingham Political Union was an acceptable model, which *The Times* itself could commend, because the local industrial context favoured a reform movement of the masses which still remained firmly under middle-class control. The history of Birmingham Radicalism is significantly different from that of the north Midlands and the north. There was no basis in its small-scale industries for Luddism, and the "father" of the Political Unions, Thomas Attwood, first gained public-prominence when he led, in 1812, a united agitation of the masters and artisans against the Orders in Council. There were undoubtedly groups of "physical force" Radicals in the Black Country in 1817–20, but— whether by good fortune or good judgement—they were never exposed by any abortive movement like the Pentridge and Grange Moor affairs.[170] As Professor Briggs has shown, Thomas Attwood was able in 1830 to "harmonize and unite" the diverse "materials of discontent" because the Industrial Revolution in Birmingham had "multiplied the number of producing units rather than added to the scale of existing enterprises." There had been little displacement of skilled labour by machinery; the numberless small workshops meant that the social gradients shelved more gently, and the artisan might still rise to the status of a small master; in times of economic recession masters and journeymen were afflicted alike.[171] Hence, class antagonism was more muted than in Manchester, Newcastle, and Leeds. Throughout the Reform Bill crisis, Attwood controlled the Birmingham Union with "such a show of good-nature" (O'Brien later recalled) "that the Brummagem operatives seemed really to believe that they would be *virtually*, though not actually, represented in the 'reformed' parliament." And, in a tribute impressive from so stern a critic, O'Brien added:

> To this body, more than to any other, is confessedly due the triumph (such as it was) of the Reform Bill. Its well-ordered proceedings, extended organization, and immense assemblages of people, at critical periods of its progress, rendered the measure irresistible.[172]

In such centres as Leeds, Manchester, and Nottingham the position of the middle-class reformers was very much more uneasy. At Manchester (as in London) rival political Unions co-existed, and from October 1831 onwards the manhood suffrage Union made the running. At Bolton in the same month the rejection of the Bill by the House of Lords resulted in a split in the Political Union, the largest (manhood suffrage) section organising a demonstration, 6,000 strong, behind the banners: "Down with the Bishops!" "No Peers!"[173] In the Midlands and the north such incidents were repeated dozens of times. "Walk into any lane or public-house, where a number of operatives are congregated together," wrote Doherty in January 1832:

and listen, for ten minutes, to the conversation. . . . In at least seven out
of every ten cases, the subjects of debate will be found to bear upon the
appalling question of *whether it would be more advantageous to attack the
lives or the property of the rich?*[174]

Indeed in the winter of 1831–2 the ridicule poured upon the Bill and upon
its attendant proceedings in the *Poor Man's Guardian* takes on a somewhat
academic air. No doubt the Rotundists were right to designate the Bill as a trap
(and as a betrayal of the Radical movement). But the well-nigh neolithic obstinacy with which Old Corruption resisted *any* reform led on to a situation in
which the nation stepped, swiftly and without premeditation, on to the threshold
of revolution. Belatedly, the *Poor Man's Guardian* adjusted its tactics, publishing
as a special supplement extracts from Colonel Macerone's *Defensive Instructions
for the People* (a manual in street-fighting).[175] Throughout the "eleven days of
England's apprehension and turmoil" which preceded the final passage of the
Bill through the Lords in May, Francis Place held his breath. On the evening
of the day when it passed, he returned home and noted:

> We were within a moment of general rebellion, and had it been possible
> for the Duke of Wellington to have formed an administration the Thing
> and the people would have been at issue.

There would have been "Barricadoes of the principal towns—stopping circulation of paper money"; if a revolution had commenced, it "would have been
the act of the whole people to a greater extent than any which had ever before
been accomplished."[176]

In the autumn of 1831 and in the "days of May" Britain was within an ace
of a revolution which, once commenced, might well (if we consider the simultaneous advance in cooperative and trade union theory) have prefigured, in its
rapid radicalisation, the revolutions of 1848 and the Paris Commune. J. R. M.
Butler's *The Passing of the Great Reform Bill* gives us some sense of the magnitude of the crisis; but his study is weakened by an insufficient awareness of
the potential openness of the whole situation, evinced in such comments as this
(upon the National Union of the Working Classes):

> . . . it disgusted sensible people . . . by its arrogant silliness, as when the
> Bethnal Green branch petitioned the King to abolish the House of Lords,
> or the Finsbury section urged the Commons to confiscate the estates of
> the 199 peers. . . .[177]

Some assessment less complacent than this is required. The fact that revolution did not occur was due, in part, to the deep constitutionalism of that part of the Radical tradition[178] of which Cobbett (urging the acceptance of half a loaf) was the spokesman; and in part to the skill of the middle-class Radicals in offering exactly that compromise which might not weaken, but strengthen, both the State and property-rights against the working-class threat.

The Whig leaders saw their role as being that of finding the means to "attach numbers to property and good order." "It is of the utmost importance," Grey said, "to associate the middle with the higher orders of society in the love and support of the institutions and government of the country."[179] The extreme care with which this line was drawn is evinced by a survey undertaken by Baines in 1831, to discover "the numbers and respectability of the £10 householders in Leeds." The results were communicated to Lord John Russell in a letter which should be taken as one of the classic documents of the Reform Bill crisis. Baines's pioneering psephological canvassers—

> stated *unanimously*, that the £10 qualification did not admit to the exercise of the elective franchise a single person who might not safely and wisely be enfranchised: that they were surprised to find how comparatively few would be allowed to vote.

In answer to Russell's enquiry as to the proportion which £10 householders bore to the rest of the population, the canvassers reported:

> . . . in the parts occupied chiefly by the working classes, not one house-holder in fifty would have a vote. In the streets principally occupied by shops, almost every householder had a vote. . . . In the township of Hol-beck, containing 11,000 inhabitants, chiefly of the working classes, but containing several mills, dye-houses, public-houses, and respectable dwell-ings, there are only 150 voters. . . . Out of 140 householders, heads of families, working in the mill of Messrs. Marshall and Co, there are *only two* who will have votes. . . . Out of 160 or 170 householders in the mill of Messrs. O. Willan and Sons, Holbeck, there is *not one* vote. Out of about 100 householders in the employment of Messrs. Taylor and Words-worth, machine-makers,—the highest class of mechanics,—*only one* has a vote. It appeared that of the working classes not more than one in fifty would be enfranchised by the Bill.

Even this estimate would appear to have been excessive. Returns made to the Government in May 1832 showed that in Leeds (population, 124,000) 355 "workmen" would be admitted to the franchise, of whom 143 "are clerks, warehousemen, overlookers, &c." The remaining 212 were in a privileged status, earning between 30s. and 40s. a week.[180]

Such surveys no doubt reassured the Cabinet, which had meditated raising the £10 franchise qualification to £15. "The great body of the people," Place wrote, "were self-assured that either the Reform Bills would be passed by Parliament, or that they should, by their own physical force, obtain much more than they contained, if they were rejected . . .[181] It is the threat of this "much more" which hung over both Tories and Whigs in 1832, and which enabled that accommodation to be made, between landed and industrial wealth, between privilege and money, which has been an enduring configuration of English society. Upon the banners of Baines and Cobden were not *égalité* and *liberté* (still less *fraternité*) but "Free Trade" and "Retrenchment." The rhetoric of Brougham was that of property, security, interest. "If there is a mob," Brougham said in his speech on the second reading of the Reform Bill,

> there is the people also. I speak now of the middle classes—of those hundreds of thousands of respectable persons—the most numerous and by far the most wealthy order in the community, for if all your Lordships' castles, manors, rights of warren and rights of chase, with all your broad acres, were brought to the hammer, and sold at fifty years' purchase, the price would fly up and kick the beam when counterpoised by the vast and solid riches of those middle classes, who are also the genuine depositaries of sober, rational, intelligent, and honest English feeling. . . . Rouse not, I beseech you, a peace-loving, but a resolute people. . . . As your friend, as the friend of my order, as the friend of my country, as the faithful servant of my sovereign, I counsel you to assist with your uttermost efforts in preserving the peace, and upholding and perpetuating the Constitution. . . .[182]

Divested of its rhetoric, the demands of the middle-class Radicals were voiced by Baines, when the Bill had been passed:

> The fruits of Reform are to be gathered. Vast commercial and agricultural monopolies are to be abolished. The Church is to be reformed. . . . Close corporations are to be thrown open. Retrenchment and economy are to be enforced. The shackles of the Slave are to be broken.[183]

The demands of working-class Radicalism were less clearly formulated. A minimum political programme may be cited from the *Poor Man's Guardian*, the organ of the National Union of Working Classes:

Extirpation of the Fiend Aristocracy; Establishment of a Republic, viz. Democracy by Representatives elected by Universal Suffrage; Extinction of hereditary offices, titles and distinctions; Abolition of the ... law of primogeniture; ... Cheap and rapid administration of justice; Abolition of the Game Laws; Repeal of the diabolical imposts on Newspapers ...; emancipation of our fellow-citizens the Jews; Introduction of Poor Laws into Ireland; Abolition of the Punishment of Death for offences against property; Appropriation of the Revenues of the "Fathers in God," the Bishops, towards maintenance of the Poor; Abolition of Tithes; Payment of every Priest or Minister by his Sect; The "National Debt" not the debt of the Nation; Discharge of the Machinery of Despotism, the Soldiers; Establishment of a National Guard.[184]

This is the old programme of Jacobinism, with little development from the 1790s. (The first principle of a declaration of the National Union, drawn up by Lovett and James Watson, in November 1831, was: "All property (honestly acquired) to be sacred and inviolable.")[185] But around this "much more" other demands accrued, according to the grievances foremost in different districts and industries. In Lancashire, Doherty and his supporters argued that "universal suffrage means nothing more than a power given to every man to protect his own labour from being devoured by others."[186] The Owenites, the factory reformers, and "physical force" revolutionaries like the irrepressible William Benbow were pressing still further demands. But, in the event, the terms of the contest were successfully confined within the limits desired by Brougham and Baines. It was (as Shelley had foreseen in 1822) a contest between "blood and gold"; and in its outcome, blood compromised with gold to keep out the claims of *égalité*. For the years between the French Revolution and the Reform Bill had seen the formation of a middle-class "class consciousness," more conservative, more wary of the large idealist causes (except, perhaps, those of other nations), more narrowly self-interested than in any other industrialised nation. Henceforward, in Victorian England, the middle-class Radical and the idealist intellectual were forced to take sides between the "two nations." It is a matter of honour that there were many individuals who preferred to be known as Chartists or Republicans rather than as special constables. But such men— Wakley, Frost of Newport, Duncombe, Oastler, Ernest Jones, John Fielden, W. P. Roberts, and on to Ruskin and William Morris—were always disaffected individuals or intellectual "voices." They represent in no sense the ideology of the middle class.

What Edward Baines had done, in his correspondence with Russell, was to offer a definition of class of almost arithmetical exactitude. In 1832 the line was drawn in social consciousness by the franchise qualifications, with the crudity of an indelible pencil. Moreover, these years found also a theorist of stature to define the working-class predicament. It appears almost inevitable that he should have been an Irish intellectual, uniting in himself a hatred of the English Whigs with the experience of English ultra-Radicalism and Owenite Socialism. James "Bronterre" O'Brien (1805–64), the son of an Irish wine merchant, and a distinguished graduate of Trinity College, Dublin, arrived in London in 1829 "to study Law and Radical Reform":

> My friends sent me to study law; I took to radical reform on my own account. . . . While I have made no progress at all in law, I have made immense progress in radical reform. So much so, that were a professorship of radical reform to be instituted tomorrow in King's College (no very probable event by the way), I think I would stand candidate . . . I feel as though every drop of blood in my veins was radical blood. . . .[187]

After editing the *Midlands Representative* during the Reform Bill crisis, he moved to London and assumed the editorship of the *Poor Man's Guardian*.

"We foresaw," he wrote of the Reform Bill, "that its effect would be to detach from the working classes a large portion of the middle ranks, who were *then* more inclined to act with the people than with the aristocracy that excluded them."[188] And in his Introduction to Buonarotti's history of the Conspiracy of Equals, he drew a parallel: "The Girondists would extend the franchise to the small middlemen (just as our English Whigs did by the Reform Bill) in order the more effectively to keep down the working classes." "Of all governments, a government of the middle classes is the most grinding and remorseless."[189]

It was a theme to which he often returned. His anger was refreshed by each new action of the Whig administration—the Irish Coercion Bill, the rejection of the 10 Hour Bill, the attack on the trades unions, the Poor Law Amendment Act.

"Previously to the passing of the Reform Bill," he wrote in 1836:

> the middle orders were supposed to have some community of feeling with the labourers. That delusion has passed away. It barely survived the Irish Coercion Bill, it vanished completely with the enactment of the Starvation Law. No working man will ever again expect justice, morals or mercy at the hands of a profit-mongering legislature.[190]

A refugee from a middle-class culture himself, he took especial pleasure in writing of his own class in terms which imitated its own drawing-room small-talk about the servant classes: "The pursuits and habits [of the middle classes] are essentially debasing. Their life is necessarily a life of low cunning and speculation . . .":

> These two classes never had, and never will have, any community of interest. It is the workman's interest to do as little work, and to get as much for it as possible. It is the middleman's interest to get as much work as he can out of the man, and to give as little for it. Here then are their respective interests as directly opposed to each other as two fighting bulls.

And he sought, with considerable genius, to twist together the tradition of ultra-Radicalism with that of Owenism, into a revolutionary Socialism, whose goals were political revolution, the expropriation of the propertied classes, and a network of Owenite communities:

> We must have what Southey calls 'a revolution of revolutions'; such an one as Robespierre and St. Just projected in France in the beginning of 1794; that is to say, a complete subversion of the institutions by which wealth is distributed . . . Property—property—this is the thing we must be at. Without a change in the institution of property, no improvement can take place.

Such a revolution (he hoped) would come, without violence, in the immediate aftermath of the attainment of manhood suffrage: "From the *laws of the few* have the existing inequalities sprung; by the laws of the many shall they be destroyed."[191]

Historians today would certainly not accept O'Brien's over-crude assimilation of the post-Reform Whig administration to the interests of the "middle class."[192] (Old Corruption had more vitality than that, as the protracted struggle for the repeal of the Corn Laws was to show.) Nor is it proper to select this one theorist (middle-class in his own origins) as expressive of the new consciousness of the working class. But at the same time, O'Brien was very far from being an eccentric at the edges of the movement. As editor of the *Poor Man's Guardian* and other journals he commanded a large, and growing, working-class audience; he was later to earn the title of the "Schoolmaster" of Chartism. His writings are a central thread through the abundant agitations of the early 1830s, providing a nexus for the old democratic claims, the social agitations (against the New Poor Law and for Factory Reform), the Owenite communitarian experiments, and the syndicalist struggles of the trade unions. O'Brien was, as much as Cobbett and Wooler in the post-war years, an authentic voice of his times.

For most working men, of course, disillusion in the Reform Bill came in less theoretical forms. The proof of the pudding was in the eating. We may see the eating in microcosm in a few of the incidents at one of the contests in the ensuing General Election—at Leeds. Here Baines, who had already used his influence to instate Brougham as the Yorkshire member, brought forward in the Whig interest Marshall, one of the largest employers in Leeds, and Macaulay (or "Mr. Mackholy" as one of the tail of Whig shopkeepers noted in his diary). Macaulay was one of the most complacent of the ideologists of the Reform Bill settlement, translating into new terms the Tory doctrine of "virtual representation":

> The higher and middling orders are the natural representatives of the human race. Their interest may be opposed, in some things, to that of their poorer contemporaries, but it is identical with that of the innumerable generations which are to follow.

"The inequality with which wealth is distributed forces itself on everybody's notice," he lamented, while "the reasons which irrefragably proved this inequality to be necessary to the well-being of all classes are not equally obvious." Mr. Marshall was not equal to him as a theorist; but, if a Radical election sheet is to be believed, he was of the view that 12s. a week was a good wage for a man with a family, he considered that the working classes might better their conditions by emigration, and:

> In Mr. Marshall's mill, a boy of 9 years of age was stripped to the skin, bound to an iron pillar, and mercilessly beaten with straps, until he fainted.[193]

The Tory candidate, on the other hand, was Sadler, leading parliamentary spokesman of the 10 Hour Movement. Oastler had launched, with the Short-Time Committees, his passionate campaign against child labour two years before. The amazing "Pilgrimage to York" had taken place in the previous April; and the 10 Hour agitation (like the Owenite agitation) continued without pause during the Reform Bill crisis months. In such a contest, therefore, Oastler could be counted upon to side with Sadler against Baines, who had conducted a mealy-mouthed defence of the mill-owners in the *Leeds Mercury*. Cobbett could be counted upon to do the same. Indeed, he gave a reference for Baines which reminds us of the latitude of the libel laws of the time:

> This great LYING PUFFER of Brougham . . . who has always taken care to have one member, at least, to do more mischief to public liberty than any other fifty members in the House of Commons; this swelled-up, greedy,

and unprincipled puffer, who has been the deluder of Yorkshire for twenty years past . . .[194]

A Tory-Radical alliance was therefore inevitable behind Sadler. It was also inevitable that the greater part of the Nonformist "shopocrat" vote would go to "Mr. Marshall Our Townsman and Mr. Mackholy the Scotchman" (as our diarist put it):

> . . . as to Sadler he never has done any good nor he never will do . . . for he has always been inventing something that has tended to injure the inhabitants of the Town of Leeds . . . he was the first promoter of the Improvement Act and that has cost the Inhabitants a manny thousands and the Burthen has cheefly fallen upon Shopkeepers and what I call the Middling Class of People . . . its true he is one of our Magestrate Party but he is not better for that . . .[195]

The working-class Radicals in Leeds maintained their independent press and organisation. The men of Leeds (they declared) who "have assembled in evil report and good report; . . . been instant in season and out of season," had now been betrayed by the men who, in the days of May, had addressed their great assemblies and promised Reform or barricades:

> Messrs. Marshall and Macaulay may . . . be very friendly to Reforms of all sorts and sizes, both in church and state; they may also be in favour of the abolition of all monopolies except their own, those of mill-men and placemen; but let the operatives of Leeds remember that if they support them, they do what they can to put legislative power into the hands of their enemies.

Moreover, the Radicals declared that the old forms of electoral bribery and influence employed by the aristocratic interest were now finding insidious new forms in the service of the manufacturing interest. Although the workers did not have votes, great efforts were made to offset the effects of 10 Hour demonstrations in favour of Sadler by compelling factory-hands to declare for Marshall and Macaulay at the hustings:

> We could name more than a dozen mills, all the hands of which have received positive orders to be in the Yard on Monday, and to hold up their hands for the Orange candidates . . . on pain of instant privation of employment. . . . They have each their stations assigned in the yard, where they are to be penned like flocks of sheep, surrounded on all sides by

overlookers, clerks and other under-strappers, for the purpose of enforcing the high mandate of the counting-house.

In the event, the scene on the hustings turned into riot, where Oastler and the 10 Hour men "rang matins on the thick skulls of the flying oranges." When Sadler was defeated at the poll, Marshall and Macaulay were burned in effigy in the same city centre where Paine had been burnt by the loyalists in 1792.[196]

This Leeds election of 1832 was of more than local significance. It had focussed the attention of factory reformers throughout the country, drawing addresses in Sadler's favour from thousands of signatories in northern towns. There is no mistaking the new tone after 1832. In every manufacturing district a hundred experiences confirmed the new consciousness of class which the Bill had, by its own provisions, so carefully defined. It was the "reformed" House of Commons which sanctioned the transportation of the Dorchester labourers in 1834 ("a blow directed at the whole body of united operatives"),[197] and who launched, with "the document" and the lock-out, the struggle to break the trade unions, whose intensity and whose significance (in both political and economic terms) is still too little understood. Against the manifesto of the masters, the Yorkshire Trades Union issued its own:

> The war cry of the masters has not only been sounded, but the havoc of war; war against freedom; war against opinion; war against justice; and war without justifying cause. . . .

"The very men," declared one Leeds trade unionist, "who had pampered Political Unions, when they could be made subservient to their own purposes, were now endeavouring to crush the Trades Unions":

> It was but the other day that the operatives were led in great numbers to the West Riding meeting at Wakefield, for the purpose of carrying the Reform Bill. At that time, the very individuals who were now attempting to put down trades' unions, were arraying them to carry by the force of numbers, a political reform which he was sure would not otherwise have been obtained from the aristocracy of this country. That reform which had thus been obtained appeared to him to have been the ultimate means of strengthening the hands of corruption and oppression.[198]

The line from 1832 to Chartism is not a haphazard pendulum alternation of "political" and "economic" agitations but a direct progression, in which simultaneous and related movements converge towards a single point. This point was the vote. There is a sense in which the Chartist movement commenced, not in 1836 with the promulgation of the "Six Points," but at the moment when the Reform Bill received Royal Assent. Many of the provincial Political Unions never disbanded, but commenced at once to agitate against the "shopocrat" franchise. In January 1833 the *Working Man's Friend* was able to announce that the fortress of middle-class Radicalism had been stormed: ". . . in spite of all the opposition and chicanery of a RAG MERCHANT MONARCHY, the Midland Union of the Working Classes was formed by the brave, but, till then, misled people of that country."[199] The characteristic ideology of Birmingham Radicalism, which united employers and journeymen in opposition to the aristocracy, the Banks, the National Debt, and the "paper-money system," was beginning to fall apart. For a time Attwood himself was carried with the new current, partly through loyalty to the regiments to which he had made large promises before. Once again, a monster demonstration gathered on Newhall Hill (May 1833), at which an attendance of 180,000 was claimed, and at which there was expressed—

> . . . a sentiment of common hatred to the parties whom, having been mainly instrumental in forcing into power, they now assembled to express their disgust of the . . . treachery which they had manifested.

The attendance was swelled by colliers from Walsall, iron-workers from Wolverhampton, outworkers from Dudley. The process of radicalisation which was to make Birmingham a Chartist metropolis had begun.[200]

But the content of this renewed agitation was such that the vote itself implied "much more," and that is why it had to be denied. (The Birmingham of 1833 was not the Birmingham of 1831: it was now the home of an Equitable Labour Exchange, it was the headquarters of the socialist Builders' Union, it housed the editorial office of the *Pioneer*.) The vote, for the workers of this and the next decade, was a symbol whose importance it is difficult for us to appreciate, our eyes dimmed by more than a century of the smog of "two-party parliamentary politics." It implied, first, *égalité*: equality of citizenship, personal dignity, worth. "Instead of bricks, mortar, and dirt, MAN ought to be represented," wrote one pamphleteer, lamenting the lot of "the miserable, so-called 'freeborn' Englishman, excluded from the most valuable right that man can enjoy in political society."[201] "Be we, of the working millions," wrote George Edmonds—

> never more seen at baby-shows, Lord Mayor penny-peeps, and gingerbread Coronations—be not present as accomplices in such national fooleries. Let the tawdry actors have all the fun to themselves.

"Like the wild Irish of old, the British millions have been too long insolently placed without the pale of social governments":

> I now speak the thoughts of my unrepresented fellow millions, the Wild English, the free-born slaves of the nineteenth century.[202]

But in the context of the Owenite and Chartist years, the claim for the vote implied also further claims: a new way of reaching out by the working people for *social control* over their conditions of life and labour. At first, and inevitably, the exclusion of the working class provoked a contrary rejection, by the working class, of all forms of political action. Owen had long prepared the ground for this, with his indifference to political Radicalism. But in the post-1832 swing to general unionism, this anti-political bias was not quietist but embattled, militant, and even revolutionary. To examine the richness of the political thought of these years would take us further into the history of general unionism—and, indeed, into the early years of Chartism—than we intend to go. They are years in which Benbow canvassed his notion of the "Grand National Holiday" in the industrial districts; in which the printing-worker, John Francis Bray, carried forward Hodgskin's ideas, in lectures to Leeds artisans, later published as *Labour's Wrongs and Labour's Remedies*; in which the Builders' Union and the Grand National Consolidated Trades Union rose and fell; and in which Doherty and Fielden founded the "Society for National Regeneration" with its remedy of the General Strike for the Eight-Hour Day. The Owenite communitarians were fertile with notions and experiments prefiguring advances in the care of children, the relations between the sexes, education, housing, and social policy. Nor were these ideas canvassed among a limited intelligentsia only; building workers, potters, weavers, and artisans were willing, for a while, to risk their livelihood to put experiments to the test. The swarming variety of journals, many of which made exacting demands upon the readers, were addressed to an authentic working-class audience. In the silk mills of the Colden Valley, isolated on the Pennines between Yorkshire and Lancashire, the Owenite journals were read.

Two themes only may be mentioned of those which arose again and again in these years. The first is that of internationalism. This was, to be sure, part of the old Jacobin heritage; and one which the Radicals had never forgotten. When Oliver tramped with the Leeds cropper, James Mann, and another revolutionary, to the rendezvous at Thornhill Lees (in 1817) he found, from their discourse, that "the recent news from the Brazils seemed to cheer them with greater hopes than ever."[203] Cobbett could always find time to add a stop-press to his journals:

> I have just room to tell you, that the people of BELGIUM, the *common people*, have *beaten the Dutch armies*, who were marched against them to compel them to *pay enormous taxes*. This is excellent news.[204]

The French Revolution of 1830 had a profound impact upon the people, electrifying not only the London Radicals but working-class reformers in distant industrial villages. The struggle for Polish independence was followed anxiously in the working-class press; while Julian Hibbert, in the Rotunda, carried a vote of sympathy with the Lyons weavers, in their ill-fated insurrection, likening them to the weavers of Spitalfields. In the Owenite movement this political tradition was extended to embrace social and class solidarities. In 1833 a "Manifesto of the Productive Classes of Great Britain and Ireland" was addressed to "the Governments and People of the Continents of Europe and of North and South America," commencing: "Men of the Great Family of Mankind . . ." By the end of the same year, the question of some common alliance between the trade unionists of England, France, and Germany had already come under discussion.[205]

The other theme was that of industrial syndicalism. When Marx was still in his teens, the battle for the minds of English trade unionists, between a capitalist and a socialist political economy, had been (at least temporarily) won. The winners were Hodgskin, Thompson, James Morrison, and O'Brien; the losers were James Mill and Place. "What is capital?" asked a writer in the *Pioneer*. " 'It is reserved labour!' cries M'Culloch. . . . From whom and what was it reserved? From the clothing and food of the wretched."[206] Hence the workers who had been "insolently placed without the pale of social government" developed, stage by stage, a theory of syndicalism, or of "Inverted Masonry."[207] "The Trades Unions will not only strike for less work, and more wages," wrote "A Member of the Builder's Union,"

> but they will ultimately ABOLISH WAGES, become their own masters, and work for each other; labour and capital will no longer be separate but they will be indissolubly joined together in the hands of the workmen and work-women.

The unions themselves could solve the problem of political power; a "Parliament" of the industrious classes could be formed, delegated directly from workshops and mills: "the Lodges send Delegates from local to district, and from district to National Assemblies. Here are Universal Suffrage, Annual Election, and No Property Qualification, instanter."[208] The idea was developed (in the *Pioneer*) of such a House of Trades:

which must supply the place of the present House of Commons, and direct the commercial affairs of the country, according to the will of the trades which compose associations of the industry. This is the ascendancy scale by which we arrive to universal suffrage. It will begin in our lodges, extend to our general union, embrace the management of trade, and finally swallow up the whole political power.[209]

This vision was lost, almost as soon as it had been found, in the terrible defeats of 1834 and 1835. And, when they had recovered their wind, the workers returned to the vote, as the more practical key to political power. Something was lost: but Chartism never entirely forgot this preoccupation with social control, to the attainment of which the vote was seen as a means. These years reveal a passing beyond the characteristic outlook of the artisan, with his desire for an independent livelihood "by the sweat of his brow," to a newer outlook, more reconciled to the new means of production, but seeking to exert the collective power of the class to humanise the environment:—by this community or that co-operative society, by this check on the blind operation of the market-economy, this legal enactment, that measure of relief for the poor. And implicit, if not always explicit, in their outlook was the dangerous tenet: production must be, not for profit, but for *use*.

This collective self-consciousness was indeed the great spiritual gain of the Industrial Revolution, against which the disruption of an older and in many ways more humanly-comprehensible way of life must be set. It was perhaps a unique formation, this British working class of 1832. The slow, piecemeal accretions of capital accumulation had meant that the preliminaries to the Industrial Revolution stretched backwards for hundreds of years. From Tudor times onwards this artisan culture had grown more complex with each phase of technical and social change. Delaney, Dekker, and Nashe: Winstanley and Lilburne: Bunyan and Defoe—all had at times addressed themselves to it. Enriched by the experiences of the 17th century, carrying through the 18th century the intellectual and libertarian traditions which we have described, forming their own traditions of mutuality in the friendly society and trades club, these men did not pass, in one generation, from the peasantry to the new industrial town. They suffered the experience of the Industrial Revolution as articulate, free-born Englishmen. Those who were sent to gaol might know the Bible better than those on the Bench, and those who were transported to Van Diemen's Land might ask their relatives to send Cobbett's *Register* after them.

This was, perhaps, the most distinguished popular culture England has known. It contained the massive diversity of skills, of the workers in metal, wood, textiles, and ceramics, without whose inherited "mysteries" and superb ingenuity with primitive tools the inventions of the Industrial Revolution could scarcely have got further than the drawing-board. From this culture of the crafts- man and the self-taught there came scores of inventers, organisers, journalists, and political theorists of impressive quality. It is easy enough to say that this cul- ture was backward-looking or conservative. True enough, one direction of the great agitations of the artisans and outworkers, continued over fifty years, was to *resist* being turned into a proletariat. When they knew that this cause was lost, yet they reached out again, in the Thirties and Forties, and sought to achieve new and only imagined forms of social control. During all this time they were, as a class, repressed and segregated in their own communities. But what the counter- revolution sought to repress grew only more determined in the quasi-legal insti- tutions of the underground. Whenever the pressure of the rulers relaxed, men came from the petty workshops or the weavers' hamlets and asserted new claims. They were told that they had no rights, but they knew that they were born free. The Yeomanry rode down their meeting, and the right of public meeting was gained. The pamphleteers were gaoled, and from the gaols they edited pamphlets. The trade unionists were imprisoned, and they were attended to prison by pro- cessions with bands and union banners.

Segregated in this way, their institutions acquired a peculiar toughness and resilience. Class also acquired a peculiar resonance in English life: everything, from their schools to their shops, their chapels to their amusements, was turned into a battle-ground of class. The marks of this remain, but by the outsider they are not always understood. If we have in our social life little of the tradition of *égalité*, yet the class-consciousness of the working man has little in it of deference. "Orphans we are, and bastards of society," wrote James Morrison in 1834.[210] The tone is not one of resignation but of pride.

Again and again in these years working men expressed it thus: "they wish to make us tools," or "implements," or "machines." A witness before the par- liamentary committee enquiring into the hand-loom weavers (1835) was asked to state the view of his fellows on the Reform Bill:

Q. Are the working classes better satisfied with the institutions of the country since the change has taken place?
A. I do not think they are. They viewed the Reform Bill as a measure cal- culated to join the middle and upper classes to Government, and leave them in the hands of Government as a sort of machine to work according to the pleasure of Government.

Such men met Utilitarianism in their daily lives, and they sought to throw it back, not blindly, but with intelligence and moral passion. They fought, not the machine, but the exploitive and oppressive relationships intrinsic to industrial capitalism. In these same years, the great Romantic criticism of Utilitarianism was running its parallel but altogether separate course. After William Blake, no mind was at home in both cultures, nor had the genius to interpret the two traditions to each other. It was a muddled Mr. Owen who offered to disclose the "new moral world," while Wordsworth and Coleridge had withdrawn behind their own ramparts of disenchantment. Hence these years appear at times to display, not a revolutionary challenge, but a resistance movement, in which both the Romantics and the Radical craftsmen opposed the annunciation of Acquisitive Man. In the failure of the two traditions to come to a point of junction, something was lost. How much we cannot be sure, for we are among the losers.

Yet the working people should not be seen only as the lost myriads of eternity. They had also nourished, for fifty years, and with incomparable fortitude, the Liberty Tree. We may thank them for these years of heroic culture.

Notes

1. Mayhew, op. cit, *London Labor and the London Poor* (1884), I, p.22

2. See esp. Mayhew, op. cit., I, p. 252 ff.

3. W. E. Adams, *Memoirs of a Social Atom* (1903), I, p. 164.

4. See especially R. K. Webb, *The British Working Class Reader, 1790–1848* (1955), the same author's article, "Working-Class Readers in Early Victorian England," *English Hist. Rev.*, LXV (1950); R. D. Altick, *The English Common Reader* (Chicago, 1957), esp. Chs. IV, VII, XI; and J. F. C. Harrison, *Learning and Living* (1961), Part One.

5. *Political Observer*, 19 December 1819.

6. Another letter ("Eliza Ludd" to Rev. W. R. Hay, 1 May 1812) commences: "Sir, Doubtless you are well acquainted with the Political History of America"; both in H.O. 40.1.

7. H.O. 42.121.

8. H.O. 42.163; *Blanketter*, 20 November 1819.

9. R. Fynes, *The Miners of Northumberland and Durham* (1923 edn.), p. 21.

10. Sherwin's *Political Register*, 17 May 1817.

11. H. O. 42.172. These correspondents, who were impatiently awaiting release from detention, knew that their mail was read by the prison governor, and were therefore especially prone to insert references to forgiveness, grace, and improving reading.

12. See J. Stanhope, op. cit., pp. 161–7.

13. Some of the earliest trade union correspondence which survives—that of the framework-knitters in the Nottingham City Archives—shows a widespread diffusion of literary attainment.

14. *First Report . . . on Artizans and Machinery* (1824), p. 25.

15. Catnach's "Trial of Thurtell," 500,000 (1823): "Confession and Execution of Corder," 1,166,000 (1828).

16. H. O. 40.1.

17. For Radical reading-rooms, see A. Aspinall, Politics and the Press (1949), pp. 25–8, 395–6; Wearmouth, op. cit., pp. 24–5, 88–9, 97–8, 111–12. For Dunning, "Reminiscences" (ed., W. H. Chaloner), *Trans. Lancs. & Cheshire Antiq. Soc.*, LIX, 1947, p. 97. For Stockport, see *Blanketteer*, 27 November 1819, and D. Read, op cit., p. 48 f. For Blackburn, W. W. Kinsey, "Some Aspects of Lancashire Radicalism," (M. A. Thesis, Manchester 1927), pp. 66–7.

18. In 1822 the circulation of the leading daily, *The Times*, was 5,730; the *Observer* (weekly), 6,860.

19. I have accepted the figures given by R. D. Altick, op. cit., pp. 381–93, although I doubt the claims for the *Voice of the People* and *Gauntlet*. For comparative figures of the orthodox press, see Raymond Williams, *The Long Revolution* (1961), pp. 184–92. For the attempts to replace the radical press with safe and improving matter, see R. K. Webb, op. cit., Chs. II, III, IV and J. F. C. Harrison, op. cit., Chs. I and II.

20. His account, covering the period 1817–1823, is mainly concerned with the first phase of the battle—the right of publication—particularly associated with Richard Carlile. The second phase, the struggle of the "Great Unstamped" (1830–5), associated particularly with the names of Carpenter, Hetherington, Watson, Cleave, and Hobson, has not yet found its historian, although see C. D. Collett, *History of the Taxes on Knowledge* (1933 edn.), Ch. II, and A. G. Barker, *Henry Hetherington* (n.d.).

21. Wickwar, op. cit., p. 315. See also ibid., pp. 38–9 for the peculiarly unfair form of persecution, the *ex-officio* information, which virtually permitted imprisonment without trial.

22. *The Two Trials of T. J. Wooler* (1817).

23. *Second Trial of William Hone* (1818), pp. 17, 45; *Proceedings at the Public Meeting* to form a subscription for Hone (1818); F. W. Hackwood, *William Hone* (1912), Chs. IX-XI; Wickwar, op. cit., pp. 58–9. An old patterer told Mayhew (I, p. 252) that despite the acquittals, it remained difficult to "work" Hone's parodies in the streets: "there was plenty of officers and constables ready to pull the fellows up, and. . . . a beak that wanted to please the high dons, would find some way of stopping them. . . ."

24. Hazlitt, *Works*, VII, pp. 176 ff. "Instead of applying for an injunction against *Wat Tyler*," Hazlitt opined, "Mr. Southey would do well to apply for an injunction against Mr. Coleridge, who has undertaken his defence in *The Courier*."

25. Sherwin's *Republican*, 29 March 1817; Carlile's *Republican*, 30 May 1823.

26. In these three years there were 115 prosecutions and 45 *ex officio* informations.

27. See below, p. 118.

28. Wickwar, op. cit., p. 231.

29. Keats to his brother George, 17 September 1819, *Works* (1901), V, p. 108. The letter continues: "This makes the business of Carlile the bookseller of great moment in my mind. He has been selling deistical pamphlets, republished Tom Paine, and many other works held in superstitious horror. . . . After all, they are afraid to prosecute. They are afraid of his defence; it would be published in all the papers all over the empire. They shudder at this. The trials would light a flame they could not extinguish. Do you not think this of great import?"

30. W. J. Linton, *James Watson* (Manchester 1880), p. 19.

31. In 1830 these taxes amounted to a 4d. stamp on each newspaper or weekly periodical, a duty of 3s. 6d. on each advertisement, a small paper duty, and a large surety against action for libel.

32. Abel Heywood, the Manchester bookseller, claimed the figure to be 750.

33. Societies for the Diffusion of "Really Useful Knowledge" were formed to assist the "unstamped." See *Working Man's Friend*, 18 May 1833.

34. See Wickwar, op. cit., pp. 40, 103–14; *Second Trial of William Hone* (1818), p. 19; for the case

of Robert Swindells, confined in Chester castle, while his wife and baby died from neglect, and his remaining child was placed in the poorhouse; Sherwin's *Political Register*, 14 March 1818, for the cases of Mellor and Pilling of Warrington, held for nineteen weeks chained to Felons in Preston Gaol, sent for trial at the Court of King's Bench in London—the 200 miles to which they had to walk—the trial removed to Lancaster (200 miles back)—and then discharged.

35. Most of Carlile's shopmen were provided with long written defences by Carlile, and this was probably so in her case.

36. See Wickwar, op. cit., pp. 222–3; *Trial of Mrs. Susannah Wright* (1822), pp. 8, 44, 56; *New Times*, 16 November 1822.

37. Wickwar, op. cit., pp. 105–7; *Independent Whig*, 16 January 1820; Cobbett's *Political Register*, 17 August 1822; *Poor Man's Guardian*, 12 November 1831; A. G. Barker, *Henry Hetherington*, pp. 12–13.

38. See Wickwar, op. cit., p. 214.

39. The counties of Lancaster, Chester, the West Riding, Warwick, Stafford, Derby, Leicester, Nottingham, Cumberland, Westmorland, Northumberland, Durham, the city of Coventry, and the county boroughs of Newcastle-upon-Tyne and Nottingham.

40. W. E. Adams, op. cit., p. 169. I am indebted to Mr. A. J. Brown for information about Ipswich. See also *Chartist Studies*, ed. A. Briggs, for Chartism in Somerset and East Anglia.

41. J. F. C. Harrison's admirable account in *Learning and Living* tends to underestimate the vigour of radical culture before 1832. The best first-hand accounts are in William Lovett's autobiography and (for Chartist times) Thomas Frost, *Forty Years Recollections* (1880).

42. Thomas Wood, *Autobiography (1822–80)* (Leeds, 1956). See also An Old Potter, *When I Was a Child* (1903), Ch. I.

43. M. L. Pearl, *William Cobbett* (1953), pp. 105–7. There were also many pirated editions.

44. *Philanthropist*, 22 June 1795.

45. T. A. Ward, op. cit., p. 196.

46. See H. O. 119.3/4 for the accusations and counter-accusations passing between Covent Garden and Drury Lane, on the one hand, and the "illegitimate" little theatres on the other, 1812–18.

47. H. O. 65.1

48. *Trades Newspaper*, 31 July, 21 August 1825 et. seq. The Editor felt called upon to apologise for carrying news of prize-fighting and animal-baiting; but the paper was governed by a committee of London trades unions, and the members' wishes had to be met.

49. Some notion of the complexity of this output can be gained from Dr. Dorothy George's very learned *Catalogues of Political and Personal Satire in the British Museum*, volumes VII, VIII, and IX and X. See also Blanchard Jerrold, *George Cruikshank* (1894), Ch. IV.

50. Southey, *Life of Wesley*, p. 558.

51. *Works*, IV, pp. 57 ff., from *The Round Table* (1817).

52. Thomas Dick, *On the Improvement of Society by the Diffusion of Knowledge* (Glasgow, 1833), p. 175. See also p. 213, where it is argued that "arithmetic, algebra, geometry, conic sections, and other departments of mathematics" are particularly godly studies since they "contain truths that are eternal and unchangeable."

53. H. O. 40.4.

54. *Political Register*, 13 January 1821. The Temperance Movement can be traced to this post-war campaign of abstinence.

55. See Wickwar, op. cit., p. 68.

56. Cf. T. Frost, *Forty Years' Recollections*, p. 20 (of the anti-Owenite propaganda of the Thirties): "It was a very common device for complainants and witnesses to say of a person charged with larceny, wife desertion, or almost any other offence, 'He is a Socialist'; and reports of all such cases had the side-head, 'Effect of Owenism.'. . . ."

57. See, for example, William Hodson in the *Social Pioneer*, 20 April 1839 (*et passim*): "Allow me, Sir, to state . . . my views upon the [Marriage] Question . . . neither *man nor woman* can be happy, until they have *equal rights*; to marry each other for a home, as if often the case now, is the buying of human flesh; it is slave dealing of the worst description. . . . I contend that all unions ought to be solely from affection—to continue the unions when that affection ceases to exist is perfect . . . *prostitution.*"

58. See Wallas, op. cit., pp. 166–72; N. Himes, "J. S. Mill's Attitude toward Neo-Malthusianism," *Econ. Journal* (Supplement), 1926–9, I, pp. 459–62; M. Stopes, *Contraception* (1923); N. Himes, "The Birth Control Handbills of 1823," *The Lancet*, 6 August 1927; M. St. J. Packe, *Life of John Stuart Mill* (1954), pp. 56–9. See also below, p. 128.

59. See J. F. C. Harrison, op. cit., pp. 43 et. seq.

60. See Wickwar, op. cit., p. 147; and Place's comment, *"Well done, hypocrite; you who are not a Christian yourself."*

61. See especially J. F. C. Harrison, op. cit., pp. 57–88, 173–8; *Mechanic's Magazine*, II and 18 October 1823; T. Kelly, *George Birkbeck* (Liverpool, 1957), Chs. V and VI; E. Halévy, *Thomas Hodgskin* (1956), pp. 87–91; Chester New, op. cit., Ch. XVII; *Trades Newspaper*, 17 July 1825; F. B. Lott, *Story of the Leicester Mechanic's Institute* (1935); M. Tylecote, *The Mechanic's Institutes of Lancashire and Yorkshire before 1851* (Manchester, 1957).

62. *Political Register*, 27 January 1820.

63. "What is the People?" from *Political Essays* (1819), in *Works*, VII, p. 263.

64. Hone said in his advertisement: "The Publisher conscientiously affirms, that there is more Original and just Thinking, luminously expressed in this Volume, than in any other Work of a living Author."

65. Cf. Cobbett's "Seigneurs of the Twist, Sovereigns of the Spinning Jenny, great Yeomen of the Yarn."

66. "Address to the Journeymen and Labourers," *Political Register*, 2 November 1816.

67. Ibid., 27 January 1820.

68. The loyalist press delighted in publishing lists of Cobbett's self-contradictions. So also, from an opposite standpoint, did his ultra-Radical opponents: see Gale Jones's damaging *Vindication of the Press, against the Aspersions of William Cobbett, including a Retrospect of his Political Life and Opinions* (1823).

69. *Political Register*, 1 September 1830. See G. D. H. and M. Cole, *The Opinions of William Cobbett*, pp. 253–4.

70. *Political Register*, June 1817, 11 April 1818, 2 October 1819; *Rural Rides*, passim; Bamford, op. cit., p. 21; Hazlitt, *Table Talk* (1821).

71. W. J. Linton, *James Watson*, p. 17. Cf. T. Frost, op. cit., p. 6: "the only books I ever saw in my father's house, besides the bible and a few old school books . . . were some odd numbers of Cobbett's *Register.*"

72. Hone's *Reformist's Register*, 5 April 1817, on Cobbett's departure to America. See, however, Wooler's angry rejoinder: "We are almost inclined to wish that Mr. Cobbett had confined himself to writing . . . upon such subjects, that he might have . . . deceived none but kitchen maids and scullions." *Black Dwarf*, 9 April, 1817.

73. *Political Register*, 2 February 1822.

74. *Political Register*, 27 January 1820.

75. *Political Register*, 30 January 1832. See also R. Williams, *Culture and Society* (Pelican edn.), pp. 32–4.

76. *Twopenny Trash* 1 October 1830.

77. *Political Register*, 28 February 1835.

78. See Asa Briggs, "The Welfare State in Historical Perspective," *Archiv. Europ. Sociol.*, II (1961), p. 235.

79. *Tour of Scotland* (1833), cited in W. Reitzel (ed.), *The Autobiography of William Cobbett*, pp. 224–5.

80. R. Carlile, *An Effort to set at rest . . . the Reformers of Leeds* (1821), p. 7.

81. W. E. Adams, op. cit., I, p. 169.

82. Philanthropus, *The Character of a Priest* (1822), pp. 4, 6.

83. *Republican*, 19 January 1821. Carlile also republished Saxby's "Killing No Murder."

84. *Republican*, 4 October 1820, 26 April 1822; see Wickwar, op. cit., pp. 213–15.

85. *Republican*, 23 August 1822.

86. See Wickwar, op. cit., p. 272.

87. *Republican*, 11 July 1823; *Devil's Pulpit*, 4 and 18 March 1831; *Prompter*, 30 August, 31 September, 15 October 1831; *Radical*, 24 September 1831; H. O. 40.25.

88. *Gorgon*, 24 April 1819. Shelley, writing *Prometheus Unbound* in 1818–19, gave to the obscure revolutionary god the name "Demogorgon": one wonders if there was any association of ideas?

89. It is not clear whether Wade accepted Place's notes as they came in, or took editorial liberties with them. Although Place assisted the *Gorgon*, he never met Wade, and the paper "was not altogether such a publication as I should have preferred." See Wallas, op. cit., pp. 204–5.

90. *Gorgon*, 20 June, 18 July, 22 August 1818.

91. *Gorgon*, 8 August 1818, and *The Extraordinary Black Book* (1831 edn.), pp. 217–8. See also A. Briggs, "The Language of Class in early 19th-century Britain," *Essays in Labour History*, p. 50.

92. Ricardo is cited in *Gorgon*, 26 September 1818.

93. Ibid., 12 September 1818. For the origins of the labour theory of value, touched upon briefly and inexpertly in this chapter, see G. D. H. Cole, *History of Socialist Thought, The Forerunners* (1953); A. Menger, *The Right to the Whole Produce of Labour* (1898); R. N. Meek, *Studies in the Labour Theory of Value* (1956).

94. Ibid., 21 November 1818.

95. Place informed the Select Committee on Artizans and Machinery (*First Report* [1824], p. 46): "no principle of political economy [is] better established than this of wages: increase of wages must come from profits."

96. *Trades Newspaper*, 31 July 1825.

97. See the Hammonds, *The Town Labourer*, pp. 138–40.

98. Ibid., p. 311; Webbs, *History of Trade Unionism*, pp. 84–5; Wallas, op. cit., p. 189; G. D. H. Cole, *Attempts at General Union*, pp. 81–2.

99. Hunt's *Address to the Radical Reformers*, 9 December 1822.

100. The paper was planned by "those Town and Country Representatives of Trades who had assembled in London to watch the progress of the late Inquiry respecting the Combination Laws." £1,000 was subscribed by the trades themselves to found the paper, and apart from the

shipwrights, the sawyers, coopers, carpenters, ladies' shoemakers, caulkers, and silk weavers appear to have been directly involved. The paper was governed by a committee of the trades.

101. See the controversy on population, commencing on 12 November 1823, and continuing through successive issues.

102. There is a legend abroad that "unemployment" was outside the semantic frame of the 1820s. Perhaps it stems from an unwise statement in G. M. Young, *Victorian England* (Oxford, 1936), p. 27, that "unemployment was beyond the scope of any idea which Early Victorian reformers had at their command, largely because they had no word for it": to which is added the authority of a footnote: "I have not observed it earlier than the sixties." In fact (as is often the case with these semantic "datings") the statement is wrong. (Cuckoos generally arrive in these islands some weeks before they are announced in *The Times*.) "Unemployed," "the unemployed," and (less frequently) "unemployment" are all to be found in trade union and Radical or Owenite writing of the 1820s and 1830s: the inhibitions of "Early Victorian reformers" must be explained in some other way.

103. *Black Dwarf*, 3 and 31 December 1823.

104. There is some suggestion that the editor's responsibilities were limited to the professional preparation of copy for press, and I have therefore assumed—perhaps erroneously—that Gast, who was Chairman of the controlling committee of trades, wrote the first editorials. Similar difficulties arise in attributing authorship to articles in the *Poor Man's Guardian* and the Owenite press.

105. See F. Place, *Illustrations and Proofs of the Principle of Population* (1822). Also see above, p. 742, n.2.

106. *Trades Newspaper*, 17, 24, 31 July, 11 September 1825. Place appears to have given assistance to an unsuccessful rival to the *Trades Newspaper*, the *Artizan's London and Provincial Chronicle* (1825).

107. *Trades Newspaper*, 21 and 28 August 1825 et. seq.

108. In the following pages I cannot hope to re-examine the thought of Owen or of the "labour economists." My purpose is to illustrate at one or two points the way theory impinged upon working-class experience and the way the new ideas were selected or changed in the process; that is, my concern is more with the sociology of these ideas than with their identity. For Hodgskin see G. D. H. Cole's edition of *Labour Defended* (1922) and E. Halévy, *Thomas Hodgskin* (1956, trans. A. J. Taylor). For a lucid and brief discussion of Owen and the labour economists, see H. L. Beales, *The Early English Socialists* (1933), Chs. IV and V; and for a fuller summary, G. D. H. Cole, *History of Socialist Thought*, I, *The Forerunners*, and M. Beer, *A History of British Socialism*, Part III.

109. R. Owen, *A New View of Society and other writings* (Everyman edn.), pp. 74, 260.

110. Sherwin's *Political Register*, 26 April, 9 August, 20 September 1817.

111. See *Independent Whig*, 24 August 1817. The only radical papers which appear to have given Owen a favourable bearing in 1817–19 were the short-lived *People* and the *Independent Whig* which sent a correspondent to New Lanark.

112. *Examiner*, 4 August 1816; see *Works*, VII, p. 97 et.seq.

113. See Owen, op. cit., pp. 148–55.

114. Sherwin's *Political Register*, 20 September 1817.

115. See, however, Engels's generous tribute to Owen in *Anti-Dühring* (1818; Lawrence & Wishart, 1936), pp. 287–92: "a man of almost sublimely child-like simplicity of character, and at the same time a born leader of men."

116. *Economist*, 4 August, 20 and 27 October 1821 et passim. For the proclamation of the Millennium, I have used the account appended in Bronterre O'Brien's edition of *Buonarrotti's History of Babeuf's Conspiracy of Equals* (1836), pp. 438–45.

117. *Economist*, 13 October 1821, 9 March 1822. See Armytage, op. cit., pp. 92–4 for a brief account of the Spa Fields experiment.

118. See "Report to the County of Lanark" (1820), in Owen, op. cit., esp. pp. 261–2.

119. An attempt was made, as early as 1796, to form a British Fraternal Society, which was to unite the resources of the benefit societies with forms of organisation derived from the Corresponding Society. It originated among the Spitalfields weavers, and it was proposed that old age and unemployed benefits should be paid, the Society should employ its own out-of-work members, and the products of silk weavers, tailors, shoemakers, &c., should be exchanged with each other. See Andrew Larcher, *A Remedy for Establishing Universal Peace and Happiness* (Spitalfields, 1795) and *Address to the British Fraternal Society* (1796).

120. E.g., the Journeymen Tobacco Pipe Manufacturers who, after an eleven-week strike in the winter of 1818–9, commenced direct manufacture in the Maze, Borough—"a friend" having "procured us a factory." See *Gorgon*, 6 and 13 February 1819.

121. Nightingale, *The Bazaar* (1816). Particularly commended was the New Bazaar, 5 Soho Square, opened that year; a Beehive Bazaar in Holborn was also mentioned.

122. *Co-operative Magazine* (1827), pp. 230–1, cited in S. Pollard, "Nineteenth-Century Co-operation: from Community Building to Shopkeeping," *Essays in Labour History*, p. 87.

123. *Crisis*, 30 June, 27 October, 8 and 15 December 1832.

124. *Lancashire and Yorkshire Co-operator*, No. 2. (date unidentified).

125. 6 March 1830; 26 November 1831. See A. E. Musson, "The Ideology of Early Co-operation in Lancashire and Cheshire," *Transactions Lancs & Cheshire Antiq. Soc.*, LXVII, 1957.

126. S. Pollard, op. cit., p. 86.

127. *Crisis* 27 October 1832.

128. J. H. Priestley, *History of Ripponden Co-operative Society* (Halifax, 1932), Ch. IV. It is not clear whether these rules date from 1833 or 1839.

129. *Common Sense*, 11 December 1830.

130. See S. Pollard, *Dr. William King* (Loughborough Co-operative College Papers, 6, 1959).

131. *Trades Newspaper*, 31 July 1825. For the quasi-co-operative corn mills founded as a result of the near-famine of 1795, see G. J. Holyoake, *Self Help A Hundred Years Ago* (1891), Ch. XI, and J. A. Langford, *A Century of Birmingham Life*, II, pp. 157–60. In some MS "Notes and Observations on Co-operative Societies" Lovett records that there were many societies, especially consumer groups, during the wars, and mentions the Spitalfields Weavers: Add. MSS., 27, 791 ff. 245, 258.

132. Ibid., 14 August 1825.

133. See, e.g. *Crisis*, 17 November 1832.

134. *Trades Newspapers*, 11 September 1825.

135. Hammonds, *The Town Labourer*, p. 312.

136. *Report of the Proceedings of a Delegate Meeting of Cotton Spinners, &c.*(Manchester, 1830)

137. *Union Pilot and Co-operative Intelligencer*, 24 March 1832.

138. See Doherty's *Poor Man's Advocate*, 21 January 1832: "The management [of the Association] has passed into the hands of the spirited and intelligent operatives of Yorkshire, where we hope the same spirit of jealousy and faction which, in a great measure, neutralized the best influence of the Association here, will be avoided."

139. See especially, G. D. H. Cole, *Attempts at General Union*; Postage, *The Builders' Union*, Chs. III to V; W. H. Warburton, *History of T. U. Organization in the Potteries* (1931), Chs. II to IV.

Some details of the "fatality" which beset the N.A.P.L. are to be found in D. Caradog Morris, "The History of the Labour Movement in England, 1825–51" (Ph.D. thesis, London, 1952).

140. For Thompson, see R. Pankhurst, *William Thompson* (1954). For accounts of the Labour Exchange, see R. Podmore, *Robert Owen* (1906), II; G. D. H. Cole, *Life of Robert Owen* (1930), pp. 260–6, and Lovett, op. cit., I, pp. 43 ff. Davenport's account is in *National Co-operative Leader*, 15 March 1851.

141. See T. Fielden, *An Exposition of the Fallacies and Absurdities of that Deluded Church generally known as Christian Israelites or "Johannas"* . . . (1850), for details of the "mysteries" of initiation and discipline at the hands of the pious sisterhood: "the woman takes the man by his privates while in his stooping attitude . . . she holds him by one hand, and gives him the stripes by the other. . . ."

142. G. R. Balleine, *Past Finding Out*, Ch. XI; ed. H. B. Hollingsworth, *Zion's Works* (1899), I, pp. 300 ff.; Zion Ward, *A Serious Call: or The Messiah's Address to the People of England* (1831).

143. P. G. Rogers, *Battle in Bossenden Wood* (1961), pp. 4, 96; *An Account of the Desperate Affray in Blean Wood* (Faversham, 1838); *Essay on the Character of Sir William Courtenay* (Canterbury, 1833); *The Lion*, 6 and 27 April 1833; *Globe*, 1 June, 10 August 1838.

144. See Armytage, op. cit., Part III, Ch. 7, "Liverpool: Gateway to Zion."

145. *Poor Man's Guardian*, 19 October 1833. See M. Morris, *From Cobbett to the Chartists* (1948), p. 87.

146. F. D. Maurice, *The Kingdom of Christ*, cited in Armytage, op. cit., p. 85.

147. Owen, op. cit., p. 269.

148. See Postgate, op. cit., pp. 72–3.

149. See S. Pollard, op. cit., p. 90.

150. *Economist*, 11 August 1821.

151. A. E. Musson, op. cit., p. 126.

152. O'Brien, op. cit., p. 437.

153. *The "Forlorn Hope," or a Call to the Supine*, 4 and 11 October 1817.

154. Add. MSS. 27791 f. 270.

155. Add. MSS. 27789. For an example of this facility in spontaneous organisation, see Prentice, op. cit., pp. 408–10.

156. See Jephson, *The Platform*, II, Ch. XV.

157. 1 October 1831.

158. *The Times*, 1 December 1830, 27 October 1831; see Jephson, op. cit., II, pp. 69, 107. During the Bristol riots, the authorities were forced to call in the leaders of the Bristol Political Union to restore order. See *Bristol Mercury*, 1 November 1831; Prentice, op. cit., p. 401.

159. Cited in Jephson, op. cit., II, p. III. The demonstration of the National Union was, in fact, pronounced seditious and prohibited. It was a risk too great to take.

160. Final Address, prefacing *Black Dwarf*, XII (1824).

161. *Poor Man's Guardian*, 10 December 1831.

162. G. Edmonds, *The English Revolution* (1831), p. 5. Edmonds went on to play an active part in the Chartist movement.

163. See A. J. C. Rüter, "Benbow's Grand National Holiday," *International Review of Social History* (Leiden), I, 1936, pp. 217 et seq.

164. W. Carpenter, *An Address to the Working Classes on the Reform Bill* (October 1831). See also the ensuing controversy in the *Poor Man's Guardian*.

165. *Poor Man's Guardian*, 25 October 1832; see A. Briggs, *The Age of Improvement*, p. 258.

166. See J. R. M. Butler, *The Passing of the Great Reform Bill* (1914), pp. 293–3, 350; Add. MSS., 27, 791 f. 51; Memorandum on "Measures to be taken to put an End to the Seditious Meetings at the Rotunda," *Wellington Despatches*, second series (1878), VII, p. 353.

167. E. G. Wakefield, *Householders in Danger from the Populace* (n.d. October 1831?).

168. While Lovett and his circle believed in the maximum of pressure short of physical force (and maintained some relations with Place), others, including Benbow and Hibbert, were preparing for an armed struggle.

169. It is interesting to speculate upon how far Place's frequent assertions as to the improvement in the manners and morals of the London populace expressed the truth, or merely the widening gulf between the artisans and unskilled, the narrowing of Place's own circle of experience, and the pushing of poverty out of the City's centre towards the east and the south. On the whole problem of metropolitan growth and demoralisation (and its "biological" foundation), see L. Chevalier, *Classes Laborieuses et classes dangereuses à Paris pendant la première moitié du XIX sièle* (Paris, 1958), which suggests many new lines of research into London conditions.

170. It is difficult to discount Oliver's circumstantial account of Birmingham contacts (Narrative in H.O. 40.9). See also evidence in H.O. 40.3 and 6.

171. See Cobbett's angry comment: "Do you imagine that the great manufacturers, and merchants, and bankers are crying for REFORM, because they have been converted to a love of *popular rights*! Bah!. . . . [Financial causes] have made them raise their wages; these they cannot pay and pay *tithes and taxes* also. . . . Therefore, are they *reformers*; therefore, they throw their lusty arms around the waist of the Goddess": *Political Register*, 17 October 1831.

172. *Destructive*, 2 February and 9 March 1833; A. Briggs, "The Background of the Parliamentary Reform Movement in Three English Cities," *Camb. Hist. Journal*, 1952, p. 293, and *The Age of Improvement*, p. 247.

173. W. Brimelow, *Political History of Bolton* (1882), I, p. III.

174. *Poor Man's Advocate*, 21 January 1832.

175. *Poor Man's Guardian*, 11 April 1832.

176. Add. MSS., 27, 795 ff. 26–7.

177. Butler, op. cit. p. 303.

178. See Gladstone's comment: "I held forth to a working man . . . on the established text, reform was revolution . . . I said, 'Why, look at the revolutions in foreign countries, meaning of course France and Belgium. The man looked hard at me and said . . . 'Damn all foreign countries, what has old England to do with foreign countries'; This is not the only time that I have received an important lesson from a humble source." J. Morley, *Life of Gladstone* (1908), I, p. 54.

179. See A. Briggs, "The Language of 'Class' in Early 19th-century England," op. cit., p. 56.

180. Baines, *Life of Edward Baines*, pp. 157–9.

181. Add. MSS. 27790.

182. See. J. R. M. Butler, op. cit., pp. 284–5.

183. Baines, op. cit., p. 167.

184. Cited in A. L. Morton and G. Tate, *The British Labour Movement* (1956), p. 59 and attributed (erroneously) to *Poor Man's Guardian*, 3 March 1831.

185. See Lovett, op. cit., I, p. 74.

186. A. Briggs, op. cit., p. 66.

187. *Bronterre's National Reformer*, 7 January 1837. O'Brien in fact was qualified in law at the Bar in Dublin.

188. *Destructive*, 9 March 1833.

189. O'Brien, op. cit., pp. xv, xx. For O'Brien, see G. D. H. Cole, *Chartist Portraits* (1941), Ch. IX; T. Rothstein, *From Chartism to Labourism* (1929), pp. 93–123; Beer, op. cit., II, pp. 17–22.

190. *Twopenny Despatch*, 10 September 1836.

191. *Destructive*, 9 March, 24 August 1833; *People's Conservative; and Trade's Union Gazette*, 14 December 1833.

192. O'Brien himself came to regret the vehemence of his dismissal of the entire "middle class," when an opportunity for alliance between the Chartists and elements from the middle class occurred in the 1840s: see Beer, op. cit., II, p. 126.

193. J. R. M. Butler, op. cit., pp. 262–5; *Cracker*, 8 December 1832.

194. *Political Register*, 24 November 1832. Cobbett was recalling the former Yorkshire county member, Wilberforce.

195. MS. Letterbook of Ayrey (Leeds Reference Library).

196. *Cracker*, 8, 10, 21 December 1832. See also A. Briggs, "The Background of the Parliamentary Reform Movement in Three English Cities," op. cit., pp. 311–14; E. Baines, *Life*, pp. 164–7; C. Driver, *Tory Radical*, pp. 197–202.

197. Speech of William Rider, Leeds stuff-weaver and later to be a prominent Chartist Leader, *Leeds Times*, 12 April 1834.

198. *Leeds Times*, 12, 17, 24 May 1834.

199. *Working Man's Friend and Political Magazine*, 5 January 1833.

200. *Report of the Proceedings of the Great Public Meeting & c.*, 20 May 1833.

201. "I.H.B.L.," *Ought Every Man to Vote?* (1832).

202. G. Edmonds, *The English Revolution* (1831), pp. 5, 8.

203. Narrative of Oliver, H. O. 40.9.

204. *Two-Penny Trash*, 1 October 1803.

205. See, e.g., *Destructive*, 7 December 1833.

206. *Pioneer*, 13 October 1833.

207. *Man*, 13 October 1833.

208. *Man*, 22 December 1833.

209. *Pioneer*, 31 May 1834.

210. *Pioneer*, 22 March 1834; see A. Briggs, "The Language of 'Class' in Early Nineteenth Century England," loc. cit., p. 68.

MARY WOLLSTONECRAFT

On the day after Mary Wollstonecraft first made love to William Godwin she retreated in concern and self-doubt. "Consider what has passed as a fever of your imagination . . . and I will become again a . . . Solitary Walker." Claire Tomalin, in her bright new biography, gives us this passage, but not that other haunting sentence: "I perceive that I shall be a child to the end of the chapter. . . ."

We are all, every one of us, in some part of ourselves children to the end of the chapter. Wollstonecraft didn't always manage her personal life wisely. Nor, when one comes to think of it, did Coleridge, De Quincey, Wordsworth, Hazlitt . . . need one go on? I have no objection to reminders that persons of genius share all the infirmities of other mortals. The particular infirmities to which they were liable often help us to understand also their genius. But it is, in the end, the plus of genius, and not the lowest common denominator of infirmity, which gives their lives importance.

I do object, on Wollstonecraft's behalf, to the inequitable treatment which she has received at the hands of historians and critics. She is seen less as a significant intellectual, or as a courageous moralist in an exceptionally exposed position, than as an "Extraordinary Woman." And the moral confusions, or personal crises, of a woman are always somehow more interesting than those of a man: they engross all other aspects of the subject. As, indeed, from the inexorable facts of the woman's "situation" they often tend to do. Wordsworth "had" an illegitimate daughter in revolutionary France: he carried her around intermittently for a few years as a private guilt, but his daughter didn't encumber him in more practical ways. Wollstonecraft also "had" an illegitimate daughter in revolutionary France: but the having was a rather different matter, and

From *New Society*, 19th September 1974, reviewing Claire Tomalin's *The Life and Death of Mary Wollstonecraft*, Weidenfeld & Nicholson. Reprinted in *Making History: Writings on History and Culture* by E. P. Thompson (New York: The New Press, 1994).

thereafter she carried her around (with the help of a loyal maid) through France, England, northern Europe. It was not a carefully guarded secret to be turned up by biographers in this century. Out-facing the "world," she walked with Fanny through the London streets.

A different matter. And it makes her life a subject peculiarly difficult to handle. We are all interested in sexual relations; we are all willing to moralise about them at the drop of a hat. And the mention of Wollstonecraft's name is like the collapse of a whole hat shop: it turns up the moralising volume-control somewhere in our intestines. We have scarcely begun to establish the facts before we begin to mix them up with our own moralising additives: scandalised, or apologetic, or admiring or condescending. What we make of her is already mixed up with what we have made of ourselves; it is something different from her own taut, unrelenting self-making.

There have been perhaps a dozen serious biographies: the first, by William Godwin, appeared within a year of her death. None of them wholly satisfies. One reason is that Wollstonecraft presents not one subject, but two: and it would take unusual versatility to unite both in a single study. From one aspect, she was one of the five or six truly significant ultra-radical intellectuals in England in the 1790s: she must be placed beside Paine and Godwin: beside the Coleridge of the *Watchman*; Flower of the *Cambridge Intelligencer*; or Thelwall of the *Tribune* and the *Rights of Nature*. In this company, she requires no manner of condescension because she happened also to be a woman. Nor did she ask for such. It was her notion that "mind has no sex"; she measured herself as an equal in the republic of the intellect.

But from another aspect, Wollstonecraft was reminded by every fact of nature and of society that she was a woman. She was not a mind which has no sex, but a human being exceptionally exposed within a feminine predicament. Long before she died, she was seized upon by friend and by enemy as an exemplar. She noted this in her late *Letters from Sweden*:

> All the world is a stage, thought I; and few are there who do not play the part they have learnt by rote; and those who do not, seem marks set up to be pelted at by fortune; or rather as signposts, which point out the road to others, whilst forced to stand still themselves amidst the mud and dust.

Not many men are expected to justify in every encounter of their lives their published professions. The author of the *Vindication of the Rights of Woman* was exposed in her every motion. The "world" observed her successively as a mannish journalist; as a rejected lover (of Fuseli); as a soured spinster (the "wrong side" of 30); as a discarded mistress (of Imlay); as the mother of an illegitimate child; as an attempted suicide.

"What" said I within myself, "this is Miss Mary Wollstonecraft, parading about with a child at her heels, with as little ceremony as if it were a watch just bought at the jeweler's. So much for the rights of women," thought I . . .

The characteristic response is that of Archibald Hamilton Rowan, the Irish patriot. It is fair to add that he became her friend, and perhaps was thus educated a little out of his prejudices.

The final episode of her life has much of the contrivance of fiction. When she married William Godwin it was much as if De Beauvoir, soon after writing *The Second Sex*, had married Sartre at the zenith of his reputation, and then had died in childbirth. What a temptation her life provides for the nudge-nudge sort of biographer. And what materials survived her. After her death, Godwin— candid, benevolent, and stricken (perhaps for the only time in his life) by emotions which he could not rationalise—thought it an act of piety to publish her *Posthumous Works*, including her letters to her feckless and foot-loose lover, Imlay. It was not an act of piety. She could not have wished it so. No rejected lover, man or woman, imploring for love in the face of equivocation or indifference could wish to be so exposed.

But there was more. Wollstonecraft's marriage to Godwin, in her last year, was conducted from independent neighbouring establishments. Godwin objected to marriage on principle, and Wollstonecraft accepted his views up to a point: they were each to continue to conduct an independent life, received friends (of either sex), and visit socially as independent persons, not as man-and-wife. Hence domestic arrangements were conducted often by letter: usually affectionate, sometimes loving, sometimes querulous or recriminatory, sometimes just arrangements for dinner or the theatre. And all that lot survives also. This is fortunate again for biographers. But I doubt how far any of us would wish to be judged—or judged in a public sense—on evidence of this casual, and essentially unconsidered, kind.

So there are two possible subjects here, and the best two biographies, hitherto, have taken opposite courses. The standard academic biography by Ralph Wardle is painstaking and, on occasion, pedestrian; but it maintains a seriousness towards its subject's intellectual identity, examining her writings with care but turning its back upon any sustained analysis of her sexual predicament. Wollstonecraft, one feels, might have approved this approach. More recently, Margaret George has published in the United States, but not, so far as I am aware, in Britain, a highly-intelligent analysis (*One Woman's Situation* Illinois, 1970) of her subject's personal evolution and predicament. Both books are to be strongly recommended, although neither, in my view, even when taken together, give a full view of Wollstonecraft's originality and stature.

I had hoped to welcome Claire Tomalin's book, and in a way I do. The books by Wardle and George are better. But Tomalin has attacked her subject with zest. She has turned up a few new facts, although her documentation is (deliberately) so sloppy that it is difficult to see what is new and what she has borrowed from Wardle and others. She has read around her subject to place her in a context: the placings succeed on occasion, when they concern personalities and not ideas. The chapter on Wollstonecraft's experiences as governess to Lord and Lady Kingsborough is perceptive—the best treatment of this which I have read. And the book flows along nicely—an inquisitive feminine narrative which readers will enjoy. The book will certainly go: it is a calculated book club choice.

It is this fact which relieves me from an inhibition against saying that I dislike it a good deal. It is a book which diminishes the stature of its subject. And, by a sick irony, it does this in ways which are supposedly characteristically feminine. Wherever Tomalin deals with central political or intellectual issues, her manner and her matter is commonplace, personalised, or crassly philistine. Her French revolution is a madly-interesting scene with swinging intellectuals followed by a predictable plebeian Terror. (In England, it was "the signal for everyone to rush to extremes.") Tomalin is against extremes, and, as the book proceeds, it becomes apparent that no one is wholly balanced and mature except the author: certainly not Wollstonecraft, for whom she is always making sophisticated psychological allowances. After all, Wollstonecraft did not have the benefit of reading Freud, Durkheim, or Kenneth Tynan. The political philosophy of Godwin and of Holcroft is sketched in boldly: "their enthusiasm for perfectibility was such that they envisaged the end of all superstition, crime, war, illness and even . . . sleep and death itself." Any attentive reader of Jilly Cooper's weekly column will know herself wiser than that: and, since this is so, Tomalin need carry her investigation of Godwin's thought no further.

It follows that Tomalin is very little interested in Wollstonecraft's thought either. She underestimates the *Rights of Man*: condescends to the *Vindication*; and she scarcely discusses the late (and important) *Letters from Sweden* at all. By contrast, she hovers lingeringly above each personal encounter or private letter, and pokes around knowingly for hidden sexual motives. While only a few lines of the *Vindication* are cited, we have passage after passage of the letters to Imlay, some of them provoking the most *interesting* questions: could there be "an allusion to a flirtation with another man here"?

The basis of Wollstonecraft's precarious independence, and the very precondition of her ever writing the *Vindication*, was secured when she was befriended by that very remarkable Dissenting publisher, Joseph Johnson, who provided her with regular work, an income, and lodgings. This is the only episode in her subject's life which has Tomalin baffled. Johnson (49) was befriending "Mary." "youngish" (28). And yet there is no evidence as to even a putative sexual encounter. For Tomalin, this is utterly improper. She implies (with no evidence) that perhaps Johnson was a homosexual; or, when he invited "Mary" to work for him, "perhaps he was in a manic moment such as come to certain asthmatics." At any rate. "Johnson's interest in women as anything other than friends was either extremely discreet or, more probably, non-existent." And (a final solution) "they played at fathers and daughters."

"Women as anything other than friends"—could our sexually hyperconscious age condemn itself more clearly than this? We know nothing about Johnson's sexual inclinations and (one might add in passing), since we do know nothing, speculation on the subject is more suited to a gossip column than a history book. What we do know about Johnson is that he was a good judge of authors: he published ultra-radical and feminist books throughout the 1790s; he was the friend of other writers with feminist sympathies—Mary Hays, William Frend, George Dyer—and his loyalty to these people and causes led him in the end to prison. When Wollstonecraft arrived on his doorstep, Johnson needed a reliable full-time editorial assistant: his need and her ability and predicament matched each other. Is it not conceivable that they actually became *friends*, agreeing to set aside or distance Tomalin's obligatory "anything other than"? It is even possible that they were "playing at" being comrades in a common political and intellectual endeavour—a game which I fear our own sophisticated world would regard with knowing disbelief.

But it was this game of egalitarian comradeship for which Wollstonecraft attempted to image the rules. Against Rousseau's sophistry, that educated women would lose their power over men, she replied: "This is the very point I aim at. I do not wish them to have power over men; but over themselves." To attempt this self-determination in her own life, entailed a disregard for convention which required qualities which can easily be labelled as domineering, wilful, egotistical. To attempt this also meant that she must suffer in her own experience as she pressed against each one of those boundaries which she had already defined in her writings. As Margaret George has written: "With that determination to be 'free' Mary proceeded to successive revelations of the limits—external and self-imposed—of her freedom." With extraordinary tenacity, she herself sought to bring those two subjects—her philosophy and her biography—into one: as Godwin wrote, she "had through life tramped on those rules which are built on the assumption of the imbecility of her sex." She was bound to suffer; and her suffering, expressed in letters never intended for publication, and in a style of self-dramatising, over-articulate "sensibility" nurtured by Rousseau's *Confessions* and the *Sorrows of Werther*, is altogether too "heavy" for the flip insensibility of our own times.

So Wollstonecraft has become a bit of a bore. Each generation does her over again in its own image. The anti-Jacobins did her as a prostitute. The bourgeois feminist did her as a bourgeois feminist. More recently, in 1947, two American Freudians (one, shamefully, a woman) did her over as a bitch motivated by penis-envy: "the shadow of the phallus lay darkly, threateningly over all that she did." As against this, Tomalin's doings are greatly preferable. Wollstonecraft—or "Mary," as she must always call her—is now seen as a premature inhabitant of our own literary and feminine north London: premature not only in the fact of living in the 1790s but also in displaying manifest immaturities which, from the composure of our advanced civilisation, we may easily detect, smile at, but make allowances for. Every mature professional woman today, who has "worked hard at" her relationships, "come to terms with" her sexuality, and who is never manic or extreme in her feminism, can recognise instantly in Tomalin's Mary that exasperating neighbour, or old college friend, who is always getting into muddles and—in the moment of denouncing us for our conventionality—falling flat on her own face. And every uninformed male reviewer can see Tomalin's Mary equally clearly. For the *Daily Telegraph Magazine*, this is the "book of the week": Mary had "an acute shortage of worldly wisdom"; "she fell in love with charming rotters"; she "gave birth to a tragic bastard"—"a magnificent and touching failure." Predictably, she leads *The Times* review page as "Poor Mary": her life is seen as a "comedy" which (we are chivalrously warned) it is too easy to laugh at.

I do not find Wollstonecraft's life funny. Nor can I see it as any kind of failure. I see her as a major intellectual, and as one of the greatest of Englishwomen. There were scores of thousands of women in the 1790s who were domineering, or who professed sensibility excessively, or who got into personal muddles; just as there were scores of thousands of men who were vain, cocksure, and who drank too much. But there was only one Wollstonecraft just as there was only one Paine. It is the plus that matters. Large innovations in thought and sensibility often arise after so many and so prolonged premonitions that they appear to us, in retrospect, as mere common-places. Paine's *Rights of Man* and Wollstonecraft's *Vindication* both have this air: it is a puzzle that no one had written them before.

But no one had. And, once written, the terms of argument were forever changed. It is difficult to know which book proposed the larger claims; but since women make up one half of the species, the honours may rest with Wollstonecraft. Her arguments, in this book and in other places, could have been made with more system. But they were not negligible: they could be repressed, but they could not be expunged. Nor were they repressed as utterly as Tomalin, in her final chapter, proposes. She has simply looked in the wrong places. She should have looked, instead, at the Shelleyan tradition carried through to Thomas Hardy and William Morris: or at Anna Wheeler and William Thompson; at Owenites and free-thinkers.

Nor is this all. Paine's book is better written, better structured. But Wollstonecraft's is the more complex sensibility. She by no means swam along easily with the current of 18th-century rationalism: she often struck across it, creating within it a romantic and critical eddy. She had suffered too much in her own human nature—and she had experienced, very closely, Paris at the height of the Terror—not to have reservations about Godwinain optimism. More than this, in the very moment of the annunciation of "bourgeois feminism" she was one of those most alert to the limitations of bourgeois political thought. As a woman, she had fully experienced the force of property rights, both in personal and in social life; and she knew the hollowness of programmes of merely-political emancipation to people held in economic dependency. Hence her writing always showed an alertness to social injustice, and—as in her *Letters from Sweden*—a disgust at ascendant commercialism. In this way, she spliced together feminism and social radicalism at the very start.

As for her life: I know that I would not have lived it so well, and I think it arrogant in any biographer to assume, too easily, that it could have been lived better. This was not, after all, north London in 1974. It was a rough time; and the place was less provided with our modern supportive amenities. (There was not, come to think of it, a Tavistock clinic to take one's horrors to, nor a social worker to advise her on her bastard child.) She fell into one or two holes; and she dug herself out, with her own nails. She never asked anyone to extricate her, except for Imlay, and she had—or do we not allow this now?—a little claim on him. Even from Imlay she would accept—if affection had died—no alms or maintenance. She went on her own way, as a solitary walker. She not only took upon herself the full consequences of her convictions, in a world whose rules she had not made, but she had the resilience to get up (she, a deserted mistress fished out of the Thames) and resume her work of imagining the rules for egalitarian comradeship once more.

We have rarely seen her equal in our history. To Tomalin's mature assessment, I prefer infinitely the words of Virginia Woolf, where she speaks of "the high-handed and hot-blooded manner in which she cut her way to the quick of life." And as Woolf well knew, high-handedness brings down its revenges. Wollstonecraft was prepared for these; but what she does not deserve is the revenge of "Poor Mary!" blazoned across a complacent press. She needs no one's condescension. She was poor in nothing. She was never beaten. And the final evidence lies in that part of her which remained a child to the end of the chapter. For that part of her—the refusal to become careful and "knowing," the resilient assent to new experience—is exactly that part which most of us are careful to cauterise, and then to protect with the callouses of our worldly-wise complicities.

THE "ANTI-SCRAPE"

FROM *WILLIAM MORRIS: ROMANTIC TO REVOLUTIONARY*

While the Eastern Question agitation was giving William Morris his first education in the workings of the political world, he was gaining insight from another direction into the depth of philistinism of his century. Even since his early days in Street's office in Oxford, when he had planned to enter the profession of an architect, Morris had fulminated in private against the excesses of "restoration." In his first lecture, *The Lesser Arts*, Morris referred to the "restoration" of ancient monuments:

> Thus the matter stands: these old buildings have been altered and added to century after century, often beautifully, always historically; their very value, a great part of it, lay in that. . . .
>
> But of late years a great uprising of ecclesiastical zeal, coinciding with a great increase of study, and consequently of knowledge of mediaeval architecture, has driven people into spending their money on these buildings, not merely with the purpose of repairing them, of keeping them safe, clean, and wind and water-tight, but also of "restoring" them to some ideal state of perfection; sweeping away if possible all signs of what had befallen them at least since the Reformation, and often since dates much earlier: this has sometimes been done with much disregard of art and entirely from ecclesiastical zeal, but oftener it has been well enough meant as regards art: yet . . . this restoration must be as impossible to bring about, as the attempt at it is destructive. . . . I scarcely like to think what a great part of them have been made nearly useless to students of art and history. . . .[1]

This is a moderate statement of the case—as moderate as ever came from Morris's pen. In fact, as Morris well knew, "restoration" was an extremely

From *William Morris: Romantic to Revolutionary* by E. P. Thompson (New York: Pantheon Books, 1955, 1977).

profitable business for a few fashionable architects. Chief among these was Sir Gilbert Scott, the perpetrator of the Albert Memorial, who died in 1878. An enormous amount of work passed through his office, over which he could hardly have exercised even the most superficial supervision. It is related of him that once on a journey he noticed a church that was being built, and enquired the name of the architect. "Sir Gilbert Scott," was the reply. "The cathedral-restoring business was very thoroughly organized by him," relates W. R. Lethaby, one of Morris's colleagues in the Society for the Protection of Ancient Buildings.[2] Describing the work done by Scott and his fellows, Lethaby writes:

> It is impossible to give any notion of the violence and stupidities which were done in the name of "restoration." The crude idea seems to have been born of the root absurdity that art was shape and not substance; our ancient buildings were appearances of what was called "style." When the architect had learned what his text-books taught of the styles he could then provide thirteenth- or fourteenth-century "features" at pleasure, and even correct the authentic old ones. Professional reports would run: "The Tudor roof is incongruous with the Early English chancel arch, and it should be replaced by a thirteenth-century roof of steep pitch." At Canterbury a wonderful twelfth-century tower was destroyed to put in its place a nineteenth-century "fifteenth-century" erection. At St. Albans eleventh-century and fifteenth-century work were both destroyed to satisfy the whims of a lawyer-lord. It never struck any one that antiquity is being old. . . . A practice of producing professional office-made versions of the art of any century which passed as the art itself was at full blast when the much-hated, much-revered Society for the Protection of Ancient Buildings was founded by Morris, Webb and Faulkner.[3]

The idea first occurred to Morris in the summer of 1876. "The sight of Burford Church being pulled about set my father to making notes for a letter of appeal for some united action," May Morris relates.[4] It is significant that he did no more about the matter until March of the next year, by which time his experience of the first successful months of the Eastern Question agitation may have given him confidence in the effectiveness of public action. His first blast was provoked by the proposed "destruction" by Sir Gilbert Scott of Tewkesbury Minster, and was printed in March, 1877, in *The Athenaeum*, a periodical which had long been raising the issue in its columns. Although the tone of his letter was scarcely diplomatic—"the architects are, with a very few exceptions, hopeless, because interest, habit, and ignorance bind them, and . . . the clergy are hopeless, because their order, habit, and an ignorance yet grosser, bind them"—it aroused an immediate response. Morris had appealed for—

an association . . . to keep a watch on old monuments, to protest against
all "restoration" that means more than keeping out wind and weather,
and . . . to awaken a feeling that our ancient buildings are not mere ecclesiastical toys, but sacred monuments of the nation's growth and hope.[5]

The Society, which Morris dubbed "Anti-Scrape," was formed in the next
month, and Morris became its Honorary Secretary. Morris's enthusiasm was
supplemented by the tact and persistence of Philip Webb. At the first annual
meeting in June the adhesion of an imposing list of notabilities was announced,
including—after some persuasion—Thomas Carlyle, as well as John Ruskin,
James Bryce, Sir John Lubbock, Leslie Stephen, Coventry Patmore, Burne-
Jones, Holman Hunt, Lord Houghton, and A. J. Mundella. A Manifesto, drafted
by Morris, together with some passages reprinted from Ruskin's *Seven Lamps
of Architecture*, were issued by the Society.

From this time until the end of his life, the Anti-Scrape never ceased to
occupy a part of Morris's time. For more than a year he acted as Secretary,
and afterwards he continued as one of the most active members of the Committee. His work included the undertaking of correspondence in the Press, and
from time to time the visiting and making of reports upon buildings due for
destruction or restoration. In the first year alone, some of the major issues
which came before the Society included Tewkesbury Minster, the restoration
of the choir at Canterbury Cathedral, the destruction of Wren's city churches,
and the rebuilding of the roof at St. Albans. In 1879, an even bigger issue came
up—the threatened replacement of the mosaics and rebuilding of the west front
at St. Mark's, Venice. The campaign to arouse European opinion on this included the presentation of a Memorial which was signed, among others, by
Disraeli and Gladstone, to the Italian Ambassador.[6] The work at St. Mark's
was stopped: but whether as a result of the pressure of the Committee, or as a
result of an independent decision of the Italian Government, became a matter
of some heated dispute.

Tact was never Morris's strong point, whether in international or parochial
affairs. Perhaps that was one of the main reasons for the success the Society
achieved. If his thundering letters sometimes only made his opponents stand on
their dignity and refuse to alter their plans, they at least had the effect of making
the next lot of restorers a great deal more wary for fear that the same outspoken
public wrath would fall upon them. The guardians of old property began to
consult the Anti-Scrape rather than the fashionable architects before forming
their plans, especially when it became known that a group of highly skilled
architects would give their free advice on behalf of the Society. On several
occasions, the Anti-Scrape helped to raise funds for essential repairs to parish
churches and other buildings in danger of decay. On other occasions, they

gladly issued publicity with the aim of finding some use for buildings in danger of destruction.

On the Committee itself Morris was a tower of strength. As a visitor for the Society, he was not such a success: and perhaps it was the restraining influence of Webb and his other colleagues which accounts for the fact that he did little visiting after the first two or three years. After visiting one church which was being thoroughly "restored," he "rushed to the window of the inn shaking his fist as the parson passed by."[7] On being shown a piece of nineteenth century Gothic carving in another cathedral, he burst out: "Why, I could carve them better with my teeth." Another anecdote does not concern an official visit for the Society, but a chance moment during the Socialist propaganda in Glasgow in the late 1880s. In the company of Bruce Glasier, Morris was on his way to a meeting when they stopped to look at the Cathedral:

> We were within a few yards of the doorway when he stopped abruptly, as if struck by a rifle ball, his eyes fixed furiously on some object in front of him. As he glared he seemed to crouch like a lion for a leap at its prey, his whiskers bristling out. "What the hell is that? Who the hell has done that?" he shouted, to the amaze, alarm, and indignation of the people near by.
>
> I looked . . . and saw at once what was the offending object. There it was . . . a sculptured memorial or sarcophagus in shining white marble jammed into the old grey stone-work of the aisle . . . completely cutting off a portion of the window above. . . . "What infernal idiot has done that?" Morris again demanded, and heedless of the consternation around him poured forth a torrent of invective against the unknown perpetrators of the crime. For the moment I thought he might actually spring upon the excrescence and tear out the hateful thing with his bare fists.[8]

But his visits did not only bring him rage. There is a pleasant description by Philip Webb of Morris's love for a certain barn in Berkshire, which illustrates the richness of the pleasure he gained from old buildings—and which, indeed, helps us to understand his rage at their destruction. Great Coxwell Barn "had great hold on William Morris's imagination." "Before I had seen it," recounts Webb,

> I laughingly scorned his determination that it was the most wonderfully beautiful example in England. When at last he exultingly carried me to it (almost tremblingly for fear of my judgement) I was obliged to agree with him that it was unapproachable in its dignity. I clearly understood in this case as in others that his insight and judgement were unfailingly right. . . .

One turned up a narrow lane ... when the ridge of the mighty roof ... rose foot by foot over the grassy bank till one got over the top of the knoll, when its whole impressiveness was clearly seen, so large in its lines as to make one draw breath sharply with wonder. There it was, dominating the farmhouse adjoining, and with nothing but the simple fields of Berkshire about them. Its magnitude, nice precision of building and dainty parts of pure architecture, all done in handsome freestone, made it as beautiful as a cathedral, but with no ostentation of building whatever: a perfectly suitable barn and nothing else. The workmen who set it up did well once and for all time. . . . "If I saw what it all meant in the quiet Berkshire landscape and its clear history of the builders and their craft, how much more must he have seen into and round it? This building and all of its like, were infinite delight to him."[9]

It may seem an unlikely road to Communism by way of Great Coxwell Barn. Nevertheless it is true that Morris's work for the Anti-Scrape contributed as much to bring him on the final stages of his journey as any other influence. In giving leadership to the Anti-Scrape he was forced again and again to examine and set into words his deepest preoccupation—the relation of the arts to society. In the controversies which sprang up around the work he was continually forced to define (and to revise) the basic assumptions which had guided his life from his Oxford days.

In the first place, Morris was brought directly into conflict with the property sanctions of capitalist society. In the negative sense, he had to fight against both commercial rapacity and views of ecclesiastical propriety. When he remonstrated with the Vicar of Burford, the Vicar replied that it was his own Church and he could stand on his head in it if he wanted to. The Dean of Canterbury, in a controversy in *The Times* in 1877, struck a rather more lofty note:

Mr. Morris's Society probably looks on our Cathedral as a place for antiquarian research or for budding architects to learn their art in. We need it for the daily worship of God.

When Wren's city churches were being threatened with destruction, Morris was able (in *The Times* of April, 1878) to call upon those same religious sentiments which had been outraged by his earlier interference:

Surely an opulent city, the capital of the commercial world, can afford some small sacrifice to spare these beautiful buildings the little plots of ground upon which they stand. Is it absolutely necessary that every scrap of space in the City should be devoted to money-making, and are religion, sacred memorials, recollections of the great dead, memorials of the past, works of England's greatest architect, to be banished from this wealthy City?[10]

But this—strong as it is—is the expression of Morris's more diplomatic self—the loyal servant of his own Society. While he might score valid points in this way, with every case that came forward he was given further and more horrifying insight into the insensibility of commercial philistinism, the absolute lack of any public conscience where questions of individual profit or loss were concerned. "Even now mere cynically brutal destruction, not veiling itself under any artistic pretence, is only too common," he reported to the First Annual General Meeting of the Anti-Scrape in June, 1878: "It is still only too commonly assumed that any consideration of Art must yield if they stand in the way of money interests."[11] The next few years gave him more than enough examples to prove this statement. He was forced to contrast the attitude of feudal society in this respect with that of industrial capitalism. This contrast—while a frequent theme of his lectures and addresses in the late 1870s—found its fullest expression in his address to the Twelfth Annual Meeting of the Anti-Scrape in 1889:

Consider London of the fourteenth century: a smallish town, beautiful from one end to the other; streets of low whitewashed houses with a big Gothic church standing in the middle of it; a town surrounded by walls, with a forest of church towers and spires, besides the cathedral and the abbeys and priories; every one of the houses in it, nay, every shed, bearing in it a certain amount of absolute, definite, distinct, conscientious art. Think of the difference between that and the London of to-day. . . .

The mind is thrown back directly to the "London, small and white and clean" of the opening of *The Earthly Paradise*. But this time it is evoked, not with a sense of nostalgia, but as an aggressive and fully-realised comparison, exposing the indifference of his own time:

Just consider what England was in the fourteenth century. The population . . . at about four millions. Think then of the amount of beautiful and dignified buildings which those four millions built. . . . Not only those churches and houses which we see, but also those which have been destroyed. . . . Those buildings . . . contained much art: pictures, metal-work, carvings, tapestry, and the like, altogether forming a prodigious mass of art, produced by a scanty population. Try to imagine that. Why, if we were asked (supposing we had the capacity) to reproduce the whole of those buildings with their contents, we should have to reply, "The country is not rich enough; every capitalist in the country would be ruined before it could be done." Is not that strange?[12]

Thus the work of the Anti-Scrape quickened and deepened his insight into the destructive philistinism of capitalist society. His friends, like Edward Burne-Jones, followed him this far, but then were content to leave it at that. If clergymen or landowners wished to destroy old works of art, they were prepared to fight them tooth and nail, to fulminate against the age, to point out that people in earlier times had viewed the matter differently. But Morris's mind worked in a different way. He was not a systematic thinker, although he forced himself on occasion to discipline his intuitions with very great logic; but, whenever he was aware of the existence of a problem, he had a quite remarkable persistence in worrying at it until he was satisfied that he had reached a solution. One of the aims of the Society (proposed in his first letter to *The Athenaeum*) was "to awaken a feeling that our ancient buildings are not mere ecclesiastical toys, but sacred monuments of the nation's growth and hope." Faced with the jealous property-rights of capitalism, he wished to argue, first, that—irrespective of their position at law—"our ancient historical monuments are national property and ought no longer to be left at the mercy of the many and variable ideas of ecclesiastical propriety that may at any time be prevalent among us"[13] and, second, to convince the public in general that they had both responsibilities and rights in relation to these buildings. Since the law denied that this was true, he was forced to ground his case upon canons of social morality unacknowledged in capitalist society.

This view of men's responsibilities towards the art of past ages was not, in the first place, his own, but had come to him through Carlyle and Ruskin. It was suggested in those passages which he reprinted for the Anti-Scrape propaganda from the *Seven Lamps of Architecture*:

It is . . . no question of expediency or feeling whether we shall preserve the buildings of past times or not. *We have no right whatever to touch them.* They are not ours. They belong, partly to those who built them, and partly to all the generations of mankind who are to follow us. The dead have still their right to them: that which they laboured for . . . we have no right to obliterate. What we have ourselves built we are at liberty to throw down; but what other men gave their strength, and wealth and life to accomplish, their right over does not pass away with their death; still less is the right to the use of what they have left vested in us only. It belongs to all their successors.

These words, Morris wrote to Ruskin, "are so good, and so completely settle the whole matter, that I feel ashamed at having to say anything else about it."[14]

"A Society like ours is nothing if it is not aggressive," he said in 1889; "therefore we have to try to convince even the most ignorant; and to do that properly, we ought to be able to get in the habit of putting ourselves in their position." In doing this, he found himself from the outset forced to rebut the charge that he wished only to preserve, in order to feed the sentiments of a handful of artists, the ruinous and the "picturesque." The interest in ancient buildings, he agreed, was "romantic"—"but what romance means is that capacity for a true conception of history, a power of making the past part of the present."[15] The romantic building "recalls to the mind the interest of the life of times past." Each attempt which he made to define in social terms the meaning of this beauty, the value of this interest in the past, brought him closer to Marxist conclusions. The beauty of the masterpieces of the past, he declared in a hundred different ways, lay in their embodiment of the aspirations of past generations of men, of their "hopes and fears," the vicissitudes of their affairs and the quality of their lives.

This conclusion forced upon him yet another series of questions. Why should men care to preserve the record of history at all? What could be learnt from the monuments of past aspirations beyond the sense of mortality, and the bitterness and degradation of the present? The answer lay in that astonishing rebirth of hope which permeated all Morris's writing and activity in these years. The masterpieces of the past were not dead relics, but a living inspiration and warning to the present, a proof of qualities in man which—however suppressed and slumbering—could not be extinguished for ever. "I love art, and I love history," he declared in a lecture delivered in 1882 in support of the Anti-Scrape—

> but it is living art and living history that I love. If we have no hope for the future, I do not see how we can look back on the past with pleasure. If we are to be less than men in time to come, let us forget that we have ever been men. It is in the interest of living art and living history that I oppose so-called restoration. What history can there be in a building bedaubed with ornament, which cannot at the best be anything but a hopeless and lifeless imitation of the hope and vigour of the earlier world? . . . Let us leave the dead alone, and, ourselves living, build for the living and those that shall live.[16]

This theme recurs in all his early addresses to the Society. But it was in a most remarkable paper read to the Society in 1884, after he had become an active Socialist, that he achieved his finest expression of his views. Our ancient architecture, he commenced—

> bears witness to the development of man's ideas, to the continuity of history, and, so doing, affords never-ceasing instruction, nay education, to the passing generations, not only telling us what were the aspirations of men passed away, but also what he may hope for in the time to come.

After discussing the distortions of past historians, presenting history without pattern or development, he referred to the modern understanding of the past, which, now that the "mists of pedantry" were beginning to lift, revealed a different picture—

> inchoate order in the remotest times, varying indeed among different races and countries, but swayed always by the same laws, moving forward ever towards something that seems the very opposite of that which it started from, and yet the earlier order never dead but living in the new, and slowly moulding it to a recreation of its former self. How different a spirit such a view of history must create it is not difficult to see. No longer shallow mockery at the failures and follies of the past, from a standpoint of so-called civilization, but deep sympathy with its half-conscious aims, from amidst the difficulties and shortcomings that we are only too sadly conscious of to-day; that is the new spirit of history; knowledge . . . has brought us humility, and humility hope of . . . perfection. . . .

The two instruments of this new knowledge of history Morris declared to be the study of language and the study of archaeology ("the record of man's creative deeds"); the preservation of this latter record was the special aim of the Society.

Morris then turned to examine the second great argument which had been brought against the Anti-Scrape. The whole case of the restorers rested upon it. Granted the beauty of the medieval buildings, they said, why could not nineteenth-century architects and craftsmen, by patient research and practice, make copies of thirteenth-century work to replace the old stone where it had decayed? Once again, Ruskin had been the first to give an answer:

> Do not let us deceive ourselves in this important matter; it is *impossible*, as impossible as to raise the dead, to restore anything that has ever been great or beautiful in architecture. That which I have . . . insisted upon as the life of the whole, that spirit which is given only by the hand and eye of the workman, can never be recalled. Another spirit may be given by

another time, and it is then a new building; but the spirit of the dead workman cannot be summoned up, and commanded to direct other hands and other thoughts.

Morris, starting from the arguments of "The Nature of Gothic," examined in detail the conditions and organization of labour in ancient, feudal, and in capitalist society. "Every architectural work is a work of co-operation," he commenced. "The very designer, be he never so original . . . [is] under the influence of *tradition*; dead men guide his hand even when he forgets that they ever existed." The closely-reasoned arguments with which Morris followed through the various changes in the skill and organization of the craftsmen cannot be summarized here. But this address is one of Morris's most important contributions to the theory of architecture. The inspired insights of Ruskin have been embodied within a coherent analysis of the techniques and productive relations of the societies within which the crafts were practised. Finally, Morris reached the point of change between the domestic industries and crafts of the eighteenth century, and modern industrial capitalism:

This strange and most momentous revolution was brought about by the machinery which the chances and changes of the world . . . *forced* on our population. You must think of this great machine industry as though on the one hand merely the full development of the effects of producing for profit instead of for livelihood, which began in Sir Thomas More's time, yet on the other as a revolutionary change from that of the mere division of labour. The exigencies of my own work have driven me to dig pretty deeply into the strata of the eighteenth-century workshop system, and I could clearly see how very different it is from the factory system of to-day . . . therefore it was with a ready sympathy that I read the full explanation of the change and its tendencies in the writings of a man, I will say a great man, whom, I suppose, I ought not to name in this company, and who cleared my mind on several points (also unmentionable here) relating to this subject of labour and its products . . .[17]

We can see here a clear example of the converging paths by which Morris was advancing towards Socialism. In the years between 1879 and 1884 he had been very active in practical work with tapestry and textiles, setting up his new workshops at Merton Abbey:[18] this work had brought him increasing insight into the contrast between the domestic and factory systems. At the same time his propaganda for the Anti-Scrape had brought him down a different path towards an understanding of the relations of the artist to his society. A few paces separated the paths, and the reading of *Capital* joined the two. Here is the explanation for the extraordinary clarity of this address.

Thus he had solved the problem, to his own satisfaction, of why restoration was impossible. The solution brought him back once again to his constant preoccupation of the time—the change and movement of history:

> Surely it is a curious thing that while we are ready to laugh at the idea of ... the Greek workman turning out a Gothic building, or a Gothic workman turning out a Greek one, we see nothing preposterous in the Victorian workman producing a Gothic one ... I may be told, perhaps, that ... historical knowledge ... has enabled us to perform that miracle of raising the dead centuries to life. But to my mind it is a strange view to take of historical knowledge and insight, that it should set us on the adventure of trying to retrace our steps towards the past, rather than give us some glimmer of insight into the future; a strange view of the continuity of history, that it should make us ignore the very changes which are the essence of that continuity. ...
>
> Surely such a state of things is a token of change—"of change, speedy perhaps, complete certainly: of the visible end of one cycle and the beginning of another."

It is important to make these views of Morris clear, since they scatter the charges of nostalgic medievalism or sentimental pedantry still sometimes levelled ignorantly at his name. In fact, it was his work for the Anti-Scrape which urged him forward from a passive to an active view of history. Persons with a false idea of the continuity of history, he told the Society in a notable passage of his address in 1889,

> are loth to admit the fatal words, "it cannot be, it has gone." They believe that we can do the same sort of work in the same spirit as our forefathers, whereas for good and for evil we are completely changed, and we cannot do the work they did. All continuity of history means is after all perpetual change, and it is not hard to see that we have changed with a vengeance, and thereby established our claim to be the continuers of history.[19]

At times Morris was despondent, saying: "It seems as if they will see what we mean just as the last old building is destroyed."[20] He was faced by that general apathy and defeatism which he himself was only shaking off, when he wrote to Georgie Burne-Jones in July, 1881:

> As to Anti-Scrape, I have little comfort there ... As to the buildings ... the destruction is not far from being complete already. What people really say to themselves is this: I don't like the thing being done, but I can bear it maybe—or certainly, when I come to think of it—and to stir in it is

such obvious suffering; so I won't stir. Certainly to take that trouble in any degree it is needful that a man should be touched with a real love of the earth, a worship of it, no less; and I think that as things go, that is seldom felt except by very simple people, and by them . . . dimly enough. You know the most refined and cultured people, both those of the old religions and those of the vague new ones, have a sort of Manichean hatred of the world (I use the word in its proper sense, the home of man). Such people must be both the enemies of beauty and the slaves of necessity, and true it is that they lead the world at present, and I believe will so till all that is old is gone, and history has become a book from which the pictures have been torn.

But the conclusion to the letter is equally revealing:

If you ask me why I kick against the pricks in this matter, all I can say is, first because I cannot help it, and secondly because I am encouraged by a sort of faith, that something will come of it, some kind of culture of which we know nothing at present.[21]

The work of the Anti-Scrape both arose from and contributed to Morris's rebirth of hope. How can we ever analyse the sources of such a change in a man's outlook? Which contributed most—the contact with Iceland, the practice of his crafts, the study of history, the concrete response to life of the poet (the "real love of the earth"), the public activity and contact with the working class? Certainly all had their part in his rising tide of confidence in the future. From the outset of his work with the Society he pleaded not for a complete halting of restoration, but for a "truce" lasting perhaps for a century, the preservation of the buildings intact until then, for the future to decide. Naturally, when he became a Socialist in 1883, he argued this with ever stronger conviction. In his address of 1884 he said plainly that capitalism was dying, and a new society coming to birth:

On the genuineness and reality of that hope the existence, the reason for existence of our Society depends. Believe me, it will not be possible for a small knot of cultivated people to keep alive an interest in the art and records of the past amidst the present conditions of a sordid and heart-breaking struggle for existence for the many, and a languid sauntering through life for the few. But when society is so reconstituted that all citizens will have a chance made up of due leisure and reasonable work, then will all society, and not our "Society" only, resolve to protect ancient buildings . . . for then at last they will begin to understand that they are part of their present lives, and part of themselves.[22]

"Although I am engaged with other societies, who might consider themselves more useful," he said in his address in 1889, "I think the work of this Society is thoroughly worth doing . . . Let us do what seems to us our duty in this matter, and let those that come after us do theirs; that will suffice; but my belief is that our descendants will thank us for our share of the work."[23]

Perhaps his most remarkable expression of confidence was in his address of ten years earlier—before he had any acquaintance with Socialism, and before he had even heard of Marx's name. "The workman of to-day is no artist," he said:

> It is the hope of my life that this may one day be changed; that popular art may grow again in our midst; that we may have an architectural style, the growth of its own times, but connected with all history.

After making his appeal for a "truce" which would leave the decision to the future, he continued:

> As for that decision of the future times of perfect and living art, I am not afraid of it . . . I believe that then the little grey weather-beaten building, built by ignorant men, torn by violent ones, patched by blunderers, that has outlived so many hopes and fears of mankind, and yet looks friendly and familiar to them—I believe that this relic of past times will be no offence to the beauty and majesty of their streets . . . Rather I believe that they will honour it the more for the many minds and hands of men that have dealt with it, and they will religiously guard it as a holy symbol of all the triumphs and tribulations of art: of art, the constant companion and expression of the life and aspirations of the world.[24]

Notes

1. "The Lesser Arts," *Works*, Vol. XXII, p. 19.

2. W.R. Lethaby, William Morris as Work-master (1901), p. 67.

3. Ibid., pp. 145–6.

4. *The Collected Works of William Morris*, 24 vols. (Longmans, 1910–15), Vol. XII, p. xiii.

5. *The Letters of William Morris to his Family and Friends*, edited by Philip Henderson (Longmans, Green, 1950), p. 86.

6. This campaign was actually organized by an independent Committee, with G.E. Street as Vice-Chairman and H. Wallis as Hon. Sec. The correspondence of the Committee is preserved in Brit. Mus. Add. MSS. 38831, and Morris's letter soliciting Gladstone's signature is preserved in Brit. Mus. Add. MSS. 44461. f.123.

7. Lethaby, op. cit., pp. 149–50.

8. J. Bruce Glasier, *William Morris and the Early Days of the Socialist Movement* (Longmans, 1921), pp. 103–4.

9. Lethaby, op. cit., p. 154.

10. *Letters*, p. 122.

11. Address to 1st Annual Meeting, S.P.A.B. May Morris, *William Morris, Artist, Writer, Socialist*, 2 vols., with an introduction to volume 2 by George Bernard Shaw (B. Blackwell, 1936).

12. May Morris, I, pp. 153–4.

13. *Letters*, p. 92.

14. *Letters*, p. 93.

15. May Morris, I, p. 148.

16. "The History of Pattern-Designing," *Works*, Vol. XXII, p. 233.

17. May Morris, I, p. 139.

18. See P. Henderson, *William Morris* (1973 edition), pp. 273–82.

19. May Morris, I, p. 152.

20. Lethaby, op. cit., p. 159.

21. *Letters*, p. 150.

22. May Morris, I, p. 145.

23. Ibid., p. 157.

24. May Morris, I, p. 124.

THE RIVER OF FIRE

FROM *WILLIAM MORRIS: ROMANTIC TO REVOLUTIONARY*

S peaking at a Socialist meeting in Oldham on July 11th, 1885, a notorious agitator declared:

> I have lived through and noted the most degrading epoch of public opinion that ever happened in England, and have seen the triumphant rule of the swindler in private and public life, the rule of hypocrisy and so-called respectability, begin to shake and totter.[1]

This agitator, normally reported in the Press as "Mr. W. Morris," should be distinguished from "William Morris, Author of 'The Earthly Paradise,' " who was still acknowledged in polite society. The transformation of the eccentric artist and romantic literary man into the Socialist agitator may be counted among the great conversions of the world. Morris was not only taking a step of far-reaching significance in his own life; nor was he only bringing the struggling Socialist pioneers their most notable recruit. He was also—if he is viewed (as he once viewed himself) as "the type of a certain group of mind" rather than as an isolated individual—taking a step which broke through the narrowing charmed circle of defeatism of bourgeois culture.

The years when this transformation took place were those between the end of the Eastern Question agitation in 1878 and the early months of 1883. Morris was by no means alone in his time in analysing the disease of capitalist society: from their different standpoints Carlyle, Ruskin, Matthew Arnold—even Dante Gabriel Rossetti and John Stuart Mill—either revolted in disgust against the ethic of capitalism or questioned its immutable economic basis. Yet all these men, the "railers against 'progress,' " were somehow held back from a final

From *William Morris: Romantic to Revolutionary* by E. P. Thompson (New York: Pantheon Books, 1955, 1977).

positive and involutionary understanding. Discussing the death of the old art in a lecture of 1881, Morris declared:

> We of the English middle classes are the most powerful body of men that the world has yet seen. . . . And yet when we come to look the matter in the face, we cannot fail to see that even for us with all our strength it will be a hard matter to bring about that birth of the new art: for between us and that which is to be, if art is not to perish utterly, there is something alive and devouring; something as it were a river of fire that will put all that tries to swim across to a hard proof indeed, and scare from the plunge every soul that is not made fearless by desire of truth and insight of the happy days to come beyond.[2]

What a remarkable insight this is! At the time Morris could do little to define the nature of this "river of fire," and yet he could see around him his most gifted contemporaries—men who had helped to lead him to this point—hesitating upon its brink. Rossetti, the inspiration of his youth, died in April, 1882, and Morris reflected upon his lack of interest in politics:

> The truth is he cared for nothing but individual and personal matters. . . . He would take abundant trouble to help one person who was in distress of mind or body; but the evils of any mass of people he couldn't bring his mind to bear upon. I suppose in short it needs a person of hopeful mind to take disinterested notice of politics, and Rossetti was certainly not hopeful.[3]

If Rossetti was without hope, Arnold (in Morris's view) fell short in another direction—determination and courage. It is true that Arnold, in his last years, was carried by his hatred of the philistines to the point of declaring "Our middle classes know neither man nor the world; they have no light, and can give none," and of appealing directly to the working class to take the remedy into their own hands. But in his lecture upon "Equality," which Morris read in the *Fortnightly Review* in 1878, he proposed as a practical programme little more than some reform in the law of bequest—"Self-Help" starting afresh with each generation, the Transport House distant ideal. Morris was impressed by Arnold's sincerity:[4] but not with his conclusions:

> With the main part . . . I heartily agree: the only thing is that if he has any idea of a remedy he dursn't mention it. I think myself that no rose-water will cure us: disaster and misfortune of all kinds, I think, will be the only things that will breed a remedy: in short, nothing can be done

till all rich men are made poor by common consent. I suppose he dimly sees this, but is afraid to say it, being, though naturally a courageous man, somewhat infected with the great vice of that cultivated class he was praising so much—cowardice, to wit.[5]

As we have seen, even John Ruskin, whom Morris called "the first comer, the inventer,"[6] drew back at this "devouring" barrier. In truth, Carlyle, Ruskin, Arnold—all were too ready to appeal to the working class to lead the nation forth in battles for objectives which they themselves had at heart, which were derived from their own special discontent, but which had little relevance to the immediate grievances under which working people were suffering. They were too inclined to see the workers as the rank and file of an Army of Light, struggling valiantly for culture or for a new morality, under the generalship of themselves and a few enlightened leaders who had broken free from the Philistine middle class.

Morris also fell into this error in the years between 1878 and 1880. At the same time as he was beginning to write and lecture for "Anti-Scrape," he started on a new series of lectures in which he sought to take the cause of art to the workers. Discussing "The Lesser Arts" in his first lecture in December, 1877, he put the case at its simplest. The flood of "cheap and nasty" products on the market was the fault of all classes of society, he declared, producers and consumers alike. In particular—

> manufacturers (so called) are so set on carrying out competition to its utmost, competition of cheapness, not of excellence, that they meet the bargain-hunters half way, and cheerfully furnish them with nasty wares at the cheap rate. . . .

The remedy must therefore lie with the producers,

> The handicraftsmen, who are not ignorant of these things like the public, and who have no call to be greedy and isolated like the manufacturers or middlemen; the duty and honour of educating the public lies with them, and they have in them the seeds of order and organization which make that duty easier.[7]

Moreover, all his researches into Gothic architecture and into the decorative arts reinforced his conviction that the true roots of these arts were in the traditional skills of the people. "History," he said in one of his most striking phrases, "has remembered the kings and warriors, because they destroyed: Art has remembered the people, because they created."[8] What was more natural

then that he should turn to the people for the rebirth of art? The only hope
for the arts lay in a future when the working class,

> the "residuum" of modern civilization, the terror of radical politicians, and
> the tool of reactionists, will become the great mass of orderly thinking
> people, sweet and fair in its manners, and noble in its aspirations, and
> that . . . is the sole hope of worthy, living, enduring art: nothing else, I
> say, will help . . .[9]

His first lecture was delivered for a body called the "Trades Guild of Learning," promoted by Professor Warr, a Positivist colleague of Marx's old Radical
friend, Professor Bessly, and for some years Secretary of the Cobden Club.
George Wardle, the Manager of the Firm, recalled (in a letter to Sir Sydney
Cockerell) that Warr established the Guild with Morris's aid because he "had
visions of moralizing the Capitalist" by means of educating the young carpenters, stonemasons, and apprentices. In the beginning, for Morris as well,

> It was rather a question of educating the workman, more especially the
> artizan or worker in some of the fine arts . . . I need hardly say there were
> very few workmen of any kind there [at the first lectures], except the men
> from Queen Square [the Firm] and that the bulk of the audience was
> formed by Morris's *clients*.[10]

Here, then, was Morris, in 1879 and 1880, even as late as 1881, standing on
the brink of the "river of fire," hesitating before the plunge. Of the real lives
of the workers he knew very little. He knew and respected the craftsmen who
worked for the Firm, and the villagers of Kelmscott: but he saw the sordid
scenes of the metropolis as an outsider glimpsing a garish interior of vice. "Look
you," he said in 1881,

> As I sit at work at home, which is at Hammersmith,[11] close to the river,
> I often hear go past the window some of that ruffianism of which a good
> deal has been said in the papers of late . . . As I hear the yells and shrieks
> and all the degradation cast on the glorious tongue of Shakespeare and
> Milton, as I see the brutal reckless faces and figures go past me, it rouses
> recklessness and brutality in me also, and fierce wrath takes possession of
> me, till I remember, as I hope I mostly do, that it was my good luck only
> of being born respectable and rich that has put me on this side of the
> window among delightful books and lovely works of art, and not on the
> other side, in the empty street, the drink-steeped liquor-shops, the foul
> and degraded lodgings. What words can say what all that means?[12]

Then indeed I fall a-wondering at the strange and slender thread of circumstances which has armed me for doing and forebearing with that refinement which I didn't make myself, but was born into. That, I say, I wonder at. . . .[13]

By the early 1880s it is clear that Morris was disappointed in the great ambitions with which he had started the Firm. In order to understand this, it must be remembered that in its origin the Firm had appeared to him not as a commercial venture and scarcely even as a strictly artistic one. It was the form taken by his "holy crusade against the age": it was intended to fight the flood of philistinism in one field of Victorian life, to inject into the very sources of production pleasurable and creative labour, to re-create conditions of artistic production found in medieval times. But the age had not flinched in the face of this form of attack. The slums grew, and the respectable suburban jerry-building thrived:

I think you will understand me . . . but too well when I ask you to re-member the pang of dismay that comes on us when we revisit some spot of country which has been specially sympathetic to us in times past . . . but where now as we turn the corner of the road or crown the hill's brow we can see first the inevitable blue slate roof, and then the blotched mud-coloured stucco, or ill-built wall of ill-made bricks of the new buildings; then as we come nearer and see the arid and pretentious little gardens, and cast-iron horrors of railings, and miseries of squalid out-houses break-ing through the sweet meadows and abundant hedgerows. . . .[14]

It might have been something if the age had ignored the Firm altogether, or fought it tooth and nail. But, instead, it had been absorbed by fashionable and wealthy circles.[15] Lady Tranmore's house, in Mrs. Humphrey Ward's novel, *The Marriage of William Ashe*, is described as reflecting "the rising worship of Morris and Burne-Jones":

Her walls were covered with the well-known pomegranate or jessamine or sunflower patterns; her hangings were of a mystic greenish blue, her pictures were drawn either from the Italian primitives or their modern followers.[16]

Moreover, Morris was enraged to find commercial manufacturers turning out cheap imitation-Morris products, including one wall-paper which he described as "a mangy gherkin on a horsedung ground."[17] "Morris" was becoming the code-word for a kind of ostentatious cultivation among a fringe of the upper and middle classes, and the designer himself was beginning to regard his own customers with increasing distaste.

From its early days the Firm had held fast to certain principles in its work: its first Manager, Warington Taylor, had (unbeknown to Morris) once lost a good contract for decorating a church because he had written on the estimate, under the item: "To providing a silk and gold altar cloth":

> Note.—In consideration of the fact that the above item is a wholly un-necessary and inexcusable extravagance at a time when thousands of poor people in this so-called Christian country are in want of food—additional charge to that set forth above, ten pounds.[18]

When Morris started the Anti-Scrape he turned down all orders for decorations or stained glass in old churches, in order not to appear to be profiting from restoration himself. In the decoration of private houses he felt even more con-strained. Philip Webb had built one of his most ambitious houses for Sir Low-thian Bell, the ironmaster, and Morris, called in to do the decoration, was so well pleased with his friend's building that he decided to attend to the work in person. One day, Sir Lowthian Bell related,

> he heard Morris talking and walking about in an excited way, and went to inquire if anything was wrong. "He turned on me like a wild animal— 'It is only that I spend my life in ministering to the swinish luxury of the rich.' "[19]

In January, 1882, he was writing to Georgie Burne-Jones:

> I have perhaps rather more than enough of work to do, and . . . am dwell-ing somewhat low down in the valley of humiliation. . . . It sometimes seems to me as if my lot was a strange one: you see, I work pretty hard, and on the whole very cheerfully, not altogether I hope for mere pudding, still less for praise; and while I work I have the cause always in mind, and yet I know that the cause for which I specially work is doomed to fail, at least in seeming; I mean that art must go under, where or how ever it may come up again. . . . It does sometimes seem to me a strange thing indeed that a man should be driven to work with energy and even with pleasure and enthusiasm at work which he knows will serve no end but amusing himself; am I doing nothing but make-believe then, something like Louis XVI's lock-making?[20]

In his designing, he was, in general, coming to favour simplicity rather than richness of finish: and when he came to lecture upon the lesser arts—in such a lecture as "Making the Best of It"—he was continually striving to translate his principles into terms of a working-class income. Fine carving, costly carpets and hangings, rich painting—all these might be desirable: but they were not the most important thing. Shoddy must be driven out first. "Simplicity of life, begetting simplicity of taste . . . is of all matters most necessary for the birth of the new and better art," he said in his first lecture. It was a constant theme of those that followed. "Simplicity of life," he said in 1881,

> is not a misery, but the very foundation of refinement: a sanded floor and white-washed walls, and the green trees and flowery meads and living waters outside; or a grimy place amid the smoke with a regiment of housemaids always working to smear the dirt together so that it may be unnoticed; which, think you, is the most refined? . . .[21]

Even the richness of the future seemed to him to be more one of quality than abundance:

> In looking forward towards any utopia of the arts. I do not conceive to myself of there being a very great quantity of art of any kind, certainly not of ornament, apart from the purely intellectual arts; and even those must not swallow up too much of life. . . . Looking forward from out of the farrago of rubbish with which we are now surrounded, [I can] chiefly see possible negative virtues in the externals of our household goods; can see them never shabby, pretentious, or ungenerous, natural and reasonable always; beautiful also, but more because they are natural and reasonable, than because we have set about to make them beautiful.[22]

"I decorate modern houses for people," he told the young Yeats,

> but the house that would please me would be some great room where one talked to one's friends in one corner, and ate in another, and slept in another, and worked in another.[23]

And to his Socialist friend, Scheu, who must often have exchanged with him anecdotes of the trade, he said:

> I would like to be able to make a good fitting boot or a good suit of clothes; not always only those things that are the toys of rich folk. As

things stand at the moment, I hang along with my creative work on to the apron-strings of the idle privileged classes.[24]

"Morris's writings about Socialism," Shaw wrote, "really called up all his mental reserves for the first time."[25] This is profoundly true: and among these writings the pre-Socialist lectures on art must be included. In preparing these lectures—writing them out in a beautiful hand with only an occasional abbreviation or correction—Morris was exercising and disciplining his mind in a way he had never done before. Nothing would be more mistaken than to suppose that the lectures were casually undertaken or easily prepared. Apart from those delivered to a general audience in support of the funds of the Anti-Scrape, Morris carefully selected his audience, going to the men practically engaged in artistic production, design, or craftsmanship. In the lectures it is possible to see his thought advancing step by step—the discovery of one conclusion, the forced-march forward to the next. In 1880 he referred to the preparation of a lecture for the "Trades Guild of Learning" as his "autumn work." Of another lecture promised to the London Institute for the following March he wrote in the same letter:

> I will be as serious as I can over them . . . the subject . . . still seems to me the most serious one that a man can think of; for 'tis no less than the chances of a calm, dignified, and therefore happy life for the mass of mankind.[26]

"I know what I want to say, but the cursed words go to water between my fingers," he wrote of another lecture. A lecture delivered early in 1881 took him the whole month of February to prepare, including—his journal suggests—eight complete days, while of another lecture he wrote: " 'tis to be a short one, but will give me a fortnight's work, I know."[27] And even after a lecture's delivery his mind was flooded with fresh problems, or he was left puzzled and bewildered:

> My audience . . . was polite & attentive; but I fear they were sorely puzzled at what I said; as might well be, since if they acted on it Nottingham trade would come to an end.[28]

In all his lectures he was moved—as in his addresses to the Anti-Scrape—by his increasing understanding of the movement of history, of the fact of class division and the class struggle. If simplicity was the aim, its attainment would liberate rich and poor alike:

A state of things that produces vices among low people, will produce, not opposing virtues among high people, but corresponding vices; if you weave a pattern on a piece of cloth, and then turn it over and look at the back of it, you will see the back of the pattern, and not another pattern: material riches bred by material poverty and slavery produce scorn, cynicism and despair.[29]

And again:

Luxury cannot exist without slavery of some kind or other, and its abolition will be blessed . . . by the freeing both of the slaves and of their masters.[30]

Or the uncompromising declaration of his first lecture of all:

Sirs, I believe that art has such sympathy with cheerful freedom, open-heartedness and reality, so much she sickens under selfishness and luxury, that she will not live thus isolated and exclusive. I will go further than this and say that on such terms I do not wish her to live . . . I do not want art for a few, any more than education for a few, or freedom for a few.

No, rather than art should live this poor thin life among a few exceptional men, despising those beneath them for an ignorance for which they themselves are responsible, for a brutality that they will not struggle with,—rather than this, I would that the world should indeed sweep away all art for awhile . . . rather than the wheat should rot in the miser's granary, I would that the earth had it, that it might yet have a chance to quicken in the dark.[31]

In truth, these lectures are less concerned with a close criticism of the arts than with a criticism of civilization itself, as measured in the perspective of history, and as revealed by the evidence of contemporary public art. The danger, he said in one lecture, is that—

the present course of civilisation will destroy the beauty of life—these are hard words, and I wish I could mend them, but I cannot, while I speak what I believe to be the truth.[32]

And in another:

Civilization . . . has let one wrong and tyranny grow and swell into this, that a few have no work to do, and are therefore unhappy, the many have degrading work to do, and are therefore unhappy . . . Of all countries ours is . . . the most masterful, the most remorseless, in pushing forward this blind civilization . . . For our parts, we think that the remedy is to be found in the simplification of life, and the curbing of luxury and the desires for tyranny and mastery that it gives birth to. . . .

If this cannot be done, the alternative must be—

the rending asunder for a time of all society by the forces of greediness and self-seeking, by the strife of man against man, nation against nation, class against class.[33]

This strife of class against class he felt still to be something only destructive — and yet still to be preferred to the gradual extinction of all art and noble aspirations in bourgeois vulgarity. If "civilization" meant no more than the attainment of comforts for the middle class, he said in 1880, then "farewell my hope!":

I had thought that civilization meant the attainment of peace and order and freedom, of goodwill between man and man, of the love of truth and the hatred of injustice . . . a life free from craven fear, but full of incident: that was what I thought it meant, not more stuffed chairs and more cushions, and more carpets and gas, and more dainty meat and drink—and therewithal more and sharper differences between class and class.[34]

If this was all that was meant by "a civilization that is too apt to boast in after-dinner speeches; too apt to thrust her blessings on far-off peoples at the cannon's mouth,"[35] then—

I for one wish we had never gone so far . . . rather than we should never be other than we are, I would we had all together been shepherds . . . among the hills and valleys; men with little knowledge, but desiring much; rough men if you please but not brutal; with some sort of art among them, genuine at least and spontaneous; men who could be moved by poetry and story, working hard yet not without leisure . . . neither malicious nor over soft-hearted, well pleased to live and ready to die—in short, men, free and equal.

No, it cannot be: it has long passed over, and civilization goes forward, swiftly, if unsteadily . . .[36]

And he declared in a passage from another lecture of 1880 which anticipates his full Socialist criticism of society:

If civilization is to go no further than this, it had better not have gone so far: if it does not aim at getting rid of this misery and giving some share in the happiness and dignity of life to *all* the people that it has created ... it is simply an organized injustice, a mere instrument for oppression, so much the worse than that which has gone before it, as its pretensions are higher, its slavery subtler, its mastery harder to overthrow, because supported by such a dense mass of commonplace well-being and comfort.[37]

"It is strange indeed", he said in 1881,

it is woeful, it is scarcely comprehensible, if we come to think of it as men, and not as machines, that, after all the progress of civilization, it should be so easy for a little official talk, a few lines on a sheet of paper, to set a terrible engine to work, which without any trouble on our part will slay ten thousand men ... and it lies light enough on the conscience of *all* of us; while, if it is a question of striking a blow at grievous and crushing evils which lie at our own doors ... not only is there no national machinery for dealing with them ... but any hint that such a thing may be possible is received with laughter or with terror, or with severe and heavy blame. The rights of property, the necessities of morality, the interests of religion—these are the sacramental words of cowardice that silence us![38]

"If we ... think of it as *men*"—it is here, in his steadfast refusal to admit that men were mere victims of circumstances of their own creating, that the influence of the Norse sagas, and their "worship of courage" can be most strongly felt, "You may think", he said at the end of 1881, that we are "mere straws" in the "resistless flood": "But don't let us strain a metaphor; for we are no straws, but men, with each one of us a will and aspirations, and with duties to fufil ..." *Action*—this is the constant theme of his lectures. In 1880 he was writing to Georgie Burne-Jones:

I do most earnestly desire that something more startling could be done than mere constant private grumbling and occasional public speaking to lift the standard of revolt against the sordidness which people are so stupid as to think necessary.[39]

Educational ventures, campaigns for the enforcement of the Smoke Act, societies like the Commons Preservation and Kyrle Societies which were dong something to prevent the worst desecrations of town and countryside, to all these he was ready to give his public support. But his analysis of society was far too profound to suppose that these efforts would do more than scratch the surface. In August, 1881, he wrote again to Georgie, who seems to have suggested that he should be satisfied with such limited forms of action:

> I don't agree with you in condemning grumbling against follies and ills that oppress the world, even among friends, for you see it is but now and then that one has a chance of speaking about the thing in public, and meantime one's heart is hot with it, and some expression of it is like to quicken the flame even in those one loves and respects most, and it is good to feel the air laden with the coming storm even as we go about our daily work or while away time in light matters. To do nothing but grumble and not to act—that is throwing away one's life: but I don't think that words on our cause that we have at heart do nothing but wound the air, even when spoken among friends: 'tis at worst like the music to which men go to battle.[40]

Here, in his lectures, then, Morris was continually reconnoitering the banks of the "river of fire" "When he spoke off-hand," one of his contemporaries recalled,

> he had a knack at times of hammering away at his point until he had said exactly what he wanted to say in exactly the words he wished to use, rocking to and fro the while from one foot to the other.[41]

The lectures were the anvil on which he beat out his thoughts. His mood varied often between hope and depression. On the one hand, he felt the gathering of the storm, that he was no longer isolated and that people were beginning to move in the same way: "it is a real joy to find the game afoot, that the thing is stirring in other people's minds besides mine," he wrote in 1881.[42] In one of the most penetrating passages of his very first lecture, he had sensed that the movement of ideas and their influence in history was more than a mere accident of individual discontent:

> I suppose that if some half-dozen men at any time earnestly set their hearts on something coming about which is not discordant with nature, it will come to pass one day or other; because it is not by accident that an idea comes into the heads of a few; rather they are pushed on, and forced to speak or act by something stirring in the heart of the world . . .[43]

On the other hand, he felt often enough powerless in the face of the unbroken capitalist facade. In the summer of 1882, with trouble at home, colonial wars abroad, a famine in Ireland, he wrote to Georgie Burne-Jones:

Indeed I am older, and the year is evil; the summerless season, and famine and war, and the folly of peoples come back again, as it were, and the more and more obvious death of art before it rises again, are heavy matters to a small creature like me, who cannot choose but think about them, and can mend them scarce a whit.[44]

Here, indeed, he might have remained, had his work for Anti-Scrape, his lectures and practice of the arts, been his only line of advance. However revolutionary his theoretical insight into the problems that most concerned him, he was likely to fall into hopelessness or nostalgia if he did not have practical confidence in the possibility of overthrowing capitalism, practical contact with the working class. This was the point at which Morris broke so decisively with both Ruskin and Arnold. "To do nothing but grumble and not to act—that is throwing away one's life." Once his mind was decided, he always looked for the most likely form of action that was at hand to realize his desires. From the time that the Eastern Question agitation had come to its sorry end, Morris had maintained his links with the radical movement of the London workers. It is true that the break-up of the E.Q.A. did not leave him in a hopeful frame of mind. Jingoism, it appeared to him, had swept the country:

The peace-party are in a very small minority . . . *there is no doubt of it* . . . For some years to come, until perhaps great disasters teach us better, we shall be a reactionary and Tory nation. I believe myself that the best way would be for all worthy men to abstain from politics for a while; so that these fools might be the sooner filled with the fruit of their own devices.[45]

But this "leave-them-to-stew-in-their-own-juice" attitude was little more than a new enthusiast making faces when he meets with his first check; and Morris was quickly shocked out of it by the events of the next year.

Imperialism was continuing its brutal advance, from the Fiji Islands to Burma, from South Africa to the Mediterranean. At the end of 1878 Disraeli and his military advisers took advantage of the Jingo spirit and the anti-Russian phobia to set to work to "rectify" the North-West Frontier of India, which (Disraeli explained) was a "haphazard and not a scientific one." The campaign thus launched in Afghanistan dragged on for several years, through disastrous setbacks and inglorious "victories." The miners' M.P., Thomas Burt, made one of his best speeches in the house at its outset.[46] The Government over-reached itself in 1879, with this war, the annexation of the Transvaal, wars against the Kaffirs and—least popular of all—against the Zulus. Had these wars been successful, no doubt the wave of Jingoism might have carried Disraeli back to power in the General Election which took place in the first months of 1880. But all were indeterminate, brutal, and expensive: and the rising disgust of the British people, which Gladstone enlisted in the rolling phrases of his "Mid-Lothian" campaigns, helped to bring a Liberal administration into power.

Imperialism, Morris saw, was the inevitable and most vicious outcome of the "Century of Commerce." He denounced it both in artistic and political terms. "While we are met here in Birmingham," he said at the beginning of 1879.

to further the spread of education in art, Englishmen in India are . . . actively destroying the very sources of that education—jewellery, metal-work, pottery, calico-printing, brocade-weaving, carpet-making—all the famous and historical arts of the great peninsula have been . . . thrust aside for the advantage of any paltry scrap of so-called commerce.[47]

At the end of January, 1880, in a lecture which was probably designed for some working-class Radical Club in connection with the election campaign, and which was devoted to combating "the tribe of Jingoes," and the slogan "Our country Right or Wrong" blazoned upon their banners, he declared:

England's place—what is England's place? To carry civilization through the world? Yes, indeed, the world must be civilized, and I doubt not that England will have a large share in bringing about that civilization.

And yet, since I have heard of wine with no grape-juice in it, and cotton-cloth that is mostly barytes, and silk that is two-thirds somach, and knives whose edges break or turn up if you try to cut anything harder than butter with them, and many another triumph of Commerce in these days, I begin to doubt if civilization itself may not be sometimes so much adulterated as scarcely to be worth the carrying—anyhow it cannot be worth much, when it is necessary to kill a man in order to make him accept it. . . .[48]

At the time when he delivered this lecture Morris was in that transitional period which he came later to describe as "a brief period of political radicalism during which I saw my ideal clear enough, but had no hope of any realization of it."[49] In the autumn of 1879 he became Treasurer of the National Liberal League, a small and largely ineffective organization which strove to keep to-gether what influence the Labour Representation League still held when the latter petered out towards the end of 1878. Its first Secretary was Henry Broad-hurst, Morris's old colleague of the "Workmen's Neutrality Committee" and also Secretary of the Parliamentary Committee of the T.U.C. To the Parlia-

mentary Committee now fell the main responsibility for the promotion of
working-men candidatures within the patronage of the Liberal Party: and the
N.L.L. seems to have been mainly designed by its promoters, Broadhurst and
its Chairman, George Howell (ex-Secretary of the Labor Representation
League), as a means of uniting the London Radical Clubs and trade unions,
together with some middle-class men, behind certain specific and short-term
democratic reforms. Its first important campaign came in the election of 1880,
when it helped to rouse the London working class behind Gladstone's platform
of "Peace, Retrenchment, Reform." Morris, still under the spell of Gladstone's
oratory, worked as a loyal electioneer in the campaign.[50] It is true that he could
not refrain from suggesting objectives more far-reaching:

> I think of a country where every man has work enough to do, and no
> one has too much: where no man has to work himself stupid in order to
> be just able to live: where on the contrary it will be easy for a man to
> live if he will but work, impossible if he will not . . . where every man's
> work would be pleasant to himself and helpful to his neighbour; and then
> his leisure . . . (of which he ought to have plenty) would be thoughtful
> and rational. . . .[51]

But these views, he said, were only personal "crochetts":

> I understand clearly that my crochett has no chance of being heard till
> Peace, Retrenchment, and Reform are abroad. . . . I intend at the coming
> election to vote for any good man and true who will help me to those,
> and to let my crochett bide its time; and others of you who are like me,
> crochetteers, I give the advice to do the same.[52]

The formation of Gladstone's ministry put the promoters of the League in
a quandary. "We have now to consider the possibility of making the League a
force: if that be not possible, better dissolve at once," Howell wrote to Broadhurst in April 26th, 1880.[53] Broadhurst had little reason to continue his interest
in the League. The honest stonemason had suffered the disaster of being elected
to Parliament himself, and, exposed to the patronizing flattery of the bourgeoisie
for the representative of the "British working man," his feet were set on the
road which led to his total surrender at Sandringham in 1884, where the Prince
of Wales even went so far as to accompany him to the village pub on the royal
estate:

> The Prince invited me to partake of the refreshment of the house, and I
> was quite ready to comply. We had, I think, a glass of ale each and sat

down in the club-room, where we found several farm labourers enjoying their half-pints and their pipes. No excitement, no distubance, no uncomfortable feeling, was envinced by those present. . . . The beer was very good and of a homely and acceptable flavour. . . . I left Sandringham with a feeling of one who had spent a week-end with an old chum of his own rank in society rather than one who had been entertained by the Heir-Apparent and his Princess.[54]

No wonder Morris was to write in a letter of this year (when lamenting the lack of real working-class leaders to make conscious the "vague discontent and spirit of revenge" of the workers):

But you see when a man has gifts for that kind of thing he finds himself tending to rise out of his class before he has begun to think of class politics as a matter of principle, and too often he is just simply "got at" by the governing classes, not formally but by circumstances. . . .[55]

However, John Hales took Broadhurst's place as Secretary and it was agreed that it was desirable "in the interests of the Liberal party generally and of the principles of Liberalism specially" that the League should continue and extend its work. Morris wrote to Broadhurst congratulating him on his election, and adding: "How to broaden and deepen the stream of radical principles, keeping meanwhile the government both alive and steady, without harrassing or frightening it,—that is the question, I fancy."[56] A programme of reforms was drawn up, including demands for detailed electoral reform and shorter parliaments, the abolition of paid canvassing, the codification of electoral law, a (vague) demand for reform of the Land Laws, the long-standing demand for municipal government for London, and—added in April, 1881, as a result of the hostility of the Tory Lords to certain of Gladstone's policies—the replacement of the House of Lords by an Elective Chamber.[57] "Unsatisfactory," Morris noted in his journal for March 26th, 1881, after attending a meeting of the League.[58] Reluctantly he was coming to admit his own disillusion in the Liberal Government and in any movement which attached itself to its tail. The momentum of imperialism was not checked in the least by the new administration: the only apparent result was the introduction of a certain indecisiveness into colonial policy, which led to further setbacks and inglorious defeats. Gladstone, his former idol, was still not overthrown: he pictured him as sincere and progressive but enchained by his more reactionary colleagues. "Politics: Not pleasant," he wrote in February, 1881:

"I don't trust the present government . . . to show as radical—Whig it is and will remain. . . . I doubt the Liberal Majority in the house, and the

Government may get timid. . . . In that case Gladstone's influence will be so shaken that the Liberal Party will fall to pieces, and good men and true must set to work to build up a Radical Party out of them and make themselves leaders out of the stones of the streets for all I can see. But . . . Gladstone is much stronger in the country than I thought for, and if he could only stop these damned little wars he might stop in till he has carried the regular liberal programme, and we should make a good step forward. But little wars with defeats and inglorious victories . . . shake a Government terribly. . . .[59]

A few days later he was even more anxious. The war was dragging on in Afghanistan: "I do think our side ought to start putting a little pressure on Government to make them do what they doubtless want to do . . . what a pity it is that there is not a proper radical club properly organized for political purposes, who could act speedily in such junctures."[60] Less than a month later affairs in the Transvaal shook Morris's confidence in Gladstone himself. During his second Midlothian campaign Gladstone had treated Disraeli's annexation with his intensest moral indignation:

If Cyprus and the Transvaal were as valuable as they are valueless, I would repudiate them because they are obtained by means dishonourable to the character of the country.

Reminded of these words now that he was in power, he explained that he had used the word "repudiate" in the sense of "dislike." Grievous as his moral revulsion might be, he could not see his way to letting them regain their independence—although the defeat inflicted by the Boers on the British troops at Majuba Hill brought morality and practice a little closer together. "I am in hopes the matter will be taken up somewhat by people outside parliament for inside it all or nearly all people seem to be behaving ill enough" wrote Morris.[61]

Perhaps it was owing to Morris's persistence that among the objects of the National Liberal League there was added, at the end of 1881, the demand for the application to foreign policy of the "same moral principles" as in private relations. Otherwise, the programme of the League[62] showed little advance on the previous year, except in its emphasis on the need for extensive reform in the laws regarding land tenure—a question very much in the air in Radical circles. But shortly after this Morris resigned as Treasurer of the League, declaring: "I do so hate—this in spite of my accounts—everything vague in politics as well as in art."[63] Shortly after his resignation the League disappeared from public view.

Much of Morris's work for the E.Q.A. and the N.L.L., then, brought him education only in a negative sense. The work of the former, Wardle recalled, introduced him "to some politicians he had not known personally before, but acquaintance did not increase any respect he may have had for them."[64] His relations with the "Lib-Lab" working-class leaders were even more important in the development of his political views. George Howell, the patient wire-puller, can never have commanded much of his respect. Henry Broadhurst was a man of more sincerity, but a typical product of a skilled craft union in a time of industrial peace. Morris had ample opportunity to observe the stages by which Howell and Broadhurst became pawns of Mundella and of his colleagues, and it is not difficult to see—behind such passages as this in a lecture of 1883—not doctrinaire opinion but the weight of Morris's own personal experience: "The Trade Unions, founded for the advancement of the working class as a class, have already become conservative and obstructive bodies, wielded by the middle-class politicians for party purposes."[65]

By 1882 his disillusion in the Liberal Party was almost complete. He wrote, of a by-election, to the Hon. George Howard (Earl of Carlisle to be), amateur artist, Liberal M.P., and colleague of his on the E.Q.A.:

> I suppose your election is the North Riding . . . I make . . . the unpolitical remarks that I hope you have a good candidate: 'tis better to be beaten with a good one than be successful with a bad one. I guess there will be a fine procession of rats before this parliament is over: that will teach us, I hope, not to run the worst man possible on all occasions. Excuse the spleen of a kind of Radical cobbler.[66]

What finally opened Morris's eyes to the impossibility of advance within the shadow of the Liberal Party was the policy of the Government in Ireland and Egypt. The introduction of the infamous Coercion Bill in 1881 had aroused Morris's anxiety, but he had softened his fears with the reflection that they "don't *intend* to use it tyranically."[67] In fact, the Minister responsible for its operation, Foster—who had spoken so nobly on the platform of the E.Q.A. five years before—employed his powers so tyranically that even a section of the Conservatives thought his actions injudicious. In Egypt the Liberal measures of "pacification" in the summer of 1882 included the shelling of Alexandria by British warships. This made the lesson complete. The Coercion Bill, the worship of Liberal "leaders" who " 'led' the party into mere Jingoism," the "Stockjob-ber's Egyptian War, quite destroyed any hope I might have had of any good being done by alliance with the Radical party."[68] "Radicalism," he wrote in June of the next year, "will never develop into anything more than Radica-lism. . . . It is made for and by the middle classes, and will always be under the control of rich capitalists: they will have no objection to its political development, if they think they can stop it there: but as to real social changes, they will not allow them. . . .[69]

The last of his illusions had perished under the criticism of practical experience. No barrier remained in his mind to prevent his acceptance of Socialist conclusions. But changes as great as this cannot be accomplished without the severest tensions. As early as the end of 1879 he was lamenting the seeming drying-up of the sources of his creative writing:

> As to poetry, I don't know, and I don't know. The verse would come easy enough if I had only a subject which would fill my heart and mind: but to write verse for the sake of writing is a crime in a man of my years and experience. . . .[70]

The great intellectual effort of his lectures must have exposed to him the facility of much of his verse. At the same period there are unexplained passages in his letters to Georgie Burne-Jones which suggest the breaking apart of old and intimate ties. In October, 1879, he wrote from Kelmscott:

> I am sitting . . . in the tapestry-room, the moon rising red through the east-wind haze, and a cow lowing over the fields. I have been feeling chastened by many thoughts, and the beauty and quietness of the surroundings, which latter, as I hinted, I am, as it were, beginning to take leave of. That leave-taking will, I confess . . . seem a long step towards saying good-night to the world.

His estrangement from his wife seems to have become more pronounced. Indeed, the sense of his personal isolation during these critical years is extreme. He was turning his back upon his own class, and this meant that he was facing the separation from many old friends and colleagues. It was only the growing sense of "the Cause" which sustained his courage. "Little by little it must come, I know," he said in 1879:

> Patience and prudence must not be lacking to us, but courage still less. Let us be a Gideon's band. "Whosoever is fearful and afraid, let him return, and depart early from Mount Gilead." And among that band let there be no delusions; let the last encouraging lie have been told, the last after-dinner humbug spoken. . . .[71]

"Every man who has a cause at heart," he said in 1881, "is bound to act as if it depended on him alone, however well he may know his own unworthiness; and thus is action brought to birth from mere opinion."[72]

In the summer of 1882, then, he was ready "to join any body who distinctly called themselves Socialists,"[73] although for a few months his action was delayed by the breakdown of his daughter, Jenny's, health,[74] his practical endeavours to relieve a famine in Ireland, and also his distrust of the ex-Tory leader of the Democratic Federation, H. M. Hyndman.[75] He had almost no acquaintance with individual Socialists, no knowledge of the theory of Socialism. In the summer of 1881 he had been enraged by the Liberal Government's prosecution of Johann Most, the German anarchist editor of the paper *Freiheit*, published from London, which had printed an article extolling the assassins of Tsar Alexander II:

> I suppose you have seen the sentence on Herr Most . . . just think of the mixture of tyranny and hypocrisy with which the world is governed! These are the sort of things that make thinking people so sick at heart that they are driven from all interest in politics save revolutionary politics: which I must say seems like to be my case. Indeed I have long known, or felt, say, that society in spite of its modern smoothness was founded on injustice and kept together by cowardice and tyranny; but the hope in me has been that matters would mend gradually, till the last struggle, which must needs be mingled with violence and madness, would be so short as scarcely to count.[76]

As for theoretical knowledge, when he took the step of joining the Democratic Federation, he later wrote: "I was blankly ignorant of economics; I had never so much as opened Adam Smith, or heard of Ricardo, or of Karl Marx."[77] In 1882 he read Henry George's *Progress and Poverty* and Wallace's *Land Nationalisation*[78] and something of Robert Owen and the French Utopian Socialists and also—it is evident from the many references—he was reading a good deal of William Cobbett, who seems to have had a pronounced influence upon the forthright polemical style of his later Socialist writings. In the winter of 1882–3 he attended a series of meetings at the Westminster Palace Chambers, organized by the Democratic Federation, on the subject of "Stepping-stones" to Socialism. The Austrian refugee Andreas Scheu, a furniture designer by trade, recalled Morris's first attendance:

> One evening, the meeting had scarcely started when Robert Banner, the book-binder, who sat behind me, passed me a note. . . . "The third man on your right is William Morris." I had never seen Morris before and looked at once in his direction. The fine, highly intelligent face of the man, his earnestness, the half-searching, half-dreamy look of his eyes, his plain unfashionable dress, made a deep sympathetic impression on me.[79]

On January 13th, 1883, he joined the Federation. In the same week he was made an Honorary Fellow of Exeter College, Oxford. His membership card for the Federation, counter signed by H. H. Champion, was simply inscribed, "William Morris, Designer."

The next few months were the true months of conversion. In one of his earliest Socialist lectures he spoke of that feeling of joy,

> when at last, after many a struggle with incongruous hindrances, our own chosen work has lain before us disentangled from all encumbrances and unrealities, and we have felt that nothing could withhold us, not even ourselves, from doing the work we were born to do, and that we were men and worthy of life.[80]

He plunged at once into the day-by-day round of activities:

> When I joined the Communist folk, I did what in me lay
> To learn the grounds of their faith. I read day after day
> Whatever books I could handle, and heard about and about
> What talk was going amongst them; and I burned up doubt, after
>   doubt,
> Until it befel at last that to others I needs must speak . . .[81]

On February 22nd, a friend noted in his diary: "He was bubbling over with Karl Marx, whom he had just begun to read in French. He praised Robert Owen immensely."[82] In March he delivered a lecture in Manchester so trenchant as to bring down the wrath of the leader-writers upon him. But nothing was more appropriate in his whole life than that one of his first public announcements that he was "one of the people called Socialists" was made with the "first comer," Professor Ruskin, in the chair. At the close of his address, in the Hall of University College, Oxford, Morris turned his appeal to the middle class:

> I have a last word or two to say in begging them to renounce their class pretensions and cast in their lot with the working men. . . . It may be that some of them are kept from actively furthering the cause which they believe in by that dread of organization . . . which is very common in England . . . more common among highly cultivated people, and . . . most common in our ancient universities. Since I am a member of a Socialist propaganda I earnestly beg those of you who agree with me to help us actively, with your time and your talents if you can, but if not, at least with your money, as you can. Do not hold aloof from us, since you agree with us, because we have not attained that delicacy of manners . . . which the long oppression of competitive commerce has crushed out of us.[83]

The reactions of the academic Podsnaps was immediate. "At the close of his address," *The Times* reported the next day,

> Mr. Morris announced himself a member of a socialist society and appealed for funds for the objects of the society. The Master of University then said to the effect that if he had announced this beforehand it was probable that the loan of the College-hall would have been refused.

Morris had crossed the "river of fire." And the campaign to silence him had begun.

What was the "river of fire," the something "alive and devouring," but the class division within society? Morris's conversion was a true conversion. It was not sudden, unannounced, a bolt out of the blue. It was in every sense a qualitative change in understanding and in action, for which all his life had prepared the way. In a certain sense he had already in his lectures advanced the theory of Socialism in relation to the decorative arts beyond any point which any other theorist had yet reached. But the final understanding was lacking. The understanding of the class struggle, submerged in many of his lectures, was only made apparent on his reading of *Capital*, in his discussions with Scheu and Bax and Hyndman, and his first Socialist activities. Once made apparent, all his previous thought came into unity, his action acquired new purpose and direction. One of his earliest Socialist lectures, in which he makes acknowledgement to Marx, shows clearly how all his old pre-occupations—his resistance to imperialism, his work for the National Liberal League—fell suddenly into place:

> Once again I tell you that our present system is not so much a confusion . . . as a tyranny: one and all of us in some way or other we are drilled to the service of Commercial War; if our individual aspirations or capacities do not fit in with it, so much the worse for them: the iron service of the capitalist will not bear the loss, the individual must; everything must give way to this; nothing can be done if a profit cannot be made of it: it is for this that we are overworked, are made to fear starvation, live in hovels, are herded . . . into foul places called towns . . . it is for this that we let half Scotland be depopulated . . . and turn its stout peasants and herdsmen into mere flunkies of idle fools: it is for this that we let our money, our name, our power, be used to drag off poor wretches from our pinched fields and our dreadful slums, to kill and be killed in a cause they know nothing of.

Imperialism he saw no longer as the outcome of ambitious statesmen and generals: "It is simply the agony of capitalism driven by a force it cannot resist to seek for new and ever new markets at any price and any risk." England is losing her favoured position in the world:

> What is to be done? . . . Conquer new markets from day to day; flatter and cajole the men of our colonies to consider themselves what they are not, Englishmen responsible for every quarrel England may lead them into: conquer valiant barbarians all over the world: rifle them rum them missionary, them into subjection, then train them into soldiers for civilization. . . .

And so to the most uncompromising paragraph of all:

> Here are two classes, face to face with each other. . . . No man can exist in society and be neutral, no-body can be a mere looker on: one camp or another you have got to join: you must either be a reactionary and be crushed by the progress of the race, and help it that way: or you must join in the march of progress, trample down all opposition, and help it that way.[84]

Here was Morris's greatest discovery—the discovery which his friends, for all their genius, could not make. Marx helped him to make it, but once it was made he accepted it as the inevitable conclusion of all his past thought. In its discovery he found his way forward both as an artist and as a man. His old dream of healing the division between artist and the people now became a vision to look forward to with certainty: that time when—

> the man of the most refined occupation, student, artist, physician . . . shall be able to speak to him who does the roughest labour in a tongue that they both know, and to find no intricacy of his mind misunderstood.[85]

The finest aspirations of the romantic revolt, which aroused his own desires for "Liberty, Equality, Fraternity" in his youth, now seemed possible of fulfilment:

> Not in Utopia, subterranean fields,
> Or some secreted island, Heaven knows where!
> But in the very world, which is the world
> Of all of us. . . .

Blake's Jerusalem might yet be built in earnest, and Shelley's Phantoms and Sages be given flesh and blood. The long romantic breach between aspiration and action was healed.

So it was that William Morris crossed the "river of fire." "How can we of

the middle classes, we the capitalists, and our hangers-on," help the workers?
he asked in January, 1884. His answer was decisive:

> By renouncing our class, and on all occasions when antagonism rises up
> between the classes casting in our lot with the victims. . . . There is no
> other way: and this way, I tell you plainly, will in the long run give us
> plenty of occasion for self-sacrifice. . . .[86]

Of his old friends, only Philip Webb and Charlie Faulkner, both of whom fully
knew his greatness, went with him. It was "the only time when I failed Morris,"
said Edward—soon to be Sir Edward—Burne-Jones many years later.[87] Swinburne, when Morris tried to enlist his aid, gave only his "sympathy":

> I do trust you will not . . . regard me as a dilettante democrat if I say
> that I would rather not join any Federation. What good I can do to the
> cause . . . will I think be done as well or better from an independent point
> of action and of view. . . .[88]

His years of revolt had ended in breakdown, and he was now the "prisoner of
Putney," beginning his thirty years of genteel retirement with the solicitor, Theo-
dore Watts-Dunton. Ruskin watched with encouragement from the further bank.
He had had one mental crisis already, and he knew his powers to be failing:

> It is better that you should be in a cleft stick than make one out of me—
> especially as my timbers are enough shivered already. In old British battles
> the ships that had no shot in their rigging didn't ask the disabled ones to
> help them.[89]

But Morris was finding new friends and comrades on every side. He was in
his fiftieth year, but he looked to the future with the excitement of youth. In
an allegorical poem, "The Three Seekers," he exorcised for the first time the
old despair, the fear of death, the restless fret of his middle years: and, in its
singing refrain, we hear the joy of his "new birth":

"There is no pain on earth," she said,
"Since I have drawn thee from the dead."

Laughing, "The world's my home," she said,
"Now I have drawn thee from the dead."

"Now life is little, and death is nought,
Since all is found that erst I sought."[90]

Notes

1. *Unpublished Letters of William Morris to the Rev. John Glasse* (Labour Monthly, 1951). "The Depression of Trade," Brit. Mus. Add. MSS. 45333.

2. "The Prospects of Architecture," *Works*, Vol. XXII, p. 131.

3. J. W. Mackail, *The Life of William Morris*, 2 Volumes (Longmans, 1899), II, p. 93.

4. May Morris, II, p. 69.

5. *Letters*, p. 113.

6. May Morris, II, p. 584.

7. "The Lesser Arts," *Works*, Vol. XXII, p. 22.

8. Ibid., p. 32.

9. From a pre-Socialist Lecture (1880), reprinted in part in May Morris, II, p. 68.

10. May Morris, II, p. 605.

11. Morris moved to Kelmscott House, Hammersmith (not to be confused with Kelmscott Manor in Lechlade) in 1878. It was Kelmscott House which became famous as a Socialist meeting-place.

12. "Art and the Beauty of the Earth," *Works*, Vol. XXII, p. 171.

13. Address to Nottingham Kyrle Society, 1881, May Morris, 1, pp. 201–2.

14. "The Prospects of Architecture," *Works*, Vol. XXII, p. 125.

15. See "The Lesser Arts" (1877): "People say to me often enough: If you want to make your art succeed and flourish, you must make it the fashion: a phrase which I confess annoys me; for they mean by it that I should spend one day over my work to two days trying to convince rich, and supposed influential people, that they care very much for what they really do not care in the least, so that it may happen according to the proverb: *Bell-wether took the leap, and we all went over.*", (*Works*, Vol. XXII, p. 13).

16. See also Mary Howitt, *An Autobiography* (1889), Vol. II, p. 170.

17. Mackail, II, p. 97.

18. Glasier, op. cit., p. 56.

19. Lethaby, op. cit., p. 94.

20. *Letters*, p. 157.

21. "The Prospects of Architecture," *Works*, Vol. XXII, p. 150.

22. "Textile Fabrics," Ibid., p. 294.

23. *Fortnightly Review*, March, 1903.

24. Andreas Scheu, *Umsturzkeime* [Seeds of Revolution] (?1920), Part III, Ch. VI.

25. May Morris, II, p. xxxvi.

26. *Letters*, p. 134.

27. Brit. Mus. Add. MSS. 45407, 45330.

28. *Letters*, p. 148.

29. May Morris, II, p. 66.

30. "The Art of the People," *Works*, Vol. XXII, p. 48.

31. "The Lesser Arts," Ibid., p. 25.

32. "The Beauty of Life," Ibid., p. 53.

33. Brit. Mus. Add. MSS. 45331.

34. "The Beauty of Life," *Works*, Vol. XXII, p. 76.

35. "Art and the Beauty of the Earth," Ibid., p. 170.

36. May Morris, II, p. 70.

37. "The Beauty of Life," *Works*, Vol. XXII, p. 65.

38. "The Prospects of Architecture," Ibid., p. 137.

39. *Letters*, p. 139.

40. *Letters*, p. 151.

41. Mackail, II, p. 7.

42. Mackail, II, p. 24.

43. "The Lesser Arts," *Works*, Vol. XXII, p. 13.

44. *Letters*, pp. 160–1.

45. *Letters*, p. 120.

46. See *Thomas Burt: an Autobiography* (1924), p. 52. Frederick Harrison and other Positivists organized a Committee to oppose the Afghan War, and Morris attended one of its meetings.

47. "The Art of the People," *Works*, Vol. XXII, p. 36.

48. Brit. Mus. Add. MSS. 45334. Some extracts from the lecture are in May Morris, II, pp. 53–62.

49. "How I Became a Socialist," *Justice*, June 16th, 1894.

50. Morris campaigned enthusiastically for Sir Charles Dilke, with the help of Burne-Jones and William De Morgan. See A.M.W. Stirling, *William De Morgan and His Wife* (1922), p. 144.

51. May Morris, II, p. 60.

52. Brit. Mus. Add. MSS. 45334.

53. Howell Collection, Bishopsgate Institute.

54. Broadhurst, op. cit., pp. 151–3.

55. May Morris, II, p. 72.

56. Morris to Broadhurst, April 4th, 1880, Brit. Lib. Polit. Science.

57. Handbill in Howell Collection.

58. Brit. Mus. Add. MSS. 45407.

59. May Morris, II, p. 581.

60. *Letters*, p. 144.

61. *Letters*, p. 146.

62. Handbill in Howell Collection.

63. Mackail, II, p. 8.

64. May Morris, II, p. 604.

65. "Art Under Plutocracy," *Works*, Vol. XXIII, p. 188.

66. *Letters*, p. 156.

67. Ibid., p. 144.

68. Ibid., pp. 176, 188.

69. *Letters*, p. 173.

70. Ibid., p. 132.

71. "Making the Best of It," *Works*, Vol. XXII, p. 117.

72. Ibid., p. 174.

73. "How I Became a Socialist," *Justice*, June 16th, 1894.

74. Jenny's breakdown shattered Morris for several months: see Mackail, II, p. 73.

75. The Federation's Radical character in 1882 is discussed by M. S. Wilkins, "The Non-Socialist Origins of England's First Socialist Organization," *Int. Rev. Social Hist.* IV, (1959), pp. 199–207.

76. *Letters*, p. 149.

77. "How I Became a Socialist," *Justice*, June 16th, 1894.

78. Morris to his daughter Jenny, November 13th, 1883, refers to Wallace's *Land Nationalisation:* "not nearly such a good book as George's but there are some nice things to remember in it," Brit. Mus. Add. MSS. 45339.

79. Scheu, op. cit.; Scheu gave a similar account to Mackail, II, pp. 95–6.

80. "The Lesser Arts of Life," *Works*, Vol. XXII, p. 269.

81. *The Pilgrims of Hope*, Section VI.

82. Mackail, II, p. 97.

83. "Art Under Plutocracy," *Works*, Vol. XXIII, p. 191.

84. Unpublished lecture, "Commercial War," Brit. Mus. Add. MSS. 45333.

85. Speech to the Kyrle Society, May Morris, I, p. 195.

86. "Art and Socialism," *Works*, Vol. XXIII, p. 213.

87. *Memorials*, II, p. 97.

88. Brit. Mus. Add. MSS. 45345.

89. Ibid.

90. *To-Day*, January, 1884.

POSTSCRIPT: 1976

FROM *WILLIAM MORRIS: ROMANTIC TO REVOLUTIONARY*

In twenty-one years (the interval between this book's first publication and this revised edition) the terrain of scholarship changes, and so also do the preoccupations of scholars. I have no intention of offering here a comprehensive bibliography of recent writing which bears on Morris studies. But some books must be mentioned and others must be discussed more carefully.

First mention may go to the William Morris Society which, over the past twenty years, has organised a valuable series of events, lectures, and publications. The Society's *Journal* carries an up-to-date bibliography, and in 1961 the Society's Honorary Secretary, Mr. R. C. H. Briggs, published a *Handlist* of Morris's addresses. A more complete list of lectures and speeches, and their dates of delivery, is to be found in Eugene D. LeMire's *Unpublished Lectures of William Morris*.[1] This presents in full for the first time ten lectures which had before been drawn upon only in my text or in May Morris's two volumes. Another interesting lecture (of 1889), and notes for a further one, have been published by Paul Meier.[2] Few important new letters have been published, apart from Morris's letters to J. L. Mahon.[3] A valuable collection of critical notices of Morris's work has been brought together by Peter Faulkner,[4] and at least two new selections of political writings have been made available.[5]

Much has been written on Morris's practice of the arts. I've done little to revise my own chapter on these, although I am aware that it is inadequate to its several themes. When so much of expert authority has been published, the wisest course for one without such expertise is reticence. An important revision to received views of Morris's influence was made by the late Peter Floud, who contested the view that the revolution in mid-Victorian taste was the consequence of "the Morris movement," and who emphasised his—sometimes idiosyncratic, sometimes conservative—part within a wider tradition of inno-

From *William Morris: Romantic to Revolutionary* by E. P. Thompson (New York: Pantheon Books, 1955, 1977).

vation.[6] Since Floud was kind enough to write to me approving of my chapter, I've let it stand, even though it follows at points the older convention. More recently there have been important new contributions from Paul Thompson, Ray Watkinson, and others.[7] Philip Henderson, in his biography of Morris, has also enlarged our knowledge of the Firm, drawing upon the correspondence of Warington Taylor and of Morris to Sir Thomas Wardle.[8] From these materials, and from others in California, a definitive history of the Firm could now be written.[9]

By contrast, twenty-one years' harvest of critical writing on Morris's poetry and prose is disappointing. Apart from one lecture by Jack Lindsay[10] and John Goode's important study (discussed at the end of this Postscript) I find little that I can recommend. This may indicate a continuing adverse judgment upon Morris's poetry, although I had expected that my own treatment of *The Defence of Guenevere* and *The Earthly Paradise* might have provoked a little comment, or at least disagreement, among scholars of English literature.[11] These chapters constitute an important part of my argument about the crisis of Romanticism in early Victorian England, and I remain as ready to defend them today as when they were first written. In one area one may detect the first signs of a "thaw" in the icy resistance to Morris: a generation nourished upon Tolkien and C.S. Lewis (himself a sympathetic critic of Morris),[12] is now willing to read with more complaisance the late prose romances. This increasing tolerance has enabled critics, whose prior interest is in Morris's political thought, to show a renewed respect for *The House of the Wolfings* and *The Roots of the Mountains*.[13] When this book first appeared, the only notice (so far as I am aware) that it received from the literary establishment was in a comminatory review in the *Times Literary Supplement*, which reported that many pages—

> are dedicated to defending the language of the saga translations and of the prose romances such as *The Earthly Paradise* [sic!] and *The Well at the World's End*. Mr. Thompson, in fact, concentrates upon just those aspects of Morris's work and thought which seem least relevant today.[14]

Criteria of relevance have now changed, and I suspect that I may today be criticised, more properly, for giving inadequate attention to the prose romances than for "defending" them to excess.

Paul Thompson's study of Morris is not limited to his work as a designer but offers a more comprehensive biography, structured around his work. Philip Henderson's new biography is strongest in its recovery of Morris's personal life and conflicts. Henderson repairs the obligatory silence of Mackail as to relations between William and Janey Morris and Dante Gabriel Rossetti, and he draws upon surviving correspondence between Janey and Rossetti which, at the time of my first writing, was not open to inspection. These letters illuminate the predicament of the three friends, but do not lead me to revise my earlier treatment. Philip Henderson is always perceptive[15] upon all matters other than Morris's political thought and action, and he often catches the nuances of personal relations better than I do: but where his interpretation rests upon Morris's poems I prefer to stand by my own account. Perhaps the most significant new evidence to come to light relates not to the Morrises but to Edward and Georgie Burne-Jones: for it now appears that during the height of Janey's and Rossetti's mutual obsession, Ned Burne-Jones was also preoccupied in a love-affair, with Mary Zambaco. Undoubtedly this will have thrown Georgie and Morris more upon each other's sympathy.[16] As for the relations between Morris and Rossetti in later years, the new evidence can lead only to mournful conclusions. Janey was beset with unexplained illnesses, perhaps of neurotic origin. Rossetti mocked at Morris in his private letters to Janey, calling him, during the Eastern Question agitation, "the Odger of the Future,"[17] while Morris commented, on Rossetti's death:

It makes a hole in the world, though I have seen so little of him lately, and might very likely never have seen him again: he was very kind to me when I was a youngster. He had some of the very greatest qualities of genius, most of them indeed; what a great man he would have been but for the arrogant misanthropy that marred his work, and killed him before his time: the grain of humility which makes a great man one of the people and no lord over them, he lacked, and with it lost the enjoyment of life which would have kept him alive, and sweetened all his work for him and us.[18]

Some part of Janey Morris's correspondence remains in private hands in the United States. It was made available to Henderson and (previously) to Rosalie Glynn Grylls (Lady Mander) for her *Portrait of Rossetti* (1964). Mrs. Grylls, as may be proper in a biographer, is always ready to extend sympathy to her subject, and, as may also be proper, she extends it also to the woman whom he loved. It needn't follow that she should feel obliged to write ungenerously about William Morris. But she loses few opportunities of doing so. She implies, in a knowing way, that Morris was a failure as a lover: his early love poems were thrown together in a few minutes snatched from tapestry or wall-paper (but Morris was at work in neither medium when *The Defence of Guenevere* poems were written). Morris was drawn to the North, Janey and Rossetti to the South, and Grylls, who is one for the South also, commiserates with Janey. If Janey was often silent (Grylls notes with mature self-congratulation) this was only because she "saw through" Morris's Socialist friends, notably Shaw. And more of all this.

I don't wish to be misunderstood. It's no part of my intention to offer a moralistic judgment on Janey's and Rossetti's behaviour. William and Janey Morris were not happy together, and in another time it might have been better if they could have separated and found other partners. But what gives offence is Gryll's implication that if Morris accepted the role of *mari complaisant* (even of a wounded and miserable one) this allows her to portray him as unmanly and as a subject for ridicule. This is one of the most ancient and most disabling of male-dominative stereotypes of sexual relations, and one which, in my own view, derives its damaging potency more from the universal dictatorship of the stereotype itself than from any inherent sexual determinations. Moreover, it is one which has been transmitted with peculiar force within feminine conventions. For generations women advised each other to condone or overlook the infidelities of their husbands, but to despise the husband who extended a similar courtesy to his wife. In short, while wishing in no way to pass judgment on Janey and Rossetti, I suggest that it was a matter of honour in Morris that he did not, in that difficult situation, act the conventional Victorian part of the "wronged" husband. For the rest, I haven't myself attempted to consult any still-unpublished letters from Janey in Mrs. Troxell's collection. I think the matter has been pried into enough.[19]

Much new work has appeared on the Socialists of the 1880s and 1890s, although little bears directly on the Socialist League. My own account inevitably concentrated on Morris's relations with Hyndman and gave inadequate attention to the S.D.F. at branch or district level. Chushichi Tsuzuki's study of Hyndman gives a fair account of his end of the story.[20] I have serious disagreements with Tsuzuki's judgements here,[21] but fewer with his capable study of Eleanor Marx.[22] At the time of writing only the first volume of Yvonne Kapp's definitive life of Eleanor Marx has appeared.[23] The next volume, due to appear very shortly, should give us the first complete study of the Avelings' work for the League and in the Bloomsbury Socialist Society: to judge by its predecessor, the book is likely to be both illuminating and persuasively partisan. And we now have fuller accounts of the activity of other colleagues of Morris in the Socialist propaganda.[24] Dona Torr's study of Tom Mann is indispensable for understanding the choppy period of new unionist upsurge and of the fragmentation of Socialist organization in the late 1880s.[25] My own study of Tom Maguire enlarges upon the history of the League in the West Riding in the same years.[26] The Fabian Society has also attracted a lot of scholarly attention.[27] And more is now known about the ideas and the indefatigable Socialist propaganda in the 1880s of George Bernard Shaw: from his diary it appears that he was delivering up to 100 lectures and talks, under various auspices, each year. And it also appears from these sources that the theoretical confrontation between Fabianism and "Morrisism" was even more conscious and prolonged than I had supposed.[28] This by no means exhausts the relevant new studies; no doubt I have overlooked work of importance; but this survey must suffice.

There remain some more substantive questions (and books) to be discussed. Several of the most recent studies of Morris or of British Socialism draw heavily upon my work, sometimes with generous acknowledgement and sometimes without. In short, my book came to be recognised as a "quarry" of information, although in one or two instances it appears that it was a suspect quarry, to be worked surreptitiously for doctoral advancement. One ought not to object to this: a quarry should release materials into the general fabric of scholarship. But what if my book was not a quarry but a construction meriting attention in its own right? And what if the stones lifted from it end up by adding only to the featureless sprawl of academic suburbia?

At least the question may be put. But one must be careful as to *how* the question is put. Several of my successors, in volumes appearing from the most reputable academic presses, are in agreement that the question can be put in only one way: my scholarship is vitiated by Marxist dogmatism. A work "of intelligent and exhaustive scholarship," in one generous account, "but it is marred by the author's intense Marxian bias." Morris's activities "are examined through the prism of the class struggle and the result is a somewhat distorted view of Morris's ideas."[29] Another finds my book "flawed by its misguided attempt to present its object as an orthodox Marxist."[30] A less generous critic notes that my book devoted "some 900 pages to demonstrate that Morris was really a Marxist."[31]

I had thought that the book was something rather different. It is, in a central respect, an argument about the Romantic tradition and its transformation by Morris. (It is of interest that I and Raymond Williams, whose important *Culture and Society* appeared three years after this book, should have been, unknown to each other, working upon different aspects of the Romantic critique of Utilitarianism.) But, leaving this aside, one has to ask whether it may not be the political commitment of Morris, and not of Marx, which has given offence to these authors? In which case my own offence has been chiefly that of showing an intense *Morrisian* bias? The question is difficult: it is true that in 1955 I allowed some hectoring political moralisms, as well as a few Stalinist pieties, to intrude upon the text. I had then a somewhat reverent notion of Marxism as a received orthodoxy, and my pages included some passages of polemic whose vulgarity no doubt makes contemporary scholars wince. The book was published at the height of the Cold War. Intellectual McCarthyism was not confined to the United States, although few in the subsequent generations understand its discreet British modes of operation. Marxist sympathies were so disreputable that they could find little expression outside of Communist publications; and the vulgarity of my own polemic[32] can only be understood against the all-pervasive and well-furnished vulgarities of the anti-Marxist orthodoxies of that time.

The climate can be illustrated by the welcome afforded my book in the non-Socialist press.[33] This welcome was mainly a silence, broken by the review in the *Times Literary Supplement*, headed "Morris and Marxism." The reviewer reported that my book was "heavily biased by Marxism" and "splenetic in tone"; the "remarkable feat" of its author is that "he manages to sustain a mood of ill-temper through a volume of 900 pages." My citations from Morris's political writings "show how fluffy were Morris's socialist views," and the book as a whole "merely serves to emphasize aspects of Morris which are better left forgotten."[34] It is clear that it was Morris, and not Thompson, nor even Marx, who must be pushed back into the silence of disrepute.

All this was (in those days) predictable. So far from dismaying one it was a tonic to one's fighting-blood: in a sense, even one's self-righteous sectarian errors were confirmed within the circular field of antagonism to such official lampoons and silences. Despite this (and perhaps because of the post-1956 "thaw") the book found its way into university and public libraries. Some years afterwards it began to find its way out again, being rather widely stolen; for several years (I am told) it has been "missing" from both the British Museum and the Bodleian, although whether through the agency of the Congress for Cultural Freedom or of readers converted by Morris to an over-literal repudiation of bourgeois property-rights (but what is bourgeois about the common use-rights of a library?) must be left undetermined. In all this, the book became typed, by enemies and even by some friends, as offering only one finding: the Morris=Marx equation. And yet the book, while perhaps offering too tidy an account of that relation, by no means contented itself with showing Morris ending his life in an orthodox Marxist terminus. The point was, rather, that Morris was an original Socialist thinker whose work was complementary to Marxism. And in repeated emphases, and in particular in the stress upon Morris's genius as a moralist, it should not have been difficult for a sensitive reader to have detected a submerged argument within the orthodoxy to which I then belonged.

But this line of argument is an uneasy one, since it focusses attention on my own intellectual evolution (and apologetics) and distracts attention from our proper concern: William Morris and his political thought. And we should return to the question already proposed: have some recent writers used the criticism of my book to mask their ulterior dislike of Morris, so that for Thompson's "intense Marxian bias" we ought really to read "Morris's uncompromising commitment to revolutionary Socialism?" For if I had really falsified my account of Morris's positions, one would suppose that these critics would go on to correct my account, in informed and accurate ways. But I don't find that this has been done. Thus Willard Wolfe, who affirms that my attempt to present Morris as a Marxist is "misguided," offers no close examination of Morris's Socialist writings, and presents, in succession, the following judgements on Morris's Socialism: (a) his lectures of the 1880s "advocated a form of Radical-individualist utopianism that was very similar to Shaw's" (p. 132 n.48);* (b) his Socialism was "ethical-aesthetic" (p. 162); and (c) Morris "must be classed among the Christian Socialist recruits" to the S.D.F. since his Socialism was "essentially religious in character" and was "grounded on an essentially Christian ideal of brotherhood" (pp. 174, 301). This may be good enough for Yale University Press, but it would have been rejected by the Editor of *Commonweal*: what it seems to argue is that Morris's Socialism was really very nice, and never rude, although it leaves unresolved the question as to how "Radical-individualist Utopianism" was reconciled with the "Christian ideal of brotherhood."

J. W. Hulse, in *Revolutionists in London*,[35] does a little better: but not much. He has had a good idea for a book and has executed that idea unevenly. His intention was to treat the inter-relations between the ideas of five remarkable men, co-habitants of London in the 1880s and 1890s—Stepniak, Kropotkin, Morris, Shaw, and Bernstein. Despite the fact that the ideas under discussion float around in a state of political weightlessness, some parts of the study are executed well. It may be because I know the subject best that I find the study of Morris to be the worst. Hulse, who knows that my book is marred by "intense Marxian bias,"[36] knows a great many more things about Morris's Socialism, although his knowledge is supported more often by assertion than by argument: thus (of the Manifesto of the Socialist League), "it incorporates several of the Marxian arguments, but the basic tone was moderate"(p. 85); of the Split:

> Morris found it necessary to make the break because Hyndman's faction was too authoritarian, too wildly militant, and too opportunistic—in short, too Marxist (p. 85).

We are also reassured that "the doctrine of the class struggle was one of the Marxian ideas that was only gradually and partially assimilated by Morris (p. 81). In short, once again Morris's Socialism is shown to have been nice; and if Marxism is defined as "authoritarian," "wild," and "opportunistic" (i.e. *not*

---

*In this Postscript I distinguish references back to the revised text of this book by placing these in italics thus (*162*), from references to the works of other authors under discussion, which are thus (p. 162).

nice) then Morris can scarcely have been associated with it unless by accident. But it is not clear that Hulse has helped us towards any precisions. Since he has evidently made no study of *Commonweal* or of the actual political movement[37] his assertions cannot be shown to be supported by anything more than academic self-esteem.

This is a pity, since Hulse does have a correction of substance to offer to my account. He argues that Morris may have been more influenced by Kropotkin and by the Communist-Anarchists than has been generally allowed: in particular in his notion of federated communes, as envisaged in "The Society of the Future" and in *News from Nowhere*. It is a fair point: the "withering away of the State" was not a major preoccupation of Engels or of the Marxist circles of the 1880s, whereas it was a preoccupation shared by Morris and Kropotkin. (Morris noted in 1887 that he had "an Englishman's wholesome horror of government interference & centralization which some of our friends who are built on the German pattern are not quite enough afraid of" [*451*]). Morris's imagination may well have been stimulated more by Kropotkin and by arguments with his followers in the League than I have suggested. But Hulse damages his own argument by special pleading and thin scholarship, thickened up with anti-Marxist rancour. His conclusion offers an eclectic's bazaar which might stand in for a dozen other contemporary academic accounts: "Morris's Socialism might best be described as catholic, borrowing from the Middle Ages and from Russian nihilism, as well as from Mill and from Marx" (p. 110). It might "best be described" in this way if the object of the exercise is polite conversation, but not if it is accurate definition: *what*, one wonders, was borrowed, and how were these unlikely elements combined? "It serves little purpose," Hulse concludes, "to insist that Morris belonged more to one branch of Socialism, or Communism, or anarchism, than to another" (p. 109). That may be so: the "claiming" or Morris for this or that tendency has less purpose than I once supposed myself. But what, surely, may serve a purpose, if we wish to attend to Morris, is to define what Morris's Socialism *was*, what were its controlling ideas, values, and strategies? And this can scarcely be done if we disregard his polemic against Fabianism on the one hand, and Anarchism on the other. By neglecting both, and by straining the case for Kropotkin's influence, Hulse ends up as only one more (muddled) claimant.

I would not have laboured my disagreements with Hulse if they didn't illustrate a very general problem of the interpretation of Morris. What is being done, again and again, is that a stereotype of Marxism in its subsequent evolution is being brought back to Morris, and the attempt is then made either to dissociate Morris from it or to assimilate him altogether to it (discarding anything unassimilable as "immaturities" or Romantic hang-overs). But the important question might be not whether Morris was or was not a Marxist, but whether he was a Morrisist; and, if he was, whether this was a serious and coherent position in its own right? The problem is illustrated, from different directions, by two studies, both more serious than any noticed up to this point: Stanley Pierson's *Marxism and the Origins of British Socialism*[38] and Paul Meier's *La Pensée Utopique de William Morris*.

Stanley Pierson does not offer a stereotype of Marxism, and his study is in most respects well-founded. He is interested in the intellectual tendencies within British Socialism between 1880 and 1900, and he takes us steadily through intellectual precursors, and thence to Hyndman, Morris, Bax, Carpenter, the Fabians, Glasier, Blatchford, Mahon, Hardie, the Anarchists, the Labour Churches. They are all put together between the same covers, informatively and often shrewdly, and they are held in place, not only by the binding, but also by a controlling argument which, summarised, is this: when Marxist ideas became a presence in British life, they operated upon a ground of native intellectual traditions: those of Utilitarianism, of Christian nonconformity, and of the Romantic tradition as mediated by Carlyle and Ruskin. No sooner had the new ideas appeared than they became subject to a process of assimilation within the older traditions: they became "attached to deeply ingrained attitudes and feelings." "Marxist theory, in any strict sense, disintegrated rapidly in the Britain of the eighties," but only through "a complex process of mediation" which diverted the native traditions into new channels. Pierson argues that in different ways both Fabianism and the Marxism of Hyndman reverted to the control of the utilitarian tradition; Morris, of course, signals the junction of the Marxist and Romantic traditions, but it was an incomplete junction ("The new system of thought was superimposed on his earlier ideas rather than integrated with them" [p. 80]), and in the result those activists most influenced by Morris "fell back on the moral sentiments released by a disintegrating [Nonconformist] religious tradition" (p. 275). "Marxist ideas entered creatively into the working-class movement only through the breakup of the distinctive synthesis which Marx had constructed" (pp. 276–7). In this breakup any inheritance from Morris came largely by way of *Merrie England*, or through the ethical and sometimes religious Socialism of Independent Labor Party evangelists like the Glasiers—a Socialism which had lost both "the cutting edge of serious theoretical analysis" and the "reach" for creative alternatives (p. 276).

This account is fair and persuasive. At one level it is an acceptable account of what took place; and Pierson only strengthens his argument when he points out that, so far from British development being unique, "later European Marxism has followed much the same pattern of breakdown and reassimilation" to national traditions (p. 278), even when the resulting mixture was sometimes acclaimed as orthodox "Marxism." But at another level, which must most concern the student of Morris, the account is less acceptable. To begin with, this intellectual history is seen in terms of the polite culture: but when we consider the problem of the relation of Socialist theory to the working-class movement in 1880–1900, the "inherited pattern of thought and feeling" which demands attention is not that of Utilitarianism, nor of Romanticism, nor even (except for certain regions) Nonconformity, but that of Labourism—that is, a class culture, already with a long history of struggle, with its own organisational forms and strategies, as well as a certain class morale, although these strategies and forms were in important ways influenced by, and sometimes subordinated to, the ideas which Pierson describes. This need not contradict Pierson's argument; for this class culture was able to assimilate the "ethical Socialism" of *Merrie England* and of some part of Morris, in ways which were not negligible but which still fell short of challenging the controlling strategies of the movement; leaving, nevertheless, a residue in terms of motivation, goal, rhetoric, "Clause Four" obstinacy and even—more than some Marxist historians are willing to allow—Socialist priorities expressed at local levels, which have contributed much to the ambiguities of the modern Labour movement and to the difficulties of its more abject parliamentary leaders.

What this raises, acutely, is the problem of ideology, and this is not a problem which Pierson addresses.[39] For the record is something more than one of intellectual "mediations" or "assimilations." Very sharp theoretical confrontations were taking place, in which emergent Socialist thought contested with the "common-sense" of Victorian liberal-capitalist society and its dominant ideological illusions. And the reminder leads us to two attendant considerations. First, in what sense did the new Socialist theory (and its strategies) constitute a critical break, or rupture, not with this or that point of liberal Victorian thought, but with the organising ideas of bourgeois Liberalism? If we argue that it did constitute such a rupture, it need not follow that the new Socialist theory was in all respects mature, coherent, and without self-contradiction;[40] it follows only that at critical points, and in certain controlling ideas, this theory was antagonistic to bourgeois ideology, and, specifically, proposed not the amelioration of the liberal capitalist state but its revolutionary transformation. It will follow that, when we attend to Pierson's arguments about "assimilation," we will be alert to see how far such assimilation went, and whether it went so far as to dissolve the revolutionary pretentions of the new theory and drag it back, across the "rupture," into an accommodation with the old: or whether it served only to confuse and constrict (perhaps in serious ways) the new. Thus Pierson may be right (I think he is) to argue that the Fabians and the Marxists of the S.D.F. (and of other European sections) shared an abbreviated notion of economic man which had a good deal in common with the utilitarian tradition. But the Fabians matched this with theories of rent and of value, of the State, and of history, and with a strategy of permeation, which clearly dragged them back across the ideological divide; whereas the S.D.F., despite all the difficulties which Hyndman presents, continued to offer, until the eve of the World War, a confused and sectarian theory of revolutionary Socialism.[41]

I'm not suggesting that there are some talismanic concepts (Marx's theory of value, the theory of the State) which allow us instantly to identify whether the controlling theory of any person or group is "bourgeois" or "revolutionary." Analysis will never be as easy as that. Still less am I suggesting that there is one single, "correct," immanent Socialist orthodoxy. I'm arguing, as I argued twenty-one years ago, that there *is* a "river of fire." One has to resist a tendency in historians of ideas to see concepts only in their lineage of inheritance and in their mutations: this was mediated by that, and that was assimilated into the other, and all this went on in a world of discourse as congenial as the reading-rooms in which we consult the old periodicals. But—and this is our second consideration—these ideas inhabited actual people in actual contexts (often contexts of serious class confrontation—Bloody Sunday, the miners' strikes, the Sudan War, the new unionism), and the ideas had work to do in the present before they were passed on down the line. It might even be asked (although this is at odds with certain notions of the academic discipline) whether certain ideas were *right?*

In the face of these considerations, doubts as to Pierson's analysis multiply. It lacks not only any argument about critical breaks between opposing intel-lectual systems, but also any sense of *politics*. We can follow the argument only as it bears upon Morris. The entry might best be through the problem of imperialism, which Pierson never faces, since imperialism is not, in his sense of the term, an intellectual tradition. But if we set ourselves in 1890, and employ hindsight, the major disaster which was bearing down upon the European So-cialist and working-class movements was the World War and the ignominious collapse of the Second International. Insofar as this disaster was the consequence of those complex processes which we group together as "imperialism," then surely the responses to these processes, and to national-chauvinist complicity within the working-class movement, will dwarf in importance Pierson's more intellectual criteria of classification? Applying this test, we find that the response of the S.D.F. to imperialism was contradictory; the response of the I.L.P. was evasive and ambiguous. The Fabian response was wholly unambiguous; indeed, at one time the Fabians were unabashed advocates of imperial "rationalisa-tion."[42] The response of William Morris was also, as I show in detail, unam-biguous and indeed prophetic.

This might suggest two things: either that Pierson's conventional description of the "Romantic" derivation of Morris's ideas (with Marxist concepts "super-imposed" upon Romanticism but not "integrated" with it) is an inadequate account: or that the Romantic tradition had possibilities of antagonism to capitalist common-sense a good deal tougher than it is usual to attribute to it. I believe that *both* suggestions are correct. For Pierson's account of Morris's political theory manages, in some way, to leave out Morris's politics: his *Commonweal* notes, his active organization, his anti-imperialist and internationalist actions, his struggle to defeat chauvinism within the movement. Pierson's inattention is such that he is able to write that Morris "virtually dissolved moral claims in aesthetic feelings" (p. 275)[43] and that "Morris carried much further the tendency (evident in Carlyle and Ruskin) toward eliminating clear acknowledgement of those impulses in men which did not harmonize with their desire for fellowship and beauty."[44] These are odd comments to make upon a thinker who argued that "the death of all art" was preferable to its survival among an elite which owed its condition to class supremacy (*664*); and who, more than any other of this time, cast his eye forward to the disasters of our century, identified the "Manichean hatred of the world" loose in the polite culture (*240*), envisaged the possibility of imperialism leading on to "a regular epoch of war" (*428*), and of the transition to Socialism proving to be "more terrible, far more confused and full of suffering than the period of the fall of Rome" (*723*), and who, finally, argued that the "tremendous organization under which we live," rather than "lose anything which really is its essence . . . will pull the roof of the world down upon its head" (*542*).[45] It's not easy to see how Pierson can derive such startlingly prophetic foresight from a consciousness which refused to acknowledge impulses in men other than their desire for fellowship and beauty. "From the Marxist standpoint," Pierson assures us, "the Socialism of Morris was regressive—a relapse into the subjectivism and idealism from which Marx has attempted to rescue earlier Socialist reformers"; in short, Morris reverted to "Utopianism" (pp. 274, 84).[46]

So there are two disagreements, and each of them is large. First, I hold, against Pierson, that certain critical and controlling Socialist concepts were not "superimposed" upon Morris's Romantic critique, but were indeed integrated with it, and in such a way as to constitute a rupture in the older tradition, and to signal its transformation.[47] Insofar as these concepts were consonant with those of Marx, and were in some cases derived directly from Marxist sources, we ought to call them Marxist. Second, I hold, against Pierson, that the Romantic tradition is not to be defined only in terms of its traditional, conservative, "regressive," "escapist," and "utopian" characteristics—and hence to be seen as a continual undertow threatening to draw Morris back to "subjectivism" and "idealism"—but contained within it resources of a quite different nature, capable of undergoing this transformation independently of the precipitate of Marx and Engels's writing. This is to say, the moral critique of capitalist process was pressing forward to conclusions consonant with Marx's critique, and it was Morris's particular genius to think through this transformation, effect this junction, and seal it with action. Nor should Pierson have been unaware that the typing of this Romantic critique as "regressive," "utopian," and "idealist" is a facile way of getting out of the problem, for an alternative way of reading that tradition had been proposed, not only in this book, in 1955, but, very cogently, by Raymond Williams in *Culture and Society* in 1958. If Pierson is right that "from the Marxist standpoint the Socialism of Morris was regressive"—and we can't know how Marx himself would have seen it—this may only be a comment on the imaginative lethargy and theoretical constriction which orthodox Marxism was undergoing from the 1880s. It need not prove (if it is true) that the juncture was impossible or that Morris was an intellectual incompetent. It might even mean that orthodox Marxism turned its back upon a juncture which it neglected to its own peril and subsequent disgrace.

I prefer to press the issue in this way, since I can now see, very much more clearly than when I first wrote this book, the danger of the other stereotype. This argues that William Morris "became *a* Marxist," was "converted *to* Marxism," &c. The danger is to be found throughout M. Paul Meier's weighty and often helpful study.[48] I'm sorry that I must take issue with him, for this major attention paid to Morris's political thought by a scrupulous French scholar is yet one more indication that this thought is alive and is not confined to a national idiom. Meier has carefully considered classical, utopian and other influences upon Morris; he has examined with the greatest care every evidence of Marxist influence upon him, either through texts or by way of conversations with Engels and with Bax,[49] and he has then assembled all the elements of Morris's writings about Communist society (and the transitional stage of Socialism) and has presented these with greater system than I (or, it must be said, Morris) attempted. All this is done lucidly and with generous respect for his subject. One can be assured that the book will put a final end to much rubbish.

But major difficulties remain. Meier offers Morris to us as an orthodox Marxist, and his notion of this orthodoxy is heavily influenced by its subsequent Marxist-Leninist definition. When Morris fails to match these requirements, Meier is able to apologise for him, with sympathetic allusion to his weaknesses in economic analysis, the lack of available Marxist texts, or to his Leftist immaturities or vestigial idealist survivals. The notion of Marxism as a correct truth is assumed throughout, and Morris is judged approvingly in terms of his approximation to this. Meier by no means intends to diminish his subject's stature or to disallow his original influence upon Socialist thought; but, in the result, he does both.

A small part of this lies in the treatment of Morris-Engels relations, already discussed in my text. The Engels-Lafargue correspondence[50] became available subsequent to my first edition: at some places, where Meier derives from it illumination, I derive only irritation. It is impossible, in my view, to study this and other evidence without concluding that on occasion Engels and the extended political family of Marx (operating largely through the German party) had a mischievous and elitist influence upon the European movement. This is perhaps only a small defect to set against the immense and positive influence of Engels's central work, and the perspicacity of many of his judgments. But this small defect rubbed rather sharply, on occasion, against Morris's shins, and (after reading the Lafargue letters) I sharpened my own judgments at one point in the revision (470–1). By 1887–8 Morris had reason to feel that his shins were raw. The actions of the "Marxists" of the League had been damaging and uncomradely; although their strategy was an improvement upon Morris's purism, it was folly in them to force matters to an issue on the least significant issue (that of parliamentary candidatures);[51] the attempt to manipulate a doctrinal unity of the European movement on the basis of the German party's programme justified Morris's irritation at Bax being "steeped in the Marxite pickle" (*471*); and (a point I had overlooked) on top of all this Morris's continued solidarity with the German party resulted, early in 1888, in his being dunned for the very heavy sum of £1,000 in a libel action.[52] Indeed, in Morris's personal encounters with the Marxist family circle, one is chiefly impressed by his forbearance.

But, questions of tactics and of personality apart, other questions remain. Meier presses the claim that Engels's subterranean influence can be sensed throughout Morris's writings; indeed, he presses this very far, and further than I can possibly follow him. Again and again, when Meier notes a congruity between Morris and Marxist text, he assumes that Morris could not have reached such a position independently, and he speculates upon a derivation—a sight of an unpublished manuscript, a mediation through Bax. Sometimes the case is well-sustained.[53] At other times it is sustained by little more than the assumption that Morris was incapable of arriving at any original "Marxist" conclusion by his own route:[54] *"Malgré notre sincère admiration pour son génie,"* Meier writes, *"et notre refus de ne voir en lui qu'un rêveur, il nous est difficile de croire qu'il ait pu s'élever tout seul à ce niveau théorique"* (p. 409).[55] At other times, again we are faced with exactly that juncture between Morris and Marxism which has been my theme. We needn't waste time on the trivial question of ascribing priority of thought to Morris or to Engels. What Meier is doing, when he insists that Morris's Socialist concepts must always be derivative from "Marxism," is, first, narrowing the notion of Marxism to a kind of family tradition—a sort of Royal Legitimacy from which alone descent may be derived—and, second, gravely underestimating the vigour of the tradition which Morris had transformed, and which still stood quite as much at his back as Hegel stood at the back of Marx.

A striking example arises in Meier's treatment of dialectical historical consciousness. He cites the famous passage from the conclusion to *A Dream of John Ball* ("I pondered how men fight and lose the battle. . . .") and notes, as I had noted, its congruity with a passage of Engels's *Ludwig Feuerbach* (722). But for Meier such a coincidence can't be accidental, and he goes on to speculate upon Morris's knowledge of unpublished sources of Marxist dialectics. This speculation has a little point to it. As Meier notes, the conclusion to Note C in the League's *Manifesto* (739) expresses a dialectical sense of historical process, written in Morris's style, although we know that the metaphor of "the spiral" is one that he owed to Bax (pp. 689–92, 693). And, as Meier also notes, there was then no available instruction-kit of Marxist dialectics. Ergo, Morris had received tuition in this, either directly from the author of *The Dialectics of Nature* (unpublished until 1925) or by way of Bax.

There are two objections to this. The first (too complex to press here) is that it is a matter of argument whether anything was gained by formalising "the dialectic" in this way. If we are thinking of contradiction, and of the "double-edged, double-tongued" process of social change, Morris had already grasped this, and was confirmed in it by his reading of *Capital*. The second is that, once Morris had reached Socialist conclusions and effected a definitive rupture with Whiggish notions of progress, he must—and did—arrive at a dialectical understanding of process, not just because he had arrived at "Marxism," but because of the whole force of the Romantic tradition that pressed behind him. Indeed, few passages of his writings have a greater sense of inevitability than the final meditations in *John Ball*. The Romantic critique is easily described as "regressive" or "nostalgic" because it is grounded upon an appeal to pre-capitalist values: and this is most specifically so in Morris, with his imaginative location of value in medieval, Old Icelandic, and Germanic contexts. As Williams has noted, Morris carries directly through into his Socialist thought some of the terms of the Romantic critique of Utilitarianism, as in the opposition of the notion of community (or "true society") to "mechanical civilization,"[56] So that it is difficult to see how Morris could have transformed that tradition if he had *not* attained to a dialectical notion (Bax's "spiral") of the reassertion at a new level and in new forms of pre-capitalist values of community and of "barbarism."[57]

Meier, in presenting Morris's thought as system, clarifies much: but he loses the understanding of its own authentic dynamic—how and where it broke through on its own. And I must insist upon the importance of my chapter, "The 'Anti-Scrape,' " a chapter which I dare say impatient Socialist readers generally skip. For this, as much as "The River of Fire," analyses Morris at the point of transforming a tradition, when he is confronted by problems which demand a solution both in practice and in theory. "The essence of what Ruskin taught us," Morris said, "was really nothing more recondite than this, that the art of any epoch must of necessity be the expression of its social life."[58] This was, please note, what Ruskin taught, and not Marx, and in 1880, when he had never so much as heard of Marx's name, Morris was writing:

> So the life, habits, and aspirations of all groups and classes of the community are founded on the economical conditions under which the mass of the people live, and it is impossible to exclude socio-political questions from the consideration of aesthetics.[59]

It was to "Anti-Scrape" that he spoke, in 1884, of the new understanding of history:

> Inchoate order in the remotest times . . . moving forward ever towards something that seems the very opposite of that which it started from and yet the earlier order never dead but living in the new, and slowly moulding it to a recreation of its former self (236).

The thought prefigures *A Dream of John Ball*, and entails the same dialectical sense of process. Bax (or Engels) may have found a name for this (the "spiral") but Morris was already immersed in the problems which it named: why was it impossible to reproduce Gothic architecture? How were the handicrafts of an earlier social order (unless by some spiral of change) to be revived? And in the same Address Morris paused to acknowledge *both* Ruskin and the Marx of *Capital*. But what he acknowledged as a debt to Marx was not some total and new revelation as to historical process but a specific understanding of the effects of the capitalist mode of production, for profit rather than use, upon the workshops of the "manufacturing system" (238). This can't be seen just as a conversion *by* Marx *to* "Marxism." It is a juncture of *two* strong traditions, and the second didn't attain to its supremacy only after assassinating the first.

    So that I can accept neither Pierson's notion that certain Marxist concepts were "superimposed" upon Morris's Romanticism, without integration; nor Meier's implicit judgment that Romanticism is co-terminous with "idealism" (in its orthodox Marxist connotation), and hence to be sloughed off when Morris became "a Marxist."[60] And if we have to choose between errors, it may be the second which is the more disabling. I may seem to be dancing on the point of a pin, but others have danced there before me. Raymond Williams, when offering in 1958 a cogent criticism of the self-contradictions of English Marxist critics (including myself) noted:

> It certainly seems relevant to ask English Marxists who have interested themselves in the arts whether this is not Romanticism absorbing Marx,

rather than Marx transforming Romanticism. It is a matter of opinion which one would prefer to happen (p. 274).

But, if we let Morris stand in for "Romanticism," these are not the only alternatives. It is possible also to envisage the Romantic tradition, transformed as it was by Morris (in part through his encounter with Marx), entering into a common Communist tradition to which it could contribute its particular emphases, vocabulary, and concerns. It was a distinctive contribution of *Culture and Society* to show how tough this long Romantic critique of industrial capitalism had been; and I would add that Williams's own writing, over two decades, has exemplified how tough a mutation of that tradition can still be, and how congruent to the thought of Marx.

At least we have to ask what could lie inside the phrase, "Marx transforming Romanticism"? This might stand for what was actually effected in Morris's own thought. Or it might only mean that Marxism could gobble Romanticism up, both beak and quill, assimilating its good faith as useful nutriment, and discarding its "sentimentalism," its moral realism, and its utopian courage as so much idealist excrement. And it is this second response which only too often appears to characterise Engels's reactions to Morris. There was a brief moment of mutual warmth at the time of the "Split," when Morris was delighted to find the Old Norse Edda on Engels's table and responded by reading him some passages from *Sigurd*: "It went off very well."[61] Thereafter the disdainful and dismissive references multiply: Engels could not be bothered to "manage" this "rich artist-enthusiast" and "sentimental socialist" (*471*). There is no evidence that he read *Hopes and Fears for Art* (1882) nor *Signs of Change* (1888), and there is evidence that he left *News from Nowhere* unread. He did read *Socialism, Its Growth and Outcome*, and signalled a tepid approval, but this was a text of the movement which he was scanning for its utility: there is not the least suggestion that he might have had anything to learn from Morris in his turn. As I noted in 1959, "while Morris strained hard and successfully to understand and absorb much of Engels's tradition, Engels made no comparable effort in Morris's direction."[62]

Marx, whose early revolt was germane to the Romantic tradition, might have met Morris more warmly. But this can't be passed off as a matter of temperament. Engels's disdain for Morris exemplifies the narrowing orthodoxy of those years, a narrowing noted not only in his own writings but in the Marxist tradition more generally. As tendencies towards determinism and positivism grew, so the tradition suffered a general theoretical closure, and the possibility of a juncture between traditions which Morris offered was denied. The Romantic critique of capitalism, however transformed, became suspect as "moralism" and "utopianism." I should not need, in 1976, to labour the point that the ensuing lack of moral self-consciousness (and even vocabulary) led the major Marxist tradition into something worse than confusion.[63] But this helps us to identify two important points about Morris's contemporary significance. First, it is more important to understand him as a (transformed) Romantic than as a (conforming) Marxist. Second, his importance within the Marxist tradition may be seen, today, less in the fact of his adhesion to it than in the Marxist "absences" or failures to meet that adhesion half-way. Morris's "conversion" to Marxism offered a juncture which Marxism failed to reciprocate, and this failure—which is in some sense a *continuing* failure, and not only within the majority Communist tradition—has more to teach us than have homilies as to Morris's great-hearted commitment.[64]

One would expect that the most significant new studies of Morris would be directed to these problems. And it is heartening to find two writers, Miguel Abensour and John Goode, whose work carries my points a great deal further. Abensour has presented a new study of the Utopian tradition, which, after a chain of subtle analysis, places exceptional emphasis upon Morris's critical (and unexhausted) significance.[65] Since M. Abensour's work will not be easily available to English-speaking readers for some time, I must report his conclusions with care. He writes from a critical position (a position of the "Left") within French Marxist culture; and he attends with especial care to what other Socialist writers have written about Morris: Guyot, Page Arnot, A. L. Morton, John Middleton Murry,[66] Williams, Meier, and myself: and none of us escapes criticism. Abensour recognises the importance of Page Arnot's *Vindication* of Morris (1934) in confronting the anti-Marxist myths of the time. But he argues that this also established the countervailing myth within the Marxist tradition, in which all that was "valuable" in Morris's thought had first to be passed through the sieve of an orthodoxy, and any bits of Utopianism too large to be pushed through the holes could be forgiven by invoking the licence afforded to a poet (p. 252). The new myth was not wrong to show that Morris was a practical and theoretical adherent to the Marxist tradition: it was wrong in passing over or apologising for significant differences of emphasis within that tradition (where Morris stood, with Domela Nieuwenhuis, on the "Left"), and in neglecting aspects of his thought which could not be assimilated. I am found less guilty of such assimilation and neglect than some others, but Abensour finds that I run aground, alongside A. L. Morton, on the problem of Utopianism; and he chides me for evasion in accepting the formula "Scientific Utopia" for *News from Nowhere* (p. 263).[67] Behind this formula he detects a rejection of the validity of the utopian mode in any form: a "Scientific Utopia" may be condoned only because it is not *really* utopian.

Abensour argues that the critique of Utopian Socialism in the *Communist Manifesto* and, even more, in Engels's *Socialism, Utopian and Scientific*, gave rise in the subsequent Marxist tradition to a doctrinal antinomy: Science (good), Utopianism (bad). At any point after 1850 Scientific Socialism had no more need for Utopias (and doctrinal authority for suspecting them). Speculation as to the society of the future was repressed, and displaced by attention to strategy. Beyond "the Revolution" little more could be known than certain skeletal theoretical propositions, such as the "two stages" foreseen in *The Critique of the Gotha Programme*. It must follow that orthodox Marxists must approach William Morris with great uneasiness. What was this throwback to Utopianism doing within the Marxist tradition at all? Perhaps his was a case of misrecognition? The usual solution was to propose a respect for Morris (for his good intentions and his more explicit political texts) beneath which was hidden a yawning condescension: Morris, who became "a Marxist" at fifty, couldn't be expected to shed all his old Romantic habits, most of which were charming or amusing; but while the form of his writings remains "utopian," the content became, in good part, "scientific"; and what can not be shown to conform to Marxist text may be passed over. The solution, in short, has been to propose that Morris was not really a Utopian at all.

These are not Abensour's words but a gloss upon his argument. And I will gloss also certain of his counter-proposals: (i) While one may assent (as he does) to the criticisms by Marx and Engels of the pre-1850 Utopian Socialists, these are local political judgments which need not condemn, once and for all, any generic utopian mode; (ii) Morris is, inescapably, a utopian Communist, not only in *News from Nowhere*, but also on the evidence of a large part of his more directly political writing, and any judgment which fails to confront this squarely is guilty of evasion; (iii) The question of Morris's relations to Marxism raises acutely the question, not as to whether Marxists should criticise Morris, but whether Marxism should criticise itself?

Let us now see, in more detail, how Abensour pursues these arguments. The conventional Marxist approach to Morris (he argues) combines an exercise of "domestication" and "repression," in which the utopian components in his thought are reduced to an expression of Scientific Socialism (p. 270). It is Meier who draws upon himself Abensour's sharpest critique. In admitting *News from Nowhere* to the Marxist canon, Meier must first pass it through a double scrutiny: first, he must extract from it certain propositions, which are then compared with propositions in Morris's more explicit political writings: then these propositions are compared, in their turn, with the texts of Marx and Engels, as "a kind of Supreme Court, alone qualified to pronounce a final verdict." The theoretical texts are thus used as a master-key to de-code the utopian work (p. 345). As a result, Meier at last "gives a name to the 'Nowhere' from which we've had news: the name of the continent is Marxism" (p. 346). But we are permitted to respond to the work only insofar as it has been found correct, by way of this double textual verification. Where it is correct, the Utopia may be said to be "scientific." Primacy is given, in Meier's analysis, to the "theory of the two stages," as found in *The Critique of the Gotha Programme*, a text which we might well be advised to hold in our right hand and study carefully, while we scan *News from Nowhere* in our left. The function of this "Scientific Utopia" is then reduced to the "illustration" of truths already disclosed elsewhere (p. 347). What Meier offers as a sympathetic appreciation of Utopianism is in effect an *exercise of closure*, confining the utopian imagination within textually-approved limits. Meier has been guilty of an exercise of theoretical repression (p. 350).

A summary would not do justice to Abensour's alternative analysis of *News from Nowhere*. But we should report certain of his general propositions. First, the scientific/utopian antinomy of Engels must be rejected. Second, a new kind of utopian writing may be found among European Socialists after 1850, prefigured by Déjacque and Coeurderoy, and of which Morris is the most notable exemplar. This new Utopianism turned away from the forms of classical Utopianism—those of juridico-political model-building (p. 296)—and turned towards a more open heuristic discourse. Third, and we are now specifically taking the case of Morris, it is possible to show how, around the body of general expectations (*"prévision generique"*) of Marxist thought, further hypotheses as to the future might be advanced by the utopian imagination—hypotheses which are neither Marxist nor anti-Marxist but simply *"a*-Marxist." Morris could (and did) take certain Marxist propositions as his point of departure, but used these as a springboard from which his imagination made a utopian leap (p. 277). If the major Marxist tradition has sought to reduce his insights back to their point of departure, that is because that tradition was becoming enclosed within a self-confirming doctrinal circularity.

What, then, is the function of the new Utopianism of Morris, if it brings back neither propositions which can be validated in relation to text, nor offers, in the classical way, a strict societal model? Communism (as Morris saw it) involved the subversion of bourgeois society and a reversal of the whole order of social life: "the attainment of that immediate end will bring about such a prodigious and overwhelming change in society, that those of us with a grain of imagination in them cannot help speculating as to how we shall live then."[68] It was not Morris's intention, in any of his utopian writings, to offer either doctrine or systematic description of the future society (pp. 295–6). He was often deliberately evasive as to "arrangements." Exactly for this reason he drew upon his Romantic inheritance of dream and of fantasy, accentuated further by the distancing of an archaic vocabulary, instead of adopting the spurious naturalism of Bellamy. His intention was to embody in the forms of fantasy alternative values sketched in an alternative way of life (p. 298). And what distinguishes this enterprise is, exactly, its *open*, speculative quality, and its *detachment* of the imagination from the demands of conceptual precision.[69] Neither in *News from Nowhere* nor in such lectures as "A Factory as It Might Be" or "The Society of the Future" is Morris offering precise "solutions." Nor does it even matter (as a first criterion) whether the reader approves of his approximations. Assent may be better than dissent, but more important than either is the challenge to the imagination to become immersed in the same open exploration. And in such an adventure two things happen: our habitual values (the "common sense" of bourgeois society) are thrown into disarray. And we enter into Utopia's proper and new-found space: *the education of desire*. This is not the same as "a moral education" towards a given end: it is, rather, to open a way to aspiration, to "teach desire to desire, to desire better, to desire more, and above all to desire in a different way" (p. 330). Morris's Utopianism, when it succeeds, liberates desire to an uninterrupted interrogation of our values and also to its own self-interrogation:[70]

> In fact, in William Morris's case, the recourse to utopian writing signifies exactly the desire to make a breakthrough, to risk an adventure, or an experience, in the fullest sense of the word, which allows one to glimpse, to see or even to think what a theoretical text could never, by its very nature, allow us to think, enclosed as it is within the limits of a clear and observable meaning (p. 347).

Nor is Abensour even willing to allow us to see this as a form of political criticism, since it is, at the deepest level, a criticism of all that we understand by "politics" (p. 341).

This remarkable study despatches the old questions into the past, and proposes new problems. Where the argument had been, "was Morris a Marxist or a not-Marxist?" it turns out that, in a major part of his Communist propaganda, he was neither. He was somewhere else, doing something else, and the question is not so much wrong as inappropriate. This explains the difficulty which all critics, except the "repressive" M. Meier, have in reducing his Socialist writings to system; and why these unsystematic writings should still challenge in such profound ways. We may say, and should say, that Morris was a Marxist *and* a Utopian, but we must not allow either a hyphen or a sense of contradiction to enter between the two terms. Above all, the second term may not be reduced to the first. Nor can we allow a condescension which assumes that the "education of desire" is a subordinate part.

I welcome Abensour's insight the more since it is the insight which, at a submerged level, structured this book when it was first written, but which I finally failed to articulate. In my emphasis upon "aspiration" within the Romantic tradition, upon "moral realism," upon Morris's repeated play on the word "hope," and in the very title of Part Four ("Necessity and Desire"), I was reaching towards a conclusion which, in the end, I turned away from out of piety towards politics-as-text and timidity before the term, "utopian." But it stares one in the face: Morris was a Communist Utopian,[71] with the full force of the transformed Romantic tradition behind him.

The pin-point upon which we have been dancing has imperceptibly enlarged, until it stretches as far as eye can see on every side. To define Morris's position as a Socialist it has proved necessary to submit Marxism itself to self-criticism: and in particular to call in question the scientific/utopian antinomy. But this self-criticism involves very much larger consequences than the local judgment as to William Morris's relation to that tradition. Indeed, "the case of Morris" may be a critical one in diagnosing the case of post-1880 Marxism. A Marxism which could not reciprocate or live without disdain alongside Morris, or which, even while "claiming" him, sought to close what he had opened and to repress his insights, was likely to find equal difficulty in co-habiting with any other Romantic or utopian mode. And "desire," uneducated except in the bitter praxis of class struggle, was likely—as Morris often warned—to go its own way, sometimes for well, and sometimes for ill, but falling back again and again into the "common-sense" or habitual values of the host society. So that what may be involved, in "the case of Morris," is the whole problem of the subordination of the imaginative utopian faculties within the later Marxist tradition: its lack of a moral self-consciousness or even a vocabulary of desire, its inability to project any images of the future, or even its tendency to fall back in lieu of these upon the Utilitarian's earthly paradise—the maximisation of economic growth. But this is to extend the argument further than is proper in this place. Let it suffice to say that this pin has a big enough point; and that to vindicate Morris's Utopianism may at the same time be to vindicate Utopianism itself, and set it free to walk the world once more without shame and without accusations of bad faith.

To vindicate Utopianism (in the sense that Abensour has proposed) does not, of course, mean that *any* (non-classical, non-juridico-political) utopian work is as good as any other. The "education of desire" is not beyond the criticism of sense and of feeling, although the procedures of criticism must be closer to those of creative literature than those of political theory. There are disciplined and undisciplined ways of "dreaming," but the discipline is of the imagination and not of science. It remains to be shown that Morris's utopian thought survives this criticism, as well as the criticism of ninety rather sombre years. I have not changed my view that it does. Raymond Williams reached a more nuanced judgment, which has been challenged by both Abensour and John Goode. Williams wrote:

> For my own part, I would willingly lose *A Dream of John Ball* and the
> romantic socialist songs and even *News from Nowhere*—in all of which the
> weaknesses of Morris's general poetry are active and disabling, if to do
> so were the price of retaining and getting people to read such smaller
> things as *How We Live, and How We Might Live, The Aims of Art, Useful
> Work versus Useless Toil,* and *A Factory as It Might Be*. The change of
> emphasis would involve a change in Morris's status as a writer, but such
> a change is critically inevitable. There is more life in the lectures, where
> one feels that the whole man is engaged in the writing, than in any of the
> prose and verse romances. . . . Morris is a fine political writer, in the broad-
> est sense, and it is on that, finally, that his reputation will rest.[72]

This is not very far from my own judgement (*717*). Nor need the question of
utopian vision necessarily be at issue here, in the examples which Williams
gives, and taking in "the broadest sense" of political writing. But Abensour
fears that Williams is leaving a way open to evasion, much as I did with
"Scientific Utopia." For the judgement might easily reduce the utopian to the
political, in its customary notation ("a fine political writer"), which may then
be judged by normal political canons.[73]

Abensour's objection rests in part upon his own fine and close reading of
News from Nowhere—of its structure and its openness—and in part upon a
criticism of Williams's neglect of the prior utopian tradition. But the questions
may be reduced to one: why should the utopian and the "political" works be
set off against each other, when so obviously they must be taken together?
Why should we be invited to pay this price at all? Williams gives up *Nowhere*
and *John Ball* too easily, as perhaps *Pilgrim's Progress* or *Gulliver's Travels* may
once have been given up by readers to whom they had become overfamiliar
furniture of the mind. And John Goode asks much the same question. It is
fascinating to observe how Abensour and Goode, working on different materials
and drawing upon the respective strengths—analytic and critical—of their respective disciplines and idioms, approach to similar conclusions.

Goode's work is readily available and I needn't report it at length.[74] He notes
of Williams's judgement that it "suggests the right order in which to read
Morris," but that as a critical judgement it "needs to be challenged," for such
drastic devaluing of Morris's creative writing would bring a change in his status,
and Williams "does not seem to realize how great that change would be." A
similar criticism is extended to me: I also offer a "split between aesthetic and
moral judgments" which "again reduces Morris's creative work to a marginal
role."[75] Goode then returns to Morris's creative writing, from *Sigurd* onwards,
but he doesn't attempt to rehabilitate this within the conventional terms of

literary criticism. What he does is to enquire into the problems which Morris had to surmount in the creative writing of his Socialist years. This writing should be seen as "a formal response to problems which are theoretically insoluble, except in terms of metaphors which are unsatisfactory and intractable in the actual historical situation" (p. 222). In this view Goode is close to the view of Pierson that "the fusion Morris effected between the romantic vision and Marxism," as one consequence, "sharpened the divorce between consciousness and objective social reality which had characterized the thought of Carlyle and Ruskin."[76] The deeper Morris's understanding became of the determinations of capitalist process, the more intransigeant became the protest against these of aspiration or "desire," the more impossible it became to clothe these aspirations within contemporary forms, and the more urgent it became for "desire" to master "necessity." Goode shares my view that despair, rather than vision, moved Morris in the first place towards revolutionary Socialism (p. 235); and while Marxism "gives his vision an historical basis, the central concept of his socialist ideology is one which has been with him from the beginning, alienation" (p. 236).[77] Not only are we entitled to use "alienation" in an analytic rather than merely descriptive way, but Goode shows that Morris was very conscious of this diagnosis, as when he wrote that "civilization has bred desires which she forbids us to satisfy, and so is not merely a niggard but a torturer also," or that "all civilization has cultivated our sensibility only to disappoint it" (p. 236).[78] "Thus Morris faced this contradiction, in a tension brought about by a vision of a Socialist future which "is in some way beyond immediate consciousness although in theoretical terms it is conceivable" (p. 238)—a tension expressed also in his own work (which Goode suggests is the true subject of the later creative writing) between "the vision of the historical potential" and the humdrum or depressing actualities of the movement. Faced with contradictions between Socialist aspiration and the overwhelming presence of capitalist actuality (with its "common-sense" signalling at every turn the "impossibility" of Socialist realisation) a general reaction within the Marxist tradition was (as Gramsci saw) a relapse into mechanical predestinarian determinism—a stamina fortified by a faith in the inevitability of the victory of "the Cause."[79] It is not only that Morris, perhaps increasingly, doubted such determinism or evolutionism;[80] it is also, as Goode very well notes, a pseudo-resolution of the problem of alienation: a resolution (or "Revolution") "achieved by forces outside himself: man's alienation will be brought to an end by alien forces" (p. 270). It is in the face of these contradictions that we should see how Morris's works "attempt, with much success, to find a mode in which the creative mind can be portrayed in its determined and determining relationship to historical actuality" (p. 222), and also how people themselves may be seen "as a determining as well as determined force" (p. 271).

This can't be done, however, within the received forms of realism. It is therefore inevitable and right that Morris should turn to new account his old Romantic inheritance of dream. "The affirmation of the responsibility of dream in a world in which consciousness has become ineradicably dislocated from the field of its existence is an assumed feature of all of Morris's socialist writings" (p. 239).

The test of Goode's defence of Morris's practice must depend not on this argument (although this argument puts us into the right critical relation to the works) but upon Goode's own very close criticism of particular works. This includes a remarkable revaluation of *Sigurd the Volsung*, which reveals hitherto unperceived levels of complexity of mythic organization in the work, but which leaves me not wholly convinced,[81] a very rich, subtle, and convincing analysis of *A Dream of John Ball*; and a significant reappraisal of *The House of the Wolfings*. In my view, although differences of local judgement of course remain, Goode emphatically sustains his challenge to Williams and myself. Henceforward these works and the "political writings" must be taken together.

But what are they to be taken as? It's here that Goode approaches to the same solution as that of Abensour, but (as it seems to me) finally takes alarm and backs away. Goode also challenges the term "Scientific Utopia"; but, as it turns out, he does so because he finds that *News from Nowhere* may neither be described adequately as "Scientific" nor as "Utopia." The work is primarily "not so much a picture of enacted values as a reversal of the rejected values of modern life" (p. 277), and it expresses the exhaustion and even pessimism in the mind of its author: "Nowhere is nowhere except as a conceptual antithesis in the mind of an exhausted activist." But why, in these clauses, does Goode insist upon such an opposition? Is it possible, in this kind of work, to reject present values without enacting alternatives? How can one be done without the other? Perhaps the weight falls on "antithesis": Nowhere's values are those of the not-present, or anti-present, they are not boldly imagined *ex-nihilo?* But it has to be shown, first, that this is so (as Goode does not); and second, that a utopian writer can proceed in any other way than by re-ordering the values of present or past, or by proposing antitheses to these. What Goode seems to be doing is, like so many before him, and like myself in 1955, running away from the acceptance of Utopianism as a valid imaginative form, because of a fright given to us by Engels in 1880.[82] Goode therefore concentrates upon one component only of *News from Nowhere* (the "never-ending contrast" between future, past, and present, which, as I noted [695], is essential to the work's structure) at the expense of all others:

It seems to me that we have, in this novel, much less a Utopia than an account of the agony of holding the mind together, committed as it is to the conscious determinants of history and the impersonal forces of change—united only in conceptual terms (p. 278).

So that, in conclusion, Goode can say that he has identified the achievement in the last creative works in that Morris "discovers forms which dramatize the tensions of the revolutionary mind." This is a part of the truth, especially of *John Ball*, and Goode is the first to have identified this part so well. But is *News from Nowhere* really to be read, responsively, only as an "agony"? And is this not a somewhat cerebral account of a work which does, indeed, enact alternative values? At least it seems a somewhat introverted judgment ("the tensions of the revolutionary mind") upon a work which succeeded rather well in communicating something very different to an audience not given to the intellectual's narcissistic obsession with his own mental agonies.[83]

I may well be wrong: but it seems to me that Goode has come to a conclusion at odds with his own evidence, and that he has done so because he leaves the problem of Utopianism unexamined. For earlier in his study he moves very close to the positions of Abensour. He warns that there is nothing "facile" in Morris's use of dream "as a convention within which to realize concretely socialist insight." Morris's use of dream is "not polemical but exploratory" (p. 246), and, again, he uses it:

> . . . not in order to escape the exigencies of the depressing actuality but in order to insist on a whole structure of values and perspectives which must emerge in the conscious mind in order to assert the inner truth of that actuality, and give man the knowledge of his own participation in the historical process which dissolves that actuality (p. 270).

This is, almost, to rehabilitate Utopianism. But not quite. For there is a little fuzz of evasion. Utopia is accepted as "convention" to realize "insight," and dream allows perspectives to emerge "in the conscious mind" which afford "knowledge." (We recall Goode's judgement that "Nowhere" is a "conceptual antithesis" and the work enacts an agony of the "mind.") What one notes is a certain tendency to intellectualise art, and to insist that it can be validated only when translated into terms of knowledge, consciousness, and concept: art seen, not as an enactment of values, but as a re-enactment in different terms of theory. What is lost is Abensour's insistence upon "the education of desire." "The role of Morris's art," Goode writes, "seems increasingly to be one which combats the tendency to collapse into a determinist act of faith by presenting the potentialities of human growth in a situation in which it is enabled and compelled to take the initiative" (p. 261). This is fine, and what this expresses is, precisely, the utopian "leap." If Goode has lingered over "initiative" he might have concluded, with Abensour, that one part of Morris's achievement lies in the open, exploratory character of Utopianism: its leap out of the kingdom of necessity into an imagined kingdom of freedom in which desire may actually indicate choices or impose itself as need; and in its innocence of system and its refusal to be cashed in the same medium of exchange as "concept," "mind," "knowledge," or political text.

Whether Utopianism succeeds in what it offers must in each work be submitted to the test of local criticism. And Goode's criticism of *A Dream of John Ball* is by far the best appreciation (and vindication) of any of Morris's Socialist works of art. His work, taken together with Abensour's, carries Morris studies into different territory. These bring, at last, news from somewhere new. That is what is important.

In this review, both of my own work and of Morris studies over the past twenty-one years, I've concentrated perhaps overmuch on one problem: the Morris/Marxism relation. I think that this is where the significant questions lie. The older attempts to assimilate Morris to Labourism, or even to Fabianism, were given a check long ago. Very clearly, the course which British Labourism has pursued in this century has not only departed from the perspectives advocated by Morris, but has led into exactly that general deadlock which he foresaw. The people must "take over for the good of the community *all the means of production*: i.e. *credit*, railways, mines, factories, shipping, land, machinery," he wrote to a correspondent in 1884; "Any partial scheme *elaborated as a scheme* which implies the existence with it side by side of the ordinary commercial competition is doomed to fail . . . it will be sucked into the tremendous stream of commercial production and vanish into it, after having played its part as a red-herring to spoil the scent of revolution."[84] In "The Policy of Abstention" in 1887 he envisaged, with some precision, the course of a parliamentary Labourism which fell into the errors of "*depending* on parliamentary agitation," which did not support "a great organization outside parliament actively engaged in reconstructing society" and which would move "earth & sea to fill the ballot boxes with Socialist votes which will not represent Socialist *men*" (*460*). At about the same time he wrote:

> They are already beginning . . . to stumble about with attempts at State Socialism. Let them make their experiments and blunders, and prepare the way for us by so doing . . . We—sect or party, or group of self-seekers, madmen, and poets, which you will—are at least the only set of people who have been able to see that there is and has been a great class-struggle going on. Further, we can see that this class-struggle cannot come to an end till the classes themselves do: one class must absorb the other.[85]

Morris already at that time envisaged "experiments" leading on to a "transitional condition" which reads uncomfortably like some passages in the history of this century:

> Attempts at bettering the condition of the workers will be made which will result in raising one group of them at the expense of another, will create a new middle-class and a new proletariat; but many will think the change the beginning of the millenium. . . . This transitional condition will be chiefly brought about by the middle-class, the owners of capital themselves, partly in ignorant good-will towards the proletariat (as long as they do not understand its claims), partly with the design both conscious and unconscious, of making our civilization hold out a little longer against the incoming flood of corruption on the one hand, and revolution on the other.[86]

In his last years Morris became reconciled to the inevitability of the course upon which Labourism was set. But, in his final lectures, he asked repeatedly "how far the betterment of the working people might go and yet stop short at last without having made any progress on the *direct* road to Communism?"

> Whether, in short, the tremendous organization of civilized commercial society is not playing the cat and mouse game with us socialist. Whether the Society of Inequality might not accept the quasi-socialist machinery . . . and work it for the purpose of upholding that society in a somewhat shorn condition, maybe, but a safe one. . . . The workers better treated, better organized, helping to govern themselves, but with no more pretence to equality with the rich, nor any more hope of it than they have now.[87]

What are being counterposed here are the alternative notions of Equality of Opportunity, within a competitive society: and of a Society of Equals, a Socialist community. Utopianism suddenly reveals itself as more realistic than "science," the exploratory historical imagination overleaps its own circumstances and searches the dilemmas of our own time with a moral insight so searching that it can be mistaken as callous. "I must tell you that my *special* leading motive as a Socialist is hatred of civilization; my ideal of the new Society would not be satisfied unless that Society destroyed civilization" (*718*).

We have to make up our minds about William Morris. Either he was an eccentric, isolated figure, personally-admirable, but whose major thought was wrong or irrelevant and long left behind by events. This could be so, although it needn't mean that we must dismiss his subsidiary interests and emphases. He will always remain of major importance in the history of the decorative arts and in the narrative history of British Socialism. And certain other themes can be taken out of his writings, which will swim up now and then into revitalised discourse: thus it has recently been noted (remarkable discovery!) that he is a pioneer of responsible "ecological" consciousness, and it has never been forgotten that he had definite and uncomfortable views on the question of work.[88] On the other hand, it may be that Morris was a major intellectual figure. As such he may be seen as our greatest diagnostician of alienation, in terms of the concrete perception of the moralist and within the context of a particular English cultural tradition. And if he was that, then he remains a contemporary figure. And it then must be important to establish the relation in which he stands to contemporary thought. And if the British Labour movement has now reached, rather exactly, the deadlock which, some ninety years ago, he foresaw, then we can expect an intense renewal of interest in his work and a number of claimants to his inheritance to come forward.

The most plausible, and most vocal, claimant is "Marxism," and that is why my discussion has turned on this point. I must confess that, when I first read M. Meier, I was thrown into depression. It seemed that one had extricated Morris, twenty-one years ago, from an anti-Marxist myth, only to see him assimilated curtly within a myth of Marxist orthodoxy. The result was not only repressive, it was also distancing and boring—Morris's portrait might now be hung safely on the wall, with *The Critique of the Gotha Programme* on his lap. But since Meier was only writing out at large certain pieties and evasions in my own original treatment, I hardly had the heart to enter the argument again. Thanks to M. Abensour and Mr. Goode I've got back my morale. We can now see that Morris may be assimilated to Marxism only in the course of a process of self-criticism and re-ordering within Marxism itself.

The question turns upon Morris's independent derivation of Communism out of the logic of the Romantic tradition; upon the character of his Utopianism; and upon the relations in which the moral sensibility stands to political consciousness. "My Socialism began," he wrote, "where that of some others ended, with an intense desire for complete equality of condition for all men." And "I became a Communist before I knew anything about the history of Socialism or its immediate aims." It was at this point that he turned to Marx and became "a practical Socialist"—"in short I was born again."[89] But to be born again did not mean renouncing his own parentage. "Ideal" and "science" continued to co-exist and to argue with each other.

"Equality is in fact our ideal," he said, and "I can only explain the fact that some socialists do not put this before them steadily by supposing that their eager pursuit of the means have somewhat blinded them to the end." This was aimed at the Fabians, whom he was then addressing.[90] In one sense this ideal could be defined simply as a negation of class society: Socialism aims at "the full development of human life set free from artificial regulations in favour of a class."[91] The implicit underlying metaphor, drawing upon the old Romantic critique of Utilitarianism, is the "organic" one: the natural growth of "life" will be set free from the artificial (or "mechanical") constraints of "civilization." Fulfilled Communist society will not depend upon a new race arising of morally-admirable people but upon the growth of a communal value-system made habitual by the absence of private property in the means of production and the attendant competition for the means of life. In "Nowhere" a "habit of life," "a habit of acting on the whole for the best" has "been growing on us"—"it is easy for us to live without robbing each other" (697). In this sense, the alternative value-systems of capitalism and socialism are seen, in ways which some contemporary anthropologists might approve, as being both supportive to and supported by the organization of economic and social life.

But this is not quite all that Morris is saying. For in another sense, his use of moral criteria and his assertions of "ideal" ends and of prior values, is *indicative* also: it indicates a direction towards which historical development may move, suggests choices between alternative directions, asserts a preference between these choices, and seeks to educate others in his preferences. These indications are never absolute and "utopian" in that sense: Morris never proposes that men may live in any way they may suppose that they might choose, according to any value-system imaginable. The indications are placed within a firm controlling historical and political argument. But they are certainly there and they are important. They are perhaps an occasion for Engels's dismissal of him as a "sentimental Socialist"—an accusation which left Morris pugnaciously unrepentant ("I *am* a sentimentalist . . . and I am proud of the title" [718]). They indicate where a crack lies between Morris's avowed and conscious positions and a moral determinism (from these relations of production, these values and this consonant morality) which has occupied much Marxist thought. In Morris's critique of capitalist society, there is no sense in which morality is seen as secondary, power and productive relations as primary. The ugliness of Victorian social relations and "the vulgarities of civilization" were "but the outward expression of the innate moral baseness into which we are forced by our present form of society . . ."[92] This moral baseness was "innate," within the societal form: "economics" and "morality" were enmeshed in the same nexus of systematised social relationships, and from this nexus an economic *and* a moral logic must ensue.

It must follow that the revolt against this logic must equally be "economic" and "moral" in character. But a moral revolt, no less than an economic one, must have somewhere to go, somewhere to point towards. And pointing must involve choosing, not between any direction one likes, but between inflexions of direction. When Morris looked forward to the society of the future, he proposed that a quarrel between desire and utilitarian determinations would continue, and that desire must and could assert its own priorities. For to suppose that our desires must be determined by our material needs may be to assume a notion of "need" itself already determined by the expectations of existing society.[93] But desire also can impose itself as "need": in class society it may be felt in the form of alienation, desire unsatisfied: in the society of the future in the form of more open choices between needs:

> We may have in appearance to give up a great deal of what we have been used to call material progress, in order that we may be freer, happier and more completely equal.[94]

And he went on, in the same lecture, to warn that differential rewards and "different standards of livelihood" accorded to different kinds of work would "create fresh classes, enslave the ordinary man, and give rise to parasitical groups," ensuing in "the creation of a new parasitical and servile class." With a quizzical glance at the determinism of evolutionary theory, he concluded:

> My hope is, that now we know, or have been told that we have been evolved from unintelligent germs (or whatever the word is) we shall con- sciously resist the reversal of the process, which to some seems inevitable, and do our best to remain men, even if in the struggle we become bar- barians.[95]

"Civilization" and "barbarism" were terms which he always employed with ironic inversion, drawing in part upon the inheritance from Carlyle and Ruskin, in part upon the very deep commitment he had learned for certain pre-capitalist values and modes. To "become barbarians" alarmed him not at all. " 'Civili- zation' " (he wrote to Georgie Burne-Jones in May 1885) "I *know* now is doomed to destruction." This "knowledge" is what he had gained as "a practical Socialist," thus being saved from "a fine pessimistic end of life" (*175*). But the assent of desire had preceded this knowledge. "What a joy it is to think of it!" his letter to Georgie continued:

> And how often it consoles me to think of barbarism once more flooding the world, and real feelings and passions, however rudimentary, taking the place of our wretched hypocrisies. With this thought in my mind all the history of the past is lighted up and lives again to me. I used really to despair once be- cause I thought what the idiots of our day call progress would go on per- fecting itself. . . .[96]

It is not a comfortable passage, after the barbarism of blood and race into which twentieth-century "civilization" in fact debouched. True, Morris would have seen this outcome, which indeed he almost predicted ("the doom of Blood and Iron in our own day" (*720*), as being no barbarism in his sense, but an authentic outcome of the logic of capitalist "civilization." But that is a little too easy as a way out from the accusation that Morris, like other alienated intellectuals, was allowing his outraged aesthetic feelings to commit him to a dangerous course of emotional arson. And we have to put his private comment to Georgie together with other private and public evidence to take a full measure. For if Morris was emphatically a revolutionary Socialist, he didn't suppose that "the Revolution" would, at one throw, "liberate" some mass of healthy "barbarism," some underground reserves of repressed desire. And if he toyed with such notions on his first commitment to "the Cause" between 1883 and 1885,[97] he was rescued from any revolutionary Romanticism (of the Swinburne variety) exactly by the sobering experience of very hard and applied mundane political agitation. Neither his audiences nor his comrades in the quarrelling Socialist sects were "barbarians" of that kind; nor, as he knew *far* better than most Victorian intellectuals, out of his immense practical experience in the decorative arts, was the "ordinary man in the street" an unspoiled vessel of true barbaric art ("Let us once for all get rid of the idea of the mass of the people having an intuitive idea of Art" (*666*). The false consciousness of "civilization" was not seen by him as masking some healthy proletarian Unconscious. Necessity itself would impel the workers into struggle, but this struggle could attain no goal unless the goal was located by desire and a strategy for its attainment prescribed by Socialist theory. First we must have "courage enough to will"; "*conscious hope*" must match the response to "commercial ruin" (*428*). Moreover, if Socialists failed to educate desire, and to enlarge this conscious hope, "to sustain steadily their due claim to that fullness and completeness of life which no class system can give them," then they would the more easily fall victim of the "humbug" of "a kind of utilitarian sham Socialism" (*429*). Or, if the existing society failed to provide even that, and "if we give it all up into the hands of necessity," the result will be a volcanic disaster (*724*).[98] The end itself was unobtainable without the prior education of desire or "need." And science cannot tell us what to desire or how to desire. Morris saw it as a task of Socialists (his own first task) to help people to find out their wants, to encourage them to want more, to challenge them to want differently, and to envisage a society of the future in which people, freed at last of necessity, might choose between different wants. "It is to stir you up not to be contented with a little that I am here tonight" (*361*).

When I say that Morris may be assimilated to Marxism only in the course of a re-ordering of Marxism itself, I don't of course imply that Marxist thinkers

have not noticed these problems or proposed solutions. But it is in this area
that (I think) the problem still lies. And "the case of Morris," and Marxism's
bewilderment before it, emphasises that the problem is unresolved. Moreover,
it should now be clear that there is a sense in which Morris, as a Utopian and
moralist, can never be assimilated to Marxism, not because of any contradiction
of purposes but because one may not assimilate desire to knowledge, and because the attempt to do so is to confuse two different operative principles of
culture. So that I've phrased the problem wrongly, and Marxism requires less
a re-ordering of its parts than a sense of humility before those parts of culture
which it can never order. The motions of desire may be legible in the text of
necessity, and may then become subject to rational explanation and criticism.
But such criticism can scarcely touch these motions at their source. "Marxism,"
on its own, we now know, has never made anyone "good" or "bad," although
a faith, arising from other sources but acclaimed as Marxism, has sustained epic
courage, and a bad faith, arising from other sources but acclaimed as Marxism,
has defiled the first premises of Marx. So that what Marxism might do, for a
change, is sit on its own head a little in the interests of Socialism's heart. It
might close down one counter in its universal pharmacy, and cease dispensing
potions of analysis to cure the maladies of desire. This might do good politically
as well, since it would allow a little space, not only for literary Utopians, but
also for the unprescribed initiatives of everyday men and women who, in some
part of themselves, are also alienated and utopian by turns.

   This won't be how all other readers see it. So it is time for me to get out
of Morris's way, and put this book to bed. I shan't revise it again. It must now
stand like this, for people to use as they will. If they want to use it as a quarry,
that's all right. The bits of Morris are what matter. But I would hope that one
part of its structure—the part least noted by its critics—might receive a little
attention before it is pulled down: that is, the analysis of Romanticism and of
its trajectory in Morris's life. I don't mean only the way in which Morris rejected
the reactionary "Feudal Socialism" of Carlyle and turned to new account the
Ruskin of "The Nature of Gothic." I mean, even more, the trajectory from the
profoundly-subjective Romanticism of Keats (in which aspiration, denied of
realisation, circulated between the integrity of the artist and the ideal artefact
of Beauty), through the sublimated rebellion of *The Defence of Guenevere*, to
the crisis of despair of *The Earthly Paradise*, in which all the values of subjective
individualism were poisoned by the taint of mortality; and thence, through the
recuperative societal myths of Icelandic saga, to the Socialist resolution.

   This trajectory may be viewed from two aspects. In Morris's own poetry it
appears as fragmentary and suggestive, but as unfulfilled. His aesthetic premises
were modified least of all, and his devotion to pre-capitalist achievements in
the visual and architectural arts re-inforced his stubborn attachment to Keatsian

and Pre-Raphaelite notions of "Beauty." This led him to his rash attempt to invent (or re-invent) a language which would put at a distance Victorian society. From this aspect we can see how Morris intended the arch of his creative writing to go. But, as I've argued sufficiently, his premises were wrong, and to attempt to "make a new tongue" in that way was to disengage from, rather than to challenge, the sensibility of his time. The attempt succeeded only when it was matched by the form of dream, when disengagement was itself a means by which criticism of the age's common-sense could be brought to bear.

From another aspect the arch is that of aspiration fulfilled. Morris's youthful Romantic rebellion was not a rebellion of individual sensibility against "society," but a rebellion of value, or aspiration, against actuality. When he stood, with young Burne-Jones, entranced by his first sight of medieval Rouen, what seized him like a passion was the sense of a whole alternative way of life: "no words can tell you how its mingled beauty, history, and romance took hold on me"(4). This mingled sense was the accent which he gave to Romanticism, and in later years he specifically identified this sense with the historical consciousness:

> As for romance, what does romance mean? I have heard people miscalled for being romantic, but what romance means is the capacity for a true conception of history, a power of making the past part of the present.[99]

Nor was this sense confined to reverie; Morris's close practical knowledge of the medieval craftsman's mode of work gave to it an unusual substance. But it also threw into deeper shadow the actuality of his own society, in which both the values and the artefacts of the past were doomed to decay. This nourished the pessimism—the impulse to use art as a means of escape—of his early middle years. And I remain convinced that these *were* years of despair, and that the acute sense of mortality within a purposeless social universe was sapping the very sources of Morris's psychic life. When his arduous quest ended in Socialist conclusions, he was able, in one motion, to re-appropriate that "power of making the past part of the present" and extend it into an imagined future. The aspirations of the past were themselves infused with new meaning: "the past is lighted up and lives again to me." For the present, "I did not measure my hope, nor the joy it brought me." (*126*). The old fear of death relaxed, as aspiration was extended, vicariously, into the future: when he imagined that society, he asked, not "How Will They Live?" but "How Shall We Live Then?" The trajectory was completed. And what was transformed was, not only his tradition, but his own personality and sensibility. So that we may see in William Morris, not a late Victorian, nor even a "contemporary," but a new kind of sensibility. If he sometimes appears as an isolated and ill-understood figure, that is because few men or women of his kind were then about—or have happened since.

If I write about Morris again it will be in my character, not as historian, but as Socialist. For I must set one misunderstanding at rest. It might seem that, in the revaluation proposed in this Postscript, I've been setting myself up as yet one more "claimant" of Morris, in the attempt to attach him to an idiosyncratic Thompsonian position. But the case is the reverse. Morris, by 1955, had claimed me. My book was then, I suppose, already a work of muffled "revisionism." The Morris/Marx argument has worked inside me ever since. When, in 1956, my disagreements with orthodox Marxism became fully articulate, I fell back on modes of perception which I'd learned in those years of close company with Morris, and I found, perhaps, the will to go on arguing from the pressure of Morris behind me. To say that Morris claimed me, and that I've tried to acknowledge that claim, gives me no right to claim him. I have no license to act as his interpreter. But at least I can now say that this is what I've been trying, for twenty years, to do.

August, 1976.

Notes

1. Detroit, 1969.

2. Paul Meier, "An Unpublished Lecture of William Morris: 'How Shall We Live Then?' " *International Review of Social History*, XVI, 1971, Part 2: "Justice and Socialism," extended notes for a lecture in 1885, in Appendix I to Paul Meier, *La Pensée Utopique de William Morris* (Paris, 1972).

3. In R. Page Arnot, *William Morris, the Man and the Myth* (1964). Professor Norman Kelvin of the Department of English, City College, City University of New York, N.Y. 10031, has for some ten years been assembling materials for a full collection of letters. Anyone with knowledge of unpublished letters is invited to get in touch with him.

4. Peter Faulkner (ed.), *William Morris: The Critical Heritage* (1973).

5. Asa Briggs (ed.), *William Morris: Selected Writings and Designs* (1962); A. L. Morton (ed.), *Political Writings of William Morris* (1973).

6. Unfortunately Floud's early death robbed us of his full conclusions: but see his articles in the *Listener*, October 7th & 14th, 1954: "Dating Morris Patterns," *Architectural Review*, July 1959; "English Chintz: the Influence of William Morris," *CIBA Review*, 1961.

7. Paul Thompson, *The Work of William Morris* (1967); Ray Watkinson, *William Morris as Designer* (1967). Also Graeme Shankland in (ed.) Asa Briggs, op. cit.; R. Furneaux Jordan, *The Medieval Vision of William Morris* (1960); A. C. Sewter, *The Stained Glass of William Morris and His Circle* (New Haven, 1975); E. Goldzamt, *William Morris et La Genèse Sociale de L'Architecture Moderne* (Warsaw, 1967).

8. Warington Taylor, Victoria & Albert Museum, Reserve Case JJ35; Sir Thomas Wardle, V. &

A. Box II 86. zz. See especially Philip Henderson, *William Morris: His Life, Work and Friends* (1967: Penguin edition 1973), pp. 105–12 (Taylor) and pp. 193–5 (letters to Wardle on dyeing).

9. Some minute-books of Morris & Co. are in the Hammersmith Public Library. Account-books, pattern-books, and other materials of the Firm are now in the private collection of Sanford and Helen Berger at their home in Carmel near San Francisco. It is unfortunate that the Firm's records should be divided by the Atlantic and between public and private hands. But scholars who can get to California will find (as I have done) that the present owners of these records are generous in providing access to them.

10. *William Morris, Writer* (William Morris Society, 1961). A brief essay in general interpretation by George Levine in (eds.) H. J. Dyos and M. Wolff, *The Victorian City* (1973), II, pp. 495–517, is also fresh and perceptive.

11. Disagreement has been expressed by Jessie Kocmanova. "Some remarks on E. P. Thompson's Opinions of the Poetry of William Morris," *Philologica Pragensia*, III, 3, 1960, and in *The Poetic Maturing of William Morris* (Prague, 1964). But I have not been convinced by her critical re-appraisals.

12. C. S. Lewis, *Rehabilitations and Other Essays* (Oxford, 1939).

13. Notably John Goode's work, discussed below. Also Lionel Munby, "William Morris's Romances and the Society of the Future," *Zeitschrift für Anglistik u. Amerikanistik*, X, 1, 1962. I find Jessie Kocmanova's studies on *A Dream of John Ball* and on the late prose romances more helpful than her studies of Morris's poetry: see *Brno Studies in English* II, no. 68, 1960 and VI, no. 109, 1966.

14. July 15th, 1955.

15. Jack Lindsay, who had the benefit of Henderson's work, as well as Meier's, also offers some perceptive suggestions in his helter-skelter biography: *William Morris: His Life and Work* (1975).

16. See Henderson, op. cit., pp. 124–5; C. Doughty and Robert Wahl (eds.), *Letters of Dante Gabriel Rossetti* (Oxford, 1965), II, p. 685; Penelope Fitzgerald, *Edward Burne-Jones* (1975), esp. chapter 10.

17. "Has Top perhaps thrown trade after poetry, & now executes none but wholesale orders in philanthropy,—the retail trade being beneath a true humanitarian? But no—without a shop he could not be the Odger of the Future!" D. G. Rossetti to Janey Morris, April 1st, 1878, cited in Jack Lindsay, *William Morris*, pp. 224–5. George Ogder, the shoemakers leader, had repeatedly fought parliamentary elections, with strong support, against both Liberal and Conservative candidates, on a Radical working-men's platform: he had died in 1877.

18. Morris to W. Bell Scott, April 9th, 1882, cited in Philip Henderson, op. cit., p. 260.

19. This judgment of mine is perhaps smug in the light of the full surviving correspondence between Rossetti and Janey Morris which has become available while these pages were in proof: *Dante Gabriel Rossetti and Jane Morris: Their Correspondence*, ed. John Bryson (Oxford, 1976). Unrevealing in some ways, these letters (the bulk of them from Rossetti) do appear to disclose the general shape of the relationship. There are several letters of 1868–70, when the mutual passion of Janey and Rossetti appears to be first fully disclosed. In 1869 Janey had her first breakdown and Morris took her to recuperate at Ems: the three friends appear to have been attempting to live through the triangular situation with mutual affection and confessional frankness: "All that concerns you" (Rossetti wrote to Janey at Ems, July 1869) "is the all absorbing question with me, as dear Top will not mind my telling you at this anxious moment. The more he loves you, the more he knows that you are too lovely and noble not to be loved . . ." In whatever way the three friends attempted to "handle" the situation, it seems clear that the attempt broke down. No letters survive for the years of crisis, 1870–75. These are the years of Morris's two Icelandic journeys—years when Janey and Rossetti were often together at Kelmscott. By the time the correspondence resumes in 1877, a sad change has come over the situation. Gabriel is preparing

to move out of Kelmscott and there are no more friendly messages (and a few sneers) for "Top." Janey appears to have entered a settled melancholia and hypochondria (the symptoms mentioned include lumbago, sciatica, neuralgia, migraine, sore throats, fevers) which matches the melancholia of Rossetti. "I hope," Gabriel writes on Christmas Eve 1879, "you will have a Xmas not too unlike a merry one." In her reply Janey says nothing about her Christmas, but writes of her daughter May: "she is excessively delicate this winter, and I think will not drag through a long life. So much the better for her!" (May was in fact to live well into her seventies.) It is altogether a sad correspondence, of two self-preoccupied people conjoined by a melancholy retrospective obsession, redeemed by reciprocal concern and respect. Much of the nature of the relationship remains unclear; one does not know how far to credit the statement of Hall Caine (which Meier has brought to light) that Rossetti told him that he had been made impotent by a serious accident (at some time during these years?); moreover, the letters reveal little of the paradoxes of Rossetti's own feeling and behavior (his mistress, Fanny Cornforth, is never mentioned). It is clear only that the relationship falls easily into no stereotype, and that an emotional distance had opened up between Morris on one hand and Janey and Rossetti on the other.

20. *H. M. Hyndman and British Socialism* (Oxford, 1961). For London, see also, Paul Thompson, *Socialists, Liberals and Labour: The Struggle for London, 1885–1914* (1967), and (for class relations generally) Gareth Stedman Jones, *Outcast London* (Oxford, 1971).

21. See my review in the *Bulletin of the Society for the Study of Labour History*, no. 3, Autumn 1961, pp. 66–71.

22. C. Tsuzuki, *The Life of Eleanor Marx, 1855–1898* (Oxford, 1967).

23. *Eleanor Marx: Family Life, 1855–83* (1972). This volume introduces Eleanor fully and also introduces Aveling.

24. S. Pierson, "Ernest Belfort Bax: the Encounter of Marxism and Late Victorian Culture," *Journal of British Studies*, 1972; Laurence Thompson, *The Enthusiasts* (1971)—on Bruce and Katherine Glasier; W. J. Fishman, *East End Jewish Radicals, 1875–1914*. New information on the Labour Emancipation League, Frank Kitz and other London pioneers is in Stan Shipley, *Club Life and Socialism in Mid-Victorian London* (History Workshop, 1972), and on London anarchism in Rudolf Rocker, *The London Years* (1956).

25. *Tom Mann and His Times* (1965).

26. "Homage to Tom Maguir," in Asa Briggs and John Saville (eds.), *Essays in Labour History* (1960).

27. Especially A. M. McBriar, *Fabian Socialism and English Politics, 1884–1918* (Cambridge, 1962); Margaret Cole, *The Story of Fabian Socialism* (1961); E. J. Hobsbawm, "The Fabians Reconsidered," in *Labouring Men* (1964). Also Wolfe and Pierson (discussed below).

28. The new sources on Shaw and the relations between Fabians and Socialist League in 1886, are discussed in Appendix II of the 1976 edition.

29. James, W. Hulse, *Revolutionists in London* (Oxford, 1970), p. 27.

30. Willard Wolfe, *From Radicalism to Socialism: Men and Ideas in the Formation of Fabian and Socialist Doctrines* (New Haven, 1975), p. 320.

31. J. Y. Le Bourgeois, "William Morris and the Marxist Myth," *Durham University Journal*, December 1976.

32. I have taken out certain passages (e.g. first edition, pp. 735–46) not because I apologise for them in 1955 but because they are not relevant to 1976.

33. In fact my book was better received than most books from Lawrence & Wishart (a Communist publishing-house), getting a generous notice from G.D.H. Cole in the *Listener* and a knockabout, but not unfair, criticism from A.J.P. Taylor in the *Manchester Guardian*.

34. July 15th, 1955.

35. Oxford, 1970.

36. By contrast Hulse offers Lloyd Wendell Eshleman (alias Lloyd Eric Grey), *A Victorian Rebel: The Life of William Morris* (New York, 1940: and, under a different title and different author, London, 1949) as "the most readily available general biography for the past quarter century . . . based on competent research and a sympathetic understanding of Morris." For Mackail's opinion, in 1940, as to Eshleman's "lack of sincerity," see Meier, op. cit., p. 303. I dissected Eshleman/ Grey's nauseous and thoroughly dishonest book in "The Murder of William Morris," *Arena*, April-May 1951; and abused it further in first edition, pp. 74–3.

37. Hulse notes (p. 17) that the S.D.F., League and Fabians "filled the columns of their respective periodicals with criticisms of the other organizations": this is rubbish, most of all for *Commonweal*. Of Bloody Sunday he notes, "it . . . needed only a few officers to disperse the crowd" (p. 93). And so on.

38. Ithaca and London, 1973.

39. This point is made forcefully in Keith Nield's review of Pierson in the *Bulletin of the Society for the Study of Labour History*, no. 27, Autumn 1973.

40. Nor need it follow that we must endorse all of Althusser's notions of "rupture." I do not.

41. We have been reminded that Hyndman's ideas were not co-terminous with those of the whole S.D.F.: see E. J. Hobsbawm, *Labouring Men*.

42. See Bernard Semmel, *Imperialism and Social Reform*, (Cambridge, U.S.A., 1960).

43. Cf. Morris: "I am not pleading for the production of a little more beauty in the world, much as I love it, and much as I would sacrifice for its sake; it is the lives of human beings I am pleading for . . ." "Art and its Producers" (1888); "Once again I warn you against supposing, you who may specially love art, that you will do any good by attempting to revivify art by dealing with its dead exterior. I say it is the *aims of art* that you must seek rather than the *art itself*; and in that search we may find ourselves in a world blank and bare, as a result of our caring at least this much for art, that we will not endure the shams of it," "The Aims of Art" (1886). See also the letter on the miners' strike of 1893, "The Deeper Meaning of the Struggle," in *Letters*, pp. 355– 7 and above, *665*.

44. See pp. 274–5. Also p. 84, where Morris is held to have tended to refuse to acknowledge "those forces in life, formerly categorized as the sinful or the tragic."

45. When I say "more than any other of his time," I am thinking of British Socialists. But it isn't easy to suggest European comparisons, unless we move to cosmic (non-Socialist) pessimists. If Engels in his last years allowed himself to confront a similar pessimistic realism, he kept it to himself.

46. Pierson is fond of this term "regressive." In another place (*The Victorian City*, eds. H. J. Dyos and M. Wolff, 1972, II., p. 879) he has Morris trying to rescue "the rural vision" by "attaching it to Marxism." "Ideological impulses within Marxism encouraged the project, but it was incompatible with the social and economic realism of that system of thought and it soon collapsed. In Morris's Socialism the Romantic regression ended virtually in anarchism . . ." The "collapse" here is not of Morris's thought but of Pierson's more nuanced appraisal in the book under discussion.

47. I prefer the term "transformation" to the term "extension," employed by Raymond Williams in *Culture and Society* (1958), p. 158, since it insists upon "rupture" as well as continuity. I argued the point rather loudly in a review of *The Long Revolution* in *New Left Review*, 9 & 10, May/ June & July/August 1961, to be reprinted shortly in my political essays (Merlin Press, 1977). Any differences between myself and Williams have (I think) diminished over the years, and neither of us would argue in exactly the same way today. The choice of terms is unimportant, but the point remains of interest.

48. An English edition of *La Pensée Utopique de William Morris* (Paris, 1972) is announced as forth-coming from the Harvester Press.

49. See also Meier, "Friedrich Engels et William Morris," *La Pensée*, no. 156, Avril, 1971, pp. 68–80.

50. F. Engels and Paul & Laura Lafargue, *Correspondence* (Moscow, 1959), 2 vols.

51. As early as July 24th, 1884 Morris wrote to Robert Thompson: "I believe (and have always done so) . . . that the most important thing to press . . . at present is the legal reduction of the working day: every working man can see the immediate advantage to him of this: the Trades Unions *may* be got to take it up . . ." This would become "an international affair," *Letters* p. 205. When the Marxists of the Bloomsbury Branch split from the League they put their best efforts exactly into the Eight Hour agitation, and not into parliamentary candidatures. Had they made this their main plank while still within the League, no break would have been necessary.

52. In brief, *Commonweal* (January 7th, 1888) publicised the exposure in the *Sozial-Demokrat* of 13 German police-spies, one of whom, Reuss, lived in England. Reuss commenced an action; Engels noted that Morris was "funky" but tried to collect evidence to support a defence. When the case was lost, Morris appears to have been allowed to carry the damages and costs out of his own purse.

53. I find helpful the suggestion that *The House of the Wolfings*, and Morris's articles on "The Development of Modern Society" in *Commonweal* (1890) may have drawn upon ideas in *The Origin of the Family*, derived from conversations with Engels or with Bax. But it still has to be shown that Morris was drawing upon Engels rather than (as John Goode has suggested) turning Morgan's *Ancient Society* to a similar account: see Meier, *La Pensée Utopique*, pp. 308, 359–65; Goode (cited below), pp. 261–5.

54. I find especially strained Meier's attribution of an influence from Marx's theses on Feuerbach (p. 347); and the notion that Morris's wholly characteristic insistence that a Communist morality must rest upon the habits induced by the general conditions of life in Communist society must depend upon knowledge of the manuscript of *The German Ideology* (unpublished until 1932): Meier, pp. 706–8.

55. The case being argued at this point is difficult. Meier ascribes a very general influence to ideas (as yet unpublished) in *The Critique of the Gotha Programme*. Possibly some of these derive from conversations with Engels, Bax, the Avelings and others, while some were of Morris's own definition.

56. Op. cit., p. 149. See also George Levine, op. cit., on the continuity of the underlying "organic metaphor."

57. In making these criticisms I should add that Meier treats well the questions of "barbarism" and "civilization" in Morris's thought: see esp. his discussion of Richard Jefferies, *After London*, and its influence (pp. 107–13) and Part III, chapter 1. But, as Goode points out, Morgan also envisaged that "civilization" contained within itself "the elements of self-destruction," since private property had become an "unmanageable power"; the "next higher plane of society" will be "a revival, in a higher form, of the liberty, equality and fraternity of the ancient *gentes*"—a view as influential upon Morris as upon Engels, who cited it at the conclusion to *The Origin of the Family*.

58. "The Revival of Architecture" (1888).

59. "The Revival of Handicraft" (1880).

60. See Meier (p. 646) where he refers to *"un passage progressif des positions idéalistes du début au materialisme marxiste de sa maturité."*

61. Engels to Laura Lafargue, November 23rd, 1884, *Correspondence* I. p. 245.

62. *The Communism of William Morris* (William Morris Society, 1965)—a lecture delivered in May 1959.

63. Since I did not myself take the point when I first wrote this book, it would be pharisaical to labour it now.

64. Cf. Asa Briggs's comment that Morris's writings "provide the material for a critique of twentieth-century Socialism (and Communism) as much as for a critique of nineteenth-century capitalism": *William Morris: Selected Writings*, p. 17.

65. M. M-H. Abensour, *"Les Formes de L'Utopie Socialiste-Communiste,"* thèse pour le Doctorat d'État en Science politique, Paris 1, 1973, esp. chapter 4. Forthcoming as *Utopies et dialectique du socialisme*. Pavot. Paris (1977?).

66. Abensour re-directs attention to Murry's neglected articles, "The Return to Fundamentals: Marx and Morris," *Adelphi*, V, nos. 1 & 2 (October-November, 1932); "Bolshevism and Bradford," *Adelphi*, IV, no. 5 (August 1932).

67. See above *693*. I accept Abensour's criticism, but have let my passage stand, as a text in this argument.

68. "How Shall We Live Then?," op. cit., p. 6.

69. *"L'utopie se détache du concept pour devenir image, image médiatrice et ouverture a la verité du désir"* (p. 329).

70. *"Sa fonction est de donner libre cours au désir d'interroger, de voir, de savoir, au desire même"* (p. 349).

71. I write "Communist Utopian" when I refuse the term "Marxist Utopian" (just as Abensour refuses "Scientific Utopia") since the term "Communist" may appertain to value-systems as well as to theoretical system in a way in which "Marxist" has ceased to do. By "Communist" I mean especially those values which Morris himself attributed to the society of the future.

72. *Culture and Society*, 1958, pp. 155–6.

73. *"Privilégiant une lecture politique, l'interprète s'expose à minimiser ou à même passer sous silence la critique de la politique dans l'oeuvre de William Morris, si fondamentale qu'elle vise une fin de la politique at que son auteur ne peut être dit un penseur politique au sens classique du terme"* (Abensour, p. 341).

74. John Goode, "William Morris and the Dream of Revolution" in John Lucas (ed.), *Literature and Politics in the Nineteenth Century* (1971).

75. Goode, pp. 222–3 and first edition of this work, *779*. In this case the judgment properly criticised by Goode as "complacent" was too pious to be allowed to stand in this revision.

76. Pierson, op. cit., p. 274. This is the only place where Pierson allows the term "fusion."

77. I strongly support Goode's judgment here, as to the unitary theme of alienation in Morris's work from youth to maturity. But I wish that Goode, in common with many English Marxists, would not use "ideology" in such a sloppy way. Morris did not have "a socialist ideology."

78. I'm aware that "alienation" is used in several senses in Marxist writing. But this sense of alienated sensibility seems permissible and consonant with some passages of Marx.

79. Goode, p. 260, citing *The Modern Prince*, 1967, p. 69.

80. Until the mid-1880s, and occasionally thereafter (e.g. *748*), Morris refers to the "new understanding of history" in terms of "evolution" of a necessary kind. It's my impression that he came to doubt this evolutionism after 1887 (see e.g. *427–30*). Engels, Bax, Aveling, Hyndman &c were all also in the habit of using evolutionary metaphors (sometimes with explicit parallels with Darwinism); and Goode notes with justice (p. 270) that some of Engels's comments on the English scene show a "merely reflexive" defeatism fortified by determinist stamina.

81. Undoubtedly no-one can approach *Sigurd* after this analysis without a new kind of respect. The

problem is that Goode can show this mythic elaboration only by extricating it from the poem's "linguistic fog" and then offering it as an analytic precis; also, how much was already given to Morris in his materials?

82. 1880 is the date of the first French edition of *Socialism, Utopian and Scientific*.

83. In the post-1929 depression Harold Laski reported that he found copies of *A Dream of John Ball* and *News from Nowhere* in the Tyneside area (which Morris had visited in 1887) "in house after house of the miners," even when most of the furniture had been sold off: see Paul Thompson, *William Morris*, p. 219.

84. Morris to Robert Thomson, July 24th [1884], Houghton Library, Harvard University, MS. Eng. 798; *Letters*, p. 205.

85. "Feudal England," *Signs of Change*, (1888), pp. 82–3.

86. *Commonweal*, Mayday issue, 1886.

87. "Communism" (1893).

88. These views are discussed lucidly by Alasdair Clayre, *Work and Play* (1974), esp. chapter 6.

89. Morris carefully emphasised this sequence in "How Shall We Live Then?" op. cit., p. 10. Cf. Raymond Williams, op. cit., p. 265: "The economic reasoning, and the political promise, came to him from Marxism; the general rebellion was in older terms."

90. "How Shall We Live Then?" p. 20.

91. William Morris, Preface to Frank Fairman, *Socialism Made Plain* (1888), p. iv. Cf. another definition by negation: "the great central power of modern times, the world-market . . . with all the ingenious and intricate system, which profit-hunting commerce has built up about it" must develop into "its contradiction, which is the conscious mutual exchange of services between equals": "How Shall We Live Then?" p. 16.

92. Preface to *Signs of Change* (1888). I am here revising a very confused discussion of moral consciousness and the Marxist tradition, in my first edition, pp. 83–5 (cut from this edition), and am replacing it with points first argued in "The Communism of William Morris," op. cit., p. 17.

93. See Morris's criticism of some "practical" Socialists: "he is thinking entirely of the conservative side of human nature . . . and ignores that which exists just as surely, its revolutionary side": *Commonweal*, February 18, 1888.

94. "How Shall We Live Then?" p. 23. Another unequivocal preference which, of course, Morris never ceased to nourish as a want, was the need for artistic expression: "For without art Socialism would remain as sterile as the other forms of social organization: it would not meet the real and perpetual wants of mankind." Preface to Ruskin's "On the Nature of Gothic" (Kelmscott Press, 1892). And ("How I Became a Socialist"): "It is the province of art to set the true ideal of a full and reasonable life before him, a life to which the perception and creation of beauty . . . shall be felt to be as necessary to man as his daily bread."

95. "How Shall We Live Then?" pp. 23–4. The last comment was perhaps a crack at Bax's notion that evolutionary changes "in the human organism" would eradicate "the coarser side of the sexual passion" (*705*), but Morris is hanging on this peg a more general irony.

96. *Letters*, p. 236.

97. See "Art and Socialism" (1884): "the change in store for us hidden in the breast of the Barbarism of civilization—the Proletariat."

98. When writing in this sense, Morris offered the alternatives of Socialism or social disaster in a way which anticipates Rosa Luxembourg's "Socialism or Barbarism."

99. May Morris, I, p. 148.

REJECTIONS AND RECONCILIATIONS

FROM "ALIEN HOMAGE": EDWARD THOMPSON AND RABINDRANATH TAGORE

Thompson had a streak of perversity in him, of contrariety. When in India or America he often defended England—or a sentimental idealization of what England, at its best, might be. At least he asked for "fairness." When in England, he defended India. He was not long back in England before he commenced his play, *Atonement*, and his first work of history, *The Other Side of the Medal*. When one of his former missionary colleagues chided him on the indiscretion of the second, he drew down on his head a vehement reply:

> Our Christianity was a bad brand. . . . I'm afraid I feel too bitterly about it. I'd like, as an individual Englishman, to do my bit of prayaschitta, if I cd. . . .
>
> I'm becoming a left-winger pretty fast, & I feel how patronizing nearly all our propaganda, political & religious & educational, must seem to an Indian. . . . I understand why my *Tagore* annoyed them; & I marvel that they bore with me in my Indian days. We are a *gauche*, crass lot.[1]

In November 1925, hearing that Tagore was ill, Thompson wrote to him to tell him that a copy of *The Other Side of the Medal* was on its way, inscribed to "R. T. An individual Englishman's act of atonement":

> I wish I were still in India. I was very ignorant, ill-informed, & John Bullish when I was there. I see better now. . . .[2]

Tagore replied (with an evident reflection upon the scandal caused in some part of the British press by the book):

From *"Alien Homage": Edward Thompson and Rabindranath Tagore* by E. P. Thompson (Delhi: Oxford University Press, 1993).

> You are in disgrace with your people just now for which you have my congratulations—and I am proud to say that my position with my own countrymen is, if anything, worse than yours, the reason being very much the same as it is in your case.[3]

The relationship seemed to be as warm as of old. But in 1926 the major book at length was published, having hung around between publishers for three years. Tagore's exceedingly hostile response we know from his letter to Rothenstein. In a sense, much of this essay has been a commentary and a defence.

I must confess that I find something still unexplained, in the violence of Tagore's reaction to the major study as contrasted with his toleration of the *gaucher*, slimmer volume. Several of his criticisms, as we have seen, were just. Others were misrepresentations—one wonders how much of the book Tagore had read? Others seem to refer back to old grievances, dating back to the earlier study. Thus Tagore complained to Rothenstein that the book insinuates "that I have an antipathy against Englishmen." Thompson had not written that, but he had written (in the first book) of "his dislike of England." Mahalanobis had questioned this in 1921 and Thompson had replied: "Tagore told me himself that he had a prejudice against England & things English, which the *Gitanjali* reception swept away. I took the statement down at the time."[4] But C. F. Andrews would not let the matter rest, telling Thompson that it was a mis-understanding arising from the "cruelly unfortunate publication of a strictly private Bengali letter written on the very night of the Debate in the H. of Lords on 'Amritsar.' I would have stopped it at once if I had known that it was going to be given to the Press. . . ."[5] This tells us less about Tagore than about Andrew's management of Tagore's image, since what the poet wrote in a private Bengali letter might have as much authenticity as a politic public statement. What Thompson did do, in the second book, was to quote an "ex-asperated" comment made by Tagore during his German tour in 1921:

> Our modern schoolmasters are Englishmen; and they, of all the western nations, are the least susceptible to ideas. They are good, honest and reliable, but they have vigorous excess of animal spirits, which seek for exercise in racing, fox-hunting, boxing-matches, etc., and they offer stub-born resistance to all contagion of ideas.[6]

There does not seem to be anything especially sinful in that. There must have been moments when a Bengali felt like making an anti-English thrust, just as the English made anti-Bengali "jests."[7] I am teasing this small point because the need to disclaim any "anti-English" sentiments in the Poet's universal heart suggests an overheated atmosphere in the Tagore circle around Santiniketan. By the 1920s the manipulation of the gurudeb's image had become an increasingly "political" operation. His published views must be sanitized and approved. One wonders if there is some clue here to the fury with which Thompson's book was received within the cult?[8] Undoubtedly Tagore was offended—and justly offended—by Thompson's over-confident critical pretensions, just as Seal had been before him. But did the poet's own circle resent even more an interloper who was getting in the way of their production of the poet to the West?

The most judicious examination of this whole question is in D. Harish Trivedi's introduction to the Oxford University Press (India) edition of the *Tagore* (1991). It seems that Tagore and his circle were deeply upset by Thompson's book and that they pursued it relentlessly. Perhaps Rani Mahalanobis attempted to intercede on Thompson's behalf, for Trivedi cites a letter to her from Tagore even more denunciatory than his letter to Rothenstein. "The very attitude of the whole book is to strike a blow at me at every step." Tagore not only denounced Thompson's book vehemently in his own intimate circle, he also wrote a savage pseudonymous critique in *Prabasi*, and enlisted others (Ramananda Chatterjee, Shanta Debi [Ramananda's daughter] and Nihararanjan Ray) to join the attack.[9] Not all the younger and more radical intellectuals in the Tagore circle could go along with this feud. The young historian, Susobhan Sarkar, noted of Thompson's book:

> We liked it very much. . . . The book had a few mild criticisms of Rabindranath. The over-sensitive Rabindranath was very angry. . . . I remember Prasantachandra [Mahalanobis] being quite embarrassed, for he had given Thompson much of his materials.[10]

After this the letters that passed between Tagore and Thompson became increasingly formal. The tide of *Prabasi* and the *Modern Review* had set against Thompson. There was a sad moment of chill in 1930 when Thompson was in the United States, and was goaded by the torrent of ill-informed American criticism into an ambivalent defence of the British record. It was an episode he lived to regret. He was jumped upon, not for the first or last time, by Ramananda Chatterjee in the *Modern Review* for "his mischievous anti-Indian propaganda work."[11] The rebuke was one which he had called down on his own head. But it cooled the welcome for him in Bengal when he revisited India in 1932. As he told Sir William Rothenstein,

> The only place where I did not meet with the most humiliating friendliness was Bengal. Tagore insisted that I was an Imperialist and had been nobbled by the India Office for anti-Indian work. Quite frankly, I think he has

treated me pretty rottenly. There were a lot of people in India, the Ma-
rathas especially, who thought the same. He has kept steady resentment
for what he considers the "detraction" of my book. . . . His appetite for
flattery has grown to absurdity since his first success. He lives amid in-
cense, and India outside Bengal and the Punjab half resents, half laughs
at it. . . .[12]

One door in Bengal, however, was never closed. And more than once our
house near Oxford was graced by the visits of a statistician of growing emi-
nence, whose head—I can still remember with a schoolboy's awe—was too
large for any English-made hat, and his charming and outgoing wife. They had
married shortly after Thompson left India in 1923, and the marriage itself was
not free from the political controversies of Calcutta. Nirmalkumari—or
"Rani"—was the daughter of the Principal of City College, and the betrothal
took place at the very moment when Principal Maitra was locked in controversy
with the young reformers of the Brahmo Samaj as to the legitimacy of different
marriage forms. The leading reformer was, of course, Mahalanobis, who took
his stand on the legality of marriage as performed according to the prescribed
rites of the Brahmo Church, whereas Maitra conformed to the practice of registration under the Act of 1872. The matter was finally resolved by the couple's
marriage by Brahmo rites without the bride's father's consent. There was now
a settled family friendship between the Thompsons and the Mahalanobises.
"You know," Thompson wrote in 1929, "we regard you as dear friends,"[13] and
I blame the women as much as the men for keeping friendship's boat afloat
through all political and intellectual storms. In 1932 in Calcutta this door was
open, and on his return Edward Thompson wrote to Rani:

> It was excessively magnanimous of you to receive a notorious enemy of
> your people under your roof. And you did not even seize the chance to
> poison him! You were very kind to me & Prasanta was his consistent self,
> generous & unselfish & eager.
>   If I were writing to Prasanta I might raise a complaint against *your*
> measures of repression against me. I now know what it is like, living
> under an Ordinance, wielded by a capricious & irresponsible power.[14]

Thompson's 1932 visit was in part sponsored by the Rhodes Trust, to in-
vestigate possibilities of cooperation between Indian and British writers, and he
met some of the younger poets around the journals *Parichaya* and *Triveni*.[15] But
the story was going around the Tagore circle that Thompson was in fact an
agent of Government.
    Thompson's brief visit to Calcutta in February 1932 perhaps represented the

nadir in the relations between the two men. There was a good meeting with Abanindranath Tagore who said: "I have few friends now, & I am not willing to lose any of them. I would rather lose ten pictures than lose you." But Thompson went to view Rabindranath's paintings in a mood of hostility:

> Tagore . . . has a *most absurd* exhibition of his paintings. Sits in a room behind, purring as he laps up the cream of praise. We saw him, but he & I were barely on speaking terms. He has slandered me all over India, & I was not going to pretend to be enthusiastic.[16]

When Tagore (who very much liked Thompson and Garratt's *The Rise and Fulfilment of British Rule in India*)[17] presented him with one of his books in 1934, Thompson thanked him warmly "because it seems to suggest that you are revising your belief that I have been, or ever shall be, an Enemy of your people."[18] "You do me an injustice," Tagore replied. "While not agreeing with all you have said or written on India, I have never questioned your sincerity or your love and affection for our people."[19]

Matters seemed to be mending and a vigorous correspondence continued in 1934 and 1935. Thompson was trying to persuade Alexander Korda to film one or two Tagore stories, and Tagore asked Thompson to revise the English version of *Gora*.[20] Amiya Chakravarty came to Oxford, commissioned by Tagore to consult Thompson on the revision and selection of his collected works.[21] Thompson promised to prepare a leading article for the *Times Literary Supplement*, which would show "the way your interests have marched from width to width."[22] But the circle around Tagore remained hypersensitive. In April 1935 Thompson wrote to Tagore that the *Modern Review*

> has excelled itself in its latest attack on me. I am sorry only because Ramananda has managed to make Bengal a closed region to me, during years when my intimate friendship with Indians from every other nation has been a steadily widening circle. Except you and Prasanta, I have no Bengali friends now.[23]

Early in 1936 some absurd misunderstanding again clouded their relations. Thompson had written a general leading article on modern Bengali poetry for the *TLS* ("A Land Made for Poetry," 1 February 1936) in response to repeated requests from Buddhadeva Bose and others around the new review, *Kabita*. It was a survey piece, which also touched on Tagore's most recent work and which, one would have thought, could not have given offence. Thompson was uneasy with the task, since his Bengali was once again rusty, and he seems to have written a letter to Mahalanobis—to be passed to the *Kabita* circle—apologizing for his lack of expertise for the work. This leader put the Tagore circle in a state of uproar once more. Amiya Chakravarty seems to have written to Tagore disparagingly about the interpretation given to one of his poems, and Tagore refused even to read the piece. Since the gurudeb had condemned the essay (unseen) all his admirers in Bengal must follow. Chakravarty sent a flustered apology to Thompson; and commented on "the sore and sensitive state into which the Indian mind, and more specially perhaps the Bengali mind, has fallen":

> Any slightest difference of opinion is at once made an occasion for heat and suspicion: respect for each other's conviction or the desire to honour the motives of fellowbeings seem to have gone overboard. One has to be careful in uttering a word in that whispering gallery which is modern India. . . .[24]

And yet, by some accounts, Chakravarty himself was as good at whispering as any. Thompson was informed confidentially by Mahalanobis that Chakravarty "for years has kept Tagore fed with mendacious reports of me, & his latest exploit was a peculiarly shabby letter about my TLS article, saying I had spread myself just to get notoriety, when I knew nothing of Bengali literature."[25] Before he had been told this, Thompson had written wearily to Prasanta:

> I have decided never to write on Indian literature again. I not only know what I have always known, that no foreigner can write or judge fairly, but I know that one is bound to give offence unwittingly. I used to believe that if one did one's best & was honest, as well as aware of the short-comings of what one wrote, much would be forgiven. But that is not so. . . .
>
> You must tell Tagore that the TLS leader was merely a flag waved to draw outside attention to the fact that good minds were functioning in Bengal. Nothing that the leader said seemed to me of the slightest value. But the gesture was meant to encourage men who—as the world is made & arranged—have to write with no encouragement from the outside, & very little from their own people.

"I do not suppose," he added, that "poets are having a much easier time in India than they are here." And "poetry is finished, so far as the West is concerned. Everything else seems unreal, beside our monstrous political & economic problems."[26]

This unnecessary misunderstanding did, however, have one unexpected result. It had long been doctrine in the Tagore circle that Thompson knew nothing about Bengali literature and scarcely understood the language. This is much what Tagore himself implied in his notorious letter to Rothenstein. Thompson himself never claimed to be an accomplished Bengali scholar,[27] but qualified scholars tell me that his notes and the letters that passed between him and Mahalanobis suggest accomplishments greater than his modesty would acknowledge. There had always been voices which contradicted the doctrine. Dineshchandra Sen gave a qualified testimonial to his translations from Ramprasad: "your ample vision is always correct and your translation of the songs is literal"—"I believe you to be now the soundest scholar of Bengali amongst the Europeans."[28] Now, as if in reaction to the detraction in Tagore's immediate circle, younger Bengali writers began to write to Thompson in his defence. "As for Ramananda Chatterjee," wrote Humayun Kabir, "he doesn't matter very much nowadays: most people are suspicious of him."[29] Now a younger circle of poets wrote to thank Thompson for his *TLS* article. "I must congratulate you on your knowledge of Bengali, which, frankly, has surprised me," wrote Buddhadeva Bose:

> What we ... liked most about your article was its clear honesty which helped you to enter into the spirit of a language & literature which must be more alien to you than English is to us.[30]

"You have been too modest about your own critical judgement," wrote Premendra Mitra. "I do not know of any present Bengali critic who could have done better justice to the subject."[31] And Sudhindranath Datta, the editor of *Parichaya*, declared that the article "reveals such a detailed knowledge of our language and literature that I cannot but condemn the modesty you assume when asked to appraise anything Bengali."[32] Flatterers (it might be suggested) who had found their own work commended in the trade-paper of Eng. Lit. Yet, between detraction and flattery, Thompson was attempting something. I do not notice many leading articles on contemporary Bengali poetry in the *TLS* today.

Late in 1936 Edward Thompson was once again in Bengal and "walked in on Prasanta Mahalanobis at the Presidency College." He was at once invited to visit Prasanta and Rani at their home in Giridih (Bihar), and from thence the three of them went to a forest officer's bungalow "in lovely wild country ... above the banks of a river, with dense forest all round." A tiger growled outside Thompson's window on the first night, and Rani made him barricade it with chairs:

> We went to Budh Gaya, where the Buddha attained enlightenment. Gaya, 5 miles away, is a foul city ... but Budh Gaya ... is the most wonderful

& peaceful place in the world. Practically no pilgrims go there; & the huge aged bo-tree after darkness just has 3 pink candles lit before it, & a few scented flowers set, by a saffron-clad monk who pauses for a few minutes in adoration. The Mahalanobises & I sat on there for hours, talking of religion & death & after death.[33]

Tagore wished to repair misunderstandings and invited him to Santiniketan, but Thompson did not wish to break in upon him at a time when Nehru was known to be visiting.[34] But Prasanta Mahalanobis was determined to lay some of the ghosts of past alienations. Thompson recorded the encounter with one such ghost in letters to Theo and to Rothenstein: "Prasanta took me, greatly loth, to call upon poor old Brajendranath Seal":

Seal broke off an ancient & deep friendship because of my earlier small book on Tagore. For 20 years we had nothing to do with each other. Then . . . Prasanta suddenly led me into his presence. The old man has had several strokes, was being fed with milk like a child, the milk streaming all over his beard. He had no idea I was coming, & he started up with a wild cry, "Ohhh! Edward Thompson!" and broke down & sobbed.

"He has been miserable all these years, ever since we ceased to be friends. 'Often & often I have thought of you.' He . . . was as like King Lear begging pardon of Cordelia as I ever saw."[35] "I have always thought him one of the 2 or 3 noblest men I have known," Thompson wrote to Tagore, "and I shall never forget what was our farewell."[36] Thompson also called on another old friend, Abanindranath Tagore, the artist—"an old man turned philosopher. Again, it was singularly moving."[37] "I think," he wrote to Rabindranath:

No nation ever produced such a group of men as this Bengali group which is now passing away. I am glad I visited Calcutta to take my farewell of such friends.[38]

If Mahalanobis was now the world-renowned statistician, Thompson had become the historian of India, novelist, and polemicist on Indian questions. His friendships now extended to Bombay, Delhi, Lucknow, and Allahabad, and to persons as various (and mutually incompatible) as Sapru, Iqbal, Ambedkar, Sastri, Jayakar, Rajagopalachari, Sarojini Naidu, and, later, Nehru. He was now sometimes called in the Indian press the "friend of India," a go-between in new fields, bumping his boots on everyone's shins as before. He made one final, and extraordinary, visit to India in October 1939, as a go-between between continents, ideologies, and individuals, spending much time with Sapru, more with

Nehru, and visiting Gandhi and the Congress Working Committee at Wardha. On a brief visit to Calcutta he was able to lay one more ghost. Calling in on Abanindranath he found that he cherished a grievance about the disappearance from view of the projected *Oxford Book of Bengali Verse*. This project had originally been Thompson's, back in 1920, but he had withdrawn when Mahalanobis and Sudhindranath Datta had been enlisted (with Tagore's help) as co-editors. For some reason, Abanindranath blamed Thompson for the project's failure. Calling at the Oxford University Press office in Calcutta with Amiya Chakravarty, they learned that the editors had mislaid the manuscript. Thompson broke his journey back from Calcutta at Asansol, where Prasanta and Rani were waiting, having driven in 90 miles by car. They had some hours together. It turned out that Prasanta, who shared some of the absent-minded foibles of the Great Seal, was himself the culprit—but the manuscript had now been found.[39] That was over fifty years ago. Now, it seems, it has been lost once more.

Notes

1. EJT to Rev. E. W. Thompson, 26 June 1924: Thompson Papers.

2. EJT to Tagore, 15 November 1925: Visva-Bharati archives.

3. Tagore to EJT, Santiniketan, 30 December 1925: Thompson Papers.

4. EJT to Mahalanobis, 26 March 1922: Visva-Bharati archives.

5. C. F. Andrews to EJT, 26 March 1922: Thompson Papers.

6. *Tagore* (1926), p. 278.

7. The offence given to Indians by English "jests" is a motif in both *Atonement* and *An Indian Day*.

8. It seems that Andrews reacted strongly against the study, saying that Thompson showed "a patronage and a superiority complex": see Hugh Tinker, *The Ordeal of Love* (OUP, Delhi 1979), p. 224.

9. Harish Trevedi, introduction to *E.J. Thompson Rabindranath Tagore, Poet and Dramatist* (OUP, New Delhi 1991). Also Prabhat Kumar Mukherjee, *Rabindrajibani* (Visva-Bharati, Calcutta, 1952), vol. 3, p. 297 (favour of Professor Mary Lago).

10. Susobhan Sarkaar, *Prasonga Rabindranath* (Calcutta, 1982), pp. 18–19, by favour of Professor Sumit Sarkar. Susobhan Sarkar and his friends were already critical of the Tagore cult. He was disturbed by the term "*Gurudeva*, used by everyone there [i.e. at Santiniketan]. . . . It smacked too much of an *asrama*. . . . Another thing that upset me was the *pranam* [foot-touching] to Rabindranath morning or evening. . . . What I disliked was that Rabindranath never tried to discourage either. . . ." Ibid., pp. 11–12.

11. *Modern Review*, September 1930.

12. EJT to Rothenstein, 14 May 1932: Houghton Library, Harvard. It is not clear to me whether EJT ever saw Tagore's earlier letter to Rothenstein, although Mukherjee, op. cit., vol. 3, p. 297, implies that he did.

13. EJT to Mahalanobis, 26 May 1929: Thompson Papers.

14. EJT to Rani Mahalanobis, 11 March 1932: Visva-Bharati archives.

15. See *A Letter from India* (1932), pp. 135–7.

16. EJT to Theodosia, Barackpur, 29 February 1932: Thompson papers.

17. Tagore to EJT, 2 August 1934: Thompson Papers. Also Tagore to Macmillans, 2 August 1934: Brit. Lib. Add. MSS 55004.

18. EJT to Tagore, 16 January 1934: Visva-Bharati archives.

19. Tagore to EJT, 6 February 1934: Thompson Papers.

20. Tagore to EJT, 10 October and 11 November 1934: Thompson Papers.

21. Tagore to EJT, 10 April 1935: ibid.

22. EJT to Tagore, 22 March 1935: Visva-Bharati archives.

23. Ibid., 28 April 1935.

24. Amiya Chakravarty to EJT, 19 May 1936: Thompson Papers.

25. EJT to Theodosia, Calcutta, 5 November 1936: ibid. Mahalanobis wrote to EJT, 10/12 March 1936: "Amiya Chakravarty had written to [Tagore] an angry letter. Amiya said many hard words about English reviewers (and I gather, you in particular). But Poet told me that he did not feel much disturbed. He said that the difficulties of language are great and there is no reason why we should expect to be clearly understood or appreciated by foreigners." Visva-Bharati archives.

26. EJT to Mahalanobis, 1 September 1936: Visva-Bharati archives.

27. EJT to Canton, 26 December 1922: ibid.

28. D. C. Sen to EJT, 10 January & 3 November 1924: Thompson Papers. Buddhadeva Bose wrote later that EJT was "so far the only reliable European writer on Bengali literature": *An Acre of Green Grass* (Bombay, 1948), p. 8.

29. Humayun Kabir to EJT, 27 May 1932: Thompson Papers. But Kabir sent to EJT a courteous, reasoned but (in my view) deservedly severe criticism of certain passages in *A Letter from India*, 1 June 1932: ibid.

30. B. Bose to EJT, 4 March 1936: ibid.

31. P. Mitra to EJT, 11 March 1936: ibid.

32. S. Datta to EJT, 5 March 1936: ibid.

33. EJT to Theodosia, 11 November 1936: ibid.

34. Tagore to EJT, 16 October 1935 and 21 October 1936, giving to EJT "a warm welcome"; "I hope you will not leave the country till you have looked us up": Thompson Papers. EJT to A. K. Chanda, 4 November 1936 (Visva-Bharati archives) explaining that he did not wish to break in upon the poet's time with Nehru. Perhaps the Mahalanobises persuaded him to visit Tagore, since he hired a car and drove up to Bolpur on November 13th: EJT to Tagore, 12 November 1936, ibid. Evidently Tagore was not there, since EJT left a diary fragment in which the entry for November 13th is "Bolpur farce."

35. EJT to Theodosia, 5 November 1936: Thompson Papers. EJT to Rothenstein, 12 August 1938: Houghton Library, Harvard.

36. EJT to Tagore's Secretary, A. K. Chanda, 4 November 1936: Visva-Bharati archives.

37. EJT to Theodosia, 4 November 1936: Thompson Papers.

38. EJT to A. K. Chanda, 4 November 1936: Visva-Bharati archives.

39. "Report by Edward Thompson" to Rhodes Trustees, typescript in Thompson Papers, December 1939.

II

Law and Custom

THE GRID OF INHERITANCE
FROM *MAKING HISTORY: WRITINGS ON HISTORY AND CULTURE*

The essays in this volume have told us a great deal about the sociological texture of given communities and about existent relationships within them, as exemplified by their inheritance practices. We have perhaps learned less about process over time, since intentions in inheritance systems, as in other matters, often eventuate in conclusions very different from those intended. If we anatomize inheritance systems in a condition of stasis, it is possible for the mind to assent to a fallacy which, in our waking hours, we know very well to be untrue—that what is being inherited remains a historical constant: "property," "ownership," or, more simply, "the land"—land which, after all, did pass on from generation to generation, which is still there for us to walk over, which may even carry today much the same kind of crops or timber or stock as three hundred years ago.

Of course we know that this constancy is illusory. In land what is being transmitted through inheritance systems is very often not so much property in the land as property in the usufruct, or a place within a complex gradation of coincident use-rights. It is the tenure—and sometimes functions and roles attached to the tenure—which is being transmitted. Perhaps a little light may be thrown backwards upon what was being transmitted by considering aspects of the decomposition of certain kinds of tenure in England in the eighteenth century.

It is difficult to estimate the proportion of landholdings governed by copyhold or by other forms of customary tenure in the years from the Restoration to the mid eighteenth century—the period which is generally accepted as the classic period for the accelerated decline of the "yeoman." We should remember that there are two different totals to be counted: the acres and the farmers. It is not difficult to find, in the early eighteenth century, manors in which the

From *Making History: Writings on History and Culture* by E. P. Thompson (New York: The New Press, 1994).

average size of customary holdings was small, so that the acreage of freehold or of land subject to non-customary economic rental greatly exceeded the acreage in copyhold, but in which the total number of customary farmers exceeded the number of freeholders or of tenants-at-will. The point is important, since the economic historian may find that the clues to expanding agrarian process lie in the "free" sector, while the social historian may find that the psychological horizons and expectations of the majority of the farming community lie still within the customary sector.[1]

Without attempting any quantitative assessment it will be sufficient, for this comment, to emphasise that the survival of customary tenure into the eighteenth century was very considerable: in very many private manors: in Church and collegiate lands: in Crown lands, forest areas, etc.[2] It is also my impression that there was, from the 1720s onwards, some revival of careful court-keeping, and considerable activity in the field of customary law. This had nothing to do with some unlocated "reaction" or with antiquarian sentiment. Customs of manors were scrutinized in new ways by stewards and by lawyers, whose employers saw property in new and more marketable ways. Where custom inhibited rack-renting, "fringe" use-rights—timber, mineral-rights, stone, peat and turves—might assume even greater importance for the manorial lord anxious to improve his revenue. In general agricultural improvement and the enlargement of the market economy meant that customary use-rights had a more valuable cash equivalent than before, if only they could be prised loose from their sociological and tenurial context.

Despite the consolidation at law of rights of copyhold in the late fourteenth and fifteenth centuries, these were not of course absolute. If copyhold could be sold, mortgaged, bequeathed in any direction (although not according to the custom of all manors), it could still be forfeited for felony and for waste: and it was on occasion so forfeited.[3] Tenures unsecured by a will or by a clear lineage of heritable descent, according to the custom of the manor, could fall back into the hands of the lord. Where tenancies for lives were predominant, as in some parts of western England, the eighteenth century may have seen greater insecurity of tenure. Such tenures were copyhold (in the sense that they were held by copy of the court roll) but they remained tenancies-at-will and subject to arbitrary fines at the entry of new lives.[4] Perhaps such insecure tenures were increasing.[5] Where fines were truly arbitrary this could effectively enforce insecurity of tenure: thus at Whiston and Caines (Worcs.) it was reported in 1825 that "the customary tenants have been copyholders of inheritance until within these hundred years. . . . But for many years past the tenants have been constrained to fine at the lord's pleasure; and some to let their inheritance be granted over their heads, for want of ability to pay such great fines as were required of them, or to try their rights with the lords." "In other Worcestershire manors there is an evident tension between "custom" in the sense of practices and expectations, and custom as enforceable in terms of law. At Hartlebury the custom is "to grant one life in possession, and three in reversion, and to alter and change at the will of the lord: when three lives are dropt the lord may grant the estate to whom he pleases; though the tenants claim the first offer."[7]

But in general customary tenures in the eighteenth century appear to have been falling away through a process of attrition rather than through any frontal assault from landowners and the law. (Since many substantial landowners themselves had an interest in copyhold, through purchase or inheritance, the form of tenure was by no means coterminous with the interests of the yeoman or husbandman.) If the lord or his steward could see an advantage in bringing the land back into hand, either to set it out again in an economic leasehold or in anticipation of enclosure, they had opportunities to hasten on the process. Fines on entry or on surrenders could be forced up, based upon the improved rather than upon the customary rents, and these could hasten a copyholder's career towards indebtedness. The well-situated copyholder could claim equal security of tenure with the freeholder. But he could of course claim no *greater* security. Both were equally subject to those vagaries of economic or familial situation which could lead them to mortgage their lands and to heap debts upon the heads of their sons. And, when we discuss inheritance systems, we should not forget that one of their important functions in some peasant and petty tenurial societies was precisely to ensure security down the generations for the landlord's or moneylender's interest upon the farmer's debt.

Customary tenure is seen, very often, in its legal status only, as defined as case-law. But custom always had a sociological dimension also, and one recognized at law in the reservation "according to the custom of the manor." This can perhaps be seen most clearly in the in-between world of Church and collegiate tenures. Such tenures did not have the security of copyhold, nor can they be regarded as tenancies-at-will. The definition is not one at law but in customary usage. The historian of the finances of St. John's College, Cambridge, comments (on the seventeenth and early eighteenth centuries):

> For some reason the College over a long period appears to have acted on the assumption that it was precluded from varying the rents of its estates. It is not possible to discover an entirely satisfying ground for this assumption. So far as is known it rests on no legal basis. . . .[8]

But he goes on to show that successive Bursars found ways of overcoming their inhibitions from the first quarter of the eighteenth century; and the increase in revenue came first of all from fines.[9]

The reason for this situation lies less in law than in a certain balance of social relations. From 1576 ("Sir Thomas Smith's Act" of 18 Elizabeth) Church and college tenures were normally limited to three lives and 21 years, with renewals expected every seventh year. Undoubtedly Church tenures, as well as royal and manorial over-rights in forest areas, had been deeply shaken in the Interregnum. After the Restoration, the Church scrutinized all tenures and raised substantial fines upon those which were confirmed. These tenants, and their children, no doubt felt that they had paid for the security of a copyhold. Their tenure had (it was argued) "by long Custom become Hereditary, purchased almost as dear as Freeholds, from the Confidence reposed in their Landlords of Renewals on customary Terms."[10] But the security of tenure was never endorsed at law. Church and college tenures remained as "beneficial" lease, in which the right of renewal at a "reasonable" fine was assumed but not prescribed.

That fines became less "reasonable" after 1720 was a consequence of the Whig ascendancy, and the greed of the Whig bishops.[11] The raising of fines of course encountered resistance: a steward will report (as one reported to St. John's from Windlesham, Surrey, in 1726) "the Homage insisted that my demands were very extraordinary."[12] On such a matter the homage could usually be overruled. But to overrule or alienate a homage was not quite as simple a matter as it may appear to our eyes—eyes which have long been habituated to seeing property-rights overruling functions and needs. These were the farmers, large and small, on the spot, and a distant corporate manorial owner found it necessary to work in some cooperation with them.[13] The steward of College or Church might encounter, on some matter of antagonistic interest, a conspiracy of silence among the tenants. In 1687 an informant wrote to the Bursar of St. John's about one estate:

> I cannot learn what life is in it, I am told by some 'tis an old woman in Suffolke and by others that two old women have their lives in it. They possibly may be dead, and the thing conceal'd. . . .[14]

The Bursar was at a loss to obtain true information about matters in other manors. When he sought to secure the help of the incumbent of the College's living at Ipsden, asking him to enquire into matters at Northstoke (Oxon) in 1683, the vicar was thrown into a paroxysm of alarm. There would be "suspision and great jealousies" if he was known to report to the College: his "affections to the College" already made him suspect. As to one enquiry:

> This is thing of so tender a nature that if there be given any shadow of suspicion I am unserviceable for ever, for it is the maxim of the country

people to be very silent to these . . . and it is in all virtue among them, to
be vindificative [sic] where their Interest is affected. . . .

Even to set this down in writing made the poor gentleman sweat: "I desire to
hear that my letter cometh safely to your hand, I shall be in paine till I am
assured thereof. . . ."[15]

A rich bishopric, like Winchester, was better equipped with a bureaucracy
of stewards, woodwards, etc., to deal with such problems. St John's (and no
doubt other colleges) got round the problem in the eighteenth century by leasing
whole manors to prosperous laymen.

But in the seventeenth century the beneficial lease still involved non-
economic mutualities, and even some paternal responsibilities. In 1610 Joan
Lingard, a widow of over seventy, was petitioning the Master of St. John's on
a delicate matter. Her tenure (described as a copyhold) was by virtue of her
widow's "free bench" in the right of her first husband. But in the interval of
twenty years since this husband's decease she had married twice more and had
been left twice more a widow. Her second and third husbands continued the
tenancy of the land, but in her widow's right. She had no issue by her first
husband, and now wished to surrender her copyhold to her eldest son, by her
second husband: her son had convenanted to reserve for her use a tenement
"together with other helpes towardes my maintenance during my life. . . ."[16]
Tenure is here being sought as descending through the widows right: presumably this was contrary to the custom of the manor, and for this reason the
permission of the Master and Fellows was solicited.

In the case of beneficial leases, renewal of tenure was not of right, but it
appears to have been difficult to refuse. We still understand only imperfectly
the tenacity and force of local custom. In a lease for three lives or 21 years
surrenders must be made and fines paid for the renewal of years or lives with
regularity. If the renewal was left over for more than seven years, the fine was
raised in proportion. The balance between custom and courtesy here is illustrated by a letter to the College in 1630 from an old student of St. John's,
soliciting charity for a poor widow, his own kinswoman. She was the relict of
a tenant whose lease was within four years of expiry, and she doubted whether
the College would renew because of the tardy application. "Peradventure," her
kinsman wrote, "you may thinke that hir husband and his son, both now with
God, had noe purpose to be suitors to your Colledge in renewing theire lease
in regard they detracted and let their lease weare out almost to the stumps."
But (he explained) her husband had had a lingering illness, had left debts, and
six small children; while the son—a seventh child—had enjoyed only one year's
tenure, during which time he had settled his father's debts, and then himself
died, leaving a widow and three children in his turn. The widow so circum-

stanced could clearly not pay the high fine due at a point so close to the expiry of the lease. The charity of the Master and Fellows was invoked, in the name of "the vowes and prayers of widdowes and fatherless children."[17]

In theory beneficial leases could be allowed to run out, unrenewed, and the Church or collegiate owner could bring all back into its own hands, in order to lease the land out once again at its "improved" or market value. This did happen on occasion, where only a few tenants were involved.[18] But it entailed an immediate loss of revenue—the existing lives and leases must be run through, and meanwhile there would be no revenue from fines.[19] This required an active, exploitive owner, or a rich one with several manors in hand. It also required an expansionist agriculture in which suitable new tenants, with capital on hand, were available. Moreover, where rights in usufruct extended over common lands—and this included upon fields held in severalty but over which lammas grazing rights existed, etc.—the tenants, if they briefed a good lawyer, could prevent the manorial owner from entering into his land until the last lease had fallen in. For the "inheritance" which we have here is that of communal use-rights, governed by the custom of the manor, and secured at law. When the College determined to regain possession of one manor in 1700, it was advised that this could not take place until the death of the last survivor— "namely the lives then in being and the last widdowe. . . ." Serjeant Wright of the Temple added: "The Tenants must now spit on their hands and live as long as they can, and the estates will be good to them to the end of the last life and widdow's estate. . . ."[20] Only then could the College accomplish its proposed rationalization, reletting the land at economic leases for 21 years.

By the early eighteenth century we have the sense that there was a deepening (albeit submerged and confused) conflict as to the very nature of landed property, a widening gap between definitions at law and in local custom—and by custom I do not mean only what the custumal may say but the denser reality of social practice. In Berkshire and in Hampshire in the 1720s, conflict over turves, grazing, timber-rights, and over the raids by deer upon the farmers' corn, contributed to episodes of armed disturbance.[21] But my point, in this comment, is only to emphasize that it is not helpful to discuss inheritance systems unless we keep always in mind what it is that is being inherited. If we refer vaguely to "land" then at once anachronistic images spring to mind of the patrimonial farm, with its ancient olives or its well-drained pastures, laboriously-built sheepfolds or spreading oaks. But in many of the farming systems under consideration inheritance of tenure was not so much the passage of land from one generation to the next (although certain closes and tenements might so pass) as the inheritance of use-rights over land (sometimes inherited only as security upon debt), some of which rights might be held in severalty, much of which was subject to at least some communal and manorial control and regulation.

There is a distinction here in social psychology. The farmer, confronted with a dozen scattered strips in different lands, and with prescribed stints in the commons, did not (one supposes) feel fiercely that he *owned* this land, that it was *his*. What he inherited was a place within the hierarchy of use-rights; the right to send his beasts, with a follower, down the lane-sides, to tether his horse in the sykes or on the baulks, the right to unloose his stock for lammas grazing, or for the cottager the right to glean and to get away with some timber-foraging and casual grazing. All this made up into a delicate agrarian equilibrium. It depended not only upon the inherited right but also upon the inherited grid of customs and controls within which that right was exercised. This customary grid was as intrinsic to inheritance as the grid of banking and of the stock exchange is to the inheritance of money. Indeed one could say that the beneficiary inherited both his right *and* the grid within which it was effectual: hence he must inherit a certain kind of social or communal psychology of ownership: the property not of his family but of his-family-within-the-commune.

Thus alongside the "Cartesian" logic of differing inheritance systems we must place the complementary logic of differing agrarian practices and tenures: and then assess the impact of the logic of the market, of capitalist agrarian practices. For what my scattered illustrations of the operation of some tenurial system shows, at the point of decomposition, is (1) the reification of use-right and its divorce from the actuality of use. An old woman whose death may be concealed is a property, albeit of uncertain value. Stints, abandoned messuages and tenements to which common rights are attached, the reversion of lives, may be bought and sold, independent of the user, just as dove-cots or pig-styes may be bought and sold for the burgage-rights attached to them. (2) The grid itself which validates the exercise of these rights is becoming increasingly insecure. The reification of the rights of some may mean in practice the limitation of the rights of the rest of the community. In extreme cases the manorial owner may be able to extinguish the grid without recourse to enclosure, although if his customary tenants know their law and have the stomach and purses to take recourse to it, the grid will survive as long as the last surviving customary tenant or his widow. As the grid becomes threatened, the small man (the copyholder or the freeholder with common rights appurtenant) must calculate his advantages. Enclosure may bring absolute freehold heritable rights, as well as the extinction of some petty customary claims over their land by the poor. But it may also threaten the equilibrium of crop and stock, in which the old grid carried many advantages. Some of these advantages were those sanctioned in practice in the village, although they could not be sustained at law.[22] (3) There is some evidence of the breaking-apart in the seventeenth and early eighteenth centuries of the agrarian inheritance system (conceived of as a body of rules enshrined in case-law) and the received customary traditions and practices of the village.

This breaking-apart lay along the lines of socio-economic cleavage, between the greater and the lesser rights of usage. Kerridge has identified the advance of capitalist process with greater security of tenure:

> To assert that capitalism throve on unjust expropriations is a monstrous and malicious slander. Security of property and tenure answered capitalism's first and most heartfelt need. Where insecurity reigned, it was because of the absence, not of the advent or presence of capitalism.[23]

No doubt, for tenures and rights of substance, the judgement is true. But to the degree that substantial usages were defined and secured, the insubstantial usages were disallowed. Kerridge (and many others) step bravely into a self-fulfilling argument, whose premises are entailed in its conclusions. Those usages which the law subsequently endorsed and secured as rights (such as heritable copyhold) are seen as genuine and lawful usages, those usages which the law subsequently disallowed are seen as pretended rights or illicit intrusions upon the rights of others. And yet it was the law itself which allowed one and disallowed the other; for it was the law which served as a superb instrument for enforcing the reification of right and for tearing down the remnants of the threadbare communal grid. At the outset of the seventeenth century the judgement in Gateward's Case both confirmed the customary rights of copyholders and disallowed those of vaguer categories—"inhabitants," "residents": if the latter were to be allowed their claims upon use-rights, then "no improvements can be made in any wastes."[24] But still in many areas indefinite rights of "inhabitants" prevailed until demographic pressure or the realities of local power resulted in their extinguishment or their tighter regulation by by-law. In many forest areas—among them Windsor, the New Forest, the Forest of Dean—large and ill-defined rights were claimed throughout the eighteenth century, and they appear to have been effectively exercised.[25] How far this situation obtained depended upon factors peculiar to each region and each manor.[26] But where the appeal was made to law the decisions moved in one direction: that of reification and limitation.

Copyhold itself, as an alienable property with a cashable monetary equivalent, had been very widely secured by the sixteenth century, partly because many men of substantial property and interest had a stake in this kind of tenure themselves. During the eighteenth century it became of more evident advantage to such men to bring into their own hands messuages which would carry at enclosure, substantial common-right values. But as the indefinite rights of the poor were excluded, so what may be called the fringe-benefits of the communal grid were extinguished. In a Chancery decision of 1741 an indefinite claim by "occupants" to enjoy the right of turbary was disallowed in the tradition of "Gateward's Case": the claim was found to be "a very great absurdity, for an occupant, who is no more than a tenant at will, can never have a right to take away the soil of the lord."[27] Similar judgements extended over other fringe rights. In 1788 the claim of "poor, necessitous and indigend householders" in Whaddon (Bucks.) to take dead wood in the local coppice was disallowed since "there is no limitation . . . the description of poor householder is too vague and uncertain. . . ."[28] The famous decision against gleaning in the same year did not of course extinguish (unless here and there) the *practice* of gleaning. What it did was to extinguish the claim of the villagers to glean *as of right*, even though that right may be seen clearly defined in dozens of early manorial by-laws.[29] Hence, at a stroke of the pen, a most ancient use-right was decreed to be uncashable at law—might one use such an ugly concept as *un*reified?

This law evolved from a Baconian and not a Cartesian mind. It is a law which resisted (as Blackstone proclaimed with proud chauvinism)[30] the influence of Justinian and of the revival of Roman law in general. Its precedents were piecemeal: it evolved with empirical caution. But behind this empirical evolution one may detect the no-less-Cartesian logic of capitalist evolution. Coke's decision in "Gateward's Case" rested less upon legal than upon economic logic— "no improvements can be made in any wastes." The judges sought to reduce use-rights to an equivalent in things or in money, and hence to bring them within the universal currency of capitalist definitions of ownership. Property must be made palpable, loosed for the market from its uses and from its social situation, made capable of being hedged and fenced, of being owned quite independently of any grid of custom or of mutuality. As between substantial rights, and even as between the greater and the lesser of such rights, the law was impartial: it was tender of property of whatever degree. What it abhorred was an indefinite sociological praxis, a *coincidence* of several use-rights, unreified usages. And this English law, following upon the heels of the Pilgrim Fathers and of the John Company, attempted to reify and translate into terms of palpable property ownership the customs and usages of whole peoples which had inherited communal grids of a totally different character.

The consequences in these cases were far-reaching. The bearing upon the problem of inheritance in England was more subtle. Any system of impartible inheritance in an agrarian system which has ceased to expand must be subject to a delicate demographic equilibrium. The fringe-benefits of the grid are not things distinct from the transmitted tenurial rights. Some laxness in the definition of rights of grazing, gleaning, firing, etc., can help to support the sons who do not inherit tenures, stock, and implements. With these benefits extinguished, the excess population may be reduced to a landless proletariat or ejected like lemmings from the community. One need not propose a simple typological model of a "swapping" equilibrium, one son inheriting, one daughter married to a tenant or freeholder, half a son or daughter remaining to be provided for. It is rather that we have to take the total context together; the inheritance customs, the actuality of what was being inherited, the character of the economy, the manorial by-laws or field regulations, the poor law. If in the fifteenth and sixteenth centuries younger children sometimes inherited beasts or implements (but no land) we must assume that they expected access to land somehow. If (as I suppose) in the same centuries communal agrarian regulation became tighter, excluding those without land from certain unacknowledged but practised grazing rights, then to the same degree what the occupier inherited became better, what the younger child had left to him became worse. The yeoman is advantaged: it is less easy for his brother to make do as a husbandman or a craftsman with a few sheep and a cow on the common. What matters then becomes the inheritance of capital, for both land and stints on the common may still be rented.

In certain areas, such as forests, the fringe-benefits may be so large as to afford a livelihood of sorts for many younger brothers, and even immigrants. This will also be so in areas where a scanty agrarian income may be supplemented by developing domestic industries and crafts. Such areas, one might suppose, favoured practices of partible inheritance—practices which cannot be deduced from the registration of tenures in the court-roll. The successor who enters upon the tenure may be seen (from the evidence of the will) to be acting as trustee for the widow[31] or, as trustee for the children whose portions are to be divided "share and share alike."[32] Forms may grow up whereby the lives in being[33] or reversionary[34] entered in the court-roll are fictitious. The actual practices of inheritance, as evidenced by wills, may be completely at odds with the recited customs of the manor: and even where custom specifically enforced the impartibility of a tenure, devices could be arranged to circumvent custom.[35]

In Windsor Forest, in the early years of the eighteenth century, there is a little evidence of such practices of partible inheritance.[36] Percy Hatch, a yeoman of Winkfield, with about 70 acres (mostly in freehold) sought in 1727 to benefit his four sons and a married daughter.[37]

In this (see table) the oldest son is clearly advantaged, although the other sons receive some money in compensation. The second son, who is charged with his sister's dowry, is also advantaged, but as between the second, third, and fourth there is clearly some notional sense of equality. Eleven acres of poor land might seem inadequate for a livelihood: but Winkfield, an extensive parish in the heart of the forest, enjoyed large grazing rights, for sheep as well as

	House	Land	Furniture	Money
1st Son	Messuage & Farmhouse "Sumertons"	27 ½ acres & 4 doles of land in common fields	Furnace Clothes-press Biggest spit Malt mill	—
2nd Son	Messuage & Farmhouse "Berkshire House"	c. 14 acres	—	£30*
3rd Son	—	11 acres	—	£20
4th Son	—	11 acres	Is executor and has residue of estate	
Daughter	—	—	Best chest of drawers	*

*The daughter was married to a substantial famer. The second son was charged to pay £60 to her husband. This presumably was her dowry, but it is not clear whether this debt was her settlement in part or in full.

cattle,[38] substantial (if contested) rights of turbary, access to timber, as well as brick-kilns (perhaps this explains the furnace?) and a little forest industry. There were several branches of the Hatch family in the parish, the eldest of which "time out of mind has had an handsome estate and good interest therein. . . ."[39] We do not know the degree of kinship of Percy Hatch to this older branch: but some degree of kinship was likely to have added a supportive social context to the younger son's struggle for a livelihood—and we know from other evidence that Winkfield parishioners defended their community's rights with the greatest vigour.[40].

Much of this rests on inference. But it may add a little flesh to the bone of the conjecture that it was in such a context, where the grid of communal inheritance was strong and where fringe-rights were indefinite and extensive, that a yeoman could risk the practice of partible inheritance without condemning his children to poverty. Below a certain minimum further partition would be ridiculous: husbandmen (in the evidence of one local study) were unlikely to divide their land.[41] But in the normal course of succession portions would not only be divided but also, through marriage, death, legacies from childless kin, be thrown together: Percy Hatch evidently held two distinct farms, one of which ("Sumerton") he left intact to his oldest son, from the other of which ("Berkshire House") he took out portions of land for his third and fourth.

If we learn more about the regions where such "egalitarian" practices were prevalent, these may throw light upon the relationship of inheritance customs to industrialisation.[42] But in fielden, arable regions, in which little extension of land-use was possible, such "share and share alike" practices would have led to economic suicide: tenure must pass as one parcel along with buildings, implements, and stock. But this certainly faced the yeoman with a dilemma. Kiernan doubts whether a love of private property can be seen as a constant in "human nature," and one may agree. But a desire to secure the expectations of one's children—to try to throw forward some grid which will support them—has at least had a long run in social history. It is here that Spufford's findings are important, for they seem to emphasize that the "yeomen" were seeking to transmit down the generations not only "land" (particular tenures) but also a social status to *all* their children. The nobility and gentry devised with care their own grid of transmission through entail and marriage settlement. Such a grid was not available to the yeoman. The merchants and professions might throw forward a grid of money. The small farmer could hope to do a little in this way himself, by bequeathing legacies as a charge upon his estate. In such cases, the moment of death was for the small man a moment of great familial financial risk. M. K. Ashby, examining the village of Bledington—a village with slight manorial presence and with a large number of freeholders—keeps a careful eye on the farmers' wills. She observes two points of change. In the early seventeenth century the wills of farmers and of widows indicate still "a world of wide family connections and affections, a valuation of persons and also of objects, goods: charitable bequests are frequent." But the movable property given away is in small amounts. "After 1675 the family recognised is the immediate group of parents and children, charity is absent and money is prominent, and in larger amounts." The second change is in accentuation of the first: by the early eighteenth century farmers "are leaving their estates burdened by very large monetary legacies, to be paid by those who inherit the land. . . . The pattern they adopt . . . is that of the owner of large estates in which, e.g. the head of the family provides for widow, daughter, and younger sons out of the receipts of a landed estate."[43] But the outpayments to be made by their heir sometimes appear as unrealistic. Mortgages must be taken up or debts incurred to meet the legacies. Possibly it is exactly in this inheritance practice that we may see the death-warrant of the yeomanry as a class? They were seeking to project forward a grid of legacies upon which the children who did not inherit land or its tenure could yet be maintained at yeoman status. In doing so they were withdrawing capital which could have been dunging their own land. Not all of this need leave the village: some would pass, by way of a daughter's portion, to another farm: some younger brothers might rent land and stints or settle to local crafts. But it would seem that the practice of laying legacies upon the heir (a practice with some analogies to the French "recall") could equally have been a way of diverting capital from the countryside to the town.

The attempt to impose large portions—perhaps approaching to some notional "share and share alike"—upon the heir led him not only into debt but into a different kind of debt from the neighbourhood borrowing often found in the traditional village. This neighbourhood petty indebtedness was itself a sort of "swapping" which often had a social as well as economic dimension: loans were exchanged among kin, neighbours, sometimes as part of a reciprocity of services. The new mortgages carried the small man into a wider and more ruthless money market quite outside his own expertise. An alert manorial owner who wished to bring tenures back into his own hands could take advantage of the same situation by granting and foreclosing mortgages upon his own copyholds: by such means the St. Johns of Dogmersfield managed in the years after the South Sea Bubble to lose a village and turn much of it into a deer-park.[44] In this case some of the tenants seem to have resorted to arson, to the shooting of cattle and the felling of trees. But so far as one can see they were victims not of forced dispossession but of "fair" economic process, of good lawyers, and of the debt incurred by the Bubble.

The old communal grid had been eaten away by law and by money long before enclosure: eighteenth-century enclosure registered the end rather than the climax of that process. The tenures which we have been discussing can be seen also as roles, functions, access to use-rights, governed by communal rules and expectations as well as by customary law. They are part of one impartible bundle, a dense socio-economic nexus. The attempt to define these by law was in itself an abstraction from that nexus. For a practice to be offensive to the community or to the homage does not provide any compelling reason at law or in cash for the practice not to continue. But opinion can be more effective than we suppose: in some parts of Ireland in the eighteenth and early nineteenth centuries there was no reason at law why a landlord might not expel his tenants and lease more advantageously to new ones. The only trouble was that the steward might be shot and the new tenants' cabins be burned down. In Hampshire in 1711 they were more polite. When Bishop Trelawny's assertive, rationalizing steward, Dr Heron, showed excessive zeal and rapacity in seizing herriots upon the death of a tenant, he was exposed by the bereaved son to public rebuke in front of his officers and strangers. This cost the steward no more than some loss of face; he should have taken it as a danger signal, an inhibition upon his action. When he failed to do so, the tenants and other episcopal officers closed against him and commenced an agitation which forced the bishop to replace his steward.[45]

Small victories like this, in defence of customary practice, were won here and there. But the campaign itself was always lost. (The bishop's next steward attained much the same ends, with a little more diplomacy and a little more care in favouring his subordinate officials.) For to the impartible bundle of communal practice capitalism introduces its own kind of partible inheritance. Uses are divorced from the user, properties from the exercise of functions. But once you break the bundle up into parts what becomes inherited is not a communal equilibrium but the properties of particular men and of particular social groups. Le Roy Ladurie speaks of the equal division by value of tenures as "egalitarian": and if we mean by this nothing more than equal division then the term need not be disputed. But he proposes to take the thought further: "spreading progressively through the rural world this current of egalitarianism will . . . finally submerge all the hierarchies of ordered society." But we have here proposed that in some parts of England the egalitarian desire of the yeoman to advantage as far as possible equally all of his children ended up, through a surfeit of mortgages, in submerging not the hierarchies of ordered societies but the yeomanry as a class. We should perhaps recall some lines of William Blake:

> Is this thy soft Family Love
> Thy cruel Patriarchal pride
> Planting thy Family alone,
> Destroying all the World beside.

And Blake adds to this a suggestion of the same logic through which the yeomen fell:

> And he who make his law a curse
> By his own law shall surely die.

For it had been these same copyholders, anxious to maintain their status within the rural hierarchy, who had taken an active part in the previous two centuries in breaking the communal bundle apart, in drawing up more stringent by-laws which advantaged the landholder and disadvantaged those without tenures, in limiting the fringe benefits of the grid, in setting use-rights to market.[46] In their anxiety as a social class to plant their own family alone they prepared the means of their own destruction.

Perhaps another characteristic of traditional tenurial society was lost. Free bench or widow's estate, as it pertained in many manors into the eighteenth century, did allow for a considerable feminine presence. Female tenure, either as free bench or in the woman's own right, does not of course prove that the agrarian and other attendant functions were always performed by the tenants: a subtenant could be put in, or the farm could be left under the control of male

kin. But we would be making a hasty judgment if we assumed that most feminine tenures were only fictionally so. This was certainly not true at the top of
society, which saw the formidable presence of such women as Sarah, duchess
of Marlborough, or of Ruperta Howe, the ranger of Alice Holt Forest. And we
must all have encountered evidence which suggests that women of the yeoman
class acquitted themselves, at the head of farming households, with equal vigour.
In the early eighteenth century a steward of St. John's was engaged in a protracted and inconclusive negotiation with one infuriating tenant, whose evasions
always left her in possession of all the points at issue: "I had rather" (he wrote)
"have business with three men than one woman."[47]

The customary grid did allow for a female presence, although usually—but
not necessarily—on condition of either widowhood or spinsterhood. There was
an eye—and in the eighteenth century a continuing eye—upon the continuity
of the familial tenure through the male line. Free bench was often conditional
upon no remarriage, and also upon chaste living—a prohibition which arose
less from Puritanism than from jealousy of the influence of new children, or of
the waste to the estate which might be committed by the stepfather. Where the
widow did not lose her tenure upon remarriage there is sometimes a suggestion
that the lord, his steward, or the homage had some kind of paternal responsibilities for overwatching the children's right. In 1635 a clergyman petitioned
St. John's on behalf of the children of William Haddlesen. In this case, the
father had willed his lease to the children, who were not yet of age; and
Haddlesen's widow "hath married very unluckely, so that if the Colledge stand
not the children's friend to lett it to some in trust for their use (for the mother
is not to be trusted) the children are like to be undunne . . ."[48] (One wonders
whether it was cases of remarriage of this kind which would have been the
particular occasion of rough music in England and charivari in France?)

Manors had different customs to make allowance for frailty or to deal with
unusual circumstances. The "jocular" customs of Enborne (Berks.) and of Kil-
mersdon (Somerset)—and probably of other places—were not as ridiculous as
they may seem. In Enborne if the woman "commits incontinency she forfeits
her Widow's estate"—

> Yet, after this, if she comes into the next Court held for the Manor, riding
> backward upon a Black Ram, with his Tail in her hand, and says the
> Words following, the Steward is bound by the Custom to re-admit her to
> her Free Bench:

> Here I am,
> Riding upon a Black Ram,
> Like a Whore as I am:

And for my Crincum Crancum,
Have lost my Bincum Bancum;
And for my Tail's game
Am brought to this Worldly Shame,

Therefore good Mr. Steward let me have my Lands again.

At Kilmesdon the recitative required was more brief, and the offender need only ride astride the ram:

For mine Arse's Fault I take this Pain,
Therefore, my Lord, give me my Land again.[49]

In other customs more rational controls or adjustments are established.[50]

One trouble with the customs of manors rehearsed between 1660 and 1800 is that we know rather little about the relation of custom to practice. And this is, mainly, because we have not bothered to find out. The Webbs noted in 1908 that there was no comprehensive study of the Lord's Court in the period 1689–1835[51] and the position remains much the same today. (Recent advances in agrarian history have inevitably been addressed more to the improving and market-oriented sectors of the economy than to the customary.) In the case of customs of the manor governing inheritance, these came into force only when the tenant died intestate and without effecting a previous surrender; and it was usual to allow a death-bed surrender, in the presence of two customary tenants, bequeathing the tenure to an heir. Hence practice and recited customs of inheritance may long have parted company. But there is a further difficulty of a different kind. Customs formally presented at a survey (for example, upon the entry of a new lord) may have recited only a small portion of the uncodified but accepted customary practices of a manor. The uncodified portion could have remained in the custody of the memories of the steward and of the homage, with reference to the case-law built up in the court rolls. Only when we find a strong body of copyholders whose customs have become insecure in the face of an invasive or absent lord do we find an attempt to codify this case-law in all its dense social particularity.[52]

Probably the practice of widow's estate or free bench is least confused by these difficulties. Since the widow normally entered upon her free bench without any fine, this constituted a bonus of years to the existent tenure. Unless the husband had some distinct reason for making an alternative arrangement, he was likely to leave the free bench to run according to the custom of the manor; and even the briefest eighteenth-century recitals of customs normally take care to establish what the custom on this important point was. Thus custom here is some indication as to practice.

Perhaps custom within the manor may even have influenced practice outside the customary sector? The customs of Waltham St. Lawrence (Berks.), rehearsed in 1735, afford to the widow full free bench during widowhood and chaste living. If she remarries or lives unchaste, she is to have one-third of the rental value of the tenure—that is, a reversion to an earlier notion of dower.[53] But if she had had issue before marriage, then she had neither free bench nor moiety.[54] Waltham St. Lawrence lies within the same hundred as Warfield, and it is interesting to find that a yeoman of Warfield, in 1721, willed eight acres of *freehold* to his widow for life, on condition that the timber was not to be wasted nor the land ploughed: if she broke these conditions "my will is that she shall thenceforth have out of the same no more than her Dower or Thirds."[55] At nearby Binfield in Windsor Forest in the same year another yeoman left all lands and tenements to his wife "during her natural life if she keep her selfe a widow but if she should happen to be married again . . . then only to have and enjoy the Thirds thereof . . ."[56] For some forest farmers, custom and practice in free bench appear to have run a parallel course.

Customs varied between one region and the next and, within each region, from one manor to another. I can offer only an impression, based on limited research into two or three districts. It would seem that by the eighteenth century free bench was one of the most secure and universal of customs, applicable both to copyholds of inheritance and tenures for lives; distinctions between customary and common law terms or between tenures of customary or demesne lands had generally lapsed, and free bench generally signified continuance in the whole tenure, not in a moiety of its profits. The customs collected in Watkins's *Treatise on Copyholds* (1825 edn.) offer no systematic sample, being such as came to the editor's hand or were sent in by correspondents. Custom is often reported in imprecise terms—"the widow has her face free bench," the manor "gives no dower." But for what the collection is worth it reports the status of widows in some sixty manors in terms which suggest that the customs were still operative or had at least survived into the eighteenth century.[57] Of these some forty show free bench, either for life or during widowhood; ten show no "dower"; ten show dower of one-third moiety; and one of one-half. The manors with free bench are drawn from fifteen countries (with Worcestershire greatly over-represented). The manors with no "dower" or moieties only are drawn from six countries: in these Norfolk is over-represented, while in Middlesex and Surrey it is probable that the custom of free bench was weak where the practice of the alternative form of security—the jointure or joint-tenancy of husband and wife—was strong.[58]

Where free bench was assured the main distinction between manors turned on the question of its continuance or discontinuance upon remarriage. At May-field (Sussex) the ancient distinction between bond-land and assert-land tenure survived: "yard-land widow, to hold during widowhood, Assert-widow during life."[59] At Littlecot (Wilts.) the widow has full widow's estate and may marry again without the loss of her tenure, but if she was a *second* wife she "can have but her widowhood."[60] At Stoke Prior (Worcs.) the widow enjoys "the moiety" of the lands "and to receive only the rent of the heir if they can agree"—any difference to be referred to the homage.[61] At Balsall (Warws.) free bench was granted to the widow if a first wife, but only one-third moiety of rents and profits if she was the second or third.[62] At Farnham, a manor with a strong homage, jealous of its privileges, the customs were rehearsed in 1707 with great vigour and detail and it is fair to assume that they were correspondent to practice and that we have in them some codification of the precedents that had come before the court. In these a surrender by the husband (even to the use of his will) bars the wife's dower: such a provision was essential if the land was to be alienable. But the husband could, by surrender in the court or surrender to the use of his will, reserve his wife's life: that is, afford her free bench in precedence to the next reversion. If he were to surrender without making any such condition then his widow "shall neither have tearmes of Life or Widow's estate; but if he die without Surrender she shall have her Widow's estate if she live sole and Chastly."[63] And, by an additional provision, "if she comes to the next court after her husband's death and pays half a fine, she becomes tenant for life, and may marry again without forfeiting her estate."[64]

These divergent customs record different solutions offered to adjust the same insoluble problems. On the one hand there is an attempt to afford security to the widow, and perhaps to her underage children. On the other hand if copyhold was to be truly alienable then no absolute security could be afforded. Moreover where tenure was expected to descend to the children, remarriage presented a threat to the line of inheritance. This also called for nice adjustments, sometimes recorded in the customs. Once again the Farnham customs of 1707 reveal a complex codification and sociological government. Where a tenant had a daughter by one wife, and a son and daughter by a second, the daughter by the second marriage had precedence over the daughter by the first, even if the son (her brother) had predeceased the tenant and never been admitted to the tenure ("yet shall his sister by his mother inherit the land . . . as heire to her brother . . . notwithstanding her elder sister by the first woman. . . ."[65] It is difficult to address Cartesian logic to this solution. It looks very much like a piece of case-law, decided by the court and then added to the custumal. What appears to be emphasized here is the transmission of the tenure with the least domestic friction: presumably the first daughter will already be likely to have left the farm, the second wife (now widowed) is likely to remain in residence with her daughter: she seems the most "natural" heir.

In any case we are not looking at any sort of sexually egalitarian customs. No "jocular" custom has yet come to light in which a fornicating old widower had to submit himself to the pain of riding into court on a goat. But we do have an accepted area of feminine presence, and this may have been an effective and creative one, and one felt, at any given time, palpably in the customary village.[66] Kerridge, who sometimes appears to hold a conspiratorial theory of tenure, in which the customary tenants are seen as constantly seeking for new ways to exploit their lords, has doubts as to the morality of the practice of free bench: it was "open to abuse in a loose and disreputable manner, as when an aged and ailing customer took a young wife merely in order that she or a third party might enjoy the holding during her expected widowhood."[67] No doubt on occasion this happened:[68] but as a general comment on the value or functions of free bench the judgment is flippant. It is even possible that habituation to this active feminine presence in areas of strong customary and yeoman occupancy served to modify sexual roles and inheritance customs more generally, even outside the customary sector.[69] Where I have compared the wills of Berkshire yeomen and tradesmen with the customs in Berkshire parishes in the 1720s and 1730s I have noted no evidence in the former of any bias against female kin,[70] and, on occasion, a little bias the other way.[71] When in 1721 the Rev. Thomas Power, the curate of Easthampstead (Berks.) sought to persuade his recalcitrant wife to sign over some messuages to him by hanging her by a leg from the window and threatening to cut the rope, so far from meeting with the applause of the neighbourhood he was subjected by some local gallants to some very rough music and to a mock execution.[72] But this no doubt is another example of "loose and disreputable" practice.

Freehold could of course also be transmitted to women: and it was so transmitted, to widows, to sisters, to daughters, and to grand-daughters. But if we accept that between 1660 and 1760 there was a severe decline in the numbers of yeomen, both free and copy, it may follow that there will also have been an equivalent decline in the effective female agrarian presence. Where lands came out of customary tenure, and were leased out again at will, they would be leased to men. A tenancy-at-will carried no widow's estate: at the most it would be allowed as a favour. Security of the customary grid was lost; and if the yeoman was only at a further point in his secular decline, the yeowoman had been served notice to quit.

As a final point I wish to return to the difference between the inheritance of a family, and inheritance of security, status, power, by a social group, caste, or class. The first depends generally upon the second. We have the particular inheritance practices of families, and the grid of law, custom, expectation, upon which these practices operate. And these grids differ greatly between social groups. What is happening is the devising of rules and practices by which particular social groups project forwards provisions and (as they hope) guarantees of security for their children. Cooper has examined the grid of the great. The moneyed class had a different grid, although it meshed in closely with that of the land. But the eighteenth century had also a third, complementary, grid for the propertied classes: that of interest, preferment to office, purchase of commissions, reversions to sinecures, placings within the Church, and so on. In this grid of nepotism and interest, possession was not all: one must also supplement possession with continuing interest and the right kind of political connections. One must both have (or find for one's child) an office and maintain the influence to exploit that office to the full. The parent might attend to the first: his child must see to the second.

Throughout the eighteenth century the grid of interest and preferment remained as a bundle of that kind. Along this grid the lesser gentry sought to secure the future of their families. The papers of the great patrons show the incessant activity of petitioners on behalf of their kin, in the attempt to secure the whole structure of the Church and State as a kind of Trust for their own class. Middle-class reformers, rallying under the banner of the "career open to talent," at the same time sought to secure the future status of their own children upon a grid of educational qualification and professional exclusiveness. Moreover, this reminds us that a privileged group could—and still can—secure its own grid while trying to tear down the grid of another. In the twentieth century the see-saw of social-democratic and conservative politics has often turned on such rivalries. But in the eighteenth and nineteenth centuries similar contests were fought which will be overlooked if we only take into account post-mortem inheritance. Sabean appears, momentarily, to have allowed this oversight to enter when he cites the case of a poor village in the Sologne and concludes from its evidence that "in the absence of property there is little tendency to develop extended kin ties." Of course if there is an absence of land and of movable property then neither of these can be transmitted through inheritance: nor are the poor in any position to "arrange for good marriages." So that Sabean's generalization may hold good for a poor peasant economy. But even for the landless rural labourer, and certainly for an urban proletariat, the critical point of familial transmission has not been *post mortem* but at the point of giving the children a "start in life." If we wish to examine inheritance and the family in the eighteenth century among urban craftsmen, we have to look, not at wills, but at apprenticeship regulations, apprenticeship premiums, and at trades in which a strong family tradition was preserved by offering a preference to sons or kin and by limiting apprentices.[73] Even among the rural poor (one suspects) the business of placing a son on a good farm, a daughter in service at the great house, occupied much effort and anxiety, and was part of the effort of transmitting to the next generation a "respectable" status, on the right side of the poor law. And in the early nineteenth century, by clipping away at apprenticeship, by repealing the Statute of Artificers, the rulers of England were threatening the inheritance system of the skilled workmen; while in 1834, by striking at all out-relief, they threatened the only grid of ultimate security known to the poor.

Of course, no guarantee has ever secured to the individual family immunity from the accidents of mutability. Remarkable as are certain continuities among aristocracy and gentry, there are many more cases of the downward turn of fortune's wheel. As Raymond Williams has recently argued, the very literary values of landed estate and settlement are often those espoused by the newly-rich anxious to pretend to the values of settlement. Penshurst, the subject of Ben Jonson's classic country house poem, raised by "no man's ruin, no man's grone," was in fact a manor which had lapsed by execution and attainder some fifty years before Jonson wrote.[74] For other poets the family and its fortune are taken as an illustration of mutability:

> And what if my descendants lose the flower
> Through natural declension of the soul,
> Through too much business with the passing hour,
> Through too much play, or marriage with a fool?
> May this laborious stair and this stark tower
> Become a roofless ruin that the owl
> May build in the cracked masonry and cry
> Her desolation to the desolate sky.

For Yeats no forethought could hold back the cyclical mutability of things:

> The Primum Mobile that fashioned us
> Has made the very owls in circles move. . . .

Yeats underestimated certain continuities, and notably the remarkable longevity of certain corporate landowners—those wise old owls, Merton College and St. John's College, Cambridge, have flown directly to us from the twelfth or thirteenth centuries. But common observation (or a brief consultation of any genealogical authority) confirms this thought: as Yorkshire people have it, from clogs to clogs in three generations. What this may conceal is that independent of the rise and fall of families, the inheritance-grids themselves have often proved to be extremely effective as a vehicle of another kind of corporate inheritance—the means by which a social group has extended its historical tenure of status and of privilege. We are busy with it still today, as accountants and lawyers devise new trusts, new hedges against inflation, setting up invest-ment trusts with one leg upon each of the four corners of the capitalist world. But we should be on our guard. We commence by examining the inheritance systems of particular families: but, over time, family fortunes rise and fall; what is inherited is property itself, the claim on the resources of a future society; and the beneficiary may be, not any descendant of that particular family, but the historical descendant of the social class to which that family once belonged.

> From *Family and Inheritance* edited by Goody, Thirsk and Thompson (Cambridge 1976), the report of a *Past and Present* Conference. These comments which arose in the course of the conference are based upon work, some of which is yet to be published: for the forest areas of Berk-shire and eastern Hampshire. *Whigs and Hunters* (London, 1975) and for some other aspects of eighteenth-century customs. "Common Right and Enclosure" in *Customs in Common*. In any case, many points are proposed here as questions, requiring further research, rather than as conclusions. My thanks are due to Jeanette Neeson and to editors and contributors to this volume for reading this comment in manuscript and for sending me valuable criticisms, some of which raised questions too complex to answer in the context of this study.

Notes

1. Since much copyhold land was itself sub-let on economic leases, it may well be true that by the eighteenth-century leasehold at rack-rent "had largely displaced all other tenancies": Eric Ker-ridge, *Agrarian Problems in the Sixteenth Century and After* (London, 1969), p. 46. But the number of occupying customary tenants remained substantial and they should not be allowed to be lost to view.

2. Here I will use the term "customary tenure" in a general (and sociological) rather than precise (and legal) definition. Copyhold need not be held according to the custom of the manor, while beneficial leases were not, at law, customary tenures although Church and collegiate manors were in fact often subject to customary practices. See Kerridge, ch. 2 for a lucid discrimination between forms of tenure, which (however) affords priority to legal definitions over customary practice.

3. Thus the Court Baron of Uphaven (Wilts.), 20 October 1742; Rinaldo Monk's copyhold cottage forfeited to the lord, he having been convicted of felony and transported: P.R.O.T.S. 19.3. Forfeiture for waste (often compounded by a fine) is more common.

4. In a copyhold of inheritance even a fine uncertain must be "reasonable"—a definition which was set by common law at around two years' improved rental. But a copyhold at the will of the lord limited fines to no such legal rationality: R. B. Fisher, *A Practical Treatise on Copyhold Tenure* (London, 1794), pp. 81–2, 90. Six or seven years' improved rental might be charged in such cases, "The only alternative left to the tenant is to pay the fine, or let the estate fall in."

5. R. B. Fisher who was Steward of Magdalen College claimed to be writing from practical knowledge of manorial usages in many parts of the country: Coke had been writing only of "pure and
genuine copyholds" but "at this time of day there is a sort of bastard species . . . a copyhold
tenure," i.e. copyhold for lives, which was to be found "in a multiplicity of manors within the
kingdom." How far this "bastard species" was of recent creation, how far it indicated a degeneration of "pure" copyhold could only be established by many local studies: ibid., pp. 14–15, 90.

6. Charles Watkins, *A Treatise on Copyholds* (4th edn, 1825), ii, pp. 549–50. It is difficult to set a
date upon the customs which Watkins's editor assembled for the 100 pages of Appendix III to
the 4th edition. Some customs cited date from the seventeenth century or earlier; but others,
including most of the Worcestershire customs, appear to have been sent in by a correspondent
in the attempt to describe contemporary or very recent practice.

7. Ibid., ii, p. 553. At Tebberton the custom as presented in 1649 was "that the lord hath always
used to grant the copyholds for three lives in possession, and three in reversion," the fines being
arbitrary; but Watkins's correspondent notes that "of late years the lord hath only granted for
two lives in possession and two in reversion, which is no invasion of the ancient custom, as
grants are entirely at the lord's pleasure." A comment on the case of Broadwas perhaps generalizes
the experience of insecurity in a number of Worcestershire manors: "these servile tenures are
inconsistent with the present times; and occasion ill-will to the lords, and uneasiness to many
honest men": ibid., ii, pp. 546, 564. It is interesting to note that the only instance of wrongful
treatment towards copyholders which Kerridge, after his very extensive searches, is able to confirm
as at least "an allegation which found some support" concerns tenants of the Dean and Chapter
of Worcester Cathedral forced, in the early seventeenth century, to take leases for years in place
of copyholds of inheritance: Kerridge, op. cit., p. 83.

8. H. F. Howard, *An Account of the Finances of St. John's College, Cambridge 1511–1926* (Cambridge,
1935), p. 47.

9. See also R. F. Scott, *Notes from the Records of St. John's College, Cambridge* (St. John's, Cambridge), Second Series, 1899–1906, no. xiv, who estimates that the usual fine for surrenders and
renewals in the seventeenth century was one year's gross or extended rent: this was raised over
the course of the eighteenth century to 1¼, 1½, and thence to two years. See also W. S. Powell
in *Eagle* (St. John's College), xx, no. 115, March 1898. By the nineteenth century the fine was
generally 2.6 of the gross letting value: St. John's College, Cambridge, calendar of archives,
drawer 100 (70): Statement of Senior Bursar at Audit for 1893. I am indebted to the Master and
Fellows of St. John's for permission to consult their calendar and archives, and to the Librarian
and Archivist for assistance.

10. Anon., *Reasons for a Law to oblige Spiritual Persons and Bodies Politick to Renew their Leases for
Customary and Reasonable Fines* (London, n.d., c. 1736).

11. Or so it is argued in *Whigs and Hunters* (London, 1975), Chapter 4, passim. The Church appears
to have introduced new tables for the assessment of fines, computed according to the interest on
the capital investment, the age of the life in being, the number of years lapsed since the last
renewal, etc., at some time between 1715 and 1720. The rules demanded 1½ years' extended
rental value for renewal of twenty-one year leases, and so in proportion for more or fewer years
out: and, in leases for lives, two years' value be insisted on for one life out, and where two are
void in proportion, or (preferably) conversion of a lease for three lives to a twenty-one-years'
lease. These tables, known as "Sir Isaac Newton's Tables," created great resentment among
tenants: they raised fines, replaced personal and flexible negotiations by a uniform rationalized
standard, and above all disallowed the tenants' claim to have established themselves by long
precedent in tenures which in effect were customary, heritable, and subject (like copyholds) to a
fine certain. See St. John's College calendar, drawer 109 (38), "Rules agreed to by the Church
of Canterbury at your Audit 1720, according to Sir I. Newton's Tables, thus allowing your

Tenants 9 per cent which they think favour sufficient": also, C. Trimnell to W. Wake, 4 July 1720, Christ Church College Library, Oxford. Arch. Wake Epist, XXI. For the case of the tenants (some of whom were substantial landholders), *Reasons for a Law, cit. supra* note 10; "Everard Fleetwood" (Samuel Burroughs). *An Enquiry into the Customary-Estates and Tenant-Rights of those who hold Lands of Church and other Foundations* (London, 1731). For the case of Church and Colleges, see *inter alia*, Anon., *Tables for Renewing and Purchasing of Cathedral Churches and Colleges* (London, 1731).

12. John Aldridge, 27 October 1726, St. John's College calendar, drawer 109 (185). For other complaints at the raising of fines, all in 1725, see ibid. drawer 109 (80), (84), (92), (99).

13. This was acknowledged by the Colleges' own defenders. Thus *Tables for Renewing, supra*, p. 55, agreed that leases "of a considerable term of years," and reasonably renewable, were beneficial to both parties "because Men of Letters and Bodies Corporate cannot so well manage their Estates as Laymen or a single Person may do, if they kept them in their own Hands, or let them out at Rack-Rent," especially where such properties were at a distance. In such circumstance a good tenant might be given favour much as if he were acting as the College's Steward: thus M. John Baber was entered as tenant of the manor of Broomhall (at Sunninghill, Berks.) in 1719: he was long in possession, and when there was an extensive fall of timber in the manor in 1766 it was resolved that "if the sale of the timber answers our expectations [we intend] to make him a present of fifty guineas for the care that has been taken of it." The sale exceeded expectations and Baber's gift was increased to £100: St. John's College archives. "Old Dividend and Fine Book." p. 66: Conclusion Book, I. pp. 176, 178.

14. Howard, *Finances of St. John's College*, pp. 71–2.

15. Rev. T. Longland to Senior Bursar, 27 November 1683, St. John's College calendar, drawer 86 (62).

16. Joan Lingard (a tenant at Staveley) to Master, ibid., drawer 94 (25). The College held certain properties through gift or purchase in which regular copyhold (rather than beneficial leases) pertained.

17. Robert Pain to Master, 26 October 1630, ibid., drawer 94 (52). The tenant in question held land in Paxton Magna (Hunts.).

18. George Davies, 3 July 1725, ibid., drawer 109 (96), concerning a few tenants at Marfleet (Yorks.): "I am of opinion it will be better for the College that they do not renew but take the estates, as they fall, into their own hands."

19. The College did not finally decide to end the system of beneficial leases until 1851. The Fellows endured a loss of revenue from fines in the 1850s, but benefited considerably from the improved income from economic rentals after the mid 1860s: "Statement of the Senior Bursar at Audit for 1893," ibid., drawer 100 (70).

20. John Blackburne to Charles Head, 27 August 1700, ibid., drawer 94 (284). This manor had come to the College as a gift from the Duchess of Somerset: Howard, *Finances of St. John's College*, pp. 98–9.

21. See my *Whigs and Hunters*, passim.

22. Thus it was said that the signatories to a petition against the enclosure of the common fields at Hooknortorf in 1773 were made up from "the smaller" proprietors "who have now an opportunity of committing trespasses on their neighbour's property with their sheep, which in so large a field cannot be altogether prevented": R. Bignall, 10 January 1773. Bodleian Library, MS Oxford,. Archd. Papers, Berks. b.5.

23. Kerridge, *Agrarian Problems*, p. 93.

24. 6 Co. Rep. 59/b. As Lord Eversley pointed out we should be careful not to confuse a legal

decision of general significance with the general adoption of it in practice: "so long . . . as a common remained open and uninclosed, the decision in Gateward's case did not practically affect the position of the inhabitants . . . (who) continued to exercise the customary user of turbary, estovers, or pasture." Lord Eversley, *Commons, Forests and Footpaths* (London, revised edn, 1910), pp. 10–12.

25. For a not exceptional example see the customs claimed in the manor of Warfield in Windsor Forest during a survey of 1735: all "tenants and inhabitants" have common pasture in all commons and wastes for all kinds of beasts "as well without stint of number, as also without restraint of any season or time of year." Rights were also claimed to dig loam and sand (and to cut heath, fern and furzes "without any leave, lycence or molestation"). Only the part of the claim inserted within brackets was objected to by the steward as an innovation on the old books of survey: Berkshire Rec. Off. D/EN M 73/1. For practice in the forest generally, see *Whigs and Hunters*, pp. 32, 239–40.

26. In the poor soils of Windsor Forest (within the Blackheath Country) and of the New Forest the family farmer came into his own, "largely in subsistence husbandry on land that working and gentlemen farmers considered unfit for their purposes": E. Kerridge, *The Farmers of Old England* (London, 1973), p. 81. In the case of the Forest of Dean the Free Miners were very fortunate that their ancient usages were *not* challenged at law in the eighteenth century since they would almost certainly have been disallowed in the spirit of Gateward's Case: see Lord Eversley, op. cit., pp. 178–9.

27. Dean and Chapter of Ely *v.* Warren, 2 Atk. 189–90.

28. Selby *v.* Robinson, 2 T.R. 759.

29. It is true that this right was controlled and regulated (like all other common rights) and often limited to particular categories of persons . . . the very young, the old, the decrepit, etc.: see W. O. Ault, *Open-Field Farming in Medieval England* (London, 1972), pp. 29–32. Ault appears to take Blackstone to task for accepting gleaning as a right of "the poor" by "the common law and custom of England" (*Commentaries*, 1772, iii, p. 212). But it would not have disturbed Blackstone to know that there is no reference to such right in thirteenth-century by-laws, "nor is there a single mention of the poor as gleaners." Custom did not rest on suppositious origin but established itself in common law by four criteria: antiquity, continuance, certainty, and reason—and "customs are to be construed according to vulgar apprehension, because customs grow generally, and are bred and brought up amongst the Lay-gents": S.C. (S. Carter), *Lex Custumaria: or a Treatise of Copy-hold Estates* (London, 1701), pp. 27–9. By such criteria gleaning by the poor was of greater antiquity, and of equal continuity, certainty and rationality as most customary tenures.

30. Blackstone, op. cit., i, section 1.

31. The form can be seen in the manor of Barrington-in-Thriplow. Benjamin Wedd is admitted (11 November 1756) according to the use of the will of his deceased father-in-law: he is charged by this will to pay an annuity of £60 to his mother-in-law: St. John's College calendar, drawer 99 (214). Such practices were of course very widespread.

32. The form may be seen in the will of William Cooke of East Hendred (Berks.), probat. 7 September 1728, who left two sons and two daughters. After small monetary legacies, the residue of his estate was left to his brothers Thomas and Edmund Cooke, in trust to divide amongst all and every of his children "share and share alike." The lives of his brothers "are in the copy of court roll by which I hold my copyhold," but the brothers are bound to surrender all rents and profits to the above used, and to distribute it among the children "share and share alike": Bodleian Library, MS Wills Berks. 20, p. 48.

33. This form was especially used in copyholds for lives, as two or three lives in being, others in reversion: one or more of the lives in being were inserted as trustees for the actual tenants, as

security that the tenure should pass on to his heirs: on occasion the actual tenant, who paid for the entry fines, was not even entered in the court roll: see R. B. Fisher, op. cit., pp. 15–16.

34. The form may be seen in the will of Timothy Lyford of Drayton (Berks.), probat. 5 December 1724: "whereas my daughter Elizabeth Cowdrey is the first reversion named in my copyhold estate in Sutton Cortney my will is that the said copyhold estate be surrendered into the hands of the Lord of the manor pursuant to a certain obligation to me entered into for that purpose with intent that my daughter Jane the wife of John Chear may be admitted tenant thereof for her own life and such other lives as she can agree for": Bodleian Library, MS Will Berks. 19, p. 239.

35. As in Knaresborough, where "it was possible . . . for a man with more than one son to make provision for the younger sons by transferring the title of part of his land to them during his lifetime, receiving back a life interest": *A History of Harrogate and Knaresborough*, ed. Bernard Jennings (Huddersfield, 1970), pp. 80, 178–9.

36. When I say "a little evidence" I mean that a little evidence has come to my hand while working on other matters. There may (or may not) be much evidence. The impressions offered in these pages are not intended as a substitute for the systematic research which I have not undertaken.

37. Bodleian Library, MS Wills Berks. 19, pp. 338–9.

38. Percy Hatch's daughter was married to William Lyford. This could have been the same William Lyford who was presented at the Windsor Forest Swanimote court in 1717 for staffherding sheep in the forest: P.R.O. L.R. 3.3. "Staffherding" (accompanying the sheep in the forest with a herdsman) was an offence since it frightened the deer and secured the best grazing for the sheep: left to their own unaided competition the deer enforced their own priorities.

39. Reverend Will Waterson, Memorandum Book, I, the Ranelagh School, Bracknell, Berks.

40. See *Whigs and Hunters*, Part I, passim: Winkfield was the epicentre of "Blacking" in the forest in the 1720s.

41. See J. A. Johnston, "The Probate Inventories and Wills of a Worcestershire Parish, 1676–1775," *Midland History* i, 1 (Spring 1971), pp. 20–33. The author finds that the husbandmen all "showed an inclination to preserve their estates intact, all leaving their land to their eldest sons": they also "favoured their male relations outside the immediate family." No other social group showed such rigidity of custom, nor a stress on primogeniture: of 87 landowners, 36 willed their land intact to a single heir, the remaining 51 left their land to 122 new owners. The parish in question (Powick) is only two miles from Worcester: rich land with opportunities for dairy farming, fruit growing, and some horse-breeding. Possibly this could be another kind of regimen in which partible inheritance was viable?

42. Bernard Jennings informs me that in the very extensive manor of Wakefield practices of partible inheritance were continued analogous to those in Knaresborough (see note 35). His researches, with the cooperation of extra-mural classes, have demonstrated a coincidence between this practice and the density of looms in different districts of the West Riding: i.e. where the holding was too small to provide a livelihood this became an incentive for the development of domestic industry (spinning and weaving), in the first place as a supplementary income. One looks forward to the publication of these findings.

43. M. K. Ashby, *The Changing English Village: a History of Bledington* (Kineton, 1974), pp. 162–4, 194–5.

44. See *Whigs and Hunters*, pp. 106–8.

45. Ibid., pp. 125–33, and "Articles against Heron" and Heron's responses, Hants. Rec. Off. Heron's reply complains that "at Waltham Court, without any Previous notice, the Son of the Widow was brought into the Room where wee dined (with some Clergymen & Strangers of Mr. Kerby's

Acquaintance all unknown to mee) to Challenge mee publickly for this unjust Seizure." This confrontation was engineered by Kerby, the Woodward, and Heron's rival.

46. I hope to substantiate these generalizations in "Common Right and Enclosure," *Customs in Common*.

47. St. John's College, Cambridge, calendar, drawer 109 (16). But Mrs. Allen who had outlived two husbands and had repudiated the debts of both—"a very sharp self interested woman"—may be untypical and may offer evidence on Le Roy Ladurie's side of the question: since she turns out to have been a "saucy Frenchwoman": and "an unaccountable Frenchwoman, and regards no body": ibid., 109 (7), (13), (14).

48. Reverend Richard Perrot to College, petitioning on behalf of a customary tenant at Marfleet (Yorks.), 2 February 1635, ibid., drawer 94 (289). The Manor Court at Farnham also took unusual care to overwatch the interest of orphans. "It is a principall poynt in the Court of this Mannor and to be remembered" that if a tenant left an orphan under age "then the next in kind and farthiest from the Land shall have the tuition and Guardianship of such an heir untill he come to the age of 14 years," when he may chose his own tenant to farm. The guardian shall pay his ward's charges and education, and account to him for the rest. But if the appropriate person as guardian "be insufficient by defect of Nature or otherwise," then the court, with the consent of the homage, could appoint a guardian. By "next of kind and farthiest from the land" I understand the closest kin who is at the same time not in the direct line of customary inheritance: e.g. an uncle or aunt on the mother's side: Farnham Custom Roll, 1707, Dean and Chapter archives, Winchester Cathedral Library. Compare the custom at nearby Woking: "If any copyholder die, his heir being within age, the custody of the body and the land of such heir shall be committed by the lord to the next of kindred of the heir to whom the land cannot descend, he being a fit person. . . .": Watkins, op. cit., ii. p. 559.

49. Josiah Beckwith's edition of Thomas Blount's *Fragmenta Antiquitatis; or Antient Tenures of Land, and Jocular Customs of Some Manors* (York, 1784) pp. 265–6. A similar custom is claimed to have existed in Tor (Devon).

50. At Balsall (Warwks.) the customs presented in 1657 included the provision: "If any female heir, being in possession of any copyhold, for lack of grace should happen to commit fornication or be begotten with child, she was not to forfeit her estate, but she must come into the lord's court" and pay a fine of five shillings: if a widow committed fornication or adultery "she is to forfeit her estate for her life, until she agree with the lord by fine to be restored": Watkins, op. cit., ii, p. 576. It is doubtful whether such customs were effective in the eighteenth century, unless in unusual circumstances; however, in 1809 Lord Ellenborough, C. J. upheld judgement for the plaintiff, thus ousting from her tenure a widow (a tenant of Lord Lonsdale in Westmorland) who had breached the custom of tenure during "her chaste viduity" by having a child: but a witness could cite only one other case in that manor in the previous sixty years (in 1753) and in that case the widow had died before the case came to an issue: William Askew *v.* Agnes Askew, 10 East. 520.

51. S. & B. Webb, *The Manor and the Borough* (London, 1908), p. 11.

52. An excellent example of this is to be found in the Farnham Customs of 1707. Here we have a strong body of customers prospering through hopfarming, claiming the security of socage tenure, but suffering from the insecurity of being a Church manor (the Bishop of Winchester). The homage recited its customs with unusual detail and precision because of continuing disputes with successive Bishops and their officers: "every new Lord brings in a new procurator who for private gains Racketh the Custom and oftentimes breaketh it. . . ." Mrs. Elfrida Manning of the Farnham Museum Society has recently discovered an almost identical Farnham Custumal of the 1670s.

53. Dower in common law was defined as a moiety and the custom that the wife shall have the whole as free bench is contrary to the maxim of common law: but the custom of each manor

remained good and overrode common law: S. Carter, op.cit., p. 34. Thus a textbook of 1701. By the 1790s the terms free bench and dower were often being used indiscriminately, although they differed: "Free bench is a widow's estate in such lands as the husband died seized of, and not of such lands as he was seized of during the coverture, whereas dower is the estate of the widow in all lands, the husband was seized of during the coverture": R. B. Fisher, op. cit., p. 26, citing 2 Atk. 525.

54. Survey and customs of Waltham St. Lawrence, November 1735, Berks. Rec. Off. D/EN M 82/A/1.

55. Will of Richard Simmons, probat. 21 April 1721, Bodleian Library, MS Wills Berks. 19, p. 100.

56. Will of Thomas Punter, probat. 21 April 1721, ibid., p. 97. But forest customs varied from parish to parish: in the neighbouring parish of Winkfield it seems that the widow could remarry and her husband enjoy her estate in her right during her life, subject to stringent provisions against waste: Rev. Will Waterson, Memorandum Book, pp. 362, 365, Ranelagh School, Bracknell, Berks.

57. I have subtracted from this "sample" some customs which evidently dated back to the early years of the seventeenth century or before, but others may well have been obsolete.

58. Watkins, op. cit., ii., pp. 477–576. The North and the North Midlands are scarcely represented in this collection.

59. Ibid., ii, pp. 501–2.

60. Ibid., ii, p. 498.

61. Ibid., ii, pp. 552–3.

62. Ibid., ii, p. 575.

63. Farnham Custom Roll, 1707, Winchester Cathedral Library.

64. This last provision is cited by Watkins, op. cit., i, p. 552, and indicates a slight modification and clarification over the 1707 Customs.

65. Farnham Custom Roll, 1707, loc. cit.

66. The effect of free bench in strengthening a feminine presence in the village in late medieval society is discussed by Rodney Hilton, *The English Peasantry in the Later Middle Ages* (London, 1975), ch. vi, esp. pp. 98–101. Many of his comments may remain apposite to districts in the eighteenth century which maintained traditions of yeoman customary occupancy: for an example of strong feminine tenure, see Matthew Imber, *The Case, or an Abstract of the Custom of the Manor of Mardon in the Parish of Hursley* (London, 1707): in this Hampshire manor, whose customs were borough English, more than 20 per cent (11 out of 52) of the copyholders were women.

67. Kerridge, op. cit., p. 83.

68. By the custom of Berkeley (Glos.) "marriage *in extremis* gives no free bench": Watkins, op. cit., ii, p. 479.

69. In the parish of Winkfield the Earl of Ranelagh founded a charity school for forty poor children. The Reverend Will Waterson, Rector of Winkfield, was also Master of the school for more than thirty years. He took in the daughters as well as the sons of the parish "poor," but noted: "Its much to be wish'd that the Girles were restrain'd from learning any thing that is not requisite in an ordinary servant, and that they were imploy'd in Spinning and makeing their own and the Boys cloths. . . . Fine work . . . serves only to puff them up with pride and vanity, and to make them slight and overlook such places as they ought chiefly to be qualified for." But Waterson, writing towards the end of his life, had perhaps become disillusioned and defensive in the face of accusations that the "charity schools are nurseries of Rebellion, and disqualify poor children for such country business . . . as they are most wanted for." For boys also (he noted) "the plow must find them employment, or they'll do nothing": but he appears to have conscientiously

afforded to the children of both sexes elementary instruction in literacy and numeracy: Waterson MS. Reading Ref. Lib. BOR/D; the passages cited were perhaps written in the early 1740s.

70. Among wills of yeomen and husbandmen in Berkshire at this time one frequently finds evidence of attention to the interests of female heirs. Thus Robert Dee of Winkfield, yeoman (probat. 10 April 1730), left two parcels of land, one of 16½ acres, the other of 2½ acres: the larger parcel was willed to his grandson, together with house and furniture, the smaller to his grand-daughter: but (in compensation) the grandson was to receive also £100, the granddaughter £200. Among freeholders, tradesmen, etc., there is some evidence of egalitarian inheritance customs: thus Joseph Collier (probat. 12 July 1737), a Reading yeoman who owned some tenements and mills: all left to his brother in trust to sell and distribute "share and share alike" among his six children (four daughters—all married—and two sons); Mary Maynard (probat, 20 May 1736) the widow of a Reading waggoner—a business which she had continued—the estate to be valued and to be distributed "share and share alike" among six children (three of each sex) as each attained the age of 21: the two oldest children (one son, one daughter) to act as executors, but the daughter to lapse her function if she marries: Bodleian Library, MS Wills Berks. 20, p. 117; 21, p. 113, p. 72 verso.

71. Thus the will of William Towsey, yeoman, of Letcombe Regis, probat. 22 August 1722, leaving to his daughter Ann Hawks £50 "to her own separate use and disposicon wholy exempt from the Power or intermedling of her husband Thomas Hawks notwithstanding the Coverture between him and my said daughter": ibid., 19, pp. 150–1.

72. See *Whigs and Hunters*, pp. 71–2. If, as I suppose, Mrs. Power was born Ann Ticknor, then she hold more than 80 acres as well as barns, orchards, cottages, etc., in the forest, in jointure with her sister: the jointure explains why the land could not fall to the Reverend Power in consequence of his avaricious coverture. (Yeomen were perfectly capable of using the devices of jointures and of trusts to safeguard their daughters' rights.) It is reassuring to note that Mrs. Power endured the hazards of her marriage and died "without doing any Act to affect" her property: Abstract of Aaron Maynard's title to four closes in Wokingham, Berks. Rec. Off. D/ER E 12.

73. For a study of artisan occupational inheritance see William H. Sewell, Jr., "Social Change and the Rise of Working-Class Politics in Nineteenth-Century Marseilles," *Past and Present*, 65, November 1974.

74. Raymond Williams, *The Country and the City* (London, 1973), pp. 40–1.

THE MORAL ECONOMY OF THE ENGLISH CROWD IN THE EIGHTEENTH CENTURY

FROM *CUSTOMS IN COMMON: STUDIES IN TRADITIONAL POPULAR CULTURE*

He that withholdeth Corn, the People shall curse him: but Blessing shall be upon the Head of him that selleth it.

—PROVERBS XI. 26

I

We have been warned in recent years, by George Rudé and others, against the loose employment of the term "mob." I wish in this chapter to extend the warning to the term "riot," especially where the food riot in eighteenth-century England is concerned.

This simple four-letter word can conceal what may be described as a spasmodic view of popular history. According to this view the common people can scarcely be taken as historical agents before the French Revolution. Before this period they intrude occasionally and spasmodically upon the historical canvas, in periods of sudden social disturbance. These intrusions are compulsive, rather than self-conscious or self-activating: they are simple responses to economic stimuli. It is sufficient to mention a bad harvest or a downturn in trade, and all requirements of historical explanation are satisfied.

Unfortunately, even among those few British historians who have added to our knowledge of such popular actions, several have lent support to the spasmodic view. They have reflected in only a cursory way upon the materials which they themselves disclose. Thus Beloff comments on the food riots of the early eighteenth century: "this resentment, when unemployment and high prices combined to make conditions unendurable, vented itself in attacks upon corn-

From *Customs in Common* by E. P. Thompson (New York: The New Press, 1993).

dealers and millers, attacks which often must have degenerated into mere excuses for crime."[1] But we search his pages in vain for evidence as to the frequency of this "degeneration." Wearmouth, in his useful chronicle of disturbance, allows himself one explanatory category: "distress."[2] Ashton, in his study of food riots among the colliers, brings the support of the paternalist: "the turbulence of the colliers is, of course, to be accounted for by something more elementary than politics: it was the instinctive reaction of virility to hunger."[3] The riots were "rebellions of the belly," and there is a suggestion that this is somehow a comforting explanation. The line of analysis runs: elementary—instinctive—hunger. Charles Wilson continues the tradition: "Spasmodic rises in food prices provoked keelmen on the Tyne to riot in 1709, tin miners to plunder granaries at Falmouth in 1727." One spasm led to another: the outcome was "plunder."[4]

For decades systematic social history has lagged in the rear of economic history, until the present day, when a qualification in the second discipline is assumed to confer, automatically, proficiency in the first. One cannot therefore complain that recent scholarship has tended to sophisticate and quantify evidence which is only imperfectly understood. The dean of the spasmodic school is of course Rostow, whose crude "social tension chart" was first put forward in 1948.[5] According to this, we need only bring together an index of unemployment and one of high food prices to be able to chart the course of social disturbance. This contains a self-evident truth (people protest when they are hungry): and in much the same way a "sexual tension chart" would show that the onset of sexual maturity can be correlated with a greater frequency of sexual activity. The objection is that such a chart, if used unwisely, may conclude investigation at the exact point at which it becomes of serious sociological or cultural interest: being hungry (or being sexy), what do people do? How is their behaviour modified by custom, culture, and reason? And (having granted that the primary stimulus of "distress" is present) does their behavior contribute towards any more complex, culturally-mediated function, which cannot be reduced—however long it is stewed over the fires of statistical analysis—back to stimulus once again?

Too many of our growth historians are guilty of a crass economic reductionism, obliterating the complexities of motive, behaviour, and function, which, if they noted it in the work of their Marxist analogues, would make them protest. The weakness which these explanations share is an abbreviated view of economic man. What is perhaps an occasion for surprise is the schizoid intellectual climate, which permits this quantitative historiography to co-exist (in the same places and sometimes in the same minds) with a social anthropology which derives from Durkheim, Weber, or Malinowski. We know all about the delicate tissue of social norms and reciprocities which regulates the life of Trobriand islanders, and the psychic energies involved in the cargo cults

of Melanesia; but at some point this infinitely-complex social creature, Mela-
nesian man, becomes (in our histories) the eighteenth-century English collier
who claps his hand spasmodically upon his stomach, and responds to elementary
economic stimuli.

To the spasmodic I will oppose my own view.[6] It is possible to detect in
almost every eighteenth-century crowd action some legitimising notion. By the
notion of legitimation I mean that the men and women in the crowd were
informed by the belief that they were defending traditional rights or customs;
and, in general, that they were supported by the wider consensus of the community. On occasion this popular consensus was endorsed by some measure of
license afforded by the authorities. More commonly, the consensus was so strong
that it overrode motives of fear or deference.

The food riot in eighteenth-century England was a highly complex form of
direct popular action, disciplined and with clear objectives. How far these objectives were achieved—that is, how far the food riot was a "successful" form
of action—is too intricate a question to tackle within the limits of a chapter;
but the question can at least be posed (rather than, as is customary, being
dismissed unexamined with a negative), and this cannot be done until the
crowd's own objectives are identified. It is of course true that riots were trig-
gered off by soaring prices, by malpractices among dealers, or by hunger. But
these grievances operated within a popular consensus as to what were legitimate
and what were illegitimate practices in marketing, milling, baking, etc. This in
its turn was grounded upon a consistent traditional view of social norms and
obligations, of the proper economic functions of several parties within the community, which, taken together, can be said to constitute the moral economy of
the poor. An outrage to these moral assumptions, quite as much as actual
deprivation, was the usual occasion for direct action.

While this moral economy cannot be described as "political" in any advanced
sense, nevertheless it cannot be described as unpolitical either, since it supposed
definite, and passionately held, notions of the common weal—notions which,
indeed, found some support in the paternalist tradition of the authorities; notions
which the people re-echoed so loudly in their turn that the authorities were, in
some measure, the prisoners of the people. Hence this moral economy impinged
very generally upon eighteenth-century government and thought, and did not
only intrude at moments of disturbance. The word "riot" is too small to encompass all this.

II

As we speak of the cash-nexus which emerged through the industrial revolution,
so there is a sense in which we can speak of the eighteenth-century bread-
nexus. The conflict between the countryside and the town was mediated by the

price of bread. The conflict between traditionalism and the new political economy turned upon the Corn Laws. Economic class-conflict in nineteenth-century England found its characteristic expression in the matter of wages; in eighteenth-century England the working people were most quickly inflamed to action by rising prices.

This highly-sensitive consumer-consciousness co-existed with the great age of agricultural improvement, in the corn belt of the East and South. Those years which brought English agriculture to a new pitch of excellence were punctuated by the riots—or, as contemporaries often described them, the "insurrections" or "risings of the poor"—of 1709, 1740, 1756–7, 1766–7, 1773, 1782, and, above all, 1795 and 1800–1. This buoyant capitalist industry floated upon an irascible market which might at any time dissolve into marauding bands, who scoured the countryside with bludgeons, or rose in the market-place to "set the price" of provisions at the popular level. The fortunes of those most vigorous capitalist classes rested, in the final analysis, upon the sale of cereals, meat, wool; and the first two must be sold, with little intermediary processing, to the millions who were the consumers. Hence the frictions of the market-place take us into a central area of the nation's life.

The laboring people in the eighteenth century did not live by bread alone, but (as the budgets collected by Eden and David Davies show) many of them lived very largely on bread. This bread was not altogether wheaten, although wheaten bread gained ground steadily over other varieties until the early 1790s. In the 1760s Charles Smith estimated that of a supposed population of about six millions in England and Wales, 3,750,000 were wheat-eaters, 888,000 ate rye, 739,000 ate barley, and 623,000 oats.[7] By 1790 we may judge that at least two-thirds of the population were eating wheat.[8] The pattern of consumption reflected, in part, comparative degrees of poverty, and, in part, ecological conditions. Districts with poor soils and upland districts (like the Pennines) where wheat will not ripen, were the strongholds of other cereals. Still, in the 1790s, the Cornish tinners subsisted largely on barley bread. Much oatmeal was consumed in Lancashire and Yorkshire—and not only by the poor.[9] Accounts from Northumberland conflict, but it would seem that Newcastle and many of the surrounding pit villages had by then gone over to wheat, while the countryside and smaller towns subsisted on oatmeal, rye bread, maslin, [10] or a mixture of barley and "gray pease."[11]

Through the century, again, white bread was gaining upon darker wholemeal varieties. This was partly a matter of status-values which became attached to white bread, but by no means wholly so. The problem is most complex, but several aspects may be briefly mentioned. It was to the advantage of bakers and of millers to sell white bread or fine flour, since the profit which might be gained from such sales was, in general, larger. (Ironically, this was in part a consequence of paternalist consumer-protection, since the Assize of Bread was intended to prevent the bakers from taking their profit from the bread of the poor; hence it was in the baker's interest to make as little "household" bread as possible, and that little nasty.[12]) In the cities, which were alert to the dangers of adulteration, dark bread was suspect as offering easy concealment for noxious additives. In the last decades of the century many millers adapted their machinery and bolting-cloths, so that they were not in fact able to dress the flour for the intermediary "household" loaf, producing only the finer qualities for the white loaf and the "offal" for a brown loaf which one observer found "so musty griping, and pernicious as to endanger the constitution."[13] The attempts of the authorities, in times of scarcity, to impose the manufacture of coarser grades (or, as in 1795, the general use of the "household" loaf), were attended by many difficulties, and often resistance by both millers and bakers.[14]

By the end of the century feelings of status were profoundly involved wherever wheaten bread prevailed, and was threatened by a coarser mixture. There is a suggestion that labourers accustomed to wheaten bread actually could not work—suffered from weakness, indigestion, or nausea—if forced to change to rougher mixtures.[15] Even in the face of the outrageous prices of 1795 and 1800–1, the resistance of many of the working people was impermeable.[16] The Guild Stewards of Calne informed the Privy Council in 1796 that "creditable" people were using the barley-and-wheat mixture required by authority, and that the manufacturing and labouring poor with large families.

> have in general used barley bread alone. The rest, making perhaps something about one-third of the poor manufactures and others, with smaller families (saying they could get nothing *but bread*) have, as before the scarcity, eat nothing but baker's bread, made of wheatmeal called seconds.[17]

The Bailiff of Reigate reported in similar terms:

> . . . as to the poor labourers who have scarce any sustenance but bread, & from the custom of the neighbourhood have always eaten bread made of wheat only; amongst these I have neither urged nor wished a mixture of bread, least they should not be nourished sufficiently to support their labor.

Those few labourers who had tried a mixture "found themselves feeble, hot, & unable to labour with any degree of vigor."[18] When, in December 1800, the government introduced an Act (popularly known as the Brown Bread Act or

"Poison Act") which prohibited millers from making any other than wholemeal flour, the response of the people was immediate. At Horsham (Sussex),

> A number of women . . . proceeded to Gosden wind-mill, where, abusing the miller for having served them with brown flour, they seized on the cloth with which he was then dressing meal according to the directions of the Bread Act, and cut it into a thousand pieces; threatening at the same time to serve all similar utensils he might in future attempt to use in the same manner. The amazonian leader of this petticoated cavalcade afterwards regaled her associates with a guinea's worth of liquor at the Crab Tree public-house.

As a result of such actions, the Act was repealed in less than two months.[19]

When prices were high, more than one-half of the weekly budget of a labourer's family might be spent on bread.[20] How did these cereals pass, from the crops growing in the field, to the labourers' homes? At first sight it appears simple. There is the corn: it is harvested, threshed, taken to market, ground at the mill, baked, and eaten. But at every point within this process there are radiating complexities, opportunities for extortion, flash-points around which riots could arise. And it is scarcely possible to proceed further without sketching out, in a schematic way, the paternalist model of the marketing and manufacturing process—the traditional platonic ideal appealed to in Statute, pamphlet, or protest movement—against which the awkward realities of commerce and consumption were in friction.

The paternalist model existed in an eroded body of Statute law, as well as common law and custom. It was the model which, very often, informed the actions of government in times of emergency until the 1770s; and to which many local magistrates continued to appeal. In this model, marketing should be, so far as possible, *direct*, from the farmer to the consumer. The farmers should bring their corn in bulk to the local pitching market; they should not sell it while standing in the field, nor should they withhold it in the hope of rising prices. The markets should be controlled; no sales should be made before stated times, when a bell would ring; the poor should have the opportunity to buy grain, flour, or meal first, in small parcels, with duly-supervised weights and measures.

At a certain hour, when their needs were satisfied, a second bell would ring, and larger dealers (duly licensed) might make their purchases. Dealers were hedged around with many restrictions, inscribed upon the musty parchments of the laws against forestalling, regrating, and engrossing, codified in the reign of Edward VI. They must not buy (and farmers must not sell) by sample. They must not buy standing crops, nor might they purchase to sell (within three months) in the same market at a profit, or in neighbouring markets, and so on. Indeed, for most of the eighteenth century the middleman remained legally suspect, and his operations were, in theory, severely restricted.[21]

From market-supervision we pass to consumer-protection. Millers and—to a greater degree—bakers were considered as servants of the community, working not for a profit but for a fair allowance. Many of the poor would buy their grain direct in the market (or obtain it as supplement to wages or in gleaning); they would take it to the mill to be ground, where the miller might exact a customary toll, and then would bake their own bread. In London and those large towns where this had long ceased to the rule, the baker's allowance or profit was calculated strictly according to be the Assize of Bread, whereby either the price or the weight of the loaf was ordered in relation to the ruling price of wheat.[22]

This model, of course, parts company at many points with eighteenth-century realities. What is more surprising is to note how far parts of it were still operative. Thus Aikin in 1795 is able to describe the orderly regulation of Preston market:

> The weekly markets . . . are extremely well regulated to prevent forestall-
> ing and regrating. None but the town's-people are permitted to buy during
> the first hour, which is from eight to nine in the morning: at nine others
> may purchase: but nothing unsold must be withdrawn from the market till
> one o'clock, fish excepted. . . .[23]

In the same year in the South-West (another area noted for traditionalism) the city authorities at Exeter attempted to control "hucksters, higlers, and retailers" by excluding them from the market between 8 a.m. and noon, at which hours the Guildhall bell would be rung.[24] The Assize of Bread was still effective throughout the eighteenth century in London and in many market towns.[25] If we follow through the case of sale by sample we may observe how dangerous it is to assume prematurely the dissolution of the customary restrictions.

It is often supposed that sale of corn by sample was general by the middle of the seventeenth century, when Best describes the practice in East Yorkshire,[26] and certainly by 1725, when Defoe gave his famous account of the corn trade.[27] But, while many large farmers were no doubt selling by sample in most counties by this date, the old pitching markets were still common, and even survived in the environs of London. In 1718 a pamphleteer described the decline of country markets as having taken place only in recent years:

> One can see little else besides toy-shops and stalls for bawbles and knick-
> knacks. . . . The tolls are sunk to nothing; and where, in the memory of

many inhabitants, there us'd to come to town upon a day, one, two, perhaps three, and in some boroughs, four hundred loads of corn, now grass grows in the market-place.

The farmers (he complained) had come to shun the market and to deal with jobbers and other "interlopers" at their doors. Other farmers still brought to market a single load "to make a show of a market, and to have a Price set," but the main business was done in "parcels of corn in a bag or handkerchief which are called *samples*."[28]

This was, indeed, the drift of things. But many smaller farmers continued to pitch their grain in the market as before; and the old model remained in men's minds as a source of resentment. Again and again the new marketing procedures were contested. In 1710 a petition on behalf of the poor people of Stony Stratford (Buckinghamshire) complains that the farmers and dealers were "buying and selling in the farmyards and att their Barne Doores soo that now the poor Inhabitants cannot have a Grist at reasonable rates for our money which is a Great Calamity."[29] In 1733 several boroughs petitioned the House of Commons against the practice: Haslemere (Surrey) complained of millers and mealmen engrossing the trade—they "secretly bought great quantities of corn by small samples, refusing to buy such as hath been pitch'd in open market."[30] There is a suggestion of something underhand in the practice, and of a loss of transparency in the marketing procedure.

As the century advances the complaints do not die down, although they tend to move northwards and westwards. In the dearth of 1756 the Privy Council, in addition to setting in motion the old laws against forestalling, issued a proclamation enjoining "all farmers, under severe penalties, to bring their corn to open market, and not to sell by sample at their own dwelling."[31] But the authorities did not like to be pressed on the point too closely: in 1766 (another year of scarcity) the Surrey magistrates enquired whether buying by sample in fact remained a punishable offence, and received a portentously evasive reply— H. M.'s Secretary is not by his office entitled to give interpretation to the Laws.[32]

Two letters give some insight into the spread of new practices towards the West. A correspondent writing to Lord Shelburne in 1766 accused the dealers and millers at Chippenham of "confederacy":

He himself sent to market for a quarter of wheat, and though there were many loads there, and it soon after the market bell rang, wherever his agent applied, the answer was " 'Tis sold." So that, though . . . to avoid the penalty of the law, they bring it to market, yet the bargain is made before, and the market is but a farce. . . .[33]

(Such practices could be the actual occasion of riot: in June 1757 it was reported that "the population rose at Oxford and in a few minutes seized and divided a load of corn that was suspected to have been bought by sample, and only brought to the market to save appearances."[34]) The second letter, from a correspondent in Dorchester in 1772, describes a different practice of market-fixing: he claimed that the great farmers got together to fix the price before the market,

> and many of these men won't sell less than forty bushels, which the poor can't purchase. Therefore the miller, who is no enemy to the farmer, gives the price he asks and the poor must come to his terms.[35]

Paternalists and the poor continued to complain at the extension of market practices which we, looking back, tend to assume as inevitable and "natural."[36] But what may now appear as inevitable was not, in the eighteenth century, necessarily a matter for approval. A characteristic pamphlet (of 1768) exclaimed indignantly against the supposed liberty of every farmer to do as he likes with his own. This would be a "natural," not a "civil" liberty.

> It cannot then be said to be the liberty of a citizen, or of one who lives under the protection of any community; it is rather the liberty of a savage; therefore he who avails himself thereof, deserves not that protection, the power of Society affords.

Attendance of the farmer at market is "a material part of his duty; he should not be suffered to secret or to dispose of his goods elsewhere."[37] But after the 1760s the pitching markets performed so little function in most parts of the South and the Midlands that, in these districts, the complaint against sample-sale is less often heard, although the complaint that the poor cannot buy in small parcels is still being made at the end of the century.[38] In parts of the North it was a different matter. A petition of Leeds labourers in 1795 complains of the "corn factors and the millers and a set of peopul which we call hucksters and mealmen who have got the corn into thare hands that they may hold it up and sell it at thare owne price or they will not sell it." "The farmers carry no corn to market but what they carre in thare pocket for thare sample . . . which cause the poore to groane very much."[39] So long it took for a process, which is often dated from at least one hundred years earlier, to work its way out.

This example has been followed to illustrate the density and particularity of the detail, the diversity of local practices, and the way in which popular resentment could arise as old market practices changed. The same density, the same diversity, exists throughout the scarcely-charted area of marketing. The paternalist model was, of course, breaking down at many other points. The Assize of

Bread, although effective in checking the profits of bakers, simply reflected the ruling price of wheat or flour, and could in no way influence these. The millers were now, in Hertfordshire and the Thames Valley, very substantial entrepreneurs, and sometimes dealers in grain or malt as well as large-scale manufacturers of flour.[40] Outside the main corn-growing districts, urban markets simply could not be supplied without the operation of factors whose activities would have been nullified if legislation against forestallers had been strictly enforced.

How far did the authorities recognise that their model was drifting apart from reality? The answer must change with the authorities concerned and with the advance of the century. But a general answer can be offered: the paternalists did, in their normal practice, recognise much of the change, but they referred back to this model whenever emergency arose. In this they were in part the prisoners of the people, who adopted parts of the model as their right and heritage. There is even an impression that ambiguity was actually welcomed. It gave magistrates in disturbed districts, in time of dearth, some room for maneuvre, and some endorsement to their attempts to reduce prices by suasion. When the Privy Council authorised (as it did in 1709, 1740, 1756, and 1766) the posting of proclamations in unreadable Gothic type threatening dire penalties against forestallers, badgers, laders, broggers, hucksters, etc., it helped the magistrates to put the fear of God into local millers and dealers. It is true that the legislation against forestallers was repealed in 1772; but the repealing act was not well drawn, and during the next major scarcity in 1795 Lord Kenyon, the chief justice, took it upon himself to announce that forestalling remained an indictable offence at common law: "though the act of Edward VI be repealed (whether wisely or unwisely I take not upon me to say) yet it still remains an offence at common law, co-eval with the constitution. . . ."[41] The trickle of prosecutions which can be observed throughout the century—usually for petty offences and only in years of scarcity—did not dry up: indeed, there were probably more in 1795 and 1800–1 than at any time in the previous twenty-five years.[42] But it is clear that they were designed for symbolic effect, as demonstrations to the poor that the authorities were acting vigilantly in their interests.

Hence the paternalist model had an ideal existence, and also a fragmentary real existence. In years of good harvests and moderate prices, the authorities lapsed into forgetfulness. But if prices rose and the poor became turbulent, it was revived, at least for symbolic effect.

III

Few intellectual victories have been more overwhelming than that which the proponents of the new political economy won in the matter of the regulation of the internal corn trade. Indeed, so absolute has the victory seemed to some historians that they can scarcely conceal their impatience with the defeated party.[43] The model of the new political economy may, with convenience, be taken as that of Adam Smith, although *The Wealth of Nations* may be seen not only as a point of departure but also as a grand central terminus to which many important lines of discussion in the middle of the eighteenth century (some of them, like Charles Smith's lucid *Tracts on the Corn Trade* (1758–9), specifically concerned to demolish the old paternalist market regulation) all run. The debate between 1767 and 1772 which culminated in the repeal of legislation against forestalling, signalled a victory, in this area, for *laissez-faire* four years before Adam Smith's work was published.

This signified less a new model than an anti-model—a direct negative to the disintegrating Tudor policies of "provision." "Let every act that regards the corn laws be repealed," wrote Arbuthnot in 1773; "Let corn flow like water, and it will find its level."[44] The "unlimited, unrestrained freedom of the corn trade" was also the demand of Adam Smith.[45] The new economy entailed a de-moralising of the theory of trade and consumption no less far-reaching than the more widely-debated dissolution of restrictions upon usury.[46] By "de-moralising" it is not suggested that Smith and his colleagues were immoral[47] or were unconcerned for the public good.[48] It is meant, rather, that the new political economy was disinfested of intrusive moral imperatives. The old pamphleteers were moralists first and economists second. In the new economic theory questions as to the moral polity of marketing do not enter, unless as preamble and peroration.

In practical terms, the new model worked in this way. The natural operation of supply and demand in the free market would maximise the satisfaction of all parties and establish the common good. The market was never better regulated than when it was left to regulate itself. In the course of a normal year, the price of corn would adjust itself through the market mechanism. Soon after harvest the small farmers, and all those with harvest wages and Michaelmas rents to pay, would thresh out their corn and bring it to market, or release what they had pre-contracted to sell. From September to Christmas low prices might be expected. The middling farmers would hold their corn, in the hope of a rising market, until the early spring; while the most opulent farmers and farming gentry would hold some of theirs until still later—from May to August—in expectation of catching the market at the top. In this way the nation's corn reserves were conveniently rationed, by the price mechanism, over fifty-

two weeks, without any intervention by the State. Insofar as middlemen intervened and contracted for the farmers' crops in advance, they performed this
service of rationing even more efficiently. In years of dearth the price of grain
might advance to uncomfortable heights; but this was providential, since (apart
from providing an incentive to the importer) it was again an effective form of
rationing, without which all stocks would be consumed in the first nine months
of the year, and in the remaining three months dearth would be exchanged for
actual famine.

The only way in which this self-adjusting economy might break down was
through the meddlesome interference of the State and of popular prejudice.[49]
Corn must be left to flow freely from areas of surplus to areas of scarcity.
Hence the middleman played a necessary, productive, and laudable role. The
prejudices against forestallers Smith dismissed curtly as superstitions on a level
with witchcraft. Interference with the natural pattern of trade might induce local
famines or discourage farmers from increasing their output. If premature sales
were forced, or prices restrained in times of dearth, excessive stocks might be
consumed. If farmers did hold back their grain too long, they would be likely
to suffer when prices broke. As for the other popular culprits—millers, mealmen, dealers, bakers—much the same logic applied. Their trades were competitive. At the most they could only distort prices from their natural level over
short periods, and often to their ultimate discomfiture. When prices began to
soar at the end of the century, the remedy was seen not in a return to the
regulation of trade, but in more enclosure, tillage of waste lands, improvement.

It should not be necessary to argue that the model of a natural and self-
adjusting economy, working providentially for the best good of all, is as much
a superstition as the notions which upheld the paternalist model—although,
curiously, it is a superstition which some economic historians have been the
last to abandon. In some respects Smith's model conformed more closely to
eighteenth-century realities than did the paternalist; and in symmetry and scope
of intellectual construction it was superior. But one should not overlook the
specious air of empirical validation which the model carries. Whereas the first
appeals to a moral norm—what *ought* to be men's reciprocal duties—the second
appears to say: "this is the way things work, or would work if the State did
not interfere." And yet if one considers these sections of *The Wealth of Nations*
they impress less as an essay in empirical enquiry than as a superb, self-
validating essay in logic.

When we consider the actual organisation of the eighteenth-century corn
trade, empirical verification of neither model is to hand. There has been little
detailed investigation of marketing;[50] no major study of that key figure, the
miller.[51] Even the first letter of Smith's alphabet—the assumption that high
prices were an effective form of rationing—remains no more than an assertion.

It is notorious that the demand for corn, or bread, is highly inelastic. When bread is costly, the poor (as one highly-placed observer was once reminded) do not go over to cake. In the view of some observers, when prices rose labourers might eat the same quantity of bread, but cut out other items in their budgets; they might even eat *more* bread to compensate for the loss of other items. Out of one shilling, in a normal year, 6d. might go on bread, 6d. on "coarse meat and plenty of garden stuff"; but in a high-price year the whole shilling would go on bread.[52]

In any event, it is well known that the price movements of grain cannot be accounted for by simple supply-and-demand price mechanisms; and the bounty paid to encourage corn exports distorted matters further. Next to air and water, corn was a prime necessity of life, abnormally sensitive to any deficiency in supply. In 1796 Arthur Young calculated that the overall crop deficiency in wheat was less than 25 per cent; but the price advance was 81 per cent: giving (by his calculation) a profit to the agricultural community of £20 millions over a normal year.[53] Traditionalist writers complained that the farmers and dealers acted from the strength of "monopoly"; they were rebutted in pamphlet after pamphlet, as "too absurd to be seriously treated: what! more than two hundred thousand people . . . !"[54] The point at issue, however, was not whether this farmer or that dealer could act as a "monopolist," but whether the producing and trading interests as a whole were able, with a long-continuing train of favorable circumstances, to take advantage of their command of a prime necessity of life and to enhance the price to the consumer, in much the same way as the advanced industrialised nations today have been able to enhance the price of certain manufactured goods to the less advanced nations.

As the century advanced marketing procedures became less transparent, as the corn passed through the hands of a more complex network of intermediaries. Farmers were selling, not in an open competitive market (which, in a local and regional sense, was the aim of the paternalist rather than the *laissez-faire* model) but to dealers or millers who were in a better position to hold stocks and keep the market high. In the last decades of the century, as population rose, so consumption pressed continually upon production, and the producers could more generally command a seller's market. Wartime conditions, while not in fact inhibiting greatly the import of grain during conditions of scarcity, nevertheless accentuated psychological tensions in such years.[55] What mattered in setting the post-harvest price was the expectation of the harvest yield: and there is evidence in the last decades of the century of the growth of a farming lobby, well aware of the psychological factors involved in post-harvest price levels, assiduously fostering an expectation of shortage.[56] Notoriously, in years of dearth the farmers' faces were wreathed in smiles,[57] while in years of abundant harvest Dame Nature's inconsiderate bounty called forth agricultural cries of "distress." And no matter how bountiful the yield might appear to the eye of the townsman, every harvest was accompanied by talk of mildew, floods, blighted ears which crumbled to powder when threshing commenced.

The free market model supposes a sequence of small to large farmers, bringing their corn to market over the year; but at the end of the century, as high-price year succeeded high-price year, so more small farmers were able to hold back supply until the market rose to their satisfaction. (It was, after all, for them not a matter of routine marketing but of intense, consuming interest: their profit for the year might depend very largely upon the price which three or four cornstacks might fetch.) If rents had to be paid, the growth in country banking made it easier for the farmer to be accommodated.[58] The September or October riot was often precipitated by the failure of prices to fall after a seemingly plentiful harvest, and indicated a conscious confrontation between reluctant producer and angry consumer.

These comments are offered, not in refutation of Adam Smith, but simply to indicate places where caution should be exercised until our knowledge is greater. We need only say of the *laissez-faire* model that it is empirically unproven; inherently unlikely; and that there is some evidence on the other side. We have recently been reminded that "merchants made money in the eighteenth century," and that grain merchants may have made it "by operating the market." [59] Such operations are occasionally recorded, although rarely as frankly as was noted by a Whittlesford (Cambridgeshire) farmer and corn merchant in his diary in 1802:

> I bought Rey this Time Twelve Month at 50s per Qr. I could have sold it 122s per Qr. The poor had their flower, good rey, for 2s 6d per peck. Parish paid the difference to me, which was 1s 9d per peck. It was a Blessing to the Poor and good to me. I bought 320 Quarters.[60]

The profit on this transaction was above £1,000.

IV

If one can reconstruct clear alternative models behind the policies of traditionalists and of political economists, can one construct the same for the moral economy of the crowd? This is less easy. One is confronted by a complex of rational analysis, prejudice, and traditional patterns of response to dearth. Nor is it possible, at any given moment, clearly to identify the groups which endorsed the theories of the crowd. They comprise articulate and inarticulate, and include men of education and address. After 1750 each year of scarcity was accompanied by a spate of pamphlets and letters to the press, of unequal value.

It was a common complaint of the protagonists of free trade in corn that misguided gentry added fuel to the flames of mob discontent.

There is truth in this. The crowd derived its sense of legitimation, in fact, from the paternalist model. Many gentlemen still resented the middleman as an interloper. Where lords of the manor retained market rights they resented the loss (through sample-sales etc.) of their market tolls. If they were landlord-farmers, who witnessed meat or flour being marketed at prices disproportionately high in relation to their own receipts from the dealers, they resented the profits of these common tradesmen the more. The essayist of 1718 has a title which is a précis of his matter: *An Essay to Prove that Regrators, Engrossers, Forestallers, Hawkers and Jobbers of Corn, Cattle, and other Marketable Goods . . . are Destructive of Trade, Oppressors to the Poor, and a Common Nuisance to the Kingdom in General.* All dealers (unless simple drovers or carters, moving provisions from one point to the next) appeared to this not unobservant writer as a "vile and pernicious set of men"; and, in the classic terms of reproval adopted by men of settled estate to the bourgeois,

> they are a vagabond sort of people. . . . They carry their all about them, and their . . . stock is no more than a plain riding habit, a good horse, a list of the fairs and markets, and a prodigious quantity of impudence. They have the mark of Cain, and like him wander from place to place, driving an interloping trade between the fair dealer and the honest consumer.[61]

This hostility to the dealer existed even among many country magistrates, some of whom were noted to be inactive when popular disturbances swept through the areas under their jurisdiction. They were not displeased by attacks on dissenting or Quaker corn factors. A Bristol pamphleteer, who is clearly a corn factor, complained bitterly in 1758 to the JPs of "your law-giving mob," which prevented, in the previous year, the export of corn from the Severn and Wye valleys, and of "many fruitless applications to several Justices of the Peace."[62] Indeed, the conviction grows that a popular hubbub against forestallers was not unwelcome to some in authority. It distracted attention from the farmers and rentiers; while vague Quarter Sessional threats against forestallers gave to the poor a notion that the authorities were attending to their interests. The old laws against forestallers, a dealer complained in 1766,

> are printed in every newspaper, and stuck up in every corner, by order of the justices, to intimidate the engrossers, against whom many murmurings are propagated. The common people are taught to entertain a very high opinion and reverence for these laws. . . .

Indeed, he accused the justices of encouraging "the extraordinary pretence, that the power and spirit of the mob is necessary to enforce the laws."[63] But if the laws were actually set in motion, they were directed almost without exception against petty culprits—local wide-boys or market-men, who pocketed small profits on trivial transactions—while the large dealers and millers were unaffected.[64]

Thus, to take a late example, an old-fashioned and crusty Middlesex JP, J. S. Girdler, instituted a general campaign of prosecutions against such offenders in 1796 and 1800, with handbills offering rewards for information, letters to the press, etc. Convictions were upheld at several Quarter Sessions, but the amount gained by the speculators amounted only to ten or fifteen shillings. We can guess at the kind of offender whom his prosecutions touched by the literary style of an anonymous letter which he received:

> We no you are an enemy to Farmers, Mealmen and Bakers and our Trade
> if it had not bene for me and another you you son of a bitch you wold
> have been murdurd long ago by offering your blasted rewards and per-
> secuting Our Trade God dam you and blast you you shall never live to
> see another harvest . . .[65]

Compassionate traditionalists like Girdler were joined by townsmen of various ranks. Most Londoners suspected everyone who had any part in handling grain, flour or bread of every kind of extortion. The urban lobby was, of course, especially powerful in the middle years of the century, pressing for an end to the export bounty, or for the prohibition of all exports in time of dearth. But London and the larger towns harboured inexhaustible reserves of resentment, and some of the wildest accusations came from this milieu. A certain Dr. Manning, in the 1750s, published allegations that bread was adulterated not only with alum, chalk, whiting, and beanmeal, but also with slaked lime and white lead. Most sensational was his claim that millers turned into their flour "sacks of old ground bones": "the charnel houses of the dead are raked, to add filthiness to the food of the living," or, as another pamphleteer commented, "the present age [is] making hearty meals on the bones of the last."

Manning's accusations went far beyond the bounds of credibility. (A critic computed that if lime was being used on the scale of his allegations, more would be consumed in the London baking than building industry.)[66] Apart from alum, which was widely used to whiten bread, the commonest form of adulteration was probably the admixture of old, spoiled flour with new flour.[67] But the urban population was quick to believe that far more noxious adulterations were practiced, and such belief contributed to the "Shude-hill Fight" at Manchester in 1757, where one of the mills attacked was believed to mix "Accorns,

Beans, Bones, Whiting, Chopt Straw, and even dried Horse Dung" with its flour, while at another mill the presence of suspicious adulterants near the hoppers (discovered by the crowd) led to the burning of bolters and sieves, and the destruction of mill-stones and wheels.[68]

There were other, equally sensitive, areas where the complaints of the crowd were fed by the complaints of traditionalists or by those of urban professional people. Indeed, one may suggest that if the rioting or price-setting crowd acted according to any consistent theoretical model, then this model was a selective reconstruction of the paternalist one, taking from it all those features which most favoured the poor and which offered a prospect of cheap corn. It was, however, less generalised than the outlook of the paternalists. The records of the poor show more particularity: it is this miller, this dealer, those farmers hoarding grain, who provoke indignation and action. This particularity was, however, informed by general notions of rights which disclose themselves most clearly only when one examines the crowd in action. For in one respect the moral economy of the crowd broke decisively with that of the paternalists: for the popular ethic sanctioned direct action by the crowd, whereas the values of order underpinning the paternalist model emphatically did not.

The economy of the poor was still local and regional, derivative from a subsistence-economy. Corn should be consumed in the region in which it was grown, especially in times of scarcity. Profound feeling was aroused, and over several centuries, by export in times of dearth. Of an export riot in Suffolk in 1631 a magistrate wrote: "to see their bread thus taken from them and sent to strangers has turned the impatience of the poor into licentious fury and desperation."[69] In a graphic account of a riot in the same county seventy-eight years later (1709), a dealer described how "the Mobb rose, he thinks several hundreds, and said that the corn should not be carryed out of town": "of the Mobb some had halberds, some quarter staffs, and some clubbs. . . ." When travelling to Norwich, at several places on the way:

> the Mobb hearing that he was to goe through with corn, told him that it should not go through the Towne, for that he was a Rogue, and Corn-Jobber, and some cry'd out Stone him, some Pull him off his horse, some Knock him down, and be sure you strike sure; that he . . . questioned them what made them rise in such an inhuman manner to the prejudice of themselves and the countrey, but that they still cryed out that he was a Rogue & was going to carry the corn into France. . . .[70]

Except in Westminster, in the mountains, or in the great sheep-grazing districts, men were never far from the sight of corn. Manufacturing industry was dispersed in the countryside: the colliers went to their labour by the side of cornfields; domestic workers left their looms and workshops for the harvest. Sensitivity was not confined to overseas export. Marginal exporting areas were especially sensitive, where little corn was exported in normal years, but where, in times of scarcity, dealers could hope for a windfall price in London, thereby aggravating local dearth.[71] The colliers—Kingswood, the Forest of Dean, Shropshire, the North-East—were especially prone to action at such times. Notoriously the Cornish tinners had an irascible consumer-consciousness, and a readiness to turn out in force. "We had the devil and all of a riot at Padstow," wrote a Bodmin gentleman in 1773, with scarcely-concealed admiration:

> Some of the people have run to too great lengths in exporting of corn. . . . Seven or eight hundred tinners went thither, who first offered the corn-factors seventeen shillings for 24 gallons of wheat; but being told they should have none, they immediately broke open the cellar doors, and took away all in the place without money or price.[72]

The worst resentment was provoked, in the middle years of the century, by foreign exports upon which bounty was paid. The foreigner was seen as receiving corn at prices sometimes below those of the English market, with the aid of a bounty paid out of English taxes. Hence the extreme bitterness sometimes visited upon the exporter, who was seen as a man seeking private, and dishonourable, gain at the expense of his own people. A North Yorkshire factor, who was given a ducking in the river in 1740, was told that he was "no better than a rebel."[73] In 1783 a notice was affixed to the market-cross in Carlisle, commencing:

> Peter Clemeseson & Moses Luthart this is to give you Warning that you must Quit your unlawfull Dealing or Die and be Damned your buying the Corn to starve the Poor Inhabitants of the City and Soborbs of Carlisle to send to France and get the Bounty Given by the Law for taking the Corn out of the Country but by the Lord God Almighty we will give you Bounty at the Expence of your Lives you Damed Roagues. . . .

"And if Eany Publik House in Carlisle [the notice continued] Lets you or Luthart put up . . . Corn at their Houses they shall suffer for it."[74] This feeling revived in the last years of the century, notably in 1795, when rumours flew around the country as to secret exports to France. Moreover, 1795 and 1800 saw the efflorescence of a regional consciousness once more, as vivid as that of one hundred years before. Roads were blockaded to prevent export from the parish. Wagons were intercepted and unloaded in the towns through which they passed. The movement of grain by night-convoy assumed the proportions of a military operation:

> Deep groan the waggons with their pond'rous loads,
> As their dark course they bend along the roads;
> Wheel following wheel, in dread procession slow,
> With half a harvest, to their points they go . . .
> The secret expedition, like the night
> That covers its intents, still shuns the light . . .
> While the poor ploughman, when he leaves his bed,
> Sees the huge barn as empty as his shed.[75]

Threats were made to destroy the canals.[76] Ships were stormed at the ports. The miners at Nook Colliery near Haverfordwest threatened to close the estuary at a narrow point. Even lighters on the Severn and Wye were not immune from attack.[77]

Indignation might also be inflamed against a dealer whose commitment to an outside market disrupted the customary supplies of the local community. A substantial farmer and publican near Tiverton complained to the War Office in 1795 of riotous assemblies "threatening to pull down or fire his house because he takes in Butter of the neighbouring Farmers & Dairymen, to forward it by the common road waggon, that passes by his door to. . . . London."[78] In Chudleigh (Devon) in the same year the crowd destroyed the machinery of a miller who had ceased to supply the local community with flour since he was under contract to the Victualling Department of the Navy for ship's biscuits: this had given rise (he says in a revealing phrase) "to an Idea that ive done much infimy to the Community."[79] Thirty years before a group of London merchants had found it necessary to seek the protection of the military for their cheese-warehouses along the river Trent:

> The warehouses . . . in danger from the riotous colliers are not the property of any monopolizers, but of a numerous body of cheese-mongers, and absolutely necessary for the reception of their cheese, for the conveyance to Hull, there to be ship'd for London.[80]

These grievances are related to the complaint, already noted, of the withdrawal of goods from the open market. As the dealers moved further from London and attended more frequently at provincial markets, so they were able to offer prices and buy in quantities which made the farmers impatient to serve the small orders of the poor. "Now it is out of the course of business," wrote Davies in 1795, "for the farmer to retail corn by the bushel to this or that poor

man; except in some particular places, as a matter of favour, to his own labourers." And where the poor shifted their demand from grain to flour, the
story was much the same:

> Neither the miller nor the mealman will sell the labourer a less quantity
> than a *sack* of flour under the retail price at shops; and the poor man's
> pocket will seldom allow of his buying a whole sack at once.[81]

Hence the labourer was driven to the petty retail shop, at which prices were
enhanced.[82] The old markets declined, or, where they were kept up, they
changed their functions. If a customer attempted to buy a single cheese or half
flitch of bacon, Girdler wrote in 1800, "he is sure to be answered by an insult,
and he is told that the whole lot has been bought up by some London con-
tractor."[83]

We may take as expressive of these grievances, which sometimes occasioned
riot, an anonymous letter dropped in 1795 by the door of the mayor of Salisbury:

> Gentlemen of the Corporation I pray you put a stop to that practice which
> is made use of in our Markits by Rook and other carriers in your giving
> them the Liberty to Scower the Market of every thing so as the Inhabitance
> cannot buy a single Artickel without going to the Dealers for it and Pay
> what Extortionat price they think proper and even Domineer over the
> Peopel as thow they was not Whorthy to Look on them. But their time
> will soon be at an End as soon as the Solders ear gon out of town.

The corporation is asked to order carriers out of the market until the townspeople have been served, "and stop all the Butchers from sending the meat
away by a Carces at a time But make them cut it up in the Markit and sarve
the Town first." The letter informs the mayor that upwards of three hundred
citizens have "positively swor to be trow to each other for the Distruction of
the Carriers."[84]

Where the working people could buy cereals in small parcels intense feeling
could arise over weights and measures. We are exhorted in Luke: "Give, and
it shall be given unto you, good measure pressed down, and shaken together,
and running over, shall men give unto your bosom." This was not, alas, the
practice of all farmers and dealers in protestant England. An enactment of
Charles II had even given the poor the right to *shake* the measure, so valuable
was the poor man's corn that a looseness in the measure might make the
difference to him of a day without a loaf. The same Act had attempted, with
total lack of success, to enforce the Winchester measure as the national standard.

A great variety of measures, varying even within county boundaries from one market-town to the next, gave abundant opportunities for petty profiteering. The old measures were generally larger—sometimes very much larger—than the Winchester; sometimes they were favoured by farmers or dealers, more often they were favoured by the customers. One observer remarked that "the lower orders of people detest it [the Winchester measure], from the smallness of its contents, and the dealers . . . instigate them to this, it being their interest to retain every uncertainty in weights and measures."[85]

Attempts to change the measure often encountered resistance, occasionally riot. A letter from a Clee Hill (Shropshire) miner to a "Brother Sufferer" declared:

> The Parliament for our relief to help to Clem [starve] us Thay are going to lesson our Measure and Wait [weight] to the Lower Standard. We are about Ten Thousand sworn and ready at any time And we wou'd have you get Arms and Cutlasses and swear one another to be true. . . . We have but one Life to Loose and we will not clem . . .[86]

Letters to farmers in Northiam (Sussex) warned:

> Gentlemen all ie hope you whill take this as a wharning to you all for you to put the little Bushels bie and take the oald measher [measure] again for if you dont there whill be a large company that shall borne [burn] the little measher when you are all abade and asleep and your cornehouses and cornstacks and you along with them. . . .[87]

A Hampshire contributor to the *Annals of Agriculture* explained in 1795 that the poor "have erroneously conceived an idea that the price of grain is increased by the late alteration from a nine-gallon bushel to the Winchester, from its happening to take place at a moment of a rising market, by which, the same money was paid for eight as used to be paid for nine gallons." "I confess," he continues,

> I have a decided predeliction for the nine-gallon measure, for the reason that it is the measure which nearest yields a bushel of flour; whence, the poor man is enabled to judge of what he ought to pay for a bushel of flour, which, in the present measure, requires more arithmetic than comes to his share to ascertain.[88]

Even so, the arithmetical notions of the poor may not have been so erroneous. Changes in measures, like changes to decimal currency, tend by some magic to disadvantage the consumer.

If less corn was being being bought (at the end of the century) in the open market by the poor, this also indicated the rise to greater importance of the miller. The miller occupies a place in popular folklore, over many centuries, which is both enviable and unenviable. On one hand he was noted as a fabulously successful lecher, whose prowess is still perhaps perpetuated in a vernacular meaning of the word "grinding." Perhaps the convenience of the village mill, tucked around a secluded corner of the stream, to which the village wives and maidens brought their corn for grinding; perhaps also his command over the means of life; perhaps his status in the village, which made him an eligible match—all may have contributed to the legend:

> A brisk young lass so brisk and gay
> She went unto the mill one day . . .
> There's a peck of corn all for to grind
> I can but stay a little time.
>
> Come sit you down my sweet pretty dear
> I cannot grind your corn I fear
> My stones is high and my water low
> I cannot grind for the mill won't go.
>
> Then she sat down all on a sack
> They talked of this and they talked of that
> They talked of love, of love proved kind
> She soon found out the mill would grind . . .[89]

On the other hand, the miller's repute was less enviable. *"Loving!"* exclaims Nellie Dean in *Wuthering Heights: "Loving!* Did anybody ever hear the like? I might as well talk of loving the miller who comes once a year to buy our corn." If we are to believe all that was written about him in these years, the miller's story had changed little since Chaucer's Reeve's Tale. But where the small country miller was accused of quaintly medieval customs—over-size toll dishes, flour concealed in the casing of the stones, etc.—his larger counterpart was accused of adding new, and greatly more enterprising, peculations:

> For ther-biforn he stal but curteisly,
> But now he was a thief outrageously.

At one extreme we still have the little country mill, exacting toll according to its own custom. The toll might be taken in flour (always from "the best of the meal and from the finer flour that is in the centre of the hopper"); and since the proportion remained the same with whatever fluctuation in price, it was to the miller's advantage if prices were high. Around the small toll-mills (even where toll had been commuted for money payments) grievances multiplied, and there were fitful attempts at their regulation.[90] Since the millers entered increasingly into dealing, and into grinding corn on their own account for the bakers, they had little time for the petty customers (with a sack or two of gleaned corn); hence endless delay; hence also, when the flour was returned it might be the product of other, inferior, grain. (It was complained that some millers purchased at half-price damaged corn which they then mixed with the corn of their customers.[91] As the century wore on, the translation of many mills to industrial purposes gave to the surviving petty corn-mills a more advantageous position. In 1796 these grievances were sufficiently felt to enable Sir Francis Bassett to carry the Miller's Toll Bill, intended to regulate their practices, weights and measures, more strictly.[92]

But these petty millers were, of course, the small fry of the eighteenth century. The great millers of the Thames Valley and of the large towns were a different order of entrepreneurs, who traded extensively in flour and malt. Millers were quite outside the Assize of Bread, and they could immediately pass on any increase in the price of corn to the consumer. England also had its unsung banalities in the eighteenth century, including those extraordinary survivals, the soke mills, which exercised an absolute monopoly of the grinding of grain (and the sale of flour) in substantial manufacturing centres, among them Manchester, Bradford, Leeds.[93] In most cases the feoffees who owned the soke rights sold or leased these to private speculators. Most stormy was the history of the School Mills at Manchester, whose soke rights were intended as a charitable endowment to support the grammar school. Two unpopular lessees of the rights inspired, in 1737, Dr. Byrom's rhyme:

> Bone and Skin, two millers thin,
>   Would starve the town, or near it;
> But be it known, to Skin and Bone,
>   That Flesh and Blood can't bear it.

When, in 1757, new lessees sought to prohibit the importation of flour to the growing town, while at the same time managing their mills (it was alleged) with extortion and delay, flesh and blood could indeed bear it no longer. In the famous "Shude-hill Fight" of that year at least four men were killed by musketry, but the soke rights were finally broken.[94] But even where no actual soke right obtained, one mill might command a populous community, and could provoke the people to fury by a sudden advance in the price of flour or an evident deterioration in its quality. Mills were the visible, tangible targets of some of the most serious urban riots of the century. The Albion Mills at Black-friars Bridge (London's first steam mills) were governed by a quasi-philanthropic syndicate; yet when they burned down in 1791 Londoners danced and sang ballads of rejoicing in the streets.[95] The first steam mill at Birmingham (Snow Hill) fared little better, being the target of a massive attack in 1795.

It may appear at first sight as curious that both dealers and millers should continue to be among the objectives of riot at the end of the century, by which time in many parts of the Midlands and South (and certainly in urban areas) working people had become accustomed to buying bread at the baker's shops rather than grain or flour in the market-place. We do not know enough to chart the change-over with accuracy, and certainly much home-baking sur-vived.[96] But even where the change-over was complete, one should not under-estimate the sophistication of the situation and of the crowd's objectives. There were, of course, scores of petty riots outside bread shops, and the crowd very often "set the price" of bread. But the baker (whose trade in times of high prices can scarcely have been an enviable one) was, alone of all those who dealt in the people's necessities (landlord, farmer, factor, carrier, miller), in daily contact with the consumer; and he was, more than any of the others, protected by the visible paraphernalia of paternalism. The Assize of Bread clearly and publicly limited their lawful profits (thereby also tending to leave the baking trade in the hands of numerous small traders with little capital), and thus pro-tected them, to some degree, from popular wrath. Even Charles Smith, the able exponent of free trade, thought the continuation of the Assize to be expedient: "in large Towns and Cities it will always be necessary to set the Assize, in order to satisfy the people that the price which the Bakers demand is no more than that what is thought reasonable by the Magistrates."[97]

The psychological effect of the Assize was, therefore, considerable. The baker could hope to enhance his profit beyond the allowance calculated in the Assize only by small stratagems, some of which—short-weight bread, adulter-ation, the mixing in of cheap and spoiled flour—were subject either to legal redress or to instant crowd retaliation. Indeed, the baker had sometimes to attend to his own public relations, even to the extent of enlisting the crowd on his side: when Hannah Pain of Kettering complained to the justices of short-weight bread, the baker "raised a mob upon her . . . and said she deserved to be whipped, there were enough of such scambling scum of the earth."[98] Many corporations throughout the century, made a great show of supervising weights and measures, and of punishing offenders.[99] Ben Jonson's "Justice Overdo" was still busy in the streets of Reading, Coventry, or London:

> Marry, go you into every alehouse, and down into every cellar; measure the length of puddings . . . weigh the loaves of bread on his middle finger . . . give the puddings to the poor, the bread to the hungry, the custards to his children.

In this tradition we find a London magistrate in 1795 who, coming on the scene of a riot in Seven Dials where the crowd was already in the act of demolishing the shop of a baker accused of selling light-weight bread, intervened, seized the baker's stock, weighed the loaves, and finding them indeed deficient, distributed the loaves among the crowd.[100]

No doubt the bakers, who knew their customers, sometimes complained of their powerlessness to reduce prices, and diverted the crowd to the mill or the corn-market. "After ransacking many bakers' shops," the miller of Snow Hill, Birmingham, related of the 1795 attack, "they came in great numbers against us. . . ."[101] But in many cases the crowd clearly selected its own targets, deliberately by-passing the bakers. Thus in 1740 at Norwich the people "went to every Baker in the City, and affix'd a Note on his Door in these words, Wheat at *Sixteen Shillings a Comb*." In the same year at Wisbech they obliged "the Merchants to sell Wheat at 4d per Bushel . . . not only to them, but also to the Bakers, where they regulated the Weight & Price of Bread."[102]

But it is clear at this point that we are dealing with a far more complex pattern of action than one which can be satisfactorily explained by a face-to-face encounter between the populace and particular millers, dealers or bakers. It is necessary to take a larger view of the actions of the crowd.

V

It has been suggested that the term "riot" is a blunt tool of analysis for so many particular grievances and occasions. It is also an imprecise term for describing popular actions. If we are looking for the characteristic form of direct action, we should take, not squabbles outside London bakeries, nor even the great affrays provoked by discontent with the large millers, but the "risings of the people" (most notably in 1740, 1756, 1766, 1795, and 1800) in which colliers, tinners, weavers, and hosiery workers were prominent. What is remarkable about these "insurrections" is, first, their discipline, and, second, the fact that they exhibit a pattern of behaviour for whose origin we must look back several hundreds of years: which becomes more, rather than less, sophisticated in the eighteenth century; which repeats itself, seemingly spontaneously, in different parts of the country and after the passage of many quiet years. The central action in this pattern is not the sack of granaries and the pilfering of grain or flour but the action of "setting the price."

What is extraordinary about this pattern is that it reproduces, sometimes with great precision, the emergency measures in time of scarcity whose operation, in the years between 1580 and 1630, were codified in the *Book of Orders*. These emergency measures were employed in times of scarcity in the last years of Elizabeth, and put into effect, in a somewhat revised form, in the reign of Charles I, in 1630. In Elizabeth's reign the magistrates were required to attend the local markets,

> and where you shall fynde that there is insufficiente quantities broughte to fill and serve the said marketts and speciallie the poorer sorte, you shall thereupon resorte to the houses of the Farmers and others using tyllage ... and viewe what store and provision of graine theye have remayninge either thrashed or unthrashed. ...

They might then order the farmers to send "convenient quantities" to market to be sold "and that at reasonable price." The justices were further empowered to "sett downe a certen price upon the bushell of everyc kynde of graine."[103] The queen and her Council opined that high prices were in part due to engrossers, in part to the "greedie desier" of corn-growers who "bee not content wth anie moderate gaync, but seeke & devise waies to kepe up the prices to the manifest oppression of the poorer sort." The Orders were to be enforced "wth out all parciality in sparing anie man."[104]

In essence, then, the *Book of Orders* empowered magistrates (with the aid of local juries) to survey the corn stocks in barns and granaries;[105] to order quantities to be sent to market; and to enforce with severity every part of the marketing, licensing, and forestalling legislation. No corn was to be sold except in open market, "unlesse the same be to some pore handicrafts Men, or Day-Labourers within the parish wherein you doe dwell, that cannot conveniently come to the Market Townes." The Orders of 1630 did not explicitly empower justices to set the price, but ordered them to attend the market and ensure that the poor were "provided of necessary Corne ... with as much favour in the Prices, as by the earnest Perswasion of the Justices can be obtained." The power to set a price upon grain or flour rested, in emergency, half-way between enforcement and persuasion.[106]

This emergency legislation was falling into disrepair during the Civil Wars.[107] But the popular memory, especially in a pre-literate society, is extraordinarily long. There can be little doubt that a direct tradition extends from the *Book of Orders* of 1630 to the actions of clothing workers in East Anglia and the West in the eighteenth century. (The literate had long memories also: the *Book of Orders* itself was republished, unofficially in 1662, and again in 1758, with a prefatory address to the reader referring to the present "wicked combination to make scarcity."[108]

The Orders were themselves in part a response to the pressure of the poor:

The Corne is so dear
I doubt mani will starve this yeare—

So ran a doggerel notice affixed in the church porch in the parish of Wye (Kent) in 1630:

If you see not to this
Sum of you will speed amis.
Our souls they are dear,
For our bodys have sum ceare
Before we arise
Less will safise . . .
You that are set in place
See that youre profession you doe not disgrace . . . [109]

One hundred and thirty years later (1768) incendiary papers were once again being nailed to church doors (as well as to inn-signs) in parishes within the same lathe of Scray in Kent, inciting the poor to rise.[110] Many similar continuities can be observed, although undoubtedly the pattern of direct action spread to new districts in the eighteenth century. In many actions, especially in the old manufacturing regions of the East and West, the crowd claimed that since the authorities refused to enforce "the laws" they must enforce them for themselves. In 1693 at Banbury and Chipping Norton the crowd "took away the corne by force out of the waggons, as it was carrying away by the ingrossers, saying that they were resolved to put the law in execution, since the magistrates neglected it."[111] During the extensive disorders in the West in 1766 the sheriff of Gloucestershire, a gentleman clothier, could not disguise his respect for the rioters who

went . . . to a farmhouse and civilly desired that they wou'd thresh out and bring to market their wheat and sell it for five shillings per bushel, which being promised, and some provisions given them unasked for, they departed without the least violence or offence.

If we follow other passages of the sheriff's accounts we may encounter most of the features found in these actions:

On Friday last a Mobb was rais'd in these parts by the blowing of Horns &c consisting entirely of the lowest of the people such as weavers, mecanicks, labourers, prentices, and boys, &c. . . .

"They proceeded to a gristmill near the town . . . cutting open Baggs of Flower and giving & carrying it away & destroying corn &c." They then attended at the main markets, setting the price of grain. Three days later he sent a further report:

They visited Farmers, Millers, Bakers and Hucksters shops, selling corn, flower, bread, cheese, butter, and bacon, at their own prices. They returned in general the produce [i.e. the money] to the proprietors or in their absence left the money for them; and behaved with great regularity and decency where they were not opposed, with outrage and violence where they was: but pilferd very little, which to prevent, they will not now suffer Women and boys to go with them.

After visiting the mills and markets around Gloucester, Stroud, and Cirencester, they divided into parties of fifty and a hundred and visited the villages and farms, requesting that corn be brought at fair prices to market, and breaking in on granaries. A large party of them attended on the sheriff himself, downed their cudgels while he addressed them on their misdeameanours, listened with patience, "chearfully shouted God Save the King," and then picked up their cudgels and resumed the good work of setting the price. The movement partook of the character of a general strike of the whole clothing district: "the rioters come into our workshops . . . and force out all the men willing or unwilling to join them."[112]

This was an unusually large-scale and disciplined action. But the account directs us to us features repeatedly encountered. Thus the movement of the crowd from the market-place outwards to the mills and thence (as in the *Book of Orders*) to farms, where stocks were inspected and the farmers ordered to send grain to market at the price dictated by the crowd—all this is commonly found. This was sometimes accompanied by the traditional round of visits to the houses of the great, for contributions, forced or voluntary. At Norwich in 1740 the crowd, after forcing down prices in the city, and seizing a keel loaded with wheat and rye on the river, solicited contributions from the rich of the city:

Early on Thursday Morning, by Sound of Horns, they met again; and after a short Confabulation, divided into Parties, and march'd out of Town at different Gates, with a long Streamer carried before them, purposing to

visit the Gentlemen and Farmers in the neighbouring Villages, in order
to extort Money, Strong Ale, &c, from them. At many places, where the
Generosity of People answer'd not their Expectation, 'tis said they shew'd
their Resentment by treading down the Corn in the Fields. . . .

Perambulating crowds were active in this year, notably in Durham and Northumberland, the West Riding, and several parts of North Wales. Anti-export
demonstrators, commencing at Dewsbury (April 1740) were led by a drummer
and "a sort of ensign or colours"; they performed a regular circuit of the local
mills, destroying machinery, cutting sacks, and carrying away grain and meal.
In 1766 a perambulating crowd in the Thames Valley called themselves "the
Regulators"; a terrified farmer allowed them to sleep in the straw in his yard,
and "could hear from his Chamber that they were telling one another whom
they had most frightened, & where they had the best success." The pattern
continues in the 1790s: at Ellesmere (Shropshire) the crowd stopping the corn
as it goes to the mills and threatening the farmers individually; in the Forest
of Dean the miners visiting mills and farmers' houses, and exacting money
"from persons they meet in the road"; in West Cornwall the tinners visiting
farms with a noose in one hand and an agreement to bring corn at reduced
prices to market in the other.[113]

It is the restraint, rather than the disorder, which is remarkable; and there
can be no doubt that the actions were approved by an overwhelming popular
consensus. There is a deeply-felt conviction that prices *ought*, in times of
dearth, to be regulated, and that the profiteer put himself outside of society.
On occasion the crowd attempted to enlist, by suasion or force, a magistrate,
parish constable, or some figure of authority to preside over the *taxation
populaire*. In 1766 at Drayton (Oxfordshire) members of the crowd went to
John Lyford's house "and asked him if he were a Constable—upon his
saying 'yes' Cheer said he sho'd go with them to the Cross & receive the
money for 3 sacks of flour which they had taken from one Betty Smith and
which they w'd sell for 5s a Bushel"; the same crowd enlisted the constable
of Abingdon for the same service. The constable of Handborough (also in
Oxfordshire) was enlisted in a similar way, in 1795; the crowd set a price—
and a substantial one—of 40s a sack upon a wagon of flour which had been
intercepted, and the money for no fewer than fifteen sacks was paid into his
hands. In the Isle of Ely, in the same year, "the mob insisted upon buying
meat at 4d per lb, & desired Mr Gardner a Magistrate to superintend the
sale, as the Mayor had done at Cambridge on Saturday sennight." Again in
1795 there were a number of occasions when militia or regular troops
supervised forced sales, sometimes at bayonet-point, their officers looking
steadfastly the other way. A combined operation of soldiery and crowd

forced the mayor of Chichester to accede in setting the price of bread. At Wells men of the 122nd Regiment began

> by hooting those they term'd forestallers or jobbers of butter, who they hunted in different parts of the town—seized the butter—collected it together—placed sentinels over it—then threw it, & mix't it together in a tub—& afterwards retail'd the same, weighing it in scales, selling it after the rate of 8d per lb . . . though the common price given by the jobbers was rather more than 10d.[114]

It would be foolish to suggest that, when so large a breach was made in the outworks of deference, many did not take the opportunity to carry off goods without payment. But there is abundant evidence the other way, and some of it is striking. There are the Honiton lace-workers, in 1766, who, having taken corn from the farmers and sold it at the popular price in the market, brought back to the farmers not only the money but also the sacks; the Oldham crowd, in 1800, which rationed each purchaser to two pecks a head; and the many occasions when carts were stopped on the roads, their contents sold, and the money entrusted to the carter.[115]

Moreover, in those cases where goods were taken without payment, or where violence was committed, it is wise to enquire whether any particular aggravation of circumstances enters into the case. The distinction is made in an account of an action at Portsea (Hampshire) in 1795. The bakers and butchers were first offered by the crowd the popular price: "those that complied in those demands were paid with exactness." But those who refused had their shops rifled "without receiving any more money than the mob chose to leave." Again, the quarrymen at Port Isaac (Cornwall) in the same year seized barley warehoused for export, paying the reasonably high price of 11s, a bushel, at the same time warning the owner that "if he offer'd to ship the Remainder they would come & take it without making him any recompence." Very often the motive of punishment or revenge comes in. The great riot in Newcastle in 1740, when pitmen and keelmen swept into the Guildhall, destroyed the town books and shared out the town's hutch, and pelted aldermen with mud and stones, came only after two phases of aggravation: first, when an agreement between the pitmen's leaders and the merchants (with an aldermen acting as arbitrator) setting the prices of grain had been broken; second, when panicky authorities had fired into the crowd from the Guildhall steps. At one house in Gloucestershire in 1766 shots were fired at the crowd which (writes the sheriff)—

> they highly resented by forceing into the house, and destroying all the furniture, windows, &c and partly untiled it; they have given out since

that they greatly repented of this act because 'twas not the master of the house (he being from home) that fired upon them.

In 1795 the tinners mounted an attack upon a Penryn (Cornwall) merchant who was contracted to send them barley, but who had sent them spoiled and sprouting grain. When mills were attacked, and their machinery damaged, it was often in furtherance of a long-standing warning, or as punishment for some notorious practice.[116]

Indeed, if we wish to call in question the unilinear and spasmodic view of food riots, we need only point to this continuing motif of popular intimidation, when men and women near to starvation nevertheless attacked mills and granaries, not to steal the food, but to punish the proprietors. Repeatedly corn or flour was strewn along the roads and hedges; dumped into the river; mill machinery was damaged and mill-dams let off. To examples of such behaviour the authorities reacted both with indignation and astonishment. It was symptomatic (as it seemed to them) of the "frantic" and distempered humours of a people whose brain was inflamed by hunger. In 1795 both the Lord Chief Justice and Arthur Young delivered lectures to the poor, pointing out that the destruction of grain was not the best way to improve the supply of bread. Hannah More added a Half-penny Homily. An anonymous versifier of 1800 gives us a rather more lively example of these admonitions to the lower orders:

When with your country Friends your hours you pass,
And take, as oft you're wont, the copious glass,
When all grow mellow, if perchance you hear
"That 'tis th' Engrossers make the corn so dear;
"They must and will have bread; they've had enough
"Of Rice and Soup, and all such *squashy* stuff:
"They'll help themselves: and strive by might and main
"To be reveng'd on all such rogues in grain":
John swears he'll fight as long as he has breath,
" 'Twere better to be hang'd than starv'd to death:
"He'll burn Squire Hoardum's garner, so he will,
"Tuck up old Filchbag, and pull down his mill."
Now when the Prong and Pitchfork they prepare
And all the implements of rustick war . . .
Tell them what ills unlawful deeds attend,
Deeds, which in wrath begun, and sorrow end,
That burning barns, and pulling down a mill,
Will neither corn produce, nor bellies fill.[117]

But were the poor really so silly? One suspects that the millers and dealers, who kept one wary eye on the people and the other on the maximisation of their profits, knew better than the poetasters at their *escritoires*. For the poor had their own sources of information. They worked on the docks. They moved the barges on the canals. They drove the carts and manned the toll-gates. They worked in the granaries and the mills. They often knew the local facts far better than the gentry; in many actions they went unerringly to hidden supplies of grain whose existence the JPs, in good faith, denied. If rumours often grew beyond all bounds, they were always rooted in at least some shallow soil of fact. The poor knew the one way to make the rich yield was to twist their arms.

VI

Initiators of the riots were, very often, the women. In 1693 we learn of a great number of women going to Northampton market, "with knives stuck in their girdles to force corn at their own rates." In an export riot in 1737 at Poole (Dorset) it was reported: "The Numbers consist of so many Women, & the Men supporting them, & Swear, if any one offers to molest any of the Women in their Proceedings they will raise a Great Number of Men & destroy both Ships & Cargoes." The mob was raised in Stockton (Durham) in 1740 by a "Lady with a stick and a horn." At Haverfordwest (Pembroke) in 1795 an old-fashioned JP who attempted, with the help of his curate, to do battle with the colliers, complained that "the women were putting the Men on, & were perfect furies. I had some strokes from some of them on my Back. . . ." A Birmingham paper described the Snow Hill riots as the work of "a rabble, urged on by furious women." In dozens of cases it is the same—the women pelting an unpopular dealer with his own potatoes, or cunningly combining fury with the calculation that they had slightly greater immunity than the men from the retaliation of the authorities: "the women told the common men," the Haverfordwest magistrate said of the soldiers, "that they knew they were in their Hearts for them & would do them no hurt."[118]

These women appear to have belonged to some pre-history of their sex before its Fall, and to have been unaware that they should have waited for some two hundred years for their Liberation. (Southey could write as a commonplace, in 1807: "Women are more disposed to be mutinous; they stand less in fear of law, partly from ignorance, partly because they presume upon the privilege of their sex, and therefore in all public tumults they are foremost in violence and ferocity."[119]) They were also, of course, those most involved in face-to-face marketing, most sensitive to price significancies, most experienced in detecting short-weight or inferior quality. It is probable that the women most frequently precipitated the spontaneous actions. But other actions were more carefully prepared. Sometimes notices were nailed to church or inn doors. In 1740 "a Mach of Futtball was Cried at Ketring of five Hundred Men of a side, but the design was to Pull Down Lady Betey Jesmaine's Mills." At the end of the century the distribution of hand-written notices may have become more common. From Wakefield (Yorkshire), 1795:

> To Give Notice
> To all Women & inhabitance of Wakefield they are desired to meet at the New Church . . . on Friday next at Nine O'Clock . . . to state the price of corn. . . .
> By desire of the inhabitants of Halifax
> Who will meet them there

From Stratton (Cornwall), 1801:

> To all the labouring Men and Tradesmen in the Hundred of Stratton that are willing to save their Wifes and Children from the Dreadfull condition of being STARVED to DEATH by the unfeeling and Griping Farmer. . . . Assemble all emeadiately and march in Dreadfull Array to the Habitations of the Griping Farmer, and Compell them to sell their Corn in the Market, at a fair and reasonable Price. . . .[120]

The small-scale, spontaneous action might develop from a kind of ritualised hooting or groaning outside retailers' shops;[121] from the interception of a wagon of grain or flour passing through a populous centre; or from the mere gathering of a menacing crowd. Very quickly a bargaining-situation would develop: the owner of the provisions knew very well that if he did not comply voluntarily with the price imposed by the crowd (and his compliance made any subsequent prosecution very difficult) he stood in danger of losing his stock altogether. When a wagon with sacks of wheat and flour was intercepted at Handborough (Oxfordshire) in 1795, some women climbed aboard and pitched the sacks on the roadside. "Some of the persons assembled said they would give Forty Shillings a Sack for the Flour, and they would have it at that, and would not give more, and if that would not do, they would have it by force." The owner (a "yeoman") at length agreed: "If that must be the price, it must be the price." The procedure of forced bargaining can be seen equally clearly in the deposition of Thomas Smith, a baker, who rode into Hadstock (Essex) with bread on his panniers (1795). He was stopped in the village street by forty or more women and children. One of the women (a labourer's wife) held his horse and having asked whether he had fallen in his price of Bread, he told her, he had no Orders to fall from the Millers, & she then said, "By God if you don't fall you shall not leave any Bread in the Town." ...

Several in the crowd then offered 9d. a quartern loaf, while he demanded 19d. They then "swore that if he would not let them have it at 9d a Loaf, they would take it away, & before he could give any other Answer, several Persons then about him took several of the Loaves off his Pads. ...." Only at this point did Smith agree to the sale at 9d. the loaf. The bargaining was well understood on both sides; and retailers, who had to hold on to their customers in the fat years a well as the lean, often capitulated at the first sign of crowd turbulence.

In larger-scale disturbances, once the nucleus of a crowd had been formed, the remainder was often raised by horn or drums. "On Monday last," a letter from a Shropshire magistrate commences in 1756, "the colliers from Broseley &c assembled with horns blowing, & proceeded to Wenlock Market. ...." What was critical was the gathering of the determined nucleus. Not only the "virility" of the colliers, and their particular exposure to consumer-exploitation, explain their prominent role, but also their numbers and the natural discipline of the mining community. "On Thursday morning," John Todd, a pitman at Heaton Colliery, Gateshead, deposed (1740), "at the time of the night shift going on," his fellow pitmen, "about 60 or 80 in number stopped the gin at the pit ... and it was proposed to come to Newcastle to settle the prices of corn. ...." When they came from Nook Colliery into Haverfordwest in 1795 (the magistrate relates that his curate said: "Doctor, here are the colliers coming ... looked up & saw a great crowd of men women & children with oaken bludgeons coming down the street bawling out, 'One & all—one & all' ") the colliers explained later that they had come at the request of the poor townspeople, who had not the morale to set the price on their own.[122]

The occupational make-up of the crowd provides few surprises. It was (it seems) fairly representative of the occupations of the "lower orders" in the rioting areas. At Witney (Oxfordshire) we find informations against a blanket-weaver, a tailor, the wife of a victualler, and a servant; at Saffron Walden (Essex) indictments against two collar-makers, a cordwainer, a bricklayer, a carpenter, a sawyer, a worsted-maker, and nine labourers; in several Devonshire villages (Sampford Peverell, Burlescomb, Culmstock) we find a spinster, two weavers, a woolcomber, a cordwainer, a thatcher, and ten labourers indicted; in the Handborough affair a carpenter, a mason, a sawyer, and seven labourers were mentioned in one information.[123] There were fewer accusations as to the alleged incitement by persons in a superior station in life than Rudé and others have noted in France,[124] although it was more often suggested that the labourers were encouraged by their superiors towards a tone hostile to farmers and middlemen. An observer in the South-West in 1801 argued that the riots were "certainly directed by inferior Tradesmen, Woolcombers, & Dissenters, who keep aloof but by their language & immediate influence govern the lower classes."[125] Occasionally, large employers of labour were alleged to have encouraged their own workers to act.[126]

Another important difference, as compared with France, was the relative inactivity of farm labourers in England as contrasted with the activity of the *vignerons* and petty peasantry. Many cereal farmers, of course, continued the custom of selling cheap grain to their own labourers, while the living-in hired farm servants shared the farmer's board. Rural labourers did participate in riots, when some other groups (like colliers) formed the original nucleus, or where some activity brought them together in sufficient numbers. When a large band of labourers toured the Thames Valley in 1766, the action had commenced with gangs at work on a turnpike-road, who said "with one Voice, Come one & all to Newbury in a Body to Make the Bread cheaper." Once in town, they raised further support by parading in the town square and giving three huzzas. In East Anglia in 1795 a similar nucleus was found from among the "bankers" (gangs "employed in cleansing out Drains & in embanking"). The bankers also were less subject to instant identification and punishment, or to the revenges of village paternalism, than were field labourers, being "for the most part strangers from different countries [who] are not so easily quieted as those who live on the spot."[127]

In truth, the food riot did not require a high degree of organisation. It required a consensus of support in the community, and an inherited pattern of action with its own objectives and restraints. And the persistence of this form of action raises an interesting question: how far was it, in any sense, successful? Would it have continued, over so many scores, indeed hundreds, of years, if it had consistently failed to achieve its objectives, and had left nothing but a few ruined mills and victims on the gallows? It is a question peculiarly difficult to answer; but one which must be asked.

VII

In the short-term it would seem probable that riot and price-setting defeated their own objects. Farmers were sometimes intimidated so far that they refused afterwards, for several weeks, to bring goods to market. The interdiction of the movement of grain within the country was likely only to aggravate shortage in other regions. Although instances can be found where riot appeared to result in a fall in prices, and instances can be found of the opposite, and, further, instances can be found where there appears to be little difference in the movement of prices in riot and non-riot markets, none of these instances—however aggregated or averaged—need necessarily disclose the effect of the *expectation* of riot upon the total market-situation.[128]

We may take an analogy from war. The actual immediate benefits of war are rarely significant, either to victor or defeated. But the benefits which may be gained by the *threat* of war may be considerable: and yet the threat carries no terrors if the sanction of war is never used. If the market-place was as much an arena of class war as the factory and mine became in the industrial revolution, then the threat of riot would affect the entire marketing situation, not only in years of dearth but also in years of moderate harvest, not only in towns notorious for their susceptibility to riot but also in towns where the authorities wished to preserve a tradition of peace. However carefully we quantify the available data these cannot show us to what level prices would have risen if the threat of riot had been altogether removed.

The authorities in riot-prone areas were often cool and competent in handling disturbance. This allows one sometimes to forget that riot was a calamity, often resulting in a profound dislocation of social relations in the community, whose results could linger on for years. The provincial magistracy were often in extreme isolation. Troops, if they were sent for, might take two, three, or more days to arrive, and the crowd knew this very well. The sheriff of Gloucestershire could do nothing in the first days of the "rising" of 1766 but attend at Stroud market with his "javelin men." A Suffolk magistrate in 1709 refrained from imprisoning the leaders of the crowd because "the Mob threatened to pull both his house and the Bridewell down if he punished any of their fellows." Another magistrate who led a ragged and unmartial *posse comitatus* through North Yorkshire to Durham in 1740, capturing prisoners on the way, was dismayed to find the citizens of Durham turn out and release two of his prisoners at the gate of the goal. (Such rescues were common.) A Flint grain exporter had an even more unpleasant experience in the same year. Rioters entered his house, drank the beer and wine in his vaults, and stood—

> with a Drawn Sword pointed upon my Daughter in Laws breast. . . . They have a great many Fire Arms, Pikes and Broadswords. Five of the Pikes they declare that four of them shall do to Carry my Four Quarters and the other my head in triumph about with them. . . .

The question of order was by no means simple. The inadequacy of civil forces was combined with a reluctance to employ military force. The officers themselves had sufficient humanity, and were surrounded by sufficient ambiguity as to their powers in civil affrays, to show a marked lack of enthusiasm for employment in this "Odious Service."[129] If local magistrates called in the troops, or authorised the use of fire-arms, they had to go on living in the district after

the troops had left, incurring the odium of the local population, perhaps receiving threatening letters, and being the victims of broken windows or even
arson. Troops billeted in a town quickly became unpopular, even with those
who had first called them in. With uncanny regularity requests for the aid of
troops are followed, in Home Office or War Office papers, after an interval of
five or six weeks, by petitions for their removal. A pitiful petition from the
inhabitants of Sunderland in 1800, headed by their Rector, asked for the withdrawal of the 68th Regiment:

> Their principal aim is robbery. Several have been knocked down and
> plundered of their watches, but always it has been done in the most violent
> and brutal manner.

One young man had had his skull fractured, another his upper lip cut off.
Inhabitants of Wantage, Farringdon, and Abingdon petitioned.

> in the name of God . . . remove the part of Lord Landaff's regiment from
> this place, or else Murder must be the consequence, for such a sett of
> Villains never entered this Town before.

A local magistrate, supporting the petition, added that the "savage behaviour
of the military. . . . exasperates the populace to the highest degree. The usual
intercourse of the husbandmen at fairs and markets is much interrupted."[130].

Riot was a calamity. The "order" which might follow after riot could be an
even greater calamity. Hence the anxiety of authorities, either to anticipate the
event, or to cut it short in its early stages, by personal presence, by exhortation
and concession. In a letter of 1773 the mayor of Penryn, besieged by angry
tinners, writes that the town was visited by three hundred "of those Banditti,
with whom we were forced to beat a Parley and come to an agreement to let
them have the Corn for one-third less than the Prime Cost to the Proprietors."
Such parleys, more or less reluctant, were common. An experienced Warwickshire magistrate, Sir Roger Newdigate, noted in his diary on 27 September
1766:

> At 11 rode to Nuneaton . . . and with the principal people of the town met
> the Bedworth colliers and mob who came hallowing and armed with sticks,
> demanded what they wanted, promised to satisfy all their reasonable de-
> mands if they would be peacable and throw away their sticks which all of
> them then did into the Meadow, then walked with them to all the houses
> which they expected had engrossed and let 5 or 6 go in search and per-
> suaded the owners to sell what was found of cheese. . . .

The colliers then left the town quietly, after Sir Roger Newdigate and two others had each given them half a guinea. They had, in effect, acted according to the *Book of Orders.*[131]

This kind of bargaining, in the first commencement of riot, often secured concessions for the crowd. But we should also note the exertions by magistrates and landowners in anticipation of riot. Thus a Shropshire magistrate in 1756 describes how the colliers "say if the farmers do not bring their corn to the markets, they will go to their houses & thresh for themselves:"

> I have sent to my Tenants to order them to take each of them some corn to the market on Saturday as the only means I can think of to prevent greater outrages.

In the same year we may observe magistrates in Devon exerting themselves in a similar way. Riots had occurred at Ottery, farmers' corn seized and sold off at 5s. a bushel, and several mills attacked. Sir George Yonge sent his servant to affix an admonitory and conciliatory paper in the market-place:

> The mob gather'd, insulted my Servant, and intimidated the Cryer. . . . On reading [the paper] they declared It would not do, the Gentlemen need not trouble themselves, for *They* would fix the Price at 4s 9d next Market Day: upon this I rode into the Town yesterday, and told both the Common people and the better sort, that if things were not quite the military must be sent for. . . .

He and two neighboring gentry had then sent their own corn into the local markets:

> I have ordered mine to be sold at 5s 3d and 5s 6d per bushell to the poorer sort, as we have resolved to keep rather above the Price dictated by the Mob. I shall send to the Millers to know if they can part with any Flour. . . .

The mayor of Exeter replied to Yonge that the city authorities had ordered corn to be sold at 5s. 6d.: "Everything was quiet immediately the farmers fell the price. . . ." Similar measures were still being taken in Devon in 1801, "some Gentlemen of the most respectable characters in the neighbourhood of Exeter . . . directing . . . their Tenantry to bring Corn to the Market, under the penalty of not having their leases renewed." In 1795 and 1800–1 such orders by traditionalist landowners to their farming tenants were frequent in other counties. The earl of Warwick (an arch-paternalist and an advocate of the leg-

islation against forestallers in its fullest rigour) rode in person around his estates giving such directions to his tenants.[132]

Such pressures as these, in anticipation of riot, may have been more effective
than has been proposed: in getting corn to market; in restraining rising prices;
and in intimidating certain kinds of profiteering. Moreover, a disposition to riot
was certainly effective as a signal to the rich to put the machinery of parish
relief and of charity—subsidised corn and bread for the poor—into good repair.
In January 1757 Reading Corporation agreed:

> that a Subscription be set on foot for Raising money to Buy Bread to be
> Distributed to the Poor . . . at a Price to be fixed much below the present
> price of Bread. . . .

The Corporation itself donated £21.[133] Such measures were very commonly
followed, the initiative coming sometimes from a corporation, sometimes from
individual gentry, sometimes from Quarter Sessions, sometimes from parish
authorities, sometimes from employers—especially those who employed a substantial labour-force (such as lead-miners) in isolated districts.

The measures taken in 1795 were especially extensive, various, and well-
documented. They ranged from direct subscriptions to reduce the price of bread
(the parishes sometimes sending their own agents direct to the ports to purchase
imported grain), through subsidies from the poor rates, to the Speenhamland
system. The examination of such measures would take us farther into the history
of the poor laws than we intend to go.[134] But the effects were sometimes curious.
Subscriptions, while quieting one area, might provoke riot in an adjacent one,
through arousing a sharp sense of inequality. An agreement in Newcastle in
1740 to reduce prices, reached between merchants and a deputation of dem-
onstrating pitmen (with aldermen mediating), resulted in "country people" from
outlying villages flooding into the city; an unsuccessful attempt was made to
limit the sale to persons with a written certificate from "a Fitter, Staithman,
Ton Tail Man, or Churchwarden." Participation by soldiers in price-setting
riots in 1795 was explained, by the duke of Richmond, as arising from a similar
inequality: it was alleged by the soldiers "that while the Country People are
relieved by their Parishes and Subscriptions, the Soldiers receive no such Benefit." Moreover, such subscriptions, while being intended to buy off riot (actual
or potential), might often have the effect of *raising* the price of bread to those
outside the benefit of subscription.[135] In South Devon, where the authorities
were still acting in 1801 in the tradition of 1757, the process can be seen. The
Exeter crowd demonstrated in the market for wheat at 10s. a bushel:

The Gentlemen and Farmers met, & the People waited their decision. . . . They were informed that no Price they shou'd name or fix would be agreed to, & principally because the principle of fixing a Price wou'd be resisted. The Farmers then agreed at 12s and every Inhabitant to have it in proportion to their Families. . . .

The Arguments of the discontented at Exmouth are very cogent. "Give us whatever *quantity* the Stock in Hand will afford, & at a price by which we can attain it, & we shall be satisfied; we will not accept any Subscription from the Gentry because it enhances the Price, & is a hardship on them."[136]

The point here is not just that prices, in time of scarcity, were determined by many other factors than mere market-forces: anyone with even a scanty knowledge of much maligned "literary" sources must be aware of that. It is more important to note the total socio-economic context within which the market operated, and the logic of crowd pressure. One other example, this time from a hitherto riot-free market, may show this logic at work. The account is that of a substantial farmer, John Toogood, in Sherborne (Dorset). The year 1757 commenced with "general complaint" at high prices, and frequent accounts of riots elsewhere:

On the 30th of April, being Market-Day, many of our idle and insolent Poor Men and Women assembled and begun a Riot in the Market House, went to Oborn Mill and brought off several Bags of Flour and divided the Spoil here in Triumph.

On the next Monday an anonymous letter, directed to Toogood's brother (who had just sold ten bushels of wheat at 14s. 10d.—"a great price indeed"—to a miller), was found in the abbey: "Sir, If you do not bring your Wheat into the Market, and sell it at a reasonable price, your Barns shall be pulled down . ."

As Rioting is quite a new Thing in Sherborne . . . and as the neighbouring Parishes seemed ripe for joining in this Sport, I thought there was no Time to be lost, and that it was proper to crush this Evil in it's Bud, in Order to which we took the following Measures.

Having called a Meeting at the Almshouse, it was agreed that Mr. Jeffrey and I should take a Survey of all the most necessitous Families in the Town, this done, We raised about £100 by Subscriptions, and before the next Market Day, our Justice of the Peace and some of the principal

Inhabitants made a Procession throughout the Town and published by the Cryer of the Town the following Notice.

> "That the Poor Families of this Town will be supplied with a Quantity of Wheat sufficient for their Support every Week 'till Harvest at the Rate of 8s p. Bushel and that if any person whatsoever after this public Notice shall use any threatening Expressions, or commit any Riot or Disorder in this Town, the Offender shall be forthwith committed to Prison."

They then contracted for wheat, at 10s. and 12s. the bushel, supplying it to a "List of the Poor" at 8s. until harvest. (Sixty bushels weekly over this period will have involved a subsidy of between £100 and £200.) "By these Means we restored Peace, and disappointed many loose, disorderly Fellows of the Neighbouring Parishes, who appeared in the Market with their empty Bags, expecting to have had Corn without Money." John Toogood, setting down this account for the guidance of his sons, concluded it with the advice:

> If the like Circumstances happen hereafter in your Time and either of you are engaged in Farmering Business, let not a covetous Eye tempt you to be foremost in advancing the Price of Corn, but rather let your Behavior shew some Compassion and Charity towards the Condition of the Poor. . . .[137]

It is within such a context as this that the function of riot may be disclosed. Riot may have been, in the short term, counter-productive, although this has not yet been proved. But, once again, riot was a social calamity, and one to be avoided, even at a high cost. The cost might be to achieve some medium, between a soaring "economic" price in the market, and a traditional "moral" price set by the crowd.

That medium might be found by the intervention of paternalists, by the prudential self-restraint of farmers and dealers, or by buying-off a portion of the crowd, through charities and subsidies. As Hannah More carolled, in the persona of the sententious Jack Anvil, when dissuading Tom Hod from riot:

> So I'll work the whole day, and on Sundays I'll seek
> At Church how to bear all the wants of the week.
> The gentlefolks, too, will afford us supplies,
> They'll subscribe—and they'll give up their puddings and pies.
> *Derry down.*[138]

Derry down, indeed, and even Tra-la-dee-bum-deeay! However, the nature of gentlefolks being what it is, a thundering good riot in the next parish was more likely to oil the wheels of charity than the sight of Jack Anvil on his knees in church. As the doggerel on the *out*side of the church door in Kent had put it succinctly in 1630:

> Before we arise
> Less will safise.

VIII

We have been examining a pattern of social protest which derives from a consensus as to the moral economy of the commonwealt in times of dearth. It is not usually helpful to examine it for overt, articulate political intentions, although these sometimes arose through chance coincidence. rebellious phrases can often be found, usually (one suspects) to chill the blood of the rich with their theatrical effect. It was said that the Newcastle pitmen, flushed with the success of their capture of the Guildhall, "were for putting in practice the old levelling principles"; they did at least tear down the portraits of Charles II and James II and smash their frames. By contrast, bargees at Henley (Oxfordshire) in 1743 called out "Long Live the Pretender"; and someone in Woodbridge (Suffolk) in 1766 nailed up a notice in the market-place which the local magistrate found to be "peculiarly bold and seditious and of high and delicate import": "We are wishing [it said] that our exiled King could come over or send some Officers." Perhaps the same menace was intended, in the South-West in 1753, by threats that "the French w'd be here soon."[139]

Most common are general "levelling" threats, imprecations against the rich. A letter at Witney (1767) assured the bailiffs of the town that the people would not suffer "such damned wheesing fat guted Rogues to Starve the Poor by such Hellish Ways on purpose that they may follow hunting horse racing etc and to maintain their familys in Pride and extravagance." A letter on the Gold Cross at Birmingham's Snow Hill (1766), signed "Kidderminister & Stourbridge," was perhaps in the mode of rhyming doggerel—

> . . . there is a small Army of us upwards of three thousand all ready to
>   fight
> & I'll be dam'd if we don't make the King's Army to shite
> If so be the King & Parliament don't order better
> we will turn England into a Litter
> & if so be as things don't get cheaper

I'll be damd if we don't burn down the Parliament House & make all
better. . . .

A letter in Colchester in 1772 addressed to all farmers, millers, butchers, shopkeepers, and corn merchants, warned all the "damd Rogues" to take care,

> for this is november and we have about two or three hundred bum shells
> a getting in Readiness for the Mellers [millers] and all no king no parlia-
> ment nothing but a powder plot all over the nation.

The gentlemen of Fareham (Hampshire) were warned in 1766 to prepare "for
a Mob or Sivel war," which would "pull George from his throne beat down
the house of rougs [rogues] and destroy the Sets [seats] of the Law makers."
"Tis better to Undergo a forrieghn Yoke than to be used thus," wrote a villager
near Hereford in the next year. And so on, and from most parts of Britain. It
is, in the main, rhetoric, although rhetoric which qualifies in a devastating way
the rhetoric of historians as to the deference and social solidarities of Georgian
England.[140]

Only in 1795 and 1800–1, when a Jacobin tinge is frequent in such letters
and handbills, do we have the impression of a genuine undercurrent of articulate
political motivation. A trenchant example of these is some doggerel addressed
to "the Broth Makers & Flower Risers" which gave a Maldon (Essex) magistrate
cause for alarm:

> On Swill & Grains you wish the poor to be fed
> And underneath the Guillintine we could wish to see your heads
> For I think it is a great shame to serve the poor so—
> And I think a few of your heads will make a pretty show.

Scores upon scores of such letters circulated in these years. From Uley (Gloucestershire), "no King but a Constitution down down down O fatall down high
caps and proud hats forever down down. . . ." At Lewes, (Sussex), after several
militiamen had been executed for their part in price-setting, a notice was posted:
"Soldiers to Arms!"

> Arise and revenge your cause
> On those bloody numskulls, Pitt and George,
> For since they no longer can send you to France
> To be murdered like Swine, or pierc'd by the Lance,
> You are sent for by Express to make a speedy Return
> To be shot like a Crow, or hang'd in your Turn. . . .

At Ramsbury (Wiltshire) in 1800 a notice was affixed to a tree:

> Downe with Your Luxzuaras Government both spiritual & temperal Or
> you starve with Hunger, they have stripp you of bread Chees Meate &c
> &c &c &c &c. Nay even your Lives have they Taken thousands on
> their Expeditions let the Burbon Family defend their owne Cause and
> let us true Britons look to Our Selves let us banish Some to Hanover
> where they came from Downe with your Constitution Arect a republic
> Or you and your offsprings are to starve the Remainder of our Days
> dear Brothers will you lay down and die under Man eaters and Lave
> your offspring under that Burden that Blackguard Government which is
> now eatain you up.
>   God Save the Poor & down with George III.[141]

But these crisis years of the wars (1800–1) would demand separate treatment.
We are coming to the end of one tradition, and the new tradition has scarcely
emerged. In these years the alternative form of economic pressure—pressure
upon wages—is becoming more vigorous; there is also something more than
rhetoric behind the language of sedition—underground union organisation,
oaths, the shadowy "United Englishmen." In 1812 traditional food riots overlap
with Luddism. In 1816 the East Anglian labourers do not only set the prices,
they also demand a minimum wage and an end to Speenhamland relief. They
look forward to the very different revolt of labourers in 1830. The older form
of action lingers on into the 1840s and even later; it was especially deeply
rooted in the South-West.[142] But in the new territories of the industrial revolution it passed by stages into other forms of action. The break in wheat prices
after the wars eased the transition. In the northern towns the fight against the
corn jobbers gave way to the fight against the Corn Laws.

There was another reason why 1795 and 1800–1 bring us into different
historical territory. The forms of action which we have been examining depended upon a particular set of social relations, a particular equilibrium between
paternalist authority and the crowd. This equilibrium was dislodged in the wars,
for two reasons. First, the acute anti-Jacobinism of the gentry led to a new fear
of any form of popular self-activity; magistrates were willing to see signs of
sedition in price-setting actions even where no such sedition existed; the fear
of invasion raised the Volunteers, and thus gave to the civil powers much more
immediate means for meeting the crowd, not with parley and concession, but
with repression.[143] Second, such repression was legitimised, in the minds of
central and of many local authorities, by the triumph of the new ideology of
political economy.

Of this celestial triumph, the Home Secretary, the duke of Portland, served as Temporal Deputy. He displayed, in 1800–1, a quite new firmness, not only in handling disturbance, but in overruling and remonstrating with those local authorities who still espoused the old paternalism. In September 1800 a significant episode occurred in Oxford. There had been some affair of setting the price of butter in the market, and cavalry appeared in the town (at the request—as it transpired—of the Vice-Chancellor). The Town Clerk, on the direction of the mayor and magistrates, wrote to the Secretary at War, expressing their "surprise that a military body of horse soldiers should have made their appearance early this morning":

> It is with great pleasure I inform you that the people of Oxford have hitherto shewn no disposition to be riotous except the bringing into the market[of] some hampers of butter and selling it at shilling a pound and accounting for the money to the owner of the butter be reckoned of that description . . .

"Notwithstanding the extreme pressure of the times," the City authorities were of "the decided opinion" that there was "no occasion in this City for the presence of a regular Soldiery," especially since the magistrates were being most active in suppressing "what they conceive to be one of the principal causes of the dearness, the offences of forestalling, ingrossing, and regrating. . . ."

The Town Clerk's letter was passed over to the duke of Portland, and drew from him a weighty reproof:

> His Grace . . . desires you to inform the Mayor and Magistrates, that as his official situation enables him in a more particular manner to appreciate the extent of the publick mischief which must inevitably ensue from a continuance of the riotous proceedings which have taken place in several parts of the kingdom in consequence of the present scarcity of Provisions, so he considers himself to be more immediately called upon to exercise his own judgment and discretion in directing adequate measures to be taken for the immediate and effectual suppression of such dangerous proceedings. For greatly as His Grace laments the cause of these Riots, nothing is more certain than that they can be productive of no other effect than to increase the evil beyond all power of calculation. His Grace, therefore, cannot allow himself to pass over in silence that part of your letter which states "that the People of Oxford have hitherto shewn no disposition to be riotous, except the bringing into Market some Hampers of Butter, and selling it at a Shilling a pound, and accounting for the money to the Owner of the Butter, can be reckoned of that description."
>
> So far from considering this circumstances, in the trivial light in which it is represented in your letter (even supposing it to stand unconnected

with others of a similar and a still more dangerous nature, which it is to be feared is not the case) His Grace sees it in the view of a violent and unjustifiable attack on property pregnant with the most fatal consequences to the City of Oxford and to it's Inhabitants of every description; and which His Grace takes it for granted the Mayor and Magistrates must have thought it their bounden duty to suppress and punish by the immediate apprehension and committal of the Offenders.[144]

Throughout 1800 and 1801 the duke of Portland busied himself enforcing the same doctrines. The remedy for disturbance was the military or Volunteers; even liberal subscriptions for cheap corn were to be discouraged, as exhausting stocks; persuasion upon farmers or dealers to lower prices was an offence against political economy. In April 1801 he wrote to Earl Mount Edgcumbe,

> Your Lordship must excuse the liberty I take in not passing unnoticed the agreement you mention to have been voluntarily entered into by the Farmers in Cornwall to supply the Markets with Corn and other Articles of Provision at reduced Prices . . .

The duke had information that the farmers had been subjected to pressure by the county authorities:

> . . . the experience I have . . . calls upon me to say that every undertaking of the kind cannot in the nature of things be justified and must unavoidably and shortly add to and aggravate the distress which it pretends to alleviate, and I will venture also to assert that the more general it could be rendered the more injurious must be the consequences by which it could not fail to be attended because it necessarily prevents the Employment of Capital in the Farming Line. . . .[145]

The "nature of things" which had once made imperative, in times of dearth, at least some symbolic solidarity between the rulers and the poor, now dictated solidarity between the rulers and "the Employment of Capital." It is, perhaps, appropriate that it was the ideologist who synthesized an hysteric anti-Jacobinism with the new political economy who signed the death-warrant of that paternalism of which, in his more specious passages of rhetoric, he was the celebrant. "The Laboring *Poor*," exclaimed Burke: "Let compassion be shewn in action,"

> . . . but let there be no lamentation of their condition. It is no relief to their miserable circumstances; it is only an insult to their miserable un-

derstandings. . . . Patience, labour, sobriety, frugality, and religion, should be recommended to them; all the rest is downright *fraud*.[146]

Against that tone the notice at Ramsbury was the only possible reply.

IX

I hope that a somewhat different picture has emerged from this account than the customary one. I have tried to describe, not an involuntary spasm, but a pattern of behaviour of which a Trobriand islander need not to have been ashamed.

It is difficult to re-imagine the moral assumptions of another social config-uration. It is not easy for us to conceive that there may have been a time, within a smaller and more integrated community, when it appeared to be "un-natural" that any man should profit from the necessities of others, and when it was assumed that, in time of dearth, prices of "necessities" should remain at a customary level, even though there might be less all round.

"The economy of the medieval borough," wrote R. H. Tawney, "was one in which consumption held somewhat the same primacy in the public mind, as the undisputed arbiter of economic effort, as the nineteenth century attached to profits."[147] These assumptions were under strong challenge, of course, long before the eighteenth century. But too often in our histories we foreshorten the great transitions. We leave forestalling and the doctrine of a fair price in the seventeenth century. We take up the story of the free market economy in the nineteenth. But the death of the old moral economy of provision was as long-drawn-the death of paternalist intervention in industry and trade. The consumer defended his old notions of right as stubbornly as (perhaps the same man in another role) he defended his craft status as an artisan.

These notions of right were clearly articulated. They carried for a long time the church's imprimatur. The *Book of Orders* of 1630 envisaged moral precept and example as an integral part of emergency measures:

> That all good Means and Perswasions bee used by the Justices in their several Divisions, and by Admonitions and Exhortations in Sermons in the Churches. . . . that the Poore may bee served of Corne at convenient and charitable Prices. And to the furtherance thereof, that the richer Sort bee earnestly mooved by Christian Charitie, to cause their Graine to be sold under the common Prices of the Market to the poorer sort: A deed of mercy, that will doubtlesse be rewarded of Almighty God.

At least one such sermon, delivered at Bodmin and Fowey (Cornwall) before the Sessions in 1630 by the Rev. Charles Fitz-Geffrey, was still known to eighteenth-century readers. Hoarders of corn were denounced as

> these Man-haters, opposite to the Common good, as if the world were made only for them, would appropriate the earth, and the fruits thereof, wholly to themselves. . . . As Quailes grow fat with Hemlocke, which is poison to other creatures, so these grow full by Dearth. . . .

They were "enemies both to God and man, opposite both to Grace and Nature." As for the dealer exporting corn in time of scarcity, "the savour of lucre is sweet to him, though raked out of the puddle of the most filthy profession in Europe. . . ."[148] As the seventeenth century drew on, this kind of exhortation became muted, especially among the Puritans. With Baxter one part of moral precept is diluted with one part of casuistry and one part of business prudence: "charity must be exercised as well as justice," and, while goods might be withheld in the expectation of rising prices, this must not be done "to the hurt of the Commonwealth, as if . . . keeping it in be the cause of the dearth."[149] The old moral teaching became, increasingly, divided between the paternalist gentry on one hand, and the rebellious plebs on the other. There is an epitaph in the church at Stoneleigh (Warwickshire) to Humphrey How, the porter to Lady Leigh, who died in 1688:

> Here Lyes a Faithful Friend unto the Poore
> Who dealt Large Almes out of his Lord[ps] Store
> Weepe Not Poore People Tho' Y[e] Servat's Dead
> The Lord himselfe Will Give You Dayly Breade
> If Markets Rise Raile Not Against Theire Rates
> The Price is Stil the Same at Stone Leigh Gates.[150]

The old precepts resounded throughout the eighteenth century. Occasionally they might still be heard from the pulpit:

> Exaction of any kind is base; but this in the Matter of Corn is of the basest Kind. It falls heaviest upon the Poor, It is robbing them because they are so. . . . It is murdering *them* outright whom they find half dead, and plundering the wreck'd Vessel. . . . These are the Murderers accused by the Son of *Sirach*, where he saith, *The Bread of the Needy is their Life: he that defraudeth them thereof is a Man of Blood.* . . . Justly may such

Oppressors be called "*Men of Blood*"; and surely will the Blood of those, who thus perish by their means, be required at their Hands.[151]

More often they were heard in pamphlet or newspaper:

To keep up the Price of the very Staff of Life at such an extravagant Sale, as that the Poor . . . cannot purchase it, is the greatest Iniquity any Man can be guilty of; it is no less than Murder, nay, the most cruel Murder.[152]

Sometimes in broadsheet and ballad:

Go now you hard-hearted rich men,
   In your miseries, weep and howl,
Your canker'd gold will rise against you,
   And Witness be against your souls. . . .[153]

and frequently in anonymous letters. "Donte make a god of your mony," the gentlemen of Newbury were warned in 1772:

but think of the por you great men do you think of gohing to heaven or hell. think of the Sarmon which preach on 15 of March for dam we if we don't make you do you think to starve the pore quite you dam sons of wors [whores]. . . .[154]

"Averishes Woman!" a corn-hoarder in Cornwall was addressed in 1795 by Cornish tinners: "We are . . . determined to assemble and immediately to march till we come to your Idol, or your God or your Mows [Moses?], whome you esteem as such and pull it down and likewise your House. . . ."[155]

Today we shrug off the extortionate mechanisms of an unregulated market economy because it causes most of us only inconvenience, unostentatious hardships. In the eighteenth century this was not the case. Dearths were real dearths. High prices meant swollen bellies and sick children whose food was coarse bread made up from stale flour. No evidence has yet been published to show anything like a classic *crise des subsistances* in England in the eighteenth century:[156] the mortality of 1795 certainly did not approach that in France in the same year. But there was what the gentry described as a distress that was "truly painful": rising prices (wrote one) "have stript the cloaths from their backs, torn the shoes and stockings from their feet, and snatched the food from their mouths."[157] The risings of the Cornish tinners were preceded by harrowing scenes: men fainted at their work and had to be carried home by their fellows in scarcely better state. The dearth was accompanied by an epidemic described as "Yellow Fever," very possibly the jaundice associated with near-starvation.[158] In such a year Wordsworth's "pedlar" wandered among the cottages and saw

> The hardships of that season, many rich
> Sank down as in a dream among the poor,
> And of the poor did many cease to be,
> And their place knew them not. . . .[159]

But if the market was the point at which working people most often felt their exposure to exploitation, it was also the point—especially in rural or dispersed manufacturing districts—at which they could most easily become organised. Marketing (or "shopping") becomes in mature industrial society increasingly impersonal. In eighteenth-century Britain or France (and in parts of southern Italy or Haiti or rural India or Africa today) the market remained a social as well as an economic nexus. It was the place where one-hundred-and-one social and personal transactions went on; where news was passed, rumour and gossip flew around, politics was (if ever) discussed in the inns or wine-shops round the market-square. The market was the place where the people, because they were numerous, felt for a moment that they were strong.[160]

The confrontations of the market in a "pre-industrial" society are of course more universal than any national experience. And the elementary moral precepts of the "reasonable price" are equally universal. Indeed, one may suggest in Britain the survival of a pagan imagery which reaches to levels more obscure than Christian symbolism. Few folk rituals survived with such vigour to the end of the eighteenth century as all the paraphernalia of the harvest-home, with its charms and suppers, its fairs and festivals. Even in manufacturing areas the year still turned to the rhythm of the seasons and not to that of the banks. Dearth always comes to such communities as a profound psychic shock. When it is accompanied by the knowledge of inequalities, and the suspicion of manipulated scarcity, shock passes into fury.

One is struck, as the new century opens, by the growing symbolism of blood, and by its assimilation to the demand for bread. In Nottingham in 1812 the women paraded with a loaf upon a pole, streaked with red and tied with black crepe, emblematic of "bleeding famine decked in Sackecloth." At Yeovil (Somerset) in 1816 there was an anonymous letter, "Blood and Blood and Blood, a General Revolution their mus be . . . ," the letter signed with a crude heart dripping blood. In the East Anglian riots of the same year such phrases as, "We will have blood before dinner." In Plymouth "a *Loaf* which had been *dipped in blood*, with a heart by it, was found in the streets." In the great Merthyr riots of 1831 a calf was sacrificed and a loaf soaked in its blood, impaled on a flagpole, served as emblem of revolt.[161]

This fury for corn is a curious culmination of the age of agricultural improvement. In the 1790s the gentry themselves were somewhat perplexed. Sometimes crippled by an excess of rich food, [162] the magistrates from time to time put aside their industrious compilation of archives for the disciples of Sir Lewis Namier, and peered down from their parklands at the corn-fields in which their labourers hungered. (More than one magistrate wrote in to the Home Office, at this critical juncture, describing the measures which he would take against the rioters if only he were not confined to his house by gout.) The country will not be secure at harvest, wrote the Lord Lieutenant of Cambridgeshire, "without some soldiers, as he had heard that the People intended to help themselves when the Corn was ripe." He found this "a very serious apprehension indeed" and "in this open country most likely to be effected, at least by stealth."[163]

"Thou shalt not muzzle the ox that treadeth out the corn." The breakthrough of the new political economy of the free market was also the breakdown of the old moral economy of provision. After the wars all that was left of it was charity—and Speenhamland. The moral economy of the crowd took longer to die: it is picked up by the early co-operative flour mills, by some Owenite socialists, and it lingered on for years somewhere in the bowels of the Co-operative Wholesale Society. One symptom of its final demise is that we have been able to accept for so long an abbreviated and "economistic" picture of the food riot, as a direct, spasmodic, irrational response to hunger—a picture which is itself a product of a political economy which diminished human reciprocities to the wages-nexus. More generous, but also more authoritative, was the assessment of the sheriff of Gloucestershire in 1766. The mobs of that year (he wrote) had committed many acts of violence,

> some of wantoness and excess; and in other instances some acts of courage, prudence, justice, and a consistency towards that which they profess to obtain.[164]

Notes

1. M. Beloff, *Public Order and Popular Disturbances, 1660–1714* (Oxford, 1938), p. 75.

2. R. F. Wearmouth, *Methodism and the Common People of the Eighteenth Century* (1945), esp. chs. 1 and 2.

3. T. S. Ashton and J. Sykes, *The Coal Industry of the Eighteenth Century* (Manchester, 1929), p. 131.

4. Charles Wilson, *England's Apprenticeship, 1603–1763* (1965), p. 345. It is true that the Falmouth magistrates reported to the duke of Newcastle (16 Nov. 1727) that "the unruly tinners" had "broke open and plundered several cellars and granaries of corn." Their report concludes with a comment which suggests that they were no more able than some modern historians to un-

derstand the rationale of the direct action of the tinners: "the occasion of these outrages was pretended by the rioters to be a scarcity of corn in the county, but this suggestion is probably false, as most of those who carried off the corn gave it away or sold it at quarter price." PRO, SP 36/4/22.

5. W. W. Rostow, *British Economy in the Nineteenth Century* (Oxford, 1948), esp. pp. 122–5. Among the more interesting studies which correlate prices, harvests, and popular disturbance are: E. J. Hobsbawm, "Economic Fluctuations and Some Social Movements," in *Labouring Men* (1964) and T. S. Ashton, *Economic Fluctuations in England, 1700–1800* (Oxford, 1959).

6. I have found most helpful the pioneering study by R. B. Rose "Eighteenth Century Price Riots and Public Policy in England," *International Review of Social History*, vi (1961); and G. Rudé, *The Crowd in History* (New York, 1964).

7. C. Smith, *Three Tracts on the Corn-Trade and Corn-Laws*, 2nd edn. (1766), pp. 140, 182–5.

8. See Fitzjohn Brand, *A Determination of the Average Depression of Wheat in War below That of the Preceding Peace etc.* (1800), pp. 62–3, 96.

9. These generalisations are supported by "replies from towns as to bread in use," returned to the Privy Council in 1796 in PRO, PC 1/33/A.87 and A.88.

10. For maslin (a mixed bread of several cereals) see Sir William Ashley, *The Bread of Our Forefathers* (Oxford, 1928), pp. 16–19.

11. See Smith, op. cit., p. 194 (for 1765). But the mayor of Newcastle reported (4 May 1796) that rye bread was "much used by the workmen employed in the Coal Trade," and a reporter from Hexham Abbey said that barley, barley and gray pease, or beans, "is the only bread of the labouring poor and farmers' servants and even of many farmers'," with rye or maslin in the towns: PRO, PC 1/33/A.88.

12. Nathaniel Forster, *An Enquiry into the Cause of the High Price of Provisions* (1767), pp. 144–7.

13. J. S. Girdler, *Observations on the Pernicious Consequences of Forestalling, Regrating and Ingrossing* (1800), p. 88.

14. The problem was discussed lucidly in [Governor] Pownall, *Considerations on the Scarcity and High Prices of Bread-corn and Bread* (*Cambridge*, 1795), esp. pp. 25–7. See also Lord John Sheffield, *Remarks on the Deficiency of Grain Occasioned by the Bad Harvest of 1799* (1800), esp. pp. 105–6 for the evidence that (1795) "there is no household bread made in London." A Honiton correspondent in 1766 described household bread as "a base mixture of fermented Bran ground down and bolted, to which is added the worst kind of meal not rang'd": HMC, *City of Exeter*, series lxxiii (1916), p. 255. On this very complex question see further S. and B. Webb, "The Assize of Bread," *Economic Journal*, xiv (1904), esp. pp. 203–6.

15. See e.g. Lord Hawkesbury to the duke of Portland, 19 May 1797, in PRO, HO 42/34.

16. See R. N. Salaman, *The History and Social Influence of the Potato* (Cambridge, 1949), esp. pp. 493–517. Resistance extended from the wheat-eating South and Midlands to the oatmeal-eating North; a correspondent from Stockport in 1795 noted that "a very liberal subscription has been entered into for the purpose of distributing oatmeal & other provisions among the poor at reduced prices—This measure, I am sorry to say, gives little satisfaction to the common people, who are still clamorous & insist on having wheaten bread": PRO, WO 1/1094. See also J. L. and B. Hammond, *The Village Labourer* (1966), pp. 119–23.

17. PRO, PC 1/33/A.88. Compare the return from J. Bouche, vicar of Epsom, 8 Nov. 1800 in HO 42/54: "Our Poor live not only on the finest wheaten bread, but almost on bread alone."

18. PRO, PC 1/33/A.88.

19. PRO, PC 1/33/;a.88; *Reading Mercury* 16 Feb. 1801. Hostility to these changes in milling, which were imposed by an Act of 1800 (41 Geo. III, c.16) was especially strong in Surrey and Sussex. Complainants produced samples of the new bread to a Surrey JP: "They represented it as disagreeable to the taste (as indeed it was), as utterly incompetent to support them under their daily labour, & as productive of bowelly complaints to them and to their children in particular": Thomas Turton to Portland, 7 Feb. 1801, HO 42/61. The Act was repeated in 1801: 42 Geo. III, c.2.

20. See especially the budgets in D. Davies, *The Case of Labourers in Husbandry* (Bath, 1795); and Sir Frederick Eden, *The State of the Poor* (1797). Also D. J. V. Jones, "The Corn Riots in Wales," 1793–1801," *Welsh Hist. Rev.*, ii, 4 (1965), App. I, p. 347.

21. The best general study of eighteenth-century corn marketing remains R. B. Westerfield, *Middlemen in English Business, 1660–1760* (New Haven, 1915), ch. 2. Also see N.S.B. Gras, *The Evolution of the English Corn Market from the Twelfth to the Eighteenth Century* (Cambridge, Mass., 1915); D. G. Barnes, *A History of the English Corn Laws* (1930); C. R. Fay, *The Corn Laws and Social England* (Cambridge, 1932); E. Lipson, *Economic History of England*, 6th edn. (1956), ii, pp. 419–48; L. W. Moffitt, *England on the Eve of the Industrial Revolution* (1925), ch. 3; G. E. Fussell and C. Goodman, "Traffic in Farm Produce in Eighteenth Century England," *Agricultural History*, xii, 2 (1938); Janet Blackman, "The Food Supply of an Industrial Town (Sheffield)," *Business History*, v (1963).

22. S. and B. Webb, "The Assize of Bread."

23. J. Aikin, *A Description of the Country from Thirty to Forty Miles round Manchester* (1795), p. 286. One of the best surviving records of a well-regulated market in the eighteenth century is that of Manchester. Here market lookers for fish and flesh, for corn weights and measures, for white meats, for the Assize of Bread, aletasters, and officers to prevent "engrossing, forestalling and regretting" were appointed throughout the century, and fines for short weight and measure, unmarketable meat, etc. were frequent until the 1750s; supervision thereafter was somewhat more perfunctory (although continuing) with a revival of vigilance in the 1790s. Fines were imposed for selling loads of grain before the market bell in 1734, 1737, and 1748 (when William Wyat was fined 20s. "for selling before the Bell rung and declaring he would sell at any Time of the Day in Spite of either Lord of the Mannor or any person else"), and again in 1766. *The Court Leet Records of the Manor of Manchester*, ed. J. P. Earwaker (Manchester, 1888/9), vii, viii, and ix, passim. For the regulation of forestalling at Manchester, see note 3 on p. 209.

24. Proclamation by Exeter Town Clerk, 28 March 1795, PRO, HO 42/34.

25. See S. and B. Webb, op. cit., passim; and J. Burnett, "The Baking Industry in the Nineteenth Century," *Business History*, v. (1963), pp. 98–9.

26. *Rural Economy in Yorkshire in 1641* (Surtees Society, xxxiii, 1857), pp. 99–105.

27. *The Complete English Tradesman* (1727), ii, pt. 2.

28. Anon., *An Essay to Prove that Regrators, Engrossers, Forestallers, Hawkers, and Jobbers of Corn, Cattle, and Other Marketable Goods Are Destructive of Trade, Oppressors to the Poor, and a Common Nuisance to the Kingdom in General* (1719), pp. 13, 18–20.

29. Bucks. CRO, Quarter Sessions, Michaelmas 1710.

30. *Commons Journals*, 2 March 1733.

31. PRO, PC 1/6/63.

32. *Calendar of Home Office Papers* (1879), 1766, pp. 92–4.

33. Ibid., pp. 91–2.

34. *Gentleman's Magazine*, xxvii (1757), p. 286.

35. Anonymous letter in PRO, SP 37/9.

36. Examples, from an abundant literature, will be found in *Gentleman's Magazine*, xxvi (1756), p. 534; Anon. [Ralph Courteville], *The Cries of the Public* (1758), p. 25; Anon. ["C. L."], *A Letter to a Member of Parliament proposing Amendments to the Laws against Forestallers, Ingrossers, and Regraters* (1757), pp. 5–8; *Museum Rusticum et Commerciale*, iv (1765), p. 199; Forster, op. cit., p. 97.

37. Anon., *An Enquiry into the Price of Wheat, Malt, etc.* (1768), pp. 119–23.

38. See e.g. Davies (below p. 335). It was reported from Cornwall in 1795 that "many farmers refuse to sell [barley] in small quantities to the poor, which causes a great murmuring": PRO, HO 42/34; and from Essex in 1800 that "in some places no sale takes place excepting at the ordinaries, where buyers and sellers (chiefly Millers and Factors) dine together . . . the benefit of the Market is almost lost to the neighbourhood"; such practices are mentioned "with great indignation by the lower orders": PRO, HO 42/54.

39. PRO, HO 42/35.

40. See F. J. Fisher, "The Development of the London Food Market, 1540–1640," *Econ. Hist. Rev.*, v (1934–5).

41. Lord Kenyon's charge to the Grand Jury at Shropshire Assizes, *Annals of Agriculture*, xxv (1795), pp. 110–11. But he was not proclaiming a new view of the law: the 1780 edition of Burn's *Justice*, ii, pp. 213–4 had already stressed that (despite the Acts of 1663 and 1772) "at the common law, all endeavours whatsoever to enhance the common price of any merchandize . . . whether by spreading false rumours, or by buying things in a market before the accustomed hour, or by buying and selling again the same thing in the same market" remained offences.

42. Girdler, op. cit., pp. 212–60, lists a number of convictions in 1795 and 1800. Private associations were established in several counties to prosecute forestallers: see the Rev. J. Malham, *The Scarcity of Grain Considered* (Salisbury, 1800), pp. 35–44. Forestalling etc. remained offences at common law until 1844: W. Holdsworth, *History of English Law* (1938), xi, p. 472. See also below, note 64.

43. See e.g. Gras, op. cit., p. 241 (". . . as Adam Smith has shown . . ."); M. Olson, *Economics of the Wartime Shortage* (North Carolina, 1963), p. 53 ("People were quick to find a scapegoat").

44. J. Arbuthnot ("A Farmer"), *An Inquiry into the Connection between the Present Price of Provisions and the Size of Farms* (1773), p. 88.

45. Adam Smith's "digression concerning the Corn Trade and Corn Laws" is in Book IV, chapter 5 of *The Wealth of Nations*.

46. R. H. Tawney takes in the question in *Religion and the Rise of Capitalism* (1926), but it is not central to his argument.

47. The suggestion was made, however, by some of Smith's opponents. One pamphleteer, who claimed to have known him well, alleged that Adam Smith had said to him that "the Christian Religion debased the human mind," and that "Sodomy was a thing in itself indifferent." No wonder that he held heartless views on the corn trade: Anon, *Thoughts of an Old Man of Independent Mind though Dependent Fortune on the Present High Prices of Corn* (1800), p. 4.

48. On the level of *intention* I see no reason to disagree with Professor A. W. Coats, "The Classical Economists and the Labourer," in E. L. Jones and G. E. Mingay (eds.), *Land, Labour and Population* (1967). But intention is a bad measure of ideological interest and of historical consequences.

49. Smith saw the two as going together: "The laws concerning corn may everywhere be compared

to the laws concerning religion. The people feel themselves so much interested in what relates either to their subsistence in this life, or to their happiness in a life to come, that government must yield to their prejudices. . . ."

50. See, however, A. Everitt, "The Marketing of Agricultural Produce," in Joan Thirsk (ed.), *The Agrarian History of England and Wales, 1500–1600*, vol. iv (Cambridge, 1967) and D. Baker, "The Marketing of Corn in the first half of the Eighteenth Century: North-east Kent," *Agric. Hist. Rev.*, xviii (1970).

51. There is some useful information in R. Bennett and J. Elton, *History of Corn Milling*, 4 vols. (Liverpool, 1898).

52. Emmanuel Collins, *Lying Detected* (Bristol, 1758), pp. 66–7. This seems to be confirmed by the budgets of Davies and Eden (see below, note 20), and of nineteenth-century observers: see *The Unknown Mayhew*, eds. E. P. Thompson and E. Yeo (1971), App. II. E. H. Phelps Brown and S. V. Hopkins, "Seven Centuries of the Prices of Consumables Compared with Builders' Wages Rates," *Economica*, xxii (1956), pp. 297–8 allow only 20% of the total household budget to farinaceous food, although the budgets of Davies and Eden (taken in high-price years) show an average of 53%. This again suggests that in such years bread consumption remained stable, but other items were cut out altogether. In London there may already have been a greater diversification of diet by the 1790s. P. Colquhoun wrote to Portland, 9 July 1795, that there was abundance of vegetables at Spitalfields market, especially potatoes, "the great substitute for Bread," carrots and turnips: PRO, PC 1/27/A.54.

53. *Annals of Agriculture*, xxvi (1796), pp. 470, 473. Davenant had estimated in 1699 that a deficiency in the harvest of one-tenth raised the price by three-tenths: Sir C. Whitworth, *The Political and Commercial Works of Charles Davenant* (1771), ii, p. 244. The problem is discussed in W. M. Stern, "The Bread Crisis in Britain, 1795–6," *Economica*, new series, xxxi (1964), and J. D. Gould, "Agricultural Fluctuations and the English Economy in the Eighteenth Century," *Jl. Econ. Hist.*, xxii (1926). Dr. Gould puts weight on a point often mentioned in contemporary apologetics for high prices, e.g. *Farmer's Magazine*, ii (1801), p. 81, that the small growers, in a year of scarcity, required their entire crop for seed and for their own consumption: in such factors as this he finds the "chief theoretical explanation of the extreme volatility of grain prices in the early modern period." One would require more investigation of the actual operation of the market before such explanations carry conviction.

54. Anon. ["A Country Farmer"], *Three Letters to a Member of the House of Commons . . . concerning the Prices of Provisions* (1766), pp. 18–19. For other examples see Lord John Sheffield, *Observations on the Corn Bill* (1791), p. 43; Anon., *Inquiry into the Causes and Remedies of the Late and Present Scarcity and High Price of Provisions* (1800), p. 33; J. S. Fry, *Letters on the Corn-Trade* (Bristol, 1816), pp. 10–11.

55. See Olson, *Economics of the Wartime Shortage*, ch. 3; W. F. Galpin, *The Grain Supply of England during the Napoleonic Period* (New York, 1925).

56. See e.g. Anon. ["A West Country Maltster"], *Considerations on the Present High Prices of Provisions, and the Necessities of Life* (1764), p. 10.

57. "I hope," a Yorkshire landowner wrote in 1708, "the dearth of corn which is likely to continue for several years to come will make husbandry very profitable to us, in breaking up and improving all our new land": cited by Beloff, op. cit., p. 57.

58. The point is noted in Anon., *A Letter to the Rt. Hon. William Pitt . . . on the Causes of the High Price of Provisions* (Hereford, 1795), p. 9; Anon. ["A Society of Practical Farmers"], *A Letter to the Rt. Hon. Lord Somerville* (1800), p. 49. Cf. L. S. Pressnell, *Country Banking in the Industrial Revolution* (Oxford, 1956), pp. 346–8.

59. C. W. J. Grainger and C. M. Elliot, "A Fresh Look at Wheat Prices and Markets in the Eighteenth Century," *Econ. Hist. Rev.*, 2nd series, xx, (1967), p. 252.

60. E. M. Hampson, *The Treatment of Poverty in Cambridgeshire, 1597–1834* (Cambridge, 1934), p. 211.

61. Adam Smith noted nearly sixty years later that the "popular odium . . . which attends the corn trade in years of scarcity, the only years in which it can be very profitable, renders people of character and fortune averse to enter into it. It is abandoned to an inferior set of dealers." Twenty-five years later again Earl Fitzwilliam was writing: "Dealers in corn are withdrawing from the trade, afraid to traffic in an article trafficking in which had render'd them liable to so much obloquy & calummy, and to be run at by an ignorant populace, without confidence in protection from those who ought to be more enlighten'd": Fitzwilliam to Portland, 3 Sept. 1800, PRO, HO 42/51. But an examination of the fortunes of such families as the Howards, Frys and Gurneys might call in question such literary evidence.

62. Collins, op.cit., pp. 67–74. In 1756 several Quaker meeting-houses were attacked during food riots in the Midlands: *Gentleman's Magazine*, xxvi (1756), p. 408.

63. Anon., *Reflections on the Present High Price of Provisions, and the Complaints and Disturbances Arising therefrom* (1766), pp. 26–7, 31.

64. Contrary to the common assumption, the forestalling legislation had not fallen into desuetude in the first half of the eighteenth century. Prosecutions were infrequent, but sufficiently evident to suggest that they had some effect upon regulating petty dealing in the open market. At Manchester (see note 23 above) fines for forestalling or regrating took place sometimes annually, sometimes every two or three years, from 1731 to 1759 (seven fines). Commodities involved included butter, cheese, milk, oysters, fish, meat, carrots, pease, potatoes, turnips, cucumbers, apples, beans, gooseberries, currants, cherries, pigeons, fowls, but very rarely oats and wheat. Fines are less frequent after 1760 but include 1766 (wheat and butter), 1780 (oats and eels), 1785 (meat), and 1796, 1797, and 1799 (all potatoes). Symbolically, the Court Leet officers to prevent forestalling jumped from 3 to 4 appointed annually (1730–1795) to 7 in 1795, 15 in 1796, 16 in 1797. In addition offenders were prosecuted on occasion (as in 1757) at Quarter Sessions. See Earwaker, *Court Leet Records* (cited in note 23), vii, and viii and ix and *Constables' Accounts* (note 68), ii, p. 94. For other examples of offences, see Essex Quarter Sessions, indictments, 2 Sept. 1709, 9 July 1711 (engrossing oats), and also 1711 for cases involving forestallers of fish, wheat, rye, butter, and, again, 13 Jan. 1729/30: Essex CRO, Calendar and Indictments, Q/SR 541, Q/SR 548, Q/SPb b 3; Constables' presentments for forestalling hogs, Oct. 1735 and Oct. 1746: Bury St. Edmunds and West Suffolk CRO, DB/1/8 (5); ditto for forestalling of butter, Nottingham, 6 Jan. 1745/5, *Records of the Borough of Nottingham* (Nottingham, 1914), vi, p. 209; conviction for forestalling of fowls (fine 13s. 4d.) at Atherstone Court Leet and Court Baron, 18 Oct. 1748: Warwicks. CRO, L2/24 23; cautions against the forestalling of butter etc., Woodbridge market, 30 Aug. 1756: Ipswich and East Suffolk CRO, V 5/9/6–3. In most Quarter-Sessional or market records the odd prosecution is to be found, before 1757. The author of *Reflections* (note 63) writing in 1766, says these "almost-forgotten and disregarded statutes" were employed for the prosecution of "some submissive hucksters and indigent or terrified jobbers," and implies that the "principal factors" have despised "these menaces," believing them to be bad law. For 1795 and 1800 see note 42; the most important cases of the prosecution of large dealers were those of Rushby, for regrating oats (1799): see Barnes, pp. 81–3; and of Waddington, convicted for forestalling hops at Worcester Assizes: see *Times*, 4 Aug. 1800 and (for conviction upheld on appeal) I East 143 in ER, cii, pp. 56–68.

65. Girdler, op. cit., pp. 295–6.

66. Collins, op. cit., pp. 16–37. P. Markham, *Syhoroc* (1758), i, pp. 11–31; *Poison Detected: or Frightful Truths . . . in a Treatise on Bread* (1757), esp. pp. 16–38.

67. See e.g. John Smith, *An Impartial Relation of Facts Concerning the Malepractices of Bakers* (n.d. [1740?]).

68. See J.P. Earwaker, *The Constables' Accounts of the Manor of Manchester* (Manchester, 1891), iii, pp. 359–61; F. Nicholson and E. Axon, "The Hatfield Family of Manchester, and the Food Riots of 1757 and 1812," *Trans. Lancs. and Chesh. Antiq. Soc.*, xxviii (1910/11), pp. 83–90.

69. *Calendar State Papers, Domestic*, 1631, p. 545.

70. PRO, PC 1/2/165.

71. See D.G.D. Isaac, "A Study of Popular Disturbance in Britain, 1714–54" (Edinburgh Univ. Ph.D. thesis, 1953), ch. 1.

72. *Calendar of Home Office Papers*, 1773, p. 30.

73. PRO, SP 36/50.

74. *London Gazette*, March 1783, no. 12422.

75. S.J. Pratt, *Sympathy and Other Poems* (1807), pp. 222–3.

76. Some years before Wedgwood had heard it "threatened . . . to destroy our canals and let out the water," because provisions were passing through Staffordshire to Manchester from East Anglia: J. Wedgwood, *Address to the Young Inhabitants of the Pottery* (Newcastle, 1783).

77. PRO, PC 1/27/A.54; A.55-7; HO 42/34; 42/35; 42/36; 42/37; see also Stern, op. cit., and E.P. Thompson, *The Making of the English Working Class* (Penguin, 1968), pp. 70–3.

78. PRO, WO 1/1082, John Ashley, 24 June 1795.

79. PRO, HO 42/34.

80. PRO, WO 1/986 fo. 69.

81. Davies, op. cit., pp. 33–4.

82. "The first principle laid down by a baker, when he comes into a parish, is, to get all the poor in his debt; he then makes their bread of what weight or goodness he pleases. . . .": *Gentleman's Magazine*, xxvi (1756), p. 557.

83. Girdler, op. cit., p. 147.

84. PRO, HO 42/34.

85. *Annals of Agriculture*, xxvi (1796), p. 327; *Museum Rusticum et Commerciale*, iv (1765), p. 198. The difference in bushels could be very considerable: as against the Winchester bushel of 8 gallons, the Stamford had 16 gallons, the Carlisle 24, and the Chester 32: see J. Houghton, *A Collection for Improvement of Husbandry and Trade* (1727), no. xlvi, 23 June 1693.

86. *London Gazette*, March 1767, no. 10710.

87. November 1793, in PRO, HO 42/27. The measures concerned were for malt.

88. *Annals of Agriculture*, xxiv (1795), pp. 51–2.

89. James Reeves, *The Idiom of the People* (1958), p. 156. See also Brit. Lib. Place MSS, Add MSS 27825 for "A pretty maid she to the miller would go," verse 2:

> Then the miller he laid her against the mill hopper
> Merry a soul so wantonly
> He pulled up her cloaths, and he put in the stopper
> For says she I'll have my corn ground small and free.

90. See Markham, *Syhoroc,* ii, p. 15; Bennett and Elton, op. cit., iii, pp. 150–65; information of John Spyry against the Miller of Millbrig Mill, 1740, for taking sometimes 1/6th, sometimes 1/7th, and sometimes 1/8th part as mulcture: West Riding Sessions papers, County Hall, Wakefield.

91. See Girdler, op. cit., pp. 102–6, 212.

92. *Annals of Agriculture*, xxiii (1795), pp. 179–91; Bennett and Elton, op. cit., iii, p. 166; 36: Geo III, c.85.

93. See Bennett and Elton, op. cit., iii, pp. 204 ff; W. Cudworth, "The Bradford Soke," *The Bradford Antiquary* (Bradford, 1888), i, pp. 74ff.

94. See note 68, above and Bennett and Elton, op. cit., pp. 274ff.

95. Ibid., iii, pp. 204–6.

96. Replies from towns to Privy Council enquiry, 1796, in PRO, PC 1/33/A.88: e.g. mayor of York, 16 April 1796, "the poor can get their bread baked at common ovens. . . ."; mayor of Lancaster, 10 April, "each family buys their own flour and makes their own bread"; mayor of Leeds, 4 April, it is the custom "to buy corn or meal, and to mix up their own bread, and to bake it themselves or get it baked for hire." A survey of bakers in the hundred of Corby (Northamptonshire) in 1757 shows that out of 31 parishes, one parish (Wilbarston) had four bakers, one had three, three had two, eight had one, and fourteen had no resident baker (four gave no return): Northants, CRO, H (K) 170.

97. Smith, *Three Tracts on the Corn-Trade*, p. 30.

98. Examination of Hannah Pain, 12 Aug. 1757, Northans. CRO, H (K) 167 (I).

99. It is notable that punishments for these offences were most frequent in years of dearth, and doubtless these were intended to have symbolic force: thus 6 presentments for false or short weight at Bury St. Edmunds sessions, May 1740: Bury St. Edmunds and West Suffolk CRO, D8/I/8(5); 6 fined for deficient weight in Maidenhead, October 1766: Berks. CRO, M/JMI. At Reading, however, surveillance appears to be fairly constant, in good years as well as bad: Central Public Library, Reading, R/MJ Acc. 167, Court Leet and View of Frankpledge. At Manchester the market officials were vigilant until the 1750s, more casual thereafter, but very active in April 1796: Earwaker, *Court Leet Records*, ix, pp. 113–4.

100. *Gentleman's Magazine*, lxv (1795), p. 697.

101. MS notebook of Edward Pickering, Birmingham City Ref. Lib. M 22.11.

102. *Ipswich Journal*, 12 and 26 July 1740. (I am indebted to D. R. W. Malcolmson of Queen's University, Ontario, for these references.) The crowd by no means mistook the bakers for their main opponents, and forms of pressure were often of considerable complexity; thus "incendiary" papers set up around Tenterden (1768) incited people to rise and force the farmers to sell their wheat to the millers or the poor at £10 a load, and threatened to destroy the millers who gave to the farmers a higher price: Shelburne, 25 May 1768, PRO, SP 44/199.

103. "A Coppie of the Councells her[e] for graine delyvrd at Bodmyn the xith of May 1586": Bodleian Library, Rawlinson MSS B 285, fos. 66–7.

104. There is some account of the operation of the *Book of Orders* in E. M. Leonard, *Early History of English Poor Relief* (Cambridge, 1900); Gras, op. cit., pp. 236–42; Lipson, op. cit., iii, pp. 440–50; B. E. Supple, *Commercial Crisis and Change in England, 1600–42* (Cambridge, 1964), p. 117. Papers illustrative of their operation are in *Official Papers of Nathaniel Bacon of Stiffkey, Norfolk* (Camden Society, 3rd series, xxvi, 1915), pp. 130–57.

105. For an example, see *Victoria County History, Oxfordshire*, ed. W. Page (1907), ii, pp. 193–4.

106. By an Act of 1534 (25 Henry VIII, c. 2) the Privy Council had the power to set prices on corn in emergency. In a somewhat misleading note, Gras (op. cit., pp. 132–3) opines that after 1550 the power was never used. It was in any case not forgotten: a proclamation of 1603 appears to set prices (Seligman Collection, Columbia Univ. Lib., Proclamations, James I, 1603); the *Book of Orders* of 1630 concludes with the warning that "if the Corne-masters and other Owners of Victuall . . . shall not willingly performe these Orders," His Majesty will "give Order that rea-

sonable Prices shall be set"; the Privy Council attempted to restrain prices by Proclamation in 1709, Liverpool Papers, Brit. Mus., Add. MS. 38353, fo. 195; and the matter was actively canvassed in 1757—see Smith, *Three Tracts on the Corn Trade*, pp. 29, 35. And (apart from the Assize of Bread) other price-fixing powers lingered on. In 1681 at Oxford market (controlled by the University) prices were set for butter, cheese, poultry, meat, bacon, candles, oats, and beans: "The Oxford Market," *Collectanea* 2nd ser. (Oxford, 1890), pp. 127–8. It seems that the Assize of Ale lapsed in Middlesex in 1692 (Lipson, op. cit., ii, p. 501), and in 1762 brewers were authorized (by 2 Geo. III, c. 14) to raise the price in a reasonable manner; but when in 1773 it was proposed to raise the price by ½d. a quart Sir John Fielding wrote to the earl of Suffolk that the increase "cannot be thought reasonable; nor will the subject submit to it": *Calendar of Home Office Papers* 1773, pp. 9–14; P. Mathias, *The Brewing Industry in England, 1700–1830* (Cambridge, 1959), p. 360.

107. See G. D. Ramsay, "Industrial *Laisser-Faire* and the Policy of Cromwell," *Econ. Hist. Rev.*, 1st series, xvi (1946), esp. pp. 103–4; M. James, *Social Problems and Policy during the Puritan Revolution* (1930), pp. 264–71.

108. *Seasonable Orders Offered from former Precedents Whereby the Price of Corn . . . May Be Much abated (1662)*—a reprint of the Elizabethan Orders; J. Massie, *Orders Appointed by His Majestie King Charles* I (1758).

109. *Calendar State Papers, Domestic,* 1630, p. 387.

110. *Calendar of Home Office Papers,* 1768, p. 342.

111. Westerfield, op. cit., p. 148

112. Letters of W. Dalloway, Brimscomb, 17 and 20 Sept. 1766, in PRO, PC 1//8/41.

113. Norwich, 1740—*Ipswich Journal,* 26 July 1740; Dewsbury, 1740—J. L. Kaye and five magistrates, Wakefield, 30 Apr. 1740, in PRO, SP 36/50; Thames Valley, 1766—testimony of Bartholomew Freeman of Bisham Farm, 2 Oct. 1766, in PRO, TS 11/995/3707; Ellesmere, 1795—PRO, WO I/1089, fo. 359; Forest of Dean—John Turner, mayor of Gloucester, 24 June 1795, PRO, WO I/1087; Cornwall—see John G. Rule, "Some Social Aspects of the Cornish Industrial Revolution," in Roger Burt (ed.), *Industry and Society in the South-West* (Exeter, 1970), pp. 90–1.

114. Drayton, Oxon—brief against Wm. Denley and three others, in PRO, TS 11/995/3707; Handborough—information of Robert Prior, constable, 6 Aug. 1795, PRO, Assizes 5/116; Isle of Ely—Lord Hardwicke, Wimpole, 27 July 1795, PRO, HO 42/35 and H. Gunning, *Reminiscences of Cambridge* (1854), ii, pp. 5–7; Chichester—duke of Richmond, Goodwood, 14 Apr. 1795, PRO, WO I/1092; Wells—"Verax," 28 Apr. 1795, PRO, WO I/1082 and the Rev. J. Turner, 28 Apr., HO 42/34. For an example of a constable who was executed for his part in a tinners' riot in St. Austell, 1729, see Rule, op. cit., p. 90.

115. See Rose, op. cit., p. 435; Edwin Butterworth, *Historical Sketches of Oldham* (Oldham, 1856), pp. 137–9, 144–5.

116. Portsea—*Gentleman's Magazine,* lxv (1795), p. 343; Port Isaac—Sir W. Molesworth, 23 March 1795. PRO, HO 42/34; Newcastle—*Gentleman's Magazine,* x (1740), p. 355, and various sources in PRO, SP 36/51, in Northumberland CRO and Newcastle City Archives Office; Gloucestershire, 1766—PRO, PC 1/8/41; Penryn, 1795—PRO, HO 42/34.

117. Anon., *Contentment: or Hints to Servants, on the Present Scarcity* (broadsheet, 1800).

118. Northampton—*Calendar State Papers, Domestic,* 1693, p. 397; Poole—memorial of Chitty and Lefebare, merchants, enclosed in Holles Newcastle, 26 May 1737, PRO, SP 41/10; Stockton—Edward Goddard, 24 May 1740, PRO, SP 36/50 ("We met a Lady with a Stick and a horn going towards Norton to raise the people . . . took the horn from her, She using very ill language all the while and followed into the Town, raising all the People she could. . . . Ordered the Woman to be taken up. . . . She all the way Crying out, Damn you all, Will You See me Suffer,

or be sent to Gaol?"); Haverfordwest—PRO, HO 42/35; Birmingham—J. A. Langford, *A Century of Birmingham Life* (Birmingham, 1868), ii, p. 52.

119. *Letters from England* (1814), ii, p. 47. The women had other resources than ferocity: a colonel of Volunteers lamented that "the Devil in the shape of Women is now using all his influence to induce the Privates to brake their attachments to their Officers": Lt.-Col. J. Entwisle, Rochdale, 5 Aug. 1795, PRO, WO 1/1086.

120. Kettering—PRO, SP 36/50: for other examples of the use of football to assemble a crowd, see R. M. Malcolmson, "Popular Recreations in English Society, 1700–1850" (Warwick, Univ. Ph.D. thesis, 1970); Wakefield—PRO, HO 42/35; Stratton—handwritten notice, dated 8 April and signed "Cato," in PRO, HO 42/61 fo. 718.

121. A correspondent from Rosemary Lane (London), 2 July 1795) complained of being awoken at 5 a.m. "By a most dreadful Groaning (as the Mob call it) but what I should call Squealing": PRO, WO 1/1089 fo. 719.

122. Broseley—T. Whitmore, 11 Nov. 1756, PRO, SP 36/136; Gateshead—information of John Todd in Newcastle City Archives; Haverfordwest—PRO, HO 42/35.

123. Witney—information of Thomas Hudson, 10 Aug. 1795, PRO, Assizes 5/116; Saffron Walden—indictments for offences on 27 July 1795, PRO, Assizes 35/236; Devonshire—calendar for Summer Circuit, 1795, PRO, Assizes 24/43; Handborough—information of James Stevens, tythingman, 6 Aug. 1795, PRO, Assizes 5/116. All 13 of the Berkshire rioters of 1766 tried by Special Commission were described as "labourers"; of 66 persons brought before the Special Commission at Gloucester in 1766, 51 were described as "labourers," 10 were wives of "labourers," 3 were spinsters: the descriptions reveal little: *G. B. Deputy Keeper of Public Records, 5th Report* (1844), ii, pp. 198–9, 202–4. For Wales, 1793–1801, see Jones, "Corn Riots in Wales," App. III, p. 350. For Dundee, 1772, see S. G. E. Lythe, "The Tayside Meal Mobs," *Scot. Hist. Rev.* xlvi (1967), p. 34: a porter, a quarryman, three weavers, and a sailor were indicted.

124. See Rudé, *The Crowd in History*, p. 38.

125. Lt.-Gen. J. G. Simcoe, 27 Mar. 1801, PRO, HO 42/61.

126. Thus in an export riot in Flint (1740) there were allegations that the steward of Sir Thomas Mostyn had found arms for his own colliers: various depositions in PRO, SP 36/51.

127. Newbury—brief in PRO, TS 11/995/3707; East Anglia—B. Clayton, Boston, 11 Aug. 1795, PRO, HO 42/35.

128. Undoubtedly detailed investigation of short-term price-movements in relation to riot will help to refine the question; but the variables are many, and evidence as to some (*anticipation* of riot, persuasion brought to bear on tenants, dealers, etc., charitable subscriptions, application of poor rates, etc.) is often elusive and difficult to quantify.

129. ". . . . a most Odious Service which nothing but Necessity can justify," Viscount Barrington to Weymouth, 18 Apr. 1768, PRO, WO 4/83, fos. 316–7.

130. Sunderland—petition in PRO, WO 40/17; Wantage and Abingdon—petition to Sir G. Young and C. Dundas, 6 Apr. 1795, ibid.

131. Penryn—PRO, WO 40/17; Warwickshire—H. C. Wood, "The Diaries of Sir Roger Newdigate, 1751–1806," *Trans. Birmingham Archaeological Soc.*, lxxviii (1962), p. 43.

132. Shropshire—T. Whitmore, 11 Nov. 1756, PRO, SP 36/136; Devon—HMC, *City of Exeter*, series lxxiii (1916) pp. 255–7; Devon, 1801—Lt.-Gen. J. G. Simcoe, 27 Mar. 1801, PRO, HO 42/61; Warwick—T. W. Whitley, *The Parliamentary Representation of the City of Coventry* (Coventry, 1894), p. 214.

133. MS diary of Reading Corporation, Central Public Library, Reading: entry for 24 January 1757. £30 was disbursed "towards the present high price of Bread" on 12 July 1795.

134. Especially useful are replies from correspondents in *Annals of Agriculture* xxiv and xxv (1795). See also S. and B. Webb. "The Assize of Bread," op. cit., pp. 208–9; J. L. and B. Hammond, op. cit., ch. vi; W. M. Stern, op. cit., pp. 181–6.

135. A point to be watched in any qualified analysis: the price officially returned from a market in the aftermath of riot might *rise*, although, as a consequence of riot or threat of riot, the poor might be receiving corn at subsidised rates.

136. Newcastle—advertisement 24 June 1740 in City Archives Office; duke of Richmond, 13 Apr. 1795, PRO, WO 1/1092; Devon—James Coleridge, 29 Mar. 1801, HO 42/61.

137. MS diary of John Toogood, Dorset CRO, D 170/1.

138. "The Riot: or, half a loaf is better than no bread, &c," 1795, in Hannah More, *Works* (1830), ii, pp. 86–8.

139. Newcastle—MS account of riots in City Archives; Henley—Isaac, op. cit., p. 186; Wood-bridge—PRO, WO 1/873: 1753—Newcastle MSS Brit. Lib. Add. MS 32732, fo. 343. Earl Poulet, Lord Lieutenant of Somerset, reported in another letter to the duke of Newcastle that some of the mob "came to talk a Levelling language, viz. they did not see why some sh'd be rich & others poor": ibid., fos., 214–5.

140. Witney—*London Gazette*, Nov. 1767, no. 10779; Birmingham—PRO, WO, 1/873; Colchester—*London Gazette*, Nov. 1772, no. 11304; Fareham—ibid., Jan. 1767, no. 10690; Hereford—ibid., Apr. 1767, no. 10717.

141. Maldon—PRO, WO 40/17; Uley—W. G. Baker, Oct. 1975, HO 42/36; Lewes—HO 42/35; Ramsbury—enclosure in the Rev. E. Meyrick, 12 June 1800, HO 42/50.

142. See A. Rowe, "The Food Riots of the Forties in Cornwall," *Report of Royal Cornwall Polytechnic Society* (1942), pp. 51–67. There were food riots in the Scottish Highlands in 1847; in Teignmouth and Exeter in November 1867; and in Norwich a curious episode (the "Battle of Ham Run") as late as 1886.

143. See J. R. Western. "The Volunteer Movement as an Anti-Revolutionary Force, 1793–1801," *Eng. Hist. Rev.*, lxxi (1956).

144. W. Taunton, 6 Sept. 1800; I. King to Taunton, 7 Sept. 1800: PRO, WO 40/17 and HO 43/12. In private letters Portland exerted himself even more forcefully, writing to D. Hughes of Jesus College, Oxford (12 Sept.) of the "unjust & injudicious proceedings of your foolish Corporation": Univ. of Nottingham, Portland MSS, PwV III.

145. Portland, 25 Apr. 1801, PRO, HO 43/13, pp. 24–7. On 4 October 1800 Portland wrote to the Vice-Chancellor of Oxford University (D. Marlow) as to the dangers of the people "giving way to the notion of their difficulties being imputable to the avarice and rapacity of those, who instead of being denominated Engrossers are correctly speaking the purveyors and provident Stewards of the Public": Univ. of Nottingham, Portland MSS, PwV III.

146. E. Burke, *Thoughts and Details on Scarcity, originally presented to the Rt. Hon. William Pitt in . . . November, 1795* (1800), p. 4. Undoubtedly this pamphlet was influential with both Pitt and Portland, and may have contributed to the tougher policies of 1800.

147. R. H. Tawney, *Religion and the Rise of Capitalism* (1926), p. 33.

148. C. Fitz-Geffrey, *God's Blessing upon the Providers of Corne: and God's Curse upon the Hoarders* (1631; reprint 1648), pp. 7, 8, 13.

149. Tawney, op. cit., p. 222. See also C. Hill, *Society and Puritanism in Pre-Revolutionary England* (1964), esp. pp. 277–8.

150. I am indebted to Professor David Montgomery for this evidence.

151. Anon.["A Clergyman in the Country"], *Artificial Dearth: or, the Iniquity and Danger of With-holding Corn* (1756), pp. 20–1.

152. Letter to *Sherborne Mercury*, 5 Sept. 1757.

153. "A Serious Call to the Gentlemen Farmers, on the present exorbitant Prices of Provisions," broadside, n.d., in Seligman Collection (Broad-sides—Prices), Columbia Univ.

154. *London Gazette*, Mar. 1772, no. 11233.

155. Letter from "Captains Audacious, Fortitude, Presumption and dread not," dated 28 Dec. 1795, "Polgooth and other mines," and addressed to Mrs. Herring, ibid., 1796, p. 45.

156. This is *not* to argue that such evidence may not be soon forthcoming as to local or regional demographic crisis.

157. *Annals of Agriculture*, xxiv (1795), p. 159 (evidence from Dunmow, Essex).

158. Letter of 24 June 1795 in PRO, PC 1/27 /A.54; various letters, esp. 29 Mar. 1795, HO 42/34.

159. W. Wordsworth, *Poetical Works*, ed. E. de Selincourt and Helen Darbishire (Oxford, 1959), v, p. 391.

160. See Sidney Mintz, "Internal Market Systems as Mechanisms of Social Articulation," *Intermediate Societies, Social Mobility and Communication* (American Ethnological Society, 1959); and the same author's "Peasant Markets," *Scientific American*, cciii (1960), pp. 112–22.

161. Nottingham—J. F. Sutton, *The Date-book of Nottingham* (Nottingham 1880), p. 286; Yeovil—PRO, HO 42/150; East Anglia—A. J. Peacock, *Bread or Blood* (1965), passim; Merthyr—G. A. Williams, "The Insurrection at Merthyr Tydfil in 1831," *Trans. Hon. Soc. of Cymmrodorion*, 2, Session 1965), pp. 227–8.

162. In 1795, when subsidised brown bread was being given to the poor of his own parish, Parson Woodforde did not flinch before his continuing duty to his own dinner: March 6th, ". . . for Dinner a Couple of boiled Chicken and Pigs Face, very good Peas Soup, a boiled Rump of Beef very fine, a prodigious fine, large and very fat Cock-Turkey rosted, Maccaroni, Batter Custard Pudding," etc.: James Woodforde, *Diary of a Country Parson*, ed. J. Beresford (World's Classics, 1963), pp. 483, 485.

163. Lord Hardwicke, 27 July 1795, PRO, HO 42/35.

164. W. Dalloway, 20 Sept. 1766, PRO, PC 1/8/41.

THE CRIME OF ANONYMITY

FROM *ALBION'S FATAL TREE: CRIME AND SOCIETY IN EIGHTEENTH-CENTURY ENGLAND*

*I Wauld Tel you My Name
but My Simplicity Will Not Let Mee.*

—NEWCASTLE COLLIER, 1765

I

The anonymous threatening letter is a characteristic form of social protest in any society which has crossed a certain threshold of literacy, in which forms of collective organized defence are weak, and in which individuals who can be identified as the organizers of protest are liable to immediate victimization. The same means may, equally, be used in pursuit of private grievance and also as an instrument of extortion: its use, for these purposes, belongs to no particular phase of social development, and it continues today. No tidy line of demarcation can be drawn between these two kinds of action, although the difference between them (in certain contexts) is self-evident. Both kinds will be examined in this essay. From the point of view of the recipient, in any case, the effect of such anonymous menaces upon his peace of mind may be much the same. It can be frightening and disturbing to receive such letters; it can induce extreme anxiety, night-watchers, suspicion of friends and neighbours, and justified forms of paranoia.

This study is based in the main upon eighteenth-century evidence. It is best to commence by explaining the nature and limits of the source from which the central evidence is drawn. *The London Gazette: Published by Authority* may seem an unlikely source for the student of plebeian history. The *Gazette*, which appeared twice weekly was, of course, the publication of the most august authority. In its pages appeared the Proclamations of King and Privy Council: arrangements of the Court: announcements of naval and military engagements: promotions and

From *Albion's Fatal Tree: Crime and Society in Eighteenth-Century England* by Douglas Hay, Peter Linebaugh, John G. Rule, E. P. Thompson, and Cal Winslow (New York: Pantheon Books, 1975).

commissions: official notices from Whitehall, the Admiralty, the War Office, the Excise: lists of bankrupts: the prorogation or summoning of Parliaments.[1]

Thus in no. 10752, late August 1767, we have notices for an election of Scottish peers to sit in the House of Lords; of a review in Madrid by the King of Spain of his garrison; of the movements of the Papal Nuncio; while from Berlin it was announced that "the Marriage of the Princess Louisa-Henrietta Wilhelmina of Brandenbourg with the Reigning Prince of Anhalt Dessau was solemnized in the Royal Chapel at Charlottenbourg by the Reverend Mr. Sack. . . . After which the French Play called *Turcaret* was acted in the Orangerie . . ." The gardens were illuminated, and there was a ball, attended by the King of Prussia, which lasted until the next morning. Immediately following, cheek-by-jowl with Princess Louisa-Henrietta Wilhelmina, there appears a rather different notice, addressed to Sir Richard Betenson of Sevenoaks, Kent:

> Sr: Your Baily or Steward proper is a black gard sort of fellow to the Workmen and if you dont discharge him You may Look to Your House being sett on fire if Stones will not Burn You damned Sun of a hoare You shall have Your throat cutt from Ear to Ear except You Lay £50 under the Second tree of Staple Nashes from his house at the frunt of the Great Gates near the Rabbit Warrin on Wensdy Morn next . . .

This was of course, like the preceding one, an official notice, although it was not inserted by the letter's author but by the Secretary of State. It will save much explanation if we cite in full the form of words within which such letters were encapsulated:

Whitehall, August 8, 1767.

> Whereas it has been humbly represented to the King, That the following threatening and incendiary letter, was on [date] received by Sir Richard Betenson . . . and containing the Words and Letters following [there follows the letter, with its orthography preserved] His Majesty, for the better discovering and bringing of Justice the Persons concerned in Writing the said threatening . . . Letter, is hereby pleased to promise His most gracious Pardon to any one of them (except the Person who actually wrote the said Letter) who shall discover his or her Accomplice . . . so that he, she, or they may be apprehended and convicted thereof.   Shelburne.

> And, as a further Encouragement, the said Sir Richard Betenson, Bart, doth hereby promise a Reward of *One Hundred Pounds* to any Person or Persons making such Discovery . . . to be paid by him upon the Convictions of . . . the Offenders.   Rich. Betenson.

The critical point here is that the *Gazette* was involved only when an official pardon was offered for information leading to a conviction: and such authority must be obtained from the Secretary of State.[2] In some cases, where a public official or public property was involved, an official reward might also be offered. More commonly, when a private citizen was threatened, he himself found the money for this reward. In order to make it more likely that the author of the letter might be detected, the letter with its original spelling and its ferocious imprecations, were often published in full.

Hence the *London Gazettes* lie, like so many bi-weekly lobster traps, on the sea-bottom of Namier's England, catching many curious literary creatures which never, in normal circumstances, break the bland surface of the waters of eighteenth-century historiography.[3] It seemed useful to go through the journal systematically from 1750 to 1820, in order both to count these letters and to examine their nature. This is the central evidence drawn upon in this study, supplemented by the use of state papers (especially between 1795 and 1802), the provincial press and other sources.[4]

For various reasons, the picture becomes very confused after 1811. A count of the years 1750–1811 shows about 284 gazetted letters or handbills (anonymous and hand-written), or an average of about 4.7 per year.[5] In fact the incidence is very much more uneven. Taking only those letters which indicate some social or economic grievance of a general character, and excluding those which are evidently the work of private blackmailers, the peak years for gazetted letters are shown in Table 1.

Table 1: Gazetted Letters

1800	35	*or*	1800–1802	49
1766	17		1766–7	27
1796	11		1795–6	17
1767	10			
1801	7			
1802	7			
1771	6			
1792	6			
1795	6			

An attempt has been made, sometimes on slender evidence, to break these 284 letters down into matters of "private" or "social" grievance. This attempt may be misguided: as the letter to Sir Richard Betenson shows, a private blackmailing letter may suggest a general grievance ("Your Baily or Steward . . . is a black gard sort of fellow to the Workmen"); a blackmailing bankrupt tradesman may have been the victim of another kind of extortion; and, equally, social protest may coexist with private grievance. Thus no absolute line of definition is suggested between "social" and other kinds of grievance. But the distinction may help to further our inquiry:

Table 2: Grievances

Crime-related[6]	13		
Clearly blackmail or private grievance	36	or	49 "private"
Clearly social, economic, political or community grievance	216		
Probably social grievance	19		235 "social"
Total	284		

I have also attempted to list the nature of the dominant threat implied by the letter (see Table 3).[7]

It will be noted that, taking (1) and (2) together, murder was the most common threat in "private" cases: approximately 71 per cent of all threats, as against 34.5 per cent in "social" cases. But, taking (3) and (4) together, and again giving approximate figures, arson is a threat most often to be found in "social" cases: 40 per cent as against 29 per cent in "private." The other kinds of threat belong wholly to the former.

Table 3: Nature of Threats

	Social	Private	Totals
1. Murder	60	20	80
2. Undisclosed ("do for you," "have your blood," etc.), implying murder	25	9	34
3. Arson *and* murder	36	3	39
4. Arson	68	9	77
5. Pulling down or blowing up buildings, attacking machinery, etc.	16	—	16
6. Arming, civil war, rebellion, treason, etc.	31	—	31
7. Mutilation of recipient	3	—	3
8. Maiming of stock, barking or felling of trees, etc.	3	—	3
9. Other	2	—	2
Totals	244	41	285

In the next table (Table 4) we leave aside (for the time being) the private cases and consider only the social, or putatively social, cases. From the inadequate evidence of the *Gazettes* one may identify these recipients of threats:

Table 4: Recipients of Threats

Gentry and nobility	44
Master manufacturers, tradesmen, millers	41
Persons holding some office (excluding mayors and JPs)	27
Mayors	23 }*
Magistrates	18
Farmers	17
Clergy	11
Excisemen	7
Blacklegs	2
General hand-written notices ("To all farmers," "Gentlemen of . . . ," etc.)	39
Others	19
Total	248

*Persons in authority = 68

The final table suggests only the most tentative categorization. Without following each case back through other sources, it is impossible from the evidence of a letter alone to have an exact notion of the grievance at issue; in any case, many letters are expressive of more than one grievance. However, the number of issues which could provoke men to utter murderous or incendiary threats is itself of interest (see Table 5).

Once again, this tabulation (which is based on the dominant grievance in each letter) is at points misleading. Thus, while only two letters are wholly concerned with the low wages of rural labourers, many of the 72 letters arising from the high price of food complain also about the level of labourers' wages. The 25 letters which each voice a distinct grievance range from agrarian protests (against tithes, in support of traditional measures, in defence of gleaning, against threshing-machines), through a scatter of political and religious grievances (anti-Papist, anti-Methodist, Welsh Nationalist) to a grievance against a "damd horing rogue."

Table 5: Particularization of Grievances

Price of bread, corn, food: against forestalling or monopolists	72
Industrial: machines, wages, blacklegs, etc.	34
Attempts to influence course of justice (some "social," some "private")	21
Politically related (local politics, sedition—but excluding most food-and-sedition letters of the 1800s)	19
Private grievances (e.g. dismissed servants)	11
Enclosure, common rights	9
Smuggling	7
Poor and poor laws	5
Poaching	5
Turnpikes	4
Press-gang	3
Volunteers	2
Militia ballot	2
Servants' vails (customary gratuities)	2
Licensing of ale-houses	2
Rural labourers' wages	2
Identified grievance, but one case only of each	25
Total	225

II

These tables indicate a little. But it is necessary to qualify impressions which they give.

First, the number of letters gazetted gives no constant index to the actual number of letters written. It simply indicates the number of occasions upon which a letter was taken sufficiently seriously both by the recipient and the Secretary of State for an official pardon to be offered. It was never a simple matter to gain this: in general this ensued only if (a) the recipient of the threat was a person who had interest with Government, or (b) evidence was offered to show that there was genuine danger that the threat might be carried out (or was part of a series of threats, one or more of which had already been carried out, as in cases of arson, riot, or destruction of machinery), or (c) the seditious nature of the document was very alarming to the authorities.

Second, these variables were given added uncertainty by the dispositions of different Secretaries of State and their underlings under various governments.

Not every administration held the same views as to the usefulness of gazetting letters. And only a minority of the recipients of such letters would have bothered to use this method of attempted control. To gazette a letter involved delay, correspondence with the Government, the expense of insertion (£3 3s. 6d. in 1800), and also the offering of a somewhat larger reward than might otherwise seem necessary. The recipients of such letters might more simply advertise immediately in their local press for information and offer a reward directly to informers, although if they acted in this way no pardon could of course be offered.[8] Finally, one may wonder how far the well-tried eighteenth-century system of pardons and rewards was of much use in dealing with an offence which (like arson) could be carried out in secret by one individual and without accomplices.

It is possible to observe some of these variables at work during the years 1795–1805. In 1795 only six letters of social protest were gazetted: but in fact the Home Office papers preserve very many more sent in by anxious correspondents. It is evident that the Government in this year did not wish to give additional publicity to the shocking and seditious sentiments of the letters. In 1796 a few more letters were advertised in the *Gazette* (eleven of social protest) but the Duke of Portland was still counselling caution. In November he wrote to say that he agreed that a handbill sent on to him by the Lord Mayor of London was most inflammatory: "Yet provided it does not appear to produce any effect, perhaps your Lordship will agree with me, that it is a proof that the prevailing good sense and disposition of the people lead them to treat it precisely in the manner we could wish."[9] Nothing would be gained by advertising it. When a seditious letter was sent to him from Yeovil in 1799 the Duke was still not inclined "to give any notoriety to it, by an advertisement in the Gazette."[10]

In 1800, however, when widespread riots and arson had made it evident that "the prevailing good sense and disposition of the people" could no longer be relied upon, and when blood-chilling "jacobinical" threats became commonplace, no fewer than thirty-five such letters were gazetted. This was still only a small proportion (certainly less than 25 per cent) of the letters sent in to the Home Office.[11] Portland's general advice was to watch, employ informers, and only if this seemed likely to succeed to advertise the letters.[12] This policy was continued through 1800 and into 1801 in cases supposed to affect the public interest.[13] By 1804 the pendulum had swung back to extreme caution. In March 1804 the Home Secretary wrote to one complainant: "I am doubtful of the expediency of publishing in the Gazette . . . the seditious paper. . . . Perhaps it wd answer the purpose better to insert in the County Newspaper the beginning and end of the paragraph in original, so as sufficiently to identify and point it out, without promulgating the pernicious sentiments which it contains. . . ."[14]

Such a compromise had been reached by other authorities rather earlier than this. In October 1800 the Birmingham authorities, who found such pernicious sentiments appearing around them daily in hand-bills, placards, and wall-chalking, could bear only to publish in the *Gazette* a proclamation commencing: "Whereas . . . several inflammatory papers (one of which begins with "Countrymen" and another with "Liberty") have been thrown in the streets, and stuck up against the walls. . . ."[15] After these years the policy of reticence was confirmed. Only three of four letters were gazetted in 1811, and about five in 1812, yet both years, as the Home Office papers show, saw fecund and ebullient epistolary activity. Thereafter it became usual to publish the fact but not the contents of a letter.

Hence the figures give only an erratic indication as to the extent of this kind of activity. What survives in the *Gazettes* is only what is left after much else has drained through the sieve. And undoubtedly scores of threatening letters were received by persons who never bothered to inform the authorities: in 1800 the Lord Mayor of London referred to such letters "of which by the bye I get a great many and disregard them."[16] Of those which were sent in, the majority were set aside ungazetted. And, further, there is the unknown and unknowable number of blackmailing or threatening letters which never came to light because the recipients kept them secret and complied with the demands made upon them. The figures which are offered above may certainly not be allowed to enter the intestines of some computer, as the quantity of meditated violence in pre-industrial England.

III

Private blackmailing, like kidnapping and some forms of hijacking, appears to be an epidemic offence which thrives on publicity. It is perhaps possible to date fairly exactly the first occasion when this offence was advertised throughout the whole country.

In the summer and autumn of 1730 threatening letters appeared, in a sensational way, in Bristol. They were thrown into workshops and houses, and dropped in the street, demanding small sums of money on threat of arson. It seems probable that some timid recipients complied. In October Mr. George Packer, who had refused several demands to pay six guineas, had his house and part of his ship-building yard fired. His family was lucky to escape with their lives. Within days threatening letters were being reported from many parts of the country. In November a Proclamation was issued, offering a pardon and the very considerable sum of £300 reward for information leading to any conviction: offenders were liable to the punishment of death under a clause in the Black Act of 1723 (see below p. 402). The Proclamation appears only to have afforded further publicity to the offence. The burning of Packer's house, Boyer noted, has "put it into the head of every abandon'd Wretch through the whole Country to take advantage thereof," and the practice of sending incendiary letters was compared to the fire which they threaten, spreading with equal speed and terror.[17] Some of the letters were clearly extortionary: a Hammersmith farmer, of whom ten guineas were demanded, and who placed some white halfpence in an unsuccessful trap, had his stacks and barn fired.[18] Others suggest the employment of the same form as a means of voicing private grievance: Mr Spragging, a raft merchant at Newark, was warned:

> Spraging, remember thou art but Dust,
> And to they Neighbour very unjust:
> Thou neither sticks at great nor small,
> Till Vengeance once does on thee fall.
> I think how soon thou wilt be undone;
> In Flames of Fire thy Rafts shall burn. . . .[19]

The Bristol offenders were never convicted.[20] But several of their imitators ended on the gallows. Convictions were secured in Lincolnshire, Kent, and Hertfordshire, and the rewards of £300 were paid out.[21] Jeremiah Fitch, a joiner, was one of these offenders. He had written to a wealthy farmer, Goodman Jenkyns of Harpenden, a letter commencing:

> This, with my Service to you, and I desire you'l, of all Love, lay me £30 at the Bottom of the Post next to Henry Hudsons ... a Friday night by Eight of the Clock, or if you do not, I'll burn your House to Ashes God dam your Blood; and God dam you Sir, if you watch, or declare this Secret to any Body dam my Blood if Death shall not be your Portion. . . .

But Goodman Jenkyns did place a watch, of four men, and Fitch was detected.[22]

Contemporaries suggested that "this is a new crime," although this seems unlikely.[23] The example of executions in several counties appears to have brought this epidemic to an end, although the offence remained in men's memories and a trickle of similar incendiary threats continue thereafter. But—as the case of Fitch shows—it was an offence easy to initiate but very difficult to bring to a successful conclusion. The blackmailer had at all costs to devise means of obtaining his pay-off without fear of detection. The stratagems proposed by some of the letter-writers of 1730 inspired a Norwich satirist:

If you do not put Six New Halfpence, in Form,
Into an Old Shoe (we speak for no Harm),
And place it upon the very Top-Stone
Of Christ Church high Spire, at Midnight, alone. . . .[24]

Since the victim was likely to inform police, or to wait up with friends and servants at the point where money was to be deposited, the blackmailer was likely to succeed only in limited conditions:

(i) If the blackmailer was actually in possession of information as to the criminal record, sexual improprieties, and so on of the victim—information which would be immensely damaging to the victim if it ever came out. These are, of course, the most successful grounds for blackmail; and for exactly the same reasons such offences rarely come to light.[25]

(ii) If blackmail was part of a widespread protection-racket, with effective and well-known means of retaliation against those who failed to comply.

(iii) If the victim could be terrified into compliance and into secrecy, by the very violence of the physical threats.

This last point helps to explain the extreme violence of style favoured by such letter-writers. The problem can be seen in a letter received by a gentleman in Ayrshire in 1775:

There are six of us who being reduced to Misery by Misfortune have pitched upon you for our Relief, Providence has made you able and it is our business to make you willing. You will therefore lay £50 Ster: below the Broad Stone on the Extremity of the South End of the Stone dike on your right hand as you go from Slophouse to Ayr and lett it be in Gold or Silver and lett it . . . ly one Week. . . .

But of course the victim was likely to set a watch upon this place, so the author detailed his own arrangements:

If you are so foolish as attempt to know who we are you are undone. One of us will uplift the Money while three stand on the Watch with a Couple of Good Pistols each and two left at home to take Vengeance on you if you disturb the rest and a Cask of Powder ready to blow up your House—So you see that Silence is equally necessary on both Sides.[26]

This subtle and highly literate letter perhaps failed to command belief: the possessors of at least six good pistols and of a cask of powder were not likely to risk their lives for £50. A more usual style is that which seeks to carry all before it by sheer vigour of style. A Northampton wine merchant received a demand for £800 "by Thursday next" (in January 1763): "If You do not do as We command You We will put You to the utmost Torture . . . You Villian of a Bitch Yo Theif I will blow out Your Brains. Dam Your Blood You Dog."[27] Other letters suggest a personal acquaintance between the author and the victim; perhaps the blackmailer had been a tradesman bankrupted by the activities of the recipient. "I have been your frend Veary Much & I hope Not to go unpade for it I am a Grate Acquintance of yours and by Nesesety is Drove to bad Ways," a Holborn apothecary was informed in 1760.[28] This correspondent only required a guinea. George Bryant, a Deptford distiller, was formally approached in 1763: "Sir to aquant you that I am in great Needsesety for a little Mony or otherwise I will be oblidgd to Shut oup Shop or Leave off Busness. . . ." £100 would meet the occasion: otherwise Mr Bryant's house would be burnt down.[29] A gentleman in Blackfriars in 1764 was told to bring £50— "Under the feet of a verry old Stone Stature with the nose of the statture broke of it is Lying at full lenth Directly Opposite the Entrance of the north door of Westminster abbe in the first Ile." The price for failure was to be the gentleman's "brains bloud"; "I am a tradesman well know by you and will return the money to you the 17th of next month."[30] When we recall the disaster of the debtors' gaol and the cavalier refusal of many gentry to pay their tradesmen's bills, we may perhaps have a context in which to place some of these forcible collections.

Except where a case actually comes to trial, there is little to be learned from such letters. Occasionally there is the suggestion of a protection-racket or general forced levy of money by some group or "gang." The smuggling trade involved sudden needs for capital to purchase stocks from an incoming ship; it also required the intimidation of informers.[31]

Suky Boswell, the servant of an Excise officer at Eastbourne, received in 1771 a letter which can have left her in no doubt as to its intention: "Suky Boswell I hav Ing a few moments to spere I thought I Could not in ploy my self better than send you a Line or to . . ." Boswell's offence was that she had been too officious on behalf of her master: "Lokeing out for your master that night he . . . went out with the Solgers." And so to the climax: "I must and will kill you Dam your blood I will Cut your throat from Ear to Ear Dam Dam and Dubbel Dam you your Liver I will brile. . . . God almyty Dam your Soul Dam God Dam y God Dam. . . ."[32] Another excise officer, at Redcar in 1774, was warned to keep off the sands: "You may as well . . . take what we give you as other officers do, and if you don't we'll sware that you take bribes, you had better take them then not dam you."[33]

No doubt such letters, in the continuous conflict between smugglers and Excise-men, served their function. They may have been effective in a much wider context than this. The stages by which an offender might be finally brought to (or from) the gallows were, as Douglas Hay shows, open at several points to influence and interest. But, since most prosecutions were privately initiated, they were open at the same points to pressure from the friends of the accused. Anonymous letters can be found which punctuate each stage. Thus, first of all, threats might be issued to intimidate a prosecutor before any action had commenced, or immediately afterwards, in the hope that the action would be withdrawn.[34] And there are also many examples of over-officious, over-zealous or avaricious prosecutors (whether public officers or private persons) receiving admonitions. The Chairman of the Surrey Sessions incurred the hostility of debtors sheltering in the sanctuary of the Southwark Mint, and was addressed as "an old over-grown unparallelled Monster of a Rogue! thou Spawn of fiery Dragons, Hell and Fury!"[35] The Collector of Excise in Bristol was ordered "to sine no more Warrants" and "P.S. Dont let Mr. Lion stand in the Pillory."[36] When in 1776 the Mayor and justices of Norwich launched a campaign to prosecute the embezzlers of yarn they were warned to drop their proceedings or "you Surtanly will be made to soufer in parson."[37]

There followed threats to the magistrates, to judges, and especially to witnesses: "by the living eternal Christ I kill you if you appear against me as a witness. . . ."[38] If the accused was convicted, threats might ensue directed at the prosecutor (to secure a pardon) or at the authorities (to set the convicted free). In 1810 a London employer received a note: "I have been in the Country. I had a letter from my Friend that you have transported him and a Nother for 10lb of Salt Peter. If I had known that you & your Cleark would have prosecuted them I would have put them & you & your Cleark out of the way I am determined on killing you both. . . . if you dont Get them Both off."[39] If prosecutor or informer were the recipients of blood-money they might be expected to be pursued more vigorously. In 1775 a London magistrate received this letter:

> Sir we are sorry to be so troublesom but last night Jones was Cast for Death at the old Bayley on the account of generall fitzroys Robery which was brought to Light by Mr. Nickalls who gave the inforemation. . . . Now Mr. Nickalls is initled to the Reward of sixty guinnies upon that occasion now mr nickalls may Depend upon it for fact that he is not longer live er then the person that is under Sentence of death . . . for we are Determined to putt an end to Nickalls is days if he stays in this metrophelus for he only did it for the Sake of the mony.[40]

Such threats are likely only to have tightened the noose around the condemned's neck since, as Hay shows, the exercise of the prerogative of mercy was supported by an elaborate ideology which might allow mercy only to flow as an act of grace from above to the properly deferential supplicant. Threats at this stage were likely only to hasten execution: and perhaps for this reason they are uncommon. But once the process of law was completed, threats might be resumed. In smaller affairs, like game prosecutions, this was common. After Rudston Calverly Rudston of Pocklington, East Yorks, had secured the conviction of four poachers in 1793 he was told: "Rudston our mallis is too great to bear therefore if you don't think proper to Return all the young's men money again we shall fier and destroy everything you have and after that you life shall pay."[41] In larger affairs, where the condemned was already executed or transported, little could be done. Several letters demand the instant cutting down and burial of a gibbeted felon.[42] And on occasion the prosecutor was followed by threats of revenge. In 1776 one Girdwood, himself at the time a prisoner in Newgate, wrote to the prosecutor of a friend:

> Sir, I am sorry to find a gentleman like you would be guilty of taking Mac Allester's Life away for the sake of two or three guineas; but it will not be forgot by one who is but just come home to revenge his cause. . . . I follow the road, though I have been out of London; but on receiving a letter from Mac Allester before he died, for to seek revenge, I am come to town. . . .

Girdwood was detected, since he passed his letter by way of a woman who sold provisions at the prison gates. He was convicted, an appeal was disallowed, and he was executed.[43]

Even small-time blackmailers tried to present themselves as one of a "gang" or confederacy; those who wrote in support of more general grievances presented themselves as one of a confederacy thirty or ninety or several thousand strong, bound by most solemn oaths to revenge their wrongs. Where smugglers or food rioters or illegal trade combinations were involved, those threats had teeth in them. After food riots in Norwich in 1766, in Halifax in 1770, in Staffordshire and Nottingham in 1800, the authorities were warned to free or respite sentence on their prisoners on pain of retribution. At Norwich sixteen men "are all sworne by a terrible great Oath" to burn the houses of the great: "the 16 Men then have gott 80 baggs made of thick paper fill'd with Pitch and Brimstone ty'd up with a Salt Peter match at the mouth of them these we are to cram into Windows houses and Woodstacks the night that any of the Prisoners is hang'd. . . ." But hanged several of the prisoners were. The Staffordshire magistrates received an eloquent letter, threatening them with murder and arson:

> ... for Wee are determined thay shall not be confined nor no one els for
> the same cause witch is only bread and that Wee will fight for to the last
> drop of our blood the heads of this Nation in general vialans and cause
> a famine among the poar whilst they themselves live in plenty. O Bread
> Bread Bread is the cry of poor Children and you have suffered the prise
> to go beyond our reach Wee desire printed Hand Bills to be put out
> concerning this Letter what you intend to do for we are either for War
> and Peace.[44]

The only reply which the author received was, of course, an advertisement in the *Gazette* offering a pardon for information leading to his apprehension, and £170 reward. Such advertisements were also inserted in the local press and were often circulated additionally as handbills or as placarded proclamations. In matters of general social grievance, this gave publicity to a curious kind of dialogue between the authorities and the crowd. Gazetting was actually courted as a means of publicity, and many authors clearly pondered their best rhetorical flourishes with the care of an author sending his first work to the press. The Mayor of Chester was addressed in 1767: "God Damn you blood, your house shall be burnt down very soon if you dont look after the Markets better": "Put this in the News Paper."[45] A letter from Stourbridge in the same year threatening to have all the gaols and prisons down with a force of upwards of 2,000 armed men concluded: "Mr. Rabley we Desire you to put in the Birmingham Gazzette . . . if you dwo not gazzette it upon our World we'l have[your house] down."[46]

In this aim some of the authors succeeded. An interesting example of this dialogue can be seen in an episode of the long struggle over prices conducted by the Spitalfields weavers in the 1760s and 1770s. The 1760s saw a long campaign of threatening notes to non-compliant weavers or masters, the destruction of silk in the looms, and so on. In 1770 several of the silk-cutters were tried at the Old Bailey on capital charges, and were executed.[47] In April 1771 the leading Crown evidence, a pattern-drawer named Daniel Clark, was seen by two weavers in Shoreditch, assaulted, chased from one refuge after another by a growing crowd, dragged and beaten through several streets in Shoreditch and Spitalfields, thrown into a pond in Hare Street Field, and there stoned to death. There followed a campaign of advertisement and counter-advertisement. The King offered a reward of £100 for the conviction of Clark's assailants. In reply David Wilmot, an active Bethnal Green magistrate, received a letter signed "One of ten Thousand": "You Scoundrel the Fellow we kill'd on

Tuesday swore away the Life of my dearest friend and if he had had a thousand Lives I would with pleasure have taken them and if you attempt to take his part as you seem to do by your Advertisement you may depend upont that You & Familly shall not exist on Month longer. . . ." The author had clearly studied the models of such letters which the *Gazette* from time to time published, for he concluded: "I shall not swear about it as is the usual Stile of these Letters but if you can believe any thing thats True take my word for this." Wilmot duly advertised this letter and offered a reward for information leading to its author. Thus encouraged, the writer sent, four days later, a letter of three times the length, with a fuller defence of those who had lynched Clark, "that detestable late Object of their revenge who was thirsting after their Blood not thro' any motive of Justice but mearly for Reward:" "We are now satisfied having put an End to the existence of that Monster in human Shape, the fear of whom kept several families in a starving Condition by keeping them from their principal Support thro the Apprehension of being Informed against." "Know this Busy Villain," Justice Wilmot was warned, "that tis not the greatest Reward in the Kings gift that shall either be the means of Detecting or Deterring the writer of these Letters and his Associates in this Affair, from pursuing with insatiable & heart felt Revenge their Designs against You. . . . P.S. you may now apply to the King for a larger reward and try to what Purpose it will be."[48]

It is clear at least that the advertisements in the *Gazette* or the local press found attentive readers among the crowd; and that individuals in the crowd saw in these a possible means of expressing grievances and demands. It is not possible, at this level of analysis, to make much more of the genus. Private blackmail is an offence found in any literate society. While the predominance of private prosecution in the eighteenth century gave some openings to pressure, through menaces, upon prosecutor and witnesses, it cannot be shown that this pressure was generally effective; and threats directed against the courts or against the authorities were likely to defeat their ends. Letters of this kind offer a pathetic and ineffectual counterpoint to the real exchanges of influence and interest passing between the great. It is only in specific contexts of conflict—smuggling, agrarian unrest, illicit trade union activity, or massive social protest—that such letters acquire importance. And here they may sometimes be seen as intrinsic to proto-democratic forms of organization, deeply characteristic of eighteenth-century social and economic relations.

IV

In a prescriptive society which, in myth if not in actuality, rested upon relations of paternalism and deference, domination and subordination, there were very many reasons why men might wish to remain anonymous. It is by no means the case that anonymity was the refuge of the poor alone. Even the gentleman, certainly the professional man, might wish to gain the ear of authority without offending an influential neighbour. Research into eighteenth-century archives gives one a sense of double vision. Among the estate papers of nobility and great gentry there are the obsequious letters of the surveyors, tradesmen, attorneys, petitioners for favour. But in the state papers we seem to meet a society of creeps and informers. Throughout the eighteenth century a percentage of the Secretary of State's in-coming mail was anonymous.

Even highly sophisticated proposals for the public good—relating to taxes, the regulation of markets, the poor laws, the excise—might be unsigned.[49] For even these might imply a criticism of some local figure of influence. More delicate matters—fingering a gentleman who was a papist or suspected Jacobite, exposing corruption in some public office—nearly always came through the post unsigned. Often an elaborate ritual of seeking protection in advance of disclosure then followed. The author, promising information on some racket, would sign his letter with initials; the Secretary of State would then advertise in the *Gazette* that if "R. S." would come forward at a definite time and place with further information he would be promised indemnity and perhaps a reward; a meeting might then take place. In the press and the public reviews the same wars of insinuation and character assassination took place under pseudonyms. The free-born Englishman crept about in a mask and folded in a Guy Fawkes cloak.

If this was so even among the higher orders, anonymity was of the essence of any early form of industrial or social protest. The threat of victimization was ever-present; the shelter which the community could afford to the known rebel against the vindictiveness of "interest" was scanty; the consequences of victimization, over the whole life of the victim, were total. Hence on scores of issues, throughout the eighteenth century and well into the nineteenth, the only protest that can be known is this minatory anonymous "voice of the poor." In the earlier decades of the eighteenth century one finds expressions of popular Jacobitism (although this favoured the ballad or the whistled air rather than the articulate letter), or the virulent "true blues" of Taunton: "Every damned Wiggish Scoundrel that does not Vote for Popham shall have his Throat cut by Christmas Day next."[50] By 1811 one finds premature "Swing" letters such as the one from labourers at Early Court near Reading: "Blood and Vengeance against Your Life and Your Property for taking away our Labour with Your Threshing Machine . . . if You do not refrain . . . we will Thresh Your Ricks with Fire & Bathe Your Body in Blood. How will the People of Reading Gase To see Early Court all in a Blase."[51] In between one can sample every grievance of the times: the press-gang, militia ballot, corrupt local courts, electoral scandals, customary rights, the licensing of alehouses.

The letters fall into two groups: those addressed to the rich, the authorities, employers; and those addressed to fellow workmen or to "the crowd." Until the 1790s the first group is very much the largest, although perhaps all that we can say is that these were the ones most often preserved and gazetted, since scribbled threats or hieroglyphs wrapped around bricks and thrown into workshops or thrust under the cottage doors of blacklegs were less likely to be advertised or kept in any archive.[52] After 1790 the second group enlarges: but we are now often seeing less a letter than a hand-written placard or a handbill. And those in the first group may be divided in the same way also, some being addressed to the rich or to the gentry of the area and perhaps posted up on a church door or by the market cross, others directed at particular individuals. The great majority of both kinds adopt a similar tone and manner of address, distinguished by the collective pronoun "we." What is offered is rarely a personal grievance, but the common sense of injustice of the poor as a whole. And the style appears to impose some controls upon the authors: they do indeed attempt to present not the personal but the collective grievance. It is this which gives exceptional interest to these documents. One can rarely prove that any letter indicates general protest rather than the voice of a crank: one is left to judge by the "feel" of the letter, its style, the particularization of grievances, as well as by the evidence of supporting actions—riot or rattening. Such evidence comes, with regularity, to hand.

With so many grievances to choose among we will limit our concern to three distinct contexts: letters concerned with industrial conflict; those arising within an agrarian context; and finally the largest group of letters and handbills—those concerned with price and food riots, which pass, in 1795 and 1800, into "jacobinical" sedition.

Letters in the first group arise from many contexts, but most belong clearly to that of early illicit trade unionism, with its summary enforcements: the destruction of the tools or materials of blacklegs or of masters taking unapprenticed men, the intimidation of opponents.[53] The Master Shipwright at Chatham, in 1764, was addressed:

Mr. Allen

Blackguard—for Gentleman I cannot call you it have wrote to lett You know without You are beter to the Shipwrights and all the Yard in genurl You will be very soon Nock't out of the Book of Life . . . You are like the rich Man wich refused to give Lazarus the Crums which fell from his tabel . . .[54]

In 1763 London master shoemakers and hosiers were threatened unless they met demands for prices: "Damn you you are worst than a highway man for you bete down prises."[55] In the late 1780s such letters came from London shoe-makers, Lancashire calico-printers and weavers in Glasgow, Manchester, and Newbury. "A Good Jurni-man Shoemaker" addressed a master thus: "You damd Insignificant Proud Impearias Rascal your are detested by every one that Works for you. . . . But I hope Soone to put an end to your pride by Eluminateing the Neighbourhood you live in . . . and if possible would Shove your damd Litle Self in to the midst of the Flames. . . ."[56] In 1794 the following notice was put under the door of the Blanket Weavers Company's hall at Witney: "This is to inform you Sirs that here is an agreement made betwene some Men that who-ever will not give the gurnimen weavers the two pence . . . take Care of your Selves or you will die and wat a thing to die for oppressing the poor."[57]

Machine-breaking or industrial arson was nearly always accompanied by let-ters. A group of such letters comes in the 1780s and 1790s, from the Lancashire cotton industry, with the calico-printers prominent.[58] The most vigorous series comes, between 1799 and 1803, from the West of England shearmen and cloth-ing workers, in their Luddite resistance to the introduction of gig-mills. The threats were directed equally against employers and against workers who defied the shearmen's regulations: "The Jurneymen Shearmen of Bradford Trowbridge Melksham Chipinham Calne and Devizes: Have a Greed to Pay you 4 that are at work. . . . if you dont leve of you may expect Shearmens Law; that is to be Cuartered. And Your flesh and Bones Burnt and your aishes Blown away with the weend I send this as a frind. . . ."[59] Such threats (as in the better-documented Luddism of the Midlands and the North in 1811–13[60]) were given added terror by repeated actions, usually against property rather than person.[61]

The letters from an agrarian context, or from the small market-town, com-menced early—the "Blacks" in the forests of Berkshire and Hampshire were using them in 1723—and, as a means of mass pressure, continued longest: the "Swing" letters of 1830 provided one climax, but similar letters accompanied arson in East Anglia in the 1840s and 1850s. They are some of the saddest examples of the genus, especially those written in the nineteenth century—the testimony of men driven to fury by the humiliations of the poor law, low wages, the abuse of charities. The eighteenth-century examples are often more complex, turning upon questions of common right, enclosure, gleaning, local customs. A few are the carefully drawn assertions of the claims of the poor. We cannot prove that these are typical; but since they are among the only surviving artic-ulate testaments of millions of the supposedly inarticulate, they deserve partic-ular attention. The best examples, such as the letter from "the Combined" of Cheshunt (1799) and that to the "Gentlemen of Ashill" (1816),[62] rank as im-portant social documents.

Some nine of the gazetted letters bear upon enclosure or common rights. During resistance to the enclosure of Holland Fen near Boston (Lines) in 1769 one promoter of enclosure was warned: "Mr Barlow as you have been one of the Head Injeneyers consarning hollandfen and you used the utmost of your power in geting the Rogish Act of Parleyment to take poors Right from them by Force and fraud . . . this is but the Binining of Sorows. . . ." The letters were delivered with gunshot through the windows, accompanied by the destruction of fences, arson of stacks, and shooting at cattle. One was signed: "An open fen for Ever."[63]

Any large-scale continuous resistance to enclosure was likely to be accompanied by letters. But, until the nineteenth century when labourers in many areas were reduced to a general level of poverty, the grievances would include those of small-holders or tenant farmers, petty graziers, townsmen with an interest in the local common. A comprehensive letter from Bicester in 1800 attacked the gentry for giving poor pay, the Volunteers, the farmers, millers, bakers, shopkeepers, hog-killers, and concluded with a protest against enclosure and the loss of winter threshing: "these Justices and Gentlemen have enclosed the Fields and the cause of laying down the flails The Devil will Whip them into Helltails." A letter from Hungerford in 1763 denounced the misappropriation of moneys which should have come to the poor from the letting of town lands: "wome You will You kepe alive and whom You will You starve to death and home You will You fatt up and home You will You put dound and now Your harts is Liftied up In Pride and You nowe that thare is no Law for a pore man but If this is not alteard I will Turn Jusstis my salfe. . . ."[64] In 1780 the grievance was still burning: the "Gentealman Consteable an Free holders" of Hungerford were again accused of taking "the Pores Wright away" and of failing to pay for the "dad Comins" (presumably the "dead" or unused grazing-rights on the common which should have been let for charity).[65]

There were other centres which appear to have had an epistolary tradition of long standing; or perhaps the magistrates in these villages and towns had a tradition of taking notice of letters. At Petworth (Sussex) demonstrations against prices took place in 1790, and copies of an eloquent rhyming manifesto were stuck to the church door, the whipping-post, and elsewhere. In 1795 a miller was warned that his mill would be pulled down, for "you Millers and Fammers one all agreed to starve us poor . . . what you can you think of yourself we do not know."[66] And during the "Swing" riots of 1830, William Stovolt was warned: "Gentlemen, take care of you cattle and yourselve for we are resolved to burn down the house of Mr. S. an perhaps whole of Petwort for when we begin God knows what the end may be for we think Petworth have had it rain long enough . . ."[67]

"When the Spirit of Riot gets into a People," a pamphleteer noted in 1739, "No one knows the Conseqence. The *Mob* had already got this *Maxim*, 'That

Adam made no *Will*; they are his Sons, and ought to have a Share of their Father's Possession' "[68] Hence in any general episode of agrarian disturbance or of food riot, a score of grievances come to the surface in these letters, supported upon a general levelling sentiment. This is true of the riot years of 1766, 1795, and 1800–1801; of the East Anglian disturbances of 1816; of the "Swing" riots of 1830 and their aftermath of arson in the 1840s. One commonly thinks of the "Rebecca" riots of the 1840s as being directed, in the main, against turnpikes; but in fact Rebecca, in her letters, proposed to settle decades of particular and of general accounts. These might affect the general rights of the tenantry or very particular offences committed by individuals: the spoiling of a salmon river, the failure to maintain illegitimate children, or (in an indictment of the Vicar of Eglwyserow, Cardiganshire), he "Feeds his sheep in this church yard with the grass growing in the putrifaction of human bodies these sheep are afterwards slaughtered for our Market at Cardigan and we have . . . been made canibals without our knowledge." His horses grazed over the tombstones and broke them; he was encroaching on common land; and had seized a chapel built by the Methodists.[69]

What marks out the agrarian letter in England, certainly after 1790 (and sometimes before), is its universal resort to the threat of arson. The threat was often carried into effect: indeed, the letter was sometimes found at the scene of the fire. Arson is so terrible and indiscriminate a crime, to the urban mind, that historians have scarcely bothered to consider this tactic of protest: first sympathy and then attention is withdrawn. But in a situation in which the gentry and the employing farmers held a total control over the life of the labourer and his family, and in which (as in 1816 and 1830) open and non-violent manifestations of protest met with executions and transportations, it is difficult to envisage what other forms of protest were left.[70] Rural arson was rarely indiscriminate, almost never took human life, and very rarely took the lives of stock. It was directed, first at the cornstack and the hayrick: next at the outhouse or barn. Since the cornstack represented a substantial part of the farmer's capital, his profit on the year's product, it was the point at which he was most vulnerable. It may be true that arson was a futile and counter-productive act, but the case has been assumed, not submitted to any test of evidence.

A most "melancholy" letter from the Rector of a Hampshire village terrorized in this way (under peculiar circumstances) in 1729 gives an insight into the "deplorable condition" into which the inhabitants could be reduced: "Our farmers, labourers, and servants are all worn out with toil, fear & watching; and as oft as night returns we are all under the dreadful apprehension of having our houses & barns fired. . . . of our corn being consumed and . . . of our selves and families perishing in the flames."[71] Examples of communities or of individuals living in the shadow of such terror were sufficiently numerous in eighteenth-and early-nineteenth-century Britain for a threat to carry conviction. Rural employers, overseers, and guardians of the poor, administrators of charities, game-preservers, and game-keepers—none of these can have been indifferent to the counter-terror of the poor.

When we turn to the largest group of gazetted letters—those dealing with food prices and marketing practices—a functional explanation may be offered with more confidence. Until we come to the years of Luddism, "Swing" and of Rebecca, undoubtedly the *annus mirabilis* for threatening letters was 1800. The more than thirty seditious letters gazetted in that year come at the end of an established tradition, which appears in every year of widespread food riot. Only one such letter was gazetted in 1756 (to a mealman in Newbury: "if you don't stop carrin the Flower to Bristoll we will knock you . . . in the Head"[72]), eleven in 1766, seven in 1767, two in 1772, only one in the great food-riot year of 1795, eight in 1796.

Many of these were less letters than notices or handbills, which served the double purpose of menacing the rich and advertising grievances and intentions to riot among the crowd. The tradition—a notice posted on a church door— goes back until at least the early years of the seventeenth century.[73] Although grievances against particular millers, dealers, and so on, are often mentioned, the notices are addressed either to fellow labourers or to the local rich in general.

The production of such letters was so habitual (in times of dearth and high prices), the grievances expressed are so authentic they are so often accompanied by the action of price-regulation or "riot," and they appear in so many parts of the country that it would be ludicrous to suggest that they are the work of "cranks." I have already discussed their function in the pattern of food riot, where it can sometimes be shown that their appearance was an effective signal to the authorities to attempt to restrain prices, to regulate the markets, to institute subsidies or activate charities, in anticipation of riot.[74] In this sense we may say that the letter or handbill was well understood by both parties in the market conflict, as one element within a regular and ritualized code of behaviour; it was ignored by the authorities at their peril.

Hence it is within this code that the letters must be read. Their intent is serious, but it may not be taken too literally. If on occasion before 1760 the crowd employed Jacobite threat ("we are wishing that our exiled King could . . . send some Officers"[75]), we need not take this as evidence of active Jacobite organization: this is simply the threat thought most likely to send the Whig authorities into a panic. If large boasts are made as to confederacy, thousands of men under oaths, and so on ("there is . . . 3 thousand all ready to fight & I'll be damd if we don't make the King's Army to shite"[76]), we need not suppose such formal confederacy, arming, or oath-taking to be true. This is an anonymous literary genre: unlike the agrarian letter which often led to the performance of exactly what was threatened (arson), this kind of letter gave rise not to insurrection, mass arson, and murder (as promised) but to controlled price-fixing action, or retaliatory action against millers and dealers, in which there was scarcely ever arson or bloodshed.

This is, indeed, one part of the interest and sometimes of the grim and conscious humour of these letters. The authors, evidently, were racking their brains and embellishing their style in the hope of striking maximum terror into the minds of the great—the great whom they often knew well, and to whom they deferred meekly in the daylight street. The letter from Middleton in 1762 and that from the miners of Clee Hill (Shropshire) give us the mode, as does the paper of 1767 "lately thrown into a Person's House at Kidderminster":

> This is to give Notis to badgers and fore Stallers of grain that there as Been sum in perticular a wocheing your Motions and ther whill Be in a wicks time some men Com ought of the Colepits by Nigt to Meak fire brans of all the abitations of the foretallers of grain but the best way to seave your selves seet the Cryer to work hand sell of all your Stock to the Poor at a Reasonable Reat. . . .[77]

The demand (to send round the crier and sell off stock to the poor at a reasonable rate) was by no means a utopian one: exactly such measures, to subsidize corn, were a customary response of the authorities to dearth. This letter was very probably the product of some collective, since similar papers "have lately been stuck up in many parts" of Kidderminster.

Until the 1790s the letters, while often levelling in tone, were directed at the particular marketing and pricing grievances of the time, with reference often to particular dealers or millers. The letters from Norwich and Swansea in 1766 and Carlisle in 1783 are good examples.[78] Norwich had active and eloquent correspondents. A gruff letter might be followed by flowery productions, in which the author represented himself as one of "a select body" sworn to fire the city:

> The City had been of a flame last night . . . but I used all the Eloquence I was Master of and got leave to write to you which is the last time I can intercede on your behalf. . . . If you have a mind to save the City and yourself Immediately on Saturday Morning alter the price of most Eatables for the present—in the interim I'll do all I durst to prevail upon them which will be impossible without such an Alteration. . . .[79]

Whether the author of this letter correctly judged the psychology of his correspondents may be in question. But there can be little doubt that the authors of a letter affixed to the pillory post in Salisbury market in 1767 judged the mentality of its recipients well:

Gentleman farmers

Farmers tack nodist form This time before It is to let

Be fore Christ mus Day sum of you will be as Poore as we if you Will not seel Cheper

This is two let you no We have stoel a Sheep, For which the reason Was be Cass you sold your Whet so dear and if you Will not loer pries of your Whet we will Com by night and set fiear to your Barns and Reecks gentleman Farm mers we be in Arnest now and That you will find to your sorrow soon.[80]

The letters of 1795 and afterwards continue to list particular grievances and to threaten identifiable men. But the seditious or levelling threats become more general and, while they remain theatrical, suggest some more serious underground culture of Painites or of "Jacobins." Chalking on the walls and pavements, which had certainly been known in London from at least the time of Wilkes, became a far more serious means of propaganda during the French Wars. James Bisset, a Brimingham reformer, noted in his reminiscences that the first chalking which he noticed on the walls of the town were in the 1780s, directed against the brutal flogging of soldiers in the Wiltshire militia. He composed a poem about wall-writing, compiled from "actual memorandums taken at the time." In 1791 (at the time of the Priestly Riots) there was "Church and King," "No Paine!" and "Damn the Jacobins." But by the mid-1790s:

... When trade was quite ruin'd, & ev'rything dead
The walls teem'd with horror, they wrote "blood or bread."
The tables began to seem turning apace:
"Church & King" was rubb'd off & gallows they'd trace,
Instead of "No Foxites," "No Priestley," "No Paine"
They next wrote "No Portland," no damned rogues in grain;
Fresh inscriptions each day on the buildings were seen:
"No Badger," "No War," and "Damn Pitt" too I ween,

"No King, Lords or Commons," "Large Loaves," "Revolution,"
"No Taxes," "No Tythes," but a "Free Constitution."[81]

In the "underground" years after 1795 the writing of a number of identical
handbills was organized in some large reform centres, and the Spenceans
adopted the means of propaganda through wall-chalking.[82] But the seditious
letters scattered across the whole country in 1800 were almost certainly the
work of freelance Painites, supported by a popular ground-swell of food riots
and anti-war sentiment. From Hitchin: "Come forth with courage and reselution
if you give way to those Villins you allways be bound under theise changs
[chains] . . . our Soupmaker may come with doctrine of fine speecheis as keeping
a cleen house and the Wife to give a smile send him to where hee come
from . . ."[83] From Clare (Suffolk): "Gentl men . . . if you do not give the men
more wags [wages] for thair time i will Be damd if we do not make france of
it."[84] From Wakefield: "Damn your old Methodist soul we will bring it down
you a Constable damn your eyes . . . if you do stint us to a quartern loaf take
care of your life damn King George the third and Billy Pitt . . . damn your Red
herrins Potatoes. . . . May England fall like dew to the ground and Jacobings
ever florish. . . ."[85] It is clear enough from the alarmed tone of the covering
letters of the magistrates who sent in to the Home Secretary such productions
that they had often found their mark. When a clergyman in Ramsbury (Wiltshire) had to copy a paper found affixed to a tree in the centre of his parish
and signed "God Save the Poor & down with George III" he could scarcely
keep his hand from trembling: "Such my Lord are the Contents of a Paper,
which chills me with Horror whilst I transcribe it."[86]

It was against such chilling papers as these that Hannah More and her friends
took up their pens. The seditious note which entered in the 1790s was never
extinguished: it was to revive in every context in which open agitation brought
the danger of persecution and victimization—notably in the Luddite years, in
1816–20, and in a context of agrarian protest. If the anonymous letter and
handbill became infrequent in other contexts after 1830, this was because it had
been displaced by the Radical or Chartist printing-press.

V

For most of the period under review the writing of such letters was a capital
offence. It was not only a crime but an extremely serious crime, and the gazetting of letters (with attendant pardons and rewards) was an index of the
gravity with which they were regarded. Such letters were normally described
as "incendiary," because they commonly threatened arson. Those who wrote

them, delivered them, circulated them, or were accomplice to any of these actions risked their lives.

The writing of threatening letters might of course be an offence within common law (as conspiracy), or come within the terms of seditious libel or of defamation.[87] The offence appears to have first come under the particular attention of the legislature in the Black Act (1723), by which any person who "shall knowingly send any letter without any name" (or with fictitious names) "demanding money, venison, or other valuable thing" became guilty of felony without benefit of clergy.[88] The terms of this act appear to have led to some uncertainty: were offenders guilty who threatened but who did not demand money or venison?[89] By 27 Geo. II c. 15 (1754) the definition was extended. Corn riots had occurred in 1753, and the preamble to the new act stated: "Whereas divers letters have been sent to several of his Majesty's subjects threatening their lives or burning their houses, which letters not demanding money, venison, or valuable effects, are not subject to the penalties of the said act. . . ." (the Black Act), the authors of letters threatening murder, or the arson of "houses, out-houses, barns, stacks of corn or grain, hay or straw" became equally guilty. In 1757 a further act was passed, directed against blackmailers, who threatened to accuse any person of crimes with a view to extorting money: but the penalty for this offence was only seven years' transportation. The position remained like this for some seventy years, until 1823, when the capital sentence entailed by the first three acts was reduced to a maximum sentence of transportation for life. This was fortunate for the "Swing" letter-writers of 1830.[90]

I have no figures which would indicate the number of commitals or convictions for these offences in the eighteenth century. Some figures for the early nineteenth century exist, and these suggest that committals were few and that there was an unusually high rate of acquittals. Thus from 1810 to 1818—years of industrious letter-writing, which take in Luddism, the East Anglian disturbances of 1816, post-war radical unrest—we have:[91]

	1810	1811	1812	1813	1814	1815	1816	1817	1818
Committals	3	—	5	2	1	2	2	1	1
Acquittals	2	—	2	—	—	1	1	1	1
Convictions	1	—	3	2	1	2	1	—	—

Figures are much the same over the next ten years: 1820 saw 6 committals and 2 convictions (both death sentences), and 1824 (the year after the ending of the death penalty) saw 7 committals and, again, 2 convictions. No other years saw so many committals. The rise in these after 1828 is significant:[92]

	1828	1829	1830	1831	1832	1833	1834	1835	1836	1837
Committals	3	4	4	62	6	12	11	15	7	3
No bills ⎫ Acquittals ⎭	2	2	3	38	2	5	6	10	7	1
Convictions	1	2	1	24	4	7	5	5	—	2

While no accurate figure can be offered, there is no evidence from any year of the eighteenth century as to either committals or convictions running at a rate which even approaches that of 1831—the aftermath of the "Last Labourers' Revolt." This is an offence whose incidence evades all quantification: it must remain a "dark figure."[93]

What remains is this case or that which research has brought (or will bring) to light from assize records or the press. The very high ratio of offences to committals arises from the extreme difficulty in detecting the offender—a difficulty much greater in letters of social protest than in blackmail cases, since the blackmailer was vulnerable at the point where he sought to collect his money. And the high ratio of acquittals to convictions suggests the difficulty of bringing the offence to proof.

Even in 1830 there were no accredited "handwriting experts." Mr. Justice Alderson, notorious for his conduct of the Winchester Special Commission in the winter of 1830–31, was nevertheless at pains to instruct the jury fairly in one case where an attorney, Henry Pollexfen, was accused of writing a threatening letter to a magistrate: "Evidence as to handwriting was in general most vague and unsatisfactory, and there was no subject on which men could be more easily deceived." He suggested that strong additional proof was required, such as the circumstances of two matching half sheets of paper.[94]

The defendant in this case was found not guilty. One wonders whether Mr. Justice Alderson remembered his own warning when, two weeks later at Salisbury, he sentenced a prosperous farmer, Isaac Looker, to transportation for life for writing to a neighbouring farmer: "Hif you goes to sware against or a man in prisson, you have here farm burnt down to ground, and thy bluddy head chopt off." Witnesses swore that Isaac Looker had said in a pub that the labourers were doing the right thing in going round to raise wages and to reduce tithes and rents, and that it was not they but the magistrates and soldiers who were creating disturbance. If the people were left alone they would do what they had to do peaceably. This evidence must have filled the minds of judges and of special jury with a strong presumption of Looker's guilt. It was then proved that the letter did in fact fit exactly to a half sheet in Looker's bureau, and that the water-mark had been divided. Several prosecution witnesses affirmed with the greatest confidence that this was Looker's handwriting, although witnesses for the defence denied this. The jury found the accused guilty. Alderson made no bones of the fact that this was also his direction. Isaac Looker's vehement protestations of innocence met with this remark: "We all know that a man who can be guilty of such an offence as that of which you have been convicted, will not hesitate to deny it as you now do. I would rather trust to such evidence as has been given in your case, than to the most solemn declarations even on the scaffold." The mention of the scaffold brought a surge of nostalgia into the judge's mind; had the death penalty still been available for this offence, he informed the farmer, he had little doubt that he would have used it. Transporting Looker for life he added: "You will be sent to a country where you will find very few worse than yourself."

Exhausted by this exercise of disciplinary rhetoric the judge retired for refreshment. In the interval the farmer's eighteen-year-old son, Edward, came forward and confessed that he had written the letter. His father had been away that day and knew nothing of it. Two of his cousins were then in prison awaiting trial for their part in the "Swing" disturbances: "I heard people talk that it would get my cousins off if threatening letters were written." Slightly discomforted, Mr. Justice Alderson immediately put Isaac Looker on trial *again*, for either writing the letters or for aiding and abetting his son. But the case could not stand up and he was acquitted. This time all the handwriting experts could see that the letter was undoubtedly in a better hand than the old farmer could command. Edward, the son, was then sentenced to seven years' transportation.[95]

This episode serves to emphasize the difficulty in securing a conviction—a difficulty perhaps increased by the reluctance of eighteenth-century juries to send a man to death for committing a few lines to paper. Since there were few convictions, if follows that there is little information as to the authors of the letters. Several examples of death were made shortly after the passage of the Black Act. The cases are pathetic ones—bungling amateurs trying their hands at blackmail. The first to be executed for the offence was probably Bryan Smith, an Irish Catholic, at Tyburn in 1725. A friend of his lay under sentence of transportation for stealing a silver spoon from a tavern: ordering a gill of Rhenish and a little sugar, the sugar was brought in a silver spoon which he had taken away. Smith wrote to the prosecutor, threatening his life if his friend was transported. As it happened, his friend's transportation was held over. A witness testified: "There was no persuading Smith but that his letter was the occasion of it. He became strangely elevated, and mightily admired his ingenuity and contrivance, as if no body but himself was able to do the like." He was encouraged to attempt his hand a second time. He set up an accomplice, who was a tailor, to whom he pretended to be in debt for £27. He then wrote to

"Baron" Antonio Lopez Suaffo a letter threatening murder and arson, signed "John Brown," demanding that Suaffo should pay off his debt to the tailor. It was a foolish contrivance. The tailor was of course arrested and held in Newgate until he turned evidence against Smith. This evidence was corroborated by "the hand-writing, spelling, imprecations and Irish blunders" of the letter. Smith was one of the first to adopt the fashion of riding in the cart to Tyburn in his shroud, which turned out to be an even greater blunder than any he had committed before. As his fellow sufferers were being attended to by the hangman, Smith slipped his head through the noose and jumped over the cart into the crowd; hopping around like a pantomime ghost in his shroud he was easily retaken.[96]

Jepthah Big, hanged at Tyburn in 1729, had tried his hand at equally silly means of extortion with equal lack of success. According to the Ordinary of Newgate he was twenty-five years old, an apprenticed gunstock-maker out of employment (given of course, in the usual ritual terms, to "drinking, swearing, whoring, &c."), whose parents had given him a good education in reading and writing. His exit at Tyburn was little more decorous than that of Smith, since he got hold of the rope and hung by his hands for a minute or two after the cart was driven away. This may have provided drama for the crowd. Both Smith and Big appear to have complained that they did not know that their offence was capital, although Big admitted that he had heard of two or three who had suffered upon the same law.[97] And, on occasion, others were to suffer upon it.[98]

What kind of men wrote the letters of social protest? Until the 1830s and 1840s convictions are so rare that the faces as well as the figures must remain dark. One would like to offer, as the type of one kind of letter-writer, William Tillotson, found guilty of sedition in 1804. Tillotson was an elderly man who, in the notion of the Crown brief, for a great part of his life had

> rambled about the country to cock fights, rush bearings, and amusements of that description, affecting to collect hare and rabbit skins and to sell trinkets, rings, and other suchlike small articles usually vended by pedlars. . . . He has been always deservedly considered a blasphemous, seditious and disaffected character, and suspected of obtaining his means of livelihood and dissipation in other ways than those which he appeared to pursue.

Tillotson, a native of Colne (Lancashire), spent the day of 6 August 1803 drinking in an inn in Grindleton, among the Clitheroe moors on the Yorkshire-Lancashire border, and "sotted all or great part of the day, singing and talking in the most blasphemous, seditious, and licentious way that can be imagined."

The boggling imagination finds that his ribald and bloodthirsty jests were aimed at King George, Mr. Pitt, and the country gentry generally.[99]

But this traitorous old man—this scandalous antithesis to the high-minded and moralistic pedlar of Wordsworth's "Excursion"—was, so far as the evidence allows us to see, no letter-writer. He belongs to an older oral tradition of sedition, whose expression took the form of riddling rhymes, songs, prophecies, and elaborate patter.[100] A more likely candidate for the "type" might be Charles Alderson, a journeyman saddler of Lowestoft, who did indeed write three seditious letters to a magistrate in 1793. The first two letters were full of passionate hostility towards the war against revolutionary France. Alderson claimed to have discovered some great secret weapon which would overthrow the Duke of York's army and enforce peace upon Britain: he was willing to reveal his secret to the magistrate if he could be assured of the latter's cooperation. When he failed to receive this reassurance he wrote a further letter, in the usual terms, threatening to lie in wait for him and punish him.

Identified, Alderson was fetched by the recipient of the letters before the Quarter Sessions at Beccles. But the threatened magistrate refused to press the case against him, on the grounds that Alderson was of "disturbed imagination." His fellow magistrates, however, would not let off the saddler so lightly and they committed him again, this time for sedition. They could certainly not tolerate leniency towards a man who had written: "I am ... well perswaded that the life of aney man in the world even the most opresed african is and ought to be of more value in the sight of one and other than all the revenues of King George the third and all his familey...." A former employer was brought forward to testify that Alderson showed no signs of insanity, except that he "used to spend much of his time and particularly Sundays in reading old Books of History."[101] It is a dangerous complaint, fully justifying any man's committal.

Alderson is not wholly untypical: his learning, his quotations from Pope, his attempts at a high literary style, can be matched in other letters; and these become rather more frequent in Luddite and post-war years, when eccentric enthusiasts and odd-balls turned their hands to elaborate epistolary menaces. Although his productions were briefer, one such man can be identified in 1836—Joseph Saville, a straw-plait manufacturer, who rattled about Cambridgeshire in a gig in which were found between 600 and 700 inflammatory letters. He was a man used to putting out work to the cottagers, and no doubt he put out some copying work as well. Letters manufactured on this scale were of necessity brief:

> Oh ye church of England Parsins, who strain at a knot and swallor a
> cammell, woe woe woe be unto you, ye shall one day have you
> reward   Swing

If you dont behave better and give the Poor Man his due I will visit you or my name is not   Swing

You clergy, ye Vipers, you love Tithes, Cummin, and Mint; ye are men-eaters and not soul savers, but Blind leaders of the Blind, twice dead, plucked up by the Roots   Swing

Saville was described as some kind of Methodist ranter, and he made no attempt to deny that he had distributed the letters. What he did deny, vigorously, was that he had any interest in politics. The officers of his parish came loyally to his defence in the local newspapers, deploring his "folly" but describing him as the author of a Sick Society and a Sunday School:

About Christmas he provides a good dinner for the poor widows; has given a large quantity of potatoes to the poor; has been the means of distributing some hundreds of bushels of coals in winter; has made a proposition for the poor to dig up the waste ground . . . for their benefit; has been one of the first to lower his tenants' rents; is a warm advocate and supporter of Bible and Missionary Societies. . . .

In his defence Saville said he was actuated simply by the words of Scripture, especially such as commenced: "Woe unto you Scribes and Pharisees. . . ." He was not the first or last to come under the notice of a Christian judiciary for taking Christian texts too literally, although, as a Scribe in some kind himself, he might have suspected that woe would be coming to him also. He was, nevertheless, most fortunate not to have come under the notice of Mr. Justice Alderson, to have had the loyal backing of his parish (it could scarcely be possible to receive a better character than that which they gave to him), and to have been tried in a county in which the disturbances had been comparatively light. He was fined £50 and imprisoned for twelve months.[102]

   This was indeed a light sentence. Other "Swing" authors received transportation (for seven or fourteen years, or for life); the same sentences were handed out in East Anglia in the 1840s; and even in the 1850s (although by now there is more evidence of clemency) two years' hard labour could be expected.[103] Such sentences fell, in the main, upon labourers—young men like Edward Looker—or, on occasions, men in some clerical occupation.[104] By the 1830s it might be possible to show that in rural England the march of intellect and the march of incendiarism went hand-in-hand. When the epidemic of "Swing" letters was at its height, a York newspaper reported that "some boys belonging to the Skidby school have been detected as the writers of the letters to the neighbouring farmers."[105] Thomas Brown, a seventeen-year-old labourer, transported for life at Lewes Assizes for the offence, pleaded that old and young Miller (both labourers) had put him up to it, since they could not write themselves.[106] For the illiterate, the fact of writing sometimes seems to carry magical powers.[107]

We are still very little closer to the authors of the letters of social protest and sedition of the eighteenth century. But when a face appears, which is rarely enough, it does not appear to be that of a crank; it is simply that of a member of the working community suffering under common grievances, perhaps set a little apart by his literary aptitude. Thomas Bannister, a yeoman farmer in Windsor Forest, who thrust some furious threatening letters through a hole in a neighbour's stable door early one January morning in 1724—an action which had been supported by window-breaking, the cutting of cart-leathers, breaking of fences and maiming of cattle—appears to have been a typical yeoman of the area, of long-settled family; and his neighbour appears to have given offence by giving evidence leading to the conviction of other local men.[108]

On occasion the correspondence of the authorities indicates a possible author, although the evidence may not have been firm enough to lead to a prosecution. In the high noon of anti-Jacobinism this kind of source must be used with extreme caution. As Wordsworth learned at Alfoxden and William Blake at Felpham, any stranger, especially one often closeted with books and paper, could easily be suspected as a revolutionary or a French spy. In 1795 the Mayor of Hastings wrote to Portland to assure him that the seditious handbills and threatening letters circulated in the town could not possibly have come from the hand of any citizens of Hastings, who had "ever been distinguished" for their attachment to the King and Constitution. But he was happy to be able to disclose the true author, a Mr. Leigh, a stranger recently settled in lodgings in the town. This man, "of middle stature, dark hair without powder tied in a queue behind, black coat and waistcoat, nankeen breeches" and a "down-cast look," may perhaps not have been a conspirator, but he was certainly the object of a conspiracy. The Mayor, the officers of the militia, the master of his lodgings, the servant-girl—all were watching his least motion. The directions on his letters were closely observed, and when the eighteen-year-old girl at his lodgings was asked to post a letter, "The girl . . . seeing one of his letters directed to *Lord Stanhope* had the curiosity to open a corner of the letter but cou'd only read the following part of a line: " 'News, you know I am here for that purpose. . . .' " The master of his lodgings kept back the next letter, with a view to its examination. The man "is employ'd generally in reading Paine's "Rights of Man," Brother's "Prophecies" . . . his conversation is extremely indecent in speaking of the King of Government and . . . he has taken infinite pains to mix with the soldiers . . . giving them money to drink &c." The Mayor added, with seeming self-contradiction, that the master of his lodgings "has got a vast deal of his writing which exactly resembles the threatening letters which I have receiv'd, but as he can easily disguise his natural hand, and seldom writes twice alike, it is impossible for me to take him up with a chance of conviction." He admitted the want of evidence, but had "not a moment's doubt of his being the Man." As he was writing this essay in criminal detection a message was brought to the Mayor indicating that the mysterious stranger had announced that he was about to leave Hastings, and on foot. No doubt he had his reasons.[109]

We may hesitate to convict this stranger in his absence. But a clerical magistrate in Gloucestershire did follow up a series of measures of detection which were more thorough. The whole episode, which illustrates the kind of "dialogue" which took place between authorities and the crowd through this medium, is worth recording in detail. On 16 July 1795, a gentleman in Uley, Gloucestershire found this note in his garden:

> O remember ye poor in distress by ye high pr^s of provision if not the consiquens will be fatall to a great many in all parishis round a bout here how do ye think a man can support a fam^{ly} by a quartern [?] flour for a shillin and here is a man in this parish do say the poore was never beter of as they be now a fatel blow for him and his hous and all his property we have all redy 5000 sworn to be true to the last & we have 510000 of ball redy and can have pouder at a word & every think fitin for ye purpose no King but a constitution down down down o fatall dow high caps & proud hats for ever dow down we all.

Another gentleman received a similar note on the same day, and a further note was found at another house a few days later. The three gentlemen conferred with the magistrate and agreed to keep the notes secret, while making inquiries. But this proved to be impossible, since two of the notes had been first picked up by labourers in the cloth manufactory, who had spread their contents abroad. The JP (the Reverend William Lloyd Baker) then issued a public statement that "some exertions which we had intention to have brought forward for the relief of the poor should be suspended for a week" in consequence of the letters. This is a nice moment in the contest for "face" in the paternalism—deference equilibrium: that is, these "exertions" for charitable relief had not yet been made—and were perhaps prompted by the letters and the fear of riot—but they must on no account seem to be hastened in response to duress. The Reverend Baker understood this game of threat and counter-threat only too well. He lived in a district in which more than one clothier's house had been burned to the ground, and his own house was provided with an alarm bell which, on a calm day, could be heard by 6,000 people.[110]

At this point subsidized food for the poor was provided in Uley. But the disgruntled correspondent was still unsatisfied, and some time afterwards left a further bulletin near the workhouse where "we distributed our provisions." This alleged that the gentlemen's subsidized bread, at 5½ lb for 1s., compared poorly with the bread provided by a baker in the parish at 6 lb for 13d. for bread "as white as snow." It compared unfavourably also with Cambridge, where the poor have a bushel of wheat for 10s.: "You blood thirsty crew . . . remember Dives and Lazerus."

The gentlemen ignored this piece of ingratitude and went on as before, ending their subsidies on 3 September: "we had great reason to imagine every one was pleased with what had been done till the fifteenth of September when the following note was found. . . .":

> The distress of the industerous people through the dearness of provisions calls aloud for an immediate consultation therefore a meeting is desired next Munday morning 21 in^t by nine o clock in the morning on hampton coman to consult what steps to take for an immediate alteration. Be pl^d to let more know it further. With it make no delay or else we all must starve immediately.

Troops were alerted, and a magistrate in the neighbourhood of Minchinhampton Common rode over the field on the day. He saw nothing; but the time had been altered, and in the afternoon some three hundred assembled, but without any leader or concerted plan. They reassembled again, with fewer numbers, on 5 October: once again they were observed by troops.

Baker and his friends now conducted a systematic investigation. Individuals from Uley who were present at the meetings were interrogated. The search was narrowed to three men, who had been especially active in recruiting attendance. Suspicion fell upon one of these, and the train of evidence was rather more convincing than in the case of the Hastings stranger. The man was known to have attended the meetings and to have solicited attendance; alehouse gossip among "the lower class of people" nominated him as the author; samples of his handwriting ("a number of bills") were collected and compared closely with that in the notes, "some of the letters being very particularly shaped." The suspect was a tailor who was born and had lived all his life in Uley: "an obscure individual" and those with whom he is connected "each is alike obscure."

But although the evidence might convince a jury, Baker and his fellow magistrates were uncertain as to how to proceed. They had at first thought of giving the tailor a severe reprimand and a warning that he was being watched, since "we were afraid that his offence did not make him actually liable to such a punishment as we wished." This was, presumably, because the letters were directed to no particular person, and they did not extort money or threaten arson or the murder of any individual, although one had warned unnamed persons to "expect to loase y^r heads without any ado" and others, which referred to arming and warfare, were clearly seditious. The fact of the two assemblies eventually decided the magistrates to refer the whole case to Portland for his opinion. In his reply Portland commended the magistrates for their vigilance, but counselled caution:

> The person in question is in so low a situation of life, and his endeavours appear to have produced so little effect in the Country that I am inclined to think it may perhaps be the best way of preventing disturbance in future to let him know that the Magistrates are well informed of his attempts & that they have it in contemplation to proceed against him, which may possibly induce him to quit the Country . . .[111]

In any case, this should deter him from repeating the practice; and, if he should do so, then "proper measures" should be taken to bring him to justice. What such proper measures would be the Home Secretary did not propose; presumably a charge of sedition would be the most likely to stick.[112]

This case shows the whole process of "dialogue" at work and illuminates the functions of the letters. It also shows that self-reliant magistrates would not inform the Government of such letters for many weeks, if at all, if they thought they could handle the matter on their own. Finally, it may point to an additional reason why the numerous letters of 1795 were given no publicity and kept out of the *Gazette*. Government was still adopting the traditional posture that serious political or seditious threat could come, not from "obscure individuals" in "low" situations of life, but from men in higher stations. A stranger with books, a portmanteau, a black coat and nankeen breeches was likely to draw more attention than a tailor in a Gloucestershire village; the information that Wordsworth and his sister were taking "views" of the Somerset coast was sufficient to send a Government agent hurrying down to Stowey. If the anonymous productions of the obscure were not accompanied by acts of arson, gunshot, or riot, then as late as 1795 Government was willing to pass them by. In 1800, when a plebeian Painite underground culture had become manifest, Portland himself was to change his stance.

One other case of such a letter-writer is fairly well documented, although in this case it is by no means so probable that the author was correctly identified. In the Somerset parish of Stogursey a letter-writer was busy between 1794 and 1800. In 1794 notices were posted on behalf of the poor of six parishes, demanding an advance of wages: if not, 360 men would "take arms." In 1795 a similar notice was stuck upon Stogursey church door. In 1800 a longer letter was thrust under the door of a market room where local gentlemen were supervising the sale of subsidized barley. What is peculiar about this letter is that, while literate and forceful, its spelling was erratic ("deturmed" for "determine," "genearel" for "general"), and yet it closed with four well-presented lines of Latin verse. Suspicion fell upon one Joseph Brown, a labourer of the parish, who was known to be a literate man. He had served briefly (1797–8) as a sergeant in the Somerset Volunteers, and one of his officers, a lieutenant-surgeon, claimed to identify his handwriting by comparing it with lists of the sick drawn up by Brown during his volunteer service. An indictment was drawn against Brown, which exists in draft, but the case rested only upon the evidence of handwriting. Moreover, while the letter was cited in full in the indictment, the lines of Latin were omitted: this suggests that no proof could be adduced that Brown knew Latin, and that, if he had a hand in the letter at all, he must have had a classically minded accomplice.[113] Unfortunately Coleridge had left Nether Stowey (some three miles from Stogursey) two years before, so that we cannot pin the Latin on him. But there were certainly other aspirants to literary honours around in the Somerset villages, as was illustrated by the handbill stuck up in the small market town of Wellington (Somerset) in 1801:

> Then raise yr drooping spirits up
> Nor starve by Pitt's decree
> Fix up the sacred Guillotine
> Proclaim—French Liberty!

Hundreds of such productions never found their way as far as the Home Office. Nevertheless, it remains something of a puzzle to know what Government thought it was doing, in 1800, in gazetting and thereby giving further publicity to so many examples of sedition. For Portland informed one correspondent that: "I must admit that I do not recollect an instance of any discovery having been effected by the offer of reward and pardon, any more than of the threats contained in incendiary letters having been carried into effect." He was, however, "persuaded . . . that advertisement . . . operated by way of prevention."[114] On one count this evidence is important: it confirms the impression that very few successful prosecutions were carried through in these years. But on another count Portland, who was writing in confidence to a friend, was making a directly misleading statement. It may be true that cases of murder rarely, if ever, eventuated from such threats. But cases of riot and of arson in direct association with threatening letters were passing through his hands every month.

Indeed, this very correspondent, W. Baker, the country MP for Hertford-shire, was in a position to contradict Portland's statement. On 15 July 1800, barns, hovels, and a quantity of grain belonging to Robert Young of Holwells, near Bishop's Hatfield, Hertfordshire, were fired. The offence was gazetted on 19 July. On the same day Farmer Young was sent a letter signed "Dr. Steady," commencing:

> I am sorry your Corn was destroyed it was what I was against but the next step will not be to destroy the Corn but you may tell all Farmers that with-hold it as you have done that their lives will be weary shorte if they do not sell their Corn much cheaper immediately and likewise the lives of that damned sett of Salesmen and forestallers of Mark Lane that keep the price up as they have done shall soon go to pott.
>
> We are more than 1000 strong in Harford Essex and London . . . we have many friends in Arms you little think of, but its Committee Night I am obliged to attend but at no public house. . . .

This letter was sent from London and could of course have come from anyone who had noted Young's address in the *Gazette*. Baker forwarded the letter to Portland and pressed for it to be gazetted. Portland, as we have seen, was reluctant. But on 11 September the farmer suffered the firing of a further stack of oats in his yard. Farmer Young, Baker reported, was "much distracted by agitation of mind," less, it would seem, on account of his losses, which were insured, than on account of the hostility surrounding him and the reputation which he had gained for avarice. Reports had been "most maliciously circulated" as to the quantity of corn which he was holding—reports which he "means to contradict in the most solemn and formal manner." "The poor man . . . is so affected . . . that his life is made truly miserable."[115]

In this case the arsonist and the author were not necessarily accomplices. But in these same months Portland must have noted cases where the two must have been directly related. Thus in Whiteparish, Wiltshire, this letter was found in February 1800:

> He that finds
> it open it and
> read it & set the
> news all over
> White-Parish

If all the Farmers in White-Parish Dont sink their
Wheat their Barns shall be burn'd and they shall be

in the middle of it, it is no use to offer no reward
for I have nobody but myself Amen.

Beneath the gazetted letter there followed the further announcement (over Portland's signature): "And whereas the above Threat (in Part) has been put in
Execution by some evil-minded Person or Persons unknown, in the wilfully
setting Fire on the Evening of . . . the 12th Instant to Two Barns, a Cow-House,
a Quantity of Hay and Straw, a Fatting Calf . . ." and other articles on a
gentleman's farm in Whiteparish, the customary offer of pardon and reward
was published.[116] Such letters could never be taken only as acts of theatre. As
young Thomas Brown was to write to Lord Sheffield in 1830, "My writing is
bad, but my firing is good my Lord."[117]

VI

If the authors of these letters were various, we must expect the styles to be
various also. Generalization does not take us far. The orthography of the letters
is interesting, although at times it may have been deliberately disguised. Very
often the dialect or lilt of regional speech can be detected beneath the letters—
West Country, or Irish, or East Anglian; these are written by men who knew
their letters, but whose writing was guided by their ear rather than by the
standards of memory and eye. There are letters as roughly hewn in the 1820s
and 1830s as in the 1760s, although when we come into the nineteenth century
there are more letters which suggest the "intellectuals" of the movement:
schoolmasters, tradesmen, clerks, artisans with a shelf of books.

One might perhaps find evidence in the letters for a footnote to the history
of popular literacy. Clearly, the arrival of a method of mass agitation which
involves notices in the market square, handbills, and chalking implies a mass
audience of whom many could read these signs. A rapid review of the letters
suggests that there is a movement outwards from the larger towns (in the 1760s,
London, Taunton, Tiverton, Plymouth, Chester, Nottingham, Norwich, and so
on) to the village or smaller market town (in the 1790s, Whiteparish, several
Essex villages, Newport [Isle of Wight], Petworth, Odiham, Bideford, Stogursey, Uley, Crediton, and others). But we have noted a letter from Clee Hill
colliers in 1767; there is another from the colliers of the north-east in 1765, and
Berkshire yeomen farmers were employing them in the 1720s. Scotland vindi-
cates its reputation for educational advancement by providing some of the earliest examples of highly polished literary production; and the pawkiness of the
Presbyterian end of Scottish culture peeps out even amidst the unkirklike imprecations, as when Lieutenant-Colonel John Crawfurd of Crawfurdland, Ayrshire was warned not to "hurt the Countrey bay the Advise of one abonible

Hure ane Adoltres woman."[118] Until the arrival of the often highly literate Rebecca, the common Welsh production showed no educational advance upon the English (but letters in the Welsh language might provide different evidence).[119] From the evidence of the *Gazette*, until 1790 the north and north Midlands were backward areas compared with the south and south Midlands, the east and, especially, the west.

Although most of the authors were guided in their spelling by ear, most also fell into that formal, mimetic style required by epistolary address. The recipient was warned that the author proposed to burn down, not his "house," but his "abitation"; blackmail pay-off must be laid in a hole in a tree on the such-and-such "inst."; the murderers promised to perform at "the first opertuerty." Such phrases, in elevating the style, seemed somehow to elevate the threat. So also did the literary flourishes which no doubt gave the authors much satisfaction. A Devon gentleman received in 1779 a letter describing him as: "A Narrow Back, Lowsey, false, Little forswareing, Little Rogue. I don't look upon thee no more than the Leaf of an Asp for he Whivers and is gone . . ."[120] The literary flourishes of the Painites of the 1790s fell too often into cliché, with "sons of liberty," "monarchical fetters," or warnings couched in the high style of a letter to the Mayor of Plymouth (1792) to "dread to come within the reach of a well pointed Poignard."[121]

The most polished letters probably belong to the last years of the tradition, at least in the towns, from 1800 to the 1830s. A Manchester cotton-master received one in 1812 which commenced: "Sir, We begin with the Language of the Prophet of old, in saying that your Destruction is at Hand, and why? because we the Cotton Spinners of this Town have been the means of raising you from the Dunghill to Independency."[122] But such writers could, on occasion, be equalled by their eighteenth-century forebears, such as one in Norwich in 1766 who, after threatening to raze the city by fire and sword, ended with a "noble Sentence of Horace" in the Latin.[123] In their form also, some of the letters followed the forms of authority or of the counting-house. A number of the hand-written bills posted in market squares adopted the "Wheareases" and flourishes of official proclamations. Others included touching epistolary formalities. A letter (Ayrshire, 1775) which went on to utter the most bloodcurdling blackmailing threats commenced: "Sir, This is perhaps the most interesting Letter you ever received as Your Life depends on your abaying its demands."[124] The Mayor of Nottingham received a letter in 1800 drawn up with impeccable attention to proprieties:[125]

Sir,
    If the Men who were taken last Saturday be not set at liberty by tomorrow night, the Shambles the Change and all the whole Square shall

be set on Fire, if you have an Army of Constables they can't prevent it
for the greasy boards will burn well—

Hoping that you will take this into consideration.

I am, your hble Servt.

Will. Johnston.

Until Ned Ludd, Captain Swing and Rebecca, there were no favoured pseudonyms. Those chosen range from "Probono Publico" to THE MONSTER. When
the chief magistrate of Tewkesbury was called upon to convene a meeting in
1795 to petition for peace, on pain of getting a bullet through his brains, the
signatories were: "Revenge, Force, Mallice, Determination."[126] The tinners of
Polgooth, Cornwall, signed their letter: "Captins Audacious, Fortitude, Presumption and dread not."[127] A Sussex complaint about small measures (1793)
was signed: "from the old devle that will have you all if you dont alter."[128]
Bloodcurdling threats in a Somerset village were over the signature:[129]

Pull grip Pull Devel
Devel take Both
Now lets Drink
My Jovel
        Soles

Letters in two Northamptonshire villages in 1800 were addressed to farmers
and dealers: "If you dornt Lower the greain whe will destroy all your Farm
with Fire . . . whe will destroy all your sheep and . . . whe will pull all your
turnips up. . . ." On the envelope, beside the addressee's name, was written:
"Walentine."[130] A letter from Newport (Isle of Wight) against the press-gang,
in 1793, signed itself simply "we ham For the rights of Tom Paine you
Bouger."[131]

There is no doubt that some of the authors enjoyed their stylistic extrava-
ganzas. Months and perhaps years of pent-up resentment and of assumed deference were released in a few lines. From Bideford (1812): "Your Carkase if
any such should be found will be given to the Dogs if it Contains any Moisture
for the Annimals to devour it."[132] Possibly it was the same author who had
warned a Bideford miller ten years previously that "the Devil will grind your
head in powder as the mill grinds Corn."[133] A Dumfries notice of 1771, which
is an excellent example of the popular "proclamation," warned forestallers, engrossers and dealers (and those "aiding or assisting to any that have hitherto
engrossed," etc.)—

To the great Hurt and prejudice of the Country, the Poor in particular,
to the violation of the Laws of God and Nature; Public Notice is hereby

given, that they from the Date hereof, desist from such sinful Practices, under Penalty of having their Houses burnt to the Ground, and punished in their Persons in Proportion to the Office they bear, viz. if a Magistrat with Mutilation, and if a Tradesman to have his Ears cut off at the Cross.[134]

A Bridgnorth writer remarked, less formally, of the farmers and millers: "we will cut off their Ears and slit their Noses as a mark that the country may know them."[135]

The highest literary style to which most authors wished to attain was not that of John Locke nor even of Tom Paine but of the Bible. The abundance of biblical reference must have been evident throughout this essay. The Old Testament lent itself easily to imprecations; and if the authors appealed to morality, as they commonly did, it was with reference to biblical text and style. Authors recalled Dives and Lazarus, compared employers or foremen to Herod, or recalled the sermons preached in church. A common posting-place was the church door; other letters were sent to clergy with the demand that they be read in church. In a Suffolk village in 1800 what appears to be verse was nailed to the church door:

> . . . the first that mix his Grain shall forfit his heid,
> For your entent is to starve us to ded . . .
> But the lord have [Raised?] our Curage so hie
> That soner than starve we fight till we die
> For the poor against the rich through out the land
> Will Conker the rich and have them at Command.
> So repent of your sins do not take it amiss
> It is your Cruelty the Cause of all this
> The day is epointed & that you will find
> The poor will have all this to share mind.

To be red in the Church by the Clargeman after surmon.[136]

This might perhaps have sounded oddly among the banns and parish notices. So also would have a letter sent round to several Essex parishes in 1800 which concluded:

> We will kill burn and destroy every thing we Come at spesely the greate landhldrs and the most sevear men in every parish to the poor. . . .

> We mean to behave well to every minester that will read this in the Church if not he is a ded man by night or by day by means we will destroay the king and his famealy and likewise the Parlerment.[137]

What is surprising about this letter is that we know that in at least one case (a dissenting meeting-house) the request was complied with.[138]

Most often the biblical reference comes through as echo or allusion. On occasion the aid of the God of Battles is summoned, as at Exeter (1801): "Fire and Sword is the word, and by the Almighty God they shall not escape our vengeance, we have cried unto Man in vain, we have now appealed unto God. . . ."[139] More often there is an appeal to a moral code of charity, grounded upon the Gospels. A gentleman, probably a mealman, in High Wycombe was warned in 1800 that it was likely that he would

> be sent to hell before the time god opinted you to live on all the Luxearys of Life and your poor nabour Clothed in Rags and starved for want of food his Children Crieing for Bread and none to give them I have yoy to Read the 12 Chapter of luke and the 8 Chapter of Amos. But you are as great a Stranger to the Gospel as you are to him that sent itt. . . .[140]

Few letters carry such explicit reference: one would imagine that in the seventeenth century citations of texts would have been more frequent. Nor does it seem, on the evidence at present to hand, that this manner of expression was often employed by the ranting or millenarial writers; although if such letters were received, the magistrates could have put them aside as the productions of cranks. The expression of faith in a hereafter, when the rich will be chastened in hell and the poor meet their reward, is met more often. The Surgeon of the *Sandwich* who had been an evidence against Richard Parker, the naval mutineer of 1797, was informed:

> Mr. Parker . . . is we hope where such infernal villains as you can never enter for hell is made for such base abominable miscreants and such as . . . yourself are vessels of wrath fitted to everlasting destruction o how will it gall your souls thro' all Eternity to See Blessed Parker full of Joy and happiness and Glory in the blissful presence of God and Christ and Holly Angels, when you will be company to devils and damned Souls, and full of wrath, Misery and Woe for ever and ever.[141]

One further stylistic device is of interest; it will already have been noticed that a number of the letters fall, at one point or another, into rough rhyming verse or doggerel. In some cases—addressed to a public at large rather than an individual—this is the ultimate in elevated style. In other cases—the examples from Wellington (Somerset) or from Maldon[142]—we have a genuine propaganda by poetry. But in other cases one suspects that one is seeing late examples of an older mnemonic tradition. This had been seen on a church door in Kent in 1603:

> The poor there is more
> Than goes from dore to dore
> You that are set in place
> See that youre profesion you doe not disgrace

These rhymes have a magical quality, like the riddle rhymes of Merlin, those of Mother Shipton, and "the late prophecy of a Cumberland cow"—

> Two hard winters, a wet spring
> A bloody summer and no king

which were circulating throughout the eighteenth century, were still alive in the 1790s, and which take us back to the rhyming riddles of the Fool in *Lear*. Joanna Southcott's writings are one corrupted end of that tradition, and they carry the incantatory quality of even bad verse. A rhymed threat at the foot of a letter carried some additional magical force:

> You will think it hard when you this reed
> But your Life must pay for it in Deed

Or, at the conclusion to an incendiary letter sent to a Newbury brewer in 1810:

> Wee will be gin at the Bell and so we will
> Contunu till you all goes to hell.[143]

VII

The anonymous threatening letter was an intrinsic component of social and individual protest in that complex society of manufacturing industry and of capitalist agricultural improvement which scholars persist in calling a "pre-industrial" society. In rural society it sometimes accompanied, punctuated, and illuminated the reasons for arson, fence-breaking, houghing of cattle, and so on. In mines, workshops, dockyards and the clothing industry it accompanied illicit trade union organization and rattening.[144] In years of high prices its function in intimidating some practices in dealing and marketing, and in stimulating charity or subsidized food, is clear. In such circumstances it sometimes performed the role of a channel of "negotiation" within the paternalist—plebeian equilibrium.

These generalizations do not take us far. Nor could we go far if we confined our examination to the forms of a subsequent phase of organization—the strike or the small printing-press—since each serves so many functions and carries so many voices. To learn more we must re-place each letter or group of letters within the specificity of its own context.

In the end, the form as such can be bound together only by two uniting themes. First, the act of sending such letters, for whatever purpose, constituted a crime; in the eyes of the law all literary styles, elevated or semi-literate, and all grievances, were reduced to a common level. And their authors were criminals, over whom hung the threat of the gallows or transportation. Second, these letters are, in many cases—and over many decades—the *only* literate expression of the "inarticulate" which has survived. The "dark figure" of the crime itself is dwarfed by the even darker figure of the plebeian consciousness through much of the eighteenth century and, in rural areas, well into the nineteenth. How did a society whose manifest ideology was that of paternalism feel from below?

Had these letters never been written we might suppose, although we would find it difficult to prove, that England between 1750 and 1810 was always a land of moderate consensus, within which the lower orders showed their gratitude towards a humane paternalism by a due measure of deference; or, if not quite this, then a society in which until the 1790s the gentry attained to such an overwhelming hegemony that their order appeared to be as unquestionable as the overarching sky. At least it has been possible to show that here and there something a little less than deference was to be found. "Lord Buckingham," a Norwich handbill writer remarked in 1793, "who died the other Day had Thirty Thousand Pounds, yeerly For setting his Arse in the House of Lords and doing nothing."[145] This sentence should perhaps be included in a footnote to the *History of Parliament*. Or again, regimental histories sometimes overlook aspects of their subject which were apparent to observers at the time. "We fear not the Soldiers," remarked an Exeter author (1801), "neither the Volunteers (vulgarly termed the Farmers Bull-Dogs)."[146]

Or, if we go back earlier in the century with expectations conditioned by much eighteenth-century historiography, it will be only with difficulty that we will recognize in "that Bich oud Clifton," Lady Clifton of Clifton Hall, Nottingham.[147] Nor will expectations as to the impartial workings of the law prepare us for such an account as that of the Southall Court of Requests (1757): "For Them Prespetrenc that You set as Comishenors have no regard of Conscience in Them for They will swear a black Cro is whit for a Six Peny Peic."[148] Or, again, a Hampshire villager sent, in 1798, a letter to Henry Chichley Plowden, which perhaps may modify orthodox views as to the ways in which commercial wealth, brought back to England, fertilized the agrarian and industrial revolutions: "You are a Damd Rogue and Damd Roguish you got your Money and a Damd Rogue you are in not paying it where it is owing you thinks to do as you did in the Indies but I am damd mistaken if you do for you killed thousands of poor Souls for to get their Wealth and now you makes a god of it."[149]

We now know enough about the actions of the eighteenth-century crowd to distrust the rather comfortable historiography dominant until recently. According to such accounts the English country gentleman was "close to the common life of the common people" and "never far from ordinary humanity": and "honour, dignity, integrity, considerateness, courtesy and chivalry were all virtues essential to the character of a gentleman, and they all derived in part from the nature of country life."[150] A writer from Witney (1767) displayed country life in a different nature: "Do not suffer such damned wheesing fat guted Rogues to Starve the Poor by such Hellish Ways on purpose that they may follow hunting horse-racing &c and to maintain their familys in Pride and extravagence."[151] And in 1800 an inhabitant of Henley-on-Thames, who had had the benefit of seeing the Volunteers in action against the crowd, offered to historians an alternative framework of analysis: "You gentleman as you are please to call Yourselves—Altho that is your Mistakes—for you are a sett of the most Damnable Roughs that Ever Existed."[152]

No doubt an author who had been ridden over by the Yeomanry wrote from a biased position. But the voices remain in one's inner ear. And they prompt one last, and important, reflection. The very vehemence of style should not mislead one to another extreme in which plebeian England in the eighteenth century is seen as made up of impotent revolutionaries, a few articulate (in the *Gazette*), the rest incoherent with wrath. For the imprecations and the vehemence are the other side to the medal of deference. They are those who come from a religious culture for whom the oath and the blasphemy carry most magical power. And they are those who cannot articulate their grievances openly, who cannot form their own organizations or circulate their own pamphlets and press, whose voices break out anonymously with intemperate force.

But we should not be misled by this. *Given the opportunity*, such insurrectionary voices could be followed by insurrectionary actions. Revolutionaries may indeed come on the streets, as in Paris by 1791, with voices like these. But *without the opportunity*, the voices could switch back once again, with remarkable suddenness, to silence or to abject dependency. This is apparent in many of the letters, especially those written before the influence of Tom Paine. It can be seen in the oscillatory tone of the letter from the commoners of Chestnut in 1799: on the one hand, the unmeasured violence of language— "Whe like birds of pray will prively lie in wait to spil the bloud" of those preparing enclosure, "whose names and places of abode are as prutrified sores in our Nostrils"; on the other hand, if instead of enclosure the same gentlemen had effected a fair regulation of common rights, then "thou instead of being contempabel whould thy Name been as Oderriferous Ointment pour'd fourth to us."

> Whe leave it for thy consideration Wheather thou would like to be sorted out from the land of the liveing or would like to have the poors hearts and there all if required for if thou proceeds to inclose our blood will boil like a pot if thou goest to regulate it then . . . will whe come and give our hearts and voices to it and to you for ever. . . .

And, behind this again, there is a resignation in the inevitability of the given social order: the poor, by threat or even by violence, are recalling the rich to certain notional duties. What the letters show is not the absence of deference in this kind of society, but something of its character and limitations. This deference has no inwardness: these writers do not love their masters, but, in the end, they must be reconciled to the fact that for the duration of their lives these are likely to remain their masters. It is like this in smaller institutions which profess paternalist values; the NCO may despise or hate his officers, the servant in the great house, or college, may despise those whom he serves, but dependence demands that certain dues of conduct and speech be paid.[153]

Hence the historian who encounters such letters as these, and then turns back to the licensed press or to the papers of the great, has a sense of double vision. On the surface all is consensus, deference, accommodation; the dependants petition abjectly for favour; every hind is touching his forelock; not a word against the Illustrious House of Hanover or the Glorious Constitution breaks the agreeable waters of illusion. Then, from an anonymous and obscure level, there leaps to view for a moment violent Jacobite or Levelling abuse. We should take neither the obeisances nor the imprecations as indications of final truth; both could flow from the same mind, as circumstance and calculation of advantage allowed. It would now seem, Richard Cobb tells us, that half the valets of pre-Revolutionary Paris, who followed the nobility servilely through the suave *salons*, were nourishing in their reveries anticipations of the guillotine falling upon the white and powdered necks about them.[154] But, if the guillotine had never been set up, the reveries of these valets would remain unknown. And historians would be able to write of the deference, or even consensus, of the *ancien régime*. The deference of eighteenth-century England may have been something like that, and these letters its reveries.

Notes

1. For a general history of the *London Gazette* (hereafter *LG*) see P. M. Ilandover, *A History of the London Gazette, 1665–1965*, 1965.

2. For the machinery of rewards and pardons, see Radzinowicz, esp. vol. II, sections 4 and 5.

3. The *Gazette* is, of course, an important source not only for imprecations but also for action, since rewards for information as to murders, smuggling affrays, arson, industrial riot, and so on also appear in its pages.

4. I am very much indebted to Mr. E. E. Dodd for his help in going through the *Gazettes* and to Mr. Malcolm Thomas, whose extensive knowledge of the Home Office papers between 1790 and 1803 has been made available to me. I was enabled to draw upon their help with the assistance of a grant in aid of research into food riots from the Nuffield Foundation in 1968–9.

5. No pretence is made as to final accuracy. Gazetted mentions of letters, which give no information as to the occasion or contents of the letters, have been omitted from this count.

6. By "crime-related" I mean attempts to influence the course of justice, threats to witnesses, and so on. There are in fact twenty-one such letters, but eight of these I have felt able to allocate to "social" grievances.

7. In some cases one letter contains several different threats, or threats appropriate to several different persons: for instance, murder to the mayor, destruction of property to the miller, arson to the farmer: this explains discrepancies in figures between Tables 2 and 3, 4 and 5.

8. For examples of local advertising, see *Aris's Birmingham Gazette* 11 August 1766, 9, March 1767; *Reading Mercury*, 10 March 1800.

9. PRO, HO 43.8, p. 144.

10. PRO, HO 43.11, P. 131.

11. No exact figure can be given. Home Office out-letter books in 1800 show the receipt of over eighty of such letters acknowledged; but a search of in-letters shows nearly 150 received in the same year. Since some enclosures were returned to the sender, some were sent on to the *Gazette* office, and others appear in War Office papers, 150 must be an underestimate of those brought directly to the Government's attention. In addition many correspondents referred in general terms to the frequency of such letters, but sent on no examples.

12. In February the Birmingham magistrates were advised to "employ some discreet and confidential agents, to observe, during the night time, in the most suspicious places"; J. King to Birmingham magistrates, 25 February 1800, PRO, HO 43.11, p. 374. Two weeks later Portland appears to have become more anxious: "I wish an early example could be made of those writing and distributing inflammatory and threatening handbills": Portland to Marquess Townshend, 10 March 1800, HO 43.11.

13. Portland did not consistently advise gazetting: for a contrary example, in this period, see his exchanges with W. Baker, MP, cited below, p. 292. And he consistently resisted gazetting (or offering a pardon and reward) in cases where the letters were of a private and scandalous, rather than public, character. To one recipient (a magistrate) he wrote that advertisement "would tend to make public the malicious and ill-founded suggestions ... without the smallest chance of bringing the authors of them to justice": see F. Adams, JP to Portland, 2 June 1800, PRO, HO 42.50 and HO 43.11, pp. 511–12. A pardon and reward could not be offered unless the interests of the country at large were involved: J. King to J. Taylor, 11 June 1800, HO 43.11, pp. 518–19.

14. This was, however, a special case, the letter in question being in Welsh, and a translation being proposed for the *Gazette*: clearly this would have afforded to it superfluous publicity: Charles Yorke to C. W. W. Wynne, 5 March 1804, PRO, IIO 43.14, pp. 434–5.

15. *Aris's Birmingham Gazette*, 6 October 1800; and ibid., 3 November 1800 for a handbill beginning: "Vive la Republic!"

16. PRO, IIO 42.51, fos. 166–8.

17. A. Boyer, *Political State of Great Britain*, vol. XL (1730), pp. 439, 497–9, 505–15, 590–93, 600; Samuel Seyer, *Memoirs Historical and Topographical of Bristol and its Neighbourhood, Bristol*, 1823, vol. II, pp. 578–9; J. P. Malcolm, *Anecdotes of the Manners and Customs of London during the Eighteenth Century*, 1810, vol. 1, pp. 145–6; LG, 17–21 November 1730.

18. Boyer, op. cit., vol. XLI (1731), p. 83.

19. Ibid., vol. XXXX, p. 508. A barber and former chandler was taken in custody on suspicion of being the author.

20. Several were tried at Bristol Assizes in March 1731, but all were acquitted for want of evidence. In 1738 the offences in Bristol appear to have resumed: Boyer, op. cit., vol. XLI, pp. 309–10; vol. LV (1738), p. 179.

21. See itemization of reward payments in PRO, T53.36, fos. 58–64, 65–7.

22. Ibid. and Boyer, op. cit., vol. XLI, p. 310.

23. Ibid., vol. XL, p. 506. Plain blackmail, supported by murderous threats, was of course known previously: indeed, men had been hanged for it in the 1720s (see p. 405). Possibly the incendiary threat was thought to be novel.

24. Boyer, op. cit., vol. XLI, pp. 90–91, reprinted from *Norwich Gazette*. The top of Christ Church spire was 309 feet from the ground: the author further warned the recipient not to station any watch on the weathercock.

25. For an example of such an affair which did come to light, see University of Nottingham, Manvers Coll. B 92. Here the Vicar of Edwinstowe (Notts.), who in 1824 had dismissed a Mr. Clark from his service, appears to have been blackmailed by an associate of Mr. Clark's who wrote: "I saw Mrs. Clark and you com out of the kitching and both go into the privy together and when you had dun what you whent for come out." But since the author did not ask for money but only for "your answer" he could not be prosecuted for felony.

26. *LG* 11538 (February 1775). Each *Gazette* was dated over a three- or four-day period, so that it is simpler to identify them by number rather than date. The date given in brackets indicates the month in which the letter was first sent, which was sometimes a few weeks before it was published in the *Gazette*. From 1785 onwards each year of the *Gazette* was paginated consecutively: Handover, op. cit., p. 59.

27. *LG* 10282 (January 1763).

28. *LG* 9971 (January 1760).

29. *LG* 10282 (January 1763).

30. *LG* 10392 (February 1764).

31. See Cal Winslow, above, pp. 154–6. A Hackney surgeon received a letter commencing: "Mr. toulmin this comes from a bloody gang of smuglers being lowe in cash and losing 3 horses within a fortnight therefore by god sir we insist upon your sending us 20 guineas. . . .": *LG* 12118 (September 1780).

32. *LG* 11128 (March 1771).

33. *LG* 11521 (December 1774).

34. See e.g. *LG* 12095 (June 1780), 12107 (August 1780).

35. See *C7* vol. XX. pp. 156–7 (February 1723).

36. *LG* 11793 (August 1776).

37. *LG* 11731 (December 1776).

38. *LG* 16341 (January 1810): see also 15017 (March 1798).

39. *LG* 16341 (February 1810).

40. *LG* 11569 (June 1775).

41. PRO, HO 42.27, fo. 722.

42. e.g. *LG* 9327 (October 1753). Archdeacon Robert Oliver of Preston was told that he "and havery Clergymans that his in this Town" were "Nothing but Heriticks and damned Souls if William Whittle that Worthy Man Angs up 10 dayes you may fully Expect to be blown to Damnation": *LG* 10616 (April 1766).

43. *R.* v. *Girdwood*, 1 Leach 142.

44. Norwich, *LG* 10690 (December 1766): see also *R* v. *Royce*, 4 Burr. 2073; Halifax, *LG* 11038 (April 1770); Staffordshire and Nottingham, *LG* 1800, p. 475 (May 1800).

45. *LG* 10720 (April 1767).

46. *LG* 10713 (March 1767); WO 1.873.

47. For documents illustrating the long conflict of the Spitalfields silk workers, see *Calendar of Home Office Papers of the Reign of George III*, 1878, vol. 1, pp. 312–13, vol. III, pp. 273–4, vol. IV, pp. 39–43.

48. *LG* 11136 and 11138 (April 1771). The first Spitalfields letter to be gazetted is in no. 10354 (October 1763).

49. A large parcel of such anonymous communications received by Robert Harley, the Earl of Oxford, in the first decades of the eighteenth century can be found in Brit. Mus. Portland Loan 29.11.

50. *LG* 10724 (April 1767).

51. *LG* 1811, p. 1760 (September 1811).

52. D.J.V. Jones in *Before Rebecca* 1973, p. 99, quotes excellent examples of these (sometimes decorated with sketches of red bulls etc.) within the context of the "Scotch Cattle" in the South Wales coal-and-iron "black domain"; and he comments (p. 100) on their extreme effectiveness in precipitating strikes, intimidating blacklegs, and so on. Very much the same effectiveness probably prevailed in the 1760s in the Spitalfields silk industry and in the West of England woollen industry around 1800. Such warnings (and occasionally those directed to gentry or employers) were sometimes accompanied by the hideous emphasis of blood-smears on the paper, a dead bird or beast on the doorstep, or even the heart of a slaughtered beast: see e.g., Yeovil, 1816, PRO, HO 42.150; E. P. Thompson, "The Moral Economy of the English Crowd in the Eighteenth Century," *Past and Present*, 50 (February 1971), p. 135.

53. The letters can be placed in the context defined so clearly by E. J. Hobsbawm in "The Machine Breakers," *Past and Present*, I (1952) and *Labouring Men*, 1963.

54. *LG* 10398 (February 1764).

55. *LG* 10287 and 10288 (February 1763).

56. *LG* 12854 (May 1787).

57. *LG* 13723 (October 1794).

58. e.g.*LG* 1785, p. 586 (December 1785); 12720 (January 1786); 1786, p. 203 (Glasgow weavers, April 1786); 1792, p. 191 (March 1792).

59. *LG* 1802, p. 386 (April 1802).

60. Good examples of Luddite letters can be found in W. B. Crump, *The Leeds Woollen Industry, 1780–1820*, Leeds, 1931, pp. 220–30 (the West Riding); J. Russell, "The Luddites," *Transactions*

of the Thoroton Society, x (1906), pp. 53–62 (Nottingham); E. P. Thompson, *The Making of the English Working Class*, Harmondsworth (1968), esp. pp. 607–8, 620, 626, 639, 643–4, 658, 784.

61. See e.g. *LG* 1802, p. 1047 (September 1802) listing offences committed in the disturbed district in the summer of 1802, including arson of ricks, interception of carts, and cutting up of cloth, firing of guns into houses, armed attacks upon gig-mills, destruction of machinery, and arson of buildings.

62. For the Ashill letter, see A. J. Peacock, *Bread or Blood*, 1965, pp. 65–6.

63. *LG* 10960 (July 1769); 10964 (July 1769); 11027 (March 1770).

64. *LG* 10287 (January 1763).

65. *LG* 12191 (May 1781).

66. *LG* 1795, p. 192 (December 1794).

67. Letter in QO/EW 51, East Sussex RO, cited in Monju Dutt, "The Agricultural Labourers' Revolt of 1830 in Kent, Surrey and Sussex," PhD Thesis, unpublished, London University, 1966, p. 375.

68. "Philalethes" [William Temple], *The Case as it now stands between the Clothiers, Weavers, and other Manufacturers, with regard to the late Riot in the County of Wilts*, 1739, p. 37.

69. Letter received by E. Lloyd Hall, 25 August 1843, in PRO, HO 45–454 (ii), fo. 468. See also H. T. Evans, *Rebecca and her Daughters*, Cardiff, 1910, pp. 34–5, 68–9, 194–5.

70. Cf. Raymond Williams, *The Country and the City*, 1973, pp. 184–5; on incendiary letters compare A. Abbiateci, *"Les Incendiaires dans la France du XVIIIᵉ Siècle, Annales E.S.C."*, xxv, (i) (January–February 1970), pp. 229–48.

71. PRO, SP 36.14 (i), fo. 125. See E. P. Thompson, *Whiggs and Hunters*, Allen Lane, 1975, chap. 10.

72. *LG* 9613 (August 1756). Such letters were certainly being written in the high-price years 1740 and 1753: see e.g. *Newcastle Journal*, 28 June 1740, reporting the committal of a man at Swaffham Bulbeck (Cambridgeshire) for sending an anonymous letter to a miller threatening to fire his mills if the price of flour did not fall; and for an example in 1753 see Newscastle papers, Brit. Mus. Add. MSS 32, 732, fo. 353.

73. *Calendar State Papers (Domestic)*, 1630, p. 387.

74. See "The Moral Economy of the English Crowd in the Eighteenth Century," *Past and Present*, 50 (February 1971), pp. 76–136, esp. the case from Sherborne (Dorset) examined on pp. 125–6.

75. For the place of such letters within the "theatre" and "counter theatre" of eighteenth-century society, see my "Patrician Society, Plebeian Culture," *Journal of Social History*, vol. 7, no. 4, Summer 1974, pp. 382–405.

76. Enclosure in PRO, WO 1.873, fos. 505–10; *LG* 10713 (March 1767).

77. *LG* 10710 (March 1767).

78. For Carlisle see, my "Moral Economy," op. cit., p. 99.

79. *LG* 10671 (October 1766) and 10690 (December 1766).

80. *LG* 10784 (November 1767)

81. James Bisset, "Reminiscences" (Birmingham Reference Library, MS 263924), pp. 74, 153–4. Compare W. Villers and others (Staffordshire magistrates in the neighbourhood of Birmingham) to Portland, 3 October 1800, PRO, HO 42.52, fos. 364–5: "Inscriptions are constantly making on the Walls and Public buildings exciting to revolt. The King's Proclamation posted up together with the Bills offering rewards for the discovery of the Authors of the seditious papers have been stain'd with a kind of paint resembling Blood . . ."

82. See Thompson, *The Making of the English Working Class*, p. 177.

83. *LG* 1800, p. 202 (February 1800).

84. *LG* 1800, p. 1308 (November 1800).

85. *LG* 1800, p. 1454 (December 1800).

86. Rev. Edward Meyrick to Portland, 12 June 1800 (and enclosure) PRO, HO 42.50. For the letter, see "Moral Economy," op. cit., p. 128.

87. See II Mod. Rep. 137, for *R. v. Woodward* (1707) and the judgement of Holt, C. J.: "every extortion is an actual trespass."

88. 9 Geo. I c. 22.

89. Under 12 Geo. I c. 34 (1727) workmen writing threatening letters to masters in the woollen industry were liable to seven years' transportation: this act was extended by 22 Geo. II c. 27 to workmen in the felt, hat, silk, mohair, fur, hemp, flax, linen, cotton, fustian, iron, or leather industries.

90. For the state of the law before repeal, see E. H. Hyde, *Treatise of Pleas of the Crown*, 1803, vol. II, pp. 1104–6; for the position at repeal, see Radzinowicz, vol. I, p. 641, and *The Charge of . . . Baron Vaughan . . . at the Special Commission at Winchester*, December 1830, pp. 13–14.

91. *PP*, 1819, VIII, pp. 125 et seq.

92. *PP*, 1826–7, XIX, pp. 187 et seq.; 1831–2, XIX; 1835, XLV. E. J. Hobsbawm and George Rude, *Captain Swing*, 1969, find (in 1830–31) forty-two names of men and women brought to trial from twenty-two counties for writing "Swing" letters. Thirteen only of these were convicted, of whom six were transported (p. 241).

93. In 1723, when the Black Act was passed, threatening messages were frequently sent in the disturbed areas of Berkshire and Hampshire: but I have found evidence of only two prosecutions. (See *Whigs and Hunters*, passim.) I have checked both the press and assize records in other periods of peak letter-writing (e.g. 1766–7, 1800) and have found scarcely any prosecutions. But evidence as to a continuing trickle of prosecutions is provided by case law: see East, op. cit., pp. 1104–26: e.g. Jepson and Springett's case (Essex, 1798), John Heming's case (Warwickshire, 1799).

94. *The Times*, 24 December 1830.

95. J. L. and B. Hammond, *The Village Labourer*, 1920 edn., pp. 271–2; *The Times*, 7 January 1831.

96. *Select Trials for Murder &c at the Old Bailey, 1734–5*, vol. II, pp. 31–4; the Ordinary's *Account*, 30 April 1725.

97. *Select Trials for Murder &c. at the Old Bailey*, vol. II, pp. 292–5.

98. For convictions in 1730–31, see above, p. 386; for the case of Girdler, above, p. 269. Peter Linebaugh notes a less amateurish blackmailer in Robert Brownjohn, for ten years a sailor, who boasted of having successfully sent a number of extortionary letters: he was executed in 1738: the Ordinary's *Account*, 8 March 1738 and *The Proceedings*, 13–16 January 1738.

99. Crown brief in PRO, TS 11.1070.5025.

100. See Keith Thomas, *Religion and the Decline of Magic*, 1971, esp. ch. 13, "Ancient Prophecies." This kind of "patter" continued well into the nineteenth century, as Mayhew testifies. Its adaptation to seditious purposes can be illustrated in a case from Bath, in 1797, when some journeymen shoemakers and a journeyman smith got into trouble for delivering inflammatory handbills at alehouses, accompanied by the "parole" (verbal patter): "that there was a Flat (meaning the King) between Two Sharps, who was Pitt and Dundas, and that the Rogue was taken in, for he had lost all his Money in the Bank of Venice": see J. Jeffreys to Portland, 11 August 1797, in PRO, HO 42.41. See also Birmingham handbill headed: "To Arms Countrymen

To Arms" (September 1800) and continuing: "Let the deep Pitt be made Level and all his bandette Beheaded. . . .": II0 42.52, fo. 363.

101. Crown brief in PRO, TS 11.460.1544.

102. "F. Singleton" (but in fact A. J. Peacock), "Captain Swing in East Anglia." *Bulletin of the Society for the Study of Labor History*, 8 (Spring 1964), pp. 13–15; *The Times* (citing *Suffolk Herald*), 23 December 1830.

103. I have had the advantage of seeing two excellent studies both of which deal with threatening letters in association with arson in East Anglia: A. J. Peacock, "Village Radicalism in East Anglia, 1800–1850," in J.P.D. Dunbadin, ed., *Rural Discontent in Nineteenth Century Britain*, 1974, and Julian Harber on incendiarism in Suffolk in the 1840s (unpublished). William Cornish of Gelderstone, who pleaded guilty to sending a threatening letter to a farmer who employed machinery in 1853, was recommended to mercy by the prosecution and received only two years' hard labour: *Norfolk Chronicle*, 23 July 1853.

104. Hobsbawm and Rudé, op. cit., pp. 131–2, 241, identify among accused "Swing" writers four labourers, a gardener, two schoolmasters, an attorney's clerk and a journeyman tailor said to be a "ranting" preacher. (The tailor was transported, but the schoolmasters and the attorney's clerk were acquitted: *The Times*, 22, 24 December 1830.) Peacock's letter-writers were mainly young labourers: Josiah How, a seventeen-year-old Huntingdonshire labourer, earning 5s. 1d. a week threatened his employer with arson in 1835 if he did not "behave better" to his labourers, and in 1844 Edmund Botwright, aged twenty-two, left a letter by the scene of a fire: "You bluddy farmers could not live if it was not for the poore, tis them that keeps you bluddy raskells alive." Harber identifies Samuel Stow, a thirty-one-year-old labourer (and poacher) of Polestead, Suffolk, transported for ten years (in 1845) for a threatening letter. Hobsbawm and Rudé (op. cit., p. 241) identify five women indicted for the offence in 1830–31; I have noted only two cases of female offenders prosecuted in the eighteenth century.

105. *The Times*, 21 December 1830. During the Cardiganshire "War of the Little Englishman" against enclosure in the 1820s, the authorities suspected that the author of anonymous letters was James Morris "formerly a Clergyman of the Established Church, but deprived of that dignity, thro' ill conduct; he keeps a School for the education of Children in the Neighborhood, and wanders from Cottage to Cottage for his Meals: he is one of the most troublesome Trespassers": D.J.V. Jones, "More Light on "Rhyfel y Sais Bach,' "*Ceredigion*, IV (1965), pp. 88–9.

106. *The Times*, 22 December 1830; J. L. and B. Hammond, op. cit., p. 286.

107. See J. R. Goody, ed., *Literacy in Traditional Societies*, Cambridge, 1968, pp. 13–17.

108. PRO, Assi 5.44 (ii); *Whigs and Hunters*, ch. 3.

109. Edward Milward, Mayor of Hastings, to Portland, 1 May 1795, PRO, HO 42.34. The letter is annotated. "Leigh is a member of L.C.S. [London Corresponding Society] & was distributing the publications of Eaton &c &c." See also HO 43.6, pp. 344, 402, and HO 42.52, fos. 304–5.

110. For Baker, see E. Moir, *Local Government in Gloucestershire, 1775–1800: a study of the justices of the peace*, Bristol and Gloucestershire Archaeological Society Records, vol. VIII, 1969, pp. 145, 150–51.

111. Portland's endorsement of the letter from Baker is more terse: "If the Writer of the Hand Bill can be *frightened* out of the Country the best way of preventing disturbance then almost seems to be . . . [rest illegible]."

112. Baker to Portland, n.d. (October 1795), PRO, HO 42.36; Portland to Baker 22 October, 1795, HO 43.7, pp. 219–20.

113. Informations and draft indictment exist in a transcript copy of "papers relating to the Stogursey

riots 1794–1801 in the possession of Lord St. Audries." This transcript is kept by the Vicar of Stogursey, to whom I am indebted for permission to quote from it.

114. Baker to Portland, 17 August 1800, PRO, HO 42.50; Portland to Baker, 24 August 1800, HO 43.12, p. 78.

115. *LG*, 1800, pp. 814, 1120–21; W. Baker to Portland, 12, 18 September 1800, PRO, HO 42.51.

116. *LG*, 1800, p. 202 (February 1800); G. J. Fort to W. Hussey, Esq., MP, 19 February 1800, PRO, HO 42.49. Another case which had been before Portland was that of barns etc. fired at Odiham (Hants.), on the land of a tenant of Sir H. P. St. John Mildmay, followed a week later by a furious letter claiming responsibility and threatening further actions: the Vicar of Odiham suspected (on the evidence of handwriting) "a man of a very fair character—employed by most of the farmers, & sufficiantly opulent not to feel the pressure of the present scarcity very severely": *LG*, 1800, p. 248; letters of Mildmay and of the Rev. J. W. Beadon in HO 42.49. Other examples of letters directly associated with arson or riot include Wedmore (Somerset) 2 April, Lewes, 17 April, Nottingham, 25 April 1800 (all in HO 42.49); Wimborne (Dorset), 19 June, Taunton district, 31 July 1800 (HO 42.50); Blandford, 9 September 1800 (HO 42.51); Haverfordwest (HO 42.53), and others.

117. J. L and B. Hammond, op. cit., p. 286.

118. *LG* 12084 (April 1780).

119. See an early Welsh Nationalist letter in *LG* 11368 (July 1773).

120. *LG* 11956 (January 1779).

121. *LG* 1792, p. 953 (December 1792).

122. Letter to Mr Kirkby, Cotton Master, Ancoats, enclosed in Holt, 22 February 1812, PRO, HO 42.120.

123. *LG* 10671 (October 1766). In 1840 a Chartist in Gloucester sent a letter to the Marquess of Normanby which must have given the author much satisfaction: the letter threatened retaliation against all those involved in the trial of John Frost and his fellow insurgents at Monmouth: "Depend on it there shall be a glorious cor-de-main-come-e-fo it shall be a proper Chef-d'oeuvre with ec-la, depend on it ye are all number'd and mark'd out—are not the poor suffering beyond anything through your damnable poor laws and going to marry your rapacious Vic to a German rat to give him 100,000 a year. . . . If you stand Versus us it shall be such a time as those of ye whom may have the chance to escape to say its Sui-gen-e-vis. Can Miss Vic think she will ever prosper to Consummate her cannubialis state by shedding the blood of those poor creatures at Monmouth . . . ?" PRO, HO 40.57, fo. 13.

124. *LG* 11538 (January 1775).

125. *LG* 1800, p. 475 (May 1800).

126. *LG* 13805 (July 1795).

127. *LG* 1796, p. 45 (December 1795).

128. PRO, HO 42.27 cited in 'Moral Economy', op. cit., p. 102.

129. *LG* 1800, p. 1093 (September 1800).

130. *LG* 1800, p. 1455 (December 1800).

131. *LG* 1793, p. 292 (March 1793).

132. PRO, HO 42.121, cited in Thompson, op. cit., p. 68.

133. *LG* 15540 (December 1802).

134. *LG* 11133 (March 1771).

135. *LG* 15327 (January 1801).

136. *LG* 1801, p. 56 (December 1800).

137. *LG* 1800, p. 814 (July 1800). These letters were found in the parishes of Finchingfield, Old Samford, New Samford, and Great Bardfield.

138. The minister excused his reading through "personal fear": see Thos Ruggles to Portland, 24 June 1800, PRO, HO 42.50. When the letter was gazetted Ruggles asked for extra copies of the journal to put on the church doors in the disaffected villages: it was felt that the official *Ga*ʒ*ette* would have more effect than the notices of the local authorities: Ruggles to Portland, 6 July 1800, ibid.

139. *LG* 15349 (March 1801).

140. *LG* 15302 (October 1800).

141. *LG* 14033 (August 1797).

142. *Calendar State Papers* (*Domestic*), 1630, p. 387.

143. *LG* 1810, p. 632 (April 1810).

144. . . . As late as 1869 or 1870 John Wilson, the Primitive Methodist pitman who was to become an MP and leader of the Durham miners, found it necessary to conduct an anonymous underground propaganda in the attempt to organize the Haswell colliery. "Mysterious notes began to appear on the pulley frames and waggons . . . on pieces of paper about three inches square"; but according to Wilson's memory his notes incited to organization ("Arise and assert your manhood") and carried no threats: John Wilson,*Memories of a Labour Leader*, 1910, p. 223.

145. *LG* 1793, p. 926 (October 1793).

146. *LG* 15349 (March 1801).

147. *LG* 10366 (November 1763).

148. *LG* 9754 (October 1757). For "Prespetrenc" I read "Presbyterians."

149. *LG* 1798, p. 76 (January 1798).

150. R. J. White, *Waterloo to Peterloo*, 1957, pp. 40–41; F.M.L. Thompson, *English Landed Society in the Nineteenth Century*, 1963, p. 16.

151. *LG* 10779 (November 1767).

152. *LG* 1800, pp. 346–7 (March 1800).

153. It is exactly in servant-master relations of dependency, in which personal contacts are frequent and personal injustices are suffered against which protest is futile, that feelings of resentment or of hatred can be most violent and most personal. Even the prospering tradesman whose prosperity depends upon concealing his true feelings from his arrogant and time-wasting customers can suffer such feelings: Francis Place testifies to this in his autobiography, which is perhaps warmer on this point than on any point of general political rights: "I knew . . . that the most profitable part for me to follow was dancing attendance on silly people, to make myself acceptable to coxcombs, to please their whims, to have no opinion of my own . . . I knew well that to enable me to make money I must consent to submit to much indignity, and insolence, to tyranny and injustice. I had no choice between doing this and being a beggar, and I was resolved not to be a beggar. . . . In short, a man to be a good tailor, should be either a philosopher or a mean cringing slave whose feelings had never been excited to the pitch of manhood": *The Autobiography of Francis Place*, ed. Mary Thale, Cambridge, 1972, pp. 216–17.

154. The managing director of the ounty Fire Office (who had much experience to draw upon) also found that the intimate dependants of the propertied were those most likely to commit acts of arson and incendiary letter-writing. He advised his agents; during the "Swing" episode: "The *servants of the sufferer*, people in his employ and even confidence, and living on his land, and near the spot fired, are very frequently found to be capable of committing these acts. A slight,

a refusal, a supposed harshness, nay, even the gratification of an envious and malicious feeling are sufficient motives with some people of this class to do these acts. Some of the most persevering attempts at house burning that we have on record have been committed by servant girls." Circular headed "To Discover an Incendiary in the Country," 24 December 1830, PRO, HO, 40.25 cited in Radzinowicz, vol. 11, pp. 450–54.

THE RULE OF LAW

FROM *WHIGS AND HUNTERS: THE ORIGIN OF THE BLACK ACT*

W e might be wise to end here. But since readers of this study may be provoked to some general reflections upon the law and upon British traditions, perhaps we may allow ourselves the same indulgence.

From a certain traditional middle ground of national historiography the interest of this theme (the Black Act and its evolution) may be evident. But this middle ground is now being eroded, from at least two directions. On one hand the perspective within which British political and social historians have been accustomed to view their own history is, quite properly, coming under challenge. As the last imperial illusions of the twentieth century fade, so preoccupation with the history and culture of a small island off the coast of Europe becomes open to the charge of narcissism. The culture of constitutionalism which flowered here, under favoured conditions, is an episode too exceptional to carry any universal significance. If we judge it in terms of its own self-sufficient values we are imprisoned within its own parochialism.

Alternative perspectives must diminish the complacency of national historical preoccupation. If we see Britain within the perspective of the expansion of European capitalism, then the contest over interior rights and laws will be dwarfed when set beside the exterior record of slave-trading, of the East India Company, of commercial and military imperialism. Or, to take up a bright new conservative perspective, the story of a few lost common rights and of a few deer-stealers strung from the gallows is a paltry affair when set beside the accounts of mass repression of almost any day in the day-book of the twentieth century. Did a few foresters get a rough handling from partisan laws? What is that beside the norms of the Third Reich? Did the villagers of Winkfield lose access to the peat within Swinley Rails? What is that beside the liquidation of

From *Whigs and Hunters: The Origin of the Black Act* by E. P. Thompson (New York: Pantheon Books, 1975).

the *kulaks?* What is remarkable (we are reminded) is not that the laws were bent but the fact that there was, anywhere in the eighteenth century, a rule of law at all. To ask for greater justice than that is to display mere sentimentalism. In any event, we should adjust our sense of proportion; against the handfuls carried off on the cart to Tyburn (and smaller handfuls than have been carried off in Tudor times) we must see whole legions carried off by plague or dearth.

From these perspectives concern with the rights and wrongs at law of a few men in 1723 is concern with trivia. And the same conclusion may be reached through a different adjustment of perspective, which may coexist with some of the same arguments. This flourishes in the form of a sophisticated, but (ultimately) highly schematic Marxism which, to our surprise, seems to spring up in the footsteps of those of us in an older Marxist tradition. From this standpoint the law is, perhaps more clearly than any other cultural or institutional artifact, by definition a part of a "superstructure" adapting itself to the necessities of an infrastructure of productive forces and productive relations. As such, it is clearly an instrument of the de facto ruling class: it both defines and defends these rulers' claims upon resources and labour-power—it says what shall be property and what shall be crime—and it mediates class relations with a set of appropriate rules and sanctions, all of which, ultimately, confirm and consolidate existing class power. Hence the rule of law is only another mask for the rule of a class. The revolutionary can have no interest in law, unless as a phenomenon of ruling-class power and hypocrisy; it should be his aim simply to overthrow it. And so, once again, to express surprise at the Black Act or at partial judges is—unless as confirmation and illustration of theories which might easily be demonstrated without all this labour—simply to expose one's own naivety.

So the old middle ground of historiography is crumbling on both sides. I stand on a very narrow ledge, watching the tides come up. Or, to be more explicit, I sit here in my study, at the age of fifty, the desk and the floor piled high with five years of notes, xeroxes, rejected drafts, the clock once again moving into the small hours, and see myself, in a lucid instant, as an anachronism. Why have I spent these years trying to find out what could, in its essential structures, have been known without any investigation at all? And does it matter a damn who gave Parson Power his instructions; which forms brought "Vulcan" Gates to the gallows; or how an obscure Richmond publican managed to evade a death sentence already determined upon by the Law Officers, the First Minister, and the King?

I am disposed to think that it does matter; I have a vested interest (in five years of labour) to think it may. But to show this must involve evacuating received assumptions—that narrowing ledge of traditional middle ground—and moving out onto an even narrower theoretical ledge. This would accept, as it must, some part of the Marxist-structural critique; indeed, some parts of this study have confirmed the class-bound and mystifying functions of the law. But it would reject its ulterior reductionism and would modify its typology of superior and inferior (but determining) structures.

First, analysis of the eighteenth century (and perhaps of other centuries) calls in question the validity of separating off the law as a whole and placing it in some typological superstructure. The law when considered as institution (the courts, with their class theatre and class procedures) or as personnel (the judges, the lawyers, the Justices of the Peace) may very easily be assimilated to those of the ruling class. But all that is entailed in "the law" is not subsumed in these institutions. The law may also be seen as ideology, or as particular rules and sanctions which stand in a definite and active relationship (often a field of conflict) to social norms; and, finally, it may be seen simply in terms of its own logic, rules, and procedures—that is, simply *as law*. And it is not possible to conceive of any complex society without law.

We must labour this point, since some theorists today are unable to see the law except in terms of "the fuzz" setting about inoffensive demonstrators or cannabis-smokers. I am no authority on the twentieth century, but in the eighteenth century matters were more complex than that. To be sure I have tried to show, in the evolution of the Black Act, an expression of the ascendancy of a Whig oligarchy, which created new laws and bent old legal forms in order to legitimize its own property and status; this oligarchy employed the law, both instrumentally and ideologically, very much as a modern structural Marxist should expect it to do. But this is not the same thing as to say that the rulers had need of law, in order to oppress the ruled, while those who were ruled had need of none. What was often at issue was not property, supported by law, against no-property; it was alternative definitions of property-rights: for the landowner, enclosure—for the cottager, common rights; for the forest officialdom, "preserved grounds" for the deer; for the foresters, the right to take turfs. For as long as it remained possible, the ruled—if they could find a purse and a lawyer—would actually fight for their rights by means of law; occasionally the copyholders, resting upon the precedents of sixteenth-century law, could actually win a case. When it ceased to be possible to continue the fight at law, men still felt a sense of legal wrong: the propertied had obtained their power by illegitimate means.

Moreover, if we look closely into such an agrarian context, the distinction between law, on the one hand, conceived of as an element of "superstructure," and the actualities of productive forces and relations on the other hand, becomes more and more untenable. For law was often a definition of actual agrarian *practice*, as it had been pursued "time out of mind." How can we distinguish between the activity of farming or of quarrying and the rights to this strip of land or to that quarry? The farmer or forester in his daily occupation was moving within visible or invisible structures of law: this merestone which marked the division between strips; that ancient oak—visited by processional on each Rogation Day—which marked the limits of the parish grazing; those other invisible (but potent and sometimes legally enforceable) memories as to which parishes had the right to take turfs in this waste and which parishes had not; this written or unwritten custumal which decided how many stints on the common land and for whom—for copyholders and freeholders only, or for all inhabitants?

Hence "law" was deeply imbricated within the very basis of productive relations, which would have been inoperable without this law. And, in the second place, this law, as definition or as rules (imperfectly enforceable through institutional legal forms), was endorsed by norms, tenaciously transmitted through the community. There were alternative norms; that is a matter of course; this was a place, not of consensus, but of conflict. But we cannot, then, simply separate off all law as ideology, and assimilate this also to the state apparatus of a ruling class. On the contrary, the norms of foresters might reveal themselves as passionately supported values, impelling them upon a course of action which would lead them into bitter conflict—with "the law."

So we are back, once again, with *that* law: the institutionalized procedures of the ruling class. This, no doubt, is worth no more of our theoretical attention; we can see it as an instrument of class power *tout court*. But we must take even this formulation, and see whether its crystalline clarity will survive immersion in scepticism. To be sure, we can stand no longer on that traditional ground of liberal academicism, which offers the eighteenth century as a society of consensus, ruled within the parameters of paternalism and deference, and governed by a "rule of law" which attained (however imperfectly) towards impartiality. That is not the society which we have been examining; we have not observed a society of consensus; and we have seen the law being devised and employed, directly and instrumentally, in the imposition of class power. Nor can we accept a sociological refinement of the old view, which stresses the imperfections and partiality of the law, and its subordination to the functional requirements of socio-economic interest groups. For what we have observed is something more than the law as a pliant medium to be twisted this way and that by whichever interests already posses effective power. Eighteenth-century law was more substantial than that. Over and above its pliant, instrumental functions it existed in its own right, as ideology; as an ideology which not only served, in most respects, but which also legitimized class power. The hegemony of the eighteenth-century gentry and aristocracy was expressed, above all, not in military force, not in the mystifications of a priesthood or of the press, not even in economic coercion, but in the rituals of the study of the Justices of the Peace, in the quarter-sessions, in the pomp of Assizes and in the theatre of Tyburn.

Thus the law (we agree) may be seen instrumentally as mediating and re-inforcing existent class relations and, ideologically, as offering to these a legit-imation. But we must press our definitions a little further. For if we say that existent class relations were mediated by the law, this is not the same thing as saying that the law was no more than those relations translated into other terms, which masked or mystified the reality. This may, quite often, be true but it is not the whole truth. For class relations were expressed, not in any way one likes, but *through the forms of law*; and the law, like other institutions which from time to time can be seen as mediating (and masking) existent class relations (such as the Church or the media of communication), has its own characteristics, its own independent history and logic of evolution.

Moreover, people are not as stupid as some structuralist philosophers suppose them to be. They will not be mystified by the first man who puts on a wig. It is inherent in the especial character of law, as a body of rules and procedures, that it shall apply logical criteria with reference to standards of universality and equity. It is true that certain categories of person may be excluded from this logic (as children or slaves), that other categories may be debarred from access to parts of the logic (as women or, for many forms of eighteenth-century law, those without certain kinds of property), and that the poor may often be ex-cluded, through penury, from the law's costly procedures. All this, and more, is true. But if too much of this is true, then the consequences are plainly counterproductive. Most men have a strong sense of justice, at least with regard to their own interests. If the law is evidently partial and unjust, then it will mask nothing, legitimize nothing, contribute nothing to any class's hegemony. The essential precondition for the effectiveness of law, in its function as ide-ology, is that it shall display an independence from gross manipulation and shall seem to be just. It cannot seem to be so without upholding its own logic and criteria of equity; indeed, on occasion, by actually *being* just. And furthermore it is not often the case that a ruling ideology can be dismissed as a mere hypocrisy; even rulers find a need to legitimize their power, to moralize their functions, to feel themselves to be useful and just. In the case of an ancient historical formation like the law, a discipline which requires years of exacting study to master, there will always be some men who actively believe in their own procedures and in the logic of justice. The law may be rhetoric, but it need not be empty rhetoric. Blackstone's *Commentaries* represent an intellectual exercise far more rigorous than could have come from an apologist's pen.

I do not know what transcultural validity these reflections may have. But they are certainly applicable to England in the eighteenth century. Douglas

Hay, in a significant essay in *Albion's Fatal Tree*, has argued that the law assumed unusual pre-eminence in that century, as the central legitimizing ideology, displacing the religious authority and sanctions of previous centuries. It gave way, in its turn, to economic sanctions and to the ideology of the free market and of political liberalism in the nineteenth. Turn where you will, the rhetoric of eighteenth-century England is saturated with the notion of law. Royal absolutism was placed behind a high hedge of law; landed estates were tied together with entails and marriage settlements made up of elaborate tissues of law; authority and property punctuated their power by regular "examples" made upon the public gallows. More than this, immense efforts were made (and Hay has explored the forms of these) to project the image of a ruling class which was itself subject to the rule of law, and whose legitimacy rested upon the equity and universality of those legal forms. And the rulers were, in serious senses, whether willingly or unwillingly, the prisoners of their own rhetoric; they played the games of power according to rules which suited them, but they could not break those rules or the whole game would be thrown away. And, finally, so far from the ruled shrugging off this rhetoric as a hypocrisy, some part of it at least was taken over as part of the rhetoric of the plebeian crowd, of the "free-born Englishman" with his inviolable privacy, his *habeas corpus*, his equality before the law. If this rhetoric was a mask, it was a mask which John Wilkes was to borrow, at the head of ten thousand masked supporters.

So that in this island and in that century above all one must resist any slide into structural reductionism. What this overlooks, among other things, is the immense capital of human struggle over the previous two centuries against royal absolutism, inherited, in the forms and traditions of the law, by the eighteenth-century gentry. For in the sixteenth and seventeenth centuries the law had been less an instrument of class power than a central arena of conflict. In the course of conflict the law itself had been changed; inherited by the eighteenth-century gentry, this changed law was, literally, central to their whole purchase upon power and upon the means of life. Take law away, and the royal prerogative, or the presumption of the aristocracy, might flood back upon their properties and lives; take law away and the string which tied together their lands and marriages would fall apart. But it was inherent in the very nature of the medium which they had selected for their own self-defence that it could not be reserved for the exclusive use only of their own class. The law, in its forms and traditions, entailed principles of equity and universality which, perforce, had to be extended to all sorts and degrees of men. And since this was of necessity so, ideology could turn necessity to advantage. What had been devised by men of property as a defence against arbitrary power could be turned into service as an apologia for property in the face of the propertyless. And the apologia was serviceable up to a point: for these "propertyless," as we have seen, comprised multitudes of men and women who themselves enjoyed, in fact, petty property rights or agrarian use-rights whose definition was inconceivable without the forms of law. Hence the ideology of the great struck root in a soil, however shallow, of actuality. And the courts gave substance to the ideology by the scrupulous care with which, on occasion, they adjudged petty rights, and, on all occasions, preserved proprieties and forms.

We reach, then, not a simple conclusion (law = class power) but a complex and contradictory one. On the one hand, it is true that the law did mediate existent class relations to the advantage of the rulers; not only is this so, but as the century advanced the law became a superb instrument by which these rulers were able to impose new definitions of property to their even greater advantage, as in the extinction by law of indefinite agrarian use-rights and in the furtherance of enclosure. On the other hand, the law mediated these class relations through legal forms, which imposed, again and again, inhibitions upon the actions of the rulers. For there is a very large difference, which twentieth-century experience ought to have made clear even to the most exalted thinker, between arbitrary extra-legal power and the rule of law. And not only were the rulers (indeed, the ruling class as a whole) inhibited by their own rules of law against the exercise of direct unmediated force (arbitrary imprisonment, the employment of troops against the crowd, torture, and those other conveniences of power with which we are all conversant), but they also believed enough in these rules, and in their accompanying ideological rhetoric, to allow in certain limited areas, the law itself to be a genuine forum within which certain kinds of class conflict were fought out. There were even occasions (one recalls John Wilkes and several of the trials of the 1790s) when the Government itself retired from the courts defeated. Such occasions served, paradoxically, to consolidate power, to enhance its legitimacy, and to inhibit revolutionary movements. But, to turn the paradox around, these same occasions served to bring power even further within constitutional controls.

The rhetoric and the rules of a society are something a great deal more than sham. In the same moment they may modify, in profound ways, the behaviour of the powerful, and mystify the powerless. They may disguise the true realities of power, but, at the same time, they may curb that power and check its intrusions. And it is often from within that very rhetoric that a radical critique of the practice of the society is developed: the reformers of the 1790s appeared, first of all, clothed in the rhetoric of Locke and of Blackstone.

These reflections lead me on to conclusions which may be different from those which some readers expect. I have shown in this study a political oligarchy inventing callous and oppressive laws to serve its own interests. I have shown judges who, no less than bishops, were subject to political influence, whose sense of justice was humbug, and whose interpretation of the laws served only to enlarge their inherent class bias. Indeed, I think that this study has shown that for many of England's governing elite the rules of law were a nuisance, to be manipulated and bent in what ways they could; and that the allegiance of such men as Walpole, Hardwicke, or Paxton to the rhetoric of law was largely humbug. But I do not conclude from this that the rule of law itself was humbug. On the contrary, the inhibitions upon power imposed by law seem to me a legacy as substantial as any handed down from the struggles of the seventeenth century to the eighteenth, and a true and important cultural achievement of the agrarian and mercantile bourgeoisie, and of their supporting yeomen and artisans.

More than this, the notion of the regulation and reconciliation of conflicts through the rule of law—and the elaboration of rules and procedures which, on occasion, made some approximate approach towards the ideal—seems to me a cultural achievement of universal significance. I do not lay any claim as to the abstract, extra-historical impartiality of these rules. In a context of gross class inequalities, the equity of the law must always be in some part sham. Transplanted as it was to even more inequitable contexts, this law could become an instrument of imperialism. For this law has found its way to a good many parts of the globe. But even here the rules and the rhetoric have imposed some inhibitions upon the imperial power. If the rhetoric was a mask, it was a mask which Gandhi and Nehru were to borrow, at the head of a million masked supporters.

I am not starry-eyed about this at all. This has not been a star-struck book. I am insisting only upon the obvious point, which some modern Marxists have overlooked, that there is a difference between arbitrary power and the rule of law. We ought to expose the shams and inequities which may be concealed beneath this law. But the rule of law itself, the imposing of effective inhibitions upon power and the defence of the citizen from power's all-intrusive claims, seems to me to be an unqualified human good. To deny or belittle this good is, in this dangerous century when the resources and pretentions of power continue to enlarge, a desperate error of intellectual abstraction. More than this, it is a self-fulfilling error, which encourages us to give up the struggle against bad laws and class-bound procedures, and to disarm ourselves before power. It is to throw away a whole inheritance of struggle *about* law, and within the forms of law, whose continuity can never be fractured without bringing men and women into immediate danger.

In all of this I may be wrong. I am told that, just beyond the horizon, new forms of working-class power are about to arise which, being founded upon egalitarian productive relations, will require no inhibition and can dispense with the negative restrictions of bourgeois legalism. A historian is unqualified to pronounce on such utopian projections. All that he knows is that he can bring in support of them no historical evidence whatsoever. His advice might be: watch this new power for a century or two before you cut your hedges down.

I therefore crawl out onto my own precarious ledge. It is true that in history the law can be seen to mediate and to legitimize existent class relations. Its forms and procedures may crystallize those relations and mask ulterior injustice. But this mediation, through the forms of law, is something quite distinct from the exercise of unmediated force. The forms and rhetoric of law acquire a distinct identity which may, on occasion, inhibit power and afford some protection to the powerless. Only to the degree that this is seen to be so can law be of service in its other aspect, as ideology. Moreover, the law in both its aspects, as formal rules and procedures and as ideology, cannot usefully be analysed in the metaphorical terms of a superstructure distinct from an infrastructure. While this comprises a large and self-evident part of the truth, the rules and categories of law penetrate every level of society, effect vertical as well as horizontal definition of men's rights and status, and contribute to men's self-definition or sense of identity. As such law has not only been imposed *upon* men from above: it has also been a medium within which other social conflicts have been fought out. Productive relations themselves are, in part, only meaningful in terms of their definitions at law: the serf, the free labourer; the cottager with common rights, the inhabitant without; the unfree proletarian, the picket conscious of his rights; the landless labourer who may still sue his employer for assault. And if the actuality of the law's operation in class-divided societies has, again and again, fallen short of its own rhetoric of equity, yet the notion of the rule of law is itself an unqualified good.

This cultural achievement—the attainment towards a universal value—found one origin in Roman jurisprudence. The uncodified English common law offered an alternative notation of law, in some ways more flexible and unprincipled— and therefore more pliant to the "common sense" of the ruling class—in other ways more available as a medium through which social conflict could find expression, especially where the sense of "natural justice" of the jury could make itself felt. Since this tradition came to its maturity in eighteenth-century England, its claims should command the historian's interest. And since some part of the inheritance from this cultural moment may still be found, within greatly changed contexts, within the United States or India or certain African countries, it is important to re-examine the pretensions of the imperialist donor.

This is to argue the need for a general revaluation of eighteenth-century law, of which this study offers only a fragment. This study has been centered upon a bad law, drawn by bad legislators, and enlarged by the interpretations of bad judges. No defense, in terms of natural justice, can be offered for anything in the history of the Black Act. But even this study does not prove that all law as such is bad. Even this law bound the rulers to act only in the ways which its forms permitted; they had difficulties with these forms; they could not always override the sense of natural justice of the jurors; and we may imagine how Walpole would have acted, against Jacobites or against disturbers of Richmond Park, if he had been subject to no forms of law at all.

If we suppose that law is no more than a mystifying and pompous way in which class power is registered and executed, then we need not waste our labour in studying its history and forms. One Act would be much the same as another, and all, from the standpoint of the ruled, would be Black. It is because law *matters* that we have bothered with this story at all. And this is also an answer to those universal thinkers, impatient of all except the *longue durée*, who cannot be bothered with cartloads of victims at Tyburn when they set these beside the indices of infant mortality. The victims of smallpox testify only to their own poverty and to the infancy of medical science; the victims of the gallows are exemplars of a conscious and elaborated code, justified in the name of a universal human value. Since we hold this value to be a human good, and one whose usefulness the world has not yet outgrown, the operation of this code deserves our most scrupulous attention. It is only when we follow through the intricacies of its operation that we can show what it was worth, how it was bent, how it proclaimed values were falsified in practice. When we note Walpole harrying John Huntridge, Judge Page handing down his death sentences, Lord Hardwicke wrenching the clauses of his Act from their context, and Lord Mansfield compounding his manipulations, we feel contempt for men whose practice belied the resounding rhetoric of the age. But we feel contempt not because we are contemptuous of the notion of a just and equitable law but because this notion has been betrayed by its own professors. The modern sensibility which views this only within the perspectives of our own archipelagos of *gulags* and of *stalags*, for whose architects the very notion of the rule of law would be a criminal heresy, will find my responses over-fussy. The plebs of eighteenth-century England were provided with a rule of law of some sort, and they ought to have considered themselves lucky. What more could they expect?

In fact, some of them had the impertinence, and the imperfect sense of historical perspective, to expect justice. On the gallows men would actually complain, in their "last dying words," if they felt that in some particular the due forms of law had not been undergone. (We remember Vulcan Gates complaining that since he was illiterate he could not read his own notice of proclamation; and performing his allotted role at Tyburn only when he had seen the Sheriff's dangling chain.) For the trouble about law and justice, as ideal aspirations, is that they must pretend to absolute validity or they do not exist at all. If I judge the Black Act to be atrocious, this is not only from some standpoint in natural justice, and not only from the standpoint of those whom the Act oppressed, but also according to some ideal notion of the standards to which "the law," as regulator of human conflicts of interest, ought to attain. For "the law," a logic of equity, must always seek to transcend the inequalities of class power which, instrumentally, it is harnessed to serve. And "the law" as ideology, which pretends to reconcile the interests of all degrees of men, must always come into conflict with the ideological partisanship of class.

We face, then, a paradox. The work of sixteenth-and seventeenth-century jurists, supported by the practical struggles of such men as Hampden and Lilburne, was passed down as a legacy to the eighteenth century, where it gave rise to a vision, in the minds of some men, of an ideal aspiration towards universal values of law. One thinks of Swift or of Goldsmith, or, with more qualifications, of Sir William Blackstone or Sir Michael Foster. If we today have ideal notions of what law might be, we derive them in some part from that cultural moment. It is, in part, in terms of that age's own aspiration that we judge the Black Act and find it deficient. But at the same time this same century, governed as it was by the forms of law, provides a text-book illustration of the employment of law, as instrument and as ideology, in serving the interests of the ruling class. The oligarchs and the great gentry were content to be subject to the rule of law only because this law was serviceable and afforded to their hegemony the rhetoric of legitimacy. This paradox has been at the heart of this study. It was also at the heart of eighteenth-century society. But it was also a paradox which that society could not in the end transcend, for the paradox was held in equipoise upon an ulterior equilibrium of class forces. When the struggles of 1790–1832 signalled that this equilibrium had changed, the rulers of England were faced with alarming alternatives. They could either dispense with the rule of law, dismantle their elaborate constitutional structures, countermand their own rhetoric and exercise power by force; or they could submit to their own rules and surrender their hegemony. In the campaign against Paine and the printers, in the Two Acts (1795), the Combination Acts (1799–1800), the repression of Peterloo (1819), and the Six Acts (1820) they took halting steps in the first direction. But in the end, rather than shatter their own self-image and repudiate 150 years of constitutional legality, they surrendered to the law. In this surrender they threw retrospective light back on the history of their class, and retrieved for it something of its honour; despite Walpole, despite Paxton, despite Page and Hardwicke, that rhetoric had not been altogether sham.

III

History and Theory

HISTORICAL LOGIC

FROM *The Poverty of Theory and Other Essays*

There will now be a brief intermission. You may suppose that the lights have been turned up and the ushers are advancing with trays of ice-cream. During this intermission I intend to discuss historical logic. Philosophers or sociologists who have a dislike or a profound disbelief in this subject are advised to withdraw to the foyer and the bar. They may rejoin us later.

It is not easy to discuss this theme. Not very long ago, when I was in Cambridge as a guest at a seminar of distinguished anthropologists, when I was asked to justify a proposition, I replied that it was validated by "historical logic." My courteous hosts dissolved into undisguised laughter. I shared in the amusement, of course; but I was also led to reflect upon the "anthropological" significance of the exchange. For it is customary within the rituals of the academy for the practitioners of different disciplines to profess respect, not so much for the findings of each other's discipline, as for the authentic credentials of that discipline itself. And if a seminar of historians were to laugh at a philosopher's or anthropologist's very *credentials* (that is, the logic or discipline central to their practice), this would be regarded as an occasion for offence. And the significance of this exchange was that it was very generally supposed that "history" was an exception to this rule; that the discipline central to its practice was an occasion for laughter; and that, so far from taking offence, I, as a practitioner, would join in the laughter myself.

It is not difficult to see how this comes about. The modes of historical writing are so diverse; the techniques employed by historians are so various; the themes of historical enquiry are so disparate; and, above all, the conclusions are so controversial and so sharply contested within the profession, that it is difficult to adduce any disciplinary coherence. And I can well see that there are things

From *The Poverty of Theory and Other Essays* by E. P. Thompson (New York: Monthly Review Press, 1978).

within the Cambridge School of History which might occasion anthropological, or other, laughter. Nevertheless, the study of history is a very ancient pursuit, and it would be surprising if, alone among the sciences and humanities, it had failed to develop its own discipline over several thousand years: that is, its own proper discourse of the proof. And I cannot see what this proper discourse is unless it takes the form of historical logic.

This is, I will argue, a *distinct* logic, appropriate to the historian's materials. It cannot usefully be brought within the same criteria as those of physics, for the reasons adduced by Popper and many others: thus, "history" affords no laboratory for experimental verification, it affords evidence of necessary causes but never (in my view) of sufficient causes, the "laws" (or, as I prefer it, logic or pressures) of social and economic process are continually being broken into by contingencies in ways which would invalidate any rule in the experimental sciences, and so on. But these reasons are not objections to historical logic, nor do they enforce (as Popper supposes) the imputation of "historicism" upon any notion of history as the record of a unified process with its own "rationality." They simply illustrate (and, on occasion, more helpfully, define) the conclusion that historical logic is not the same as the disciplinary procedures of physics.

Nor can historical logic be subjected to the same criteria as analytic logic, the philosopher's discourse of the proof. The reasons for this lie, not in historians' lack of logic, as in their need for a different *kind* of logic, appropriate to phenomena which are always in movement, which evince—even in a single moment—contradictory manifestations, whose particular evidences can only find definition within particular contexts, and yet whose general terms of analysis (that is, the questions appropriate to the interrogation of the evidence) are rarely constant and are, more often, in transition alongside the motions of the historical event: as the object of enquiry changes so do the appropriate questions. As Sartre has commented: "History is not order. It is disorder: a rational disorder. At the very moment when it maintains order, i.e. structure, history is already on the way to undoing it."[1]

But disorder of this kind is disruptive of any procedure of analytic logic, which must, as a first condition, handle unambiguous terms and hold them steadily in a single place. We have already noted a propensity in philosophers, when scrutinising "history's" epistemological credentials, to place "facts" as isolates upon their table, instead of the historians' customary materials—the evidence of behaviour (including mental, cultural behaviour) eventuating through time. When Althusser and many others accuse historians of having "no theory," they should reflect that what they take to be innocence or lethargy may be explicit and self-conscious *refusal*: refusal of static analytic concepts, of logic inappropriate to history.

By "historical logic" I mean a logical method of enquiry appropriate to historical materials, designed as far as possible to test hypotheses as to structure, causation, etc., and to eliminate self-confirming procedures ("instances", "illustrations"). The disciplined historical discourse of the proof consists in a dialogue between concept and evidence, a dialogue conducted by successive hypotheses, on the one hand, and empirical research on the other. The interrogator is historical logic; the interrogative a hypothesis (for example, as to the way in which different phenomena acted upon each other); the respondent is the evidence, with its determinate properties. To name this logic is not, of course, to claim that it is always evidenced in every historian's practice, or in any historian's practice all of the time. (History is not, I think, unique in failing to maintain its own professions.) But it is to say that this logic does not disclose itself involuntarily; that the discipline requires arduous preparation; and that three thousand years of practice have taught us something. And it is to say that it is this logic which constitutes the discipline's ultimate court of appeal: *not*, please note, "the evidence," by itself, but the evidence interrogated thus.

To define this logic fully—and to reply to certain of Popper's objections— would require writing a different, and more academic, essay, with many instances and illustrations. In addressing myself more particularly to the positions of Althusser it may be sufficient to offer, in defence of historical materialism, certain propositions.

1) The immediate object of historical knowledge (that is, the materials from which this knowledge is adduced) is comprised of "facts" or evidences which certainly have a real existence, but which are only knowable in ways which are and ought to be the concern of vigilant historical procedures. This proposition we have already discussed.

2) Historical knowledge is in its nature, a) provisional and incomplete (but not therefore untrue), b) selective (but not therefore untrue), c) limited and defined by the questions proposed to the evidence (and the concepts informing those questions) and hence only "true" within the field so defined. In these respects historical knowledge may depart from other paradigms of knowledge, when subjected to epistemological enquiry. In this sense I am ready to agree that the attempt to designate history as a "science" has always been unhelpful and confusing.[2] If Marx and, even more, Engels sometimes fell into this error, then we may apologise, but we should not confuse the claim with their actual procedures. Marx certainly knew, also, that History was a Muse, and that the "humanities" construct knowledges.

3) Historical evidence has determinate properties. While any number of questions may be put to it, only certain questions will be appropriate. While any theory of historical process may be proposed, all theories are false which are not in conformity with the evidence's determinations. Herein lies the disciplinary court of appeal. In this sense it is true (we may agree here with Popper)

that while historical knowledge must always fall short of positive proof (of the kinds appropriate to experimental science), false historical knowledge is generally subject to *dis*proof.[3]

4) It follows from these propositions that the relation between historical knowledge and its object cannot be understood in any terms which suppose one to be a function (inference from, disclosure, abstraction, attribution or "illustration") of the other. Interrogative and response are mutually determining, and the relation can be understood only *as a dialogue*.

Four further propositions may now be presented at greater length.

5) The object of historical knowledge is "real" history whose evidences must necessarily be incomplete and imperfect. To suppose that a "present," by moving into a "past," thereby changes its ontological status is to misunderstand both the past and the present.[4] The palpable reality of our own (already-passing) present can in no way be changed because it is, *already*, becoming the past for posterity. To be sure, posterity cannot interrogate it in all the same ways; to be sure, you and I, as experiencing instants and actors within our present, will survive only as certain evidences of our acts or thoughts.

While historians may take a decision to select from this evidence, and to write a history of discrete aspects of the whole (a biography, the history of an institution, a history of fox-hunting, etc.), the real object remains unitary. The human past is not an aggregation of discrete histories but a unitary sum of human behaviour, each aspect of which was related in certain ways to others, just as the individual actors were related in certain ways (by the market, by relations of power and subordination, etc.). Insofar as these actions and relations gave rise to changes, which become the object of rational enquiry, we may define this sum as historical *process*: that is, *practices* ordered and structured in rational ways. While this definition arrives in response to the question asked,[5] this does not "invent" process. We must take our stand here, against Goldmann, and with Bloch. The finished processes of historical change, with their intricate causation, actually occurred, and historiography may falsify or misunderstand, but can't in the least degree modify the past's ontological status. The objective of the historical discipline is the attainment of that history's truth.

Each age, or each practitioner, may propose new questions to the historical evidence, or may bring new levels of evidence to light. In this sense "history" (when considered as the products of historical enquiry) will change, and ought to change, with the preoccupations of each generation, or, as it may be, each sex, each nation, each social class. But this by no means implies that the past events themselves change with each questioner, or that the evidence is indeterminate. Disagreements between historians may be of many kinds, but they remain as mere exchanges of attitude, or exercises of ideology, unless it is agreed that they are conducted within a common discipline whose pursuit is objective knowledge.

To this proposition it is necessary to add a rider. When we speak of the "intelligibility" of history, we may mean the understanding of the rationality (of causation, etc.) of historical process: this is an objective knowledge, disclosed in a dialogue with determinate evidence. But we may also imply the "significance" of that past, its meaning *to us*; this is an evaluative and subjective judgement, and to such interrogatives the evidence can supply no answers. This does not entail the conclusion that any such exercise is improper. We may agree (with Popper) that each generation, each historian, is entitled to express a "point of view," or (with Kolakowski) that we are entitled to attribute such "immanent intelligibility" to history as an "act of faith," provided that we are clear that this rests, not upon scientific procedures, but upon a "choice of values."[6]

We may agree not only that such judgements as to the "meaning" of history are a proper and important activity, a way in which today's actors identify their values and their goals, but that it is also an *inevitable* activity. That is, the preoccupations of each generation, sex, or class must inevitably have a normative content, which will find expression in the questions proposed to the evidence. But this in no way calls in question the objective determinacy of the evidence. It is simply a statement as to the complexity, not just of history, but of ourselves (who are simultaneously valuing and rational beings)—a complexity which enters into all forms of social self-knowledge, and which requires in all disciplines procedural safeguards. It is, exactly, within historical logic that such attributions of meaning, if covert and improper, are exposed; it is in this way that historians find each other out. A feminist historian will say, or ought to say, that this history-book is wrong, not because it was written by a man, but because the historian neglected contiguous evidence or proposed conceptually-inadequate questions: hence a masculine "meaning" or bias was imposed upon the answers. It is the same with the somewhat intemperate arguments which I and my Marxist colleagues often provoke within the academic profession. The appeal is not (or is rarely) to a choice of values, but to the logic of the discipline. And if we deny the determinate properties of the object, then no discipline remains.

But I cannot leave this rider while giving the impression that the attribution of "meaning," as valued-significance, is only a matter for regret, a consequence of human fallibility. I think it to be greatly more important than that. I am not in the least embarrassed by the fact that, when presenting the results of my own historical research, I offer value judgements as to past process, whether openly and strenuously, or in the form of ironies or asides. This is proper, in one part, because the historian is examining individual lives and choices, and not only historical eventuation (process). And while we may not attribute value to process, the same objections do not arise with the same force when we are considering the choices of individuals, whose acts and intentions may certainly be judged (as they were judged by contemporaries) within the due and relevant historical context.

But this is only a special case of a more general question. Only we, who are now living, can give a "meaning" to the past. But that past has always been, among other things, the result of an argument about values. In recovering that process, in showing how causation actually eventuated, we must, insofar as the discipline can enforce, hold our own values in abeyance. But once this history has been recovered, we are at liberty to offer our judgement upon it.

Such judgement must itself be under historical controls. The judgement must be appropriate to the materials. It is pointless to complain that the bourgeoisie have not been communitarians, or that the Levellers did not introduce an anarcho-syndicalist society. What we may do, rather, is identify with certain values which past actors upheld, and reject others. We may give our vote for Winstanley and for Swift; we may vote against Walpole and Sir Edwin Chadwick.

Our vote will change nothing. And yet, in another sense, it may change everything. For we are saying that these values, and not those other values, are the ones which make this history meaningful *to us*, and that these are the values which we intend to enlarge and sustain in our own present. If we succeed, then we reach back into history and endow it with our own meanings: we shake Swift by the hand. We endorse in our present the values of Winstanley, and ensure that the low and ruthless kind of opportunism which distinguished the politics of Walpole is abhorred.

In the end we also will be dead, and our own lives will lie inert within the finished process, our intentions assimilated within a past event which we never intended. What we may hope is that the men and women of the future will reach back to us, will affirm and renew our meanings, and make our history intelligible within their own present tense. They alone will have the power to select from the many meanings offered by our quarrelling present, and to transmute some part of our process into their progress.

For "progress" is a concept either meaningless or worse, when imputed as an attribute *to* the past (and such attributions may properly be denounced as "historicist"), which can only acquire a meaning from a particular position in the present, a position of value in search of its own genealogy. Such genealogies *exist*, within the evidence: there have been men and women of honour, courage, and "foresight," and there have been historical movements informed by these qualities. But in spite of Goldmann's authority, we must argue, not that "historical reality changes from epoch to epoch with modifications in the hierarchy of values," but that the "meaning" which we attribute to that reality changes in this way.

The "rider" to my proposition has taken us a little out of our way. The proposition concerned the objectivity of "real" history. We seem to return, again and again, to the narrowing circuits of this epistemological whirlpool. Let us try to advance.

6) The investigation of history as process, as eventuation or "rational disorder," entails notions of causation, of contradiction, of mediation, and of the systematic organisation (sometimes structuring) of social, political, economic and intellectual life. These elaborate notions[7] "belong" within historical theory, are refined within this theory's procedures, are thought within thought. But it is untrue that they belong *only* within theory. Each notion, or concept, arises out of empirical engagements, and however abstract the procedures of its self-interrogation, it must then be brought back into an engagement with the determinate properties of the evidence, and argue its case before vigilant judges in history's "court of appeal." It is, and in a most critical sense, a question of dialogue once more. In the sense that a thesis (the concept, or hypothesis) is brought into relation with its antithesis (atheoretical objective determinacy) and a synthesis (historical knowledge) results we might call this the dialectics of historical knowledge. Or we might have done so, before "dialectics" was rudely snatched out of our grasp and made into the plaything of scholasticism.

Historical practice is above all engaged in this kind of dialogue; with an argument between received, inadequate, or ideologically-informed concepts or hypotheses[8] on the one hand, and fresh or inconvenient evidence on the other; with the elaboration of new hypotheses; with the testing of these hypotheses against the evidence, which may involve interrogating existing evidence in new ways, or renewed research to confirm or disprove the new notions; with discarding those hypotheses which fail these tests, and refining or revising those which do, in the light of this engagement.

Insofar as a notion finds endorsement from the evidence, then one has every right to say that it *does* exist, "out there," *in* the real history. It does not of course actually exist, like some plasma adhering to the facts, or as some invisible kernel within the shell of appearances. What we are saying is that the notion (concept, hypothesis as to causation) has been brought into a disciplined dialogue with the evidence, and it has been shown to "work"; that is, it has not been *dis*proved by contrary evidence, and that it successfully organises or "explains" hitherto inexplicable evidence; hence it is an adequate (although approximate) representation of the causative sequence, or rationality, of these events, and it conforms (within the logic of the historical discipline) with a process which did in fact eventuate in the past. Hence it exists simultaneously both as a "true" knowledge and as an adequate representation of an actual property of those events.

7) Historical materialism differs from other interpretive orderings of historical evidence not (or not necessarily) in any epistemological premises, but in its categories, its characteristic hypotheses and attendant procedures,[9] and in the avowed conceptual kinship between these and the concepts elaborated by Marxist practitioners in other disciplines. I do not see Marxist historiography as being attendant *on* some general corpus of Marxism-as-theory, located somewhere else (perhaps in philosophy?). On the contrary, if there is a common ground for all Marxist practices then it must be where Marx located it himself, in historical materialism. This is the ground from which all Marxist theory arises, and to which it must return in the end.

In saying this, I am not saying that Marxist historians are not indebted for certain concepts to a general Marxist theory which extends itself towards, and draws upon the findings of, Marxists at work in other fields. This is evidently the case; our work goes on in a continual exchange. I am disputing the notion that this is a Theory, which has some Home, independently of these practices: a self-validating textual Home, or a Home in the wisdom of some Marxist party, or a Home in purified theoretical practice. The homeland of Marxist theory remains where it has always been, the real human object, in all its manifestations (past and present): which object however, cannot be known in one theoretical *coup d'oeil* (as though Theory could swallow reality in one gulp) but only through discrete disciplines, informed by unitary concepts. These disciplines or practices meet at each other's borders, exchange concepts, converse, correct each other's errors. Philosophy may (and must) monitor, refine, and assist the conversation. But let philosophy attempt to *abstract* the concepts from the practices, and build from them a Home for Theory independently of these, and far removed from any dialogue with theory's object, then we will have—the theatre of Althusser!

It follows that if Marxist concepts (that is, concepts developed by Marx and within the Marxist tradition) differ from other interpretive concepts in historical practice, and if they are found to be more "true," or adequate to explanation, than others, this will be because they stand up better to the test of historical logic, and not because they are "derived from" a true Theory outside this discipline. As, in any case, they were not. Insofar as I am myself deeply indebted for certain concepts to Marx's own practice, I refuse to evade responsibility by falling back upon his authority or to escape from criticism by leaping from the court of appeal. For historical knowledge, this court lies within the discipline of history and nowhere else.

Appeal may take two forms: a) evidential, which has been sufficiently discussed, and b) theoretical—to the coherence, adequacy, and consistency of the concepts, and to their congruence with the knowledge of adjacent disciplines. But both forms of appeal may be conducted only within the vocabulary of historical logic. The court has been sitting in judgement upon historical materialism for one hundred years, and it is continually being adjourned. The adjournment is in effect a tribute to the robustness of the tradition; in that long interval the cases against a hundred other interpretive systems have been upheld, and the culprits have disappeared "downstairs." That the court has not yet found decisively in favour of historical materialism is not only because of the ideological *parti pris* of certain of the judges (although there is plenty of that) but also because of the provisional nature of the explanatory concepts, the *actual* silences (or absent mediations) within them, the primitive and unreconstructed character of some of the categories, and the inconclusive determinacy of the evidence.

8) My final proposition brings a fundamental reservation to bear upon Althusserian epistemology, and also upon certain structuralisms or functional systems (e.g. Parsonian sociology) which periodically attempt to over-run the historical discipline. Certain critical categories and concepts employed by historical materialism can only be understood *as historical categories*: that is, as categories or concepts appropriate to the investigation of process, the scrutiny of "facts" which, even in the moment of interrogation, change their form (or retain their form but change their "meanings"), or dissolve into other facts; concepts appropriate to the handling of evidence not capable of static conceptual representation but only as manifestation or as contradiction.

The construction of historical concepts is not of course a special privilege peculiar to historical materialism. Such concepts arise within the historians' common discourse, or are developed within adjacent disciplines. The classic concept of the crisis of subsistence[10] proposes a rational sequence of events: as, for example, poor harvest $\rightarrow$ dearth $\rightarrow$ rising mortality $\rightarrow$ the consumption of next year's seed $\rightarrow$ a second poor harvest $\rightarrow$ extreme dearth $\rightarrow$ a peak in mortality, accompanied by epidemic $\rightarrow$ a sharply rising conception-rate. The concept of the familial development cycle proposes a particular three-generational sequence within the same peasant household, modified by the particular conditions of land tenure and inheritance practice. These concepts, which are generalised by logic from many examples, are brought to bear upon the evidence, not so much as "models" but rather as "expectations." They do not impose a rule, but they hasten and facilitate the interrogation of the evidence, even though it is often found that each case departs, in this or that particular, from the rule. The evidence (and the real event) is not rule-governed, and yet it could not be understood without the rule, to which it offers its own irregularities. This provokes impatience in some philosophers (and even sociologists) who consider that a concept with such elasticity is not a true concept, and a rule is not a rule unless the evidence conforms to it, and stands to attention in one place.

Historical concepts and rules are often of this order. They display extreme elasticity and allow for great irregularity; the historian appears to be evading rigour as he disappears into the largest generalisations at one moment, while at the next moment he disappears into the particularities of the qualifications in any special case. This provokes distrust, and even laughter, within other disciplines. Historical materialism employs concepts of equal generality and elasticity—"exploitation," "hegemony," "class struggle"—and as expectations rather than as rules. And even categories which appear to offer less elasticity—"feudalism," "capitalism," "the bourgeoisie"—appear in historical practice, not as ideal types fulfilled in historical evolution, but as whole families of special cases, families which include adopted orphans and the children of typological miscegenation. History knows no regular verbs.

It is the misfortune of Marxist historians (it is certainly our special misfortune today) that certain of our concepts are common currency in a wider intellectual universe, are adopted in other disciplines, which impose their own logic upon them and reduce them to static, a-historical categories. No historical category has been more misunderstood, tormented, transfixed, and de-historicised than the category of social class;[11] a self-defining historical formation, which men and women make out of their own experience of struggle, has been reduced to a static category, or an effect of an ulterior structure, of which men are not the makers but the vectors. Not only have Althusser and Poulantzas done Marxist history this wrong, but they then complain that history (from whose arms they abducted this concept) has no proper theory of class! What they, and many others, of every ideological hue, misunderstand is that it is not, and never has been, the business of history to make up this kind of inelastic theory. And if Marx himself had one supreme methodological priority it was, precisely, to destroy unhistorical theory-mongering of this kind.

History is not a factory for the manufacturer of Grand Theory, like some Concorde of the global air; nor is it an assembly-line for the production of midget theories in series. Nor yet is it some gigantic experimental station in which theory of foreign manufacture can be "applied," "tested," and "confirmed." That is not its business at all. Its business is to recover, to "explain," and to "understand" its object: real history. The theories which historians adduce are directed to this objective, within the terms of historical logic, and there is no surgery which can transplant foreign theories, like unchanged organs, into other, static, conceptual logics, or vice versa. Our objective is historical knowledge; our hypotheses are advanced to explain this particular social formation in the past, that particular sequence of causation.

Our knowledge (we hope) is not thereby imprisoned within that past. It helps us to know who we are, why we are here, what human possibilities have been disclosed, and as much as we can know of the logic and forms of social process. Some part of that knowledge may be theorised, less as rule than as expectation. And exchanges may and should take place with other knowledges and theories. But the exchange involves vigilance, as the theoretical coin of one discipline is translated into the currency of another. Philosophy ought not to stand on every frontier like a huckster, offering spurious "universal" bank-notes current in all lands. It might, instead, operate a watchful *bureau de change*.

Those propositions of historical materialism which bear upon the relation between social being and social consciousness, upon the relations of production and their determinations, upon modes of exploitation, class struggle, ideology, or upon capitalist social and economic formations, are (at one pole of their "dialogue") derived from the observation of historical eventuation *over time*. This observation is not of discrete fact seriatim but of *sets* of facts with their own regularities: of the repetition of certain kinds of event: of the congruence of certain kinds of behaviour within differing contexts: in short, of the evidences of systematic social formations and of a common logic of process. Such historical theories as arise (not of themselves, but, at the other pole of the dialogue, by arduous conceptualisation) can not be tested, as is often supposed, by calling a halt to process, "freezing" history, and taking a static geological section, which will show capitalism or class hierarchies at any given moment of time as an elaborated structure.[12] In investigating history we are not flicking through a series of "stills," each of which shows us a moment of social time transfixed into a single eternal pose: for each one of these "stills," is not only a moment of being but also a moment of becoming: and even within each seemingly-static section there will be found contradictions and liaisons, dominant and subordinate elements, declining or ascending energies. Any historical moment is both a result of prior process and an index towards the direction of its future flow.

There are well-known difficulties, both in explaining historical process and in verifying any explanation. "History" itself is the only possible laboratory for experiment, and our only experimental equipment is historical logic. If we press improper analogies with experimental sciences, we will soon find out that the whole business is unsatisfactory. History never affords the conditions for identical experiments; and while, by comparative procedures, we may observe somewhat similar experiments in different national laboratories (the rise of the nation state, industrialization) we can never reach back into those laboratories, impose our own conditions, and run the experiment through once again.

But such analogies have never been helpful. The fact that the difficulties of historical explanation are immense should surprise no-one. We inhabit the same element ourselves (a present becoming a past), a human element of habit, need, reason, will, illusion, and desire, and we should know it to be made up of obstinate stuff. And yet there is one sense in which the past improves upon the present, for "history" remains its own laboratory of process and eventuation. A static section may show us certain elements (A, B, and C) in mutual inter-relationship or contradiction; eventuation over time will show us how these relationships were lived through, fought out, resolved, and how ABC gave rise to D; and this eventuation will, in turn, throw light back upon the ways in which the elements were previously related and the strength of the contradiction.

In this sense the eventuation confirms or disproves, hardens or qualifies, the explanatory hypothesis. This is a bad laboratory in one sense: that the event took place in this way may be the consequence of some contingent element (X) overlooked in the explanation; thus ABC + X may have eventuated in one way (D), but ABC + Y would have eventuated differently (E); and to overlook this is to fall into the familiar error of arguing *post hoc ergo propter hoc*. This is a besetting problem of all historical explanation, and philosophers who have glanced at our procedures have made a hearty meal of it. But they overlook the fact that in another sense "history" is a good laboratory, because process, eventuation, is present within every moment of the evidence, testing every hypothesis in an outcome, providing results for every human experiment that has ever been conducted. Our logic is fallible. But the very multiplicity of experiments, and their congruence to each other, limit the dangers of error. The evidence as to any particular episode may be imperfect: there will be plenty of gaps when we consider eventuation in the form of discrete facts in series: but (at least in less distant history)[13] sufficient evidence survives to disclose the logic of this process, its outcome, the characteristic social formations, and how ABC in fact gave rise to D.

We may make this point more clear if we consider a problem, not from the past, but from the historical present. The Soviet Union is such a problem. In order to explain one aspect of this problem—who holds power and in what direction is political process tending?—a number of explanatory hypotheses are proposed. For example, the Soviet Union is a Workers' State (perhaps with certain "deformities") capable of ascendant self-development, without any severe internal struggle or rupture of continuity: all "short-comings" are capable of self-correction, owing to the guidance of a proletarian party, informed by Marxist Theory, and hence blessed with the "know-how" of history. Or the Soviet Union is a state in which power has fallen into the hands of a new bureaucratic class, whose interest it is to secure its own privileges and continued tenure of power—a class which will only be overthrown by another proletarian revolution. Or the Soviet State is the instrument of a historically-specific form of forced industrialization, which has thrown up an arbitrary and contingent collocation of ruling-groups, which may now be expected to be the agents of the "modernization" of Soviet society, bringing it into tardy and imperfect conformity with that true model of modern man: the United States. Or (which is closer to my own view) the Soviet State can only be understood with the aid of the concept of "parasitism," and whether or not its ruling groups harden into a bureaucratic *class*, or whether episodic reform can be imposed upon them by pressures of various kinds (from the needs and resistances of workers and farmers, from intellectual dissenters, and from the logic arising from their own inner contradictions, factional struggles, and incapacity to perform essential functions, etc.) remains, historically, an unfinished and indeterminate question, which may be precipitated into one or another more fully-determined direction by contingencies.

There is a real and important sense in which these (or other) hypotheses will only find confirmation or refutation in the *praxis* of eventuation. The experiment is still being run through, and (much as Althusser dislikes Engels's Mancunian colloquialism) "the proof of the pudding will be in the eating." The result, when brought within the scrutiny of future historians, may appear to confirm one hypothesis, or may propose a new hypothesis altogether. Any such "confirmation," if it should arise, can never be more than approximate: history is not rule-governed, and it knows no sufficient causes: and if future historians suppose otherwise they would be falling into the error of *post hoc ergo propter hoc*. The hypotheses, or the blend of ideology and of self-knowledge, which we, or the Soviet people, adopt in this present will themselves enter as an element within eventuating process. And if some different "contingency" had impinged upon these elements (for example, if a Third World War had arisen from the Cuba crisis), then all would have eventuated differently, the military and security forces would have been immensely strengthened, and a different hypothesis might then appear to have explanatory force.

But this is not as devastating a qualification as may at first appear. For it will be *as* matters eventuate, *as* the "experiment" works out, which will afford to future historians immense additional insight as to the critical relations structuring Soviet society, which underlie the appearances of our historical present. The "result" will afford to them additional insight into which formidable elements (perhaps the State ideology of Marxism-Leninism) were to prove, in the event, to be fragile and in decline, and which inarticulate, loosely-structured elements pre-figured an emergent opposition. The historians of the future, who will know *how* things turned out, will have a powerful aid to understanding, not why they *had* to turn out in that way, but why in fact they did: that is they will observe in the laboratory of events the evidence of determination, not in its sense as rule-governed law but in its sense of the "setting of limits" and the "exerting of pressures."[14] And today's historians stand in exactly the same position in relation to the historical past, which is, simultaneously, the object of investigation and its own experimental laboratory.

That historical explanation cannot deal in absolutes and cannot adduce sufficient causes greatly irritates some simple and impatient souls. They suppose that, since historical explanation cannot be All, it is therefore Nothing; it is no more than a consecutive phenomenological narration. This is a silly mistake. For historical explanation discloses not how history *must* have eventuated but why it eventuated in this way and not in other ways; that process is not arbitrary but has its own regularity and rationality; that certain kinds of event (political, economic, cultural) have been related, not in any way one likes, but in particular ways and within determinate fields of possibility; that certain social formations are—not governed by "law" nor are they the "effects" of a static structural theorem—but are characterised by determinate relations and by a particular logic of process. And so on. And a great deal more. Our knowledge may not satisfy some philosophers, but it is enough to keep us occupied.

We have left our eighth proposition behind, and we may now rehearse it once again. The categories appropriate to the investigation of history are historical categories. Historical materialism is distinguished from other interpretive systems by its stubborn consistency (alas, a stubbornness which has sometimes been doctrinaire) in elaborating such categories, and by its articulation of these within a conceptual totality. This totality is not a finished theoretical "truth" (or Theory); but neither is it a make-belief "model"; it is a developing *knowledge* albeit a provisional and approximate knowledge with many silences and impurities. The development of this knowledge takes place both within theory and within practice: it arises from a dialogue: and its discourse of the proof is conducted within the terms of historical logic. The actual operations of this logic do not appear, step by step, on every page of a historian's work; if they did, history books would exhaust all patience. But this logic should be implicit in each empirical engagement, and explicit in the way in which the historian positions himself before the evidence and in the questions proposed. I do not claim that historical logic is always as rigorous or as self-conscious as it ought to be; nor that our practice often matches our professions. I claim only that there is such logic. And that not all of us are wet behind the ears.

Notes

1. "Sartre Aujourd'hui," *l'Arc*, no. 30, translated in *Telos*, 9 (1971), pp. 110–16.

2. One part of this claim has come from authentic efforts to establish "scientific" procedures of investigation (quantitative, demographic, etc.); the other part has stemmed from academic humbug, as "social scientists" have sought to maintain parity with scientific colleagues within edu-

cational structures (and in the face of grant-awarding bodies) dominated by utilitarian criteria. The older, "amateurish," notion of History as a disciplined "Humanity" was always more exact.

3. J. H. Hexter's "reality rule"—"the most likely story that can be sustained by the relevant existing evidence"—is, in itself, a helpful one. Unfortunately it has been put to work by its author in increasingly unhelpful ways, in support of a prior assumption that *any* "Marxist" story *must* be unlikely.

4. For a prime example of this misunderstanding, see B. Hindess and P. Q. Hirst, *Pre-Capitalist Modes of Production* (London, 1975), p. 312.

5. This does not mean that "history" may be seen *only* as process. In our time historians—and certainly Marxist historians—have selected process (and attendant questions of relationship and causation) as the supreme object of inquiry. There are other legitimate ways of interrogating the evidence.

6. Leszek Kolakowski, "Historical Understanding and the Intelligibility of History," *Tri-Quarterly*, 22, Fall 1971, pp. 103–17. I have offered a qualification to this argument in my "Open Letter to Kolakowski."

7. See Sartre's interesting distinction between the "notion" and the "concept," cited above, p. 110. But, notwithstanding this, I will continue to use both.

8. By "concepts" (or notions) I mean general categories—of class, ideology, the nation-state, feudalism, etc., or specific historical forms and sequences, as crisis of subsistence, familial development cycle, etc.—and by "hypotheses" I mean the conceptual organization of the evidence to explain particular episodes of causation and relationship.

9. One helpful elucidation of these procedures is in E. J. Hobsbawn, "Karl Marx's Contribution to Historiography," in R. Blackburn (ed.), *Ideology in Social Science* (1972).

10. For which we are particularly indebted to French historical demography.

11. I have recently re-stated my position in "Eighteenth-Century English Society: Class Struggle without Class?" *Social History*, III, no. 2 (May, 1978). See also E. J. Hobsbawn, "Class Consciousness in History," in I. Meszaros (ed.), *Aspects of History and Class Consciousness* (1971), and C. Castoriadis, "On the History of the Workers' Movement," *Telos*, 30, Winter 1976–77.

12. Such static "models" may of course play a useful part in certain kinds of investigation.

13. The problem of "gaps" in the evidence as to ancient societies is discussed in M. I. Finley, *The Use and Abuse of History* (1971), pp. 69–71.

14. See Raymond Williams, *Marxism and Literature*, and the important chapter on "Determination."

MARXISM AND HISTORY

FROM *THE POVERTY OF THEORY AND OTHER ESSAYS*

W hat is all this about? It would be simple to dismiss the whole argument on the grounds that Althusser has proposed a spurious question, necessitated by his prior epistemological confusions. This is, in fact, a large part of the answer, and a sufficient answer to Althusser, and it can be briefly stated. He has proposed a pseudo-opposition. On the one hand, he presents Theory (and *Capital* itself) as "occurring exclusively in knowledge and concerning exclusively the necessary order of appearance and disappearance of concepts in the discourse of the scientific proof" (*R.C.* 114). On the other side, across from this rather grand project, he presents the petty projects of "empiricism," which constitute "ideology." Engels is trying to muddle the two, which would be disastrous (the mark of the empiricist Beast!), since the discourse of the proof must, as a pre-requisite, demand the fixity and unambiguity of concepts. But we have already seen that Althusser's notion of "empiricism" is false, and that it imposes the canons of philosophy upon quite different procedures and disciplines. We need follow this argument no further.

Even within its own terms, Althusser's argument offers self-contradictions and evasions. Thus he tells us that "we have every right to say that the theory of Marxist political economy derives from the Marxist theory of history, as one of its regions"; but he also tells us (see p. 14) that the theory of history, even now, 100 years after *Capital* "does not exist in any real sense." So that in one of its "regions" Marxist political theory was derived from "an absent theory." This goes along with the evasion of the evident fact that in *other* of its regions, this political economy was derived, very directly, from empirical engagement, either directly (from the mountain of blue books, etc., etc., to which Marx pays such generous tribute,[1]) or less directly, by intense and critical scrutiny of the empirically-based studies of other writers.

From *The Poverty of Theory and Other Essays* by E. P. Thompson (New York: Monthly Review Press, 1978).

So that Althusser set out with a bad argument, and he rigged the terms to make it look better. Engels would appear to have been arguing two propositions. First, the inherently "approximate" nature of all our concepts, and especially of those necessarily "fixed" concepts which arise from and are brought to the analysis of changing, *un*fixed social development. This may be a "banality" in its "obviousness" to a philosopher, who supposes that it "is only another way of saying that the abstraction as such is abstract," an "admirable *tautology*" which rarely leaves Althusser's lips. But, to a historian or an economist, it is (while "obvious" as theory) exceptionally complex in fact: it is an obviousness which can only too easily be forgotten in practice, and of which we need reminders.

Moreover, Engels is not just saying that concepts and their "real object" are different. It is true that he overstates his case in a moment of exasperation at the old bourgeois scholastics and the new "Marxist" schematists on every side: "to science definitions are worthless." We understand his exasperation only too well. But the point of his letter to Schmidt is to argue, (a) that because all concepts are approximations, this does not make them "fictions," (b) that only the concepts can enable us to "make sense of," understand and know, objective reality, (c) but that even in the act of knowing we can (and ought to) know that our concepts are more abstract and more logical than the diversity of that reality—and, by empirical observation, *we can know this too*. We cannot understand European medieval society without the concept of feudalism, even though, with the aid of this concept, we can also know that feudalism (in its conceptual logic) was never expressed "in full classical form"; which is another way of saying that feudalism is a heuristic concept which represents (corresponds to) real social formations, but, in the manner of all such concepts, does so in an overly purified and logical way. The definition cannot give us the real event. In any case, Engels's words are clearer than my gloss. What they come back to, as so often in these last letters, is the cry for "dialectics," whose true meaning is to be found less in his attempt to reduce these to a formal code than in his practice. And an important part of this practice is exactly that "dialogue" between concept and evidence which I have already discussed.

Engels's second point concerns the nature of specifically *historical* concepts, concepts adequate to the understanding of materials which are in continuous change. Althusser exclaims against the notion that "the theory of Political Economy is affected even in its concepts by the peculiar *quality* of real history (its "material" which is 'changing')." The short answer to this is that if the real object of this knowledge is changing, and if the concepts cannot encompass the process of change, then we will get extremely bad Political Economy. Not only Marxist but orthodox bourgeois Political Economy had an arsenal of such concepts of change (laws of this and that, rising and falling rates of the other, even the mobilities of supply and demand). What Althusser means to exclaim against is an irreverence to the fixity of categories. Engels says not only that the object changes but that the *concepts themselves* must be "subject to change and transformation." For Althusser capitalism must be one thing: or another thing: or nothing. It cannot be one thing now, and another thing tomorrow. And if it is one thing, then the essential categories must remain the same, however much "play" there may be inside them. If the categories change as the object changes, according to a "coefficient of mobility," then science or Theory are lost; we drift among the tides of phenomena, the tides themselves moving the rudder; we become (as Marx accused the students of Ranke) the "valets" of history.

But it is not clear that Engels has set us adrift like this. The offensive words (in my view) are not "concepts . . . are subject to change and transformation" (for that may well indicate, and *does* indicate for Engels, the strenuous theoretical-empirical dialogue entailed in transformation), but the preceding words, "their mental reflections."[2] And Engels may equally be signalling—and, I think, is signalling in his discussion of the concept, feudalism—the particular flexibility of concepts appropriate in historical analysis: that is, the necessary generality and elasticity of historical categories, as expectations rather than as rules. I have had occasion enough to observe in my own practice that if a category as generous as "the working class" is improperly hardened by theoreticians to correspond to a particular historical moment of class presence (and an ideal moment at that), then it very soon gives false and disastrous historical/ political results; and yet without the (elastic) category of class—an expectation justified by evidence—I could not have practised at all.

So that I think that Engels is talking good sense, that Althusser has misrepresented him, and is talking no sense at all. But, nevertheless, it is true that a real problem remains. We cannot just say that Engels is right and Althusser wrong. Althusser has mis-stated the problem, but at least we may admit that he has pointed to the area where the problem lies. The problem concerns, from one aspect, the differing modes of analysis of *structure* and of *process*. And, from another aspect, the status of "Political Economy" and, hence, the status of *Capital*. We will take it from the second aspect first.

We must commence, at once, by agreeing that *Capital* is not a work of "history." There is a history of the development of the forms of capital inscribed within it, but this is rarely developed within the historical discipline, or tested by the procedures of historical logic. The historical passages are something more than "instances" and "illustrations," but something less than the real history. We will explain this more fully in a moment. But we must say at once that Marx never pretended, when writing *Capital*, that he was writing the history of capita*lism*. This is well known, but we will offer reminders. Marx hopes (as is apparent from the *Grundrisse* notebooks) that his work would "also offer the key to the understanding of the past—a work in its own right which, it is to be hoped, we shall be able to undertake as well."[3] This hope was not fulfilled. The work which was completed was that described (to Lassalle in 1858) as "a critique of the economic categories or the system of bourgeois economy, critically presented"; and it dealt (he told Kugelmann) with "capital in general." The first volume "contains what the English call 'the principles of Political Economy.' " And its title was : *Capital, a Critique of Political Economy.*[4]

One way of proceeding may be to stand back from the structure for a moment, and enquire what kind of structure it is. First, we must note that some part of the power of the work comes not from its explicit procedures, and from its disclosure of its object, but from choices as to values (and their vigorous and relevant expression) which could not possibly be deduced from the conceptual procedures themselves, and which are not the object of study. That is, Marx does not only lay bare the economic processes of exploitation, but he also expresses (or presents his material so as to evoke) indignation at suffering, poverty, child labour, waste of human potentialities, and contempt for intellectual mystifications and apologetics.

I comment on this, neither to commend it nor to condemn it, although the relevance may appear later. Since Marx's choice of values could be justified only with reference to a "region" which Althusser curtly dismisses as "ideology," we might have to explain (even condone) it as a vestige of bourgeois moralism, even humanism. Certainly, no such vestiges appear with Althusser and Balibar: when they have "read" *Capital* it has been disinfested of all this. We may, or we may not, prefer the first to the second "reading" of *Capital*; the point is that, in this significant respect, they are different books.

Second, it may follow from this, and I think it *does* so follow, that if we disinfest *Capital* in this way of all "moralistic" intrusions, a very considerable part of that work—the major part—could be taken *just as* "what the English call 'the principles of Political Economy' ": an analytic critique of the existing "science," and an exposition of an alternative "science," of economic functions, relations, and laws. That is, if we did not (for exterior "reasons" of value) disapprove of exploitation, waste, and suffering, then we would find ourselves presented with an alternative lawed structure of economic relations. To be true, the reader whose interests lay with "capital" would find its conclusions pessimistic; for the system is presented as moving rapidly towards a final crisis (which has not yet eventuated). But this could not afford any "scientific" reasons for disagreement.

These two considerations are not introduced for "moralistic" purposes. They help us to take a sighting of *Capital* within the intellectual context of its moment of genesis. And they remind us that the notions of *structure* and of *system* were not inventions of Marx (although one might suppose so from some contemporary statements). We had, as is well known, in eighteenth-century Britain very marvellous structures, the admiration of the world and the envy of the French. In particular, the constitutional structures were exemplary, and had perhaps been provided to the British by God:

> Britain's matchless Constitution, mixt
> Of mutual checking and supporting Powers,
> Kings, Lords and Commons. . . .

Or, in the familiar clockwork analogy, as employed by William Blackstone: "Thus every branch of our civil polity supports and is supported, regulates and is regulated, by the rest. . . . Like three distinct powers in mechanics, they jointly impel the machine of government in a direction different from what either, acting by itself, would have done. . . ."

God, as Bacon had pointed out, worked by second causes, and these causes, whether in nature, in psychology or in the constitution, often appeared as *sets* of interacting causes (structures). The sets that mechanical materialism proposed followed the paradigm of the clock, or of the mill. The constitutional set was governed by the rule of law. But bourgeois Political Economy (from Adam Smith forward) discovered a different set, seen now more as a "natural process," whose nexus was the market, where intersecting self-interests were mediated, under the government of that market's laws. By the time that Marx confronted it, this Political Economy had become, by way of Malthus, Ricardo, and the Utilitarians, a very sophisticated structure indeed, rigorous in its procedures and inclusive in its claims.

Marx identified this structure as his major antagonist, and he bent the whole energies of his mind to confounding it.[5] For nearly twenty years this was his major preoccupation. He had to enter into each one of the categories of Political Economy, fracture them, and re-structure them. We can see the evidences of these encounters in the *Grundrisse* notebooks of 1857–8, and it is customary to admire their exhaustive ardour. And I do so admire them. But I cannot altogether admire them. For they are evidences also that Marx was *caught in a trap*: the trap baited by "Political Economy." Or, more accurately, he had been sucked into a theoretical whirlpool, and, however manfully he beats his arms and swims against the circulating currents, he slowly revolves around a vortex which threatens to engulf him. Value, capital, labour, money, value, reappear again and again, are interrogated, re-categorised, only to come round once more on the revolving currents in the same old forms, for the same interrogation.[6] Nor am I even able to agree that it *had* to be like this, that Marx's thought could only have been developed in this way. When on considers the philosophical breakthrough of the 1840s, and the propositions which inform the *German Ideology* and *Communist Manifesto*, there would appear to be indications of stasis, and even regression, in the next fifteen years. Despite the significance of the *economic* encounter in the *Grundrisse*, and despite the rich hypotheses which appear in its interstices (as to pre-capitalist formations, etc.), there is something in Marx's encounter with Political Economy which is obsessive.

For what was this "Political Economy"? It did not offer a total account of society or of its history; or, if it pretended to do so, then its conclusions were entailed in its premises. These premises proposed that it was possible, not only to identify particular activities as "economic," but to isolate these as a special field of study from the other activities (political, religious, legal, "moral"—as the area of norms and values was then defined—cultural, etc.); where such isolation proved to be impossible, as in the impingement of "politics" or "law" *upon* "economic" activity, then such impingement might be seen as improper interference with "natural" economic process, or as second-order problems, or as the fulfilment of economic goals by other means.

It might also be proposed (although not necessarily) that economics, and, with Malthus, demography, were first-order problems, and that these determined (or, in a "free" state, should and would determine) social development as a whole. These "underlay" the elaborate superstructures of civilization, determining the wealth of nations and the pace and direction of progress. Thus isolated, economic activities became the object of a "science," whose primary postulates were interests and needs: self-interest at a micro-level, the interests of groups ("agriculture" and "industry") or even of classes ("Labour" and "Capital") at a macro-level, the groups and classes being defined according to the economic premises of the science. To develop such a science with rigour demanded accurate definition and fixity of categories, a mathematical logic, and the continuous internal circulation and recognition of its own concepts: its conclusions were acclaimed as "laws."

This is the structure of "Political Economy." From the outside, in the 1840s, it appeared to Marx as ideology, or, worse, apologetics. He entered within it in order to overthrow it. But, once inside, however many of its categories he fractured (and how many times), the structure remained. For the premises supposed that it was possible to isolate economic activities in this way, and to develop these as a first-order science *of society*. It is more accurate to say that Marx, at the time of the *Grundrisse*, did not so much remain within the structure of "Political Economy" as develop an *anti*-structure, but within its same premises. The postulates ceased to be the self-interest of men and became the logic and forms of capital, to which men were subordinated; capital was disclosed, not as the benign donor of benefits, but as the appropriator of surplus labour;

factional "interests" were disclosed as antagonistic classes; and contradiction displaced the sum progress. But what we have at the end, is not the overthrow of "Political Economy" but *another* "Political Economy."[7]

Insofar as Marx's categories were anti-categories, Marxism was marked, at a critical stage in its development, by the categories of Political Economy: the chief of which was the notion *of* the "economic," as a first-order activity, capable of isolation in this way, as the object of a science giving rise to laws whose operation would over-ride second-order activities. And there is another mark also, which it is difficult to identify without appearing to be absurd. But the absurdities to which this error has been taken in the work of Althusser and his colleagues—that is, the absurdities of a certain kind of static self-circulating "Marxist" structuralism—enable us to risk the ridicule. There is an important sense in which the movement of Marx's thought, in the *Grundrisse*, is locked inside a *static, anti-historical structure.*

When we recall that Marx and Engels ceaselessly ridiculed the pretensions of bourgeois economy to disclose "fixed and eternal" laws, independent of historical specificity; when we recall the movement *within* the structure, the accumulation of capital, the declining rate of profit; and when we recall that Marx sketched, even in the *Grundrisse*, capital in terms of the development of its historical forms, then the proposition seems absurd. After all, Marx and Engels enabled historical materialism to be born. And yet the proposition has force. For once capital has emerged on the page, its self-development is determined by the innate logic inherent within the category, and the relations so entailed, in much the same way as "the market" operates within bourgeois Political Economy, and still does so within some "modernization theory" today. Capital is an operative category which laws its own development, and capital*ism* is the effect, in social formations, of these laws. This mode of analysis must necessarily be anti-historical, since the actual history can only be seen as the expression of ulterior laws; and historical evidence, or contemporary (empirically-derived) evidence, will then be seen as Althusser sees it, as instances or illustrations confirming these laws. But when capital and its relations are seen as a structure, in a given moment of capital's forms, then this structure has a categorical stasis: that is, it can allow for no impingement of any influence from any other region (any region not allowed for in the terms and discourse of this discipline) which could modify its relations, for this would threaten the integrity and fixity of the categories themselves.

This is an extraordinary mode of thought to find in a materialist, for capital has become idea, which unfolds itself in history. We remember so well Marx's imprecations against idealism, and his claims to have inverted Hegel, that we do not allow ourselves to see what is patently there. In the *Grundrisse*—and not once or twice, but in the whole mode of presentation—we have examples of *unreconstructed* Hegelianism. Capital posits conditions *"in accordance with its immanent essence,"*[8] reminding us that Marx had studied Hegel's Philosophy of Nature, and had noted of "the Idea as nature" that "reality is posited with immanent determinateness of form."[9] Capital posits this and that, creates this and that, and if we are to conceive of capital*ism* ("the inner construction of modern society") it can only be as "capital in the totality of its relations."[10]

It is true that Marx reminds us (or is he reminding himself?) that "the new forces of production and relations of production" of capital "do not develop out of *nothing* . . . nor from the womb of the self-positing Idea." But he goes on, immediately, to add:

> While in the complicated bourgeois system every economic relation pre-supposes every other in its bourgeois economic form, and everything pos-ited is thus also a presupposition, this is the case with every organic system. This organic system itself, as a totality, has its presuppositions, and its development to its totality consists precisely in subordinating all elements of society to itself, or in creating out of it the organs which it still lacks.[11]

The "organic system" is then its own subject, and it is this anti-historical stasis or *closure* which I have been indicating. The "it" inside this organism is capital, the soul of the organ, and "it" subordinates all elements of society to itself and creates out of society "its" own organs.

The point is not only that in the light of this kind of lapse Engels's warnings to Schmidt are necessary and salutary: concepts and economic laws have no reality "except as approximation": "Did feudalism ever correspond to its con-cept?" There is a point of greater importance. For Marx has moved across an invisible conceptual line from *Capital* (an abstraction of Political Economy, which is his proper concern) to *capitalism* ("the complicated bourgeois system"), that is, the whole society, conceived of an "organic system." But the whole society comprises many activities and relations (of power, of consciousness, sexual, cultural, normative) which are not the concern of Political Economy, which have been *defined out of* Political Economy, and for which it has no terms. Therefore Political Economy cannot show capital*ism* as "capital in the totality of its relations": it has no language or terms to do this. Only a historical materialism which could bring all activities and relations within a coherent view could do this. And, in my view, subsequent historical materialism has *not* found this kind of "organism," working out its own self-fulfilment with inexorable idealist logic, nor has it found any society which can be simply described as "capital in the totality of its relations." "We" have *never* let it get so far as that: even Fascism, which might be offered as "its" most ferocious manifestation, would then have to be glossed as an expression of its irrationality, not of its inherent rational logic. But historical materialism has found that Marx had a most profound intuition, an intuition which in fact *preceded* the *Grundrisse*: that the logic of capitalist process has found expression within all the activities of a society, and exerted a determining pressure upon its development and form: hence entitling us to speak of capitalism, or of capitalist societies. But this is a very different conclusion, a critically different conclusion, which gives us an organicist structuralism on one side (ultimately an Idea of capital unfolding itself) and a real historical process on the other.

This is only a part of the *Grundrisse*, of course. And, of course, Marx conceived of himself, pugnaciously, as a materialist. In his introduction he vindicated his method, of proceeding from abstractions to the concrete in thought; and his method was largely vindicated in the results: only by the fiercest abstraction could he crack those categories apart. But he also discounted, in cavalier fashion, the inherent dangers of the method. Hegel went astray because, proceeding by this method, he "fell into the illusion of conceiving the real as the product of thought unfolding itself out of itself." It seemed so easy to cast this silly illusion aside, but to proceed by much the same method. But if Marx never forgot that thought was not self-generating but was "a product, rather, of the working-up of observation and conception into concepts,"[12] this mode of abstraction could still give him, on occasion, capital as the unfolding of its own idea.

I think that, for ten years, Marx *was* in this trap. His delays, his carbuncles, cannot all be attributed to the bourgeoisie. When he came to write *Capital* the trap had been in some part sprung. I am not expert enough to describe his partial self-deliverance, but I would suggest four considerations. First, the trap was never fully closed. Marx had conceived of capital*ism* in historical terms in the 1840s, continued to do so, by fits and starts, in the *Grundrisse*, and these were also years in which applied and concrete political analysis continued to flow from his pen. Second, and alongside this, he continued to develop, not only in his historical but also in his practical political experience, as a historical actor in his own part, and in observing the growth, flux, and recession of working-class struggles in Europe. These two considerations are self-evident.

The other two may be more controversial. For the third, I would emphasize once again the important influence of *The Origin of Species* (1859). I am aware that my admiration for Darwin is regarded as an amiable (or guilty) eccentricity, and that there is a general mind-set among progressive intellectuals which attributes to Darwin the sins of teleological evolutionism, positivism, social Malthusianism, and apologias for exploitation (the "survival of the fittest") and of racism.[13] But I am not convinced of these objections, and, to be honest, I am not even convinced that all these critics have read *The Origin of Species*, nor read informed scientific evaluations of it. I know very well how Darwin's ideas were put to use by others, and I also know of his subsequent (rather few) lapses. But what is remarkable in his work is the way in which he argues through rigorously, and in an empirical mode, the logic of evolution which is *not* a teleology, whose conclusions are *not* entailed in their premises, but which is still subject to rational explanation.[14] In any case, my admiration, whether innocent or not, was certainly shared by Engels and Marx. Marx read the book in December 1860, and at once wrote to Engels: "Although it is developed in the crude English style, this is the book which contains the basis in natural history for our view." To Lassalle he wrote in the next month, the book "is very important and serves me as a basis in natural science for the class struggle in history. . . . Despite all deficiencies, not only is *the death-blow dealt here for the first time to 'teleology' in the natural sciences but their rational meaning is empirically explained.*"[15]

There are two important recognitions here: first, Marx recognized, grudgingly, that the empirical method, however "crude," however "English," had educed a substantial contribution to knowledge; second, Marx recognised in the *non-teleological* explication of a rational logic in natural process "a basis . . . for our view," indeed "a basis in natural science for the class struggle in history." There is surely a recognition here that this "basis" had *not* been provided before (in the *Grundrisse*), and even the suggestion that Marx was aware that his abstractionist mode of procedure was not proof against such teleology? It is not that Marx supposed that Darwinian analogies could be taken unreconstructed from the animal to the human world: he very soon reproved a correspondent who, with the aid of Malthus, was supposing that.[16] It is rather a question of method, in which Darwin's work was taken as exemplar of the rational explication of the logic of process, which, in new terms, must be developed in historical practice. And I cannot see that we have any licence to pass this off as some momentary fancy. Still, in 1873, Marx took the trouble to send to Darwin a copy of *Capital*, inscribed by him as a gift from "his sincere admirer."[17]

It is at this time (1860) that the work of fashioning the *Grundrisse* into *Capital* commenced. And this leads me to my fourth consideration. It appears to me that Marx was more self-critical of his earlier work than many commentators allow. I will not delay to puzzle over the various hints that survive as to his own self-dissatisfaction.[18] But in my view the writing of *Capital* involved a radical re-structuring of his materials, in ways partly influenced by *The Origin of Species*. It is argued (for example, by Martin Nicolaus, the editor of the *Grundrisse*) that the changes may be attributed to Marx's desire to make his work more "popular," more "concrete," and hence more widely available to the revolutionary movement; but "the *inner* structure of *Capital* is *identical* in the main lines to the *Grundrisse*." In the first, "the method is visible; in *Capital* it is deliberately, consciously hidden . . ." I do not think so. And I think even less of the attempt to explain away Marx's letter to Engels (15 August 1863), in which he writes of the slow progress of *Capital*, and explains that he has "had to turn everything round," as meaning that "he had to overthrow virtually all of previous Political Economy." The phrase is this: "when I look at this compilation now and see how I have had to turn everything round and how I had to make even the *historical* part out of material of which some was quite unknown": and it cannot bear this construction. The "overthrow" of previous political economy had been done, already, in the notebooks (*Grundrisse*) of 1857–8; what was new was "the historical part" and the "turning around" of the rest.[19]

This turning round, I am arguing, involved not only adding a historical dimension to the work, and much greater concrete exemplification (derived from empirical investigation) but also attempting to bring under control and reduce to the rational explication of process the "idealist" (even self-fulfilling, teleological) formulations derived from the abstractionist mode. What comes into *Capital* in a new way, is a sense of history, and a concretion of exemplification (accompanied, we recall, by "extraneous" expressions of wrath).

And yet Nicolaus is not wholly wrong; in some part—and that part specifically the anti-structure of "Political Economy"—the structure of *Capital* remains that of the *Grundrisse*.[20] It remains a study of the logic of capital, not of capitalism, and the social and political dimensions of the history, the wrath, and the understanding of the class struggle arise from a region independent of the closed system of economic logic. In that sense *Capital* was—and probably had to be—a product of theoretical miscegenation. But miscegenation of this order is no more possible in theory than in the animal kingdom, for we cannot leap across the fixity of categories or of species. So that we are forced to agree with seven generations of critics: *Capital* is a mountainous inconsistency. As pure Political Economy it may be faulted for introducing external categories; its laws cannot be verified, and its predictions were wrong. As "history" or as "sociology" it is abstracted to a "model," which has heuristic value, but which follows too obsequiously ahistorical economic laws.

Capital was not an exercise of a different order to that of mature bourgeois Political Economy, but a total confrontation *within* that order. As such, it is both the highest achievement of "political economy," and it signals the need for its supersession by historical materialism. To say the former is not to diminish Marx's achievement, for it is only in the light of that achievement that we are able to make this judgement. But the achievement does not *produce* historical materialism, it provides the preconditions for its production. A unitary knowledge of society (which is always in motion, hence a historical knowledge) cannot be won from a "science" which, as a presupposition of its discipline, isolates certain kinds of activity only for study, and provides no categories for others. And the structure of *Capital* remains marked by the categories of his antagonist, notably *economy* itself. In this sense it is true that in *Capital* "history" is introduced to provide exemplification and "illustration" for a structure of theory which is not derived from this discipline. However reluctantly, we must go half-way towards the positions of Althusser and Balibar. But we need not go all the way, for these "illustrations" would have been of no value if they were *wrong*, snatched from "history's" received accounts, and not both researched ("I had to make even the *historical* part out of material of which some was quite unknown") and interrogated in new ways.

It is more true to say that the history in *Capital*, and in attendant writings, is immensely fruitful *as hypothesis*, and yet as hypothesis which calls in question, again and again, the adequacy of the categories of Political Economy. We find here a veritable cornucopia of hypotheses, informed by consistent theoretical propositions (the determining pressures of the mode of production), hypotheses which historical materialism has been setting to work ever since. But setting them to work has not involved only "testing" them or "verifying" them,[21] it has also entailed revising and replacing them. Even Marx's more elaborated historical hypotheses (for example, as to the struggle to lengthen the working day, or as to the enclosure movement in England and its relation to labour supply for industry), as well as his more cryptic or more complex hypotheses (for example, as to the transition from feudalism to capitalism, or as to the British "bourgeois revolution," or as to "oriental despotism" and the "Asiatic mode of production") have always undergone, in historical materialism's own discourse of the proof, either reformation or very much more radical change.[22]

How could it be otherwise? To suppose differently would be to suppose, not only that everything can be said at once, but that immanent Theory (or Knowledge) found its miraculous embodiment in Marx, not fully mature to be sure (it had yet to develop to Althusser's full stature), but already perfectly-formed and justly-proportioned in all its parts. This is a fairy-story, recited to children in Soviet primary classes, and not even believed by them. *Capital*, volume I, is rich in historical hypotheses; volumes II and III are less so; the "anti-structure" of Political Economy narrows once again.[23] Marx's hope of himself developing historical materialism in practice remained, very largely, unfulfilled. It was left to the old clown, Frederick Engels, to make some attempts to remedy that; and his essay in historical anthropology, *The Origin of the Family* (Darwin's influence again!) is generally taken by Marxist anthropologists today to exemplify the infancy rather than the maturity of their knowledge.

In his final years, the Engels looked around in alarm, and noted the gathering consequences of their great omission. There are "many allusions" to the theory of historical materialism in *Capital* (he wrote to Bloch in 1890), and "Marx hardly wrote anything in which it did not play a part." But he wrote nothing in which it played a leading part, and Bloch was directed to *Anti-Dühring* and *Ludwig Feuerbach* as the places in which might be found "the most detailed account of historical materialism which, so far as I know, exists." And, in the same year, to Conrad Schmidt, "All history must be studied afresh, the conditions of existence of the different formations of society must be individually examined before the attempt is made to deduce from them the political, civil-legal, aesthetic, philosophic, religious, etc., notions corresponding to them. Only a little has been done here up to now. . . ."

It is sobering to reflect upon how many human activities (for none of which Political Economy afforded categories) are comprised within this sentence. But Engels was in an increasingly sober mood:

> Too many of the younger Germans simply make use of the phrase, historical materialism (and *everything* can be turned into a phrase), in order to get their own relatively scanty historical knowledge (for economic history is still in its cradle!) fitted together into a neat system as quickly as possible, and then they think themselves something very tremendous.

So that not only historical materialism, but the region of it most immediately proximate to *Capital*, economic history, Engels could see to be "still in its cradle." It now seemed to him, with gathering urgency, that what was wrong with Marx's uncompleted life-work, *Capital*, was that it was not historical *enough*. To Mehring, in 1893:

> There is only one other point lacking, which, however, Marx and I always failed to stress enough in our writings and in regard to which we are all equally guilty. We all, that is to say, laid and were bound to lay the main emphasis at first on the derivation of political, juridical and other ideological notions, and of the actions arising through the medium of these notions, from basic economic facts. But in so doing we neglected the formal side—the way in which these notions come about—for the sake of the content.

"It is the old story," Engels continued: "Form is always neglected at first for content." But this failure had given purchase to the criticism of "the ideolotgists," with their—

> Fatuous notion . . . that because we deny an independent historical development to the various ideological spheres which play a part in history we

also deny them any effect in history. The basis of this is the common undialectical conception of cause and effect as rigidly opposite poles, the total disregarding of interaction. . . .

The letters are familiar, and it may be wondered why I rehearse them. I do this now to emphasise, first, that Engels clearly acknowledged that Marx had *assumed* a theory of historical materialism which he had neither fully posed nor begun to develop. For some part of its proposition we are, indeed, dependent upon Engels's late letters. Althusser ridicules these letters, but we should note a curiosity in the fact that he can, in the same moment, borrow notions ("relative autonomy," "in-the-last-instance determination") of central importance to his thought from passages which lie cheek-by-jowl in the same letters which he lampoons. I will add that these letters were as familiar to me and to fellow practitioners in historical materialism in 1948 as in 1978, and that this was where we started *from*. We did not have to wait upon Althusser to learn that the *critical* problems lay in the area of "relative autonomy," etc.; these phrases pointed towards the problems which we then set out in our practice to examine. I will come back to this question, since it indicates a very different Marxist tradition from that of Althusser.

The second reason for rehearsing these letters is that we find in them that Engels is (as I think) correctly indicating the area of the largest (and most dangerous and ambiguous) of the real silences left by Marx's death—and shortly to be sealed by his own. But in the same moment, in the very terms in which he discusses this absent theory he reveals the inadequacy of its terms. For "political, juridical, and other ideological notions" cannot be derived from "economic facts" within a discourse of Political Economy so exciting that its very definitions of the "economic" affords to these extraneous evidences no entry. And the notion that the concepts of Marxism should be historical categories and "subject to change and transformation" would play havoc with the credentials of Marxism as an exact "science" of the capitalist mode of production. So that Engels is saying, in effect, that historical materialism and Marxist Political Economy have failed to find a common junction and a theoretical vocabulary capable of encompassing both process and structure: that Marxism is in danger of becoming imprisoned within the categories of *Capital*; but that the pressure of incipient historical materialism can be seen within its structure (in its *inconsistencies* as much as its hypotheses), which pressure he could authenticate (from Marx's other work and from their long common project). He wished, in these final letters, to give to historical materialism a charter of liberation from the structure of the old *Grundrisse*, but he could not solve the theoretical problems thus entailed nor find the terms to do so. Subsequent historical materialism, in its practice—although insufficiently in its theory—has sought to serve under this charter of liberation. Althusser and his colleagues seek to thrust historical materialism back into the prison of the categories of Political Economy.

I think that contemporary Marxist economists are right to note that "in *Capital* . . . Marx repeatedly uses the concept of the circuit of capital to characterise the structure of the capitalist economy"—and, more than that, of capitalist society more generally.[24] But historical materialism (as assumed as hypothesis by Marx, and as subsequently developed in our practice) must be concerned with other "circuits" also: the circuits of power, of the reproduction of ideology, etc., and these belong to a different logic and to other categories. Moreover, historical analysis does not allow for static contemplation of "circuits," but is immersed in moments when all systems go and every circuit sparks across the other. So that Engels is in this sense wrong: it is not true that he and Marx "neglected the formal side—the way in which these notions come about—for the sake of the content." It was, rather, the over-development of the formal side, in the "anti-structure" of Political Economy, which in its genesis and form was derived from a bourgeois construction, and which confined the real historical content into impermissible and unpassable forms.

Our concern must now be to approach this problem from a different aspect: the alternative heuristics of "structure" and of "process." But, first, may we take a brief adieu of our old clown? It is now *de rigueur* to make old Engels into a whipping boy, and to impugn to him any sign that one chooses to impugn to subsequent Marxisms. All this has now been written out, and by many hands, and I need not go over it all again.[25] I am willing to agree that several of the charges stick. Thus I think it is true that in his writings (i) Engels gave credibility to epistemological "reflection theory,"[26] (ii) he introduced a paradigm of "natural process" (a misapplied Darwinism) in his anthropological and historical work, which drifted towards a positivist evolutionism, (iii) he certainly introduced—as did, with equal certainty, Marx—historicist notions of lawed and pre-determined development. These are heavy charges, although I cannot accept the pleadings which always find Marx and Lenin innocent and leave Engels alone in the dock. And to these I have added my own, more marginal, charges, as to Engels's unfortunate and ill-considered influence in the formative British socialist movement.[27] But when all this has been said, what an extraordinary, dedicated, and versatile man he was! How closely he followed his own times, how far he risked himself—further, often, than Marx—in engagements with his contemporary historical and cultural thought, how deeply and passionately he was engaged in a movement which was spreading to the five continents, how generously he gave himself in his last years to the papers of his old friend and to the incessant correspondence of the movement! If we must learn, on occasion, from his errors, then he would have expected this to be so. And it is, least of all, for the "revisionist" letters of his last decade that he is to be cast as a whipping boy.

It is taken to be a truism by the young that older is worse than younger, but I cannot see that Engels exemplifies that general case. The "General," in his last decade, did not renege upon the propositions of his youth; rather, he dwelt nostalgically upon "the salad days" of the 1840s, and in the wisdom and foreboding of age he noted that there was something in the young movement of the 1880s and 1890s which was turning away from the intuitions of his and Marx's original theses. If he is to be punished, he should be punished for these late letters of qualification and of warning least of all. That the letters proposed, but did not answer, many problems can be agreed; but if the warnings had been fully attended to, then the history of Marxism might have been different. I will not allow Frederick Engels to be cast as a senile clown after all. He should be taken, until his last year, as he would have wished: his great sanity, his errors, his breadth of understanding (but his excessive "family" possessiveness) of the movement, all inter-mixed.

Notes

The editions of Louis Althusser's work cited in the text are: *L. & P.—Lenin and Philosophy* (New Left Books, 1970); *P. & H.—Politics and History* (New Left Books, 1977); *R.C.—Reading Capital* (New Left Books, 1970); *C.W.—*Karl Marx, Frederick Engels, *Collected Works* (Lawrence & Wishart, in progress); *Grundrisse* (Pelican, 1973).

1. *Capital* (1938), p. xviii.

2. It is significant that Althusser passes over the most serious epistemological error of Engels ("reflection theory") without any critique. For critique would have involved him in (a) a consideration of the whole problem of "dialogue," (b) in a consequent critique of Lenin (see note 6), and (c) in a self-critique which must have led on to a self-destruct, since his own epistemology (with Generalities I arising unbidden and unexamined) is a kind of "theoreticist" reflection-theory, reproduced in idealist form.

3. *Grundrisse*, p. 461.

4. Book I of *Capital* ("Capitalist Production") of course appeared in advance of Books II and III, and was sub-titled, in the English edition edited by Engels, "A Critical Analysis of Capitalist Production."

5. When I made this self-evident point in 1965 I was sternly rebuked for my "incredibly impoverished vision of Marx's work": Perry Anderson, "Socialism and Pseudo-Empiricism," *New Left Review*, 35 (January–February 1966), p. 21. I had not then read the *Grundrisse*. The point is surely now established beyond any reach of argument?

6. Marx to Lassalle, 22 February 1858: "The thing makes very slow progress because as soon as one tries to come to a final reckoning with questions which one has made the chief object of one's studies for years, they are always revealing new aspects and demanding fresh consideration." (*Selected Correspondence*, p. 224). But seven years before Marx had assured Engels that "in five

weeks I will be through with the whole economic shit." He would then throw himself "into a new science. . . . I am beginning to be tired of it." Cited in David McLellan, *Karl Marx, His Life and Thought* (1973), p. 283.

7. I am of course aware that this is a contentious area in which a hundred books and theses have been deployed. I am only reporting my own considered conclusion. Althusser also sees *Capital* as a work of Political Economy (Marxist Science), although he sees this as a merit: "the theory of Political Economy, of which *Capital* is an example . . . considers one relatively autonomous component of the social totality" (*R.C.* 109). He also allows that, if chapter one of *Capital* is not read in *his* sense, it would be "an essentially Hegelian work" (*R.C.* 125–6). He repeatedly insists that the object of *Capital* is neither theory nor social formations, but the capitalist mode of production (e.g. *L. & P.* 76, p. 23; *P. & H.*, p. 186). Colletti sees the problem (is Marx making a critique of *bourgeois* Political Economy, or is he criticizing Political Economy as such?) as remaining unresolved: "Interview," *New Left Review*, 86 (July–August 1974), pp. 17–18; Castoriadis, examining much the same problem, flatly concludes that Marxist economic theory is untenable: "Interview," *Telos*, 23 (1975) esp. pp. 143–9.

8. *Grundrisse*, p. 459. My italics.

9. *C.W.* I, p. 510.

10. *Grundrisse*, p. 276. Roman Rosdolsky, *The Making of Marx's "Capital"* (London, 1977) has made a definitive analysis of the Hegelian structure of the *Grundrisse* and of the central status of the concept of "capital in general," a status which remains central in *Capital*. The question arises throughout, but see especially p. 41–52, 367–8, and his correct emphasis (p. 493) that "the model of a pure capitalist society in Marx's work . . . represented a heuristic device, intended to help in the illustration of the developmental tendencies of the capitalist mode of production, free from 'all disturbing accompanying circumstances.' " See also I.I. Rubin, *Essays on Marx's Theory of Value* (Detroit, 1972), p. 117.

11. Ibid., p. 278. Such passages are licenses for Althusser's view of history as a "process without a subject."

12. Ibid., p. 101. There is of course now an immense literature on the Hegel–Marx relationship. Althusser's attempt to deny the Hegelian influence upon *Capital* has not survived it. For my purposes I wish to stress the strong and continuing Hegelian influence in these critical years: for 1857–8, see McLellan, op. cit., p. 304; for circa 1861–2 see "Marx's Précis of Hegel's Doctrine of Being in the Minor Logic," *International Review of Social History*, XXII, 3, 1977; and also T. Carver, "Marx and Hegel's *Logic*," *Political Studies*, XXII, 1976, and Rosdolsky, op. cit., passim.

13. See e.g. Anderson, "Socialism and Pseudo-Empiricism," pp. 19–21.

14. When Gareth Stedman Jones, "Engels and the End of Classical German Philosophy," *New Left Review*, 79 (May–June 1973), refers (p. 25) to "the Darwinist laws of evolution," it is not clear to me which *laws* are being referred; although it is true that Engels, in *Dialectic of Nature*, saw evolutionary process as exemplifying dialectical laws: as Darwin did not.

15. *Selected Correspondence*, pp. 125–6. My italics. Engels had previously written to Marx that Darwin had "finished off" teleology, and spoke of his "magnificent attempt . . . to demonstrate historical development in nature."

16. Ibid., p. 198. McLellan, for some reason, renders Marx's "death-blow" to teleology as a blow to "*religious* teleology" (which Marx does *not* say). But he also usefully documents Marx's subsequent criticisms of Darwin, pp. 423–4. These vary from comments on the ideological intrusion of notions of competition ("Hobbes's *bellum omnium contra omnes*") to the (very different) complaint that "in Darwin progress is merely accidental." Lawrence Krader is the only authority known to me who has made a scholarly and exact definition of the point at issue: "The opposite of a teleological, directed law of nature and man attracted Marx to the conceptions of Darwin": see *The Ethnological*

Notebooks of Karl Marx (Assen, 1974), esp. pp. 82–5, also pp. 2, 354–5, 392–3. While Engels certainly employed more unconsidered analogies between natural evolution and historical process than did Marx, the attempt of many recent Marxologists to dissociate Marx from their common admiration of Darwin is absurd.

17. See Gerratana's helpful (but over-reverent) essay, "Marx and Darwin," *New Left Review*, 82 (November–December 1973), pp. 79–80. However, the supposition that Marx had wished to dedicate a volume of *Capital* to Darwin has now been shown to be in error. (Darwin's correspondent, on that occasion, was Edward Avelin.) See Margaret A. Fay, "Did Marx Offer to Dedicate *Capital* to Darwin?" *Journal of History of Ideas*, XXXIX, January–March, 1976.

18. Thus Marx's reminder to himself, at one point in the *Grundrisse*, "to correct the idealist manner of this analysis."

19. Nicolaus (*Grundrisse*, p. 60) follows Rosdolsky here. Since Rosdolsky's work has been acclaimed in some quarters as definitive, it is necessary to make a critical comment on his very serious and scrupulous study. His discussion of the whole question of the historical dimension of *Capital* is confined to one footnote (p. 25, n. 56), dismissive of the phrase "turn everything round," and to brief discussions of primitive accumulation in which Marx's historical and empirical analyses are commended for "liveliness and persuasiveness" (p. 61) but scarcely considered further. In short Rosdosky shows little interest in historical materialism, sees the Hegelian structure ("capital in general") of *Capital* as always a merit, and hence does less than justice to critics (including Marxist critics): notably to Rosa Luxembourg. I am not competent to comment on Rosdolsky's status as an economic theorist; but one must regret that he can see *Capital* only as a heuristic academic exercise in economic theory, that his study contains *no* discussion of Darwin or of the intellectual and political context more generally. In short, it is a serious but profoundly ahistorical work.

20. As Rosa Luxembourg wrote in a private letter from prison: "the famed Volume I of *Capital* with its Hegelian Rococo ornamentation is quite abhorrent to me": *Briefe an Freunde*, p. 85, cited Rosdolsky, pp. 492–3. As Althusser exalts exactly these "Rococo" elements into "Science" I find myself coming to share Luxembourg's abhorrence of them.

21. Thus Balibar (*R.C.*, p. 202) declares that *Capital* sets the "hypothesis" of historical materialism to work "and *verifies* it against the example of the capitalist social formation." A good example of Balibar's general nonsense. A historical hypothesis could only be "verified in historical investigation: and (as he and Althusser repeat *ad nauseam*) *Capital*'s object is the capitalist mode of production and not "the capitalist social formation."

22. The "historical" chapters of *Capital* have inevitably had a stronger formative influence upon the British tradition of Marxist historiography than that of any other country; and for the same reason, a slavish adoption of Marx's hypotheses was replaced fairly early by a critical apprenticeship to them. An interesting case is the suggestive final chapter of Volume One on "Primitive Accumulation," which raised questions which were re-examined by M. H. Dobb, *Studies in the Development of Capitalism* (1946), which in turn gave rise to controversies which are resumed and discussed by John Saville, *Socialist Register*, 1969. But Saville's discussion leaves open areas (accumulation through "colonial plunder") which are being re-opened from several directions (Wallerstein, Perry Anderson, and Indian Marxist historians such as Irfan Habib), who demand renewed attention to Britain's imperial and colonial role. The point is that they are those hypotheses of Marx which are most alive which continue to undergo interrogation and revision.

23. Marx was himself, on occasion, careful to indicate the limits of this structure. Thus *Capital*, Volume Three (Chicago, 1909), p. 37, commences by speaking of "the life circle of capital," and characterizes Volume One as an analysis of the capitalist productive process "without regard to any secondary influences of conditions outside it." On p. 968: ". . . the actual movements of competition belong outside of our plan . . . because we have to present only the internal orga-

nization of the capitalist mode of production, as it were, in its ideal average." And so on. On other occasions he was less careful.

24. Ben Fine and Laurence Harris, "Controversial Issues in Marxist Economic Theory," *Socialist Register*, 1976, p. 141.

25. One must also note Sebastiano Timpanaro's defense of Engels, *On Materialism* (New Left Books, 1976).

26. In any case, the positivist credentials of the natural sciences have themselves long been at the center of controversy—a controversy which Caudwell anticipated in *The Crisis in Physics* and in *Further Studies in a Dying Culture*.

27. In my *William Morris, Romantic to Revolutionary* (Merlin Books, revised edition, 1977).

IV

Reading and Writing History

HISTORY FROM BELOW

It is one of the peculiarities of the English that the history of the "common people" has always been something other than—and distinct from—English History Proper. In countries which have had ascendant revolutionary or populist traditions, the rhetoric of democracy has saturated historiography. In English History Proper the people of this island (see under Poor Law, Sanitary Reform, Wages Policy) appear as one of the problems Government has had to handle. To this day many academic history schools languish under the Norman yoke, and the seed of William the Bastard occupies the Chairs.

Hence, until recently, "Labour History" has been defined by its antagonism to this orthodoxy. This has been far more than a difference in subject-matter. It can be seen in styles and methods: in the Marxists and mavericks attracted to it. Edouard Bernstein, the Webbs, Theodore Rothstein, the Hammonds, H. N. Brailsford—none falls into a conventional academic place. And several of those who gave, in recent years, the greatest impetus to Labour history were teachers who, like R. H. Tawney, G. D. H. Cole, Dona Torr, and Mr. H. L. Beales, had an unusually wide, participatory relationship with an audience far outside the groves of academe. They addressed themselves to Ruskin College, Left Book Club and Communist Party, the Workers' Educational Association, early paperback publishing, the Rationalist Press Association (Professor Asa Briggs, as President of the W.E.A., inherits a part of the tradition).

It was an engaged tradition. It paid for this engagement in a lack of scholarly resources. The country with the oldest Labour movement in the world has no library or institution devoted to its study. Only in the past few years have Transport House and two or three of the large unions taken seriously in hand the preservation of the wealth of records in their basements and regional offices.

From *The Times Literary Supplement*, April 7, 1966.

A commentary on the status of Labour history here might be derived from the activities, over a span of fifty years, of that gifted bookseller, the late Leon Kashnor. Between the wars and into the 1950s he concentrated almost exclusively upon building up splendid collections of early economic theory, English Jacobinism, Chartism, and so on, which he sold in Moscow, the United States, Amsterdam, Japan, Australia, and to the Feltrinelli Institute in Milan. Not one collection was sold in this country.

Fortunately, London is well served. There is the great accretion of material at the British Museum: the Goldsmiths' Collection at London University: and the collection, first initiated by the Webbs, and extended by a succession of scholars and librarians, at the London School of Economics. But no provincial library has materials to compete with the best of the Kashnor collections. And any English historian wishing to engage in serious comparative study had best get a ticket to Wisconsin, Columbia, Moscow, Milan (should the Feltrinelli Institute reopen), or to the Institute for Social History in Amsterdam. Nor is there the least sign of any change in the situation, unless it be for the worse: for the American appetite for books becomes more ferocious as the supply diminishes year by year. One London bookseller who specializes in the field, and whose prices are notorious, scarcely bothers now to let English librarians have a sight of his catalogues. And when some of the manuscripts and books of the Chartist and Republican, W. J. Linton—one of the line of radical engravers that runs from Blake and Bewick through to Walter Crane—came on the market several years ago, they were spirited off quietly to Milan and to the United States.

Despite all this, Labour and trade union history are now thickly-populated fields; and in the last six years the Society for the Study of Labour History (with its Scottish associate) has brought together scholars from the older committed tradition with scholars who find this commitment strange or even improper. The Society owes a great deal to the first editors of its *Bulletin*, Professor Sidney Pollard and Dr. Royden Harrison, who have established for it a reputation for careful documentary and bibliographical work.

Much recent work has consisted in filling in the blank spaces and correcting the outlines of the maps left by the Webbs and G. D. H. Cole (John Saville has indeed been engaged for some years in preparing a biographical dictionary of Labour, which found its origin in notes left by Cole). There have been published since 1949 no fewer than nine volumes on the national or regional organization of the miners: J. E. Williams's exhaustive study of *The Derbyshire Miners* and E. W. Evans's study of the Welsh miners' leader, *Mabon*, are among the more interesting. A number of well-made histories of particular unions or industries have been added to the shelf: among them *The Foundry Workers*

(J. Fyrth and H. Collins), *The Lace-Makers' Society* (N. H. Cuthbert), and *The Railwaymen* (P. Bagwell, on the N.U.R.). Sidney Pollard's weighty *History of Labour in Sheffield* has shown the value of a regional approach, the trade unions being seen, not from the perspective of national H.Q. or Annual Conference, but within a densely documented industrial context.

An influence which can be clearly seen in some contemporary work is that of history-as-industrial-relations. Where the old magnificent-journey, or From-Tolpuddle-to-Lord-Tom-Noddy, approaches still lingered on into post-war years, the new Delectable City is seen to be a state of affairs in which a rationalized and disciplined trade union movement, governed by an automated, forward-looking T.U.C. (which turns on all proper occasions to qualified academic advisers for its policy-briefing), gets itself thoroughly integrated with the organs of the State and of the employers, enforcing an impeccable wages policy, and curbing the Trouble-makers in our Midst. A difficulty with this myth, as with all myths, is that it can only be persuasive by leaving a lot of the actual history out. The early and stormy histories of the unions are seen as teething troubles: the manifest political concern of early T.C.U. and Trades Councils are seen as an improper distraction from the authorized path. While this framework may occasionally be detected in the first volume of the sober and soundly-documented new history of trade unionism from 1889 by H. A. Clegg, Alan Fox, and A. F. Thompson, the authors are careful to keep it within control: while there is loss, in a diminished perspective of the political and social context of the labour *movement*, there is a compensating gain in the close understanding of industrial and administrative context. Nor is it inevitable that the study of industrial relations should lead one to the goal of the Wilsonian Corporate State. V. L. Allen has handled some of the same historical material to a different purpose: B. Pribicevic has brought the concern of a Yugoslav scholar for workers' control to the examination of the shop stewards' movement, 1910–22 (this general field has recently attracted other graduate researchers); while perhaps the most original of all the new studies in trade union history is H. A. Turner's *Trade Union Growth, Structure and Policy*. In this study of the Lancashire cotton unions, Professor Turner combines in a new way narrative, comparative, and structural analysis. It is s book which provokes the reader to re-examine established conclusions far beyond the author's own theme.

Those who wish to keep abreast of the published work should consult the bibliography in H. M. Pelling's neat hold-all Pelican *History of Trade Unionism*: or, for an admirable critical analysis, E. J. Hobsbawm's "Trade Union Historiography" in the Society's *Bulletin*, Spring, 1964. Dr. Hobsbawm's own *Labouring Men*, with its fine study of the gas-workers, is itself the most important book to appear subsequent to his own article.

When we turn from trade union to labour history, the subject loses coherence. One could, of course, point to the accumulation of work within the general area charted by Cole. (The Historical Association has just published a helpful survey by F. M. Mather of recent work on the Chartist movement.) It may be more useful—although this must mean passing over much valuable work in the traditional area—to suggest some of the ways in which the older conventions of Labour history are now breaking down.

The subject has become so blurred at the edges that, at the very moment when Labour history has found institutional expression in its own society, the value of the term is being called in question. One shift in interest is from the institutions of Labour (and its approved leaders and ideology) to the culture of labouring people.

What used to be Labour history can in fact become a great testing-ground for historical sociology. This does not mean—and it would be deplorable if it did mean—the wooden taking-over of unprocessed terminology and categories from one favoured school of sociology, and imposing these upon existent historical knowledge. Where this is done, it is damaging to both disciplines. It is far more a question of mutual interpretation, by which the historian finds in contemporary sociology writing new problems, or new ways of looking at old problems, pursues his research with a mind which is both fertilized by sociological concepts and distrustful of sociological categories, coming up with results which (one hopes) may in their turn add an historical dimension to sociological theory.

There is some evidence of this kind of work at the moment in France, Italy, and the United States: and, apart from *Annales E.S.C.*, the journals which are worth following include *Comparative Studies in Society and History; Le Mouvement Sociale, Sociologie et Travail*, and *Economic Development and Cultural Change*. In a somewhat more empirical way it is happening in England also. One result of the dissolution of an institutional definition of Labour history is that temporal boundaries suddenly fall open once again. Just as some sixteenth and seventeenth-century historians are throwing bridges forward to the industrial revolution, so some of us have ceased to "start" with 1789, or 1832, and are tunnelling backwards towards them. Thus Christopher Hill's study of "The Uses of Sabbatarianism" in *Society and Puritanism in Pre-Revolutionary England* touches in important ways upon the theme of the puritan ethic and work-discipline. This was a theme also of a conference held by *Past and Present* two years ago, at which Keith Thomas delivered a suggestive paper on "Work and Leisure in Pre-Industrial Society." But this relates also to a growing preoccupation among economic historians with early factory discipline, exemplified by notable studies by N. McKendrick (upon Wedgwood) in the *Economic History Review* and Pollard ("The Adaptation of Labour" in his *Genesis of Industrial Management*).

We have only started: once the problem is seen in this way the connexions propose themselves on every side. I have myself suggested that it is possible to look upon early Methodism in the same perspective, and thereby to move out of the Halevian Methodism-or-Revolution framework. The theme connects also, although more distantly, with the functions of Sabbatarianism and of the Temperance Movement in Victorian England, to which Brian Harrison has for several years been addressing research. And, by an even more indirect route, it may relate to the interesting research into Victorian sexual mores which Peter Cominos has published in the *International Review of Social History*. It relates, moreover—although here we cross over to a theme which may be independently defined—to the nature of popular disturbance from the seventeenth to the early nineteenth centuries (one thinks of the recent work of George Rudé, Barrie Rose, A. J. Peacock, G. A. Williams, D. V. J. Jones, and Hobsbawm, among others) and to the ways in which the social character of the crowd appears to change as we enter the industrial revolution, old patterns of behaviour (such as the class price-fixing food riot) die away, and new patterns of institutionalized agitation emerge.

At this point, of course, not only the old temporal but also the old provincial definitions must fall away. Work-discipline or food riots cannot be studied as English phenomena in the way that the Grand National Consolidated Trades Union or the Fabian Society must. English historians are learning from French historiography and techniques of examining disturbance: and they are fortunate in having Rudé and Richard Cobb as interpreters. (It should be said, however, that comparative study is deceptive if it is pressed forward too hastily: the similarities often leap from the history, whereas the differences are disclosed only after careful research: and several of the English chapters in Rudé's popular *The Crowd in History*—those on Luddism, Chartism, and even on English food riots—are based upon research which is deficient by the high standards which he himself had set.)

If we return to the theme of work-discipline, or of changing familial roles, leisure patterns, and community values during industrialization, the field for comparative study seems unending. It is only necessary to turn, for example, to Walter Elkan's studies of labour adaptation in Uganda, or Beate Salz's study of Ecuador (in *Economic Development and Cultural Change*) for parallels with seventeenth- and eighteenth-century England or Ireland to leap from the page. Acquaintance with anthropological studies of peasant and tribal markets, such as Bohannan and Dalton's *Markets in Africa*, prompts one to look again at the entire complex of markets and fairs in pre-industrial England, and to view it not only as an economic but also as a social nexus.

As yet few historians have done more than indicate this area of comparisons (as Professor Habbakuk and Dr. D. C. Coleman have done); and for their part, such American sociologists as Professors Hoselitz and Wilbert Moore, who write about problems of labour adaptation in UNESCO publications, have been content with a few inexact historical reminiscences. Worse than this, some Western sociologists are prepared to telescope into a few comforting phrases a hundred and more years of painful transitional conflict, to offer homilies to developing countries about "rationality" and "achievement and mobility aspirations," and to discourage all sympathetic analysis of early labour movements by attaching to them supposedly objective (but in fact profoundly value-loaded) terms like "disturbance-symptoms."

Today this comparative area is a challenging one, and one in which the historical discipline is most required. Tomorrow—or perhaps next Friday fortnight—the subject will suddenly become fashionable, and we shall hear about it on the Third Programme. At that point its credentials will have to be examined very closely. For this is likely to mean a prodigious proliferation of pretentious jargon, while historical research, which is tedious and undramatic, limps slowly behind. But if the sociology of industrialization could do with more history, the economic history of the industrial revolution is patently in need of some sociology.

Of course, some of the most valuable and rigorous work in the quantitative aspects of Labour history has appeared, and continues to appear, in the *Economic History Review* and the *Journal of Economic History*. My animus against these distinguished journals is by now notorious: but since they have their own pages, and a dozen Departments of Economic History (a good half of which are severely oriented towards the quantification of economic growth) from which to defend themselves. I may make my point once again. Among recent studies which have appeared, we are informed that Speenhamland was a form of beneficent welfare provision dealing with chronic under-employment: that the suggestion that the handloom weavers turned massively towards radicalism and Chartism is an untested hypothesis: and that the notion that the common people suffered through enclosure is a sentimental exaggeration. All these studies are of interest: but in the first case there is no evidence that the author has consulted the records of one overseer of the poor: in the second, not one of the relevant bundles in the Public Record Office, which provide overwhelming evidence as to the political affiliations of the weavers, seems to have been untied: and in the third case, one must remark that all these Departments of Economic History have not, it would seem, in the decades of their existence thought it worth while to encourage one research student to examine the quite extensive evidence (enclosure riots, petitions, anonymous letters, the throwing down of fences) as to popular discontent with enclosure.

At a certain point one ceases to defend a certain view of history; one must defend history itself. A quantitative methodology must not be allowed to remain uncriticized which obliterates (as "literary" or as "a-typical") whole categories of evidence. The industrial revolution entailed not only a change in the rate of economic growth; it also entailed far-reaching changes in the way of life of the people. Economic concepts such as "time-preference" and the "backward sloping labour supply curve" are (somewhat clumsy) attempts to describe wider sociological problems.

Dr. R. M. Hartwell has recently written, in a methodological study: "there is no help for the historian of the industrial revolution in sociology." If it is meant by this that the only significant history of the industrial revolution is a quantitative history of growth, purged of all social content, then the statement is self-validating. The very attempt to introduce sociological evidence must be inadmissible, since this evidence would challenge the authority of the court, or at least its claim to all-embracing jurisdiction. And if this misunderstands the intention, then this is, at the least, the impression given by the general direction of much eminent and orthodox work. In the Preface to Volume VI of the *Cambridge Economic History of Europe*, the editors explain that the first volumes deal with population, territorial expansion, transport, and technological change; the second volume will concern itself with the factors of production, and the entrepreneurial and managerial functions; while the third (and most distant) volume "will be devoted mainly to economic and fiscal policies, and perhaps also to the social changes involved with the economic development of the modern world." In that "perhaps" we have the poor bloody infantry of the industrial revolution, without whose labour and skill it would have remained an untested hypothesis. It is extraordinary that economic history which, in Professor Postan's younger days, was a most substantial threat to Eng. Hist. Prop. should have become its contemporary incarnation. Fortunately, the long and suggestive essay of the major contributor to the first volume, Professor David Landes, takes—as does Phyllis Deane in her book, *The First Industrial Revolution*—a somewhat wider brief than do the editors.

I have developed this theme of industrialization at disproportionate length because it may illustrate certain questions of method: the potentialities of the social history of labour, once it has broken from its older institutional mould, and some of the intellectual and institutional resistances. But illustrations might well have been taken from many other areas. Comparative history is already beginning to take on some substance. It has brought a revived interest in millenarial movements in Britain in the nineteenth century. J. F. C. Harrison, his brain—alas!—drained to Wisconsin, is completing a comparative study of Owenite thought and communities in Britain and the United States; Henry Collins and Chimen Abramsky's study of the British context of the First International was a substantial contribution to an international discussion.

The history of popular culture, also, continues to attract an interest which carries over from historical to literary studies: there are signs that it may pass on soon from the study of the Labour press and popular reading-matter to an overdue reappraisal of folk-lore and ballad. Harold Silver and Brian Simon have both filled in our knowledge of the Socialist (Owenite) and Labour influence upon the evolution of popular education. Another developing area is the study of popular religion—not so much the large national study or history of particular churches and sects as the micro-study into the social composition and effective role of Methodism in Cornwall or Shropshire, or the Salvation Army in London. The influence of French historiography—and notably of Chevalier's *Classes Laborieuses, Classes Dangereuses*—can be seen in several graduate theses in progress: it is likely to result in important work in the neglected social history of nineteenth-century London, and perhaps in advances in demographic studies and in the social history of crime. Moreover, such influences as this can be detected in work which, at a first view, might appear to remain fairly within the conventional territory of Labour History.

Just as H. A. Turner examines a conventional subject (the cotton unions) in a highly original way, so Royden Harrison, in his *Before the Socialists*, takes a theme from the heartland of Labour history, subdues whatever new techniques seem to him to be valid and appropriate to his controlling historical intelligence, and brings a new sense of significance and force back into political analysis. In such a chapter as "The 10th April of Spencer Walpole," which discusses the balance of class forces on the eve of the 1867 Reform Bill, and the different ideological positions held among proponents and opponents of Reform, there is—not an aping of Marx—but a savour of the tempered intelligence of the old man himself.

Harrison, who has also written about those spokesmen of Labour who did *not* support the North during the American Civil War, may remind us of one other way in which conventional Labour history is breaking down. There is a growing concern to examine political and social manifestations which are not in any "approved" line of Labour evolution. Horatio Bottomley was, after all, as influential in his time over the minds of some working people as was Ernest Bevin: and for every Jacobinical artisan in England in the 1790s there were probably half-a-dozen who roared out bellicose anti-Gallican ballads. The grow-ing body of work on Social Darwinism (one thinks of Bernard Semmel's notable chapter on "The Co-efficients") has made this kind of blind eye towards working-class or even Fabian sin no longer tenable. And, equally, there are a score of places where Labour history is ultimately inexplicable unless we know a great deal more about *not*-Labour history. Despite the work of Pelling, Tsu-zuki, Poirier, Bealey, Miliband, Mrs. Cole, and others on the origins of the Labour Party, we cannot really understand the whole period between 1880 and 1914 until a great deal more is known about the Liberal, the Conservative, and the plain apathetic working man. Paul Thompson, in a study in *Past and Present* of London's Working-Class Radicalism at the end of the century, has begun to fill in this vacuum.

I have passed over much work, and scarcely touched upon the very different problems of twentieth-century historiography. What is happening now, in what used to be Labour history, is not a disintegration so much as a liberation. So long as it was confined within the old conventions, it was in some senses an alter ego of Eng. Hist. Prop. Now that it feels confident enough to move outwards from the base which Cole and his successors secured, it becomes more dangerous to the established constitutional and parliamentary-political Thing, because more pervasive. Certainly, in modern English historiography it is a very lively impulse indeed. Perhaps it will prove most healthy for it if it remains somewhat disestablished, with an extra-mural audience still partly in mind. Oth-erwise it may become successful: grow fat and adopt Norman habits in its turn.

AGENDA FOR RADICAL HISTORY

FROM *MAKING HISTORY: WRITINGS ON HISTORY AND CULTURE*

I feel like an impostor here, because for six years now my trade has been submerged in peace activity, and I have to explain to you the position I speak from now. It's been six years, not just of doing this or that every now and then for peace, but, with the exception of two short spells of teaching in this country, total, full-time activity. In five years I've addressed more than five hundred meetings, attended endless committees, visited as an emissary of the peace movement nineteen or twenty different countries. I've had in my own house a weight of correspondence which has buried any possibility of work. Much of it has been fascinating papers, letters dropping out of different parts of the world. A very curious rebirth of internationalism is taking place in a very curious way, not coming through the normal structures of political parties or institutions. Partly by accident a few names got thrown up a few years ago and became widely known—of which mine was one. People found out the address, and the letters come to me.

Some letters have to be attended to very urgently. They may come from the other side; they may come from Hungarian independents or persecuted Soviet peaceniks; they may come from the United States peace movement; they may come from Canada or Australia or wherever. And this has meant that I really have evacuated perforce my trade as a historian for a long time.

I don't even have a valid ticket to the British Library or the Public Record Office. As I passed the New York Public Library this morning, I felt a knife inside me—the sense of how long it was since I had been able to work among the bounty that is there. I am at least five years behind in my reading, including the reading of the work of close friends, colleagues, and former students. I'm trying to return, but there is no guarantee of certainty. This is not a position one can easily walk out of. I have to tell you that when I was attempting to

From *Making History: Writings on History and Culture* by E. P. Thompson (New York: The New Press, 1994).

get on this year with *Customs in Common*,—I suddenly had to turn aside and to try and master all the weird acronymic vocabulary and technology of the Strategic Defence Initiative, and to edit and (in part) write a book on *Star Wars*.

But this has also involved exchanges between East and West of a very interesting and perhaps potentially very important kind. I'm not recommending others to follow my course. Although one way to liberate me, if you want to do so, is for more hands to be engaging in this international work. I know some of you will be doing this. But I hope all those hands will not start writing letters to me!

I'm not apologizing. When in our country, as in yours, professional groups started forming their own anti-nuclear organisations, historians had a bit of a problem because, unless they were post-Hiroshima, there really wasn't very much history that historians could actually contribute (they thought) to the anti-nuclear movement. But at length someone came up with the right banner for Historians against Nuclear Weapons: "Historians Demand a Continuing Supply of History." And they're right. Because under the criticism of this shadow of nuclear war, all talk of history and culture becomes empty. Even in this city, one of the densest population centres in the world, which is now to become a home base for a nuclear armed pirate Armada, the colleges and the faculties here have to consider their position. I'm therefore not in any mood to offer advice to future historians.

If, or as, I return to my trade, my preoccupations are rather personal: William Morris said to Burne-Jones when he was my age, "the best way of lengthening out the rest of our days now, old chap, is to finish off our old things." And perhaps there is a sense in which three of us on this platform are doing that and needn't apologize for it. We are completing and enlarging work which was commenced in some cases forty or more years ago. A certain breakthrough in British radical history, associated particularly at that point with the Marxist tradition, took place some 45 years ago. (I'm sorry to use military imagery.) We are still exploiting the terrain that was opened up with that breakthrough. For me in 1940 as a school student it came through the work of Christopher Hill: his first brief study of 1640. I sat down at the age of 16 to write for the sixth form history society a paper on the Marxist interpretation of history and the English civil war, leafing through Christopher's work, and Bernstein, and Petagorsky, and Winstanley's pamphlets and such Leveller tracts as I could get, and some Marx, Engels and Plekhanov. And there followed upon this other breakthroughs: one thinks of Eric's magnificent essay on "The Tramping Artisan." The rest of us followed through that gap.

My own "old things," most of which are half or more than half written, include the studies of 18th century social history, custom, practice, and popular culture, which I call *Customs in Common*, some of which has already been published; my half-written book on William Blake; my work on the Romantics in England in the 1790s—young Wordsworth, young Coleridge, and the assertion and defeat of the cause of women's rights; and I also have a book I hope to do on an odd corner of the Balkans in World War II.

If and when I return, will it be with a different eye? I think it may. I have to say honestly, without any sense of particular criticism, or of any large theoretical statement, that I'm less and less interested in Marxism as a Theoretical System. I'm neither pro- nor anti- so much as bored with some of the argument that goes on. I find some of the argument a distraction from the historical problems, an impediment to completing my work. Perry Anderson and I had an argument—or rather I had an argument with Althusser some ten years ago, and Perry, in a generous and constructive way, commented on this argument in his *Arguments in English Marxism*. I've been asked why didn't I reply to Perry? I feel no need to reply to Perry. I think he had many important and interesting things to say. I think we'd call it a draw. And I bequeath it to you to continue that argument, if it needs to be continued.

I will just say there were two terrible things which Perry did: he defended Walpole, and he showed insufficient respect for Jonathan Swift. Those two points I might like to argue some time, particularly because I regard *Gulliver's Travels* as the most savage indictment of the reasons of power that has ever been written. It still has a vitality of an extraordinary kind. And if, for political reasons, we try to devalue that, then somehow our categories are too limited.

There is a political problem here of a very straightforward kind. I find it difficult to say what my relationship to the Marxist tradition is, because, in Mrs. Thatcher's Britain, the popular press puts down *any* form of radicalism as "Marxist." If I can give one illustration: four or five years ago I was with my daughter and we stopped the car and went for a walk in an Oxfordshire wood. And we had our dog with us, who'd seen a pheasant. Fortunately we got the dog back on the lead when the gamekeeper came along with a gun. He said this wood was owned, not by a Lord now, but by some huge banking or investment institution, and we were trespassing and so on and so forth. As a deferential Englishman I was about to retreat. Unfortunately my daughter turned out to be a freeborn Englishwoman. She started to give him quite a lot of sass about civil rights and the law of trespass. Whereupon the gamekeeper said, "What are you then, *Marxists*?" In a situation like that, no-one is going to deny they're a Marxist.

I feel happier with the term "historical materialism." And also with the sense that ideas and values are situated in a material context, and material needs are situated in a context of norms and expectations, and one turns around this many-sided societal object of investigation. From one aspect it is a mode of production, from another a way of life. Marxism has given us a universal vocabulary, although there are some surprises that are going to come to us. A friend of mine was in the Soviet Union last year. After a historical seminar in which he was discussing questions of class struggle and class relations, he was taken aside quietly—not by "dissidents," but by members of the Soviet historical profession, who told him, "serious scientists no longer use the concept of class in the Soviet Union." In so far as an opening between East and West comes, we may find that the teeth of the children have been so much set on edge by the sour doctrinaire ideology of the Stalinist past that the discourse becomes very difficult.

I think the provisional categories of Marxism to which Perry has referred— those of class, ideology, and mode of production, are difficult but still creative concepts. But, in particular, the historical notion of the dialectic between social being and social consciousness—although it is a dialectical interrelationship which I would sometimes wish to invert—is extraordinarily powerful and important. Yet I find also in the tradition pressures towards reductionism, affording priority to "economy" over "culture"; and a radical confusion introduced by the chance metaphor of "base and superstructure." I find a lot in the Marxist tradition—there are many Marxisms now—marked by what is ultimately a capitalist definition of human need, even though it was a revolutionary upside-downing of that definition. This definition of need, in economic material terms, tends to enforce a hierarchy of causation which affords insufficient priority to other needs: the needs of identity, the needs of gender identity, the need for respect and status among working people themselves. I do indeed agree with all the speakers here upon the need to try and see history as a whole cloth, as an objective record of causally interrelated activities, while agreeing also with Perry that the concept of cause is extraordinarily difficult, toward which we always attain to only approximate understanding.

I think the renewed emphasis upon power and power relations, especially in history, is right. Some studies of "culture" forget the controlling context of power. And yet so many of the great problems of the 20th century, something that has called itself "Marxism" has had so little helpful to say about. The tenacities of nationalism; the whole problem of Nazism; the problem of Stalinism; of the Chinese cultural revolution; of the Cold War today, which in my view is not acting out a conflict between modes of production or economies but is acting out a conflict from an outworn ideological script which threatens indeed to be terminal to all modes of production alike. I think we've had an insufficient vocabulary for examining the structure of power relations through symbolism, from the awe of empire or monarchy to the awe today of nuclear weapons. Our concern increasingly must be with finding the "rationality" of social unreason. That is not throwing up one's hands and saying "anything can happen in history"—but, rather, finding the "reasons" of social unreason. To give an example among the few articles I've had time to read recently the one which fascinated me most of all, completely outside my field, was an article in *Past & Present* (May 1985) by Inga Clendinnen on "The Cost of Courage in Aztec Society."

And where, again, from the materialist vocabulary do agency, initiatives, ideas, and even love come from? This is why I'm so concerned with Blake and Blake's quarrel with the Deists and the Godwinian utilitarians. His political sympathies were with so many of their positions; and yet in the end he said there must be an affirmation, "Thou Shalt Love." Where does the affirmative, "Thou Shalt Love," come from? This argument with necessitarianism continues Milton's old argument with predestinarianism and prefigures today's argument with determinisms and structuralisms—which themselves are ideologically-inflected products of a defeated and disillusioned age. If we can de-structure the Cold War, then a new age of ideas may be coming, as in the 1790s or the 1640s.

I have nothing else to say except that our radical impulses are really hemmed in in many ways. We've said little about this, but we all know it. I don't know exactly how things are in the States, but, in the last ten years in Britain I feel very much a closing-down of the situation. A lack of originality. A playing safe. A job situation which is so difficult that one senses a loss of vitality, a cramping of the radical initiative. And this comes partly from straight political ideological pressures.

This symposium may seem rather like an Anglo-Marxist invasion of Manhattan. I remember that there was a *Collége Des Hautes Etudes*, which had the generous welcome of the New School during World War II; I wonder whether we are the forerunners of a British college in exile in refuge from Mrs. Thatcher?

I don't want to tell anyone how to write history. They must find out in their own way. Those of us on the platform are as much subject to our own time's formation and determinations as any others. If our work is continued by others, it will be continued differently. What's radical in it demands some relations between the academy and active experience, whether in the forms of adult education or the kind of work which MARHO and the *Radical History Review* do here in Manhattan, and some distrust of easy assimilation by the lost society, an awareness of the institutional and ideological determinations of the societies in which we work, which are founded upon unreason, or on the reasons of power and the reasons of money.

Wollstonecraft in the 1790s said "mind has no sex." I know that some contemporary feminists want to revise the position, because the mind is situated very much within a gender context. But I think we want to remember Wollstonecraft's astonishing courage in saying exactly that in the 1970s. When she said "mind has no sex," she both demanded entry into the whole world of the mind for her gender, and she also refused any privilege for her gender. If I can use an analogy, radical history should not ask for any privilege of any kind. Radical history demands the most exacting standards of the historical discipline. Radical history must be good history. It must be good as history can be.

Note: The New School for Social Research, learning that all the contributors would be in New York at the same time, invited Eric Hobsbawm, Christopher Hill, Perry Anderson, and myself to take part in a public discussion, on 20 October 1985. This is my contribution. My thanks are due to the New School and to Margaret C. Jacob who initiated the dialogue. The other contributions will be found in *Radical History Review*, no. 36, 1986.

A SELECTION OF FURTHER READINGS

For a fuller select bibliography of published works until 1993, including pamphlets and articles, see Harvey J. Kaye and Keith McClelland "E. P. Thompson: A Select Bibliography" in John Rule and Robert Malcomson, eds., *Protest and Survival: Essays for E. P. Thompson* (New York: The New Press, 1993). Of the many obituaries and later articles published, see particularly:

Palmer, Bryan. *E. P. Thompson: Objections and Oppositions*. London and New York: Verso, 1994.

Hobsbawm, E. J. "Edward Palmer Thompson," in *Proceedings of the British Academy* 90 (1996): 521–39.

Sarkar, Sumit. "The Relevance of E. P. Thompson." In *Writing Social History*. Delhi and New York: Oxford University Press, 1997.

Books and Collected Essays

William Morris: Romantic to Revolutionary. London: Lawrence & Wishart, 1955; New York: Monthly Review Press, 1961; rev. ed., London: Merlin Press, 1977; New York: Pantheon Books, 1977.

The Making of the English Working Class. London: Victor Gollancz, 1963; New York: Pantheon Books, 1964; 2nd ed. with a new postscript, Harmondsworth, England: Penguin, 1968; 3rd ed. with a new preface, 1980.

Whigs and Hunters: The Origins of the Black Act. London: Allen Lane, 1975; New York: Pantheon Books, 1975; reprinted with a new postscript, Harmondsworth, England: Penguin, 1977.

The Poverty of Theory and Other Essays. London: Merlin Press, 1978; New York: Monthly Review Press, 1978.

Writing by Candlelight. London: Merlin Press, 1980.

Zero Option. London: Merlin Press, 1982; published in the United States as *Beyond the Cold War: A New Approach to the Arms Race and Nuclear Annihilation*. New York: Pantheon Books, 1982.

Double Exposure. London: Merlin Press, 1985.

The Heavy Dancers. London: Merlin Press, 1985; New York: Pantheon, 1985. The American edition incorporates *Double Exposure* but excludes selected essays of the British edition.

The Sykaos Papers. London: Bloomsbury, 1988; New York: Pantheon, 1988.

Customs in Common. London: Merlin Press, 1991; New York: The New Press, 1991.

Witness Against the Beast: William Blake and the Moral Law. Cambridge: Cambridge University Press, 1993; New York: The New Press, 1993.

Alien Homage: Edward Thompson and Rabindanath Tagore. Delhi and New York: Oxford University Press, 1993.

Posthumously Published

Persons and Polemics: Historical Essays. London: Merlin Press, 1994; published in the United States as *Making History: Writings on History and Culture*. New York: The New Press, 1994.

Beyond the Frontier: The Politics of a Failed Mission. Edited by Dorothy Thompson. Woodbridge, Suffolk: Merlin Press, 1994; Stanford, Calif: Stanford University Press, 1994.

The Romantics: England in a Revolutionary Age. Rendlesham, England: Merlin Press, 1997; New York: The New Press, 1997.

Collected Poems. Edited and with an introduction by Fred Inglis. Newcastle-on-Tyne, England: Bloodaxe Books, 1999.